Dynamic Physical Education for Secondary School Students

Dynamic Physical Education for Secondary School Students

THIRD EDITION

Robert P. Pangrazi

Arizona State University

Paul W. Darst

Arizona State University

Allyn and Bacon

Boston   London   Toronto   Sydney   Tokyo   Singapore

Senior Editor: Suzy Spivey
Editorial Assistant: Lisa Davidson
Marketing Manager: Quinn Perkson
Production Administrator: Deborah Brown
Editorial-Production Service: P. M. Gordon Associates, Inc.
Design and Electronic Composition: Denise Hoffman
Composition Buyer: Linda Cox
Manufacturing Buyer: Megan Cochran
Cover Administrator: Suzanne Harbison

Copyright © 1997 by Allyn and Bacon
A Viacom Company
160 Gould Street
Needham Heights, MA 02194

Internet: www.abacon.com
America Online: keyword: College Online

Earlier editions were published in 1985 and 1991.

Library of Congress Cataloging-in-Publication Data
Pangrazi, Robert P.
    Dynamic physical education for secondary school students / Robert P. Pangrazi and Paul W. Darst. — 3rd ed.
        p.   cm.
    Includes bibliographical references and index.
    ISBN 0–205–19982–8
    1. Physical education and training—United States—Curricula.
2. Physical education and training—Study and teaching (Secondary)—
United States.   3. Physical education and training—Study and
teaching (Secondary)—Canada.   I. Darst, Paul W.   II. Title
GV365.P36   1997
613.7'0973—dc20   96–13396
                                                               CIP

Printed in the United States of America
10 9 8 7 6 5 4 3   01 00 99 98 97

Brief Contents

Detailed Contents

CHAPTER 6   Creating an Effective Learning Environment   110

CHAPTER 7   Management and Discipline   133

Section IV Developing a Total Program

CHAPTER 11 Students with Disabilities   208

CHAPTER 12 Legal Liability and Proper Care of Students   227

CHAPTER 13   Intramurals, Sport Clubs, and Athletics   241

CHAPTER 14   Public Relations   256

Section V Implementing Instructional Activities

CHAPTER 15   Introductory Activities   267

Preface

The physical activity habits among middle school and high school students continue to receive public attention. In many districts and secondary schools, physical education programs are being reduced or done away with altogether. The reasons being given are funding problems, concern about elective courses, and the need for students to address core subjects during the school day. We maintain that physical education is a basic component of a student's education. These concerns are clearly reflected in our revision of *Dynamic Physical Education for Secondary School Students*.

Highlights of the Third Edition

The third edition of *Dynamic Physical Education for Secondary School Students* expands the understanding of the rudiments of curriculum and instruction in physical education and constitutes a major revision.

New information on recent trends and issues, planning and management strategies, curriculum development, and maintenance of an effective learning environment are the focus of this revision. Chapter 2, a review of research that supports the need for physical education in a student's total curriculum, has been updated. New sections document the impact of physical activity on students, the incidence of hypokinetic diseases, and long-term effects of exercise during school years. Also discussed are new guidelines for safety regarding exercise.

In addition, we have reduced the overlap and repetition of ideas common to middle school and high school programs and have addressed specific ideas that pertain separately to each level. We also offer practical ideas for both the beginning and the experienced teacher.

Key Concepts and Outcomes

At the beginning of Chapters 1 to 17, purpose statements describe the intent and focus of the chapter, followed by key concepts highlighting ideas, beliefs, and principles that are basic to the material to be covered. Concluding these chapters are expected outcomes listing knowledge, understanding, and fundamental concepts that should be acquired after reading the chapter. These key concepts and expected outcomes help students gain a better understanding of each chapter.

Curriculum Planning

The examination of curriculum models in use in various school districts has been introduced in this edition in a new Chapter 3, showing strengths and weaknesses of each model. Chapter 4, which outlines specific steps of curriculum design of a physical education program, focuses on characteristics of students' growth and development at middle school and at high school level and the impact these characteristics have on the design of the curriculum. An understanding of these chapters will help teachers realize the importance of a philosophical framework to support a curriculum.

Instructional Effectiveness

Planning plays an important role in effective teaching. Chapter 5 covers planning for success through daily lesson and unit plans and practical strategies for beginning and experienced teachers that organize meaningful and sequential learning experiences. Chapter 6 presents ways of organizing the instructional environment, development of instructional cues, and aspects of class performance. A substantial section in Chapter 6 assists teachers in adapting instructional tasks to individual needs and effectively communicating these tasks. This edition also includes points on designing and implementing procedures for student cooperation.

Chapter 7 includes many new activities and techniques for managing and disciplining students in a positive way. This area is a principal concern of teachers and parents that has not been covered in detail in physical education textbooks. Teachers are shown how to reinforce desired behavior and how to develop a positive, yet assertive, discipline style. Punishment, although discouraged, is discussed, and guidelines for acceptable use are presented.

This edition reflects our continuing determination to ensure that teachers perform their duties in a manner that is technically correct and in line with current research. The chapters on pedagogy reflect a body of knowledge related to effective teaching and indicate that it is no longer acceptable to "teach as we were taught." In Chapter 8, the depth of coverage of teaching styles is increased in an effort to help teachers understand when it is best to use different teaching styles, and practical examples help students visualize how different teaching techniques may increase the quality of how and what they learn. New sections on mastery learning and cooperative learning have also been added.

Assessment and Evaluation.   Chapter 9 has been updated to help teachers develop a systematic self-evaluation approach for improving their teaching and includes the setting of realistic goals and methods for gauging accomplishment. Methods of systematic observation of instruction are discussed in a straightforward, easily implemented manner. Also included are a number of combination systems for observing teacher/student effectiveness.

Chapter 10 includes a broad and comprehensive examination of grading in secondary schools. An in-depth look at objective and subjective methods for evaluating physical skills is presented with ideas on evaluation of knowledge, attitudes, and values. This chapter also surveys the pros and cons of grading physical education in secondary schools and examines many different points of view.

Students with Disabilities.   Continued emphasis is placed in this revision on integrating students with disabilities into physical education settings. Chapter 11 offers a step-by-step approach to the development of the IEP (individualized education program) and presents guidelines for screening and assessment, and criteria for placement of students in the least restrictive environment, with emphasis on a positive and constructive approach. A section of practical ideas for modifying activities to ensure maximal student success is included. Finally, specific disabilities with accompanying requisite instructional procedures are described in detail.

Legal Liability.   The important aspects of legal liability, not often covered in secondary physical education textbooks, are defined in Chapter 12 and include unsafe situations teachers should avoid and a checklist for analyzing situations that might result in a lawsuit.

Physical Fitness

As the debate regarding physical activity and the secondary school population continues, the new data on the importance of physical activity for middle and high school students have resulted in a new focus on fitness. Chapters 15 and 16 give increased coverage to this issue. Many new introductory activities and fitness routines, including warm-up exercises, have been added in this edition. Directions and guidelines for implementing the Prudential Fitnessgram and other fitness testing issues are included. Chapter 17 concentrates on wellness and the basic components of lifetime fitness. These chapters emphasize the interconnectedness of fitness and health.

Potpourri

The purpose of the units of activity presented in Chapters 18 to 22 is to help teachers understand the different approaches and teaching devices that can be used in activity presentations. Included with each unit are practical ideas for skill work, lead-up activities, and other specific learning activities. The instructional units are divided into five categories: mini-units, team sports, individual sports, dual sports, and outdoor adventure activities. This division helps students view the need for including units of instruction from all areas in their total curriculum. Finally, a number of suggested readings for each activity are offered so students can secure in-depth information written by experts.

Supplements

The Instructor's Manual/Test Bank, prepared by the authors, is available to assist instructors preparing for class. The manual includes the purpose, key concepts, expected outcomes, and instructional formats for each chapter of the text. The test bank contains true/false, multiple choice, and essay questions arranged by chapter. In addition, over 100 transparency masters are included for creating visuals to accentuate key topics from the text. A computerized test bank is available in IBM and MacIntosh versions. Lesson Plans, written and field-tested by Dr. Carol Casten of California State University/Dominguez Hills, have been added as a supplement to this revision and provide many practical ideas for beginning and experienced teachers.

Kudos

This textbook is the result of the help of many people. We are most appreciative of the professional staff at Allyn and Bacon. Special thanks go to our editor, Suzy Spivey, and her assistant, Lisa Davidson, for their guidance and support.

A number of teachers, including John Tamburino and Dan McGee of the Kyrene School District, Tempe, Arizona, and Steve Fedorchek and Ken Coyle of the Tempe School District, Tempe, Arizona, helped field-test and evaluate the instructional units. Belinda Stillwell added valuable information to the field hockey section.

Special thanks also go to our reviewers, who helped guide this revision. They include Larry Albertson, University of Wisconsin, River Falls; Ron McBride, Texas A & M University; and John Pearson, Central Washington University.

Unreserved thank-yous go to our wives, Debbie and Charlene, for their constant support and patience.

RPP
PWD

Dynamic Physical Education for Secondary School Students

1 Physical Education in the Secondary School

PURPOSE

To establish the place of contemporary physical education in the secondary schools by defining what physical education is and what it should accomplish for students. The chapter also examines current issues and directions about activities, policies, procedures, requirements, and problems related to successful secondary school physical education programs.

KEY CONCEPTS

- The public has many different ideas about what physical education is and what it should accomplish.
- Physical education programs vary considerably across the country for many reasons.
- Physical education is an educational process that focuses on developing knowledge, attitudes, and behavior about physical activities.
- Physical education is an important and legitimate concern of our schools.
- The goals of physical education help students incorporate physical activity into their lifestyle, develop motor skills, improve fitness and wellness, enhance social skill and self-concept, and increase knowledge.
- Secondary school physical education programs are continually evolving and changing because of many forces in society.
- Requirements and laws, conceptual fitness models, interdisciplinary courses, independent study options, the use of off-campus facilities, the private sports industry, coaching conflicts, and other issues have had an impact on physical education programs.
- Successful programs provide a positive learning environment, allow students variety and choice of activities, provide in-depth instruction, and integrate activity programs.

Physical education can be a positive and exciting experience for participants. Secondary students can receive an opportunity to choose among activities such as cycling, golf , rock climbing, tennis, racquetball, and wilderness survival. Many programs in high schools offer elective choices, including sailing, scuba diving, martial arts, Frisbee, and yoga. Modern fitness centers with a variety of machines and equipment for working on various aspects of health-related physical fitness are becoming available to students. Short 2 to 3 week minicourses as well as semester-long, in-depth units are being designed by creative teachers to meet student needs and desires. New program offerings include adventure and wilderness courses that teach caving, rock climbing, stream fishing, and backpacking as part of the physical education program. Middle schools are offering a wide variety of short units, including team handball, new games, initiative challenges, ropes courses, modified lacrosse, Frisbee skills, bicycling, and orienteering, so that students can find activities they enjoy.

Many programs are emphasizing a positive and humane atmosphere. Strict dress codes are being relaxed, and students are being given a voice about the clothes they wear for activities. Instructional procedures include learning stations in which students work on different tasks at different levels. Teachers move about the gymnasium, giving information to, correcting, encouraging, and praising students. Students are being asked for input about the type of activities they would like to see offered. Physical fitness activities may include many choices such as exercise step aerobics, rope jumping, circuit training, obstacle courses, partner resistance activities, stationary bicycles, rowing machines, stair-climbing machines, or running an orienteering course (Figure 1.1). These activities are arranged and presented so all students can find personal satisfaction and success. All ability levels of students are provided with challenging and successful activities that encourage them to expand their physical limits and develop a level of personal success and confidence.

So, is this how the public perceives physical education today? What is physical education? Ask this question and an infinite number of different answers will arise. People have varied images of the physical education environment. Some envision a class in which students dress in the required uniform and exercise in straight lines under the watchful eye of a regimental instructor. Accompanying this image is a negative atmosphere where running laps and exercise are used as punishment for dress code infractions or misbehavior. Others might view physical education as a subject to be avoided because of crowded classes, smelly locker rooms, forced showers, and a lack of time for changing clothes. Athletically inclined participants often remember physical education as a time for playing sports on a daily basis. Little or no organized teaching or learning occurred, but the opportunity to play with peers was their physical education experience.

These memories of physical education create a public perception that might be described as follows: Students are hurried into their gym clothes only to wait at attention for dress inspection. Next, never-changing group calisthenics and stretching are followed by a lap around the track. Students then choose up sides and play the traditional game of the day, that is, flag football, basketball, softball, and volleyball. The final activity of the day is showering in four minutes with a mandatory shower inspection to make sure that all students are wet. Variety in the curriculum, student input and choice of activities, coed activities, and individualized instruction are seldom a part of the program they remember.

Sadly, the public's perception of physical education often diminishes the importance of the program in the total school curriculum. Even though physically active forms of sport and play can have a positive impact on students, many adults still hold a negative view of physical education. Even more unfortunate, these perceptions of physical education still exist in schools across the country. Physical miseducation is a dragon that rears its ugly head for

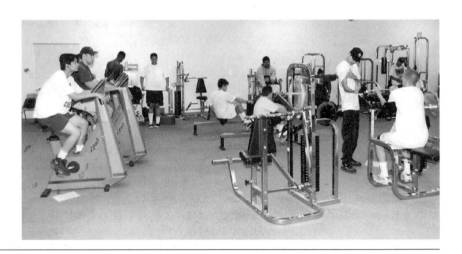

FIGURE 1.1 Fitness center activities

various reasons, and it is extremely tough to slay. These programs create a situation where young adolescent students never get the valuable opportunity to experience a quality physical education that could significantly impact their lives (Rink, 1993).

Clearly, physical education implies widely differing experiences to the public. It is easy to see why many people have misunderstood physical education. Programs vary significantly from place to place and situation to situation. Knowledge, attitudes, and behaviors toward physical activity are strongly influenced by the type of physical education program students experience. Consequently, in developing an effective physical education program, teachers must have a clear understanding of what physical education is and what it should be doing in school settings.

FIGURE 1.2 Students working cooperatively

WHAT IS PHYSICAL EDUCATION?

Physical education is a learning process that focuses on increasing knowledge and affecting attitudes and behaviors relative to physical activities, including exercise, sports, games, dance, aquatic activities, and outdoor adventure activities. It can occur inside or outside the schools. It can be formal or informal. It might include a father teaching his son or daughter how to play golf or a player receiving information from the coach of the soccer team. It could be a gymnast taking private lessons or a mother explaining pacing to her offspring during a 10-k run. It can be a youth explaining the rules of football to his grandfather or a wife teaching her husband how to play racquetball. It is a group of 7th graders learning to play badminton in a middle school or high school students learning the concepts of health-related fitness in a classroom setting. Physical education is the passing of information, attitudes, and skills from one person to another (Figure 1.2).

Physical education is an important component of the overall school program. It is an integral part of the total educational program that contributes, primarily through physical activity experiences, to the total growth and development of all students. Physical education is an instructional program that gives attention to all learning domains—psychomotor, cognitive, and affective. Three outcomes of physical education are unique and can only be accomplished through an effective physical education program. The first outcome is the achievement of a **personalized level of physical fitness**. Second is the development of **competency in a variety of physical skills** to ensure that students can function effectively in lifetime physical activities. The third outcome requires that students acquire **requisite knowledge related to motor-skill performance and fitness maintenance**. If these outcomes are not accomplished in physical education classes, they will not be realized elsewhere in the school curriculum. Physical education instructors have a responsibility to develop and teach a systematically organized curriculum for kindergarten through grade 12 that favorably influences all students and enhances their physical activity habits. Students deserve a thoughtful program of physical education that contributes to their quality of life and an active lifestyle. The transmission of knowledge, skills, and attitudes toward this end is physical education.

PHYSICAL EDUCATION PROGRAM OBJECTIVES

Current public opinion continues to ask schools to accomplish more while resources to support programs dwindle. Educational critics continually cite the ineffectiveness of school programs in meeting general goals. Physical education programs are included in this criticism, particularly in the area of youth fitness and inactivity. There is pressure for physical educators to teach a program that will stimulate students to strive toward an active lifestyle. Often, physical educators set objectives and expectations that are unrealistic and difficult to achieve. The instructional objectives of the program need to give obvious direction to the program. In addition, it is quite possible that the number of objectives should be narrowed to a few major goals that can be achieved and evaluated.

Program objectives are the framework of the program. They determine the focus and direction of the physical education program. Accomplishment of objectives must make a significant contribution to the overall goals of schools and society—the development of a well-rounded individual capable of contributing to a democratic society. Quality programs are organized around objectives and move students toward achievement of stated goals. Two major types of objectives are used to guide physical education programs. **Institutional objectives** determine the direction and focus of the program and provide teachers with a clear and constant direction for instruction. Institutional objectives determine the content and focus of a physical education program. **Student-centered objectives** provide students with target goals in terms of student behavior. These student-centered objectives are determined and written after the institutional objectives have been determined.

The booklet *Outcomes of Quality Physical Education Programs* (NASPE, 1992) was developed by the National Association for Sport and Physical Education (NASPE). This publication is useful for teachers designing, implementing, and evaluating physical education curriculum. The booklet lists 20 major outcomes for a physically educated person in 5 categories, including psychomotor, cognitive, and affective domains (Figure 1.3). In addition to the outcomes, specific student benchmarks are listed for kindergarten, 2nd, 3rd, 6th, 8th, 10th, and 12th grade students. The benchmarks are examples of types of learning that can be evaluated. The benchmarks are not meant to include all objectives of a program, but rather to give teachers a minimum standard of assessment. The benchmarks also give teachers an indication of when various learning can be evaluated at the specific grade level. The benchmarks represent reasonable levels of achievement and give direction to systematic approaches to evaluation.

Generally, experts agree that these 5 areas constitute categories for the major objectives of physical education that form the framework for physical education programs. The objectives determine the focus and direction of the physical education program. In this chapter, each of these major objectives as well as an additional one, social-emotional skills and positive self-concept, will be discussed in greater detail. Though social-emotional skills and positive self-concept can be incorporated under the "values" outcome in the NASPE model, many experts feel that it is a major objective worthy of individual consideration. The following objectives (Pangrazi and Dauer, 1995) find general agreement among experts regardless of the curriculum model used (Figure 1.4).

Motor Skills and Movement Competence

OBJECTIVE: *The physical education program will help students become competent in a variety of motor skills and movements.*

All people want to be skilled and competent in the area of motor performance. The school years are the opportune time to teach motor skills because students have time and the predisposition to learn. People tend to repeat activities they do well or find rewarding. Success is a great motivator. If students improve their volleyball bumps, Frisbee sidearm throws, or tennis serves, chances are great that they will repeat the activity and incorporate it into their lifestyle. Skill development does not occur overnight or in a 3-week unit. Students should be counseled about procedures and opportunities for developing physical skills outside the school program. Teachers provide a support system for students as their skills improve and the positive benefits of physical activity begin to appear. Students change their attitudes toward physical activity when personal skill levels improve. Students expect instant success, and teachers can help them learn that physical skill development is not easy and demands long, continuous effort. The role of teachers is to help students find individual levels of success—success that is unique to each person.

The range of skills presented in physical education should be unlimited. Since students vary in genetic endowment and interest, it is important that they have an opportunity to explore and learn about their abilities in many types of physical skills. The hierarchy of skill development progresses from fundamental motor skills to specialized skills. Components of motor skill development and movement competence follow.

A PHYSICALLY EDUCATED PERSON:

HAS learned skills necessary to perform a variety of physical activities

1. . . . moves using concepts of body awareness, space awareness, effort, and relationships.
2. . . . demonstrates competence in a variety of manipulative, locomotor, and nonlocomotor skills.
3. . . . demonstrates competence in combinations of manipulative, locomotor, and nonlocomotor skills performed individually and with others.
4. . . . demonstrates competence in many different forms of physical activity.
5. . . . demonstrates proficiency in a few forms of physical activity.
6. . . . has learned how to learn new skills.

IS physically fit

7. . . . assesses, achieves, and maintains physical fitness.
8. . . . designs safe, personal fitness programs in accordance with principles of training and conditioning.

DOES participate regularly in physical activity

9. . . . participates in health enhancing physical activity at least three times a week.
10. . . . selects and regularly participates in lifetime physical activities.

KNOWS the implications of and the benefits from involvement in physical activities

11. . . . identifies the benefits, costs, and obligations associated with regular participation in physical activity.
12. . . . recognizes the risk and safety factors associated with regular participation in physical activity.
13. . . . applies concepts and principles to the development of motor skills.
14. . . . understands that wellness involves more than being physically fit.
15. . . . knows the rules, strategies, and appropriate behaviors for selected physical activities.
16. . . . recognizes that participation in physical activity can lead to multicultural and international understanding.
17. . . . understands that physical activity provides the opportunity for enjoyment, self-expression, and communication.

VALUES physical activity and its contributions to a healthful lifestyle

18. . . . appreciates the relationships with others that result from participation in physical activity.
19. . . . respects the role that regular physical activity plays in the pursuit of life-long health and well-being.
20. . . . cherishes the feelings that result from regular participation in physical activity.

FIGURE 1.3 Definitions and outcomes of the physically educated person

From *Outcomes of Quality Physical Education Programs* with permission of the American Alliance for Health, Physical Education, Recreation, and Dance, 1900 Association Drive, Reston, VA 22091. Copyright 1992 by AAHPERD.

I. MOTOR SKILLS AND MOVEMENT COMPETENCE

Fundamental Motor Skills

Locomotor Skills	*Nonlocomotor Skills*	*Manipulative Skills*
Walking	Bending	Striking
Running	Twisting	Rolling
Hopping	Turning	Kicking
Skipping	Rocking/swaying	Catching
Jumping	Balancing	Bouncing
Leaping	Stretching	Trapping
Sliding	Pushing	Throwing
Galloping	Pulling	

Movement Concepts Skills

Body awareness
Space awareness
Qualities of movement
Relationships

Rhythmic Movement Skills

Performance of motor skills in a rhythmic manner

Specialized Motor Skills

Specific skills used in sports, stunts and tumbling, apparatus, and specialized manipulative activities such as rope jumping

II. HEALTH-RELATED PHYSICAL FITNESS AND WELLNESS

Knowledge of health-related fitness components

Ability to do fitness self-testing

Participation in regular fitness activity

Identification of personalized fitness activities

Understanding of wellness components

III. HUMAN MOVEMENT PRINCIPLES

Know basic kinesiological principles including stability, force, and leverage.

Understand elementary principles of physiology including body composition, training zone, and strength development.

IV. SOCIAL SKILLS AND POSITIVE SELF-CONCEPT

Develop interactive skills including the ability to lead and follow, develop decision-making skills, and exchange ideas with other students.

Acquire cooperative skills such as following directions, accepting individual differences, and the ability to be a member of a team.

Exhibit sportsmanship behavior including a sense of fair play, self-discipline, and winning and losing with dignity.

V. LIFETIME PARTICIPATION IN ACTIVITY

Develop competency in a variety of specialized motor skills. Participate in activities that are suited to personal competencies.

Understand the social and physical benefits of lifetime activity.

FIGURE 1.4   Objectives of physical education

From R. P. Pangrazi and V. P. Dauer. 1995. *Dynamic Physical Education for Elementary School Children.* 11th ed. Boston: Allyn & Bacon. pp. 3–4. Copyright © 1995 by Allyn & Bacon. Reprinted with permission.

Fundamental Motor Skills

Fundamental skills are those utilitarian skills that people use to enhance the quality of life. The designation *fundamental skills* is used because skills are basic to a fully functioning individual. These skills help students to function in the environment around them. These skills are divided into three categories: locomotor, nonlocomotor, and manipulative. The majority of these skills should be learned during the elementary school years.

1. *Locomotor skills* Locomotor skills are used to move the body from one place to another or to project the body upward, as in jumping and hopping. These skills also include walking, running, skipping, leaping, and galloping.

2. *Nonlocomotor skills* Nonlocomotor skills are performed in-place without appreciable spatial movement. They include bending, stretching, pushing and pulling, raising and lowering, twisting and turning, shaking, bouncing, circling, and so on.

3. *Manipulative skills* Manipulative skills are developed through object handling. This manipulation of objects leads to hand–eye and foot–eye coordination, which are particularly important for tracking items in space. Manipulative skills form the important basis for many game skills and lifetime activities. Propulsion (throwing, striking, kicking), receipt (catching) of objects, rebounding or redirecting an object in flight (such as volleyball) are basic to this set of skills.

Movement Concepts Skills

Students need to learn about the classification of movement concepts, which include body awareness, space awareness, qualities of movement, and relationships. It is not enough to learn only the fundamental skills; students need to perform these skills in a variety of settings. For example, students are asked to run in different variations, in different directions, at different levels, and along different pathways. They can learn to move slowly or quickly or to make a series of strong movements. Movement themes form the foundation of movement experiences necessary for developing specific fundamental skills. Through this process, students develop an increased awareness and understanding of the body as a vehicle, for movement, and for the acquisition of a personal vocabulary of movement skills. These skills are usually taught in elementary and middle school

years. They are used in the secondary school years without instruction and practice; it is usually assumed they have been overlearned in the earlier grades.

Rhythmic Movement Skills

Individuals who excel in movement activities possess a strong sense of rhythmic ability. Rhythmic movement involves motion that possesses regularity and a predictable pattern. The aptitude to move rhythmically is basic to skill performance in all areas. A rhythmic program that includes aerobic dance, folk and square dancing, rope jumping, and rhythmic gymnastics offers a set of experiences that help attain this objective.

Specialized Motor Skills

Specialized skills are used in various sports, games, and other areas of physical education, including adventure activities, apparatus activities, tumbling, cooperative activities, swimming, dance, and so on. When developing specialized skills such as tennis strokes, racquetball serves, or softball fielding techniques, progression is attained through planned instruction and drills. These skills have critical points of technique, and proper teaching emphasizes correct performance. In most cases, these skills are not well-learned until the middle and high school years.

Health-Related Physical Fitness and Wellness

OBJECTIVE: *The physical education program will provide students an opportunity to participate in activities designed to develop and maintain health-related physical fitness commensurate with individual needs. Students will also develop an understanding of how to maintain adequate fitness and wellness throughout adulthood.*

Physical educators provide experiences for students that lead to successful encounters with exercise and regular physical activity. Proper development in this area implies a focus on regular physical activity that results in a fitness level that motivation and heredity allow. This emphasis leads to improved health-related physical fitness (Corbin, Pangrazi, and Welk, 1994). This includes cardiovascular efficiency, flexibility, body fat reduction, and muscular strength and endurance. Recent physical fitness test batteries focus on the development of criterion-related health standards associated with reduced health risk rather than skill-related fitness based on normative standards (Cooper Institute for Aerobic Research, 1992).

Students need to experience activities that demonstrate the benefits of physical fitness on a first-hand basis. Student participation in activity choices and the opportunity to offer input about the fitness program helps create a personalized program. Learning how to develop and arrange suitable fitness routines that positively impact health is an important higher order objective. Physical fitness development is similar to physical skill development in that it requires time, energy, and self-discipline. Students need to be aware of the factors that influence fitness development. Eating habits, types of activities, heredity, and frequency of activity are just a few of the factors that students must learn. Physical education programs play an important role in helping students develop activity habits that will benefit their physical health.

Allotting a portion of each class to fitness activities helps students understand what is necessary for fitness enhancement. Learning about fitness is much more than facts; students need the participation experience in order to make fitness activities a habit. Many people know the facts about fitness but are not participating in regular physical activity. This is not to say that knowledge is unimportant, but rather that regular physical activity in a person's lifestyle is a top priority for a physical education program. A positive experience in fitness activities can help students develop attitudes that ensure an active adult lifestyle. Programs are not successful if students leave school with a dislike for physical activity. Establishing a desire in students to maintain fitness and wellness throughout their adult years is an important outcome.

Human Performance Principles

OBJECTIVE: *Students will experience a broad variety of activities and develop an understanding of human performance principles. Students will develop an understanding of their strengths and limitations in the motor performance arena and know how to select activities that assure safety.*

A physical education program should provide students with a wide range of knowledge about many areas. A knowledge component is intertwined with all objectives. Indeed, accomplishing any objective is difficult if students do not have a certain amount of knowledge. For example, getting students to enjoy tennis without understanding the rules, strategies, and etiquette is difficult, and most people will not incorporate an aerobic activity into their lifestyle without understanding the possible health-related benefits.

As students increase their knowledge of physical activities, they should also increase their enjoyment and participation. This is unfortunately not always the case. Many people understand the rules, regulations, and benefits of physical activity and yet have not incorporated any activity into their lifestyles. This is why physical education programs must do more than just provide students with knowledge about physical activity. Students must experience success while participating in these activities.

The school years should be the years of opportunity—the opportunity to explore and experience many different types of physical activity. Students should be able to find physical activities that provide personal satisfaction and success. The curriculum should be expansive rather than restrictive. It should allow students to better understand their strengths and limitations and to establish the types of activities they prefer and dislike. Related to this experience is the opportunity to learn basic concepts of movement and physical activity. Students should leave school knowing about center of gravity, force, leverage, stability, and other factors related to efficient movement. Learning basic principles and concepts of physical activity especially with reference to how physical activity contributes to good health and wellness is important in this knowledge objective. Understanding the genetic diversity among people, such as body physiques, muscle fibers, cardiovascular-respiratory endurance, and motor coordination, is requisite for helping students evaluate their physical capabilities. Specifically learning how to assess personal fitness and activity levels, how to plan activity levels, and how to make informed decisions about physical activity and fitness are all important objectives in this domain.

The *Basic Stuff Series* developed by the National Association for Sport and Physical Education (NASPE, 1987) is an example of information related to human performance and physical activity. The series is designed for physical education teachers, and a booklet is available for each of the following areas: exercise physiology, humanities related to physical activity, kinesiology, motor development, motor learning, and psychosocial aspects of physical activity. The intent of the series is to promote the inclusion of these human performance principles in the physical education curriculum.

Related to understanding principles of human performance is knowing how to safely participate in activity. The school has both a legal and moral obligation to provide a safe environment. Safety must be actively taught, and activities must be conducted in a safe environment. Instructional procedures in activity must pay attention to safety factors, and active supervision is necessary to guide students in safe participation. Students must leave school with an understanding of safety principles of human movement.

Social Skills and Positive Self-Concept

OBJECTIVE: *The physical education environment will help students acquire desirable social-emotional standards and ethical concepts. In addition, physical education instruction will offer experiences that help students develop a positive self-concept.*

Physical activity environments provide a number of unique opportunities for students to experience and develop social-emotional skills. Getting along with other people, being part of a team, accepting an official's judgment, losing the final game of a tournament, dealing with peers who have varying levels of ability, or changing clothes in a crowded locker room are just a few of the many experiences that may occur in a physical education class. These are important experiences for students. Physical educators have a responsibility to help guide and direct students in understanding these various social-emotional behaviors.

All students need to understand and internalize the merits of participation, cooperation, competition, and tolerance. Good citizenship and fair play help define a desirable social atmosphere. A teacher who listens, shows empathy, and offers guidance can help students differentiate between acceptable and unacceptable ways of dealing with others and expressing feelings. Students need to develop an awareness of how they interact with others and how the quality of their behavior influences others responses to them. If students do not receive feedback about negative behavior from teachers and peers, they may not realize that the behavior is inappropriate. Establishing reasonable limits of appropriate student behavior followed by consistent enforcement of those limits will help students understand the parameters of acceptable behavior.

Cooperation precedes the development of competition and should be emphasized in the physical education environment. If people do not cooperate, they are unable to play competitive games. The nature of competitive games requires cooperation, fair play, and sportsmanship. When these are not present, the joy of participation is lost. Various cooperative activities can teach students that all participants are important and needed. As the nature of competition comes into clearer focus, teachers can help students temper the win-at-all-costs philosophy and to understand that all participants can not win.

Teachers help students develop positive attitudes toward learning by teaching an understanding of various student ability levels, the role of winning and losing, and making an effort to succeed. Positive and concerned instruction has a powerful impact on students' attitudes and self-concepts. A positive teacher communicates to students that they are loved, capable, and contributing individuals. Not only must teachers understand students, but students should understand themselves, because self-understanding has a powerful influence on human behavior. The self-concept that a student develops is vital to the learning process. If students believe they belong, that they are important people, and that their successes outweigh their failures, they are given momentum toward developing a desirable self-concept. Encouraging students to provide positive feedback to each other will help students feel positive about their efforts.

The ability to move with grace, confidence, and ease helps students perceive themselves in a positive manner. Achieving self-satisfying levels of skill competency and fitness can also make students feel confident and assured. The self-concept is related to perceived physical skill competence. If students perceive themselves to be competent in a physical activity setting, they will want to participate in physical activity outside of the school environment. On the other hand, if they feel incompetent, they will avoid activity at all cost in an attempt to maintain their self-esteem and avoid embarrassment.

Lifetime Participation in Activity

OBJECTIVE: *Through physical education, students will learn physical skills that allow them to participate in and enjoy physical activity now and throughout their adult years.*

An important objective of a secondary school physical education program is to help students incorporate physical activity into their lifestyles. This requires that curriculum, instruction, and teachers have a positive impact on student's knowledge, attitudes, and skill behaviors relative to physical activities. A successful physical education program is not measured by the current level of knowledge or the physical skills of students nor by the number of participants on the varsity athletic teams. Certainly it is not the number of victories that the football or basketball teams accumulate. The ultimate measure of success is the number of students who participate in physical activities such as exercise, sport, dance, and outdoor adventure activities throughout their lives.

The basic considerations for lifetime activity are several. Sallis (1994) classifies the factors that influence people to be active in four categories: psychological, social, physical-environmental, and biological. Physical education programs should foster those factors, which are often referred to as the determinants of active learning. Psychological determinants are among the most powerful. For example, students must derive enjoyment through activity so they will seek further participation. To this end, students must become proficient in a variety of motor skills. Also, most adults will not participate in activities unless they have an adequate level of perceived competence. Since learning new motor skills takes a great deal of time and repetition, adulthood often prohibits busy adults from developing a level of skill competence to assure play without embarrassment. Students also need a rationale basis for play. This can be established through activity orientations that can be transferred to other situations. Such activities should include a variety of games suitable for small groups and sport activities adapted to local situations.

Social influences include factors such as having family and peer role models, having encouragement from significant others, and having the opportunities to participate in activity with others in one's social group. Physical environmental factors include adequate programs and facilities, adequate equipment and supplies, safe outdoor environments, and available opportunities near home and at school. Included are adequate school opportunities in physical education, intramurals, and after-school recreation and sports programs. Biological factors include age, gender, ethnic, and socioeconomic status.

Without proper planning and systematic arrangement of the learning environment, the probability of developing positive student attitudes and physically active lifestyles is greatly reduced. Secondary curriculum plans and instructional strategies should be concerned with developing learning environments that help students enjoy physical activities for a lifetime.

PERSPECTIVES INFLUENCING PHYSICAL EDUCATION

Though physical education programs vary widely across the United States, most endorse similar goals and objectives. These goals and objectives are greatly influenced by current social and professional perspectives. Most curriculum models are based on a wide variety of goals and objectives emanating from a wide variety of models. Nevertheless, some programs orient their programs more closely to one perspective than another. Therefore, an understanding of these perspectives will help the reader better understand how curriculums reflect the social needs of a society.

The Social-Historical Perspective

Early physical education in the United States was dominated by European gymnastics and highly organized and disciplined calisthenics programs. Many of the early leaders were European immigrants, primarily from Germany and Sweden, who brought these formal programs with them and implemented them first in colleges and then in the public schools. These systems included formal and structured exercises centered on development of the body. Some have called this an "education of the physical" focus.

In the early 1900s, a major shift in perspective began to occur. As education in general altered its perspective based on the teachings of John Dewey and others, physical education shifted as well. Two of Dewey's cardinal aims of education stressed the promotion of health and a worthy use of leisure time. People became interested in using sports and games to foster these two aims. The school curriculum became a logical place to include these sports and games. Jesse F. Williams (1927), whose text was published in numerous editions, was one of several leaders who did much to change the perspective of American physical education at this time. Williams and others championed democratic ideals and the concepts of sportsmanship and teamwork. Thus, the strong focus on team sports in physical education was started. This focus is called an "education through the physical" approach. This perspective did not negate the importance of physical fitness and "education of the physical," but it did place a strong emphasis on social development through physical education. This perspective was perpetuated by followers of these early leaders and continues to have currency in the secondary physical education field.

The Cultural-Sports Perspective

Since the turn of the century, sports have become not only a diversion for millions of Americans who are participants, but for millions of American spectators (Eitzen and Sage, 1986). Youth sports are now highly organized and have large participant rates. Collegiate and professional sports have become big business. In 1972, Title IX of the Educational Amendments Act was enacted to provide greater access for girls and women in sports. With the shift from more formal gymnastics to more "American" activities such as football, basketball, and softball, sports became central to the programs of physical education. Since sports are part of the American culture, the development and appreciation of sports skills was logically accepted as a part of American education. This perspective accounts for the emphasis on sports in the expanded curriculum, which includes interscholastic and intramural programs.

The Public Health Perspective

A renewed emphasis on physical fitness occurred in the 1950s due to the publication of the Kraus-Weber tests comparing fitness levels of American and European students on strength and flexibility. The public became concerned about the comparable weakness of U.S. students. In response to this concern, President Dwight Eisenhower established the President's Council on Physical Fitness and Sport, an agency that promotes physical fitness not only for students but also for citizens of all ages. This was the beginning of a fitness boom that has continued to this day. In recent years, more and more evidence indicates that the lack of regular physical activity among adults is a primary risk factor for heart disease and a major contributor to other diseases as well. Data now exist to show that students who are active are more likely to be active later in life, and those who are active during school years have health benefits that extend to later life (Raitakari et al. 1994).

The document *Healthy People 2000: National Health Promotion and Disease Objectives* (U.S. Public Health Service, 1990) was released by the government as a strategy to improve the health of all Americans. Many of the target goals are directed toward improving the health status of American youth. Several of the objectives in the physical activity and fitness area emphasize increasing the amount of time students participate in light to moderate activity. Based on this evidence, several public health experts have called for the use of physical education as a public health tool (Sallis and McKenzie, 1991). They suggest that implementation of programs designed to promote lifetime physical activity in the schools will reap important public health benefits, including reduced morbidity and mortality from hypokinetic conditions such as heart disease, back pain, obesity, diabetes, high blood pressure, and cancer. The public health perspective has considerable impact on curriculum and instruction in physical education. This perspective gave impetus to the recommendation within *Healthy People 2000* that there be an increase in physical education in schools by the year 2000.

ISSUES AFFECTING PHYSICAL EDUCATION PROGRAMS

A number of trends and related issues impact the development of secondary school physical education programs. Some of the factors to be considered when developing a program are discussed in the following section.

State and Local Physical Education Requirements

Each state department of education sets requirements for physical education (NASPE, 1993). Policies differ dramatically from state to state. Some require a number of minutes per week for each grade level, whereas others specify a number of days per week. Several states do not have any physical education requirement. Each school district usually sets requirements designed to fit within the requirements defined by the state department of education. Consequently, district policies can vary dramatically and still be within state guidelines. As an example, in Arizona, there is no requirement at the state level for physical education, yet most Arizona high schools have at least a 1-year physical education requirement. Other Arizona schools have a 2- or 3-year requirement, whereas others offer only an elective physical education program. The state requirement will significantly affect the curriculum, the students, and the teachers.

Designing local requirements can often be a positive practice for physical education programs because it lends stability and credibility at the district level. For example, some districts are developing requirements that facilitate a selective/elective type of curriculum. This involves specifying requirements by activity category, such as team sports, lifetime sports, gymnastics, aquatics, recreational activities, and dance. For example, students might be required to complete 12 activities in 1 year. The requirement might be that 3 of the activities must be team sports, 3 must be lifetime sports, and 1 each must be selected from the areas of dance, aquatics, and gymnastics. The remaining activity choices would be left to the student. This procedure gives students choices within a requirement and ensures that students will receive a variety of activities as well as the opportunity to choose according to their interests. Students have choice but not total freedom, so a balanced curricular approach is assured.

Coeducational Classes

Title IX of the Educational Amendments Act of 1972 has had a significant impact on most secondary school physical education programs. The law is based on the principle that school activities and programs are of equal value for both sexes. Students should not be denied access to participation in school activities on the basis of gender. This law has stirred up much debate and controversy. Interpretations and details continue to be studied by school districts, state departments of education, and the judicial system.

Legal ramifications mandate equal access to physical education activities for both males and females (Figure 1.5). Separate classes for males and females have been reduced in most schools. This does not imply that both sexes must wrestle together, share locker facilities, or have the same activity inter-

ests. It does mean that males can participate in a dance class or females can elect a strength training class when they have interest in these respective areas. In principle, the law also means that instruction is provided by the most qualified person regardless of sex.

The law does allow schools to group students by ability, even if the result is groups consisting of primarily one sex. The law also allows teachers to segregate sexes during the game or competitive aspect of contact sports such as wrestling, basketball, football, ice hockey, and others. Teachers must also be sure that grading standards or procedures are not having an adverse effect on one sex, because this is a specified regulation of Title IX. Standards must be equally fair to both sexes.

Title IX has created some challenges for physical educators. Teachers have been forced to teach students of the opposite sex. Grading procedures, safety, locker room policies, and sexuality issues are a few of the areas that teachers have had to rethink with coeducational classes. For some, these changes have been interesting, exciting, and challenging, but for others the law has brought about negative feelings. For the latter, Title IX has been the cause of all that is wrong with today's physical education programs.

Amidst all of the controversy, it is important to examine the objectives of the physical education program and to focus on developing a situation that will meet the requirements of Title IX. There are new challenges, but this is a small price to pay for inequalities that have existed in terms of opportunities for learning and participating in sport and physical education. Law or no law, physical education is im-

FIGURE 1.5   Coed class

portant for all students regardless of gender. There are also clear advantages to coeducational programs in the areas of social development, activity offerings, and instructional quality. Teachers should be responsible for all students in their classes, regardless of ability, gender, or race.

Students with Disabilities

Public Law 94-142, the Education of All Handicapped Children Act, was signed in 1975 by President Ford. This law ensures that all youngsters with disabilities receive an appropriate public education that serves their unique needs. Physical education has been specified as an important part of the curricula or individualized education program (IEP) for students with disabilities. The IEP contains extensive information covering the student's present status, program objectives, learning activities, and evaluation procedures.

The law has compelled physical educators to develop specialized classes and programs for many students with disabilities. Other students are mainstreamed into the regular physical education program as part of the least restrictive environment advocated by P.L. 94-142. School districts are required to hire qualified instructors for these programs, as well as to encourage current teachers to develop skills for providing meaningful experiences for mainstreamed children with disabilities.

The law can create challenges for physical educators in planning, organizing, managing, and evaluating daily and yearly programs for students with disabilities. In most situations, the teacher must establish learning environments concurrently for students with and without disabilities. Regardless of the law, the issue is a moral necessity. Physical education is as important to students with disabilities as it is to the other students. All students deserve physical education experiences regardless of their ability or disability.

Interdisciplinary Courses

In some secondary schools, physical education is combined with other disciplines such as health, biology, geology, and geography. In these programs, students have opportunities to learn about subjects such as drugs, alcohol, diseases, safety, first aid, hunting and fishing, taxidermy, rock formations, and environmental concerns. Emphasis is placed on combining physical skill development with knowledge. For example, students can learn about the flora and fauna of an area while concurrently learning camping and backpacking skills. This is the basic thesis of many outdoor education programs in which several disciplines are integrated to teach students about the outdoors.

This approach also balances the acquisition of knowledge and physical skill development and offers interesting opportunities for students and teachers. Teachers can take advantage of geographical locations, different learning environments, and the interests of students living in these areas. The physical education teacher can team teach with teachers from other subject areas such as biology, zoology, or geography. In this way many interesting learning experiences can be developed. A downside of this approach is that the time available for physical skill development is usually reduced in favor of more knowledge time, thus reducing the opportunity to become competent in physical skills.

Independent Study Coursework

Independent study programs give students an opportunity to earn physical education credit for advanced study or off-campus courses that are not available in the basic curricula. Students might have the opportunity to earn credit for off-campus study involving surfing, ice skating, horseback riding, bowling, golf, and other disciplines. These programs are usually available to students only after they have completed basic requirements. Some type of monitoring and weekly check-in procedure is arranged, with the student, parent, and teacher agreeing to a contract. Many of these programs also contain a fitness component, and students must show some evidence of maintenance or improvement in the fitness area (for example, body composition or cardiovascular endurance).

Most independent study options require students to keep a log of their activity with an anecdotal record of skill work, games, scores, opponents, and evaluation procedures. Written work is usually required on rules, etiquette, current personalities, research areas, or officiating. If problems occur with students not completing their work, they are returned to the regular program or are dropped from the independent study program. Some schools have special independent study areas in the library or in a room close to the gymnasium where students can check out materials or view videotapes and loop films. The independent study program offers possibilities for advanced study and can add an exciting dimension to the curricula. Students often develop self-management skills and become self-motivated because they select activities that appeal to them and are primarily responsible for what they learn from the experience.

Instruction in Community Facilities

Another trend that can be positive for school programs is the use of community facilities. This approach allows schools to use community bowling alleys, golf courses, ski slopes, and skating rinks to enhance the physical education program. Many schools bus students to a bowling alley or golf course once a week. Sometimes schools provide transportation and participation funds; in other cases, students pay the expenses. Funding can also be provided through car washes, candy sales, and raffles. Programs and procedures are limited only by a teacher's ingenuity and creative direction.

Community facilities can add a valuable dimension to secondary programs. Physical educators can broaden their areas of competency or find other professionals who have requisite expertise. A noted physical educator once asked a physical education teacher who taught at a school situated near a beautiful lake, "Do you teach swimming, boating, and sailing here?" "No," replied the teacher, "we don't have the facilities." Finding a way to use community resources for the betterment of students is surely possible. Qualified personnel from the community often want to share their expertise.

Private Sports Instruction

Opportunities for sports and fitness instruction in the private sector continue to expand rapidly. These programs are responsive to the demands of consumers. Gymnastics clubs, soccer leagues, Pop Warner football, motocross bicycle racing, little league baseball, and racquet clubs are a few examples of programs that are available to students. Students receive in-depth instruction, practice with adequate equipment, have many competitive opportunities, and receive trophies, T-shirts, and similar rewards. Private instruction programs must meet the demands of consumers or lose their clientele. Often, such programs use quality equipment, the newest techniques, and instructors who are highly skilled and excellent teachers. Many of these instructional programs will

offer strong competition for physical education programs because of their ability to provide personalized instruction.

Private-sector instructional programs can create problems for school-based physical education programs. The first problem is that private instruction creates a wide range of backgrounds, experiences, and abilities among students who are participating in school physical education. Students from middle- and upper-class families may have a wealth of experience in sports such as tennis, golf, soccer, and gymnastics, whereas students from lower income families might not be able to finance private instruction. Another problem is that it can be difficult to develop a gymnastics unit that is meaningful to 8th grade students who have had 5 years of intensive training at a private sports academy. This same point can be illustrated by comparing students involved in a soccer league for several years with students who have never played the game. Teachers face a difficult challenge when trying to motivate students with such diverse backgrounds.

A second concern relates to public opinion. As opportunities in the private sector increase, public support for the school physical education curricula may lessen. Some people currently believe that secondary school physical education programs can be eliminated because there are adequate opportunities available in the private sector. "Let students learn physical activities outside the school setting so there is more time and money for academic subjects" is a viewpoint often voiced. An opposing viewpoint argues that private instruction opportunities are available only to the upper middle class and that lower socioeconomic groups will have limited opportunities. The trend toward private instruction is continuing to grow and the possibility is strong that the private sports industry may become a serious competitor of school programs. Physical educators face the challenge of developing quality programs that provide meaningful learning experiences for all students regardless of background.

Conceptual Physical Fitness Programs

A development that started at the college level and has slowly filtered down to the secondary school level is called the conceptual approach. An example of the conceptual approach is the *Fitness for Life* program by Corbin and Lindsey (1996). This approach has been called a lecture-laboratory method. Students spend time receiving information in a lecture situation and then try out or test the information on themselves or on peers in a laboratory setting. Emphasis is placed on information, appraisal procedures, and program planning. Students are expected to understand the "how, what, and why" of physical activity and exercise. They learn to use diagnostic tests in areas such as cardiovascular endurance, muscular strength and endurance, flexibility, body composition, and motor ability.

A variety of conceptual programs have been field-tested in various situations. In some schools, concepts make up the entire physical education program, while in others, the concepts may be only a portion of the requirement, such as a semester class or 6-week unit. Several books are available with lesson sequences and other instructional materials such as slide-tape lectures, scripts, review questions, tests, lesson masters, overhead transparencies, and laboratory experiments.

The conceptual approach is currently popular for several reasons. First, many believe that an academic approach focused on knowledge and cognitive growth instead of on physical skill is a more respectable educational endeavor. Others believe that when student knowledge is increased, attitudes and behaviors will also change, causing physical activity to be incorporated into the student's lifestyle. This is not a proven phenomenon. Increasing a person's knowledge does not ensure a change in behavior, and students must also experience and attempt physical activity and fitness as well as understand conceptually. Conceptual learning is an important part of a physical education program, but physical skill development must also receive strong emphasis.

Fitness versus Skill Development

As noted previously, two major outcomes for the physically educated person are physical skill and fitness development. A debate over program emphasis has continued for years, with some saying that physical education's principle concern should be skill development and others suggesting that physical fitness development is the most important concern. Central to the problem is available time. Because minimal time is available for physical education instruction and because physical education has such ambitious objectives, competition for time is of great concern.

Much of the skill-fitness debate might be reduced if more time were available for teaching physical education because most physical educators ac-

knowledge the importance of both outcomes. They merely differ on emphasis. It is now clear that even with additional time, physical education programs cannot make every student skillful in every sport nor can they provide enough activity to guarantee fitness for every student. For this reason, many physical educators favor an emphasis on skill development in the early school years followed by allowing personal choice of skills to be learned in the later grades. They also acknowledge the importance of taking time to teach students about fitness and active lifestyles throughout the physical education program.

Equipment, Facilities, and Class Size

A continuing problem that physical educators at all levels face is inadequate equipment and facilities. For some reason, many administrators believe that physical education classes can be larger in number and yet manage with less equipment than an academic class. They fail to realize that it is impossible to learn to dribble a basketball without having access to a basketball on a regular basis. Students become frustrated and bored when standing in line waiting for a turn to dribble the ball. Teachers have a frustrating situation when 40 students are scheduled to play on 6 tennis courts. Economic conditions make these problems difficult, and physical educators must strive to get a fair share of the budget. Students are not asked to learn to read and write without books, paper, and pencils. Physical education is as important as other discipline areas and should receive an equal share of the budget dollar.

Legal Liability

Many lawsuits appearing in various aspects of society are of concern to physical educators. Teachers are not immune to liability lawsuits as evidenced by an increasing number of cases of parents and students suing teachers, administrators, and school boards. This situation is unnerving when teachers attempt new activities or use new teaching techniques that involve any type of risk. Many teachers and administrators have become extremely cautious and conservative about activities that contain an element of risk, yet often many of these activities are actually safer than those traditionally included in the curriculum. Teachers may refuse to offer new activities for fear of a lawsuit. Ultimately, students become the victims in this process because programs become limited in scope.

Teachers certainly need to acquire adequate knowledge about safety and instructional procedures before implementing a new activity. Legal ramifications must be understood when developing a broad and balanced curriculum. With proper information and careful planning, the instructional risks of various activities can be minimized. If sound policies and procedures are followed on a daily basis, teachers should not worry about legal liability. An in-depth discussion of legal liability can be found in Chapter 12.

Teaching and Coaching Conflicts

The public often has a difficult time separating the physical education program from the athletic program. The athletic program is concerned with recruiting, coaching, and administering teams that will compete against other school teams. These goals are significantly different from the goals of the secondary school physical education program, yet athletics and physical education are often linked because the programs share facilities, equipment, fields, and teachers. In addition, pressure often comes from the local community to produce winning teams. Pressure to develop outstanding physical education programs is not nearly as strong, and the visibility of the two programs is markedly different. This creates a difficult situation for the teacher-coach. The coach may support the concept of an outstanding curriculum, but may not find enough time and energy to do both causing physical education to take a back seat. This problem has no simple solution. Many teachers want to work in both programs. The pressure to produce winners is apparent, and the individual instructor will determine the quality of the physical education program that is implemented. Many people do excellent work in both areas, but it is not an easy task.

CHARACTERISTICS OF SUCCESSFUL PHYSICAL EDUCATION PROGRAMS

There are many ways to design and implement a quality physical education program. As discussed earlier a number of factors can impact physical education programs. A wide spectrum of objectives make accomplishment of a successful physical education program a difficult challenge for physical educators.

However, the best way to reach this goal is to simply develop a sound program and teach it effectively. The following are characteristics that seem to be found in successful programs regardless of the model or design of the curriculum.

A Positive Learning Environment Exists

The instructor is the most important factor in the learning environment. Regardless of the teaching method or curriculum design, a perceptive, analytical teacher is paramount to student learning. An effective teacher creates a teaching-learning atmosphere that is both positive and caring. Instructional procedures are planned carefully so students experience immediate success. The instructor's reactions to student failure are kept minimal and momentary. Instruction focuses feedback and reactions on positive student behaviors rather than using a "correction complex" that responds only to students' mistakes. Effective teachers realize they must take an active role in the teaching-learning process by demonstrating, participating, encouraging, giving feedback, and hustling. Students are influenced significantly by someone who has incorporated physical activities into his or her lifestyle.

Competent teachers use positive methods to discipline, teach, and motivate. Students are taught to enjoy physical education instead of learning to avoid the environment. Running and exercise are not used as a form of punishment. Students are rewarded for competitive efforts even if their team happens to lose on a given day. Teachers use students' first names and interact with all students on a daily basis. Students are offered a degree of choice and freedom in the learning process in an effort to increase student motivation.

Research on teaching continues to provide information about ways effective teachers impact the teaching-learning process (Siedentop, 1991). Modeling behavior is an effective strategy for influencing specific types of student behavior. Guidelines concerning how to model have long been available. Students want to see models of persons who have incorporated physical activity in their lifestyles. Teachers can discuss their exercise habits with students and allow students to see them participating in and enjoying physical activity. Influential teachers are aware of the powerful effect their behavior has on students and use modeling to help students develop healthy activity habits.

Enthusiasm is another behavior that promotes a positive environment. Evidence shows that this difficult-to-define behavior is a teaching skill associated with student learning. Teachers need to display their love of and excitement for physical activity and their joy in teaching. Expecting students to perform well is another critical factor in developing a positive atmosphere for teaching. If students are expected to be unmotivated and troublesome, then the possibility is strong that these behaviors will occur. If students are expected to learn and work hard, then the chance is better that they will. Evidence shows that teachers' expectations for students will come to fruition.

Physical educators need to look carefully at the effects of policies and procedures used in programs. If procedures discourage students to be active, they should be reevaluated. If dress codes and grading procedures are causing students to develop avoidance behaviors, acceptable alternatives must be developed. The overall atmosphere of the physical education environment has a strong impact on students and on their attitude toward physical activity. When students leave the physical education environment, they should have a good feeling about physical activity and a desire to return for more.

Student Choice Is Offered

The elective approach to physical education curricula refers to allowing student choice for an optional or elective year of physical education or to allow students to select between several activity options during each activity interval. For example, students can select either tennis, weight training, or soccer during the first 3-week unit, and either racquetball, archery, or flag football during the second 3 weeks and so on. The choice can occur not only during the optional class but also during a required class. The choice process starts in some schools as early as the middle school, while in others it does not begin until high school. This type of program gives students an opportunity to choose activities of personal interest to them, and to avoid activities in which they have little interest. Surveys have shown that some students would not elect an extra class of physical education because they wanted to avoid one or two specific units of activity such as swimming, gymnastics, or wrestling. Students would sacrifice an entire year of physical education to avoid certain activities. To circumvent this behavior, curriculum planners design elective programs in which students can choose from a number of activities.

Another advantage of the elective approach is that students will be more motivated when they have influenced the selection of learning activities. Fewer problems occur in the areas of participation and discipline. More students involved in the program can also mean more support for teachers, equipment, and facilities. Flexibility in class size is yet another advantage. Certain activities can easily accommodate more students, depending on the equipment and facilities. For example, golf and tennis might have smaller classes than soccer and flag football.

Finally, considering the above advantages, many teachers are motivated and enthusiastic about teaching in this type of program. An elective program can improve the motivational level of both students and teachers. Any educational practice that can affect the teaching-learning environment should be considered when developing programs in secondary school physical education. Problems do have to be worked out concerning grades, registration procedures, teaching attitudes, and class roll procedures. There are, however, several solutions available to a teaching staff that believes in the advantages of the approach.

Elective programs can be an influence in a positive direction. A number of secondary school physical education programs that have converted to elective programs have experienced an increase in students. Teachers point out that an elective program offers advantages such as increased student participation, enthusiasm, and motivation, as well as increased enthusiasm and motivation of teachers. Students in the 10th grade and above should be able to select all of their physical activities and not be forced into activities that they are not interested in learning or dislike. Students in middle school might be restricted to choosing from categories of activities such as team sports, lifetime sports, fitness activities, dance, aquatics, and adventure activities. This would ensure a measure of breadth in activity experiences. If possible, they should be permitted to choose from a number of activities in each category. In the fitness area, for example, they might choose aerobic dance, weight training, or jogging. In the lifetime sport area, the choices might be tennis, golf, or bowling.

A Wide Variety of Activities Are Available

The variety of physical activities available to consumers has expanded in recent years. New and exciting activities such as Frisbee, aerobics, yoga, and rock climbing are included in programs across the country. A broad-based program increases the possibility that all students will find an enjoyable physical activity. Physical education programs should offer as many activities as possible. A balance among team sports, individual sports, dance, aquatics, outdoor activities, and physical conditioning activities should be a major program goal. The following categories illustrate the wide range of activities that can be incorporated into an exemplary program.

Lifetime Sports

In the past 25 years, the most significant change in secondary school physical education offerings has been the inclusion of the "lifetime" or "carryover" sports. These sports are primarily individual or dual activities that can be used for a lifetime as opposed to team sports that are difficult to continue after the school years. A major factor in the development of the lifetime sports concept was the Lifetime Sports Education Project (LSEP) sponsored by the American Alliance for Health, Physical Education, Recreation, and Dance (AAHPERD). The LSEP originally focused on bowling, archery, badminton, tennis, and golf. Instructional materials and teaching clinics were developed by the LSEP to encourage physical educators to expand their curriculum.

Lifetime sports have become tremendously popular and have been expanded to include a host of new activities such as Frisbee, racquetball, and squash. The AAHPERD estimates that 75% of the nation's secondary schools emphasize lifetime sports in their physical education programs. This expanded offering has provided many participation opportunities for students and adults who are not interested in traditional team sports. Secondary school physical education programs are better able to serve all students when a wide variety of lifetime sports are offered, since different students are successful with different activities.

Outdoor Adventure Activities

Another category of activity gaining popularity in the past 15 years are the outdoor adventure or wilderness sports. Backpacking, rock climbing, orienteering, and bicycling are just a few of the activities in this category. These activities are similar to the lifetime sports and are primarily individual or dual activities that can be enjoyed over a lifetime. The emphasis is on risk and excitement in using the earth's

natural environments such as snow, water, mountains, ice, rivers, and wilderness areas. Exploration, travel, and adventure are important elements in these activities. To train students in outdoor adventure skills, many schools are developing on-campus facilities such as climbing walls, rope courses, and orienteering sites, as well as using nearby community environments such as ski slopes, parks, rivers, and mountains. These activities emphasize competition with oneself and the environment in contrast to competition with other people. This is an attractive feature for many students. Outdoor adventure activities can also be enjoyed with family and friends during expanded leisure hours. They give people an opportunity to get away from the city and experience the natural environment in a time of vanishing wilderness areas.

Health-Related Physical Fitness Activities

A combination of the running craze, the wellness movement, and the fitness renaissance that has emerged across the nation is rekindling interest in physical fitness types of activities. Aerobic rhythmic exercise, Jazzersize, step aerobics, body sculpting, jogging, weight training (Figure 1.6), and weight-control classes are extremely popular with secondary students and adults. Fitness centers are being built in high schools and shared with community partners after school hours. Schools are offering a variety of classes called step aerobics, shipshape class, systematic conditioning, and aerobics, which emphasize such topics as nutrition, obesity, coronary heart disease, flexibility, and strength. The Cooper Institute for Aerobic Research and AAHPERD have developed a new health-related fitness program (1995) that focuses on increasing activity in everyday activities. The program places emphasis on increasing the amount of daily and moderate activity.

Eastern-Influenced Activities

Eastern philosophy has had some influence on secondary school programs. Various forms of the martial arts, including judo, karate, aikido, kendo, and tae kwan do, are popular at the college and university level and are slowly filtering into the secondary school curricula. Yoga, transcendental meditation, relaxation techniques, and self-defense classes are common in many high school and junior high school programs.

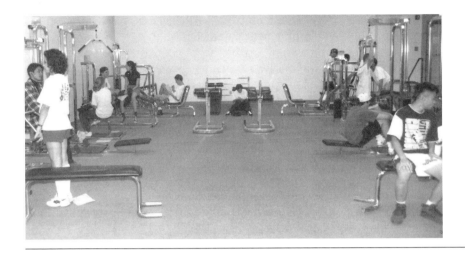

FIGURE 1.6   Weight-lifting class

New Team Sports

Finally, the development of new or modified team sports is continuing in many schools. Activities such as team handball, global ball, speed-a-way, broomball, flickerball, angleball, modified lacrosse, and pillow polo are a few of the newer team sports that are popular in various areas of the country. Some of these are new activities, whereas others are modifications of existing sports. They add another positive dimension to programs because of the increased variety and opportunities for success with certain types of students.

New team sport activities provide many interesting and exciting challenges for both students and instructors. In teaching almost any activity, there may be problems with safety, liability, competent instruction, equipment, and teacher's comfort zones, but the advantages of offering new team sports are well worth the problems encountered. A wide variety of activities should enhance the objective of developing in all students a positive attitude toward a lifetime of physical activity.

Students Receive In-Depth Instruction

Some high schools offer different levels of instruction such as beginning and intermediate classes. Some schools use the classifications of beginning, team, and recreational. Three-week units are being offered for beginning basketball, team basketball, and recreational basketball. The beginning class covers dribbling, passing, pivoting, rebounding, and so forth, while the team class includes such areas as offensive strategy, zone defenses, and techniques on beating a half court trap. The final recreational class allows opportunity for team play and tournaments. Students can take 3 units in a progressive, systematic procedure. An advantage of this approach is that teachers can do a better job of instruction because classes are more homogeneous in motivation and ability. Students usually feel more comfortable in a group in which similar attitudes and abilities prevail.

In grades 10 to 12, programs should offer intermediate and advanced levels of instruction. Students at these developmental levels choose one or two activities in which they want to excel. Advanced instruction is different from a free-play recreational situation that is commonly found in many programs. Depth refers to organized instruction rather than simply increasing the amount of participation time. Physical educators must move away from the notion that physical education programs should focus only on beginning levels. Many students do not participate in intramurals, sport clubs, athletics, or outside-school programs, and therefore the physical education program may be the only opportunity to receive in-depth instruction for students. A high level of skill development usually increases a person's tendency to repeat and enjoy activity.

The length of activity units has shortened over the past decade, especially at the middle school level. In quality programs, 6- to 9-week units are becoming obsolete. In many middle school programs, 2- to 3-week units are the norm. These shorter units enable physical educators to expand the breadth of their programs and to give students an introduction to a wider variety of activities. Some people question this trend because of the reduction in depth of instruction, but students can choose to develop depth in an activity in the high school years. Short units also reduce boredom and frustration, which are common problems among middle school students. With increased program breadth, educators have a better opportunity to provide students with some type of physical activity that they can currently enjoy and continue to use.

Depth in an activity is made available in high school curricula by allowing students to choose a semester-long unit. This specialized approach is part of an elective or optional program instead of a required program. Semester-long classes give students a chance to gain in-depth skill in an activity of their choice after they complete the required program. Many schools are offering semester or year-long units focusing on popular activities such as dance, gymnastics, tennis, and physical conditioning. The middle school program provides breadth of activity, while the high school program gives students the opportunity to develop a high level of skill competency.

Diagnostic and Counseling Practices Are Evident

Students in middle school need guidance and counseling to direct them toward activities that match their interests and physical abilities. Teachers can help students understand their physical strengths and shortcomings and the possibilities for alleviating problems. This means data collection and the procedures for interpreting the data to students and parents. Obese students, for example, might be channeled into activities in which they can find success and feel competent. Students with strong upper bodies might be encouraged to try gymnastic activities. Activity counseling can help students make wise decisions about activities that are well-suited to their abilities.

High school students also need to learn about the benefits of physical activity and the types of activities available. They can use counseling in several other areas such as behavioral self-modification techniques to aid them in the change and maintenance of fitness habits. Students should understand environmental factors and obstacles that work against

their attempts to participate in physical activities. Employment parameters, marriage, children, and climate are factors that affect activity lifestyles. Learning to keep records, set goals, and establish reinforcement procedures can help students with their activity habits. Another important area of activity counseling deals with changing interests and activities of people as they grow older. Many adults have been conditioned to think that physical activity is only for the young. This attitude needs to be changed in light of the revelation that numerous benefits are derived from being active at all age levels. Fitness and play activities are important regardless of age.

Some secondary schools have designed a series of compulsory units that require students to assess their physical abilities and make decisions about physical activities that offer them success and remediate weaknesses. A counseling program helps channel students into physical education activities that can enhance their strengths and alleviate weaknesses. The testing and counseling procedures should be set up in a systematic, organized fashion. A physical education advisor should be assigned to each student to guide her or him through the process in an attempt to give students information on which they can base sound decisions about their future. Counseling students combined with the previously described elective program is an effective way to fuse students' interests with their physical ability requirements. This model provides a blend of information about physical activity and gives students experiences in improving physical skills and physical fitness. Students should leave the program with approach tendencies for physical activity instead of avoidance behaviors.

All Activity Programs Are Integrated

Activity programs such as sport clubs, intramurals, and interscholastic athletics can effectively help students improve their skills and become more proficient. Such programs also provide opportunities for young people to meet others with similar interests. A variety of important qualities can be experienced through these programs (for example, teamwork, dedication, perseverance, deferred rewards, and loyalty). These qualities should be nurtured in today's youth.

Outside school activity programs include youth sport, YMCA, parks and recreation, and private sport programs. When possible, physical educators should contribute to the leadership aspects of programs that augment physical education. Strong leadership ensures the quality of these programs and guards against possible abuses. Unqualified leaders with inappropriate program goals can lead to a discouraging experience for young, immature students. Programs must be developed with the idea of fostering a love of physical activity in students (rather than promoting escape or avoidance behaviors). Physical educators should help parents, other teachers, and adults organize these programs with the proper goals in mind.

EXPECTED OUTCOMES

After reading this chapter, you should be able to

- Describe why people have misconceptions about physical education.
- Define physical education.
- Describe the goals of physical education.
- Defend physical education as a legitimate educational concern.
- Suggest specific strategies for accomplishing the goals of physical education.
- Describe various trends in physical education.
- Describe the ways that activities are arranged and packaged within the physical education curriculum.
- Point out several advantages and disadvantages to conceptual approaches, interdisciplinary courses, and independent study options.
- Cite reasons for different school districts having varying requirements for physical education.
- Explain several strategies for dealing with challenges in the secondary school that affect physical education.
- Describe the characteristics of successful physical education programs.

REFERENCES AND SUGGESTED READINGS

AAHPERD. 1988. *Physical Best*. Reston, VA: AAHPERD.

AAHPERD and Cooper Institute for Aerobics Research. 1995. *The You Stay Active Handbook*. Reston, VA: American Alliance for Health, Physical Education, Recreation, and Dance; and Dallas Cooper Institute for Aerobics Research.

Cooper Institute for Aerobics Research. 1992. *Fitness Test Administration Manual*. Dallas: Cooper Institute for Aerobics Research.

Corbin, C., and Lindsey, R. 1996. *Fitness for Life*. 4th ed. Glenview, IL: Scott, Foresman & Co.

Corbin, C. B., Pangrazi, R. P., and Welk, G. 1994. Toward an understanding of appropriate physical activity levels for youth. *Physical Activity and Fitness Research Digest* 2(2): 1–8.

Darst, P., and Armstrong, G. 1991. *Outdoor Adventure Activities for School and Recreation Programs*. Prospect Heights, IL: Waveland Press.

Eitzen, D. S., and Sage, G. 1986. *Sociology of North American Sport*. Dubuque, IA: Wm. C. Brown.

NASPE. 1987. *Basic Stuff Series*. Reston, VA: AAHPERD

NASPE. 1992. *Outcomes of Quality PE Programs*. Reston, VA: AAHPERD

NASPE. 1993. *Shape of the Nation 1993: A Survey of State Physical Education Requirements*. Reston, VA: AAHPERD.

Pangrazi, R. P., and Dauer, V. P. 1995. *Dynamic Physical Education for Elementary School Children*. 11th ed. Boston: Allyn and Bacon.

Raitakari, O. T., Porkka, K. V. K., Taimela, S., Telams, R., Rasanen, L., and Viikari, J. S. A. 1994. Effects of persistent physical activity and inactivity on coronary risk factors in children and young adults. *American Journal of Epidemiology* 140(3): 195–205.

Rink, J. 1993. What's So Critical? In J. E. Rink (ed.). *Critical Crossroads: Middle and Secondary Physical Education*. Reston, VA: NASPE. 1–6.

Sallis, J. F. 1994. Influences on physical activity of children, adolescents, and adults or determinants of active learning. *Physical Activity and Fitness Research Digest* 1(7): 1–8.

Sallis, J. F., and McKenzie, T. L. 1991. Physical education's role in public health. *Research Quarterly for Exercise and Sport* 62: 124–137.

Siedentop, D. 1991. *Developing Teaching Skills in Physical Education*. 3rd ed. Palo Alto, CA: Mayfield Publishing Co.

U.S. Public Health Service. 1990. *Healthy People 2000: National Health Promotion and Disease Objectives*. Washington, D.C.: U.S. Government Printing Office.

Williams, J. F. 1927. *The Principles of Physical Education*. Philadelphia: W.B. Saunders.

2 The Impact of Physical Activity on Adolescents

PURPOSE

To offer an overview of the impact of physical activity on the growing adolescent. The chapter also looks at important research and cites empirical evidence supporting the value of an active lifestyle in promoting optimum growth and development in secondary school students.

KEY CONCEPTS

- Growth patterns of students are controlled by genetic makeup at birth.
- A student's body type can affect the quality of motor performance.
- Students mature physically at different ages and speeds.
- Physical education programs should be developed for all levels of physical maturity not just early maturing students.
- Physical activity levels of students can impact body composition, skeletal structure, and aerobic power.
- Obese students seldom perform motor skills to the same degree as normal weight students.
- The school environment is not providing enough time and organized activity to develop an adequate level of fitness in students.
- Physical education programs should be developed for all skill levels of students not just the gifted athletes.
- Physical education programs should be defended based on motor skill development and the understanding and maintenance of physical fitness.
- Students who are physically active at an early age are usually active adults.

Adolescence is a time of rapid growth and development. **Adolescence** is defined here as occurring somewhere between the ages of 8 and 19 for females and 10 to 22 years for males (Malina, 1986). There is much variation in the actual onset of adolescence and entry into adulthood. However, it is during that period of time when the body matures physically and sexually.

THE GROWING ADOLESCENT

Growth patterns are generally controlled by genetic makeup at birth. Although unhealthy parents or poor dietary practices can have a negative impact on proper growth and development, the focus in this section is on normal maturation common to the majority of youngsters. Youngsters follow a general growth pattern; however, each individual's timing is unique. Some students will be advanced physically for their chronological age, whereas others will be identified as slow maturers. Only when aberration from the norm is excessive should teachers and parents become concerned.

Growth Patterns

Teachers and parents have an interest in the growth patterns of youngsters. When heights and weights are plotted on a graph from year to year, a distance curve can be developed. These curves (Figure 2.1) give an indication of how tall and heavy young people are during a specific year of life. Another method of examining growth patterns is to look at a growth velocity curve. The velocity curve is quite useful because it reveals how much a youngster grows on a year-to-year basis (Figure 2.2). Children go through a rapid period of growth from birth to age 5. From age 6 to the onset of adolescence, growth becomes slow but steady. During adolescence, rapid growth occurs again until adulthood is reached. Females reach the adolescent growth spurt first, and grow taller and heavier during the 6th and 7th grade years. Males quickly catch up, however, and grow larger and stronger. Growth charts based on a larger and more recent sample of youngsters have been de-

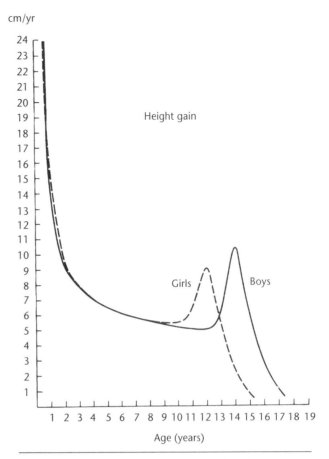

FIGURE 2.2 Growth velocity curve for height

From J. M. Tanner, R. H. Whitehouse, and M. Takaishi. 1966. *Archives of Diseases in Childhood* 41: 467.

veloped by the National Center for Health Statistics (Figures 2.3 and 2.4). These charts can be consulted to identify both height and weight percentiles for youngsters aged 2 to 18. They help teachers verify any marked differences among teenagers from a so-called normal population.

Body Physique

A student's physique can affect motor performance. Sheldon, Dupertuis, and McDermott (1954) developed the original scheme for identifying physiques based on the contribution of different components to the body as a whole. The components are termed **endomorphy**, **mesomorphy**, and **ectomorphy**. Each component is assessed individually from standardized photographs. Rating is done on a 7-point

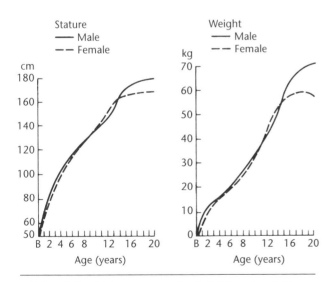

FIGURE 2.1 Distance curves for height and weight

From R. Malina. 1975. *Growth and Development: The First Twenty Years in Man.* Minneapolis, MN: Burgess. p. 19.

scale with 1 being the least expression and 7 the most expression of the specific component. The ratings of each component give a total score that results in identification of an individual's somatotype.

In general, youngsters who possess a mesomorphic body type perform best in motor activities requiring strength, speed, and agility. The mesomorph is characterized by a predominance of muscle and

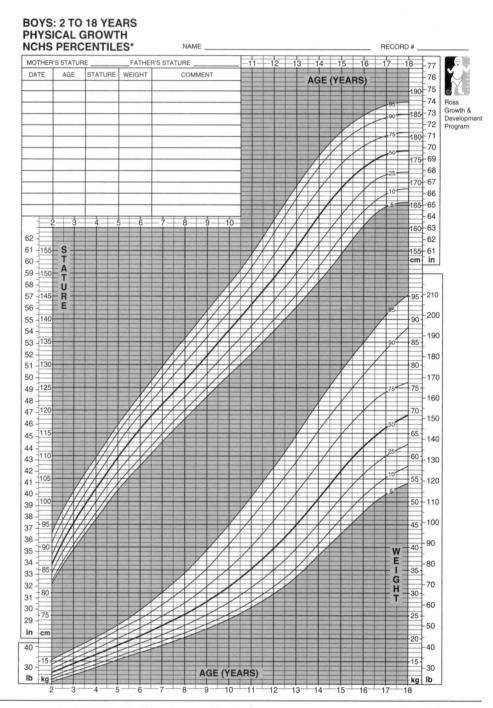

FIGURE 2.3 Physical growth percentiles for boys 2 to 18 years

From P. V. V. Hamill, T. A. Drizd, C. L. Johnson, R. B. Reed, A. F. Roche, and W. M. Moore. 1979. Physical growth: National Center for Health Statistics percentiles. *American Journal of Clinical Nutrition*, 32: 607–629. Data from the Fels Research Institute, Wright State University School of Medicine, Yellow Springs, OH. Used with permission of Ross Laboratories, Columbus, OH.

bone and is often labeled "muscled." These students usually perform well in team sports because these activities require strength, speed, and agility. The ectomorph is identified as being extremely thin, with a minimum of muscle development, and is characterized as "skinny." These students may perform poorly in activities requiring strength and power but do well in aerobic endurance activities such as jogging, cross-

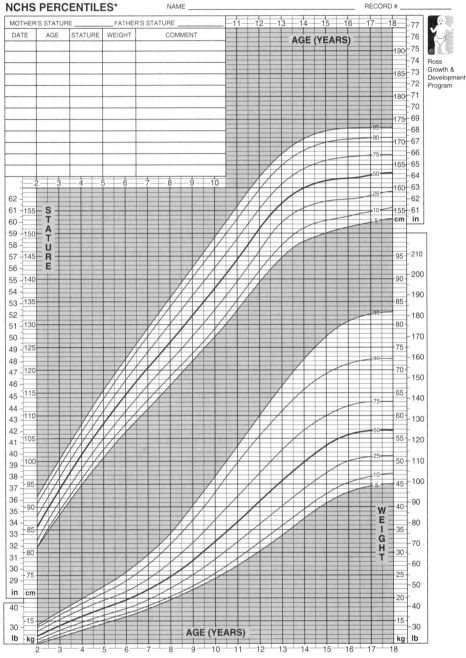

FIGURE 2.4 Physical growth percentiles for girls 2 to 18 years

From P. V. V. Hamill, T. A. Drizd, C. L. Johnson, R. B. Reed, A. F. Roche, and W. M. Moore. 1979. Physical growth: National Center for Health Statistics percentiles. *American Journal of Clinical Nutrition*, 32: 607–629. Data from the Fels Research Institute, Wright State University School of Medicine, Yellow Springs, OH. Used with permission of Ross Laboratories, Columbus, OH.

country running, and track and field. The third classification is the endomorph, who is soft and round, with an excessively protruding abdomen. These youngsters are usually regarded as obese and often perform poorly in many areas, including aerobic and anaerobic skill-oriented activities. The obese student is generally at a disadvantage in all phases of the physical education program.

Physique Changes Caused by Growth

During adolescence, growth in weight and height accelerates rapidly. Males grow faster than females and for a longer period of time. Most females reach peak growth velocity around the age of 11, whereas males do not peak until 13 years of age. It is common to see females grow larger than males in early adolescence; however, males will catch up and surpass them. In addition, males broaden at the shoulders relative to their hips, whereas females broaden at the hips relative to the shoulders. The key difference in growth patterns between the maturing sexes lies in the area of body somatotype. There are more endomorphic body types among females than males. Among males, the mesomorphic body type becomes much more common. Males become stronger and increase the amount of muscle tissue, whereas females increase the percentage of body fat. This change in body physique impacts the athletic performances of both sexes. Somatotyping can help teachers understand how a student's physique directly affects motor performance. It also shows that youngsters are dramatically different, necessitating that instruction accommodate individual differences.

Physical Maturity

The concept of maturity is used often by teachers in physical education. Usually, students are identified as being early, late, or average maturers, with teachers referring to social maturity rather than the physical maturity of the youngster. Physical maturity, however, has a strong impact on a student's performance in physical education. The most commonly used method to identify the degree of maturity is to compare chronological age with skeletal age. Ossification (hardening) of the bones occurs in the center of the bone shaft and at the ends of the long bones (growth plates). The rate of ossification gives an accurate indication of a youngster's degree of maturation.

Physical maturation or skeletal age (which can be identified by X-raying the wrist bones and comparing the development of the subject's bones with a set of standardized X-rays) gives a truer sense of the student's physical maturity (Gruelich and Pyle, 1959; Roche, Chumlea, and Thissen, 1988). If chronological age is greater than skeletal age, the youngster is said to be a **late** (or **slow**) **maturer**. On the other hand, if skeletal age is advanced beyond chronological age, the student is labeled an **early** (or **fast**) **maturer**.

Early-maturing students of both sexes are generally heavier and taller for their age than average- or late-maturing students. Obese youngsters (endomorphs) are often more mature for their age than are normal-weight youngsters. Early-maturing youngsters also have larger amounts of muscle and bone tissue due to their larger body size. However, the early maturer also carries a greater percentage of body weight as fat tissue (Malina, 1980). Late-maturing youngsters usually catch up to early maturers in height but not in weight. In addition, an early-maturing student in elementary school will also be an early maturer in secondary school. Generally, early-maturing males have mesomorphic physiques, and early-maturing females are characterized by endomorphy. These differences in body size and composition probably account for male–female performance differences in activities that require strength and power.

The motor performance of males is related to skeletal maturity, and more mature youngsters usually perform better on motor tasks (Clarke, 1971). For females, however, motor performance appears not to be related to physiological maturity. In fact, a study by Malina (1978) found that in females, late maturation is commonly associated with exceptional motor performance. Because many sports require size and strength, for males it is likely that early maturers have a strong advantage in athletic endeavors. This points out the need to design a physical education curriculum that will meet the needs of both early and late maturers. Units of instruction that emphasize activities relying less on strength and size and more on aerobic capacity, agility, balance, and coordination need to be included. Programs often place importance on learning at the same rate or participating in activities with other students regardless of skill level, even though this practice may be detrimental to the development of students who are developing at a faster or slower rate. Teachers sometimes expect all youngsters to be capable of performing the same activity at the same time, regardless of maturation. Unfortunately, students do not mature at the same rate and are therefore not at similar levels of readiness to learn. If physical education is for all students, the curriculum needs to offer successful experiences for less mature youngsters.

PHYSICAL ACTIVITY AND GROWTH

It appears that activity has no impact on the stature of maturing students (Malina, 1986). On the other hand, regular training does not have a negative effect on growth and development. Some people have theorized that strenuous physical activity disrupts normal developmental patterns, but there is no evidence to support such concerns.

Involvement in activity impacts the body composition of participants. The long-term effect of such activity is not known, however, and it is quite possible that once students quit participating they may return to a body type similar to nonexercisers. A number of studies with teenagers show that short-term training has a strong impact on muscular development (Rowland, 1990). Strength training causes muscular hypertrophy in teenagers in a manner similar to adults. However, if the activity is not continued, lean body mass decreases, and fat levels slowly increase.

Activity affects skeletal growth. Vigorous activity can improve internal bone structure so that bones are much more resistant to pressure, tension, and ultimately, to breakage. The bones increase in diameter and density in response to activity. Inactivity for prolonged periods causes demineralization and makes the bones more prone to fracture. This increased bone density developed during adolescence can help guard against osteoporosis in adult life (Haymes, 1986).

Vigorous activity appears to cause the bones to grow to a shape that is mechanically advantageous for muscle attachments (Rarick, 1973). The skeletal system is not totally rigid and responds to stress by changing its posture. This mechanical advantage may allow participants to perform physical challenges at a higher level in later years when sport activities are more meaningful. This phenomenon may explain why a small person can throw a baseball as fast as a larger person with longer arms (levers). A better mechanical advantage allows the smaller person (with shorter levers) to generate an increased force.

Even though activity enhances skeletal density, it does not appear to affect the rate of skeletal maturity. Youngsters who are most mature at an early age will be most mature when evaluated later in adolescence. Exercise assures optimum growth of bones in maturing youngsters. Care must be taken to assure that injury to the growth plates of the bones does not occur due to excessive pressure. Strength development should be administered in a progressive and reasonable manner.

Aerobic Capacity

Maximal aerobic power is an individual's maximum ability to use oxygen in the body for metabolic purposes. The oxygen uptake of an individual, all other factors being equal, determines the quality of endurance-oriented performance. Aerobic power increases with chronological age during the elementary school years in males and females at a similar rate, even though males exhibit higher levels as early as the age of 5 (Bar-Or, 1983). At the age of 12, oxygen uptake continues to increase in males and stops improving in females after the age of 14. Since maximal aerobic power is closely related to lean body mass, this tapering off in aerobic power among older females is explained by an increase in reproductive body fat. When aerobic power is related to muscle mass, and adjustments are made for body fat differences, differences in aerobic power are virtually nonexistent between the sexes.

Another method for viewing aerobic power in youngsters is to adjust their maximum oxygen uptake on a per-kilogram-of-body-weight basis. When adjusted in this manner, it shows little change for males (no increase) and a continual decrease for females (Bar-Or, 1983). Again, this decrease among females is in large part due to an increase in body fat and a proportionate decrease in lean body mass. This lack of increase raises the question as to whether training youngsters increases their aerobic performance.

It appears that, in adolescents, aerobic power can be increased 10 to 20% through training. Even though training increases aerobic power, it probably should not be the primary goal of the fitness program. Lifetime fitness entails being involved in moderate aerobic activities on a regular basis. The physical education program should be designed to enhance health and well-being rather than show only an increase in aerobic capacity. Cultivation of positive attitudes toward activity and participation in regular moderate aerobic activity are important goals. Attitudes toward fitness are more important than training and testing youngsters to see if they can reach their maximum capacity and physical limits. Few adults ever exercise for a lifetime at a level that is overly demanding and physically exhausting.

The Impact of Obesity on Aerobic Capacity

Obese students seldom perform physical activities on a par with leaner youngsters (Bar-Or, 1983). In part, this is because of the greater metabolic cost for an obese youngster. Obese students require a higher oxygen uptake capacity to perform a given task. Unfortunately, their capacity is usually lower than that of normal-weight youngsters, which means that they must perform at a higher percentage of their maximum capacity. Obese students move at a higher percentage of their aerobic capacity, so they have less reserve and perceive greater exertion (Bar-Or and Ward, 1989). This lack of reserve probably explains why these youngsters perceive aerobic tasks as demanding and unenjoyable. The task is more demanding for obese students.

Obesity takes a great toll on aerobic power because of the greater metabolic cost of exercise. Obese youngsters must perform at a higher percentage of their maximal oxygen uptake. Usually, their maximal uptake values are lower than those of lean youngsters. This allows for less reserve and results in higher perceived exertion for obese students. These reactions contribute to the well-known perception among teachers that "obese youngsters don't like to run." This reaction is irrelevant because it doesn't solve the problem. To deal with this paradox, teachers must accept that the obese student is working harder and that work loads must be adjusted accordingly. Because the obese student is working harder than the normal-weight youngster, it is necessary to understand that aerobic demands will not be similar. There is no acceptable premise, physiological or psychological, for asking all youngsters to run the same distance regardless of ability.

Workloads need to be based on time rather than distance. Lean and efficient runners should be expected to move farther than obese youngsters during a stipulated time period. All students do not and should not have to do the same amount of exercise. Just as one would not expect 6th graders to perform the same workload as that of high school seniors, it is unreasonable to expect obese students to be capable

of workloads similar to those of lean, ectomorphic youngsters. Exercise programs for obese subjects should be designed to increase caloric expenditure (emphasize amount of time moving) rather than improve cardiovascular fitness (intensity of the movement) (Rowland, 1991). The intensity of the activity should be secondary to the amount of time the student is involved in some type of moderate activity.

Weight Control

Body composition refers to the varying amounts of muscle, bone, and fat within the body. Over half of the fat stored in the body is stored in a layer just below the skin. This is the reason that skinfolds are used to estimate the amount of fat carried within the body. On the basis of data gathered for a large study conducted between 1976 and 1980 by the National Center for Health Statistics (1986), between 13 and 26% of youngsters are overweight, depending on gender and race. An additional 4 to 12% are superobese. This totals 17 to 36% of students who are obese or superobese.

Obesity not only decreases a youngster's aerobic performance, but it also has a negative impact on motor performance. The study of obesity in adolescents has produced some disturbing findings. Many obese people appear to have a decreased tendency for muscular activity. As weight increases, the impulse for physical exertion decreases further. As youngsters become more obese, they find themselves in a cycle that appears to be out of control. In most cases, physical activity appears to be the crucial factor in dealing with weight control. In comparisons of the diets of obese and normal youngsters, no substantial difference in caloric consumption was usually found. In fact, in some cases, obese youngsters actually consumed less food than did normal-weight youngsters (Corbin and Fletcher, 1968).

The lack of physical activity is common among obese youngsters. In a study of 9th grade females (Johnson, Burke, and Mayer, 1956), females who were obese ate less but also exercised two-thirds less (in total time) than did normal-weight females. Movies taken of normal-weight and overweight teenagers (Corbin and Fletcher, 1968) demonstrated a great difference in the activity level of the two groups, even though diets were quite similar. A number of researchers have identified the effectiveness of increased activity in reducing obesity (Eisenman, 1986). Wilmore (1994) identifies inactivity as a far more significant factor in the development of obesity than overeating. Increasing activity is a key factor and must be accompanied by an attitudinal shift. Students need to develop positive feelings about the role of exercise in maintaining an optimum weight level. Many educators feel it is best to deal with obese youngsters in a positive fashion rather than trying to solve their problem through increased and mandated exercise. If the treatment is not successful, students may feel as though they are failures and be strongly opposed to future activity programs.

Adults often make the statement: "Don't worry about excessive weight; it will come off when the student reaches adolescence." The opposite is usually true, however. Eighty percent of obese preadolescents grow into obese adults; however, 96% of obese teenagers become obese adults (Johnson, Burke, and Mayer, 1956). Youngsters clearly do not grow out of obesity; they grow into it. Student obesity needs to be challenged at an early age, and this challenge must come from increased movement and activity. In addition, it is important to understand that many obese students are victims of their home environment. For example, Griffiths and Payne (1976) selected 4- and 5-year-old youngsters for study based on their parents' level of obesity. At the time of the study, the youngsters were of similar body composition. Youngsters of obese parents were, however, less active and also ate less than did the offspring of leaner parents. If the behavior continued, these youngsters of obese parents would probably become obese due to lack of activity. Students are not in total control of their destiny, and solving problems of obesity are difficult at best. There are no easy answers, and to solve such complex problems as obesity, parents, nutritionists, counselors, nurses, and physicians need to be involved in the process.

The advantage of using physical activity to treat obesity is that it increases energy expenditure and may suppress appetite (Wilmore, 1994). In contrast to rigid diets, exercise will minimize the loss of lean body mass and stimulate fat loss. Physical activity is inexpensive, easy to do in a variety of situations, and often a positive social experience.

Strength Development

During elementary school muscular strength increases linearly with chronological age (Malina, 1980; Beunen, 1989) until adolescence, at which time a rapid increase in strength occurs. Strength is related to body size and lean body mass. When differences in strength between the sexes are adjusted

for height, there is no difference in lower body strength from age 7 through 17. When the same adjustment between the sexes is made for upper-body strength, however, males have more upper extremity and trunk strength (Malina, 1980). Males and females compete on somewhat even terms in activities demanding leg strength, particularly if size and mass are similar. On the other hand, in activities demanding arm or trunk strength, males have a definite advantage, even if they are similar to females in height and mass. These considerations are important when pairing students for competition. Problems can occur when students are paired with another who is considerably taller and heavier and therefore stronger.

MUSCLE FIBER TYPE AND PERFORMANCE

The number of muscle fibers that an individual possesses is genetically determined. An increase in muscle size is accomplished by an increase in the size of each muscle fiber. The muscled look of an individual is determined first by the number of fibers and second by the size of the fibers. Skeletal muscle tissue contains fibers that are fast contracting (**fast twitch [FT]**) and others that are slow contracting (**slow twitch [ST]**) (Saltin, 1973). The percentage of fast- versus slow-contracting fibers varies from muscle to muscle and among individuals. The percentage of each type of muscle fiber is determined during the first weeks of postnatal life (Dubowitz, 1970). Most individuals are believed to possess a 50:50 split; that is, half of the muscle fibers are FT and half are ST. A small percentage of people have a ratio of 60:40 (in either direction), and researchers have verified that some people possess an even more extreme ratio.

What is the significance of variation in the ratio of muscle fiber type? The ST fibers have a rich supply of blood and related energy mechanisms. This results in a slowly contracting, fatigue-resistant muscle fiber that is well suited to endurance-type (aerobic) activities. In contrast, the FT fibers are capable of bursts of intense activity but are subject to rapid fatigue. These fibers are well suited to activities demanding short-term speed and power (such as pull-ups, standing long jump, and shuttle run). The ST fibers would facilitate performance in the mile run or other endurance-oriented activity. On the other hand, the same student may do poorly in a physical education program dominated by team sports that place a premium on quickness and strength. Designing a program that offers activities demanding a wide range of physical attributes (that is, endurance, balance, flexibility) is thus essential.

STRENGTH AND MOTOR PERFORMANCE

Strength is an important factor in performing motor skills. A study by Rarick and Dobbins (1973) identified and ranked the factors that contribute to the motor performance of students. The factor identified as most important was strength or power (or both) in relation to body size. Youngsters who demonstrated high levels of strength in relation to their body size were more capable of performing motor skills than were those with lower strength levels.

Deadweight (fat) was the fourth-ranked factor in the motor performance study and was weighted in a negative direction. The more obese students were, the less proficient they were at performing motor skills. Deadweight acts as a negative factor in motor development because it reduces the student's strength in relation to body size. Obese students may be stronger than normal-weight youngsters in absolute terms, but they are less strong when strength is adjusted for body weight. This lack of strength causes obese students to perceive a strength-related task (such as push-ups or sit-ups) as much more difficult than the same task might seem to normal-weight peers. The need for varied work loads accompanied by teacher understanding and empathy is important to assure all students the opportunity for success in strength-related activities. Strength must be developed so youngsters have the tools to find success in motor development activities.

ACTIVITY AND HEALTH

During the past decade, the interest in physical fitness and increased awareness of the benefits derived from an active lifestyle have spawned a wide assortment of health clubs, a vast array of books and magazines concerning exercise and fitness, a weekly smorgasbord of distance runs and triathlons. Exercise equipment has been streamlined, and apparel is available for virtually any type of physical activity. Unfortunately, the nation's enthusiasm for physical

activity has not affected physical education programs. Only about one-third of our youth participate daily in school physical education programs nationwide (Ross, Pate, Corbin, Delpy, and Gold, 1987), and that amount is both declining and insufficient.

The need for activity as an integral part of a healthy lifestyle is strong. Rather than encourage increased activity among youth, many schools have focused on physical fitness testing. This excessive concern about the fitness levels of youth has resulted in a need to "train students to pass fitness tests" to meet district standards. When fitness results become more important than participation in regular activity, students learn that it is more important to focus on short-term goals (fitness test results) rather than a long-term lifestyle (daily activity). Health goals for the nation for the year 2000 (U.S. Public Health Service, 1990) are primarily based on increasing daily levels of physical activity, not fitness levels. Many of the goals directly target schools or programs that can take place within the school setting. These goals are stated in terms of activity objectives rather than fitness objectives, and emphasis is placed on reducing inactivity and increasing light to moderate physical activity.

Emphasis needs to be placed on developing physical education programs that cause lifestyle changes in physical activity levels so as to improve health-related fitness. (Simons-Morton, Parcel, O'Hara, Blair, and Pate, 1988; Sallis and McKenzie, 1991). Whereas fitness testing has anointed a few gifted students and failed the majority of others, developing programs that change the activity patterns of youth will allow all the opportunity for success and long-term health. Youngsters should be recognized for their willingness to participate rather than their reticence to be tested.

Heart Disease

Coronary heart disease affects over 5 million people and accounts for 1.5 million heart attacks each year (McGlynn, 1990). The yearly medical costs associated with heart disease in America amount to over $26 billion (Freedson, 1986). Surely, there can be no greater rationale for increasing the amount of exercise for junior and senior high school students. It has long been believed that heart disease is of geriatric origin and manifests itself only in older adults. In a study by Glass (1973), 5,000 youngsters in the Iowa public schools were examined over a 2-year period.

Of these students, 70% had symptoms of coronary heart disease, including 7% who had extremely high cholesterol levels, a large percentage with high blood pressure, and at least 12% who were obese.

In examining the developmental history of heart disease in humans, Dr. Kenneth Rose (1968) identified the first signs as appearing around the age of 2. The good news is that he also determined that the disease process is reversible until the age of 19. Unfortunately, if youngsters' exercise habits are not altered, they may be burdened with high blood pressure and/or obesity as they mature into adults. There are no longitudinal studies to document that early control of coronary heart disease risk will reduce the onset of premature death in adult life (Gilliam, MacConnie, Greenen, Pels, and Freedson, 1982). However, it appears that youngsters with high blood pressure, lipids, and obesity tend to retain those high levels into adulthood.

Students are not naturally active during a typical school day. A study by Gilliam, Katch, Thorland, and Weltman (1977) documented the fact that youngsters do not voluntarily engage in high-intensity activity. By the authors' definition, high-intensity activity occurred when the heart rate was elevated to at least 60% of its maximum. The heart rate of youngsters was monitored to see how much time during a 12-hour period was spent in high-intensity activity. Less than 2% of the time was spent by youngsters in high intensity activity, and 80% of the time was spent in low-intensity activity. Researchers also found that females were even less active than males.

Gilliam et al. (1977) conducted a study that showed the school environment decreases the physical activity of youngsters. Compared to summer activity, youngsters' activity patterns decreased during the school year. A related finding showed that if females were given the opportunity, they would increase their activity to those levels comparable to or above those of most moderately active males. The authors concluded that daily activity patterns can be changed and coronary heart disease decreased through increased cardiovascular activity.

Obesity and Diabetes Mellitus

There are other diseases associated with a lack of physical activity. One of the areas of grave concern is the high incidence of obesity among youngsters. Closely related to the obesity problem is that of diabetes mellitus. About 1.5 per 1,000 youngsters (ages 0

to 15 years) are afflicted with this serious ailment. Properly administered exercise programs can be an effective approach for positively influencing this chronic disorder among youth. Diabetic youth who are physically active show lower levels of blood glucose and a more stable metabolism than sedentary youngsters (Larrson, 1984). The fitness of diabetic teenagers, caused by lack of exercise, is lower than that of nondiabetic students. This probably occurs because nurses and teachers fear exercise-induced hypoglycemia (Larrson, 1984). Proper management of diet and insulin is a key factor, which usually means assuring that the energy intake is increased while the insulin dose is maintained. Unfortunately, teenagers usually decrease the amount of their voluntary activity on entering middle and senior high school.

Lack of Flexibility and Trunk Strength

A lack of flexibility and trunk strength has been a recurring problem regardless of the source of testing and research. This lack often leads to poor posture and lower back pain (Plowman, 1993). Programs have to accomplish more than aerobic fitness; the need for strength and flexibility is equally important. The need is clear: develop healthy youngsters today who are capable of maintaining a healthy lifestyle during adulthood.

The evidence shows that many youngsters are not healthy. Even though few youngsters die of heart disease and related health problems such as obesity and diabetes mellitus, there is a need for concern. For too long, parents and teachers have assumed that because teenagers seldom complain about their health status, they are healthy. Physical educators owe youngsters a legacy of personal fitness. A physical education program without a strong fitness component is taking away the only opportunity that youngsters will have to learn to maintain their health.

EFFECTS OF PHYSICAL EDUCATION ON STUDENTS

One of the more difficult questions to answer about physical education programming is: what long-term effects do physical education programs offer students? Many physical educators speak loudly about the many benefits of their program with little evidence in hand. This has led some administrators and parents to doubt some of the wilder claims. An excellent chapter on different studies dealing with a number of benefits can be found in the text *Physical Activity and Well-Being* (Vogel, 1986). The unfortunate fact revealed by this study is that most studies conducted have not adjusted for maturity of students and thus provide little or no evidence. The need for longitudinal studies of youngsters in physical education programs is obvious. Related to this problem are the dearth of studies related to middle and senior high school programs. The majority of the research deals with elementary school students.

Within the limitations of the studies reviewed by Vogel (1986), Figure 2.5 shows the impact of physical

education on the development of various parameters. Many of the studies reviewed had weaknesses and would need to be replicated in a similar manner in order to assure similar effects. Also, due to the limitations of the studies, it is possible the effects cannot be generalized to other populations. If the reader is interested in finding supporting data for a physical education program, a review of the chapter mentioned previously is suggested.

SKILL LEVEL AND PHYSICAL EDUCATION

Students who feel physically incompetent usually drop out of physical education, and when they leave school, have a negative opinion of an active lifestyle. Dropping out of physical education commonly occurs at the middle school level, although the process often begins in the elementary school years. Dropping out of activity due to lack of skill competency during elementary school is most unfortunate. Predicting who will be an outstanding athlete in junior or senior high school by observing elementary school performance is, in fact, quite difficult. In a study by Clarke (1968), coaches rated males who were outstanding athletes. Of the males who were rated as outstanding between the ages of 9 and 15 years, only 25% received this rating at the elementary and middle school age. Of the males, 45% were rated as outstanding at the elementary school level, but not at the middle school level; and 35% of the group were rated as outstanding in middle school, but not in elementary school. Thus, only 25% of the predictions were correct. Most people would not take a risk if the odds were against them 75% of the time. Teachers, however, often label youngsters at an early age, even though their predictions may be incorrect 3 out of 4 times.

This lack of predictive ability among teachers emphasizes the need for the physical education program to keep youngsters enthusiastic until they are capable of performing successfully. The purpose of a physical education program is not to develop athletes, and the program should not be presented so that it allows the athletically gifted to excel and prosper at the expense of less-talented youngsters. Physical education is for all youngsters. Gifted youngsters have a myriad of opportunities to enhance their skills. However, students who are less skilled have

---

Convincing Evidence Supports Improvement in the Following Areas

1. Student physical activity levels
2. Aerobic fitness
3. Knowledge related to healthy lifestyles
4. Motor performance
5. Muscular endurance
6. Muscular power
7. Muscular strength
8. Physical fitness

Some Evidence Supports Improvement in the Following Areas

1. Flexibility of the hip and spine
2. Selected measures of perceptual motor performance (however, no evidence supports the effect of perceptual-motor performance on academic achievement)
3. Movement speed
4. Cardiovascular health factors including cholesterol, risk-factor reduction, and blood pressure

No Evidence Supports Improvement in the Following Areas

1. Agility-coordination
2. Alterations in height, weight, or girth
3. Alteration of nutritional practices
4. Acceleration or retardation of the maturation process
5. Self-concept or personality
6. Anaerobic fitness

FIGURE 2.5 The Impact of Physical Education on Growth and Development

only the physical education program to help them develop and improve. To reiterate, trying to identify athletes at an early age in a physical education setting is not only inaccurate but may be detrimental to their future development.

INTELLECTUAL DEVELOPMENT AND PHYSICAL EDUCATION

For years, physical educators have attempted to demonstrate a relationship between physical education and improvement in a student's intellectual development. If intellectual development or academic achievement could be linked to physical education, the profession might rank higher as an educational priority. However, according to Shephard (1984a), "Strong proof is lacking." Shephard identifies the many limitations of such investigations, which include

1. Studies of special populations such as the mentally handicapped or athletes.
2. "Halo" effects, because teachers reward star performers with higher marks.
3. Self-image gains by athletes due to teacher and peer praise.
4. Short duration of training programs.
5. Possible side effects from curtailment of academic instruction.
6. Use of retrospective data relating observed academic performance to measures of activity or physical ability.

Thomas and Thomas (1986) offer a clear and concise summary statement about activity and intellectual ability: " . . . attempts to improve or remediate cognitive function through the use of movement are not theoretically sound, nor does this approach have any empirical support in the research literature." A relationship to other academic areas should not be a requisite for a physical education program. Physical education makes unique contributions to the total school curriculum: motor skill development and the understanding and maintenance of physical fitness. Since these contributions cannot be developed elsewhere in the curriculum and contribute to the physical well-being of youngsters, convincing administrators and parents that intellectual development is enhanced by physical education should not be necessary. Physical educators can justify inclusion of the program on the basis of its unique contributions: The public has shown support for a physical education program if it aids, nurtures, and shows concern for the physical development of **all** students.

A study that has created much interest is the Trois Rivieres regional experiment (Shephard, 1984b). The study provides a well-conceived design for increased physical education programming. Even though students received more time for physical education (and less for academics), their academic performance was not decreased. These results counter the objection that more physical education will result in poorer academic performance because less time is spent in the classroom. Administrators need to consider this study, particularly today, when many schools have a back-to-basics emphasis. This emphasis usually means "back to the classroom," without physical activity or the arts. One wonders if this lack of concern for the body, our "home to the brain," is detrimental to total development of students. The ability to read is unimportant if one's health has degenerated. No priority in life is higher than physical well-being.

EFFECT OF EXERCISE DURING THE SCHOOL YEARS

Many experts believe that the physical activity undertaken during the school years has a lifetime impact. Saltin and Grimby (1968) conducted a research project to learn whether the benefits of childhood activity carried over to adult life. They compared the ability to adjust to effort of 3 groups of subjects aged 50 to 59. One group comprised former athletes who had not participated in activity for over 20 years and who worked in sedentary jobs. A second group consisted of former athletes who kept up a regular training and exercise program during their adult years. The third group consisted of individuals who were not athletes in youth and who were inactive as adults. Results showed that the nonathlete group was capable of the least effort (measured by maximal oxygen uptake). The group that was active during youth but took part in little activity during adulthood scored significantly higher than did the nonathlete group. The athlete group that had maintained training scored a great deal higher than the other two groups. This study shows that functional capacity as an adult is partly a result of activity performed during the growing years.

GUIDELINES FOR EXERCISING YOUNGSTERS SAFELY

Two areas of concern for physical educators who are responsible for exercising youngsters are (a) the avoidance of physical injury or harm and (b) the maintenance and development of positive attitudes and feelings about exercise. Few, if any, healthy students are permanently injured by exercise. However, when exercise is not conducted properly or is pushed to excess, emotional problems can arise. The following sections offer guidelines for offering students exercise in a safe and positive manner.

Moderation

Moderation is the best way to ensure that youngsters grow up enjoying different types of physical activity. Moderate exercise, coupled with opportunities to participate in recreational activity, help develop a lasting desire to move. Educators are sometimes concerned that a student may be harmed physiologically by too much or too vigorous activity. To date, there is no evidence that a healthy student can be harmed through vigorous exercise. This does not mean that a student is capable of the same unadjusted physical work load as an adult. Evidence does indicate, however, that youngsters can withstand a gradual increase in work load and are capable of work loads comparable to those of adults when the load is adjusted for height and size.

Years ago, there was concern about a theory (Hurlock, 1967) that the large blood vessels did not grow in proportion to other body parts. This, it was theorized, placed the heart and the circulatory system under stress during strenuous exercise. This myth has been rebuked, and research has now established that fatigue causes healthy youngsters to stop exercising long before any danger to health occurs (Shephard, 1984a). In addition, the student's circulatory system is similar in proportion to that of an adult and is not at a disadvantage during exercise.

Exercising in Warm Climates

It is possible to exercise youngsters in hot climates. The arrival of warm weather does not mean that exercise must stop, but certain measures should be used to avoid heat-related illness. Youngsters are not little adults, and they do not adapt to extremes of temperature as effectively as adults for the following physiological reasons (Bar-Or, 1983; American Academy of Pediatrics, 1991):

1. Youngsters have a higher surface area/mass ratio than adults. This allows a greater amount of heat to transfer between the environment and the body.
2. When walking or running, youngsters produce more metabolic heat per unit mass than adults produce. Youngsters are not as efficient in executing movement patterns, so they generate more metabolic heat than do adults performing a similar task.
3. Sweating capacity is not as great in some teenagers as in adults, resulting in a lowered ability to cool the body.
4. The ability to convey heat by blood from the body core to the skin is reduced in youngsters because of a lower cardiac output at a given oxygen uptake.

These physiological differences demonstrate that youngsters are at a disadvantage compared to adults when exercising in an environment where the ambient air temperature is higher than the skin temperature. In addition, the physical maturity of teenagers varies a great deal, so it is quite possible that some youngsters are similar to adults, whereas others are still childlike in terms of their maturation level.

Individuals can and do acclimatize to warmer temperatures. However, youngsters appear to adjust to heat more slowly than adults (Bar-Or, 1983). Often, teenagers do not instinctively drink enough liquids to replenish fluids lost during exercise. The American Academy of Pediatrics (1991) offers the following guidelines for exercising youngsters in hot climates.

1. The intensity of activities that last 30 minutes or more should be reduced whenever relative humidity and air temperature are above critical levels. Figure 2.6 shows the relationship between humidity and air temperature and when it is necessary to moderate activity demands.
2. When beginning an exercise program in a warmer climate, the intensity and duration of exercise should be restrained initially and then increased gradually over a period of 10 to 14 days to accomplish acclimation to the effects of heat.

Relative Humidity Level	Air Temperature (°F)
40 %	90
50	85
60	80
70	75
80	70
90	65
100	60

FIGURE 2.6 Weather guide: When the relative humidity and air temperature exceed the corresponding levels, intense activity should be curtailed.

3. Before prolonged physical activity, participants should be fully hydrated. During the activity, periodic drinking (for example, 5 ounces of cold tap water every 30 minutes for a student weighing 88 pounds) should be enforced.

4. Clothing should be lightweight and limited to one layer of absorbent material to facilitate evaporation of sweat and to expose as much skin as possible. Sweat-saturated garments should be replaced by dry ones. Rubberized sweat suits should never be used to produce weight loss.

The Academy identifies youngsters with the following conditions as being at a potentially high risk for heat stress: obesity, febrile (feverish) state, cystic fibrosis, gastrointestinal infection, diabetes insipidus, diabetes mellitus, chronic heart failure, caloric malnutrition, anorexia nervosa, sweating insufficiency syndrome, and mental retardation.

Distance Running

The question often arises as to how much and how far youngsters should be allowed to run, particularly in a competitive or training-for-competition setting. Since parents, teachers, and coaches seldom see the long-term effects of distance running, they often show little concern or willingness to limit the amount of activity. However, the American Academy of Pediatrics (1991) has identified possible problems that could arise. Lifetime involvement in a sport often depends on the type of early participation and gratification gained. Psychological problems can result from setting unrealistic goals for distance running by youngsters. A student who participates in distance running primarily for parental gratification may tire of the activity after a time and quit, or the student may continue and chafe under the coaching or parental pressure. In either case, psychological damage can occur causing the student to become discouraged and unwilling to participate, either immediately or in the long run. Participants should be allowed to participate for the enjoyment of running without fear of teacher, parental, or peer rejection or pressure. A student's sense of accomplishment, satisfaction, and appreciation by peers, parents, and coaches will foster involvement in running and other sports during school years and in later life.

A position taken by the International Athletics Association Federation (IAAF) Medical Committee (1983) in part states: "The danger certainly exists that with over-intensive training, separation of the growth plates may occur in the pelvic region, the knee, or the ankle. While this could heal with rest, nevertheless definitive information is lacking whether in years to come harmful effects may result." In view of this position, it is the opinion of the IAAF Medical Committee that training and competition for long-distance track and road-running events should not be encouraged. Up to the age of 12, it is suggested that not more than 800 meters (one-half mile) be run in competition. An increase in distance can be introduced gradually, with a maximum of 3,000 meters (nearly 2 miles) in competition for 14 year olds.

Fitness Testing Considerations

A common practice is to test students at the start of the school year in the mile run/walk. Many students may not have ample conditioning to participate safely in the activity. In addition, in many parts of the country, the start of the school year is hot and humid, adding to the stress placed on the cardiovascular system. If testing is deemed necessary, it is recommended that the test be done near the end of the school year after youngsters have had the opportunity to be conditioned. If this is not possible, at least allow youngsters 4 to 6 weeks of activity to achieve proper conditioning. Rowland (1990) recommends starting with a one-eighth mile run/walk and gradually building to a mile run/walk over a 4-week period. A better alternative is to use the PACER (Progressive Aerobic Cardiovascular Endurance Run) aerobic fitness test (Figure 2.7) (see p. 281), which can be administered indoors and does not require completing a mile distance run. The PACER offers similar validity and reliability as the mile run/walk.

FIGURE 2.7 The PACER fitness test avoids many of the pitfalls of the mile run

Strength Training

Strength training for preadolescent youngsters has generated widely differing opinions among educators. Many worry about safety and stress-related injuries, and others question whether such training can produce significant strength gains. Accepted thinking for some time has been that prepubescents are incapable of making significant strength gains because they lack adequate levels of circulating androgens. Research evidence is continuing to build that contradicts this point of view. A study by Cahill (1986) demonstrated significant increases in strength among 18 prepubescent males. A study by Servedio et al. (1985) showed strength training created significant strength gains in shoulder flexion among prepubescent youngsters. Weltman et al. (1986) conducted a 14-week, 3 times a week program using hydraulic resistance training (circuit training using 10 different stations) in 6- to 11-year-old boys. Results showed an 18 to 37 percent gain in all major muscle groups. It seems that strength can be increased through strength training in prepubescent youngsters. However, the way prepubescent youngsters gain strength differs from how adolescents and adults do (Tanner, 1993). In preadolescent students, it appears that strength gains occur from motor learning rather than muscle hypertrophy. Youngsters develop more efficient motor patterns and recruit more muscle fibers but show no increase in muscle size (Ozmun, Mikesky, and Surburg, 1991).

Note that the term *strength training* is used here to denote the use of barbells, dumbbells, or machines as resistance. It is in sharp contrast to weight lifting or power lifting, which is a competitive sport for the purpose of determining maximum lifting ability. There is strong agreement among experts that strength training is acceptable for youngsters, but weight lifting is highly undesirable and may be harmful. In a statement of strength training recommendations, the American Orthopedic Society for Sports Medicine (AOSSM) (Duda, 1986) states: "(1) competition is prohibited, and (2) no maximum lift should ever be attempted." In addition, AOSSM recommends a physical exam, proper supervision by knowledgeable coaches, and emotional maturity on the part of the participating youngster. Safety and prevention of injury is a serious consideration for teachers interested in strength training for youngsters. Educators must consider seriously whether strength training is an appropriate activity for a typical class of youngsters in a physical education class. The majority of injuries were caused by the major lifts, the power clean, the clean and jerk, the squat lift, or the dead lift (Tanner, 1993). These lifts often are competitive and performed in an uncontrolled (ballistic) manner and should not be used with youngsters. If knowledge and expertise are limited, strength training programs should be avoided. A knowledgeable instructor is required to provide an effective and safe program.

There are no studies that examine the long-term effects of strength training in youngsters. In addition, many experts worry about highly organized training programs that place great emphasis on relative gains in strength. A strength training program should be only one component of a comprehensive fitness program for youngsters. The National Strength and Conditioning Association (NCSA) (1985) recommends that 50 to 80% of the prepubescent athlete's training must include a variety of different exercises such as agility exercises (for example, basketball, volleyball, tennis, tumbling) and endurance training (for example, distance running, bicycling, swimming).

If a decision is made to develop a strength program, it should be done in a thoughtful and studied manner. Proper supervision and technique are key ingredients in a successful program. Program prescriptions recommended by AOSSM and NSCA are

1. Training should occur two or three times a week for 20- to 30-minute periods.

2. No resistance should be applied until proper form is demonstrated. Six to 15 repetitions equal 1 set; 1 to 3 sets per exercise should be done.
3. Weight or resistance is increased in 1- to 3-pound increments after the prepubescent does 15 repetitions in good form.
4. Maximal lifts should not be performed until youngsters are at least 16 to 17 years old.

EXPECTED OUTCOMES

After reading the chapter, you should be able to

- Explain the differences in the 3 standard body types.
- Discuss how physical maturity affects the physical skills of students.
- Identify the impact of regular physical activity on adolescent students.
- Describe the general health and activity status of students in American schools.
- Explain the harmful effects that obesity can have on the health and well-being of a student.
- Defend physical education with research and empirical evidence that is available.
- Identify principles to follow for exercising students safely in warm climates.
- Describe a safe approach for weight training and distance running for adolescent students.

REFERENCES AND SUGGESTED READINGS

American Academy of Pediatrics. 1982a. Risks in long-distance running for children. *The Physician and Sportsmedicine* 10(8): 82–86.

American Academy of Pediatrics. 1982b. Climatic heat stress and the exercising child. *The Physician and Sportsmedicine* 11(8): 155–159.

American Academy of Pediatrics. 1991. *Sports Medicine: Health Care for Young Athletes*. 2nd ed. Elk Grove Village, IL: American Academy of Pediatrics.

Bar-Or, O. 1983. *Pediatric Sports Medicine for the Practitioner*. New York: Springer-Verlag.

Bar-Or, O., and Ward, D. S. 1989. Rating of perceived exertion in children. In O. Bar-Or (ed.). *Advances in Pediatric Sport Sciences*. Vol. 3. Champaign, IL: Human Kinetics Publishers.

Beunen, G. 1989. Biological age in pediatric exercise research. In O. Bar-Or (ed.). *Advances in Pediatric Sport Sciences*. Vol. 3. Champaign, IL: Human Kinetics Publishers.

Cahill, R. R. 1986. Prepubescent strength training gains support. *The Physician and Sportsmedicine* 14(2): 157–161.

Clarke, H. H. 1968. Characteristics of the young athlete: A longitudinal look. *Kinesiology Review* 3: 33–42.

Clarke, H. H. 1971. *Physical Motor Tests in the Medford Boy's Growth Study*. Englewood Cliffs, NJ: Prentice-Hall.

Corbin, C. B., and Fletcher, P. 1968. Diet and activity patterns of obese and non-obese elementary school children. *Research Quarterly* 39(4): 922.

Dubowitz, V. 1970. Differentiation of fiber types in skeletal muscle. In E. J. Briskey, R. G. Cassens, and B. B. Marsh (eds.). *Physiology and Biochemistry of Muscle as a Food*. Vol. 2. Madison, WI: University of Wisconsin Press.

Duda, M. 1986. Prepubescent strength training gains support. *The Physician and Sportsmedicine* 14(2): 157–161.

Eisenman, P. 1986. Physical activity and body composition. In V. Seefeldt (ed.). *Physical Activity and Well Being*. Reston, VA: AAHPERD.

Freedson, P. S. 1986. Cardiorespiratory Diseases. In V. Seefeldt (ed.). *Physical Activity and Well Being*. Reston, VA: AAHPERD.

Gilliam, T. B., Katch, V. L., Thorland, W. G., and Weltman, A. W. 1977. Prevalence of coronary heart disease risk factors in active children, 7 to 12 years of age. *Medicine and Science in Sports and Exercise* 9(1): 21–25.

Gilliam, T. B., MacConnie, S. E., Greenen, D. L., Pels, A. E., and Freedson, P. S. 1982. Exercise program for children: A way to prevent heart disease? *The Physician and Sportsmedicine* 10(9): 96–101, 105–106, 108.

Glass, W. 1973. Coronary heart disease sessions prove vitally interesting. *California AHPER Journal* (May-June), 7.

Griffiths, M., and Payne, P. R. 1976. Energy expenditure in small children of obese and non-obese parents. *Nature* 260: 698–700.

Gruelich, W., and Pyle, S. 1959. *Radiographic Atlas of Skeletal Development of the Hand and Wrist*. 2nd ed. Stanford, CA: Stanford University Press.

Hastad, D. N. 1986. Physical fitness for elementary school children. *Educational Theory* 1: 12–14.

Haymes, E. M. 1986. Nutrition and ergogenic aids. In V. Seefeldt (ed.). *Physical Activity and Well Being*. Reston, VA: AAHPERD.

Hurlock, E. B. 1967. *Adolescent Development*. New York: McGraw-Hill.

International Athletics Association Federation (IAAF). 1983. Not kid's stuff. *Sportsmedicine Bulletin* 18(1): 11.

Johnson, M. L., Burke, B. S., and Mayer, J. 1956. The prevalence and incidence of obesity in a cross section of elementary and secondary school children. *American Journal of Clinical Nutrition* 4(3): 231.

Larrson, Y. 1984. Physical performance and the young diabetic. In R. A. Boileau (ed.). *Advances in Pediatric Sport Sciences*. Champaign, IL: Human Kinetics Publishers.

Malina, R. M. 1978. Physical growth and maturity characteristics of young athletes. In R. A. Magill, M. H. Ash, and F. L. Smoll (eds.). *Children and Youth in Sport: A Contemporary Anthology*. Champaign, IL: Human Kinetics Publishers.

Malina, R. M. 1980. Growth, strength, and physical performance. In G. A. Stull and T. K. Cureton (eds.). *Encyclopedia of Physical Education, Fitness, and Sports*. Salt Lake City, UT: Brighton Publishing.

Malina, R. M. 1986. Physical growth and development. In V. Seefeldt (ed.). *Physical Activity and Well-Being*. Reston, VA: AAHPERD.

McGlynn, G. 1990. *Dynamics of Fitness*. Dubuque, IA: Wm. C. Brown Publishers.

National Center for Health Statistics. 1986. *Health, United States, 1986*. DHHS Pub. No. (PHS) 97-1232. Public Health Service, Washington, D.C.: U.S. Government Printing Office, December, 1986.

National Strength and Conditioning Association. 1985. Position paper on prepubescent strength training. *National Strength and Conditioning Association Journal* 74: 27–31.

Ozmun, J. C., Mikesky, A. E., and Surburg, P. R. 1991. Neuromuscular adaptations during prepubescent strength training (abstract). *Medicine and Science in Sports and Exercise* 23(4): S31.

Plowman, S. A. 1993. Physical fitness and healthy low-back function. *Physical Activity and Fitness Research Digest* 1(3): 1–8.

Rarick, L. G. (ed.). 1973. *Physical Activity, Human Growth and Activity*. New York: Academic Press.

Rarick, L. G., and Dobbins, D. A. 1975. Basic components in the motor performances of children six to nine years of age. *Medicine and Science in Sports* 72: 2.

Roche, A. F., Chumlea, W. C., and Thissen, D. 1988. *Assessing the Skeletal Maturity of the Hand-Wrist: Fels Method*. Springfield, IL: Thomas.

Rose, K. 1968. To keep people in health. *Journal of the American College Health Association* 22: 80.

Ross, J. G., and Gilbert, G. G. 1985. The national children and youth fitness study: A summary of findings. *Journal of Physical Education, Recreation, and Dance* 56(1): 45–50.

Ross, J. G., Pate, R. R., Corbin, C. C., Delpy, L. A., and Gold, R. S. 1987. What is going on in the elementary physical education program? *Journal of Physical Education, Recreation, and Dance* 58(9): 78–84.

Rowland, T. W. 1990. *Exercise and Children's Health*. Champaign, IL.: Human Kinetics Publishers.

Rowland, T. W. 1991. Effects of obesity on aerobic fitness in adolescent females. *American Journal of Disease in Children* 145: 764–768.

Sallis, J. F., & McKenzie, T. L. 1991. Physical education's role in public health. *Research Quarterly of Exercise and Sport* 62: 124–137.

Saltin, B. 1973. Metabolic fundamentals of exercise. *Medicine and Science of Sports* 5: 137–146.

Saltin, B., and Grimby, G. 1968. Physiological analysis of middle-aged and old former athletes, comparison with still active athletes of the same ages. *Circulation* 38(6): 1104.

Servedio, F. J., Bartels, R. L., Hamlin, R. L. et al. 1985. The effects of weight training, using Olympic style lifts, on various physiological variables in prepubescent boys (abstract). *Medicine and Science in Sports and Exercise* 17: 288.

Sheldon, W. H., Dupertuis, C. W., and McDermott, E. 1954. *Atlas of Men: A Guide for Somatotyping the Adult Male at All Ages*. New York: Harper & Row.

Shephard, R. J. 1984a. Physical activity and child health. *Sports Medicine* 1: 205–233.

Shephard, R. J. 1984b. Physical activity and "wellness" of the child. In R. A. Boileau (ed.). *Advances in Pediatric Sport Sciences*. Champaign, IL: Human Kinetics Publishers.

Simons-Morton, B. B., Parcel, G. S., O'Hara, N. M., Blair, S. N., and Pate, R. R. (1988). Health-related physical fitness in childhood: Status and recommendations. *American Review of Public Health* 9: 403–425.

Tanner, S. M. 1993. Weighing the risks: Strength training for children and adolescents. *The Physician and Sportsmedicine* 21(6): 105–116.

Thomas, J. R., and Tennant, L. K. 1978. Effects of rewards on changes in children's motivation for an athletic task. In F. L. Smoll and R. E. Smith (eds.). *Psychological Perspectives in Youth Sports*. New York: Hemisphere Publishing.

Thomas, J. R., and Thomas, K. T. 1986. The relation of movement and cognitive function. In V. Seefeldt (ed.). *Physical Activity and Well-Being*. Reston, VA: AAHPERD

U.S. Public Health Service. 1990. *Healthy People 2000: National Health Promotion and Disease Prevention Objectives*. Washington, D.C.: U.S. Government Printing Office.

Vogel, P. 1986. Effects of physical education programs on children. In V. Seefeldt (ed.). *Physical Activity and Well-Being*. Reston, VA: AAHPERD.

Weltman, A., Janney, C., Rians, C. B., Strand, K., Berg, B., Tippitt, S., Wise, J., Cahill, B. R., and Katch, F. I. 1986. The effects of hydraulic resistance strength training in pre-pubertal males. *Medicine and Science in Sports and Exercise* 18: 629–638.

Wilmore, J. H. 1994. Exercise, Obesity, and Weight Control. *Physical Activity and Fitness Research Digest* 1(6): 1–8.

Wilmore, J. H., and McNamara, J. J. 1974. Prevalence of coronary disease risk factors in boys, 8 to 12 years of age. *Journal of Pediatrics* 84: 527–533.

3 Curriculum Models

PURPOSE

To identify different curriculum models in use today and to understand how models evolve from a value orientation of teachers. Allied to this purpose is an analysis of characteristics of the various models.

KEY CONCEPTS

- Curriculum models provide a basis for making decisions about objectives, content, structure, sequence, and evaluation.
- Three different approaches can be used for building and implementing a curriculum.
- Curriculum models evolve from a dominant value orientation. The dominant value orientations are subject matter, student development, and social-cultural goals.
- The multi-activity model is the most popular curriculum structure.
- Outdoor adventure models offer a variety of unique activities and off-campus travel.
- Sports education is a combination of physical education, intramurals, and athletics.
- Knowledge concepts models emphasize an academic approach to physical education.
- Social development models emphasize getting along with others and becoming responsible citizens.
- Outcomes-based models identify skills and knowledges to be acquired by students.

Curriculum models provide an overall philosophy that underlies the physical education curriculum. Curriculum models include a set of beliefs and goals that evolve from a theoretical framework or value base. These models provide the basis for organizing objectives and content, structuring and sequencing activities, and evaluating the curriculum plan. The scope and sequence of activities for the instructional program evolve from the curriculum model (see Chapter 4). Models predict interrelationships between content and the instructional process. An understanding of popular curriculum models and how they can be adapted to unique situations facilitates the development process. When building a quality physical education curriculum, different approaches can be used:

1. A curriculum that is functioning in another school can be incorporated into a new setting. The program can be accepted in total with only minor changes for local school or community preferences.
2. Adaptation of an existing curriculum to meet the local interests, preferences, and school priorities is a second alternative. The existing model is modified by incorporating local interests, preferences, and school philosophies into a restructured program.

39

3. A new model is constructed, coordinating ideas from many sources to form a unified program. This is the most difficult and time-consuming challenge and requires breadth of experience and a clear understanding of the curriculum process.

A curriculum model is a framework that evolves from a value base that focuses on subject matter, student development, social-cultural goals, or some combination of all three of these areas. **Value orientation** is a set of personal and professional beliefs about physical education that provide a basis for determining curricular decisions. Each of the curriculum models discussed in this chapter have a singular and dominant value orientation. However, since physical educators usually have several value orientations, the majority of physical education programs reflect a blend of different curriculum models. For example, a chosen model might include lifetime participation in physical activities, developing sports skills, acquiring fitness knowledge, improving social skills, acquiring disciplinary knowledge, or a combination of several of these orientations.

When developing or revising an existing curriculum, the value orientation of the physical education staff toward the existing curriculum and proposed changes is an important consideration (Jewett, Bain, and Ennis, 1995). Determining the value orientation of the curriculum involves consideration of three major components: the **subject matter** to be learned, the **students** for whom the curriculum is being developed, and the **society** that has established the schools. The design of the curriculum determines the primary focus of the curriculum. For example, is there a need to place greater emphasis on subject matter development and understanding than on student development or social-cultural goals? Priorities in the curriculum vary depending on the value orientations of the physical educators involved in the planning.

Physical educators who place highest priority on subject-matter mastery include an emphasis on sports, dance, outdoor adventure activities, physical fitness activities, and aquatics activities. This curriculum orientation places strong emphasis on learning skills and gaining knowledge so students have the opportunity to learn the subject matter and continue active participation for a lifetime.

Instructors who favor a student-centered approach focus on activities that develop the individual student. Emphasis is on helping students find activities that are personally meaningful. Student autonomy and self-direction are important goals. Instruction and curricula emphasize personal development and individual excellence over subject matter or broad social and cultural goals. Other professionals strive to create social change toward equal opportunity and emphasize social reconstruction for a better society. Instruction emphasizes lifetime sport skills and nontraditional activities such as cooperative games and group activities in an attempt to foster problem solving and interpersonal skills. Skill development is directed toward future application and the improvement of society.

Most often, physical educators have multiple value orientations and develop a curriculum model that incorporates several beliefs. The discussion that follows examines a number of popular curriculum models. Understanding how different models give direction to the curriculum helps teachers work in unity toward the pursuit of program objectives. Each of the different models discussed provides different options and outcomes. For teachers, the following questions should be examined prior to the selection of a model:

- Does the model express a point of view about subject matter that is consistent with mine?
- Does the model express a point of view about student learning that I believe?
- Does the model express a point of view about our school's role in accomplishing social-cultural goals?
- Is the model workable for my community and school setting?
- Can I implement instructional strategies I value within this model?

MULTI-ACTIVITY–BASED MODEL

The most common curriculum model in use today at the secondary level is a multi-activity-based approach that focuses on physical fitness, sport, gymnastics, aquatics, and dance. The multi-activity model uses units of physical activity or sport as the basic core of the curriculum. A primary focus is placed on learning motor skills, especially sports skills rather than personal development or social-cultural goals. These activities provide the content of the model and the structure or format of the curriculum. Units vary in length from 2 weeks to 1 year depending on program philosophy. Middle schools usually offer shorter units that assure variety and introduction to skills, whereas high schools have longer units that focus on skill competency. Included activities change depending on the desires of society and needs of students. Most often, activities are classified in the following categories:

1. Team sports: basketball, softball, or soccer.
2. Individual or lifetime sports: gymnastics, tennis, or Frisbee.
3. Dance: folk, square, modern, or country swing.
4. Physical fitness activities: jogging, weight training, or aerobics.
5. Recreational games: horseshoes, shuffleboard, or table tennis.
6. Outdoor adventure activities: bicycling, skiing, or orienteering.
7. Aquatics: swimming, skin diving, or water sports.

The activity based curriculum is usually arranged with a balance of activities from these categories (Figure 3.1), however, it is possible to concentrate the

Team Sports	Individual/Dual Activities	Recreational Pursuits	Nontraditional Activities
Baseball	Aquatics	Angling	Equestrian
Basketball	Diving	Backpacking-hiking	European handball
Football	Swimming	Bowling	Korfball
Flag	Synchronized	Camping	Rhythmic
Touch	swimming	Canoeing	gymnastics
Hockey	Water safety	Cycling	Rugby
Field	Archery	Dance	Surfing
Floor	Badminton	Folk	Water polo
Lacrosse	Conditioning	Modern	
Soccer	Aerobic dance	Square	
Softball	Circuit training	Social	
Speedball	Jogging	Initiatives	
Volleyball	Slimnastics	Orienteering	
	Fencing	Rappelling	
	Golf	Sailing	
	Gymnastics		
	Tumbling		
	Acrosport		
	Handball		
	Paddleball		
	Squash		
	Martial arts		
	Aikido		
	Judo		
	Karate		
	Scuba diving		
	Skiing		
	Snow		
	Water		
	Skin diving		
	Table tennis		
	Tennis		
	Trampoline		
	Weight lifting		
	Wrestling		
	Yoga		

FIGURE 3.1
Activity categories

Models 2/5

Provide:
- For organization of subjects + content
- Structuring/ sequencing for activities
- For evaluation of curriculum plan.

focus on one category of activity such as the outdoor adventure activities. In most cases, activities are included on the basis of a number of mediating factors such as student interest, teacher interest and expertise, community interest, class size, facilities, equipment, and climate. Activities in the curriculum generally follow the preferences of society, usually with a significant time lag. The arrival of "new" activities in physical education curricula—such as activities reflecting the fitness renaissance, the wellness movement, the interest in outdoor adventure activities, or the Eastern influence in the martial arts and yoga—are usually indicative of the desires of the people whom the program serves. Instructors have to stay aware of student activity interests and trends in society in order to update the curriculum. To attract students to the program, a variety of "current and popular" activity categories need to be offered. Since students have different competencies and interests, most want to be able to participate in activities related to their personal abilities. Offering a wide range of instructional units makes the program more appealing to the entire student body.

Instruction in a multi-activity curriculum proceeds from introductory lessons to advanced and specialized courses. Students are most often grouped by grade level than by ability or developmental level. In most situations, students proceed through a sequence of required physical activities throughout the school year. Including an elective format allows students to choose activities they want to learn. An example might be to allow students to make choices from various categories of activities such as electing a certain number of team sports, lifetime sports, or physical conditioning units. Even though choices are limited by categories, this format usually enhances the interest, enthusiasm, and motivational level of both students and teachers.

The activity-based model is popular because it allows for diversity and flexibility in meeting the changing interests and desires of today's students. This model provides the opportunity for students to explore, experiment, and experience a wide variety of physical activities. The model also provides indepth units that help students gain sufficient skill competency for adult participation. There are many opportunities for students to compete with others, the environment, or against themselves in different units.

Some argue that the multi-activity model utilizing short units offers exposure to a variety of activities but does not allow ample time to develop competency or mastery of skills and knowledge (Ennis, 1993). At the high school level, short units restrict learning opportunities, and most educators advocate semester-long classes as a minimal time requirement to ensure development of adequate levels of competency. Short units of instruction are usually presented in middle school so that students can experience many different activities and learn about their areas of personal interest and competency. The flow of the curriculum from middle school to high school goes from short units to long units; from searching for areas of competency to achieving high levels of competency.

Centennial Middle School (grades 6 to 8) in central Arizona offers a multi-activity curriculum model where the students choose a block of units every 6 weeks. Classes meet daily, and students participate in 3 different units during the 6-week block. Students are taught by the same instructor for 6 weeks and then choose a new set of units and instructor for the next 6 weeks. The daily and weekly format of the lessons are consistent, and the students experience choice with a wide variety of units in the multi-activity model. Gender composition and ability levels of students in each class are dictated from choices made by students. Students are encouraged to explore and experience a wide variety of units to find activities they enjoy because of personal competencies (see Figure 3.2).

Panama Central High School in New York uses a multi-activity curriculum that offers students a broad choice of activities (Olson, 1984). Emphasis is on lifetime sports, team sports, self-testing activities, and aquatics. Classes for grades 9 to 12 are taught on a 3/2 swing schedule (3 days one semester, 2 days the next semester). The 40-week school year is divided into 4 10-week physical education units. The teaching staff is able to offer 3 activities during each 10-week period. Students choose their classes every 10 weeks from the 3 different activities that are offered. At the end of each year, students have completed 4 units and at graduation, 16 units. Upper-class students are given priority for choices when the demand is too great for a selected activity. Figure 3.3 illustrates the 4-year sequence.

An example of an elective multi-activity model for high school students that places emphasis on lifetime activities is the Eaton model (Portman and McCollum, 1995). The program is designed for students who have completed required physical education classes. The curriculum includes a balance of activities from "traditional" and nontraditional sports.

No. of Units	Introductory Activity	Fitness Activity	Lesson Focus	Game
1	Orientation and simple games			
2	Basic movements (e.g., start, stop, pivot)	Teacher leader	Soccer skills	Lead-up soccer
3	Walk, trot, sprint	Stretching	Soccer skills	Soccer
4	Partner over and under	Form running	Volleyball skills	Lead-up volleyball
5	Run, stop, pivot	Circuit training	Volleyball skills	Volleyball
6	Marking	Exercise to music	Hockey skills	Lead-up hockey
7	Tag games	Astronaut drills	Hockey skills	Hockey
8 (9)	Flash drill	Aerobic conditioning	Flag football skills	Football related
9	Mirror drill	Squad leader	Team handball skills	Lead-up team handball
10	New leader warm up	Obstacle course	Team handball skills	Team handball
11	Jumping and hopping skills	Continuity drills	Rope jumping skills	Scatter baseball
12	Rooster hop	Dyna-band exercises	Lacrosse skills	Lead-up lacrosse
13	Follow the leader	Stretching and partner resistance	Lacrosse skills	Lacrosse
14	Group agility drills	Parachute fitness	Basketball skills	Lead-up basketball
15	Manipulative skills	Fortune cookie fitness	Basketball skills	Basketball
16	Vanishing beanbags	Hexagon hustle	Tennis skills	Lead-up tennis
17	Move, change direction, pose on signal	Four corners	Tennis skills	Tennis
18	Ball activities	Squad leader exercises with task cards	New games	New game activities
19	Partner movements	Aerobic fitness	Rhythms-dance	Dance
20	Moving to music	Aerobic fitness	Rhythms-dance	Dance
21	Stretching	Jogging	Track and field skills	Relays
22	Stretching	Jogging	Field skills	Relays
23	Personal choice	Partner fitness	Softball skills	Lead-up softball
24	Personal choice	Athletic movements	Softball skills	Softball
25	Throwing and catching on the move	Circuit training with sport challenges	Recreational games	Recreational games
26	Shuttle drills	Marking	Badminton skills	Lead-up badminton
27	Pyramid power	Obstacle course	Badminton skills	Badminton
28	Following activity	Fortune cookie	Frisbee skills	Frisbee golf
29	Throwing and catching	Grass drills with partner resistance	Flickerball-speedway-gatorball	
30	Weave drills	Interval training	Flickerball-speedway-gatorball	
31	Move and perform a stretch	Rope jumping	Cooperative activities	Group games
32	Move and perform a fitness task	Rope jumping with partner resistance	Golf skills/pillow polo	Golf/pillow polo related
33	Rolling hoops	Light pace running	Golf skills/pillow polo	Golf/pillow polo related
34	Stretching	Jogging	Orienteering	Relays
35	Stretching and jogging		Fitness testing	

FIGURE 3.2 Centennial yearly plan

Whenever and wherever possible, offer these courses on alternate years. However, unforseen circumstances may require changing the course sequencing.

Year 1	Year 2	Year 3	Year 4
First 10 Weeks			
A. Speedball	A. Golf	A. Speedball	A. Field hockey
B. Field hockey	B. Boating & hunter's safety	B. Archery	B. Running for fitness–aerobics
C. Archery	C. Soccer	C. Floor hockey	C. Soccer
Second 10 Weeks			
A. Basic swimming	A. Recreational swimming	A. Basic swimming	A. Recreational swimming
B. Volleyball	B. Recreational games	B. Basketball	B. Bowling
C. Weights & fitness	C. Weights & fitness	C. Cross-country skiing	C. Weights & fitness
Third 10 Weeks			
A. Lifesaving	A. Competitive swimming	A. Lifesaving	A. Synchronized swimming
B. Gymnastics	B. Power volleyball	B. Handball	B. Recreational games
C. Weights & fitness	C. Weights & fitness	C. Weights & fitness	C. Gymnastics
Fourth 10 Weeks			
A. Bowling	A. Tennis	A. Golf	A. Tennis
B. Softball	B. Softball	B. Softball	B. Softball
C. Handball & ping pong	C. Basic fishing	C. Squash	C. Camping

FIGURE 3.3 Panama Central Senior High School 4-year sequence

Reprinted with permission from Gary M. Olson, Panama Central School, Panama, NY.

Traditional sports include tennis, golf, ping pong, shuffleboard, horseshoes, and paddleball. Nontraditional sports include horseback riding, 3-person volleyball, ground school for sky diving, hiking and camping, orienteering, wilderness camping, hunting safety, scuba diving, alpine skiing, and fly fishing. Community support is obtained from subject-matter experts in the private sector who help with instruction and offer the use of community facilities and funds. Field trips are arranged for off-campus facilities such as ski areas and the local YMCA pool for scuba instruction.

Outdoor Adventure Activities Model

Another variation of the multi-activity model is the outdoor adventure model. Some popular activities in this model are cycling, orienteering, backpacking, skin/scuba diving, canoeing, cross-country skiing, downhill skiing, caving, rock climbing and rappelling, group initiatives, and ropes course activities. Some schools include a limited number of short units (either elective or required) as part of the multi-activity program, whereas others offer an entire semester of adventure activities. Most often, high schools offer a year-long elective course designed with a variety of outdoor adventure pursuits. The program might include a year-long elective wilderness adventure class in the physical education program that includes instruction and field trips for rock climbing, rappelling, caving, beginning and advanced backpacking, and day hikes. Usually, the focus of these programs is on the development of basic skills requisite for participation in these activities. Another approach is to offer group initiative and cooperative activities that help students learn group and individual problem-solving skills under stressful situations.

Adding outdoor adventure activities to the multi-activity model creates significant change for teachers, students, administrators, and parents. Many of the activities must be done off-campus. For example, rock-climbing areas, wooded or desert locations, caves, rivers, and lakes can be utilized. Establishing a nearby off-campus environment with various outdoor facilities can provide a variety of teaching areas for these activities. The units can culminate with an off-campus trip during the school day or as an after-school or weekend trip with parents involved. The trips give students an opportunity to learn and experience activities that are different from regular school offerings. Afterschool, weekend, and vacation period times are often used for these classes.

Safety and liability problems related to these activities require special safety and insurance arrangements. Many administrators and parents show little concern about injuries related to athletic programs such as football, wrestling, and gymnastics, but are cautious about implementing adventure activities that appear risky. Most of the activities require funding for specialized equipment, such as compasses, climbing ropes, and camping gear. Teachers must show evidence of having proper qualifications because of the expertise required for high-risk activities.

With the problems created by outdoor adventure activities, why take the time and do the extra work? Because, in most cases, secondary students are highly motivated and enthusiastic about the activities. There are many reasons for this increased interest. Some students enjoy the novelty of the activities, others like the risk and excitement, the challenge of the environment, or the opportunity to make decisions, while still others like the social opportunities without competition between people. Other students are attracted to the lifetime participation emphasis and the opportunities that exist within the community. The activities offer the opportunity to travel, explore new areas, and enjoy competition with an environment of wind, water, snow, mountains, and woods. These activities satisfy the goals of physical education and are worth the extra effort.

Physical educators need to dispel four myths that often block the introduction of outdoor pursuits into the physical education curriculum (Parker and Steen, 1988). These myths are:

1. The school must be located near major outdoor areas or state parks.
2. The teacher must have advanced skill levels in outdoor activities.

3. There are insurmountable obstacles regarding safety, legal liability, and insurance.
4. The cost of outdoor pursuits is too expensive for schools.

Schools and physical educators can overcome these problems in a number of ways. By starting small and being creative and innovative, much can be accomplished. Many of the activities are easy to implement and can be started on campus with a limited budget. With proper training and supervision, students can experience a safe and rewarding experience with outdoor activities.

Deer Valley High School in Phoenix, Arizona, has offered an elective outdoor adventure curriculum with two different tracts. The first tract is an outdoor adventure activities course that gives students an opportunity to enjoy and learn about Arizona's outdoors. Students learn the fundamental skills of backpacking, fishing, hunting, camping, and wilderness first aid. Field trips are set up during the school day, after school, and over weekends. Students make choices on which and how many field trips they are going to take. Some of the activities and trips that have been used include hiking in a riparian area, fishing and camping in the high desert, desert awareness activities at the Sonora Desert Museum in Tucson, trap or skeet shooting and gun safety at a shooting range, pheasant hunting at a local hunting club, field archery at a range, and basic horsemanship skills at local horse stables.

The advanced class is called the wilderness adventure class and includes more demanding and advanced skills in rock climbing, backpacking, caving, orienteering skills, and skiing activities. Students select field trips from the following choices: hiking at Mt. Humphrey in Flagstaff, backpacking into the Havasupai Falls area of the Grand Canyon, orienteering at the North Mountain Park course, rock climbing in the McDowell Mountains, cave exploring in the Tucson area, cross-country and downhill skiing in Flagstaff, and backpacking and rock climbing at Weaver's Needle in the Superstition Mountains. These classes are elective and meet daily to work on the skills involved and prepare for the various field trips. Students pay a special class fee to pay for travel expenses and extra equipment the school is not able to supply (Figure 3.4).

Austin O'Brien High School in Calgary, Alberta, Canada, offers a variety of outdoor adventure activities as part of their curriculum. Students elect units on canoeing, sailing, kayaking, basic rock climbing,

Deer Valley High School Outdoor Adventure Schedule

Date(s)	Day(s)	Activity	Destination	Depart	Return Approx.	Fee	Comments	Type of Tran
Sept. 19	Friday	Day hike	Wet Beaver Creek—Sedona	7 A.M.	5 P.M.	Paid	Bring a swimming suit and old tennis shoes Don't forget water and your lunch	SB
27–28	Sat.–Sun.	Fishing/camping trip	Payson area	8 A.M.	8 P.M.	$20	Great place to fish and swim—may need license	CV
Oct. 7	Tuesday	Desert awareness	Sonora Museum—Tucson	8 A.M.	5 P.M.	Paid	This is the best desert museum in the Southwest	SB
24	Friday	Gun safety	Black Canyon Range	8 A.M.	2 P.M.	Paid	Bring your own shells—adults needed	SB
25	Saturday	Trap/skeet competition	Black Canyon Range	8 A.M.	2 P.M.	$10	Includes 2 rounds of shooting and prizes Bring your own shells	SV
Nov. 15	Saturday	Pheasant hunt	Salt Cedar Preserve	7 A.M.	2 P.M.	$15	Bring own gun and shells—must have adult with each student—you keep pheasants you shoot	CV
26	Wednesday	Field archery	Black Canyon Range	8 A.M.	2 P.M.	Paid	Compound Bows OK—adults needed Wear tennis shoes	SB
Dec. 9	Tuesday	Horsemanship	Pointe Stables	8 A.M.	1 P.M.	Paid	Wear jeans and tennis shoes or boots	SB
12	Friday	Horsemanship	Pointe Stables	6 P.M.	10 P.M.	Paid	All parents are invited and needed for potluck under the stars—guests of students are welcome	None
Jan. 31	Saturday	Downhill skiing	Flagstaff	6 A.M.	8 P.M.	$???	Rent boots, skies, and poles in Phoenix	CB
Feb. 7	Saturday	Cross-country skiing	Flagstaff	6 A.M.	6 P.M.	Paid	Bring gloves, hat, change of clothes—over dress	CV
March 6	Friday	Rock climbing	South Mountain Park	8 A.M.	5 P.M.	Paid	Bring chocolate chip cookies for instructor	SB
28	Saturday	Rock climbing	McDowell Mts.	6 A.M.	6 P.M.	Paid	Bring chocolate chip cookies for instructor	SV
April 4–5	Sat.–Sun.	Caving/day hike	Tucson Area	6 A.M.	8 P.M.	$25	Bring change of clothes and plastic bag	PV
16	Thurs.	Map and compass	North Mountain Park	8 A.M.	2 P.M.	Paid	Bring water, lunch, hat, sunglasses, notebook, ruler, and pencil	SB
25	Saturday	Day hike	Superstitions	6 A.M.	5 P.M.	Paid	Bring water, hat, sunglasses, and lunch	SB
May 8	Friday	Day hike	Mt. Humphreys	5 A.M.	9 P.M.	Paid	Bring warm clothing, rain gear, lunch, water, hat	SB
14–18	Th.–Mon.	Backpacking trip	North Rim—Grand Canyon	4 P.M.	4 P.M.	$30	Advanced hike—30 miles—qualifying hike will be Thurs., May 7th, 6 P.M. Squaw Peak Park	CV

SB—School bus   CB—Commercial   SV—School van   CV—Commercial

REMINDER!! Unless someone takes your place, there will be *no refunds* on non-paid field trips for *any reason*. Non-paid field trips are limited by number. Participants will be selected by physical conditioning and/or class grade-point average.

FIGURE 3.4 Deer Valley yearly plan

Physical Education 30B
Austin O'Brien High School

1. Learn-to-sail program—Lake Wabamum
2. Walleyball
3. Bicycle mechanics course and Elk Island Tour
4. Curling
5. Archery
6. Rifle target shooting (trap and skeet)
7. Camping and hiking program
8. Cross-country skiing
9. Tennis
10. Social dance
11. Badminton
12. Racquetball
13. Bowling
14. Downhill skiing
15. Volleyball and pickleball
16. Coaching certification level-one theory

FIGURE 3.5   Austin O'Brien example

orienteering, outdoor survival, wilderness camping, backpacking, and cross-country skiing. A senior-level elective physical education class includes the yearly sequence of activities shown in Figure 3.5, including outdoor adventure and several popular lifetime activities.

Lake Forest High School in Lake Forest, Illinois, offers a multi-activity outdoor adventure curriculum for juniors and seniors. A wide variety of activities are available to the students. A sample of the yearly sequence of activities and the day-to-day progressions are included in Figure 3.6.

[Darryl Siedentop]

SPORTS EDUCATION MODEL

The sports education model is an activity-based approach developed by Siedentop (1994), with the primary objective being to help students become skilled sports participants and good sportspeople. The model is a combination of physical education, intramurals, and interscholastic athletics. It allows students, regardless of ability level, to experience the positive values of sports in a manner similar to being involved in an interscholastic sports program. The goal of the sports education model is to help students experience such qualities as working to reach deferred goals, teamwork, loyalty, commitment, perse-

verance, dedication, and concern for other people. The model emphasizes the importance of teams, leagues, seasons, championships, coaches, practice, player involvement, formal records, statistics, and competitive balance. These characteristics are usually emphasized in sport programs but not in a physical education program. This model gives all students a chance to experience a quality competitive sports program that is organized and supervised by an unbiased physical educator who will protect the important values of sport. Students learn to compete and be good competitors. A desired outcome is that students become competent, literate, and enthusiastic sports participants who want to play sports at local, national, and international levels.

Siedentop (1994) identifies 6 characteristics that make the sports education model different from more traditional approaches to physical education:

1. Sports education involves seasons rather than units.
2. Students quickly become members of teams.
3. There is a formal schedule of competition.
4. There is usually a major culminating event.
5. Records are kept and publicized.
6. Teachers assume the role of coaches.

Each season begins with instruction and development of team strategies according to teams' strengths and weaknesses. The teacher helps organize the class into teams, elect a student captain, and provides instruction for team members about skill development. Teams take the initiative to organize practice, decide on players' positions, and determine strategies for playing other teams. Students assume more responsibility as the program evolves, and they begin to understand its goals.

The program can be implemented in several ways, depending on the situation and the comfort zone of the teacher. It might be accomplished in a single class with one teacher and one class. It could involve several classes that meet during the same period of the day. It could also be implemented with classes that meet during different periods of the day with competition scheduled at a common time. Another implementation style involves practicing during the regular class period followed by competition outside of class.

Depending on student interests, available facilities, and school schedule, different activities can be selected for the program. Traditional team sports and individual sports such as basketball, volleyball, flag football, soccer, softball, badminton, gymnastics, cross-country running, or track and field can be se-

Sample Curriculum for
Outdoor Adventure Education Course

Weekdays		Optional Weekend Outings	
September			
2–5	Introduction—Basic camping backpacking equipment	19–20	Cycling overnight Ecology-biology
8–12	Cycling		Light hike
15–19	Cycling and camping		Sensory activities
22–26	Climbing		Star study
29–10/3	Climbing		
October			
6–10	Climbing and rappelling	17,18,	Climbing
13–17	Climbing and rappelling trip planning	and 19	Canoeing—sailing
20–24	Climbing		Fishing
27–31	Orienteering		Belaying
			Rappelling
			Star study
November			
3–7	Angling and casting		
10–14	Backpacking and cooking		
17–21	First aid		
24–26	Water safety		
December			
1–5	Winter camping	5–6	Winter camping overnight
8–12	Shooting (riflery)		Star study
15–19	Shooting		Orienteering
January			
5–9	Cross-country skiing		
12–16	Cross-country skiing and snowshoeing		
19–23	Testing and wrap up		

FIGURE 3.6   Lake Forest High School example of yearly plan

lected. The sports could be modified into activities such as 3-person volleyball, 3-person basketball, or over-the-line softball. Lifetime sports such as tennis, bowling, or golf are popular choices, with other possibilities being less-common activities such as ultimate Frisbee, bicycling courses, orienteering meets, speed-a-way, team handball, floor or field hockey, and modified lacrosse.

If several teachers are working together, students have several choices for leagues that are of interest to them. The leagues vary in length from 3 to 4 weeks to 9 to 10 weeks depending on student interest, facilities, and the school schedule. Students have the opportunity to participate in approximately 5 to 12 leagues in a year of physical education. The seasonal schedule for a school could adhere to grading peri-

Spring Semester
Outdoor Adventure Education Course

Weekdays		Weekend Outings	
February			
1/31–4	Introduction and cross-country skiing		
7–11	Cross-country skiing		
14–18	Cross-country skiing and snowshoeing		
21–25	Riflery		
March			
2/28–4	Riflery and casting and angling		
7–11	Winter camping		
14–18	Conservation of energy and diet		
21–25	Backpacking and equipment		
28–4/1	First aid		
April			
4–8	No school		
11–15	Map and compass		
18–22	Climbing		
25–29	Climbing		
May			
2–6	Climbing	20, 21, and 22	Climbing
9–13	Climbing		Rappelling
16–20	Climbing		Sensory activities
23–27	Cycling		Star study
30–6/3	Cycling	28–29	Cycling overnight
			Ecology-biology
			Sensory activities
			Light hike
June			
6–10	Wrap–up		

FIGURE 3.6 Continued

ods; for example, 6- or 9-week grading periods could drive seasons for the leagues (Figure 3.7). All leagues include aspects of sports (Siedentop, 1994) including seasons, team affiliation, formal competition, culminating events, record keeping, and festivity. Leagues and rules of competition can be modified to ensure students are successful. For example, volleyball and basketball leagues could have choices for 3-on-3 competition in addition to the 5-on-5 format. There could be a boys' league, a girls' league, or a coed league. Participation is required for all students, and developmentally appropriate competition that is equated is implemented. Students handle all roles in the units including coaching, scorekeeping, statisticians, equipment managers, and refereeing. The teacher's role is to ensure the sports environment is

Seasonal Schedule for Sport Education

Semester	Seasons	Team Sports	Individual Sports
Fall	Fall 9 weeks	Flag football Cross country	Tennis Archery Table tennis
Fall	Early winter 9 weeks	Volleyball Soccer	Fencing Bowling Badminton Racquetball
Spring	Late winter 9 weeks	Basketball Swimming	Fencing Bowling Racquetball Riflery
Spring	Spring 9 weeks	Baseball Softball Track and field	Badminton Golf Archery

FIGURE 3.7 Seasonal schedule for sports education model

From Donna Dugas, *Sport Education in the Secondary Curriculum.* In D. Siedentop (ed.). *Sport Education.* Champaign, IL: Human Kinetics Publishers. p. 107. Copyright © 1994 by Daryl Siedentop. Reprinted by permission.

protected and students learn the values of fair play, equal competition, and the skills, rules, and etiquette of the sport. Students are involved as coaches and instructors for their teams. Students select uniforms, team names, starting lineups, substitution patterns, and practice arrangements and times. Records are kept and posted in public areas, and awards are given for a variety of student accomplishments in addition to winning games or matches. Siedentop, Mand, and Taggart (1986) offer an example of using 3-person teams in a volleyball league setting.

Three-Person Volleyball

This model is for a middle or junior high school setting in which 2 teachers share classes that total 50 to 70 students. Three-person volleyball is played with a junior-size volleyball, with a 7-foot net, and a 15 by 40 foot court.

The class meets 4 days per week, and the volleyball season is designed for 8 weeks or a total of 32 sessions. With 64 students, this class has 2 volleyball leagues. One league is for skilled players, and the other is for less-skilled players. (Note that there are other legitimate ways of dividing students for competition.)

The first week is devoted to practice and instruction. Four students of varying levels of skill are selected to assist the teachers in assigning students to teams. After 3 days of observation, the students are assigned to teams, 4 students to each team. The teams are then assigned to 2 leagues of 8 teams each. On the fourth day of class, students begin to receive instruction and practice as a team. One teacher takes administrative responsibility for each league.

During the second week, the students have 2 practice days and 2 scrimmage days. Scrimmage days allow teachers to make sure that rules are understood and to teach refereeing as a skill. During the third week, a double round-robin league play begins for each league; there are 2 match days and 2 practice days. From the third through the seventh weeks, students have 3 match days and 1 practice day per week. During the eighth week, there is a championship tournament involving all 16 teams.

During match days students participate in a warm-up period followed by a timed match (the duration of the match is determined by the length of the teaching period), for example, 22 minutes. All matches start and stop at the same time. There is a signal every 5 minutes for substitutions. Students referee their own games, with referees being those students not playing at the moment. Referees also keep score. The winner of each match is the team with the most points at the final time signal. Standings can be kept in terms of total points scored or win-loss records (or some combination of the 2). The teachers observe games and make notes for individual players and teams in terms of skills and strategies to be worked on at subsequent practice sessions. Team captains are responsible for seeing that a certain portion of practice sessions is devoted to those notes. In other practice sessions, all teams and players practice certain skills and strategies as directed by the teachers.

Students get to choose a name for their team and adopt a uniform (as long as it meets the standards set by the teachers for physical education clothing). Each Monday, the league standings are posted along with other items concerning the league. If team play in any league is very unequal, the teachers and the 4 student representatives can, at the end of the first round of play, make personnel changes in teams so as to equalize competition for the second round (pp. 196–197).

KNOWLEDGE CONCEPTS MODELS

In a knowledge concepts model, primary focus is on knowledge and cognitive understanding through the various subdisciplines of physical education. Students learn the *how* and the *why* of physical activity through involvement in problem-solving experiments. Less emphasis is placed on *doing* activities in these models. Students still spend time with activities in the gym and on playing fields, but they also spend time in a classroom with lectures, overheads, worksheets, and films similar to a classroom teacher in a more academic subject. Time is set aside for laboratories designed to help students discover important conceptual knowledge (see Figures 3.8, 3.9, 3.10, and 3.11). Knowledge objectives have long been listed as a primary concern of physical education, but they are attended to with much emphasis. The rules, strategy, and history of a sport are given at the end of each unit of activity. Some experts believe school physical education will survive only if it becomes more academically oriented (Ennis, 1993; Harageones, 1993; and Vickers, 1993). The argument is for more intellectual rigor in our physical education curricula.

A current compendium of knowledge that can be used to implement this type of model is the *Basic Stuff Series* (NASPE, 1987). This series of booklets is a compilation of knowledge gleaned from the subdisciplines of physical education organized into an applied format for teachers. A booklet is available for each of the following areas: exercise physiology, humanities in physical education, kinesiology, motor development, motor learning, and psychosocial aspects of physical education. The intent of the series is to promote the inclusion of subdisciplinary knowledge in physical education curricula, grades K through 12. Series I focuses on knowledge concepts from the subdiscipline, and Series II provides learning experiences teachers can use to teach concepts.

The *Basic Stuff Series* booklets are arranged around student motives or purposes for participating in physical activity. Common student motives identified and discussed include achievement (doing better), health (feeling good), appearance (looking good), social interaction (getting along), and coping with the environment (surviving). Secondary schools can use the conceptual knowledge for units in each subdiscipline. For example, an instructional unit on biomechanics focuses on the following topics: balance, spin and rebound, center of gravity, force production, Newton's laws of motion, and the use of biomechanics in various sport skills. The student motives or purposes can serve as an individual unit or as part of a unit. A curriculum based on this model offers a balance of activities from these areas, and students are encouraged to select activities that best fit their perceived motives. A curriculum based on student motives devotes time to discussing values, motives, and knowledge concepts, with the primary focus on knowledge. Harrison, Blakemore, Buck, and Pellett (1996) describe several variations for implementing concepts into a curriculum: (1) Integrate the concepts into regular activity-based units, (2) include several separate units on concepts to supplement activity-based units, and (3) teach concepts only on special occasions such as rainy days or shortened periods.

Some argue that a curriculum based on concepts is more academic and easier to defend to a school board. Other educators feel knowledge-based discussions divert too much time from physical skill development. Balancing these areas of emphasis is important because instructional time for knowledge and skill is limited. If one area is emphasized, then another area has to be reduced or eliminated. Knowledge concepts are important, but if the increased em-

Name _____   Date _____

Instructor _____   Period _____

Activity 4.35 Check It Out—Dribbling

Observing and evaluating dribbling technique

There are two ways to see if someone is skillful. One is to look at results; how long did he or she take to dribble through a set of cones. The other way is to observe if the person's body moved in the most effective way using correct form.

Below is a form checklist. Select a classmate and watch him or her dribble a soccer ball. Check each element listed on the chart. It may take a number of kicks before you can see everything. When you have completed the list, share it with your partner.

Dribbling a Soccer Ball

1. Eyes and head are up at all times.   Yes _____   No _____
2. The ball is in front of, and close to, the body.   Yes _____   No _____
3. The ball is dribbled off the inside of the foot, never the toe.   Yes _____   No _____
4. Body is over the ball.   Yes _____   No _____

Repeat your observation of your partner. This time look at only one element at a time. After each observation tell your partner if he or she did that part correctly. If your partner did not, repeat dribbling until that part is correct, then move on to the next part.

5. How did it feel to make corrections and help a classmate dribble better? _____

_____

_____

_____

6. (Ask your partner to write here.) How did you feel when you were being told what you were doing correctly or incorrectly? _____

_____

_____

_____

7. Did this help you to understand how to dribble a soccer ball and do it better? _____

8. How did you feel when you were asked to repeat the dribble? _____

_____

_____

_____

FIGURE 3.8   Dribbling a soccer ball worksheet

From T. Spindt et.al. 1993. *Moving with Skill*. Dubuque, IA: Kendall/Hunt. p. 109.

Name _____ Class _____ Date _____

Skill-Related Fitness

Purpose: To learn about skill-related fitness.

Procedure:

1. Try each of the activities on page 6 of your textbook.
2. As you do each activity, think about what part of fitness the activity best represents. Also think about how one part of skill-related fitness differs from another. The activities are not intended as tests of your fitness but are intended to give you a general idea of the nature of each fitness part. See how close you come to doing each activity.
3. After you have tried each activity, place a check on the line to show that you have attempted the activity. These activities will not be scored.

Skill-Related Fitness

Activity	Attempted
Line jump (Agility)	_____
Backward hop (Balance)	_____
Double-ball bounce (Coordination)	_____
Knees to feet (Power)	_____
Coin catch (Reaction time)	_____
Double heel click (Speed)	_____

Discuss Your Results

1. Which of the above activities did you have the most difficulty performing? the least? _____

_____

_____

_____

_____

2. How might improving skill-related fitness benefit someone not interested in sports? _____

_____

_____

_____

_____

FIGURE 3.9 Skill-related fitness worksheet

From C. Corbin and R. Lindsey. 1993. *Fitness for Life.* Glenview, IL: Scott, Foresman & Company. p. 8.

Student's Name: _____

Practice several overhand and underhand volleyball serves. Try putting different types of spins on both of the serves. Complete the following questions:

1. Where do you have to contact the ball to make it spin to the right? _____
   _____

2. Where do you have to contact the ball to make it spin to the left? _____
   _____

3. Can you serve the volleyball with backspin toward you? _____
   _____

4. Can you serve the volleyball with topspin away from you? _____
   _____

5. Can you serve the volleyball with no spin? _____
   _____

6. Please explain where you must strike the volleyball in order to get the proper spin as described in questions 3, 4, and 5. _____
   _____

7. Please describe the flight of the volleyball with the spins described in questions 3, 4, and 5. _____
   _____
   _____

8. How can these different spins impact your ability as a volleyball player? _____
   _____
   _____

9. Please relate this concept of spin to baseball, softball, racquetball, tennis, or basketball, and give a specific example of the use of spin in these activities. _____
   _____
   _____

10. What conclusion can you make about the use of force in creating spin on an object? _____
    _____
    _____

FIGURE 3.10 Volleyball Serves—Problem-Solving Questions

Name _____　Date _____

Period _____　Instructor _____

Activity 3-2　Center of Gravity and Stability

Objective:　To observe how balance and stability are affected by the constantly moving center of gravity in the human body.

Directions

1. Assume a position on your hands and knees. Place your hands no greater than 3 inches apart. Position your knees no greater than 3 inches apart as shown.

2. Now have a partner attempt to push you over. Be sure to maintain the starting position.

3. Next assume a position on your hands and knees. Make any adjustments that you feel you need to make you more stable.

4. Have your partner attempt to push you over.

   A.　Was it harder or easier on the second stance? _____

   _____

   B.　What did you do to your base of support in the second stance to make it more stable? _____

   _____

   C.　State the principle of stability that you used in order to be more stable in a kneeling position. _____

   _____

   D.　Describe at least 3 examples from sports or dance that make use of this principle of stability.

3 inches

FIGURE 3.11　Center of gravity and stability worksheet

From G. Spindt, W. Monti, and B. Hennessy. 1991. *Moving for Life*. Dubuque, IA: Kendall/Hunt. p. 49.

phasis reduces time available for physical skill development, an important program objective may be slighted. Knowing about physical activities is not the same as experiencing them. If students are going to incorporate activities into their lifestyles, they need an opportunity to gain knowledge and develop competency in several physical activities.

Fitness Education Model

The fitness education model is most consistent with the public health perspective of physical education and is an example of a knowledge concepts model. The model has gained popularity in many universities, colleges, and high schools (Corbin and Lindsey,

1996a; Johnson and Harageones, 1994). The model focuses on imparting physical fitness concepts to students. The theory is that at some point in a student's education, it is important to devote a course to the knowledge concepts related to the physical education objectives: *Is* active, *Has* knowledge, *Values* regular activity, and *Is* fit (see Chapter 1, objectives section). Evidence suggests that fitness education courses are effective in promoting knowledge, improving attitudes about activity, and altering lifestyle activity patterns later in life (Brynteson and Adams, 1993).

A popular fitness model is the *Fitness for Life* approach (Corbin and Lindsey, 1996a). This approach to physical education and fitness development places instructional emphasis on lecture, laboratory experiments, and exercise programs for use in adulthood. Lessons help students learn facts about fitness and physical activity so they can be good consumers, program planners, and problem solvers. Students participate in both classroom activities and gymnasium or outdoor fitness activities. They receive experiences with self-testing procedures in order to establish a fitness profile. A variety of fitness activities and routines are taught that can be done individually or in groups for a lifetime of regular activity. The *Fitness for Life* program teaches answers to the following central questions:

1. Why is physical activity important to every person?
2. How should physical activity take place?
3. What forms of physical activity are available?

The objectives for this model are arranged in a hierarchical order called the "stairway to lifetime fitness" (Figure 3.12) (Corbin and Lindsey, 1996a). The rationale is that if students climb the lifetime fitness stairway, they will be more likely to be active throughout life. Information and activities are provided on a number of topics including cardiovascular fitness, strength, endurance, flexibility, fat control, skill-related fitness, correct ways to exercise, and how to plan an exercise program. Students learn to diagnose and solve personal fitness problems. They have opportunities to develop exercise programs to remediate health concerns.

Several options are available for incorporating fitness for life into a school curriculum. Common alternatives are to offer a 1- or 2-semester program using the *Fitness for Life* model (Corbin and Lindsey, 1996a). Some schools, such as Mainland High School in Daytona Beach, Florida, combine teaching knowledge concepts with participation in a modern school fitness center equipped with the latest fitness machines and technology (Wood, Fisher, Huth, and Graham, 1995). Gilbert High School, in Gilbert, Arizona, offers an elective "Super Circuit" class using a fitness circuit developed by the Universal Company in Iowa. Students work out on the super circuit every other day and participate in lifetime sports such as tennis, golf, and racquetball during other days (see Figure 3.13).

Thirteen states have adopted a statewide requirement for a fitness concepts course. In addition, the province of New Brunswick in Canada and the Department of Defense Dependent Schools worldwide

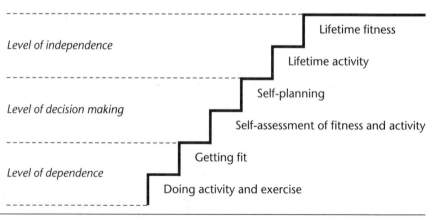

FIGURE 3.12 Stairway to lifetime fitness

From C. Corbin and R. Lindsey. *Fitness for Life.* 4th ed. Copyright © 1996 by Scott, Foresman & Company.

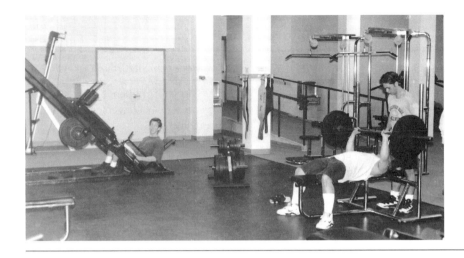

FIGURE 3.13 Students working out on weight machines

have added such a requirement (Watson, Sherrill, and Weigand, 1994). A wide variety of curriculum and instructional materials are available to teachers, such as books for students, lesson plans for teachers, slides, lesson masters, overhead transparencies, review questions, laboratory experiments, and test materials (Corbin and Lindsey, 1996b). The recommended content for a high school *Fitness for Life* class is shown in Figure 3.14. This model is based on 2 days per week in the classroom and 3 days in an activity setting. Students learn the concepts of healthy activity and apply these concepts by designing fitness activities and self-assessing personal fitness.

Another similar knowledge concepts approach to secondary curriculum focuses on the components of human wellness (see Chapter 17 for a variety of wellness activities). The wellness model is more comprehensive than the fitness concepts approach. Units of instruction in wellness include stress management, alcohol and drug abuse, nutrition, weight control, physical fitness, coping skills, personal safety, environmental awareness, behavioral self-control, and problem-solving skills related to these specific topics. Wellness is viewed by many as an important state of health that is an ongoing process throughout life. It is a preventive approach to health and expands the fitness concepts model. To maintain wellness, students need requisite information and skills. Advocates of this program point to numerous health problems that abound in our society. A healthy lifestyle for all students is the major objective of this model.

Both the wellness and the fitness education models focus primarily on knowledge and under-standing of physical fitness and wellness. People who advocate these models find the emphasis on knowledge to be an advantage because it adds credibility to a program. The down side is the increased time spent on lecture and analysis resulting in less time for learning physical skills. Students need information, but they also need successful encounters with physical activity and time allotted for practicing and performing physical skills. Determining exactly how much time should be spent on knowledge acquisition and how much on physical skill development is difficult. Schools using a concepts approach offer a balance of physical activity and knowledge concepts. For example, a common approach is to offer several units on wellness activities (including fitness) to supplement or complement physical activities units.

SOCIAL DEVELOPMENT MODEL

Hellison (1985, 1995) developed a curriculum model that focuses on enhancing social competence, self-control, responsible behavior, and concern for others. Emphasis on fitness and the development of sport skills and knowledge is reduced in order to accomplish the primary goal of social competence. Sports and physical activities are used as a means of accomplishing social goals. The basic philosophy of the social development model is that social problems in society have created situations that requires schools to offer this type of focus. Professionals subscribing to this model believe that many students are

Discussion Topics

Table of Contents	Self-Management/Group Discussion
1. Fitness and wellness for all	Building self-confidence
2. Safe and smart physical activity	Making activity convenience
3. How much is enough?	Examining goals
4. Getting started in physical activity	Building positive attitudes
5. Benefits of physical activity	Reducing risk factors
6. Cardiovascular fitness	Finding social support
7. Physical activity and fat control	Adjusting to uncontrollable factors
8. Muscular endurance	Thinking success
9. Strength	Building intrinsic motivation
10. Flexibility	Eliminating irrational beliefs
11. Skill-related fitness	Evaluating popular activities
12. Choosing physical activities	Logging activities
13. Making consumer choices	Setting goals
14. Program planning	Managing time
15. Fitness and the future	Preventing relapse
16. A wellness perspective	Relapse prevention
17. Nutrition	Saying no
18. Stress management	Controlling competitive stress

Activity-Based Topics

Fitness Focus	Self-Assessment	Activity
1. Starter program	Exercise basics	SRF/HRF
2. Fitness games	Fitnessgram (2 tests)	Safe exercise
3. Continuous exercise	Fitnessgram (2 tests)	Jogging
4. Cooper's aerobics	Ht/Wt & sit reach	Circuit exercise
5. Aerobic dance	Healthy back test	Exercises for back/pos
6. Jump rope	Step test	Target zones
7. Line exercises	Skinfolds/BC tests	Resistance tr. tech.
8. Light weight circuit	Muscular end. tests	Calisthenics workout
9. Partner exercise: str.	IRM/grip	Resist. training
10. New games	Flexibility tests	Stretching exercises
11. Sport stars	SRF tests	Supplemental weights
12. Jolly ball	SRF tests	Rubber band exercise
13. Step aerobics	Fitness reassessment	Coop. aerobics
14. Homemade weights	Fitness reassessment	Your personal plan
15. Home calisthenics	Blood pressure/hip-waist	Your exercise circuit
16. Walking for wellness	Walking test	Your fitness club
17. Fitness trail	Posture test	Isometrics
18. Frisbee golf	Stress assessment	Relaxation exercises

FIGURE 3.14 Contents for a fitness-for-life class

From C. Corbin and R. Lindsey. 1996. *Fitness for Life Teacher's Resource Manual.* 4th ed. Glenview, IL: Scott, Foresman & Company.

disruptive and difficult to manage, making it the school's responsibility to provide better social development training. This model has been field-tested with troubled or alienated youth and general student bodies.

In this model, students proceed through 6 developmental levels of social competence. Different students enter at different levels and proceed upward through the steps. Students are encouraged to rate themselves on each of the levels and compare their ratings with their teacher's ratings (see Figure 3.15).

Discussion between teacher and students examines perceptions of how students are progressing. The following are the levels of social development.

Level 0: Irresponsibility. Students do not participate and are totally unmotivated and undisciplined. They interrupt and intimidate other students and teachers. They make excuses and blame others for their behavior. Teachers find it difficult to manage or accomplish much with these students.

Definition of Ratings		Student	Teacher	
	Date	*Rating*	*Rating*	*Comments*
0 Little self-control Not involved Uses put-downs Irresponsible Disruptive				
1 Under control, not involved Not participating Not prepared Nonproductive				
2 Under control, involved when teacher directed Frequently off task Needs prompting Needs frequent reminders				
3 Self-responsibility Works independently Self-motivated Positive attitude				
4 Caring Cares about others Involved with others Sensitive to needs of others				
5 Going beyond Leadership Additional responsibility Helping teacher				

FIGURE 3.15 Social development checklist

Level 1: Self-control. Students at the self-control level can control themselves without the direct supervision of the teacher and do not infringe on the rights of other students or the teacher. They can begin to participate in class activities and enhance their learning.

Level 2: Involvement. Level 2 involves student self-control and desired involvement with the subject matter of fitness, skills, and games. Students are enthusiastically involved in the program without constant prompting or supervision of the teacher.

Level 3: Self-responsibility. Students at level 3 begin to identify their interests and start to make choices within the parameters of the program. Motivation and responsibility are characteristics of these students. They start to take more responsibility and explore options for their lives outside the program. This stage represents a start of their own identity.

Level 4: Caring. The caring stage has students moving outside themselves and showing concern for other students and the teacher. Students are cooperative, helpful, and show a genuine interest in the lives of others. They are concerned about the world around them.

Level 5: Going Beyond. The highest level is characterized by student leadership and additional responsibility for program decisions. Students get involved with the teacher on decisions that will affect all students in the program. Students become co-workers with teachers.

This model can be implemented in different ways depending on the specifics of the school situation and the type of students. Hellison (1985) suggests an option that uses a daily program with 2 days spent on sport skills and game activities, 2 days on individual physical fitness routines, and 1 day on cooperative and sharing activities for social development. Each day, teachers begin or end a class with a "self-control" activity or strategy that reminds students of the important social goals of the class (self-control, involvement, self-responsibility, and caring). Examples of strategies available to the teacher are teacher talk, modeling, reinforcement, reflection time, student sharing, the talking bench (where 2 students go to work out a problem), student checklists, student achievement records, and behavior con-

tracts between the student and the teacher (see Figures 3.16 and 3.17). Many specific strategies are available to the teacher for each of the social development levels.

OUTCOMES MODEL

A recent trend caused by the public's concern for accountability is to mandate an outcomes-based model for physical education curricula. Not only is the model mandated, but in some states the actual outcomes are delineated and expected to be accomplished by teachers. Minimum skills and knowledge are identified and form the framework of the curriculum. Standards are identified in terms of performance or behavioral objectives for students. Performance objectives are statements of what students are expected to perform, the conditions under which the performance is to occur, and the criteria for acceptable performance (see p. 79). Teachers use the performance objectives to guide class learning experiences. Teachers are held accountable for seeing that students reach the minimum objectives.

The booklet *Outcomes of Quality Physical Education Programs* (NASPE, 1992) was developed by the National Association for Sport and Physical Education, affiliated with the American Alliance for Health, Physical Education, Recreation, and Dance. These materials are geared to help teachers move toward an outcomes-based model with specific emphasis on student learning and authentic assessment procedures. Twenty major outcomes for a physically educated person are listed under 5 categories covering the psychomotor, affective, and cognitive learning domains (see Chapter 1). In addition to the outcomes, specific student benchmarks are listed for kindergarten, 2nd, 4th, 6th, 8th, 10th, and 12th grade students. The benchmarks are examples of types of learning that can be evaluated (see Figures 3.18 and 3.19). The benchmarks are not meant to be all inclusive, but rather to give teachers a minimal standard for assessment. They also give teachers an indication of when various learning should be expected to occur and when to evaluate (by grade level).

NASPE has recently published a physical education content standards document with assessment procedures and recommendations (NASPE, 1995). These standards are an outgrowth of the NASPE *Outcomes* (1992) materials and help teachers identify what students should know and be able to do as a re-

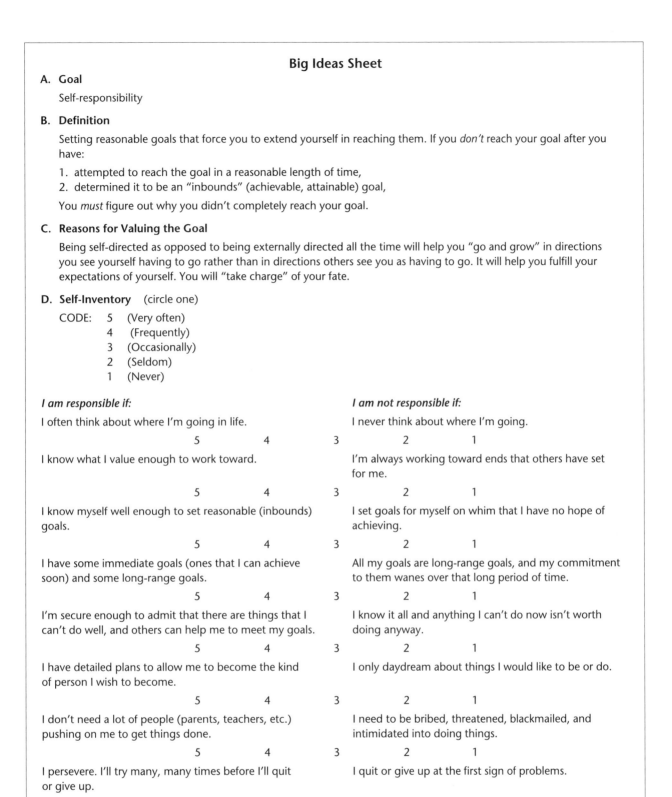

Big Ideas Sheet

A. **Goal**

Self-responsibility

B. **Definition**

Setting reasonable goals that force you to extend yourself in reaching them. If you *don't* reach your goal after you have:

1. attempted to reach the goal in a reasonable length of time,
2. determined it to be an "inbounds" (achievable, attainable) goal,

You *must* figure out why you didn't completely reach your goal.

C. **Reasons for Valuing the Goal**

Being self-directed as opposed to being externally directed all the time will help you "go and grow" in directions you see yourself having to go rather than in directions others see you as having to go. It will help you fulfill your expectations of yourself. You will "take charge" of your fate.

D. **Self-Inventory** (circle one)

CODE: 5 (Very often)
          4 (Frequently)
          3 (Occasionally)
          2 (Seldom)
          1 (Never)

I am responsible if:

I often think about where I'm going in life.

     5   4   3

I know what I value enough to work toward.

     5   4   3

I know myself well enough to set reasonable (inbounds) goals.

     5   4   3

I have some immediate goals (ones that I can achieve soon) and some long-range goals.

     5   4   3

I'm secure enough to admit that there are things that I can't do well, and others can help me to meet my goals.

     5   4   3

I have detailed plans to allow me to become the kind of person I wish to become.

     5   4   3

I don't need a lot of people (parents, teachers, etc.) pushing on me to get things done.

     5   4   3

I persevere. I'll try many, many times before I'll quit or give up.

     5   4   3

I take responsibility for my failures and successes.

     5   4   3

I look realistically at why I failed, when I do fail.

     5   4   3

I am not responsible if:

I never think about where I'm going.

     2   1

I'm always working toward ends that others have set for me.

     2   1

I set goals for myself on whim that I have no hope of achieving.

     2   1

All my goals are long-range goals, and my commitment to them wanes over that long period of time.

     2   1

I know it all and anything I can't do now isn't worth doing anyway.

     2   1

I only daydream about things I would like to be or do.

     2   1

I need to be bribed, threatened, blackmailed, and intimidated into doing things.

     2   1

I quit or give up at the first sign of problems.

     2   1

I blame others for goals I've failed to achieve.

     2   1

I don't give much thought to why I did not meet goals I've set for myself.

     2   1

FIGURE 3.16 *Big Ideas Sheet* on self responsibility—level 3

From D. Hellison. 1985. *Goals and Strategies for Teaching Physical Education.* Champaign, IL: Human Kinetics Publishers. pp. 88–89.

Big Ideas Sheet

A. Goal

Caring

B. Definition

We are not hermits. We look to others to fill many of our emotional, social, and physical needs. Likewise, we can fill these needs for others.

C. Reasons for Valuing the Goal

Realization of the fact that you need other people will help you build ties with others. Other people will value you if you help them in meeting their goals, just as you feel a tie toward anyone that assists or helps to make you feel good.

D. Self-Inventory   (Circle one)

CODE: 5   (Very often)
        4   (Frequently)
        3   (Occasionally)
        2   (Seldom)
        1   (Never)

I understand caring if:

I'm quiet when the teacher is talking.

    5   4   3   2   1

I helped someone recently.

    5   4   3   2   1

I let people help me learn new or difficult things in PE and other classes.

    5   4   3   2   1

I compliment people on things that they do well.

    5   4   3   2   1

I thank people who have helped me.

    5   4   3   2   1

I'm humble about the talents I have.

    5   4   3   2   1

I shared something with someone recently.

    5   4   3   2   1

I stuck up for or found something good about someone everyone else was putting down.

    5   4   3   2   1

I can accept compliments graciously.

    5   4   3   2   1

I don't understand caring if:

I talk and interfere with others' rights and responsibility to teach.

I can't remember the last time I helped someone.

I don't let people help me because I'll look weak or inferior to that person.

I never compliment anyone because they'll think they have the one-up on me.

I don't thank anyone because I'm too tough and cool.

I flaunt my talents and wipe them on others.

I never share anything because I might not get it back or they might not repay me.

I like getting into a group and tearing someone apart that everyone agrees is a jerk.

I can't accept compliments from others because I think they're trying to get something from me.

FIGURE 3.17   *Big Ideas Sheet* on caring—level 4

From D. Hellison. 1985. *Goals and Strategies for Teaching Physical Education.* Champaign, IL: Human Kinetics Publishers. pp. 138–139.

NASPE Physical Education Outcomes Project

EXAMPLES OF BENCHMARKS—EIGHTH GRADE

As a result of participating in a quality physical education program it is reasonable to expect that the student will be able to:

HAS	8	1. Explore introductory outdoor pursuit skills (e.g., backpacking, rock climbing, hiking, canoeing, cycling, ropes courses).
HAS	8	2. Combine skills competently to participate in modified versions of team and individual sports.
HAS	8	3. Perform a variety of simple folk, country, and creative dances.
HAS	8	4. Use basic offensive and defensive strategies while playing a modified version of a sport.
HAS	8	5. Practice in ways that are appropriate for learning new skills or sports on his/her own.
1S	8	6. Correctly demonstrate various weight training techniques.
IS	8	7. Sustain an aerobic activity, maintaining a target heart rate, to achieve cardiovascular benefits.
IS	8	8. Improve and maintain appropriate body composition.
IS	8	9. Participate in an individualized fitness program.
DOES	8	10. Identify and follow rules while playing sports and games.
KNOWS	8	11. Recognize the effects of substance abuse on personal health and performance in physical activity.
KNOWS	8	12. List long-term physiological, psychological, and cultural benefits that may result from regular participation in physical activity.
KNOWS	8	13. Describe principles of training and conditioning for specific physical activities.
KNOWS	8	14. Describe personal and group conduct, including ethical behavior, appropriate for engaging in physical activity.
KNOWS	8	15. Analyze and categorize activities and exercise according to potential fitness benefits.
KNOWS	8	16. Analyze offensive and defensive strategies in games and sports.
KNOWS	8	17. Evaluate the roles of exercise and other factors in weight control.
VALUES	8	18. Feel satisfaction on days when engaging in physical activity.
VALUES	8	19. Enjoy the aesthetic and creative aspects of performance.
VALUES	8	20. Respect physical and performance limitations of self and others.
VALUES	8	21. Desire to improve physical ability and performance.

FIGURE 3.18 Examples of benchmarks—8th grade

From NASPE. 1992. *National Outcomes of Quality Physical Education.* Reston, VA: AAHPERD. p. 14.

sult of a quality physical education program. The document also establishes user-friendly guidelines for assessment procedures that can be used in association with 7 content standards. These materials help teachers move toward an outcomes-based approach with their curriculum.

Outcomes-based models place focus on what students should know and perform at various grade levels. Emphasis is on measurable outcomes of student performance rather than subjective criteria. Students can progress at different speeds, but this is not a concern as long as minimal outcomes are reached. The

NASPE Physical Education Outcomes Project

EXAMPLES OF BENCHMARKS—TENTH GRADE

As a result of participating in a quality physical education program it is reasonable to expect that the student will be able to:

HAS	10	1. Demonstrate basic competence in physical activities selected from each of the following categories: aquatics; self-defense; dance; individual, dual, and team activities and sports; and outdoor pursuits.
HAS	10	2. Perform a variety of dance (folk, country, social, and creative) with fluency and in time to accompaniment.
IS	10	3. Assess personal fitness status in terms of cardiovascular endurance, muscular strength and endurance, flexibility, and body composition.
IS	10	4. Design and implement a personal fitness program that relates to total wellness.
DOES	10	5. Participate in a variety of game, sport, and dance activities representing different cultural backgrounds.
DOES	10	6. Participate cooperatively and ethically when in competitive physical activities.
DOES	10	7. Participate in several outdoor pursuits indigenous to the geographic area.
KNOWS	10	8. Identify participation factors that contribute to enjoyment and self-expression.
KNOWS	10	9. Compare and contrast offensive and defensive patterns in sports.
KNOWS	10	10. Discuss the historical roles of games, sports, and dance in the cultural life of a population.
KNOWS	10	11. Categorize, according to their benefits and participation requirements, activities that can be pursued in the local community.
KNOWS	10	12. Analyze and compare health and fitness benefits derived from various physical activities.
KNOWS	10	13. Analyze and evaluate personal fitness profile.
KNOWS	10	14. Use biomechanical concepts and principles to analyze and improve performance of self and others.
VALUES	10	15. Appreciate and respect the natural environment while participating in physical activity.
VALUES	10	16. Enjoy the satisfaction of meeting and cooperating with others during physical activity.
VALUES	10	17. Desire the enjoyment, satisfaction, and benefits of regular physical activity.

FIGURE 3.19   Examples of benchmarks—10th grade

From NASPE. 1992. *National Outcomes of Quality Physical Education.* Reston, VA: AAHPERD. p. 15.

outcomes-based model is designed to move from programs that merely expose students to activities toward mastery of specific outcomes. When planning outcomes-based curricula, physical educators have to decide which learning outcomes are most important and design instructional experiences that help students reach such outcomes. The accomplishment of outcomes is reported to parents, administrators, and school board members to ensure continued support for the physical education program.

EXPECTED OUTCOMES

After reading the chapter, you should be able to

- Explain how curriculum models are used by physical educators.
- Discuss the common value orientations in physical education curriculum models.

- List and describe the popular categories of activities commonly used in the multi-activity model.

- Discuss the problems of implementing an outdoor adventure activity model in a high school.

- Describe the pros and cons of a sports education model for secondary school physical education.

- Explain the characteristics of a knowledge concepts curriculum model.

- Understand how the *Basic Stuff Series* can be integrated into a knowledge concepts model.

- List the different levels of social development in Hellison's model.

- Describe how outcomes-based models can be personalized to assure learning for all students.

REFERENCES AND SUGGESTED READINGS

Brynteson, P., and Adams, T. M. 1993. The effects of conceptually based physical education programs on attitudes and exercise habits of college alumni after 2 to 11 years of follow-up. *Research Quarterly for Exercise and Sport* 64: 208–212.

Corbin, C., and Lindsey, R. 1996a. *Fitness for Life*. 4th ed. Glenview, IL: Scott, Foresman & Company.

Corbin, C., and Lindsey, R. 1996b. *Fitness for Life Teacher's Resource Manual*. 4th ed. Glenview, IL: Scott, Foresman & Company.

Darst, P., Beauchamp, L., and Thompson, L. 1989. What's going on in high school physical education: A descriptive study. Paper presented at the AAHPERD convention, Boston.

Ennis, C. 1993. Can we really do it all? Making curriculum choices in middle and high school programs. In J. E. Rink (ed.). *Critical Crossroads: Middle and Secondary Physical Education*. Reston, VA: NASPE. 13–23.

Harageones, E. G. 1993. If we're going to get out of the sandtrap, we've got to get on the ball: fitness education is our responsibility. In J. E. Rink (ed.). *Critical Crossroads: Middle and Secondary Physical Education*. Reston, VA: NASPE. 33–36.

Harrison, J. M., Blakemore, C. L., Buck, M. M., and Pellett, T. M. 1996. *Instructional Strategies for Secondary Physical Education*. 4th. ed. Dubuque, IA: Wm. C. Brown.

Hellison, D. R. 1985. *Goals and Strategies for Teaching Physical Education*. Champaign, IL: Human Kinetics Publishers.

Hellison, D. R. 1995. *Teaching Responsibility Through Physical Activity*. Champaign, IL: Human Kinetics Publishers.

Jewett, A. 1980. The status of physical education curriculum theory. *Quest* 32: 163–173.

Jewett, A., and Bain, L. (eds.). 1987. The purpose process curriculum framework: A personal meaning model for physical education. Special Monograph. *Journal of Teaching in Physical Education* 6(3): 195–366.

Jewett, A., Bain, L., and Ennis, K. 1995. *The Curriculum Process in Physical Education*. Dubuque, IA: Wm. C. Brown and Benchmark.

Jewett, A., and Mullan, M. 1977. *Curriculum Design: Purposes and Processes in Physical Education Teaching-Learning*. Reston, VA: AAHPERD.

Johnson, D. J., and Harageones, E. G. 1994. A health fitness course in secondary physical education: The Florida experience. In R. R. Pate and R. C. Hohn, *Health and Fitness through Physical Education*. Champaign, IL: Human Kinetics Publishers.

Melograno, V. J. 1996. *Designing the Physical Education Curriculum*. Champaign, IL: Human Kinetics Publishers.

NASPE. 1987. *Basic Stuff Series*. Reston, VA: AAHPERD

NASPE. 1992. *Outcomes of Quality Physical Education Programs*. Reston, VA: AAHPERD,

NASPE. 1995. *Moving into the Future–National Standards for Physical Education*. St. Louis: Mosby.

Olson, G. 1984. Physical education for the small school system. In R. P. Carlson (ed.). *Ideas II for Secondary School Physical Education*. Reston, VA: AAHPERD.

Parker, M., and Steen, T. 1988. Outdoor pursuits and physical education: Making the connection. *Newsletter of the Council on Outdoor Education* 30(1): 4.

Portman, P., and McCollum, R. 1995. Eaton high school lifetime P.E. *Teaching High School Physical Education* 1(2): 9.

Siedentop, D. 1991. *Developing Teaching Skills in Physical Education*. 3rd ed. Palo Alto, CA: Mayfield Publishing Co.

Siedentop, D. 1994. *Sports Education*. Champaign, IL: Human Kinetics Publishers.

Siedentop, D., Mand, C., and Taggart, A. 1986. *Physical Education—Teaching and Curriculum Strategies for Grades 5–12*. Palo Alto, CA: Mayfield Publishing Co.

Vickers, J. 1993. While Rome burns: Meeting the challenge of the new reform movement in education. In J. E. Rink (ed.). *Critical Crossroads: Middle and Secondary Physical Education*. Reston, VA: NASPE. 47–59.

Watson, E. R., Sherrill, A., and Weigand, B. 1994. Curriculum development in a worldwide school system. *Journal of Physical Education, Recreation, and Dance* 65: 17–20.

Wood, K., Fisher, C., Huth, T., and Graham, P. 1995. Opening the door to tomorrow's classroom. *Teaching High School Physical Education* 1(1): 1, 3–5.

4 Developing and Implementing a Curriculum

PURPOSE

To understand curriculum terminology and the basic set of prescribed steps to follow in developing a written curriculum guide.

KEY CONCEPTS

- There are prescribed steps to follow in the development of a curriculum guide.
- There are major elements common to all curricula.
- The formal curriculum is usually organized around a major theme, called an organizing center.
- Activities in curricula are articulated in a horizontal and vertical plane.
- Curriculum construction should follow a program philosophy and the desires of society.
- Characteristics and developmental levels of the students are considered when determining program objectives.
- Many factors affect physical education curriculum in a positive or negative way. These factors include the following: educational philosophy, the administration, the community, the climate, facilities, laws, schedules, and budget.
- Curriculum planners determine areas of instructional emphasis and select appropriate activities.
- Activities are arranged into units for each year and from year to year.
- Curriculum is evaluated and modified from year to year.

Physical education teachers are often involved in curriculum design and modification. The process in a secondary school can be complex and involves many factors and people. One of the first steps is to understand the confusing vocabulary of educators. Part of the confusion over curriculum vocabulary arises from various meanings attributed to the same term. Because the cooperation of many people is necessary to develop a quality curriculum in a secondary school, it is especially important to speak the same language. This chapter focuses on the presentation and analysis of steps necessary for developing a curriculum guide. The steps can help teachers when they are called upon to prepare a curriculum for a specific school setting.

The formal curriculum guide should be written in an organized, systematic manner. The steps described in this chapter can help teachers establishing a quality, meaningful, and well-planned curriculum guide. Most curriculum guides start with a definition of physical education and a discussion of the values of the physical education department. The following is an example of a philosophical statement.

> Physical education is a process that focuses on increasing students' knowledge and affecting their attitudes and behaviors in a positive manner relative to physical activity. It is an instructional program with developmental goals and achievable outcomes. Physical education focuses primarily on psychomotor goals but also makes a valuable contribution to affective and cognitive learning domains. It is an important part of each student's overall educational experience because of the unique contributions in the following areas:
>
> 1. The development of physical skills that can be used for a lifetime of enjoyment and recreation.
> 2. The development and maintenance of a personalized level of health-related physical fitness.
> 3. The acquisition of knowledge that is necessary to be successful and to enjoy the various physical activities and fitness routines.
> 4. The development of a positive attitude toward regular physical activity and physical fitness participation.

STEP 1: INCLUDE ELEMENTS COMMON TO ALL CURRICULA

A curriculum is designed to give sequence and direction to the learning experiences of students. Different approaches may be used to select and identify essential activities, but the selective criteria are based ultimately on the philosophic values of those involved in curriculum development. The curriculum specifies program content in terms of objectives and activities for students. There are elements that are common to all curricula regardless of subject-matter content. The guiding document must include and plan for the following elements.

Formal Course of Study

The traditional manner for discussing or viewing curriculum is that of a separate, **formal course of study**. The focus of this definition is on a planned in-class program. Examples of this include the history, math-

ematics, music, or physical education curricula. Each academic area has a sequence of courses and specific topics or activities within each course. These courses of study are carefully planned and arranged so the stated objectives are accomplished. Curriculum emphasis, study, and research have focused primarily on this perspective. Teachers in physical education and subject areas channel the majority of their professional efforts into this curriculum aspect.

The formal curriculum is an overall plan for all class instructional activities. It contains the *scope, sequence*, and *arrangement* of learning activities for each school year. The scope of the curriculum delineates the content for each year and assures that the content of the program will be covered in a systematic and accountable fashion. The scope should offer as many activities as possible that will help accomplish established objectives of the curriculum. The sequence of activities is arranged progressively throughout the year and from year to year. Each succeeding year in the curriculum should build on program activities offered in previous years. Sequence assures that there will be articulation of instruction between grades. Sequence is also concerned with the order in which skills and units are arranged. For example, units within a year should build upon units from previous years and units taught earlier in the current year. Figure 4.1 is an example of a page from a scope and sequence chart. The formal curriculum is intended to guide teachers in developing and conducting learning experiences that give students an opportunity to acquire knowledge, attitudes, and behaviors identified as goals or objectives. It is the "what" and "why" of education as opposed to the "how." The "how" is referred to as instruction.

Planning for curriculum and instruction cannot be separated because they are interdependent. For example, the accomplishment of curriculum objectives is significantly affected by the instructional emphasis. A direct or task style of instruction has a different impact on students than a problem-solving or process-oriented approach. The length, content, and organizational design of a unit influences the type of instruction that will be most effective. Teachers need to know how curriculum and instruction affect each other so the two areas can be planned together.

Formal curriculum is usually organized around major themes, often called *organizing centers*. The most common organizing centers for physical education curricula are movement forms, sport, and physical activity. Commonly included are units on basketball, softball, square dancing, and jogging. Programs

	PRESCHOOL	ELEM.	MIDDLE	SENIOR	K	1	2	3	4	5	6	7	8	9	10	11	12
C. Archery																	
1. History															I	I	R
2. Safety—Rules—Strategy															I	I	R
3. Equipment															I	I	R
4. Shooting															I	I	R
D. Badminton																	
1. History															I	I	R
2. Safety—Rules—Strategy	I	P							I	R					I	I	R
3. Equipment	I	P							I	R					R	R	R
4. Skills	I	P							I	R					R	R	R
a. Grip	I	P							I	R					R	R	R
b. Serves	I	P							I	R					R	R	R
c. Strokes	I	P							I	R					R	R	R
E. Bowling																	
1. History												I	R		I	I	R
2. Safety—Rules—Strategy		I	R									I	R		I	I	R
3. Equipment		I	R									I	R		I	I	R
4. Skills		I	R									I	R		I	I	R
a. Grip		I	R									I	R		I	I	R
b. Approach		I	R									I	R		I	I	R
c. Delivery		I	R									I	R		I	I	R
F. Cross-Country Skiing																	
1. History															I	I	R
2. Safety—Rules—Strategy		I	R												I	I	R
3. Equipment		I	R												I	I	R
4. Skills		I	R												I	I	R
a. Kick glide		I	R												I	I	R
b. Stop		I	R												I	I	R
c. Turns		I	R												I	I	R
d. Poling		I	R												I	I	R
e. Climb		I	R												I	I	R
G. Curling																	
1. History															I	I	R
2. Safety—Rules—Strategy															I	I	R
3. Equipment															I	I	R
4. Skills															I	I	R
a. Delivery															I	I	R
b. Sweeping															I	I	R
H. Golf																	
1. History															I	I	R
2. Safety—Rules—Strategy															I	I	R
3. Equipment															I	I	R
4. Skills															I	I	R
a. Grip															I	I	R
b. Full swings															I	I	R
c. Approach shots															I	I	R
d. Putting															I	I	R

I—Introduce: initial instruction of psychomotor, cognitive, and affective skills that are explained, demonstrated, and practiced.
R—Review and reinforce continued instruction of skill level improvement and increased knowledge of techniques.
P—Proficiency: the attainment of an individual's maximum skill level through instruction and practice.

FIGURE 4.1 An example of a page from a scope and sequence chart

Courtesy of LaCrosse, WI, Public Schools.

often follow an eclectic philosophy that focuses on several themes from several of these areas. Additional organizing centers used in physical education include:

1. Physical fitness components such as cardiovascular efficiency, strength, and control of body fat.
2. Wellness knowledge and activities involving stress management, nutrition, weight control, substance abuse, personal safety, physical fitness, environmental awareness, and behavioral self-control.
3. Movement themes such as propelling, catching, striking, and balancing.
4. Analysis of movement elements such as force, time, space, and flow.
5. Student motives such as appearance, health, and achievement.
6. Disciplinary knowledge from such areas as biomechanics, motor learning, exercise physiology, and sports philosophy.
7. Social development themes such as competition, cooperation, emotional control, and sportsmanship.

Yearly and year-to-year curriculum plans serve as guides for teachers. Curricula are articulated in two planes, horizontal and vertical. Horizontal articulation includes the yearly plan and is concerned with arranging activities for the school year. Vertical articulation is concerned with scope and sequence for all of the school years, in this case grades 6 through 12. Both reflect the overall philosophy of the program and are organized to accomplish desired outcomes. The curriculum offers direction to both teachers and students and should be a frequently used reference.

A yearly plan avoids the pitfall of running out of time or activities. It gives departments of physical education a singular purpose and eases the burden when equipment and facilities are shared. It is beneficial when instructors agree on units that should be taught and on the amount of time consigned to each unit. Each instructor then has a curriculum with similar content, differing only in the order of presentation of units. This allows effective use of equipment and facilities that have to be shared in most secondary school settings.

Another important reason for yearly planning concerns curriculum evaluation. Evaluation would be difficult if each teacher taught a unique curriculum. Similarly, if there is no yearly plan, determining the strengths and weaknesses of the curriculum becomes difficult. Which physical fitness activities were popular? Which physical fitness activities were the least popular? Why do students choose not to participate in the program? What activities should be added or deleted? Which activities are of high interest or low interest? These and other questions can be answered when the curriculum framework is known. In turn, parts of the curriculum can be modified and evaluated later. There is no substitute for a stable and well-planned curriculum.

Total Program

Physical education programs should not be designed without regard to other related programs and experiences. Currently, the **total physical education program** (Figure 4.2) (Siedentop, Mand, and Taggart, 1986) is defined as all experiences and activities where students engage and learn about physical activity and sports. In addition to formal physical education classes, this definition includes athletics, intramurals, sport clubs, noon-hour aerobics, drop-in fitness centers, and any other after-school activity that impacts students. For years, activities outside the formal course of study were called **extracurricular** because they were viewed to be "extra" to the main, formal curriculum. In recent years, these extracurricular activities have been referred to as **cocurricular** in order to give them a more equal status. Students and parents certainly do not view these activities as "extra" to the main function of the school. In fact, many would argue that these activities are the most important. The term *cocurricular* gives more status to all physical activities and helps people understand that these activities are important contributors to a school's overall goals.

Cocurricular programs are an integral part of the basic physical education program. The programs

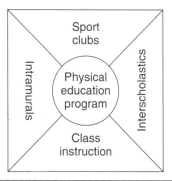

FIGURE 4.2

Model of a total physical education program

serve a valuable function by offering additional opportunities for students to participate in physical activities and develop positive activity habits. All students should be able to find success in one or several of these programs. Students can gain a variety of experiences depending on the specific situation (for example, winning, losing, teamwork, friendships, deferred goals, perseverance, and dedication). The experience depends in part on how each program is developed and emphasized.

Many schools use the physical education program to physically train students for the athletic program. In these situations, athletes lift weights year round and receive physical education credit for athletic program participation. These athletes become highly specialized and usually do not have an opportunity to learn other lifetime sports skills. The athletic program has different goals and should not be offered in lieu of the physical education program. Both programs should be unique and contribute to the total school experience. Physical educators need to take leadership roles in all activity programs to assure that proper goals for each are stressed and protected.

Athletic, intramural, and sport club programs can develop interest and enthusiasm for the physical education curriculum. Efforts should be made to coordinate offerings in the curriculum with offerings from athletics, intramurals, and sport clubs. A student taking a basic middle school basketball class may decide to play intramural basketball or to try out for the freshman team. A student in the school ski club may elect to take skiing in the physical education curriculum. A student playing intramural tennis may improve enough to make the varsity tennis team. Equipment and facilities can be bought, developed, and shared by all groups. These programs can complement each other in a number of ways if a cooperative effort is made by program leaders. Physical educators should use their experience and knowledge of these programs to help recruit and use leaders from the school and community. For example, a math or science teacher can direct the intramural program or organize a sailing club for students. Parents might work with a teacher to organize a backpacking or fishing club.

⌣ Functional Curriculum *is ALT-PE*

The third element common to a curriculum is the **functional** curriculum. The term refers to the actual amount of instructional lesson time a student spends on the specific subject matter. This time is called aca-

·Faculty
·Planning/Organize

demic learning time *(ALT)* and is being studied extensively in physical education environments (van der Mars, Darst, Vogler, and Cusimano, 1995). Time spent dribbling, passing, or shooting a basketball with a low error rate is high ALT, whereas time spent waiting in line, changing clothes, or rotating stations is not included in ALT. Studies show that many physical education environments are characterized by low rates of ALT. In some classes, no more than 15% of class time was spent engaged in ALT (Siedentop, 1991).

The functional curriculum and the concept of ALT are representative of an objective approach, which uses data to make decisions about curriculum and instruction. This approach provides a strategy for improving the quality of physical education programs for students at all levels. It provides for improvement in areas that have historically been tied to untested assumptions and hypotheses.

Hidden Curriculum

The **hidden** curriculum (Jewett, Bain, and Ennis,1995) is found in all areas of the school and cuts across stated curriculum objectives. The hidden curriculum are all of the unplanned and unrecognized values that are imparted through the educational process. Often, teachers and administrators do not realize how their behavior toward students, the policies and procedures used, and decisions regarding funding, activities, schedules, and personnel impact students. Because they are not aware of their behavior, discrepancies or inconsistencies exist between what teachers say and what they actually do. Their implicit values are not consistent with their explicit philosophy. Areas of hidden values include the development of student approach tendencies; the roles of females in sport and exercise activities; teachers' attitudes toward winning and losing; teachers' treatment of various social groups, races, and genders; and administrators' allocation of funds within the physical education program.

Physical educators often evaluate the contributions of specific activities in the written course of study. However, they may neglect to consider how aspects of the hidden curriculum such as dress codes, showering policies, grading techniques, discipline procedures, instructional strategies, or teaching behaviors impact learning. An example of this situation is illustrated by a teacher purporting to develop positive attitudes in students toward physical activity but forcing students to run laps or do push-ups for lack of effort or failure to "dress out" properly. Using negative grading schemes or overly critical instructional procedures that cause students to do everything possible to escape or avoid the environment are unwritten and hidden behaviors that impact student performance. The hidden curriculum of the school can contribute to the development of positive approach or negative avoidance tendencies of the students. Students continually evaluate school and the process of learning. Efforts must be made to study and develop the hidden curriculum to positively effect what students learn.

Articulated Curriculum: Grades K–12

Often, physical education curricula are developed in parts. There is usually a curriculum for the elementary school level, one for middle school, and another for the senior high school. Each curriculum is written and organized independently of the others. A district-wide plan that considers factors such as state requirements, facilities, scheduling, and equipment is seldom developed. In many cases, elementary physical education specialists do not know middle and senior high school physical education teachers, let alone have an understanding of the curriculum taught at each level. Teachers operate autonomously without concern for or knowledge of what is done at other levels. This leads to a fragmented program that shows little articulation between levels. Time, energy, and learning activities may be wasted, duplicated, or omitted in a curriculum that is not vertically articulated.

Elementary School Program

Elementary school physical education programs place emphasis on expanding the activity experiences of students. Youngsters enter kindergarten with similar skills. The elementary curriculum strives to offer a wide variety of activities to assure that students have the opportunity to experience success. In addition, a wide variety of activities assures that students will be involved in short units of instruction in order to minimize long bouts of failure. If units are short, students who don't like a certain activity or feel like failures know they will not have to continue the activity for an extended time. In addition, the wide variety of short units assures that all students will find some activity they enjoy, increasing their opportunity to experience success.

Middle School Program

In middle school, this variety of units continues, and the units are short to assure that students will not have to excessively endure an activity they dislike. A balanced curriculum places equal emphasis on all activities in the curriculum consistent with the program objectives and goals. Activities are included if they meet the needs and interests of all learners. For example, a design that offers 4 or 5 team sports during the year does not meet the needs of students who do not like team sports, are uninterested in the sports offered, or prefer individual activities.

Another important consideration in organizing the middle school curriculum is the matter of sequence. Organized correctly, sequence assures that students receive instruction in a progressive manner from kindergarten to graduation. Skills and knowledge are learned in a sequential manner, so material previously taught contributes to current learning. An example of a lack of sequence is teaching youngsters basketball skills in the first grade and continuing to teach these same skills until students leave school. It would be unthinkable to give youngsters a calculus book in first grade, ask them to repeat the material for 12 years, and then assume they have learned calculus through repetition.

Sequence in the middle school years ensures that units of instruction are organized and designed expressly for this level. Emphasis on strategy and advanced skill should be minimized because students at this age enter a rapid growth curve that reduces the ability to learn motor skills. Asking students to split their concentration on skill performance and strategy reduces the odds they will learn either. As an example, think back to learning to drive a car for the first time. It was difficult to concentrate on the fine motor skills involved in driving while thinking about the rules of the road. After driving skills were overlearned, it was possible to think about many other things, that is, putting on makeup, playing the radio, and so on. Frustration and fear can be the result of this type of overload. Until a skill is overlearned, concentration should be on skill performance. When the skills become overlearned, students can concentrate on the cognitive aspect of sport strategy. Most middle school students have not overlearned skills, thus, strategy should be a minor part of instruction.

When developing scope and sequence for middle school students, it is difficult to design a sequence that is perfect for all youngsters. Students are grouped (whether it be by grade, age, or developmental level), and every group is characterized by a range

FIGURE 4.3   One-on-one teaching is most effective

of differences. To expect students to strictly follow a predetermined sequence is unrealistic. Effective teachers modify the sequence depending on the capabilities of the student. The best teaching is one-on-one when activities and instruction are in line with student ability level. Regardless, scope and sequence are important because they lend general direction to instruction.

High School Program

Senior high school physical education curricula vary greatly from state to state and from large urban schools with 8 to 10 physical education teachers to small rural schools with 1 or 2 teachers. Local school districts have the ultimate responsibility for developing a program that meets state guidelines. State requirements are different, and some school districts allow a number of substitutions for physical education. Some districts have a 4-year requirement, whereas others do not have any requirements. Another district may have a 3-year requirement but allow substitutions such as cheerleading, athletics, orchestra, or band to fulfill the requirement. The variations and possibilities are endless. Nevertheless, the high school program should build upon the middle school program.

At the high school level, quality programs come in many sizes and shapes. A small high school in upstate New York, a large urban high school in eastern

Pennsylvania, or a medium-sized high school in central Arizona can all have a quality program within their existing frameworks. Some programs will have more students, more teachers, more facilities, and better equipment. Requirements, schedules, and administrative support may be quite different in each situation. Quality programs are not, however, a function of large facilities, abundant equipment, extensive physical education requirements, numerous teachers, or small class sizes. Outstanding high school programs are developed by a group of hardworking, dedicated professionals who are doing their best with given resources. There is strong leadership and purpose found in successful programs. A continual effort must be made to improve programs and to change those aspects that are detrimental to accomplishing goals. A sense of excitement must be found within the program. Curriculum developers can work positively within the existing framework to change existing parameters that cause difficulties.

The high school years offer the educational system an opportunity to polish and improve its product: students who are productive individuals in society. To assure the physical education program contributes to this long-term objective, it is important to understand the growth and development of students and implications these characteristics have on designing a well-planned curriculum. A quality experience for the entire K through 12 sequence emphasizes individual success, physical fitness, exploration, guidance and counseling, self-testing, monitoring, physical skill development, requisite knowledge, wellness concepts, choice within a requirement, and preparation for a lifetime of physical activity. It is important that the high school curriculum build vertically on the middle school curriculum and the middle school curriculum build on the elementary curriculum.

Curriculum planners need an understanding of the impact these common curriculum elements have on students in terms of overall objectives. For example, a teacher who does not look carefully at the effect of an imposed dress code may have problems with student participation. Grading procedures will have a powerful impact on students' attitudes toward physical education and physical activity participation. A well-developed formal curriculum plan will be ineffective if low rates of ALT are prevalent in classes. The absence of coeducational activities, lifetime sports, or dance activities deprives students of a well-balanced curriculum. A physical education program without after-school participation opportunities such as ski clubs, intramurals, or weight training programs is missing an important component. A teacher's emphasis on winning can have a negative effect on students when the losing team always runs an extra lap or performs some extra duty. Physical educators must consider carefully these curriculum elements when policies, procedures, yearly plans, daily plans, and other aspects of dealing with students are formulated. Specific suggestions are made throughout this text with respect to each of these common elements.

STEP 2: EXAMINE THE DESIRES OF SOCIETY

Years ago, people banded together and decided to set aside land and build schools because they wanted their children to acquire certain information, attitudes, and skills in a systematic manner from professionally prepared teachers. These people had certain ambitions for themselves and their youth. Even though society has changed dramatically since that time, and much new information has been discovered, people still have a number of expectations related to what they desire for their children. Many of these desires have direct implications for curriculum construction in physical education. Therefore, curriculum planners need to analyze the desires of society.

Desire to Be Physically Fit, Healthy, and Attractive

Being fit, healthy, and attractive is especially important to physical educators because of the contribution that physical activity makes in these areas. Proof that activity aids in achieving weight control, cardiovascular efficiency, flexibility, and strength is well documented. The public is aware of the humiliation and problems that individuals face throughout life if they are obese, weak, or unattractive. Physically fit people feel positive and successful and portray a positive image to others. These successes add up to a positive self-concept. In contrast, obese people often have difficulty with simple daily activities like dressing, sitting, and walking. They may have a negative self-image and often cannot participate in or enjoy many activities.

Desire to Play

Play has been frequently discussed as an important behavior that permeates all cultures in a variety of forms. Sports, dance, and various types of physical activity are serious forms of play. Many other forms of play, including music, drama, and art, are also important in society. Indeed, play is as important to most people as work, and an enjoyable play life is as valuable as a productive work life. In fact, to many, play is the most important aspect of their life. It is what they would call "paradise" or "the good life." They look forward to a round of golf, a jog along a canal, or a backpacking trip in the mountains. Physical education can make a significant contribution to this universal desire to play.

Desire for Knowledge

The human race continues to search for knowledge in all areas. People are curious about the world around them. Physical education has an extensive body of knowledge that contains various subfields. These are exercise physiology, kinesiology, motor learning, history of sport, philosophy of sport, sport psychology, and sport sociology. Many opportunities and areas of physical education are available to satisfy this desire for information.

Desire for Success, Approval, and Satisfaction

People tend to repeat activities that provide them with success. They also tend to avoid activities in which they are not successful. Various types of success usually lead to recognition, approval, or self-satisfaction. People participate in activities in which they are successful because feelings of success lead to satisfaction and happiness. Physical activities are in this category and thus make a significant contribution to one's life.

Desire for Social and Emotional Competence

Most people are concerned about how other people feel about them. People want to be accepted, respected, and liked. Adults want their children to develop acceptable social and emotional skills so that they can enjoy life. Schools are the major social agency in our culture. Information is imparted in the school setting regarding dating, mental health, sex education, nutrition, driver education, and many other important areas. Physical education offers unique opportunities in this social-emotional area because of the nature and arrangement of its subject matter. Competitive situations (involving winning, losing, and accepting referee decisions) and coeducational activities (with emphasis on movement skills) provide a rich source of social and emotional experiences for youth. Physical education teachers can have a tremendous impact on students in these areas.

Desire to Compete

Most societies are competitive. Indeed, competition is present in almost all aspects of our culture. People learn to compete at an early age, and many employers believe that the best competitors are the most successful workers in the business world. Adults want their children to be competitors and winners. In many youth sport leagues, children are encouraged at an early age to compete for league championships, trophies, and adult approval. In bicycle motocross racing, 5-year-old children in beginning, novice, and expert classes race around a track in pursuit of victories, trophies, and points that may bring them a funding sponsor so they can travel across the country to more races. Some people believe that this early competitive experience is beneficial for youngsters, but others seriously question these practices. Regardless of the stand taken, most societies are competitive. The competitive nature of sports and physical activity requires physical educators to take a stand on competition. Physical education programs can have a strong influence on youth and their ability to compete.

Desire for Risk, Adventure, and Excitement

Perhaps because of increased urbanization, mechanization, and impersonal, fast-paced lifestyles, many people are turning to high-risk adventurous activities for fun. Physical activities such as rock climbing, skiing, white-water canoeing, and backpacking are increasing in popularity and give people an opportu-

nity to do something new, risky, and exciting. The physical education curriculum can provide many experiences to satisfy this desire.

Desire for Rhythmic Expression

Most people enjoy listening to and moving to rhythmic sounds. Many forms of rhythmic activity have been popular in a wide variety of cultures throughout history. They can include many forms of dance, such as folk, square, and aerobic, as well as sport movements, such as jumping rope, running hurdles, or exercising to music. Rhythms can be both enjoyable and motivational. A variety of rhythmic activities is an important part of a physical education curriculum.

Desire for Creative Expression

People look for ways to express their autonomy and individuality. Clothes and hairstyles are popular ways to reveal oneself to the world. Play and leisure time is another opportunity for self-expression. The work world often puts limits on individuality stimulating people to channel their creative and individual desires into play or leisure pursuits. Physical activities provide numerous possibilities for creative outlets structured by the rules that govern the activities. In basketball, students enjoy trying to develop Michael Jordan-like acrobatic shots or Kevin Johnson-like drives to the basket, passes, and assists. In gymnastics, the opportunity to develop a creative routine to music or to perfect new moves may be challenging. New plays and defenses are created in football. The challenges are unlimited, and the opportunities for creative expression appeal to students. Physical education curricula should be planned carefully to help satisfy this desire.

STEP 3: STUDY THE CHARACTERISTICS AND DEVELOPMENTAL LEVELS OF STUDENTS

This step of curriculum construction examines the developmental level and characteristics of students for whom the curriculum is being designed. A cynical teacher once said, "Teaching would be a good job if it weren't for students." Without students, there would be no need for teachers, teaching strategies, or curriculum. Students are the most important factor to consider when developing a physical education curriculum. Potential teachers will be effective teachers if they understand the characteristics and abilities of their students. This can be accomplished by reading information, talking with students and parents, and carefully observing students.

Characteristics are those typical or distinctive features of students that represent a given developmental or age level. As students grow and develop, certain characteristics appear and disappear. Within a specific age range, most students will exhibit similar characteristics. There will always be extreme ends of the normal curve regarding developmental levels. Students will vary in height, weight, social abilities, and in many other areas at each chronological age.

Developmental characteristics are usually defined by chronological age. The problem with this approach is that 4 or 5 different developmental age levels may exist within a given chronological age range (that is, 7th grade may contain students who have developmental ages ranging from 10 to 14 years old). Most schools, however, group students by chronological age rather than developmental level because of administrative ease. Physical education teachers must be aware of the wide range of developmental levels that exist at a given grade level. These developmental differences affect physical abilities and performance in physical activities.

Student characteristics are categorized into physical, social, emotional, and intellectual areas. Curriculum planners carefully consider all areas because physical education programs contribute to all 4. Some physical educators mistakenly believe their program contributes only to the physical area, but physical activities are not learned in a vacuum—students are also involved mentally, socially, and emotionally. The characteristics of students are important to understand when determining the types of activities, the length of units, the amount of student choice, and the content to be emphasized.

The characteristics of middle school students are different from those of senior high students, and their developmental levels need to be considered as separate entities. It is difficult to sort out characteristics by each of the 4 categories. In the following sections on middle and senior high school students, 2 areas will be discussed: the physical area and a combination of the social, emotional, and intellectual areas.

The middle school curriculum is an important link in the total school curriculum. National statistics indicate that 70% of the students in grades 7 and 8 have physical education as often as 3 days per week from a trained specialist (Ross, Pate, Corbin, Delpy, and Gold, 1987). The middle school years represent the first time students are able to make personal decisions about what they like and dislike. Decisions made are often irreversible and last a lifetime. Middle school is a time when students choose to avoid physical activity whenever possible. Since teachers and administrators know this is a difficult time for youngsters, it is important to keep students turned on toward activity through a well-organized and expertly taught program. It is often difficult to find a curriculum that is designed expressly for the adolescent student. Curriculums for middle school students may be watered down high school programs or an extension of the elementary school curriculum. Neither program suits adolescents; they need a program that is designed to meet traits and characteristics that are unique to their stage of development.

Never again will youngsters have to experience as many major changes as they do during middle school. Youngsters at this level want to be independent but still desire the security of authority. This places teachers in a situation where they are consistently challenged and questioned but expected to exert direction when necessary. Understanding the developmental characteristics of these youngsters is requisite to effective instruction. The following sections discuss characteristics and follow with a discussion of the implications of various traits.

Physical Characteristics— Middle School

Rapid and Uneven Growth

Middle school students go through a rapid and uneven growth spurt. Girls enter this spurt about 1.5 years earlier than boys and are usually taller and more mature early in this period. Once boys experience the growth spurt, they pass girls in height and weight. The final result is a wide range of physical maturity that had gone unnoticed in the elementary school years.

✓ **IMPLICATIONS:** *Teachers need to recognize the number of problems caused by this rapid and uneven growth. Girls are often stronger, faster, and larger than boys. Boys may feel uneasy about this growth difference be-*

tween the sexes as well as among themselves. Activities have to be adjusted to account for the size and skill differences. Teachers can expect that boys who have not entered puberty will not be as strong and quick as more mature youngsters and will feel uneasy about competing in physical contact sports. Girls who are developmentally advanced or retarded may feel insecure and not want to participate in physical education activities. Teachers must take time to discuss this wide variation in maturity and help youngsters understand they are normal. In addition, students need to be nurtured as they learn how their physical size and development influence their choice of participation in various physical activities.

Decreased Predisposition to Learn Motor Skills

The range of motor ability levels increases among students and the skill level differences of students become increasingly apparent. Motor abilities develop slowly due to the increase in growth velocity. Awkwardness, poor coordination, low strength, and low endurance are common during rapid growth spurts. As students go through puberty they develop secondary sexual characteristics. Boys experience facial hair, pubic hair, a voice change, and genital and shoulder development. Girls develop breasts, pubic hair, a widening of the hips, and an accumulation of body fat.

IMPLICATIONS: *When growth velocity is high, the predisposition to learn motor skills is decreased. This makes the middle school years a difficult time to teach new skills that are tough to master. Combined with an unwillingness to fail in front of peers, students try to avoid activity or avoid learning new skills if they fear embarrassment. A focus on individual and dual activities will help to minimize the risk of public failure. In addition, all units of instruction should be started in a manner that assures student success. This helps minimize the tendency of adolescents to speak negatively (and loudly) about their dislike of the unit when they are failing. Finally, students develop musculature and add body fat, which changes the body's center of gravity and perceptual awareness. The result of these changes is decreased performance in activities requiring balance and body coordination.*

Changes in Physical Traits

Boys become stronger and gain endurance. Girls often gain an advantage over boys in the areas of balance and flexibility. Posture is sometimes a problem with youngsters who are embarrassed about their

height. Ossification of the bones is usually not complete.

IMPLICATIONS: *Physical performance differences between sexes is obvious to students. This increased awareness of physical differences demands that teachers discuss the differences and the importance of posture and lifetime fitness. An understanding of different body types and their impact on physical performance is important so students can begin to select activities that are well suited to their particular build and physique. Because of incomplete bone ossification, it may be a good time to avoid heavy physical contact sports in order to avoid permanent damage to the skeletal system. Learning to participate with others regardless of ability level is an important outcome because this is a time when students form cliques. This can lead to a separation of sexes and friends with differing skill levels, which is undesirable and may be self-limiting as students mature.*

Social, Emotional, and Intellectual Development—Middle School

Independence and Peer Groups

Students have a strong need for independence and are often torn between adult and peer values. Peer groups, providing the standards for behavior, represent independence because of the absence of adults. Leaders, followers, and loyalty start to evolve through group dynamics. Fighting with parents and peers is common at this age, as is competitiveness.

IMPLICATIONS: *Independence is an important trait that students need to learn. If students do not learn independence, they become liabilities to society since they cannot make decisions that contribute to the betterment of the society. Thus, it is important to provide situations that will allow youngsters to make decisions in a somewhat structured setting. They can learn the consequences of their decisions and behavior without finding themselves in a life-threatening situation. Offering opportunities for leadership skill development helps youngsters develop their decision-making skills. Participation in game and sport activities fosters an understanding of the importance of rules in maintaining an environment that is acceptable to all participants.*

Emotional Instability

Moods change quickly, for this is an emotional and unpredictable period. Students often become angry, fearful, and are easily upset.

IMPLICATIONS: *The moodiness of middle school students is often precipitated by their rapid development and lack of experience in dealing with new social situations. Teachers must strive to be even-tempered and unruffled by students' consistent mood changes. Students want great freedom to express their behavior and desires, but expect teachers to be perfect models. It is a time when teachers must display patience and direction without excessive force. Teacher modeling of desirable behavior helps avoid troubling double standards: expecting students to do as they are told regardless of the teacher's behavior.*

Social Awareness

Students are interested in improving themselves, especially in the physical area. Weight training, body building, and figure control or body sculpting are of special interest. Strong concerns about size and abilities are common. Grooming, clothes, and appearance become important since students are overly self-conscious about their bodies. Romantic interests begin at this age, and students try to impress each other in various ways. Girls are usually ahead of boys socially and begin to date older boys. Social activities become important, and dances, movies, parties, and athletic events serve as social meeting places.

IMPLICATIONS: *Discussions about physiological changes help students accept varying student sizes, limitations, and individual differences. Allowing students to express themselves without ridicule or embarrassment encourages self-acceptance. A number of social activities can be provided for students so they learn proper social behavior in a variety of settings.*

Intellectual Development

Intellectual development continues throughout this period. Students can concentrate longer, are able to understand more complex concepts, and are better able to follow directions. An interest in the "why" of physical activity occurs. Daydreaming and fantasizing are lessening for many students. The variety of student activities decreases continually throughout this period and into adulthood. Students begin to make decisions about areas in which they want to specialize. This has strong implications for future sport and physical activity participation. A strong interest in risk, excitement, and adventure is common.

IMPLICATIONS: *Intellectual development among students can be exciting for teachers since interaction can be meaningful and challenging. Students need to be told*

why they are being taught certain activities rather than simply told to do it, "because I said so." Helping students become familiar with their physical abilities so they can make wise and thoughtful choices about activities that match their skills increases understanding. Students in middle school often try high-risk activities and end up making poor decisions due to their desire to show off and impress others. It is important that safety procedures have been thoroughly covered so students understand the consequences of their behavior.*

Middle school is often a challenging and difficult time for students. They are confused by their changing physical appearance and the transition process from childhood to adulthood. Many important decisions are being made about their careers and goals for life. For physical education teachers the situation is extremely challenging and can be quite frustrating and demanding as well as rewarding. Physical education can play a significant role in these students' lives.

Physical Characteristics— High School

Increases in Motor Ability and Coordination

Most students have finished their growth spurt and are approaching physical maturity. Bone growth and the ossification process are complete for most students. Sexual characteristics reach maturity for both boys and girls. Students are beyond the period of physical awkwardness and become more comfortable with their physical abilities. Motor ability and coordination improve more quickly during this time period.

IMPLICATIONS: *This is an excellent time for students to improve existing motor skills and learn new skills. Students are more comfortable trying new physical skills and performing in front of peers. Teachers can move students through instructional progressions at a much faster rate.*

Modification of Physical Traits

There are continued increases in strength, endurance, and speed. Boys surpass girls in height and weight. Boys continue to develop muscularity, while most girls level off in this area.

IMPLICATIONS: *Teachers need to help students understand that physical differences among students impacts* *skill performance. Students need guidance toward activities they will successfully be able to participate in within their physical limits. Developing a sensitivity for participation with others at various ability levels is an important learning.*

Social, Emotional, and Intellectual Development—High School

Social Awareness

Social activities such as dances, parties, athletic events, and clubs dominate the lives of high school students. Students are concerned with dating, going steady, getting a job, marriage, and a career. Peer groups are important and help provide behavioral standards in areas such as dress, grooming, and interests. Peer groups teach students loyalty to a group yet independence from adults. Students still have a difficult time deciding between adult and peer values, and conflicts exist between adults and students. Competition increases with an emphasis on grades, athletics, and dating. Students are still concerned about size, strength, and physical ability but show more interest in cosmetic fitness than health-related fitness.

IMPLICATIONS: *High school is not a time to force students into activities that do not interest them. There should be many opportunities for choice. Dress requirements, time for changing clothes, and grooming time are important issues where students should have input into the physical education course requirements. Students enjoy opportunities to express their opinions and ideas with regard to various issues. Weight lifting, aerobics, body building, figure control, and other popular fitness activities are attractive to these students.*

Emotional Development

Most students have completed the puberty cycle and are comfortable with their bodies and the direction of their lives. There are fewer mood swings and students seem to be more stable emotionally. Problems with fighting, extreme competitiveness, and arguing over issues start to diminish.

IMPLICATIONS: *Students need additional experiences with emotional control. They need to understand the necessity of emotional control in physical education environments and in other aspects of life. Effective adult models of emotional control allow students to witness acceptable behavior patterns. Teachers who talk about*

emotional control in class and behave differently during an interscholastic basketball game offer little credibility to their students.

Intellectual Development

Students are approaching their intellectual potential. Their memories and abilities to reason, concentrate, imagine, and think conceptually have improved and continue to develop. Students have experienced the knowledge explosion and changing American values. Many students experience broken homes, single-parent families, multiple moves, drugs, and early sexual activity. Students look for risk, excitement, and adventure. They have a large base of knowledge and experience by the time they reach this period. Students express strong concern about security, attention, affection, self-worth, and intellectual improvement. There is a continued narrowing of interests and an emphasis on specialization in activities where they perceive themselves to be competent.

IMPLICATIONS: *Teachers need to be sensitive to the increasing intellectual abilities of their students. A focus on the "why" of physical education and the objectives of the program is often demanded. Students need to be able to choose activities they want to learn. Units should be longer to assure in-depth instruction. The curriculum should include units that incorporate risk, excitement, and adventure. Students also want to understand the cognitive concepts of activities as well as to improve their physical skills. The senior high school years are important in transforming adolescents into adults. Students must face the realities of the world and make decisions about education, careers, marriage, religion, politics, and lifestyles. Teachers have a responsibility for imparting information, attitudes, and skills.*

STEP 4: DETERMINE PROGRAM OBJECTIVES

Program objectives give direction to the curriculum guide. After a curriculum model has been selected and students considered, planners determine what specific objectives are going to be emphasized. For example, is the model going to focus on 1 or 2 areas such as outdoor adventure activities, knowledge concepts, or physical fitness? Is the model going to be focused on a multi-activity arrangement with a wide variety of short units to ensure breadth of exposure to all students? Are longer units going to be made available for depth of learning? Will students have a choice of activities or will the yearly sequence of units be required? The model is a philosophic view, whereas objectives are clear statements of direction. The objectives for the program should evolve from the desires of the people whom the program serves. Objectives should be formulated with the desires of both the public (parents and students) and physical education professionals integrated. Objectives need to be based on the knowledge and understanding of professional educators.

Some physical educators feel that program objectives should be narrowed to focus on the accomplishment of a few important objectives (Siedentop, Mand, and Taggart, 1986; Ennis, 1993). It is difficult to accomplish a wide variety of objectives, and an excess of program goals may prevent accomplishment of any goals. The type of program and the amount of emphasis within each program is determined by teachers, administrators, facilities, and the support available in each situation. A new curriculum at the secondary level cannot be all things to all people. It takes time and patience to start and to gain the type of support necessary. It is important to make the new curriculum successful; think big but start small and progress slowly toward the goals.

Institutional Objectives *Broad*

Objectives are behavioral goals to be reached by the students in a program. They provide focus and direction for the program. There are 2 types of objectives that are necessary for the curriculum. They are called **institutional** and **student-centered** objectives. Institutional objectives are general in nature and determine the direction of the program as desired by the school district. They specify the long-term goals of the program. These objectives are written in the 3 learning domains: psychomotor, cognitive, and affective. The following are examples of general institutional objectives that can be used as overall curriculum objectives.

Affective Domain
1. Students will incorporate physical activity into their lifestyles on a regular basis.
2. Students will display a positive attitude toward physical activity.
3. Students will develop social and emotional skills that will enable them to be responsible sports participants.
4. Students will feel good about their physical selves.

Psychomotor Domain
5. Students will develop an appropriate level of health-related physical fitness.
6. Students will develop specialized sport skills so that they can enjoy lifetime sports.

Cognitive Domain
7. Students will acquire knowledge about sports, games, dance, exercise, and fitness.
8. Students will develop a basic understanding of the underlying principles of movement.

Student-Centered Objectives *Specific*

After general institutional objectives have been determined, student-centered objectives are constructed. These objectives are written in specific behavioral or performance terms. They specify the physical skills, knowledge, and attitudes students will possess when they finish various units and daily lessons. The following are examples of specific behavioral or performance objective.

Psychomotor Domain
1. The student will run 1.5 miles in 12 minutes.
2. The student will do 35 push-ups in 1 minute.
3. The student will bump the volleyball 12 consecutive times against the wall above a 10-foot line.

Cognitive Domain
4. The student will identify 5 exercises that develop low-back flexibility.
5. The student will determine a training heart rate for a 15-year-old female.
6. The student will identify 3 exercises that develop the abdominal muscles.

Affective Domain
7. The student will demonstrate a positive attitude toward Frisbee activities by practicing during free time.
8. The student will demonstrate an understanding of cooperation by working with teammates in soccer games.
9. The student will show a positive attitude toward lifetime activity by joining the school's jogging club.

Overall institutional objectives for the curriculum are written in general terms, but unit plans and daily lesson plans usually use specific student-centered objectives with precise behavioral definitions.

Mastery Learning

The sum of daily lesson objectives equals all of the objectives for one unit, and the sum of all unit objectives equals the total curricular objectives. Specific behavioral objectives that are useful for lesson and unit plans are discussed in the planning and teaching styles chapters (Chapters 5, 6, and 8). For a review of the general objectives of physical education that can be used for institutional objectives, refer to Chapter 1.

STEP 5: CONSIDER FACTORS AFFECTING CURRICULUM IMPLEMENTATION

A number of factors impact the development and implementation of the curriculum. These include the specific parameters for each school and district, that is, the people, the programs, and the facilities. These factors determine the success or failure of a program. If all factors are not considered and accounted for, the odds of the program failing increase.

Philosophy and Abilities of Teachers

Since a secondary school physical education program involves several people, it is important that members of the department have a unified philosophy of physical education. Physical educators have to be able to answer the following questions for students, faculty, administrators, school board members, and community members. An existing curriculum cannot be effectively changed or a new one developed without agreement on the philosophy of the program. The following philosophical questions need to be answered:

1. What is physical education?
2. What are the objectives of physical education?
3. What activities should be used to accomplish these objectives?
4. How should these activities be arranged and packaged?
5. What policies and procedures should be used as guidelines?

Philosophy can be a problem when teachers do not want to change and choose not to expand their "comfort zone." Physical education curricula continue to evolve and change. A teacher who clings to a philosophy that was developed years earlier may be teaching a curriculum that is causing escape or avoidance tendencies in students. Physical educators should constantly evaluate their philosophy of physical education and make efforts to bring the curriculum in line with that philosophy. Compromises can be worked out privately when differences of opinion exist. A well-conceived philosophy based on sound educational principles is a positive factor in curriculum construction.

An important factor in hiring staff members should be their teaching competence and how their abilities blend with the existing staff's competencies. A positive situation exists when a staff has a wide variety of activity interests and abilities. It is also a plus if teachers are willing to expand their teaching abilities through in-service training and additional course work. Physical activity interests and abilities of the staff are important factors in curriculum development.

The number of staff members is another important consideration in curriculum construction. If a choice needs to be made between staff and equipment, an increase in staff size is desirable. An additional teacher means reduced class sizes, more activity offerings, and an increase in student-teacher contact. If physical educators believe their subject matter is as important as any other curriculum area, they will defend the concept of a teacher-student ratio in physical education equal to the ratio in math, science, or English classes.

The School Administration

The support of school administrators has a significant impact on the physical education curriculum. Physical education teachers need to communicate the goals of the program to administrators. Since many administrators have misconceptions about physical education, communication between staff and administration is important. In most cases, administrators will agree with and support the philosophy of the physical education staff if they perceive it to be built on sound educational principles. The support of school administrators yields positive dividends over time because administrators have the power to influence situations and implement strategies. The following are areas where administrative support is necessary:

1. Determining the number of staff members and class size.

2. Hiring staff to fill specific departmental needs.
3. Constructing or developing facilities and teaching areas (for example, racquetball courts, weight room, parcourse, or swimming pool).
4. Purchasing equipment and teaching aids (for example, golf clubs, bowling sets, loop films, or jump ropes).
5. Supporting innovative ideas or new activities (for example, pilot unit on orienteering, an off-campus cross-country skiing lesson, or a team-teaching presentation of a golf unit).
6. Maintaining existing teaching stations (for example, watering the fields, cleaning the gymnasium, or repairing weight machines).
7. Supporting professional development with in-service workshops, professional conferences, and current literature.
8. Providing useful and meaningful feedback to teachers on their teaching performance (for example, collecting data on management time, productive time, active learning time, or behavior patterns).

Community Influences: People and Places

Physical educators have to understand the importance of community influences. Occupations, religions, educational levels, cultural values, and physical activity habits of the citizenry are factors that can affect curriculum development. Parents have a strong influence on activity interests and habits of their children. By secondary school age, students have acquired specific habits that need to be considered as they develop the program. Parents in a suburban, upper-class community will be quite different from those in an urban, inner-city community.

The geographic location and climate contribute to the types of activities that should be included in the curriculum. The terrain of the mountains, deserts, or plains combined with weather conditions of each area have an effect on people's activity interests. Extremely hot or cold climates influence what activities can be arranged in the curriculum and at what time of the year they are scheduled. Cross-country skiing, bicycling, and outdoor swimming are examples of such activities. In addition, the climate influences how an activity is taught. For example, outdoor jogging during midday in September in central Arizona is next to impossible because of the extreme heat. Plans and alternatives for rainy and cold climates must also be developed by curriculum planners. There are many ways to help educate the public

and gain citizens' support. Chapter 14 discusses procedures for enhancing public relations.

Facilities and Equipment

Available teaching facilities will dictate, in part, the activities that can be offered in the curriculum. Facilities include on-campus and off-campus areas in the neighboring community. On-campus facilities are areas such as the gymnasium, wrestling room, weight room, tennis courts, field space, and hallways. Off-campus facilities can include a golf driving range, a horseback riding stable, a sailing pond, a stream for canoeing, a community swimming pool, or a hiking trail in a nearby park. Equipment includes materials such as bats, balls, tennis racquets, badminton birds, jump ropes, and records.

It is important to continually strive for ways to improve and expand existing facilities and equipment. On-campus facilities can be increased by using a foyer area for aerobic dance, adapting an old storage area for golf, or expanding a locker room into a weight room. A creative look at existing facilities may provide new teaching areas. Off-campus facilities can open a new world of teaching environments. Many areas may be close by, within walking distance, whereas others may require transportation. Many schools are now busing students to nearby bowling alleys, ski slopes, and hiking areas. When off-school facilities are used, the legal liability aspects of each situation need to be reviewed.

Equipment can be added using departmental funds or special funds raised by students for physical education. Some types of equipment can be made by school maintenance departments or by students as industrial arts projects. Safety factors should be checked carefully in all cases. In some units, students can bring equipment from home, such as tennis racquets, racquetballs, or bicycles. Curriculum planners have to be creative and consider every possibility for expanding the facilities and increasing equipment.

Laws and Requirements

The laws, regulations, and requirements at the national, state, and local levels are another factor demanding consideration. Physical educators must understand various regulations in order to develop programs that comply with the laws. However, these laws and regulations were developed by people and are subject to change. People can modify laws if the legislation is not helping programs achieve their objectives. Appropriate procedures are available to change laws and government regulations, and educators must become actively involved in the process when change is necessary.

At the national level, Title IX of the Educational Amendments Act of 1972 and Public Law 94-142 have had a significant impact on physical education curriculum. Specifics of these laws, as discussed in Chapter 1, are still being debated and interpreted differently by school districts, state departments of education, and the judicial system. Physical educators need to evaluate these laws carefully and develop curricula that are in compliance. Each state department of education has regulations and guidelines governing the physical education requirements for that particular state.

School Organization Pattern

The schedule or organizational pattern of the school will have an impact on implementation of the curriculum. There are 2 basic types of schedules: the **block** or traditional schedule and the **flexible** schedule. The block or traditional schedule (Figure 4.4) divides the school day into 5 or 6 equal time blocks or periods. Each class, such as math, science, or physical education, meets for the same length of time on each day of the school week. The advantage of the traditional schedule is that it is easier to set up, more economical, and easier to administer. Students are in the same class at the same time each day. This provides students and administrators with a stable routine.

Flexible schedules (Figure 4.5) provide a varying length of time for classes depending on the nature of the subject matter and the type of instruction given. A biology lecture might meet 3 days a week for 45 minutes, while a laboratory for biology would meet for 1.5 hours. A flexible schedule would allow physical education students to travel to a local ski slope and meet for a 3-hour block of time 1 day a week. Schools use different flexible schedules to meet the needs of students involved. In physical education, a flexible schedule can provide time for travel off-campus, the option of grouping students for different types of instruction (large or small groups), or the use of limited and specific types of equipment. Some administrators and teachers complain about "dead spots" of time in a flexible schedule. Students may have 15 minutes of free time between classes, which causes concern because they need a place to congregate and may abuse the use of the free time. Many schools have provided a "commons" area where students can gather during these intervals.

Period	Time	Monday	Tuesday	Wednesday	Thursday	Friday
Homeroom	8:00–8:15					➤
1	8:15–9:10	General math				➤
2	9:15–10:10	English				➤
3	10:15–11:10	Biology				➤
Lunch	11:15–11:45					➤
Study hall	11:45–12:15					➤
4	12:15–1:10	Physical education				➤
5	1:15–2:10	History				➤
6	2:15–3:10	Home economics				➤

FIGURE 4.4   Block or traditional schedule

Module	Time	Monday	Tuesday	Wednesday	Thursday	Friday
1	8:00–8:15	English	Industrial arts lab	English	Biology lab	English
2	8:15–8:30	English	Industrial arts lab	English	Biology lab	English
3	8:30–8:45	English	Industrial arts lab	English	Biology lab	English
4	8:45–9:00	General math	Industrial arts lab	General math	Biology lab	General math
5	9:00–9:15	General math	Industrial arts lab	General math	Biology lab	General math
6	9:15–9:30	General math	Industrial arts lab	General math	Biology lab	General math
7	9:30–9:45	Biology lecture	Industrial arts	Biology lecture	Industrial arts	Open
8	9:45–10:00	Biology lecture	Industrial arts	Biology lecture	Industrial arts	Open
9	10:00–10:15	Biology lecture	Industrial arts	Biology lecture	Industrial arts	Open
10	10:15–10:30	History	Typing	History	Typing	History
11	10:30–10:45	History	Typing	History	Typing	History
12	10:45–11:00	History	Typing	History	Typing	History
13	11:00–11:15	Open	Typing	Open	Typing	Open
14	11:15–11:30	Lunch	Lunch	Lunch	Lunch	Lunch
15	11:30–11:45	Lunch	Lunch	Lunch	Lunch	Lunch
16	11:45–12:00	Physical education	Open	Physical education	English lab	Physical education
17	12:00–12:15	Physical education	Open	Physical education	English lab	Physical education
18	12:15–12:30	Physical education	Open	Physical education	English lab	Physical education
19	12:30–12:45	Physical education	Open	Physical education	English lab	Physical education
20	12:45–1:00	Physical education	Open	Physical education	English lab	Physical education
21	1:00–1:15	Physical education	Open	Physical education	English lab	Physical education
22	1:15–1:30	Typing lab	Open	Open	Open	Open
23	1:30–1:45	Typing lab	Open	Open	Open	Open
24	1:45–2:00	Typing lab	General math lab	Open	History lab	Open
25	2:00–2:15	Typing lab	General math lab	Open	History lab	Physical education
26	2:15–2:30	Typing lab	General math lab	Open	History lab	Physical education
27	2:30–2:45	Typing lab	General math lab	Open	History lab	Physical education
28	2:45–3:00	Open	General math lab	Open	History lab	Physical education
29	3:00–3:15	Open	General math lab	Open	History lab	Physical education

FIGURE 4.5   Flexible schedule

Coeducational Classes

The issue of coeducational classes continues to be controversial. Many schools have all physical education classes assigned with 50% boys and 50% girls. Other schools conduct a few coeducational units such as square dance, volleyball, or track and field, but offer the majority of units segregated by sex. Still other programs allow students to choose classes based on interest, so the class composition has no fixed gender percentage. In some schools, boys and girls are segregated and never taught together during physical education. This is an unfortunate and unacceptable situation, yet physical educators continue to take stands on both sides of the issue. A great deal has been written on the subject, and many coeducational programs have been highly successful with boys and girls learning together. The authors' experiences in this area have led to positive feelings about coeducational classes. Program objectives can be accomplished in a coeducational format. Students in grades K through 6 are usually integrated in physical education classes, and there is reason to believe that they should be able to move into a coeducational format in the middle and senior high school programs.

Problems have to be solved, such as dress, grading, puberty, comfort zones of teachers, attitudes, interest development, learning about individual differences, increasing activity choices, and improving instructional quality. Sensitive teachers working together can develop an exciting and challenging program for boys and girls. Wrestling or other contact sports are not advocated, but a balanced program that is based on the characteristics and interests of students can be effectively implemented. The complaints that many people espouse can be solved by teachers who have a strong desire to make the program work. The bottom line: regardless of the legality of the situation, teachers have a moral and educational obligation to offer coeducational classes. If both sexes do not learn to play together in a variety of activities at the middle school level, they will undoubtedly never develop the necessary respect and understanding of differences required for successful participation.

Budget and Funding

Budget and funding procedures differ among school districts; however, the physical education department head is usually involved in developing and sub-mitting the budget. Understanding the funding procedures and planning an aggressive strategy for obtaining an adequate budget is a necessity for a quality program. Physical educators should seek parity with other school departments in terms of class size and equipment. Students cannot learn to read and write without materials and supplies, and they cannot learn physical skills without the necessary equipment.

In addition to the basic departmental budget, funds may be available through outside sources. Sometimes the athletic and physical education departments can share equipment. With tight budgets, this is an effective way to cut costs. Various community and parent groups, such as the Lions or Rotary Club, may help with short-term funding for special facility or equipment needs such as a weight room, racquetball courts, or tennis racquets. Some schools allow departments to have special fund-raising campaigns involving students and faculty. Car washes, candy sales, or admission to special sports demonstrations are useful projects for generating funds. The best programs are not always the ones with the most funding, but adequate funding is necessary to produce a quality curriculum.

STEP 6: SELECT INSTRUCTIONAL ACTIVITIES

Historically, the physical activity interests of the public have strongly influenced physical education curriculum. As people's interests have changed, programs have evolved from an early fitness-oriented model to a team sports approach and, finally, to an emphasis on individual lifetime activities and health-related fitness activities. Popular activities, such as weight lifting, aerobics, outdoor adventure activities, and lifetime activities, have filtered into physical education because such activities fulfill program goals.

The activity interests of society and students are an important consideration in curriculum construction. A curriculum formulated without concern for the interests of students may not accomplish objectives or develop positive student attitudes. In addition to popular new activities, different communities generate special interest in areas such as golf, tennis, or sailing, while others may focus more on basketball, baseball, or football. Geographic location, economics, and the background of the community members impact the activity interests of students and units included in the curriculum.

Consider the Activity Interests of Students

Program planners should examine student interests and activities being offered. Too often, programs are based on the activity interests of teachers, administrators, and parents, rather than students. Often, teachers will not teach activities in which they are not skilled. The activity comfort zone of teachers can be narrow and the curriculum limited. Lack of variety may cause students to develop escape or avoidance behaviors in physical education. They may like physical activity but not like the activities presented or the methods of instruction. Effective teachers learn to expand their teaching repertoire of activities and methods to better meet students' needs.

When the activity interests of students are not considered, students may avoid taking physical education. For example, teachers at an inner-city school may try offering units on lifetime activities such as golf, bowling, and archery and then find out that only a few students may register because of the expense of the activities. In another example, if all of the units in the curriculum are required during an optional year of physical education, some students may avoid the entire year because they do not wish to take 1 or 2 of the specific units. In other words, students will avoid an entire year because of 1 or 2 compulsory activities. As a minimum, the program should offer students 4 or 5 activity choices. The high school program is not the time to force students into activities in which they have little or no interest.

Determine Student Interests

Surveys or checklists can be used to gather data about student activity interests. Surveys completed in the spring help determine the curricular offerings for the following fall and spring semesters. The survey can be administered every other year to all demographic groups within the schools (that is, boys, girls, athletes, nonathletes, various racial groups, and various grade levels). As many students as possible should be surveyed to ensure valid information. Ideally, the survey can be administered in a class or homeroom period (math, science, or English) so all students have the opportunity to respond. Many schools have

access to data processing and computers, and a specialist may be available to help set up programs for data analysis. Student interests can be analyzed by age, sex, or racial group.

A survey instrument should include all possible physical activities that contribute to the objectives of physical education. It is important to avoid restrictive thinking when listing activity offerings in a survey. For example, the lack of a pool, racquetball courts, ski slopes, or various types of equipment for specific activities need not prohibit an educator from including these activities on the survey. Travel to off-campus facilities in the nearby community may be possible in the future. Most communities have nearby golf driving ranges, racquet clubs, bowling alleys, pools, ski slopes, or wooded areas that can be used for the school program. Data collected from surveys can be used to support the need for expanding physical facilities such as adding a pool, racquetball courts, tennis courts, or a weight lifting room. If student interest is evident, administrators may be convinced that facilities and equipment, course offerings, or new teachers should be added to the physical education program.

An example of an interest survey is shown in Figure 4.6. The instrument can be revised every other year, with new activity trends included. Professional and popular literature help provide information about the new activity patterns and habits. Interests in the community can be determined by looking at various recreation programs offered through the YMCA, the parks and recreation department, private clubs, community leagues, and corporations. Facilities available such as bowling alleys, golf courses, ski slopes, and swimming pools provide additional information about interests in the community.

Select a Variety of Activities

Appropriate activities are selected for the purpose of accomplishing program goals. Activities should blend the desires of society with the objectives of the program and the interests of the students. Effective program planners understand that the interests of students are not the sole basis for a curriculum. Students should not make all decisions on the courses and activities in the curriculum because they are not trained in educational programming. This does not mean, however, that activities selected by the educator cannot be interesting or enjoyable. For example,

Physical Activity Interest Survey

Name _____

Grade _____   Age _____   Sex _____

Athletic team _____

Instructions: Which of the following physical activities or sports would you be most interested in taking as a course in the physical education program? Please list your top 5 choices on the line provided. Place a number 1 in front of your highest choice, a number 2 in front of your next choice, and so on, until you reach choice number 5. Remember to make only 5 choices.

Aquatic Activities
_____ Lifesaving, water safety
_____ Skin and scuba diving
_____ Surfing
_____ Swimming, diving
_____ Water sports (polo, volleyball, basketball)

Individual Activities
_____ Archery
_____ Badminton
_____ Fencing
_____ Frisbee
_____ Golf
_____ Gymnastics
_____ Handball
_____ Racquetball
_____ Recreational games (bowling, horseshoes, shuffleboard, etc.)
_____ Roller-skating
_____ Skateboarding
_____ Squash
_____ Tennis
_____ Track and field

Physical Conditioning Activities
_____ Aerobic dance
_____ Body conditioning, weight control
_____ Martial arts (judo, karate, kendo, etc.)
_____ Weight training
_____ Yoga

Outdoor Adventure Activities
_____ Backpacking
_____ Canoeing, kayaking
_____ Cycling (bicycling)
_____ Fishing
_____ Horseback riding
_____ Hunting
_____ Ice skating
_____ Outdoor survival
_____ Orienteering
_____ Rock climbing
_____ Sailing
_____ Skiing (cross country)
_____ Skiing (downhill)
_____ Snow shoeing

Rhythmic Activities
_____ Ballet
_____ Country swing dance
_____ Disco
_____ Folk and square dance
_____ Jazz dance
_____ Modern dance
_____ Social dance

Team Activities
_____ Baseball
_____ Basketball
_____ Field hockey
_____ Flag football
_____ Ice hockey
_____ Lacrosse
_____ Soccer
_____ Softball
_____ Speedball-speed-a-way
_____ Team handball
_____ Volleyball
_____ Wrestling

Directions for the teacher: Remind students to select only 5 choices, using the numbers 1–5 on the lines beside the activities. When analyzing the data, it is helpful to transpose numbers 1 and 5 and numbers 2 and 4. In other words, a 1 becomes a 5 and a 5 becomes a 1. A 2 is worth 4 and a 4 worth 2. The numbers are added for each activity. The activities with the most points are the most popular and those with the least points are the least popular.

FIGURE 4.6 Physical activity interest survey

students going through the adolescent growth spurt should be offered a wide variety of physical activities to provide them with success in basic skills like running, dribbling, and throwing. The short and varied units prevent excessive failure and boredom for students at this developmental level. Conversely, a high school student would benefit from an opportunity to choose a semester unit in modern dance, tennis, racquetball, or another area that is highly specialized and in line with her or his interest.

The competencies of teachers are a consideration when designing the curriculum. However, activity selection should not be based solely on the interests or teaching competencies of teachers directing the programs. Teachers often bring a set of competencies to the program and then fail to learn new skills. These competencies may be related to activities that are not popular in our society today. Thus, the need exists for teachers to continually expand their activity knowledge and expertise.

The curriculum planner should provide a **balance** of activities from different categories. Common categories emphasized are team sports, lifetime sports, physical conditioning, dance activities, aquatic activities, adventure activities, and self-testing activities. An important point is to assure that all students have experience with several activities selected from as many categories as possible in each school setting. Too often, the curriculum is heavily tipped toward team sports because of class size, facilities, equipment, or the instructor's lack of interest or ability in other areas. An unbalanced curriculum is not appropriate for students who are interested in activity categories not offered. For example, many students enjoy Frisbee, orienteering, modern dance, or skin diving. They may not enjoy football, basketball, wrestling, or volleyball. If the curriculum is unbalanced, these students will not have access to potentially fulfilling activities. Teachers must make every effort to offer a balanced program.

Finally, activities should be selected based on the objectives of the program. The skillful curriculum planner chooses activities that influence the habits of people in both the health-related and play areas. Activities cannot be justified unless they are fulfilling program goals. Initially, students who are not interested in health-related fitness may have to be positively directed toward those activities. They need a gentle push to engage in the activities until the reinforcing aspects of physical exercise have developed a "positively addicted" person. All students need to find activities for play and health-related fitness in the physical education curriculum. Physical education programs can take a leadership role in trying to shape activity preferences, and teachers should select activities with this goal in mind.

The most often found category of activity in the schools is team sports. Many physical educators claim these are the most popular activities with students and are the most economical activities in terms of facilities and equipment. More often than not, they are popular with vocal students who are skilled in such sports. Less-skilled students are intimidated and afraid to admit that they don't like team sports for fear they will not be liked by their more-skilled peers. In addition, team sports units are only more economical (in terms of required equipment) when they are improperly taught. To teach basketball or softball with 3 or 4 balls assures that the majority of students will be standing rather than practicing skills in a semi-individualized manner.

More teachers are teaching a variety of lifetime sports such as racquetball, tennis, badminton, bowling, and golf. These activities have more carry-over value for later life since they do not require a number of teammates for participation. Popular activities such as aerobic dance, martial arts, jogging, and outdoor adventure activities like backpacking, canoeing, and rock climbing are increasing. Successful programs develop a balance of team sports, lifetime sports, physical fitness, dance, aquatic, and currently popular activities. Curricula that offer an activity balance have a higher potential for positively affecting *all* students within the school.

Integrate After-School Activities

Athletics, intramurals, sport clubs, YMCA and YWCA leagues, and parks and recreation programs offer students many opportunities for programs after school. Interest and motivation for specific activities usually increases during the time of the year when the activities are played professionally. Physical educators can capitalize on this heightened interest period by coordinating the physical education sequence of activities with after-school programs. For example, a track and field unit can be scheduled to end when the city track meet sponsored by the parks and recreation department occurs. Soccer can be offered in the fall in conjunction with the popular YMCA soccer leagues. Basketball can be coordinated with the school intramural program, and wrestling offered before an AAU wrestling tournament. Coordinating activities with all after-school programs can be challenging, but the effort will be worthwhile in terms of student motivation.

Adjust for Weather and Facilities

Many activities have to be coordinated with weather conditions and the availability of equipment and facilities. Skiing, sailing, ice skating, and other outdoor activities require specific weather conditions that occur only at certain times of year. Some schools have outdoor pools available during the early fall and late spring periods. Off-campus facilities may be available only during certain times of the year due to climate or public interest in the activity (such as golf ranges, bowling alleys, or surfing beaches). All factors should be checked carefully before making the final arrangement of activities.

Consider Proficiency Levels

Many high schools are attempting to offer different proficiency levels for various activities. This implies sections for **beginners, intermediates,** and **advanced** levels of instruction for the most popular activities. Grouping students by ability and experience can offer efficient teaching and learning situations for teachers and students. Students may be more comfortable with others who are near their ability level. Students can skip a level if they are proficient at the earlier level. The following are descriptions that can be used for different levels of instruction:

- *Beginning level.* Introductory units for the development of the basic skills and knowledge of the activity.
- *Intermediate level.* Team units for learning and practicing the basic team concepts of the activity.
- *Advanced level.* Recreational units that allow the students to focus on competitive game activity.

Offer Choice

The **choice concept** can be used with any length unit and any type of organizational schedule in a coeducational or segregated setting. A curriculum that increases the level of motivation of both students and teachers creates a positive environment for both teachers and students. Allowing for choice offers the following advantages:

1. Increased student motivation and enthusiasm and a desire to take more physical education because of a higher interest level.

2. Fewer problems with dressing, participation, and discipline.
3. Better use of teaching expertise and the development of specialists.
4. Improved instruction over a period of time.
5. Increased teacher motivation and enthusiasm.

A trend, which started at the high school level and has filtered down to middle school programs, allows students to choose activities in physical education. Classes are open to both sexes, depending on personal interests. Using this approach, male and female teachers work together and decide who is better qualified to teach a specific activity. Each teacher develops 2 or 3 specialties and teaches those specialties to different classes of students, rather than teaching all activities to the same students.

Students choose at the beginning of each semester. This design has been used coeducationally with males and females allowed to select all activities except contact sports. If more than 3 teachers are available, students have the opportunity to make choices from a broader selection. An example of alternating 4- and 5-week units in a coeducational curriculum with choices for students follows.

First Semester
First 9 weeks
    Volleyball, yoga, or soccer (4 weeks)
    Flag football, archery, or tennis (5 weeks)

Second 9 weeks
    Gymnastics, volleyball, or badminton
    (4 weeks)
    Basketball, team handball, or field hockey
    (5 weeks)

Second Semester
Third 9 weeks
    Aerobics, speed-a-way, or basketball
    (4 weeks)
    Wrestling, orienteering, or volleyball
    (5 weeks)

Last 9 weeks
    Softball, track and field, or badminton
    (4 weeks)
    Swimming, Frisbee games, or yoga (5 weeks)

Some schools vary this approach by developing requirements by activity categories to ensure that breadth is provided. For example, students take a certain number of team sports, lifetime sports, conditioning activities, dance units, aquatics, or recreational activities. This concept is referred to as a

choice within a requirement. Depending on the number of units offered, students are required to take a specified number of activities from each category. If the program offers 24 3-week units over a 2-year period, the requirements might include:

> 1 unit of wellness concepts
> 2 units of aquatics
> 2 units of dance
> 4 units of physical conditioning
> 6 units of lifetime sports
> 6 units of team sports
> 3 units of elective activities
> 24 units total

STEP 7: ARRANGE UNITS INTO A LONG-TERM PLAN

After selecting and structuring the activities, the next step is to sequence them over the length of the school year, from the first year to the second year, and so on until the students have graduated. There are many ways to sequence activities, but all long-term plans contain the following basic organizational elements.

Horizontal versus Vertical Articulation

There are 2 major concerns when arranging and sequencing activities. The first is **horizontal articulation,** which deals with activities that are to be taught during the school year for a specific grade level. Horizontal organization of the curriculum is most often done by physical educators. It describes to instructors what activities are to be taught, when they are to be taught, and how long they will be taught. Without this organizational scheme, teachers have little direction and knowledge about how to help students achieve desired goals.

Vertical articulation is less often considered by curriculum planners. It delineates what activities will be taught at different grade levels. When done correctly, the vertical curriculum demands that teachers at elementary, middle, and senior high schools be keenly aware of what is being taught at each respective level. In physical education, a common practice has been to teach the same activities, in much the same manner, year after year. Important concepts such as sequence, progression, and continuity have

been ignored as teachers at different grade levels work autonomously. Effective vertical articulation assures that related knowledge, skills, and attitudes are distributed over the 10- to 12-year school career of students. School districts with well-developed curricula continually coordinate the efforts of physical educators at all levels.

Depth versus Breadth

Breadth in a curriculum refers to the offering of many short units throughout the year. A curriculum that offers 18 2-week units illustrates breadth of curriculum. **Depth** refers to the offering of fewer but longer units. A curriculum that offers 4 units, each of which is 9 weeks long, has depth in these activities. Depth can be added to a curriculum by offering intermediate- and advanced-level units in addition to beginning units. Generally, a middle school program provides activity breadth, while the senior high school program focuses on depth. Departmental philosophy on the concepts of depth and breadth influences the length of units and the arrangement of varying levels of units.

The length of an activity unit can vary from 1 week to 1 year. Developmental level and interests of students affect the length of a unit, as does the school schedule and the number of days per week that a class meets. The number of class meetings per week is a key factor in deciding the length of a unit. A 3-week unit that meets daily offers 15 sessions, whereas a 3-week unit that meets twice a week allows only 6 sessions. Although both are 3-week units, there is a big difference in the amount of actual class time for instruction.

At one end of the spectrum is an arrangement of long units of activity focused on a few activities. Students take 4 to 8 activities in a year. An example is the following:

> First 9 weeks—Flag football or soccer
> Second 9 weeks—Basketball
> Third 9 weeks—Wrestling
> Last 9 weeks—Softball or track and field

Another design uses 6-week units:

> First 6 weeks—Swimming
> Second 6 weeks—Volleyball
> Third 6 weeks—Basketball
> Fourth 6 weeks—Gymnastics
> Fifth 6 weeks—Track and field
> Last 6 weeks—Softball

Another design is to offer 2 units during each 9-week grading period. One unit is 5 weeks and the other 4 weeks. In this way, students take 8 units per year. Two examples of this approach are as follows.

Program A

First 9 weeks
    Soccer (5 weeks)
    Flag football (4 weeks)

Second 9 weeks
    Tennis (5 weeks)
    Basketball (4 weeks)

Third 9 weeks
    Volleyball (5 weeks)
    Tumbling (4 weeks)

Last 9 weeks
    Track and field (5 weeks)
    Softball (4 weeks)

Program B

First 9 weeks
    Field hockey (5 weeks)
    Speed-a-way (4 weeks)

Second 9 weeks
    Volleyball (5 weeks)
    Dance (4 weeks)

Third 9 weeks
    Basketball (5 weeks)
    Gymnastics (4 weeks)

Last 9 weeks
    Tennis (5 weeks)
    Track and field (4 weeks)

At the opposite end of the spectrum is an arrangement using short 2- and 3-week units that offer students 12 to 18 different activities during the year. The following is an example:

Weeks	Activity
1–3	Swimming
4–6	Volleyball
7–9	Tennis
10–12	Flag football
13–15	Dance
16–18	Basketball
19–21	Badminton
22–24	Tumbling
25–27	Recreational games
28–30	Speed-a-way
31–33	Track and field
34–36	Softball

Some experts argue that units should be a minimum of 10 to 12 weeks, with in-depth instruction available for those activities of interest to students. They believe that short units (2 to 4 weeks) offer minimal time and provide little change in skill level. Pangrazi, Darst, Fedorchek, and Coyle (1982) advocate short units for middle school students, because of the developmental characteristics of these students, and longer units for high school students. Middle school youngsters, who are going through puberty, a rapid growth spurt, and a period of slow motor development, need successful experiences with a wide variety of activities. At a time when students find it difficult to tolerate failure, longer units can lock students into a frustrating or boring experience for a long period of time. Variety and novelty in a success-oriented atmosphere are important motivational keys for this age group. Students can find success in short units when emphasis is on exploration and on learning about one's personal strengths and weaknesses. Finally, because a majority of students are still trying to identify their strengths and weaknesses, this is possibly the last opportunity they will have to experience a wide variety of activities. Mini units of instruction (see Chapter 18) can be used to offer variety and help maintain student interest. The middle school years should not be a time of specialization and refinement but, rather, a time of exploration.

Learning environments can be productive when units are changed often. Students and teachers are excited when a new activity begins. Long units can turn into a prolonged class tournament without structured skill work. Some students, usually unskilled, may feel they are placed in tournament play and forced into highly competitive situations without the opportunity to develop adequate skill level. This only adds to the frustration for less-skilled students. Finally, some teachers advocate long units to minimize their preparation duties and requisite instructional competency. The fewer units taught, the less planning and knowledge needed. This rationale is difficult to accept if the needs and interests of students are kept in focus.

Progression and Continuity

Activities are arranged from simple to complex. The arrangement should move from safe activities to activities with a controlled element of risk and danger. Proper steps, intervals, or sequences between activities help students be successful and develop positive attitudes. Curriculum planners build on students' previous skills and knowledge. This can be done both within the year (horizontally) and between the years (vertically). For example, team handball uses skills from soccer, basketball, and volleyball and can be taught after these 3 units. Intermediate basketball should build on beginning basketball activities, and soccer in the middle school should build on soccer experiences learned in elementary years.

STEP 8: EVALUATE AND MODIFY THE CURRICULUM

The final and on-going step in maintaining an effective curriculum is evaluation. Program evaluation that focuses on the institutional objectives of the program is called summative evaluation. Summative evaluation provides information about how well the curriculum as a whole affects students. Differentiating between curriculum and instruction is difficult. These areas intertwine, and a program will not improve without constant evaluation in both areas.

Evaluating curriculum involves looking at 3 aspects: the curriculum itself, the performance of the students, and the effectiveness of the instructor. To evaluate curriculum, summative evaluation can be completed using a variety of checklists, rating scales, and self-appraisal instruments. Student responses can be analyzed and their performance evaluated with knowledge tests, fitness tests, performance objectives for physical skills, attitude and self-concept inventories, and free-time activity questionnaires (see Chapter 10). Instruction and teaching procedures can be evaluated using several coding instruments and devices (see Chapter 9).

Curriculum evaluation should offer insight into accomplishment of program goals and offer direction for future modifications. Figure 4.7 is an example of evaluation questions that can be used in the evaluation process. Figure 4.8 is a formal instrument that can be used to evaluate programs on a point basis. The list of items presented can be a self-evaluation tool for analyzing the program. Each item should be rated according to the scale explained at the top of the form.

Curriculum Evaluation Questions

1. Are students incorporating physical activity into their lifestyles?

2. Are students returning to optional programs after they have completed the mandatory years?

3. Are students acquiring competency in physical skills?

4. Do students understand the concepts of developing and maintaining personal fitness for a lifetime?

5. Are students reaching a desirable level of physical fitness through participation in the program?

6. Do students possess the requisite knowledge required to participate in a wide variety of sports, games, and exercises?

7. Have students acquired social and emotional skills necessary for productive participation in school and society?

8. Does the curriculum leave students with a broad understanding of the wealth of physical activities available to them (balance)?

9. Does the curriculum allow students to leave school with a high level of competency in a few activities (depth)?

10. Does the curriculum follow a progressive sequence within the school year as well as between school years (horizontal and vertical curriculum)?

FIGURE 4.7 Curriculum evaluation questions

Program Evaluation

0 points: Unacceptable. There is no compliance with the stated criteria.

1 point: Inadequate coverage. There is doubt about any compliance and little attention is paid to the stated criteria.

2 points: Adequate coverage. It is apparent that attention has been given to the criteria; however, there is room for improvement.

3 points: Excellent coverage. The program is exemplary in meeting the stated criteria.

Read each criterion, determine the extent to which there is compliance, then write in the appropriate scale score. If there is doubt about meeting certain criteria, list the lower of the two scores.

Philosophy and Program Implementation

_____ 1. A written statement is available that describes the philosophy and principles on which the program is based.

_____ 2. Physical education is seen as an integral part of the total school curriculum and receives support similar to any other area of the school curriculum.

_____ 3. The program is constructed based on the desires of its constituency.

_____ 4. A written and updated version of a K–12 curriculum guide is available for the conduct and implementation of the program.

_____ 5. The physical education curriculum delineates horizontal and vertical structure. Teachers know what is to be taught during the school year as well as what is taught at different grade levels.

_____ 6. Activities are listed in units of instruction in proper progression and sequence.

_____ 7. Daily lesson plans are developed from the units of instruction and provide direction for instruction.

_____ 8. Physical education is regarded as an instructional program with emphasis on educating the child in contrast to providing time for tournaments or free play.

_____ 9. Students are taught the "how and why" of physical activity. Emphasis is placed on cognitive learning as well as on psychomotor learning.

_____ 10. All students take part in a regular program of physical education. Substitution of music, driver education, and athletics for physical education does not occur.

_____ 11. Programs at the junior high school level emphasize variety and exposure to a large number of activities.

_____ 12. The high school program allows students to elect the activities in which they choose to participate.

_____ 13. Students with handicaps can participate fully in the program and are offered a wide range of opportunities.

_____ 14. Students with medical problems are identified and monitored for follow-up examinations regularly.

_____ 15. A physician's written statement is the only way students are permanently excused from physical education.

_____ 16. The school has a nurse trained to treat accidents.

_____ 17. Provisions are made for dealing with students desiring to be excused from physical education classes. The plan is consistent and educationally sound.

_____ 18. The grading system used in physical education is consistent with that used in other curriculum areas.

_____ 19. There are provisions for public relations and sharing the program with parents. Demonstrations and information are shared regularly with the public.

_____ 20. The physical education faculty has a plan for professional growth that includes in-service training, professional meetings, university course-work, conferences, and independent study.

_____ 21. Instruction is regarded as a dynamic process and is analyzed through self-evaluation and by outside personnel. Evaluations take place at regular intervals.

_____ 22. Intramurals are seen as an outgrowth of the physical education program. A wide variety of activities is offered for student participation.

_____ 23. The athletic program is seen as a separate entity and not as an end result of or goal for the physical education program.

_____ 24. Teachers separate physical education instruction and athletic coaching. Physical education is taught for the student body and athletics are offered for those students who excel.

Comments:

Curriculum Analysis

1. The physical education program provides learning experiences to help each student attain the following:

_____ a. A personalized level of physical fitness and body conditioning.

_____ b. Specialized sport skills in a wide variety of activities.

_____ c. Knowledge of rules, techniques, and strategy related to individual, dual, and team sports.

FIGURE 4.8 Formal program evaluation instrument

_____   d. Desirable social standards and ethical behavior.

_____   e. Knowledge and practice of safety standards for self and others.

_____   f. Competence in activities that can be used for leisure pursuits.

_____   g. Knowledge and practice of concepts leading to human wellness.

_____   2. Activities are progressively organized and adjusted to suit the maturity and skill levels of youngsters.

_____   3. Students are treated with dignity and encouraged to participate in all phases of the program.

_____   4. The program offers a variety of activities that will be attractive to all students. This includes skilled and unskilled, low-fit, and handicapped students.

_____   5. Each daily lesson has a portion (10-15 min) of time devoted to physical fitness development.

_____   6. An up-to-date library of physical education books, filmstrips, and related materials is available for students and teachers.

_____   7. There is an aquatic program available in the school or community so all students have the opportunity to learn to swim.

_____   8. Indoor and outdoor teaching stations are available for instruction.

_____   9. The yearly curriculum is written. It is reevaluated each year, and modifications are made that facilitate attainment of objectives.

_____ 10. Units of instruction vary in length depending on the maturity and skill level of students. Block plans for each unit are developed and include skill instruction on a regular basis.

_____ 11. Lead-up games are taught to students in order to isolate and develop specific skills that need to be learned.

_____ 12. Student input is welcomed. Instruments designed to monitor student interests and desires are administered on a regular basis.

_____ 13. Students are allowed to make choices about the types of activity they want to learn.

_____ 14. Units that focus on self-assessment are offered during the freshman year. Results are used to help students find the types of activities they want to participate in for a lifetime.

Comments:

Facilities, Equipment, and Supplies

_____   1. Maximum use of facilities for physical education instruction is apparent.

_____   2. Outdoor facilities meet the basic acreage standard of 5 acres plus 1 acre for each additional 100 students.

      3. Outdoor facilities include the following:

_____   a. Areas where different games and activities can be conducted without interference.

_____   b. Areas for court games.

_____   c. Backstops and goals for softball, soccer, and basketball, team handball, and field hockey.

_____   d. Suitable fencing for safety and control.

_____   e. Outdoor grassy areas that are free from rock, sprinkler heads, and other hazards that might cause injury.

      4. Indoor facilities meet the following standards:

_____   a. They are clean, sanitary, and free from hazards.

_____   b. They are well lighted, well ventilated, heated, cooled, and treated for proper acoustics.

_____   c. They are surfaced with a nonslip finish and include painted game area lines.

_____   5. Periodic inspection of all facilities and equipment, both indoor and outdoor, is conducted, and a written report sent to the appropriate administrators.

_____   6. Storage facilities are adequate for supplies and portable equipment.

_____   7. Adequate provision is made for off-season storage of equipment, apparatus, and supplies.

_____   8. An office is provided for the physical education instructors that has a telephone for emergencies and clear vision into the locker room areas.

_____   9. Basic supplies are sufficient for all instructional units. This includes a piece of equipment for each student when necessary.

_____ 10. Equipment necessary to teach units properly is available. This includes tumbling mats, basketball goals, volleyball standards and nets, gymnastic equipment, and so forth.

_____ 11. Personal storage lockers are available for students.

_____ 12. Adequate room is available for students for changing into proper physical activity attire.

_____ 13. Equipment and supplies necessary for the testing and evaluation program are available.

_____ 14. Tape recorders, record players, and records are available in sufficient number for the rhythmic program.

_____ 15. An adequate yearly budget is available for equipment repair, replacement, and development of new units of instruction.

Comments:

FIGURE 4.8   Continued

EXPECTED OUTCOMES

After reading the chapter, you should be able to

- Describe elements common to all curriculums.

- List and discuss commonly used organizing centers in secondary school physical education.

- Cite specific examples of the functional curriculum and academic learning time.

- Suggest ways the hidden curriculum can impact attitudes students have about school, learning, and physical activity.

- List and discuss the steps of curriculum construction.

- Explain the difference between institutional and student-centered objectives.

- Describe various factors that must be considered when developing a physical education curriculum.

- Explain the physical, social, emotional, and intellectual differences between middle and senior high school students.

- Discuss the following concepts as they relate to curriculum construction: horizontal and vertical progression, balance, depth, breadth, choice, and choice within a requirement.

- Give several examples of how curriculum can be evaluated.

REFERENCES AND SUGGESTED READINGS

Benson, J. 1982. An alternative direction for middle school physical education. *The Physical Educator* 39(2): 75–77.

Ennis, C., 1993. Can we really do it all? Making curriculum choices in middle and high school programs. In J. E. Rink (ed.). *Critical Crossroads: Middle and Secondary Physical Education*. Reston, VA: NASPE. 13–23

Harrison, J. M., Blakemore, C. L., Buck, M. M., and Pellett, T. M. 1996. *Instructional Strategies for Secondary Physical Education*. 4th ed. Dubuque, IA: Wm. C. Brown.

Jewett, A., Bain, L., and Ennis, K. 1995. *The Curriculum Process in Physical Education*. Dubuque, IA: Wm. C. Brown and Benchmark.

Melograno, V. J. 1996. *Designing the Physical Education Curriculum*. Champaign, IL: Human Kinetics Publishers.

Pangrazi, R., Darst, P., Fedorchek, S., and Coyle, K. 1982. The needed link: A physical curriculum designed exclusively for junior high students. *The Physical Educator* 39(2): 71–74.

Ross, J. G., Pate, R. P., Corbin, C.B., Delpy, L. A., and Gold, R. S. 1987. What's going on in elementary physical education? *Journal of Physical Education, Recreation, and Dance* 58(9): 78–84.

Siedentop, D. 1991. *Developing Teaching Skills in Physical Education*. 3rd ed. Palo Alto, CA: Mayfield Publishing Co.

Siedentop, D., Mand, C., and Taggart, A. 1986. *Physical Education—Teaching and Curriculum Strategies for Grades 5–12*. Palo Alto, CA: Mayfield Publishing Co.

van der Mars, H., Darst, P. W., Vogler, E. W., and Cusimano B., 1995. Novice and expert physical education teachers: Maybe they think and decide differently . . . but do they behave differently? *Journal of Teaching in Physical Education* 14(3): 340–347.

Wuest, D., and Lombardo, B. 1994. *Curriculum and Instruction: The Secondary School Physical Education Experience*. St. Louis: Mosby.

5 Planning for Effective Instruction

PURPOSE

To describe the various stages of planning associated with assuring quality instruction and to explain the components of a 3-part lesson plan. Essential elements of effective instruction and process-related issues are also addressed.

KEY CONCEPTS

- Planning is important to assure that a thoughtful and creative lesson will be developed.
- It is important to know a student's previous experiences before a particular lesson to integrate with past and future instruction.
- Lessons should offer necessary instruction that maximizes the amount of productive practice time.
- The planned learning experience should be based on the developmental level of students.
- Students will learn little unless there is quality instruction and many opportunities for practice.
- Cognitive development can be enhanced by involving students in the selection of content and implementation of the lesson.
- Practice should occur as soon as possible after students have had the opportunity to perform the skill correctly.
- If individual learning is to be the outcome, then each student should have a piece of equipment with which to work.
- The lesson should be directly related to the unit of instruction and based on activity progressions.
- Lesson plans follow a consistent format and can be analyzed by asking a series of key questions.

A major objective of physical education is to improve skill performance. Students participate in physical education to become physically educated. If they go to a math class, they expect to learn math. Students deserve an educational experience rather than a recreational one. When developing a lesson plan, the following points help form the underlying foundation of the planning effort.

Is there a purpose to the lesson? The lesson should be designed to improve the skill performance of students. What is the purpose of the total program, the unit, and the lesson plan? If the lesson presentation does not contribute to the skill development of participants, what is the purpose? Knowing why an activity is taught and how it contributes to the objectives of the program give direction to instruction.

Is instruction part of the lesson? Instruction is an observable action. There are many different methods for accomplishing instructional goals, but there must be instruction. Instruction can take many forms, such as working individually with students, evaluating a student's progress on a mastery learning packet, developing task cards, or conducting group instruction. Regardless of the method used, instruction must be a regular and consistent part of the lesson. Physical education goes beyond the recreational aspects of activity. A major problem with a recreational approach is that "the rich get richer and the poor get poorer." In other words, if "the ball is rolled out" for basketball games, skilled players handle the ball more and dominate less-skilled players. Unskilled students are under pressure during competitive situations and find it difficult to think about technique and proper performance when they are concentrating on strategy and not making mistakes. Recreational game situations usually benefit students who are skilled.

Does the lesson integrate with past and future instruction? A sound secondary school physical education program should be built on the foundation of the elementary school physical education curriculum. Many school districts do not have adequate communication between elementary and secondary program organizers. Each section may act autonomously, without regard for what is taught in other grades. Secondary curriculum planners should consider elementary school program goals, activities, and teaching procedures. The transition from elementary to secondary programs will be smoother if learning activities and teaching procedures progress with continuity. Knowing what youngsters learned in elementary and middle school programs makes it easier to articulate instruction with previous experiences of students.

Well-planned lessons reflect progression of activities and between lessons. Skill development activities taught throughout a unit help assure that practice opportunities are sequential and regular. A common approach is to bunch all instruction into the first day or two of a unit. This makes it difficult for unskilled students to develop motor skills because there is little instruction and opportunity for skill correction after the start of the unit.

The philosophy of the teacher determines whether effective planning will occur. Does the teacher believe that youngsters must learn on their own, and the responsibility for learning is the student's? Or does the teacher believe that student and teacher share the burden of learning in an environment where both are determined to reach educational goals? A teacher's plan for skill development will strongly affect student learning. If instructors fail to assume responsibility for teaching and refining skills, who will?

PLAN FOR QUALITY INSTRUCTION

The importance of lesson planning cannot be overemphasized. Instructors at the middle and senior high school level are, at times, criticized for their lack of planning. A cycle of not planning can begin when student teachers observe master teachers doing little, if any, planning. The emphasis placed on developing meaningful lesson and unit plans in professional preparation courses appears unnecessary when a master teacher teaches without the aid of thoughtful planning. The beginning teacher is unable, however, to meaningfully judge the effectiveness of the master teacher because of a lack of perspective and experience. The master teacher has taught the material for many years and has evolved a method of presentation through trial and error. It is possible to present a lesson without planning, but the quality of the lesson can be improved through research, preparation, and a well-sequenced plan.

A strong case for planning can be made if a teacher desires to be creative and develop the ability to interact well with students. Teachers, regardless of their experience and ability, have many elements to remember while teaching. When presenting a lesson, many situations occur that are impossible to predict. For example, dealing with discipline problems; the need to modify the lesson spontaneously; relating to students by name; offering praise, feedback, and reinforcement; and developing an awareness of teaching behavior patterns occur regularly. If the content of the lesson is planned, written, and readily available, greater emphasis can be placed on other, equally important phases of teaching.

Lesson planning is unique to each teacher. The competency of the individual in various activities will determine the depth of the lesson plan. More research and reading will have to be done for a unit activity in which a teacher has little experience. If a teacher is unfamiliar with a unit and still refuses to plan, the quality of instruction may be poor. Solid planning helps overcome a lack of competency and demonstrates the willingness to change and learn new skills and knowledge. Planning increases the effectiveness of the instructor. Regardless of the content of the lesson, consider the following points when developing a plan:

1. Learning physical skills takes practice and repetition. Each lesson should be organized to maximize the amount of meaningful participation and to minimize the amount of teacher verbalization and off-task student behavior.

2. Practice combined with instruction and meaningful feedback assures skill development. Instructional sequences and procedures to increase the amount of feedback can be written into the lesson plan. Key points to be learned may require regular and specific feedback to ensure that correct learning patterns occur.

3. Lesson plans allow for differing ability levels of the students. Build a range of activities into each lesson plan so that students can progress at varying rates, depending on their level of skill. List the activities in progression to simplify presentation and enhance learning.

4. Requisite equipment should be noted in the lesson plan. This prevents the problem of being in the middle of a lesson only to find that needed equipment was not procured. The initial placement of equipment and how it is distributed and put away are tasks that are planned before teaching.

5. Minimize time needed for management activities with prior planning. List whether students are to be in small groups or partnered, the type of formation required, and how these procedures will be carried out.

6. List outcomes of the lesson. The direction of the lesson is assured when both instructor and students know where they are going. Outcomes can be written in brief form and stated clearly so that students know what they are expected to learn.

7. Since lesson plans are personal, they can be written in code. All information need not be written out in longhand. For example, many teachers often write their lesson plan on 4 ´ 6 inch cards, which can be carried easily and used with minimal distraction. The card contents reflect the instructor's thoughts and planning that have occurred before the actual teaching session.

8. Estimate time needed for various activities in the lesson. For example, the amount of time for roll call, warm-up activity, fitness development, and lesson focus should be estimated. The time schedule need not be inflexible, but it should be followed closely enough so that planned activities are taught.

9. Planning is an important phase of teaching. Few teachers instruct for more than 4 to 5 hours per day. If an 8-hour day is expected of other workers, instructors should expect that part of their remaining working time will be used for planning. Consider a comparison with coaching. All successful coaches spend a great deal of time planning, observing films, and constructing game plans. The game may not last more than an hour or 2, but many hours of planning take place before the contest. Teachers of physical education should recognize the need to spend time each day planning for 4 to 5 hours of teaching. The results of a well-planned lesson are rewarding to both students and teacher.

10. Plan for successful experiences for students. The plan should include enough challenge to motivate and enough variety to maintain interest. A balance of safety and challenge is required in the school setting.

DESIGN EFFECTIVE PRACTICE SESSIONS

Students can listen to an instructor, read books, watch gifted athletes, and still not improve their motor skill performance. Without practice activities and skill drills, participants demonstrate little improvement in performance. Americans have a fetish for buying books that discuss how to improve everything from aerobics to Zen. Many people spend a great deal of money for private lessons and then never practice on their own. Students do not learn new skills if the lesson does not provide opportunity for skill practice. Of all the elements that go into learning new skills, correct practice is the most critical and necessary. A well-planned lesson assures necessary instruction and maximizes the amount of productive practice time for the learner (Figure 5.1).

There are reasons why students do not receive enough time for practice in a lesson. It may be that

FIGURE 5.1   Students practicing at stations

the amount of equipment is limited, and students have to wait to take their turn. Consider the time wasted standing in line waiting for a turn. Contemplate the following example. Students are organized into groups of 9. They are to practice basketball shooting skills. Unfortunately, only one ball is available for each group of 9 students. Assume that it takes 20 seconds to shoot 3 shots and recover the ball. Each student in the group will have to stand in line nearly 3 minutes before receiving a turn. If the drill continues for 15 minutes, each student only receives a little more than 1½ minutes of practice. Small wonder students do not learn how to shoot correctly when such drills are used.

Another factor that may limit practice time is lack of space. Youngsters may have to rotate in and out of a game rather than playing in 2 or more games. It is important to utilize activities that maximize participation and avoid eliminating students. Often, the least-gifted student is eliminated first and stands on the side waiting for a new game or activity. Students learn little, if anything, from standing in line or waiting to return to an activity.

There are times when a high-risk activity dictates minimizing practice time. An example is stunts and tumbling. In this case it might be necessary that students be tightly supervised on an individual basis. However, in most cases, activities taught in a physical education class are not high risk in nature, and a lack of practice time is usually the result of poor planning.

Another criterion to consider when organizing lessons is to arrange the environment so effective practice can occur. Whenever possible, drills should provide for private and sensitive practice settings.

Students should not be placed in a setting where they have to make mistakes in front of peers. Not all of this can be prevented, but much can be done to enhance the quality of the setting. Students undoubtedly have friends who accept their errors much more willingly than others. Many drills are best done with a friend in a one-on-one setting. It may be possible to assign individual homework or to allow students to work at a personalized pace with the guidance of a mastery packet. Whenever possible, ease the burden of learning new skills by reducing the fear of failure and embarrassment.

Quality control within practice sessions is important for quality learning. Drills in practice sessions must be related to the desired skill outcome. At times, drills can cause skills to be learned incorrectly. For example, assume students are learning to dribble a basketball. To teach dribbling in context, students are broken into squads and have a dribbling relay that requires dribbling the length of the floor, making a basket, and returning. Unfortunately, this drill will result in improper skill development since students will be concentrating on winning the relay rather than on dribbling. Many students will worry about making the basket, others will be more concerned about speeding down and back, and others may be preoccupied with failing in front of their peers. Few students will focus on dribbling the ball under control using proper form. The result is a situation in which all the wrong things are learned.

When developing practice drills, eliminate distractions. What elements prevent students from correctly practicing the skills? Is this drill designed to offer effective and productive practice, or is it just a way of keeping students busy? What stipulations can be made to assure students practice correctly? Does the drill provide a lead-in to actual use in an activity, or is it useful in and for itself? Examine each drill and modify it accordingly when it appears that desired skill outcomes are not being enhanced.

PLAN FOR STUDENT SUCCESS

When planning a lesson, the skills and abilities of students need to be considered if success is going to be an integral part of the presentation. This understanding results in drills and activities that are challenging but not threatening. Whether an activity is challenging or threatening is based on the student's perception, not the instructor's. An activity is challenging if the learner believes it is difficult but achievable. It is threatening if the learner perceives it to be impossible. The same drill could be challenging to some students and threatening to others. Trying to sort out how students perceive various activities makes teaching a difficult task.

Proper instruction allows students to progress at different rates of learning. There are times when the group must be taught as a whole. However, the more opportunities offered for individual or partner practice, the greater the chance for self-paced learning. Activities can and should be monitored to see how students are progressing. It might be possible to do a placheck (a rapid scan of the class; see Chapter 9) that indicates the number of students on task. Usually if students find an activity too difficult, they will avoid it. The percentage of students off-task increases quickly, offering visible feedback. If students complain loudly, the activity should be carefully reviewed. Often, if given the opportunity, students will offer productive and effective modifications.

One of the strengths of pretesting or self-testing before a unit is to gain valuable feedback about the experience and capability of the class. It helps teachers avoid assuming that students know something, only to find such assumptions incorrect. A caution here: It is easy to get engrossed in evaluation to the point that it consumes much instruction time. Achieve a balance between completing sufficient diagnostic work for effective teaching and wasting too much time. Students learn little in an evaluation setting; they show what they already know. If the majority of class time is spent on evaluation, students have little opportunity to develop new skills.

A final word on experience and skill levels. Regular success is necessary if students are expected to enjoy an activity for a lifetime. An instructor can force students to do just about anything within the educational setting. If forced into activities that result in frequent failure, students will probably learn to dislike or avoid them in the future. To give students lifetime skills and attitudes, monitor and adjust lessons regularly. Maintain a sensitivity to the learner's perceptions and feelings, and teach with concern for each student as an individual.

TEACH THE STUDENT AS A WHOLE PERSON
Intellectual
Social
Physical

When planning learning experiences, remember people learn as whole beings. One does not learn a new skill in the psychomotor domain without developing some allied cognitive and affective outcomes. For example, if people are taught to dribble low and near the floor, they will wonder why it should be learned this way. They are integrating the activity cognitively into their total selves. At the same time, they are developing a related feeling about the skill (for example, "I'm good at this skill," or "I'm never going to use this skill").

Teachers can enhance the effectiveness and duration of instruction by integrating educational goals in all domains. Tell students why they are learning new skills or performing them in a certain fashion. Learning in the cognitive area may involve knowing when to use a certain skill or how to correct errors in an activity. It involves decision making based on facts and information gathered from various sources. Cognitive development emphasizes the importance of helping students understand as contrasted to just "doing it because I told you to" (Figure 5.2).

The performing arts (physical education, music, and drama) offer a number of opportunities for affective domain development. There are many occasions to learn to share, express feelings, set personal goals, and function independently. Teamwork, learning to be subordinate to a leader, and being a leader can be learned. Teach the whole person. It is discouraging to hear teachers say, "My job is just to teach skills. I'm not going to get involved in developing attitudes. That's someone else's job." Physical educators have an excellent opportunity to develop positive attitudes and values. The battle may be won, but the war

FIGURE 5.2 Checking for student understanding

lost if teachers produce youngsters with good skill development but negative attitudes toward physical activity and participation.

Experiences can be enriched by encouraging students to discover ways of improving techniques or remedying problems they are having in skill performance. They can be given opportunities to help each other diagnose and improve techniques. Strategies for game situations can be developed through group discussions and planning. The point is to enrich and enhance learning situations so students are able to internalize them in a personalized and meaningful manner. A golden rule does not have to be taught in every lesson, but little is learned if teachers fail to offer integrated presentations on a regular basis.

Teach for Cognitive Development

Cognitive development can be enhanced by involving students in organizing the content and implementation of the lesson. This is not to suggest that students will decide what, when, and how learning will take place, but rather they will become involved in improving the structure of the learning tasks. The following are some of the advantages to involving the learner in the instructional process:

1. Learners usually select experiences that are in line with their abilities and skill levels.
2. When learners help make a decision, they accept some of the responsibility for learning. It is easy to blame others for failure if a learner is not involved in some of the decisions. Personal involvement means accepting the responsibility to make decisions and see that they are implemented.

3. Most people feel better about an environment in which they have some input. Positive self-concepts usually result in a situation where learners help determine their destiny.
4. When lessons fail because incorrect decisions were made, the learner shoulders some of the blame. This helps develop decision-making skills that focus on personal responsibility.

Decision making and involvement in the learning process must be learned. People must have the opportunity to make decisions and be placed in a situation where they can realize the impact of their decisions. The opportunity for making incorrect as well as correct decisions must be allowed. There is no decision making involved when correct decisions are the only conclusions accepted and approved by the teacher. Soon, students begin to choose not to make decisions at all rather than risk making an incorrect choice.

Responsibility is learned. The stakes are lower if students are allowed to make decisions at a young age. This involves allowing the learner to make decisions and to choose from alternatives. Allowing students to make choices should be done in a gradual and controlled manner by using some of the following strategies.

1. ***Present a limited number of choices.*** This allows the teacher to control the ultimate outcome of the situation but offers students a chance to decide how the outcome will be reached. This may be a wise choice when learners have had little opportunity for decision making in the past. New teachers who have little experience with their students should allow for student input using this model.

2. *Allow students the opportunity to modify an activity* The learner is allowed to modify the difficulty or complexity of the skill being practiced. If used effectively, it will allow learners to adapt the activity to suit their individual skill levels. Involving them in this process can actually reduce the burden of deciding about exceptions and student complaints that "It is too hard to do" or "I'm bored." It becomes the student's responsibility to personalize the task. Options allowed could be to change the rules, the implement being used, the number of players on a team, or the type of ball or racquet. Some examples are:

  a. Using the slower-moving family ball rather than a handball.
  b. Increasing the number of fielders in a softball game.
  c. Lowering the basket in a basketball unit.
  d. Decreasing the length of a distance run or the height of hurdles.

3. *Offer tasks that are open-ended.* This approach allows students the most latitude for deciding on the content of the lesson. In this situation, they are given a task, and it is their responsibility to solve it. The teacher decides the educational end, and students decide the means. As students become adept in using this approach, they can develop a number of alternatives. Examples that might be used at this level are:

  a. "Develop a game that requires 4 passes before a shot at the goal."
  b. "Develop a floor exercise routine that contains a forward roll, backward roll, and cartwheel."
  c. "Develop a long rope jumping routine that involves 4 people and 2 pieces of manipulative equipment."

This approach is called problem solving because there is no predetermined answer (see Chapter 8). This technique is effective in helping students apply principles they have learned previously to new situations. Ultimately, the problem is solved through a movement response guided by cognitive involvement.

Enhancing the Affective Domain

Youngsters' feelings about a subject determine their level of motivation and affect the long-range effectiveness of instruction. Little is gained if students participate in a class yet leave hating it. It is possible to design experiences that will improve the opportunity for positive attitudes and values to develop. When developing a lesson plan, evaluate its impact on the attitudes of students. Will the planned experience result in a positive experience for students? Few people develop positive feelings after participating in an activity where they were embarrassed or failed miserably. Ponder some of the following situations and the attitudes that might result:

• Think of the situation where a teacher asks everyone to run a mile. Overweight students are slowest and run while the the rest of the class waits for them to finish. These students cannot change the outcome of the run even if they wanted to. Failure and belittlement occur every day. Small wonder they come to dread fitness testing.

• How do students feel who have been asked to perform in front of the rest of the class even though they are unskilled? The added stress probably results in a poorer than usual response.

• What feelings do students have when asked to pitch in a softball game and are unable to throw strikes? Might they do everything possible to avoid this situation in the future?

Students need to know that teachers care about their feelings and want to prevent placing them in embarrassing situations. Sometimes, teachers have the idea that caring for students indicates weakness. This is seldom the case. Teachers can be firm and demanding as long as they are fair and considerate. To knowingly place students in an embarrassing situation is never justified and results in the formation of negative attitudes.

It is difficult, if not impossible, to develop a lesson that will assure positive development of the affective domain. Attitudes and values are formed based in large part on how students are treated by teachers and peers. When enhancing the affective domain, how one teaches is more important than what one teaches. Students want to be acknowledged as human beings with needs and concerns. They want to be treated in a courteous and nonderogatory manner. If teachers fail to sense how students feel, they are not able to adjust the learning environment in a positive direction. More often than not, the best way to discover how students feel is to ask them. The majority will be honest. If a teacher can accept student input without taking it personally, the result is an atmosphere that produces positive attitudes and values.

CONSIDER PRE-INSTRUCTIONAL DECISIONS

Pre-instructional decisions are basic to the success of a lesson. They are rather mundane, which causes many teachers to avoid thinking about them. However, they are as important as planning the content of the lesson. In fact, if this phase of the lesson is not carefully considered, it may be impossible to effectively present the content.

Determining the Instructional Format

How students are grouped for instruction is a decision that is made early in the lesson-planning process. More than one arrangement can be used in a single lesson. The objectives and nature of the instructional experiences, plus the space and equipment available, determine the type of grouping. There are 3 basic schemes, with numerous variations and subdivisions.

Large-Group Instruction

Large-group instruction demands that all students respond to the same challenge, whether as individuals, partners, or members of a group. This format allows the teacher to conduct the class in a guided progression. The single-challenge format is convenient for group instruction and demonstration because all students are involved in similar activities. Pacing is a problem with no easy solution, since effective instruction must be personalized to meet each student's needs. Student differences are recognized, yet the assumption is made that a central core of activity is acceptable for students of the same age.

Small-Group or Station Instruction

In the small-group (or station) format, the class is divided into 2 or more groups, each working on a different skill or activity. Some system of rotation is provided, and the students change from one activity to another. Dividing a class into groups for station teaching is valuable at times, particularly when supplies and apparatus are limited. This arrangement can save time in providing apparatus experiences, because once the circuit is set, little change in apparatus is needed. The participants are changed, not the apparatus. Some system of rotation is instituted, with changes either on signal or at will. Sometimes all sta-

tions are visited during a single class session, and in other cases, students make only a few station changes per session.

Class control and guidance may be a problem with the small-group format, since stopping the class to provide instruction and guidance is not practical. Posting written guidelines at each station can help students be more self-directed. The instructions should include rearranging the station before moving on. These measures preclude the teacher from dividing his or her efforts over a number of stations. If a station has a safety hazard (for example, rope climbing), the teacher may wish to devote more attention there.

Individual Skill Instruction

In the individual skill format, students select their skills from a variety of choices and rotate at will to new skills. They can get equipment themselves or choose from pieces provided. The most effective format is when students work independently. It allows everyone to work on skills at a comfortable rate. In addition, it allows students to select a variety of skills and activities based on their competency level.

Use of Equipment

In many situations, equipment is a limiting factor. Teachers need to know exactly what equipment is available and in working condition. By determining how much equipment is available, the teacher can properly structure the lesson and group students. For example, if there are only 16 paddles and balls for a class of 30, some type of sharing or station work will have to be organized.

How much equipment is enough? If it is individual-use equipment such as racquets, bats, and balls, there should be 1 per student. If it is group-oriented equipment such as gymnastics apparatus, there should be enough to assure waiting lines of no more than 4 students. Too often, teachers settle for less equipment because they teach the way they have been taught. For example, consider a teacher who is teaching volleyball and has plenty of volleyballs. Rather than have students practice individually against the wall or with a partner, the students are divided into 2 long lines and only 1 or 2 balls are used. Most of the time is spent waiting in line rather than practicing.

If equipment is limited, it is necessary to adapt instruction. Be careful about accepting limited equipment without expressing concern since many administrators believe that physical educators are always capable of "making do." Communicate with the educational leader regularly, and explain the importance of equipment for effective instruction. Ask parent-teacher groups to help with fund-raising to purchase necessary equipment. Math teachers are not expected to teach math without a book for each student, and physical educators should not be expected to teach without adequate equipment. When teachers settle for less, they get less.

How can you get by with a dearth of equipment? The most commonly found solution is to teach using the small-group format. This implies dividing students into stations where each group has enough equipment. For example, in a softball unit, some students might practice fielding, others batting, others making the double play, and so on. Another approach is to divide the class in half and allow 1 group to work on 1 activity while another is involved in an unrelated activity. For example, due to a shortage of racquets and balls, one-half of the class could be involved in practice while the other half plays half-court basketball. This approach is less educationally sound and increases the demands made on the instructor.

Another approach is to use the peer review approach. While 1 student practices the activity, a peer is involved in offering feedback and evaluation. The 2 share the equipment and take turns in practice and evaluation. The final approach is to do what is most commonly done: design drills that involve standing in line and waiting for a turn. In most cases, this is least acceptable from an educational standpoint.

The initial setup of equipment depends on the focus of the lesson. For example, the height of the basket can be reduced to emphasize correct shooting form. The height of the volleyball net can be lowered to allow spiking practice. Nets can be placed at different heights to allow different types of practice. Equipment and apparatus can be modified to best suit the needs of the learner. There is nothing sacred about a 10-foot basket or regulation-sized ball. If modifying the equipment will improve the quality of learning, do it.

Use of Time

A number of decisions related to time need to be made prior to instruction. How time allotted for a lesson is utilized influences instructional outcomes. The amount of time allowed for fitness and skill de-velopment directly influences what is accomplished in a physical education program. For example, if a teacher decides to use 10 additional minutes per lesson for fitness development, the result will be an increase of nearly 30 hours of time devoted to physical fitness during the school year.

The pace of a lesson is related to time. Skillful teachers know when to terminate practice sessions and move on to new activities. Students become bored and begin to display off-task behavior when practice sessions are excessively long. Knowing when to refocus their attention on a different task is important. In most cases, it is better to err on the short side than to allow practice to the point of fatigue and boredom. A rule of thumb is to refocus or change the task when 5 or more students go off-task. If it is necessary to extend the length of the practice session, try the following:

1. *Refocus the class.* Ask the class to observe another student's performance, or explain the importance of the skill and how it will help their game-time performance.

2. *Refine or extend the task.* Stop the class and ask them to improve their technique by focusing on a phase of their performance. Try challenging with a more difficult variation. This approach usually redefines the challenge and is a more difficult variation of the skill they were practicing.

3. *Stop and evaluate.* Stop the class and take time to evaluate performance. Students can work with a partner and check for key points. Emphasis is placed on evaluating and correcting performance. Practice resumes after a few minutes of evaluation.

Pacing is affected depending on who directs the lesson: teacher or student. When teachers direct the pace, timing is controlled by the instructor and students are expected to perform the task at the same time. Determining whether a presentation should be teacher or student paced depends on the type of skill being taught. If the skill is closed in nature (only one way to perform or respond), teacher pacing appears to be most effective. Teacher pacing can be accompanied by verbal cues and modeling behavior. It is effective for learning new skills because cues and visual imagery help learners develop a conception of the pattern to be performed. Student pacing allows learning to progress at different rates. It is effective when open skills are being learned and a variety of responses are preferred or encouraged.

Use of Space

A mistake some teachers make is to take a class to a large area, tell them the task, and fail to define the practice space. The class spreads out in an area so large the teacher finds it impossible to communicate and manage the class. The size of the space is dictated by the type of skills being practiced. Regardless of the size of the space, the practice area should be delineated. An easy way is to set up cones around the perimeter of the area. Chalk lines or natural boundaries can also signal restraining lines.

The amount of instruction to be offered affects the size of the practice area. If students are learning a closed skill and need feedback and redirection regularly, it is best they stay in close proximity to the instructor. An effective approach is to establish a smaller area in which students receive instruction and then return to the larger area for practice.

Dividing available space into smaller areas can maximize student participation. An example is a volleyball game where only 10 students can play on the one available court. Dividing the area into smaller courts will allow more students to participate. A related consideration when partitioning spaces is safety. If playing areas are too close together, it is possible that players from one area might run into those in the other area. An example is softball fields where the ball might hit a player in another area. In most cases, the safety of students can be ensured by careful planning.

Use of Instructional Devices

Instructional devices include a variety of materials, equipment, or people—any of which supplement, clarify, or improve certain instructional procedures. These devices can be used to present information, stimulate different senses, provide information feedback, restrict movements, control practice time, or aid in evaluation and motivation. The devices may be simple, such as targets taped on the wall or cones to dribble around in basketball (Figure 5.3), or they may be more sophisticated, such as videotapes, videotape recorders, or ball machines for tennis.

Teachers can use instructional devices that enhance the teaching-learning process. Because most public school environments have a large student-to-teacher ratio, it is difficult to find enough time for each student. Instructional devices help impart more information and improve the motivational aspects of the class. A number of challenging and success-ori-

FIGURE 5.3   Instructional devices

ented activities can be developed using instructional devices. The following are examples:

1. In basketball, tape targets on a wall for various types of passes. Use a stopwatch to time students dribbling through a course of boundary cones. Pictures, diagrams, and handouts can provide students with graphic information on various skills and rules.

2. In volleyball, hoops, or jump ropes, tape on the floor can be used as targets for setting, bumping, or serving. Extend a rope across the top of the net to help students hit serves above or beneath the rope to ensure height, accuracy, or velocity. Videotapes are available to provide instruction for various volleyball skills.

3. In tennis, empty ball cans are used as targets for working on serves. A tennis ball suspended on a small rope that can be adjusted up or down on a basketball hoop teaches students the "feel" of extending the arm for serves and overhead shots. A list of performance objectives for partners can give direction to a tennis class.

4. In track and field, a student leader can run a station on low hurdles by timing heats and providing corrective feedback. A string stretched between two chairs can help students practice jumping for height in the long jump. Laminated diagrams of the release angle of the shot put combined with a discussion can give students important information.

5. In badminton, targets can be placed in various sections of the court. Suspend shuttlecocks on a light rope to practice overhand shots. A rope suspended on high jump standards will force students to get the proper height on clear shots.

6. In flag football, a punting station can use a goal post for height and accuracy, boundary corners for placement accuracy, and a stopwatch for hang time. A swinging tire or a hoop suspended from a tree or goal post can be used for passing accuracy, and boundary cones for passing distance. Blackboards, magnetic boards, and overhead projectors are useful for diagraming plays and defensive strategy. Student leaders can supervise each station, record the completion of various skills, and provide corrective feedback for each student.

A creative teacher uses instructional devices in many different ways. These devices certainly do not replace the teacher but help supplement the teaching-learning environment. Effective teachers continually try to add devices that motivate students, provide more feedback, or increase practice attempts. Teachers with a limited budget can create instructional devices with such basic components as a roll of tape, several ropes, string, and hoops. An extensive budget does not always produce the best learning environments. An ingenious teacher can develop effective instructional aids. Students seem to enjoy the challenge and success related to practicing with various types of instructional devices. Variety and novelty thus enhance the teaching-learning situation.

DESIGN MEANINGFUL UNIT PLANS

Units of instruction offer a method for organizing and presenting activities over a stipulated period of time. Without units, it is difficult to offer scope and sequence for various instructional activities throughout the year. Units vary in length depending on the age and ability of students and the design of the curriculum. Most units focus on physical activity or movement forms such as team sports, lifetime sports, dance, or physical conditioning. However, some units are developed to emphasize a concept or idea such as cardiovascular efficiency, body composition, flexibility, or strength.

When unit plans are developed, a wide variety of sources should be reviewed to assure the unit is comprehensive. Units of instruction usually reflect a range of activities gathered from materials produced by experts. Another plus of unit plans is that they give teachers a plan for how instruction should proceed. This prevents fragmentation. An instructor with a coherent unit plan does not simply teach from day-to-day and hope that everything will somehow fit together in the end.

Elements of a Unit Plan

There are many different ways to write and organize units of instruction. Most plans contain the following elements, even though they may be titled differently or listed in a different order.

Objectives of the Unit

Objectives should be written before organizing the activities and experiences. The objectives state what the students are expected to know on completion of the unit. Students should be made aware of what they are expected to learn. Objectives are usually listed for the 3 learning domains. For example, what cognitive understandings should students have, and will they be tested in these areas? What are the social and emotional concepts students should develop through participation in this unit? Finally, what skills, techniques, and game strategies should be learned on completion of the unit?

Skills and Activities

This section is the instructional core of the unit and is organized according to unit objectives. Specific skills to be developed, drills to facilitate skill development, lead-up games to be taught, and culminating experiences are listed in this section. Scope and sequence are also integrated into this section to assure a meaningful presentation. When activities are listed in proper sequence, instructionally sound and legally safe lessons are more easily written. The learning experiences may be listed as desirable student outcomes to assure simple translation by student and teacher.

Instructional Procedures

Instructional procedures determine how activities will be presented to assure the maximum amount of learning. Points included are instructional techniques, observations on the efficient use of equipment, necessary safety procedures, and teaching formations.

Equipment, Facilities, and Instructional Devices

Listing equipment and facilities needed for instruction allows the teacher to quickly see what is available and whether other teachers are using it for a unit being taught concurrently. If facilities or equipment need to be modified (for example, lowering goals or deflating balls), this should be listed also.

Culminating Activities

This section identifies how the unit will be concluded. A tournament between selected teams, an intraschool contest, or a school demonstration playday could be implemented. In any case, the unit should finish with an activity that is enjoyable to students and leaves them with a positive feeling toward the unit of instruction.

Evaluation

The final plan section outlines how student progress is monitored. Monitoring can be carried out by the instructor, or students can be given guidelines for self-evaluation. Written tests can be administered to evaluate the knowledge gained through instruction. Skill tests to assess the level of performance and skill development can be selected. An attitude inventory could measure the impact of the unit on the affective area of learning.

Another phase of evaluation involves asking students to comment on the unit and its method of presentation. This should be done in writing rather than verbally because some student comments may anger or belittle the teacher. Student evaluations can offer direction for modifying the unit and making it more effective in the future.

Suggested Weekly (Block Plan) Schedule

The purpose of a block plan is to distribute the activities of the unit into weekly segments. This gives the teacher a sense of timing and an indication of what should be taught and when. A block plan alleviates problems such as insufficient time to teach the desired activities or insufficient activities to fill up the time frame. It eases the burden of writing lesson plans because the material to be taught is identified and sequenced into a meaningful time frame. Daily lesson plans are developed by following the outline of the block plan.

Figure 5.4 is an example of a block plan for a unit on racquetball. A number of examples of block plans are included in Chapters 19 to 22.

Bibliography and Resources

The bibliography contains materials used by students and teacher. Students are given a list of materials they can peruse if they desire more information. Location of materials should be identified. Teachers may have a separate list and collection of resources they use for instruction. For example, pamphlets on nutrition or physical fitness, available films, bulletin-board materials, and textbooks could be included in the resource section.

The following outline is an example of a skeleton structure for designing unit plans.

I. Title and grade level

II. Analysis and description of setting
A. Previous experiences and exposure to activity
B. Limiting factors: class size, class organization, mixed grades, facilities and equipment, period of day class meets
C. Rationale for including the activity

III. Objectives
A. General unit objectives
B. Specific behavioral objectives
1. Psychomotor (physical performance) skills
2. Knowledges, rules, and strategies
3. Attitudes and values

IV. Organization
A. Time (length of unit)
B. Space available
C. Equipment and supplies
D. Basic grouping of students
E. Number of groups

V. Content
A. Introduction of the activity
B. Rules
C. Skills (diagram all drills)
D. Activities and lead-up games
E. Skill tests
F. Written tests
G. Block plan for entire unit
H. Grading procedures

VI. References and resources

Introduction	Review	Review	Review	Review
What is racquetball?	Grip, forehand, backhand	Serves, rules	Forehand, backhand	Backwall shots
Grips—ready position	Equipment	*Teach*	*Teach*	*Teach*
Forehand stroke		Backwall shots	Court position	Ceiling shots
Backhand stroke	*Teach*	Hinders	Kill shots	Passing shots
Class procedures	Serves—Drive, Z			
Practice bounce and hit	Lob	*Activities*	*Activities*	*Activities*
		Backwall practice	Performance objectives or short game	Ceiling games 1, 2, or 3 shots
Rule of the day	*Activities*	Serve practice	Rule of the day	
	Serves—practice	Rule of the day		
	Bounce and hit			
	Rule of the day			
Review	*Teach*	*Review*	*Review*	*Review*
Problem rules	Cutthroat	Problem areas	Rules	Kill shots
Serve strategy	Doubles			
Court coverage		*Activities*	*Activities*	*Activities*
	Activities	Performance objectives	Performance objectives	Rotation work-up
Activities	Performance objectives	5 and out	Regular game	
Accuracy drills	8-ball rally	Ceiling games	Cutthroat or doubles	
Drive serve	Rotation work-up			
Lob serve				
Backhand				
Backhand games				
1 or 2 shots				
Activities	*Review*	Written exam	*Activities*	Final performance objectives work
Performance objectives	Rules, strategy	*Activities*	Performance objectives	Review course objectives
Backhand games	Shots, serves	Performance objectives	Tournament games	Final games
Regular game	*Activities*	Tournament games	Cutthroat or doubles	
Tournament	Performance objectives			Return exam
	Tournament games			

FIGURE 5.4 Racquetball block plan

DESIGN A DAILY LESSON PLAN

A daily lesson plan format provides teachers and students a measure of stability. A consistent daily instructional format offers routine and structure. Lesson plans offer a systematic approach to teaching so all activities are covered during the year. The amount of time spent on different parts of the lesson can be predetermined. Most lesson plans cover 3 parts; a warm-up activity, a fitness component, and the lesson focus.

Major Instructional Components

Introductory (Warm-Up) Activity

The introductory activity occupies 3 to 5 minutes of the total lesson. The purpose of this part is to prepare students for activity. Students require a few minutes to become emotionally involved in the activity after sitting in classes. Introductory activities (Chapter 15) require minimal organization and place demands on large muscle movement. The activities may be an integral part of the fitness routine or a separate entity. In either case, the introductory activity is used to raise the heart rate, warm up the body, and stretch the muscles in anticipation of fitness development activity. Teachers can change the introductory activity each week to add variety to the warm-up procedure.

Fitness Activity

Fitness activities take 15 to 20 minutes and focus on the development of physical fitness. Instruction centers on developing major components of fitness, especially flexibility, muscular strength and endurance, body composition, and cardiovascular endurance. A wide variety of fitness routines are offered so students can learn to select methods acceptable to them in adulthood. Graduating from school knowing many ways to develop and maintain physical fitness is a program objective that will allow students to self-select lifetime fitness activities. A successful experience in fitness activities is motivating and creates positive attitudes. An in-depth discussion of physical fitness and examples of routines are found in Chapter 16.

Application

Lesson Focus and Culminating Activity

3+4

The lesson focus and culminating activity last 25 to 30 minutes, depending on the length of the period. This is the instructional part of the lesson with major emphasis on skill development, cognitive learning, and enhancement of the affective domain. This phase of the lesson contains skills to be taught, drills, and lead-up activities, all of which culminate in games and tournaments.

Content of the Lesson Plan

Instructional Activities

Specific skills and activities to be taught need to be listed in the lesson plan. These are listed in proper progression to assure that instruction builds on previously learned skills. Progression also helps assure that activities are presented in a safe manner. The skills and related activities need not be written out in detail. Write enough so it is easy to comprehend the activities when teaching.

Organization and Teaching Hints

A list of instructional procedures can help teachers conceptualize prior to the lesson what details need to be prepared, including how the equipment is organized, what formations to use, key points of instruction to share with students, and the specific feedback used. New instructional procedures can be recorded after a lesson and maintained for the next time the lesson is taught.

Expected Student Outcomes

Prior to the lesson, establish what students are expected to experience, learn, and perform. Curriculum objectives can be listed to give direction to instruction. With careful planning of expected student out-

comes, teachers can offer a wide variety of experiences throughout the school year to help students develop in all domains—psychomotor, cognitive, and affective.

ANALYZE THE COMPLETED LESSON PLAN

There are different approaches to writing lesson plans, but regardless of the style used, the plan should include the necessary elements for assuring effective instruction. The following questions can help teachers analyze a lesson plan to assure that it is both comprehensive and effective.

Have you included the following?
1. Title, length of lesson, and facility
2. A list of equipment, supplies, and instructional devices
3. Objectives of the lesson
4. References for further information

Does the instructional process do the following?
1. Provides for continuity with previous lessons
2. Reviews past material through lead-up activities
3. Communicates to students why the material is important for them to learn
4. Builds motivational techniques into the presentation
5. Provides for students with varying interests and abilities
6. Includes the special student

Does the lesson plan cover the following points?
1. Provides for warm-up, offers students a physical fitness activity, and includes an instructional component
2. Outlines new material clearly and with enough depth
3. Progresses from simple to complex skill development
4. Progresses from known activities to the unknown
5. Includes notations for demonstrations and use of instructional devices
6. Includes key questions and points that should be covered
7. Combines physical education activities with other academic areas when possible

Does the lesson plan meet the following criteria?

1. Readable and easily used by others
2. Usable during the actual instructional process
3. Designed for evaluation of curriculum effectiveness

Regardless of the format used, the plan should cover these areas. This ensures that the lesson plan augments the instructional process and provides for students of different abilities.

EXPECTED OUTCOMES

After reading this chapter, you should be able to

- Describe the role of planning in preparing for quality instruction.

- Understand the relationships between instruction and the developmental and experiential level of the students.

- Identify the characteristics of effective practice sessions.

- List pre-instructional decisions that must occur before the actual delivery of the lesson.

- Articulate how students can become involved in developing the learning experience.

- Describe ways in which learning in the affective domain can be enhanced.

- Discuss the various parts of a meaningful unit plan.

- Understand the rationale for the three components of a lesson and describe characteristics of each.

REFERENCES AND SUGGESTED READINGS

Harrison, J. M. 1987. A review of the research on teacher effectiveness and its implications for current practice. *Quest* 39: 36–55.

Harrison, J. M., Blakemore, C. L., Buck, M. M., and Pellett, T. M. 1996. *Instructional Strategies for Secondary Physical Education*. 4th ed. Dubuque, IA: Wm. C. Brown.

Melograno, V. J. 1996. *Designing the Physical Education Curriculum*. Champaign, IL: Human Kinetics Publishers.

Pangrazi, R. P., and Dauer, V. P. 1995. *Dynamic Physical Education for Elementary School Children*. 11th ed. Boston: Allyn & Bacon.

Pangrazi, R. P., and Dauer, V. P. 1995. *Lesson Plans for Dynamic Physical Education*, 11th ed. Boston: Allyn & Bacon.

Parker, J. 1995. Secondary teachers' views of effective teaching in physical education. *Journal of Teaching in Physical Education* 14(2): 127–139.

Sariscsany, M. J., Darst, P., and van der Mars, H. 1995. The effects of three teacher supervision patterns on student on-task and skill performance in secondary physical education. *Journal of Teaching in Physical Education* 14(2): 179–197.

Siedentop, D. 1991. *Developing Teaching Skills in Physical Education*. 3rd ed. Palo Alto, CA: Mayfield Publishing Co.

van der Mars, H., Vogler, W., Darst, P., and Cusimano, B. 1994. Active supervision patterns of physical education teachers and their relationship with student behavior. *Journal of Teaching in Physical Education* 14(1): 99–112.

Wuest, D., and Lombardo, B. 1994. *Curriculum and Instruction, The Secondary School Physical Education Experience*. St. Louis: Mosby.

6 Creating an Effective Learning Environment

PURPOSE

To present effective methods for enhancing communication between teacher and student by using instructional cues, demonstrating, modeling, and providing meaningful feedback. To understand basic policies and procedures for creating a safe and stimulating environment for learning.

KEY CONCEPTS

- Movement learning time should not be sacrificed for the sake of promoting an "academic" environment.
- Communication is enhanced by securing the undivided attention of the entire class.
- There are certain types of verbal and nonverbal interactions that suggest to students that the teacher is unwilling to listen and is primarily interested in imposing his or her feelings on class members.
- Instructional cues are words or phrases that illicit quick and efficient communication to the learner regarding proper technique in the performance of a particular skill or movement.
- Demonstration of physical skills by the teacher is used to increase the student's understanding of movements.
- An important outcome of a systematic physical education program is its ability to present students with an opportunity to take risks and overcome fear.
- Effective instruction is enhanced by a teacher who paces the lesson in a way that keeps students interested, yet not frustrated.
- One of the more difficult tasks for a teacher is to address the needs of individual students by providing instruction to an entire class.
- Providing students with accurate feedback is a beneficial part of the instructional setting.
- Effective policies and procedures establish a safe and efficient setting that enhances the student's ability to concentrate on learning.

Competent teachers create a learning environment where students want to learn and practice skills. Such an environment is characterized by a sensitive and caring teacher who uses a variety of techniques to foster learning in all students. It is a fallacy that teachers treat all students alike. More often than not, effective instructors have the ability to determine how students want and need to be treated. Some students may respond to subtle encouragement, whereas others will require a more direct approach.

This section helps teachers develop a repertoire of teaching skills that allow them to meet the needs of all students in a class. Notice the word *all* in the previous sentence; many teachers can help students who want to learn; however, only the best teachers are capable of motivating students who don't particularly like the subject matter. This is the challenge: teach all students regardless of their intrinsic desire to learn. A good place to begin is with the skill of listening. Few traits enhance the learning environment more than effective listening by the teacher. A student's self-worth is enhanced when a teacher listens and acknowledges his or her feelings and concerns.

DEVELOP EFFECTIVE LISTENING SKILLS

For most teachers, listening skills are more difficult to learn than speaking skills. Instructors are taught to impart knowledge to students and have practiced speaking for years. Many students view teachers as people who teach you but do not care about your point of view. Poor communication is usually due to a breakdown in listening rather than speaking. There is a lot of truth in the adage, "People were given 2 ears and 1 mouth; to facilitate listening twice as much as they speak." The following points should be integrated into the teaching style of instructors.

1. *Develop active listening skills.* Good listeners convince the speaker that they are interested in what is being said. Much of this is done through nonverbal behavior such as eye contact, nodding the head in agreement, facial expressions, and moving toward the speaker. Active listening shows students that their ideas and thoughts count and that they have some input into their destiny.

2. *Determine what the student is trying to say.* Many students are not capable of clearly expressing their feelings, particularly if they have deep concerns. The words expressed may not signal clearly what the student is feeling. For example, a teenager may say, "I hate P.E." In most cases, students do not hate all phases of physical education; rather, it may be that something more immediate is the problem. An effective response might be, "You sound upset, are you having a problem you want to discuss?" This

makes students feel as though their feelings are important to the teacher, and also allows for an opportunity to clarify their concerns. It also prevents the teacher from internalizing the student's emotion and responding in a heated manner, such as "I don't care whether you like it or not, get on task!"

3. *Practice paraphrasing what the student said.* Paraphrasing is restating what was said to you, including the feelings detected, in your own words. For example, the teacher might respond, "Do I hear you saying that you are frustrated and bored with this activity?" If the paraphrasing is correct, it makes the student feel validated and understood. If the interpretation is incorrect, the student has an opportunity to restate the problem. In addition, it offers the teacher an opportunity to understand clearly how students perceive various situations.

4. *Allow students to tell you how they feel.* Teachers who listen to students learn more about their feelings. It is important to let students know that you will listen and then to practice doing so. If you are an effective listener, you hear things that are not always positive. For example, students may tell you honestly which activities they enjoy and which they do not. They may tell you how you made them feel when you criticized them. This type of communication is constructive if it can be accepted by the teacher objectively. It gives the teacher consistent and ongoing evaluation. Even though it may not be a valid criticism of the program or procedures, it does offer opportunity for program and instructional improvement. A word of caution: If a teacher finds it difficult to accept such communication, it is probably best to tell students this feeling. It may be necessary to avoid such interaction with students if it affects the confidence of the teacher.

5. *Develop an awareness of situations that promote effective communication.* Certain types of verbal interaction convince students that the teacher is unwilling to listen. Some of the more common examples are:

   a. *Preaching or moralizing.* This is often manifested by telling others they "should know better than that!" Obviously, students make mistakes since they are young and learning. A big part of learning is making mistakes and knowing how to avoid such situations in the future. Teachers who expect such mistakes are not shocked by student misbehavior and are able to deal with it in a rational manner.

b. *Threatening.* Threats are often used to control students. They are usually ultimatums given to students to terminate undesirable behavior, even though the teacher knows that they will be impossible to carry out. For example, the threat, "If you do not stop that, I'm going to kick you out of class," is difficult to enforce. Most teachers are not in a position to expel students. If students hear enough idle threats, they soon learn to ignore and mock the teacher. As a reminder, it is not a threat if the misbehavior can and will be rectified consistently.

c. *Ordering and commanding.* If teachers appear to be bossy, students begin to think they are nothing more than pawns to be moved around the area. Try to develop patterns of communication that ask students to carry out tasks. Courtesy and politeness are requisites for effective teacher-student relationships. In addition, if teachers want to be treated with respect, they need to treat others similarly.

d. *Interrogating.* When there is a problem such as a fight between students, teachers often try to figure out who started the fight rather than deal with the feelings of the combatants. Very little is gained by trying to solve "who started it." Students will usually shirk the blame and suggest that it was not their fault. A much better solution is to begin by acknowledging feelings, "You know fighting is not accepted in my class, you must have been very angry to place yourself in this predicament." This allows students to talk about their feelings rather than place the blame on the other person. It also tells them that even when they do something wrong, the teacher cares about them.

e. *Refusing to listen.* This technique usually manifests itself by "Let's talk about it some other time." There are situations when this response is necessary. However, if it is always the case, students will begin to avoid interaction with the instructor.

f. *Labeling.* In this situation, the teacher tells students, "Stop acting like fools," or "You're behaving like a bunch of animals." This is not only degrading, but it dehumanizes youngsters. In most cases, labeling is done because teachers think it will improve performance. In actuality, it is usually destructive and leaves a person with a negative feeling about the teacher.

REFINE COMMUNICATION SKILLS

The teaching-learning process involves the exchange of information between teachers and students. Effective communication occurs both ways: teachers with students and students with teachers. Communication behaviors can take many different forms. Different types of communication include a lecture on the strategy of a zone defense in basketball, directions for moving the class to 4 different stations for skill work, information feedback on a student's skill attempts, questions about the rules of a game, praise for lining up quickly at the end of class, or a smile for a well-executed lay-up. Forms of communication can involve a number of sensory modes including the visual, verbal, and tactile. Visual cues involve demonstrations, videotapes, and pictures. The teacher's gestures, facial expressions, or thumbs-up signs are a nonverbal type of visual communication. Indeed, some experts suggest that much of what students learn is picked up through nonverbal means. Verbal communication involves lectures, discussions, directions, and other spoken words. Tactile communication encompasses physical contact such as manually manipulating a student's arms or legs for swimming instruction or physically restricting a student's arm position in archery.

Effective teachers utilize efficient communication skills. Information is communicated in a minimum of time. Information is effective when it is expressed in a vocabulary understood by students. Use a variety of sensory modes because students process information in different ways. Enunciate verbal information clearly so students can comprehend. Encourage students to communicate with each other during physical education classes. Students can provide peers with important information for developing skills. Student communication can also be verbal, visual, or tactile.

Questions are an important communication form in the teaching-learning process. Use questions to evaluate the effectiveness of their lectures, demonstrations, or other types of instructional materials, including reading sheets, books, and pamphlets. Encourage students to ask questions because this fosters communication. The use of questions in a lesson must be planned carefully with an objective in mind. There are different categories of questions for specific goals (Siedentop, 1991). Recall questions focus on memory. Convergent and divergent questions require an analysis and a conclusion in a specific direction, such as problem-solving or guided-discovery styles. Value questions give students an opportunity to present an opinion that is neither right nor wrong.

IMPROVE COMMUNICATION BETWEEN TEACHER AND STUDENTS

The communication techniques a teacher uses will impact student motivation. Teachers who take a positive approach to communication with students and establish a warm, caring environment are effective. A positive approach to student motivation is recommended because of the long-term effects on both students and teachers. Teaching and learning are more enjoyable when students and instructors can look forward to participating in a positive environment and feel better about learning, teaching, and the overall school atmosphere at the end of the day. The positive approach seems to enhance the overall motivation of both teachers and students over a longer period of time.

Students often judge the quality of a teacher on attributes unrelated to the teacher's knowledge of subject matter. Various speech habits and the teacher's style of presentation can add to or detract from instructional effectiveness. Students eventually tune out teachers who shout commands, speak like drill sergeants, or repeat certain phrases. Students want to understand and be understood. The following points facilitate the process of communication between student and teacher.

1. *Describe specific behaviors rather than the person as whole.* For example, "I can't understand why you do stupid things like that" judges the person as a whole and leaves the feeling of worthlessness. It is much more effective to suggest that, "You need to listen when I am talking." This deals with behavior the student can improve and avoids undermining self-worth. In addition, most people will feel that you are interested in helping them improve rather than in belittling them.

2. *Put yourself in the student's shoes.* How would you feel if someone embarrassed you in front of the class? How do you feel when you are inept while trying to learn a new skill? These and other emotions often make listening difficult for youngsters. What conditions are necessary to make it easy for you to accept constructive feedback? Excessive feedback

may stress a youngster and cause a reduction in performance. Offer feedback in small doses. If you are going to suggest ways to improve performance, do so on a personal basis and leave the student to practice without scrutiny. To ask students to change and then stand over them until they do so may cause resentment and internal pressure.

3. *Identify your feelings about students.* At times teachers send mixed messages to students. They may be unhappy with the student because of a situation unrelated to class performance yet unwilling to discuss the real issue. Instead, they respond with unkind feedback about a skill performance. Their negative feelings are then transferred to the youngsters regarding their performance in class. This was not the teacher's intent but the result of pent-up feelings over an unrelated issue. Students perceive negativity from a teacher. Take responsibility for communicating how you feel (albeit negative), but make sure that it is directed toward the undesirable behavior.

4. *Accentuate the positive.* When phrasing the instructional points of a lesson, stress the positive. For example, tell students to "Make a sharp cut," rather than saying, "Don't round off your cut." An easy way to emphasize the why of an activity is to say, "Do this because . . . " If there are several different and acceptable ways to perform the movement patterns, be explicit. Show students various ways and discuss reasons for the differences. Students like to know the correct technique, even if it is beyond their sphere of accomplishment. Explain only enough, however, to get the activity under way successfully.

5. *Speak precisely.* Limit the use of open-ended directives, and substitute those with precise goals. Instead of saying, "How many times can you . . . ?" or "See how many times you can . . . ," give students a definite target goal. Use directives like, "See if you can . . . 5 times without missing," or "Show me 5 different ways you can . . . " Ask students to select a target goal. Using measurable and attainable goals is especially important when teaching slow learners or special education students.

6. *Focus on repetition of correct performance.* Doing an activity in many different ways or doing it many times is a first step in the learning process, not an ultimate goal. Ask students to pick the best way to practice. Teach students how to self-motivate themselves; they need to learn to assess when they are becoming bored and need to move to a different skill or activity.

7. *Optimize speech patterns.* Certain teacher mannerisms may require attention and change. Avoid sermonizing at the least provocation. Excessive reliance on certain words and phrases, such as "okay," "all right," and the irritating "and uh," are unappealing to students. Many adolescents begin to listen for repetitive speech patterns rather than listening to what the teacher is expressing. Acquire a broad vocabulary of effective phrases for indicating approval and good effort, and vary verbal patterns.

8. *Conduct cognitive discussions in the classroom.* Whenever possible, lengthy discussions should be held in the classroom for reasons of comfort and student expectations. Students expect to move in the activity area, whereas they have learned to sit and interact cognitively in the classroom. Rules can be explained, procedures and responsibilities outlined, and formations illustrated on the blackboard. If discussions will last longer than 1 or 2 minutes, it is best to place students in a comfortable setting and use instructional aides such as overheads, handouts, and films.

9. *Treat all responses to questions with dignity.* The teacher should respect students' responses and opinions and avoid humiliating a student who gives a wrong answer. Pass over inappropriate answers by directing attention to more appropriate responses. Or, tell students that they have offered a good answer but the question is not the right one. Remind them to save the answer and then go back to the students when it is correct for another question. Refrain from injecting personal opinion into the instructional question-answer process. At the end of the discussion, a summary of important points may be of value.

IMPROVE INSTRUCTIONAL COMMUNICATION

Many words can be spoken, but little is accomplished if students do not understand what has been said. Communication implies more than words; it assumes understanding has occurred. The following points can enhance the effectiveness of instruction:

1. *Develop a stimulating speaking style.* It is not necessary to be an outstanding speaker, yet it is important to be interesting and exciting. The chance for effective communication improves if students want to listen to a teacher. Use the voice effectively; alter the intensity, raise and lower the pitch, and change the speed of delivery. Use nonverbal behavior to emphasize important points. In addition, keep discussions short and to the point so that students are willing to stop what they are doing and listen.

2. *Use a "teaser" to create interest.* If a concept is somewhat difficult to comprehend, set the stage by briefly describing what is to follow and why it is important. This may require repeating instructions if students are having trouble comprehending. Students may miss the first part of the discussion before they realize what the teacher is expressing.

3. *Build on previous learning experiences.* Whenever possible, try to tie the discussion to previous skills and knowledge students have mastered. It can be effective to show students how a skill is similar (or dissimilar) to one learned earlier. Transfer of learning can be optimized if students understand the relationship to their previous experiences.

4. *Present the material in proper progression.* Teach skills in the sequence in which they will be performed. There are exceptions where a teacher may want to focus on a critical step first and then build around it. For example, in dance, a teacher may teach step patterns and then put them together to complete the dance. However, in most cases the progression should mimic the sequence of performance. Adolescents usually assume that the order in which activities are presented is the correct progression.

5. *Model correct and incorrect examples.* Most adolescents learn physical skills more quickly by observing rather than listening. This mandates modeling desirable and/or incorrect examples. For example, students will comprehend more quickly if they are shown the correct way to pivot and 1 or 2 incorrect examples of pivoting. Often, teachers talk students through all skills and movements. When possible, combine instruction with demonstration to improve the efficiency of the communication.

6. *Check for understanding.* Checking for understanding helps the teacher monitor the clarity of communication. A most efficient way is to ask a question and have students respond with an observable behavior. For example, "Raise your hand if you do not understand how to land correctly," or " See me if you do not understand how the game is played."

7. *Separate management and instructional episodes.* Much emphasis has been placed on maintaining short episodes of communication and focusing on cues that are easily understood. A special point of attention: Teachers often combine management activities with instructional activities. For example, during a presentation of a new game, the teacher says the following: "In this game, we will break into groups of 5. Each group will get a ball and form a small circle. On the command go, the game will start. Here is how you play the game . . . " At this point, a lengthy discussion of game rules and conduct is given. By this time, most students have forgotten the management strategies. It is more effective to move the class into the game formation and then discuss the activity. This serves 2 purposes: It reduces the length of the episode and makes it easier for the class to conceptualize how the game is played. In addition, it avoids the tendency for students to become unfocused, thinking about whom they want for a partner instead of listening to the rules. Teach students one thing at a time.

Nonverbal Communication

Nonverbal communication is an important way of telling students what behavior is acceptable. Nonverbal communication is effective because it is interpreted by students and often perceived as more meaningful than words. For example, beginning teachers often have a difficult time making their feelings align with their body language. They may be pleased with student performance, yet portray a less than pleased message (for example, frowning or placing hands on hips). Another common example occurs when teachers want to assert themselves and gain control of a class. They often place their hands in their pockets, stand in a slouched position, and back away from the class. This nonverbal behavior signals anything but assertiveness and gives students mixed messages (Figure 6.1).

Nonverbal behavior can be used to praise a class effectively: The thrust of a finger into the air to signify "number 1," thumbs up, a high 5, shaking hands, and so on. Nonverbal behavior can also be negative; for example, hands on the hips, finger to the lips, frowning, and staring. In any case, effective use of nonverbal behavior can increase the validity and strength of verbal communication.

When using nonverbal communication, consider the customs and mores of different cultures. It is the teacher's responsibility to learn how youngsters respond to different types of gestures. For example, Hmong and Laotian adolescents may be touched

FIGURE 6.1 Nonverbal reinforcement for a job well done

on the head only by parents and close relatives. A teacher who pats a student on the head for approval is interfering with the youngster's spiritual nature. The OK sign, touching thumb and forefinger, is an indication of approval in the United States. However, in several Asian cultures, it is a "zero," indicating the student is not performing properly. In many South American countries, the OK sign carries a sexual connotation. Teachers new to an area should ask for advice when expressing approval to youngsters from other cultures.

To make nonverbal behavior convincing, teachers can watch their behavior and then practice necessary modification. An effective method is to practice in front of a mirror and display different emotions. Another is to work with someone who does not know you well. If this person can identify the emotions demonstrated by the nonverbal behavior, they most likely will be effective in a teaching situation. Using a videotape recorder can be an effective tool for self-analysis. A teacher can self-analyze how he or she looks when under stress, when disciplining a student, or when praising.

IMPROVE SKILL PERFORMANCE WITH INSTRUCTIONAL CUES

Instructional cues are words that quickly and efficiently communicate to the learner proper technique and performance of skills or movement tasks. Adolescents learning skills need a clear understanding of critical skill points since motor learning and cognitive understanding of the skill must be developed simultaneously. Often, teachers carefully plan skill and movement activities, yet fail to plan for the instructional cues to be used during skill practice. The result may be a class that does not clearly understand technique and points of performance. When developing instructional cues, consider the following points.

Use Accurate Cues

If the cue is going to help the learner perform a skill correctly, it must be precise and accurate. It needs to lead the learner in the proper direction and be part of a comprehensive package of cues. All instructors teach activities they know little about. Few, if any, teachers know everything about all activities. There are textbooks and media aids available for reference. These resources delineate the key points of the skill (Fronske, 1996). Other options include asking other teachers who have knowledge or videotaping an activity and analyzing points of performance where students have the most difficulty. In any case, cues are developed through study, practice, and experience. Even a beginning teacher needs to possess ample learning cues for teaching preliminary experiences.

Use Short, Descriptive Cues

Sometimes cues are made more comprehensive and lengthy than necessary. Many teachers teach as they were taught in high school. They remember a class where the teacher told them everything they needed to know at the start of the unit and let them practice without instruction for the rest of the period. This assumes students can comprehend a long list of instructions and correctly apply them to skills. If this is not the case, students spend the rest of the unit performing skills incorrectly. An incorrect motor pattern practiced for a long period is difficult to correct later.

To avoid confusing and overwhelming the learner, choose a small number of cues for each lesson. The cues should contain key words and should be short. They should help the learner focus on one phase of skill during practice. For example, when teaching batting, a cue might be: "Keep your head in and eyes on the ball." The purpose of this cue would be to avoid overswinging and pulling the head away from the path of the ball. Other examples of hitting cues might be:

"Step toward the target."
"Keep your elbows away from your body."
"Shift weight from rear to front foot."

One way to examine the effectiveness of the cues is to see if they communicate the skill in total. Have all the critical points of batting been covered or is the skill being done incorrectly in certain phases? In most skills, the performance can be broken into 3 parts: preparing to perform, performing the skill, and following through. Focus cues on one phase at a time because it is difficult for students to remember more. Descriptive words are most effective with adolescents, particularly if they have an exciting sound. For example, "Snap your wrists," "Twist the upper body during the follow through," or "Explode off the starting line." In other situations, make the voice influence the effectiveness of the cue. For example, if a skill is to be done smoothly and softly, the teacher can speak in a soft tone and ask students to "let the movement floooooow " or to "move smooooooothly across the balance beam." Cues are most effective when voice inflections, body language, and action words are used to signal the desired behavior.

Integrate Cues

Integrate cues to combine parts of a skill and to utilize words that focus on the skill as a whole. These cues depend on prior cues used during the presentation of a skill and assume that concepts delineated in earlier phases of instruction were correctly understood. Examples of integrating cues might be:

"Step, rotate, throw"
"Run, jump, and forward roll"
"Stride, swing, follow-through"

Integrated cues are a set of action words that help students sequence and time parts of a skill. These cues are reminders of the proper sequence of skills and the mental images of the performance. Depending on the rhythm of the presentation, the cues can signal the speed and tempo of the skill performance. In addition, they can serve as a specialized language that allows the student and teacher to communicate effectively.

DEMONSTRATE AND MODEL SKILLS

Most students learn easier if they see a demonstration of a skill or technique. The adage, "a picture is worth a thousand words," holds true in physical education. Demonstrations can illustrate variety or depth of movement, show something unique or different, point out items of technique or approach, illustrate different acceptable styles, and show progress. Another important reason for demonstrating is to help develop credibility with students. For example, many students may question whether a skill can be performed until they see the teacher or another student do it. Secondary school students are notorious for their "show me" attitudes; a demonstration will help show that the skill is in their range of ability.

FIGURE 6.2   Demonstrating skills with a partner

Teacher Demonstration

Be sure that the class can see and hear the performance. When explaining technique, highlight key points of performance. Show the proper starting position and verbalize the instructions from that point on, or provide a more complete, point-by-point demonstration. Terminology should be clear and techniques demonstrated within the student's skill level. The more complex a skill is, the more demonstration needed. Questions can be raised during the demonstration, but avoid allowing the question-answer period to take up too much time.

Student Demonstration

Student demonstration is an effective teaching technique because it interjects the students' ideas into the lesson. As students practice and move, the class can be stopped for a demonstration. If the demonstration is unsatisfactory, go to another student without comment or reprimand, saying only, "Thank you, Jessica. Let's see what Seth can do." Or simply direct the adolescents to continue practicing. Selecting several students to demonstrate is usually preferable, so that others can observe varied approaches. If partner or small-group work is undertaken, the same principle holds (Figure 6.2).

If You Can't Demonstrate

Because of physical and skill limitations, some teachers cannot demonstrate. Few teachers can perform all physical activities well. Even a skilled teacher needs to devise substitutions for an effective instructor demonstration. Through reading, study, and analysis of movement, teachers can develop an understanding and knowledge of the activities. Even if performing the activity is impossible, teachers must know how an activity is done. In addition, visual aids and media can offer meaningful orientation. Select skilled students to help demonstrate.

IMPLEMENT EFFECTIVE INSTRUCTIONAL METHODOLOGY

A component of effective teaching is an instructional environment that facilitates learning. A number of instructional behaviors can be demonstrated to show that an activity area is safe and productive. Planning assures students an opportunity to learn skills in a positive setting. Each of the areas discussed below can be integrated into the lesson plan prior to the presentation of the lesson.

Create a Safe Environment

A safe environment is a prerequisite for effective teaching. Safety results from behaviors taught by the teacher. "Safety first and everything else second" should be the motto of every teacher. It is possible a teacher will be removed from the teaching profession if accidents occur due to faulty planning and lack of foresight. Over half the injuries in schools occur in physical education classes; if they are due to poor planning and preparation, a teacher may be found liable and responsible for such injuries (see Chapter 12).

Teachers must foresee the possibility of hazardous situations that result in student injury. Safety inspections should be conducted at regular intervals (see Chapter 12). Apparatus that has not been used for a while should be inspected. Rules are only the beginning with students; safe and sensible behavior needs to be taught and practiced. For example, if students are in a gymnastics unit, they must receive instruction and practice in developing proper methods of absorbing momentum and force. It may even be necessary to practice safety, as in taking turns, spotting, and using the apparatus as directed.

Safety is assured when curricular presentations are listed in proper progression. Injuries are avoided when students perform only those activities for which they are prepared. A written curriculum can assure a safety committee or court of law that proper progression and sequencing of activities was used. In addition, proper progression of activities generates a feeling of confidence in students, since they feel they have the necessary background to perform adequately.

Use Active Supervision

Observation of class performance is critical in assuring students stay on task and practice activities correctly (van der Mars, Vogler, Darst, and Cusimano, 1994). This requires supervision of students in an active manner; that is, positioning oneself so that eye contact can be maintained with all students. Students have a tendency to stay on task if they know someone is watching. This mandates staying out of the center of the area. It is quite common to observe teachers placing students in a circle and then standing in the center of the formation. Not only is it impossible to see all students, but it is difficult for youngsters facing the back of the teacher to hear.

Since students cannot hear and there is little eye contact with half of the class, the teacher may not be aware of an accident or misbehavior.

Some teachers assume they must move to the same location in the teaching area when giving instructions because students will listen only when they are on or near this spot. Not only is this incorrect, but it can result in some rather negative consequences. Students who choose to exhibit deviant or off-task behavior usually move away from the instructor. Because the teacher's movement patterns are predictable, deviant students are farthest from the teacher in a position that is difficult to observe. In addition, it is possible the teacher may never move into certain areas, causing some students to believe the teacher does not like them. Active supervision requires the instructor to move around the perimeter of the area. Another reason for moving in an unpredictable manner is to keep students on task. For example, when using a number of teaching stations, some teachers move from station to station in a predictable manner. Students may perform the tasks while the teacher is watching, but move off task as soon as the teacher moves to the next station. The bottom line: actively move in a random fashion so students cannot anticipate where you will be observing next.

Active supervision demands movement and effective observation. If you develop a plan for reaching all students, they will think you are concerned about them. In addition, it is important to place yourself in an optimum position to observe skill performance. For example, if you are observing kicking, stand to the side rather than behind the student. A judgment that needs to be made when observing performances is how long to stay with a single group or student. If you get overly involved with a student, the rest of the class may move off task. On the other hand, if contacts are short and terse, the student may not benefit from the interaction. Learn to pace instructional feedback by giving 1 or 2 pointers and moving to another student.

Develop a Plan for Active Supervision

Experts who work with beginning teachers know they often "look at students but do not see." When teachers do not have a plan for actively supervising behavior, they usually are not able to recall whether students exhibited the behavior. To keep all students on task, it is important to develop a plan for monitoring this behavior. A practical plan might be to scan the class from left to right at regular intervals and observe the number of students who are performing the assigned task. When teaching a class of 25 to 35 students, it usually takes 4 to 6 seconds to scan an entire class. If done faster, the teacher may not be able to internalize the results of the scan. A number of variables can be evaluated through systematic observation: Students responding to a start or stop signal (response latency), key points of skill performance, adherence to safety procedures, and on-task performance.

Design a plan for active supervision. This plan should include where to stand for observation, how long to stay with each student, and how to move through the instructional area. One approach to assure all students receive personal contact is to check off the names of students who were addressed during the lesson. This can be done immediately after the lesson with a roll sheet or at a later time if the lesson is recorded. Often, teachers find they do not make regular contact with certain students and make excessive contact with others. This leads to feelings of favoritism or concern that "the teacher does not like me." It is difficult to interact with all students in a single physical education lesson, however, in a 1- or 2-week period, all students should receive feedback and attention.

Teacher movement should be planned since it affects supervisory effectiveness. To facilitate learning to move, divide the teaching area into 4 equal parts and set a goal of moving into each area a certain number of times. Give instructions and reinforcement from all quadrants. A nonparticipating student can be used to chart movement. See Chapter 9 for an example of an observation recording chart.

Maintain the Flow of the Lesson

An important phase of effective instruction is pacing the lesson to keep students interested, yet not frustrated. The following points can improve the flow of a lesson toward desired goals.

Minimize Verbalization and Increase Activity

It is easy to become engrossed in instruction and lose sight of student interest. Students enter class expecting to be involved in activity. If a teacher spends 5 minutes with roll call followed by 5 or 10 minutes of lecture, students lose interest and motivation. Move the class into activity first and give instructions later. This gets students immersed in the activity so they will be more receptive to listening.

Sometimes teachers become angry about misbehavior and spend a few minutes talking about the need to be model students. Much of the "sermon" will be general in nature and reflect the instructor's anger. Lecturing students has little impact. If misbehavior has occurred, let the class start practicing, speak to the misbehaving students one-to-one, and resume instruction. Often, a whole class is lectured when only a few students were at fault. This forces the majority of students to listen to something that has little or no meaning to them, and they may think it is unfair to scold the entire class. Time spent talking to the entire class prevents meaningful skill practice. Minimize excessive talking and maximize productive and on-task practice.

Maintain the Focus of Instruction

It is easy to become derailed when an interesting event occurs in class. Lesson plans are designed to guide the instruction toward desired objectives. When teachers constantly allow students to "sidetrack" them to more interesting topics, goals may not be reached. Experienced teachers know some students will intentionally try to move them away from the tasks at hand in order to participate in activities they prefer. Effective teachers maintain their momentum toward objectives and still show interest in student ideas. Sometimes it is necessary to deviate from planned objectives and take advantage of the "teachable moment." However, this should be the exception, not the rule. Students know the teacher is responsible for guiding the content of the lesson, and they expect it.

Maintain the Pace and Continuity of Instruction

Effective lessons flow in a consistent and well-planned manner. There are many transitions during a lesson: organizing students into groups, changing from one part of the lesson to another, and issuing and putting away equipment. Students should perceive transitions as an integral part of the instruction. If a transition is excessively long, it interrupts instructional momentum and students may begin to misbehave. Minimize time spent on transition since it detracts from accomplishing the lesson's goals.

Pace of instruction affects the flow of the lesson (Siedentop, 1991). How often should a teacher break into practice sessions to clarify a point or refocus instruction? Usually, there is a natural break in practice episodes when students become bored or fatigued and begin to move off task. This signals time to refocus. If, after an instructional episode, most of the class are not performing the task correctly, stop and clarify the situation. However, if a teacher stops the class frequently without concern for learning, the result is a lesson without flow and continuity. Students become frustrated, feeling that they never have enough time to master a task.

Activity instruction demands continuity so learners understand the purpose of performing various activities. For example, instructors break activities into parts while knowing how the skill as a whole is performed. Students also need to know how the various parts of a skill fit together. This should occur within the same lesson. It is expecting too much of students to have them practice parts for 1 or 2 weeks and then put them together as a whole. Integrate the activity or drill into the ultimate focal point: the accomplishment of the skill or activity.

Individualizing Instruction

A difficult task is to meet the individual needs of students even though the majority of instruction is conducted as a group activity. It is obvious, even to the least experienced teacher, that the ability levels of students vary widely. As students mature, their range of ability increases, making it more difficult to meet all of their needs. In addition, many students participate in extracurricular activities such as baseball, basketball, and private tutoring in various sports. This range of experiences places greater responsibility on the instructor to modify tasks so that all students can find success. The following methods can be used to individualize instruction and keep students on task.

1. *Modify the conditions.* In this situation, the task is modified to help students find success. For example, it may mean moving partners closer together if they are learning tennis skills, using a slower-moving object such as a family soft ball, increasing the size of the target, changing the size of boundaries or goal areas, allowing students to toss and catch individually, or increasing the size of the striking implement. An optimum rate of error and success should be the goal of individualized instruction. When stu-

dents find little success, they may exhibit off-task behavior to draw attention away from their subpar performance. This behavior is a clear indicator to the teacher that the error rate is too high and is preventing learning.

2. *Increase challenge through self-competition.* When the success rate is too high, students become bored and avoid continued practice. This calls for increasing challenge by adding personal competition to the task. Challenge gifted students to see how many times they can perform without missing, break a personal record, or be allowed to use the skill in group competition. The challenge can be increased by asking gifted performers to use a faster-moving object, accomplish higher levels of performance, or increase the distance or size of the goal. Students respond best to challenges; a task is a challenge when it is slightly above their current skill level.

3. *Offer different task challenges.* Students do not have to work on the same tasks simultaneously. It is desirable to present a number of tasks of varying complexity so that students of varying abilities develop personal challenges. Task cards or station teaching allows students the opportunity to learn at an optimum rate. In cases where specialized sport skills are being taught, it is particularly important to offer different tasks. For example, students who have limited upper body strength find inverted balances to be difficult, if not impossible. Balance activities utilizing the legs could be substituted, allowing all students to work on balance skills through different activity challenges.

4. *Encourage higher levels of performance.* Another solution for individualizing instruction is to refine the performance of skilled individuals. Fine points of technique can be used to offer greater challenge. For example, during throwing instruction, less gifted students may be learning proper footwork, whereas skilled throwers are working on distance, accuracy, or velocity of throws.

UTILIZE EFFECTIVE INSTRUCTIONAL FEEDBACK

Instructional feedback is used by effective teachers to assure student learning. Used properly, it can enhance a student's self-image, improve the focus of performance, result in individualized instruction, increase the rate of on-task behavior, and improve understanding. The following points offer direction for improving the quality of feedback used in the instructional setting.

Positive, Corrective, and Negative Feedback

Most teachers use corrective feedback to alter student performance. Unless a teacher utilizes a negative approach, little negative feedback (such as "That was a lousy throw") is used. Instead, they offer corrective feedback focusing on inaccurate phases of the performance (or related behavior). This is usually expected by students; however, if it is the only type of feedback offered, youngsters begin to perceive it as negative. The danger of overusing corrective feedback is that it creates a climate where students worry about making errors for fear the instructor will embarrass or belittle them. In addition, excessive correction may cause youngsters to think that no matter what they do correctly, the teacher never recognizes their effort.

Focus on the positive points of student performance. This creates a positive atmosphere where students are willing to accept a challenge and risk error or failure. Teachers who use positive feedback usually feel better about their students since they look for strengths in performance and use this as a foundation for skill improvement. Most physical education instructors rely heavily on corrective feedback, and the observation has been made that many physical educators have a correction complex. Corrective statements are appropriate if the learning environment has a balance of positive and corrective feedback. Siedentop (1991) recommends that an educational environment have a 3:1 or 4:1 ratio of positive feedback to corrective feedback. A higher ratio of positive feedback certainly enhances the overall positive atmosphere of the class. Since the use of corrective feedback comes easily for most teachers, it is usually necessary for them to practice increasing the amount of positive feedback used with students.

Use a Variety of Information Feedback

Information feedback is what students receive after they have completed a skill attempt. Feedback on the results of many skill attempts is obvious as, for example, in the case of golf swings, basketball shots, or baseball swings. It is inherent in the activity, and students know immediately the results of the skill attempt. Feedback on the form or topography of skill behavior is, however, difficult to attain. Provide students with useful information feedback on how well they are performing a skill.

A teacher usually gives feedback immediately after a skill attempt has been made. Teachers need to plan carefully for information feedback in classes. Planning for feedback should include determining the specific skill behaviors that a teacher is trying to foster. The feedback should be prescriptive in nature so that it helps to eradicate errors. Many different things tell students that they are performing at an acceptable level. Feedback statements can be general, specific, verbal, or nonverbal. Including a student's first name with the feedback is a meaningful way to make students realize that the teacher is aware of them and is sincere about their skill development. The following are some examples of different types of feedback:

Corrective or Prescriptive
"Get the shot put angle up to 42 degrees."
"Bend your knees more and uncoil."
"Adjust your grip by spreading your fingers."
"Accelerate through the ball."
"Keep your wrists stiff and start the action with your shoulders."
"Transfer your weight as you contact the ball."

Positive General
"Good job."
"Way to go."
"Nice defense."
"All right, Jim."
"Very nice hustle."
"Interesting question, Mike."
"OK, class."

Positive Specific
"Good angle of release."
"Perfect timing on the outlet pass."
"Way to hit the soft spot in the 1-3-1 zone."
"Great job looking off the undercoverage."
"That's the way to vary your serves. It keeps them off-balance."
"Mike, good job keeping your head down."

Nonverbal Positive or Corrective
Winking or smiling.
Thumbs up or down.
Pat on the back.
Clapping the hands.
Facial gestures.
Making a "V" sign.
Shaking the fist.

Plan a variety of feedback, including statements that use first names and give specific positive information, and nonverbal messages. Variety is necessary to avoid satiation and redundancy. Feedback should be directed at key points of the specific skill, and the terminology should be appropriate to the student's age and developmental level.

Offer Feedback to All Class Members

Teachers have many students in class and must decide on the length of feedback episodes and the number of students to contact. It may depend on the skill being taught. For example, if it is a skill that students learn quickly, the best model may be to move quickly from student to student, assuring there are no major dysfunctions. A systematic approach where all students are quickly observed or a random approach of moving and looking for students having problems can be used. This fast-moving approach allows contact with many students during the lesson. In addition, it helps keep students on task since they know the teacher is moving and watching the class regularly. The drawback to this approach is that little opportunity for in-depth feedback occurs. If skills are complex and refinement is a goal, taking more time with students is usually more effective. This means watching a student long enough to offer highly specific and information-loaded feedback. The end result is high-quality feedback to a fewer number of students.

When giving feedback to students, avoid close scrutiny of the student at the completion of the episode. Students become tense if a teacher tells them how to perform a skill correctly and then watches to see if they do it exactly as instructed. Students are willing to try new and risky ways of performing if they are allowed to practice without being closely observed by the teacher or class. In short, observe carefully, offer feedback, move to another student, and recheck progress at a later time.

Group or Individual Feedback?

In school settings, much feedback is group oriented. The most common method is to stop and offer feedback to all youngsters. This is the fastest method, but it also allows the most room for misinterpretation. Some students may not understand the feedback, while others may not listen since it does not seem relevant to them. It is more effective to direct feedback (positive only) at a student so the rest of the class can hear it. This allows feedback to "ripple" through the class, offering instructional feedback to the rest of the class. Use this approach in a manner that avoids student failure in front of the rest of the class. An example would be, "Sarah is hitting the tennis ball at its peak when she serves."

In addition, feedback should focus on the desired task. For example, if students are asked to catch a batted ball in front of their body, it clouds the issue if the teacher offers feedback on the quality of throw. If catching is the focus, feedback should be on catching so that students continue to concentrate on that skill. An example of feedback in this setting is, "Watch the way Michelle keeps her body in front of the ball when catching ground balls." A final clarification: it is not necessary to have students watch other students to accomplish the desired outcome. In fact, it is effective only if the performer is capable of showing the skill correctly. If this approach is used exclusively, less skilled (or shy) performers will never have an opportunity to receive feedback from the class. It can be just as effective to tell the class how well a student was doing and move on, for example, "Mike always keeps his head up when dribbling."

Offer feedback to students as soon as possible after the performance. If delayed feedback is offered, allow opportunity for immediate practice so students can apply the information. Little is gained and much lost if students are told how to improve and then leave class without opportunity for practice. Few, if any, students will remember the suggestions. If the end of class is approaching, it is probably best to limit feedback and work on situations that can be practiced immediately. Other problems can be solved at the next class.

DEFINE POLICIES AND PROCEDURES

The development and implementation of a quality physical education program require that policies and procedures are determined, communicated, and applied consistently to all students. Effective programs utilize a set of written guidelines that are presented to students on the first day of school and reinforced continually throughout the year. Policies and procedures are evaluated constantly to determine if they continue to contribute to program objectives. An excellent curriculum is not effective without a well-developed set of policies and procedures and an ongoing revision process.

Guidelines in the form of a handbook or booklet for all students, parents, and administrators should be distributed. The handbook should be brief, clear, and succinct, and no more than 10 pages. Information in the handbook is discussed with a requisite that students discuss the information with their parents. A form indicating parents have read the guidelines is signed and returned to the physical education teacher (Figure 6.3). Many students and parents have misconceptions about the nature of physical education, and clarifying all aspects of the program will limit future problems.

The physical education handbook should cover the following areas:

1. Philosophy of the program
2. Curriculum objectives
3. Program scope and graduation requirements
4. Uniform and dressing requirements
5. Showers and towels
6. Locks and lockers
7. Attendance and participation
8. Excuses and make-up procedures
9. Equipment
10. Grading procedures

Philosophy and Objectives

Communicating the department's views and objectives for the program is important. (Refer to Chapter 1 for a general discussion of physical education and program objectives.) There are many disparate views of physical education (such as strictly as a physical training program or a training ground for the athletic program), and many know little about new approaches to physical education. A short 1-page discussion about philosophy and objectives helps parents and students understand the nature and importance of the program.

Ovation High School Physical Education Department
Ovation, AZ

Dear Parents:

This booklet contains the policies and procedures of the physical education department. We would like you to read carefully and discuss the program regulations with your son or daughter. These policies and procedures are important for making the learning environment a pleasant experience for all students.

We desire to have all students leave physical education classes with a positive attitude and the urge to be physically active throughout their lifetime. If you have any questions about the curriculum or the policies and procedures of the department, please call me at 925-4724.

Please sign the slip at the bottom of the sheet and have your child return it to school.

Thank you.

Sincerely,

_____

Physical Education Teacher

- -

We have read the booklet and understand the policies and procedures.

_____   _____
Parent   Student

_____
Date

FIGURE 6.3 Letter to parent regarding policies and procedures

Program Scope and Graduation Requirements

An understanding of how physical education fits into the graduation requirements of the school needs to be clarified. Schools in each state require varying amounts of physical education for graduation. In some districts, physical education credit is awarded for participation in athletics, cheerleading squads, marching band, ROTC, and driver education classes. Whether such activities should be allowed as substitutes for physical education has long been a subject of debate. Maybe the best way to answer the question of which activities should be awarded physical education credit is to examine the objectives of the program. If an activity fulfills program objectives, then credit should be awarded for participation in that activity. If the activity does not contribute to objectives, then physical education credit should not be awarded. Athletics, marching band, ROTC, and driver education are all important and valuable experiences for students, but they do not contribute to the objectives of physical education.

It is easy to understand why some people argue the physical benefits of the marching band or the skills developed while playing on a basketball team. These are, however, only a small portion of the objectives of a quality physical education program. Students need to learn a variety of lifetime sports and fitness activities and receive knowledge about health, exercise, and nutrition. This information is only imparted to students and their parents through a physical education program.

Another important aspect of the program scope relates to coeducational classes. Many parents have had little or no experience with sexually integrated physical education classes, and convincing them of the benefits of coeducational classes may be difficult. Parents and students need to expand their comfort zones regarding this issue. The departmental handbook can begin "socializing" people to the idea of male/female classes.

Uniforms and Dress Requirements

Students should be encouraged to change into active wear for physical education classes. The importance of comfort, safety, and hygiene of uniforms is a plus. Many schools still require a specific uniform and enforce strict dress codes. Uniforms and dress codes can create problems and be a source of controversy. Students often avoid physical education environments simply because of a dress code requirement, yet these same students will admit they enjoy physical activities and would take a class if no dress code existed. The benefits of having all students dress alike may not be worth developing escape and avoidance behaviors in students.

Controversy over uniforms and dress codes should not develop into a critical issue. If the school favors a dress code, a student committee can be formed each year to select a new uniform. Clothing companies can provide several available options with school colors, emblems, or mascots. Students then decide which uniform they desire or can be given the option of buying a different type of uniform. Several choices should be available. Adolescence is a time of growing independence, and allowing students to select their physical education attire is not detrimental to the accomplishment of program objectives.

In addition, each physical activity class is different and can require specialized clothing that is appropriate for the activity. Rock climbing or horseback riding classes may require the wearing of long pants for safety. Aerobics, yoga, and the martial arts necessitate specialized clothing for freedom of movement.

Another problem is the legality of an imposed dress code. Some states stipulate that if a specific dress code is required, the school must purchase uniforms for those students unable to do so. Dress codes can create problems for students with specific religious beliefs that forbid wearing gym attire. Other students may have physical deformities or embarrassing conditions they wish to keep covered. For example, a student who has a severe case of acne on his back may not want to go swimming without a shirt.

These problems reveal why a flexible policy on uniforms and dress requirements may be the best approach. The perceived advantages of a strict dress code—developing discipline, school spirit, and cooperation; enhancing the identification of teams; reducing discrimination against poorer or wealthier students; and reducing unit cost of attire because of large orders—are debatable and seldom worth the problems generated. Teachers and students should both influence the decisions on dress requirements, and teachers should have the flexibility to make decisions that facilitate the learning process of each individual in each situation.

A department policy regarding students who cannot afford a uniform or a change of clothes is necessary. Often, a special fund can be made available through candy or bake sales. The parent-teacher association may be able to provide funds through one of its projects. Sometimes used or unclaimed clothes can be cleaned and worn by students who cannot afford to buy a uniform. A policy on the laundering of gymnasium clothes is probably one of personal choice, as is the laundering of regular street clothes. If hygiene problems occur, students (and if necessary, parents) can be confronted. Students should identify their gym clothes with permanent ink or name tags because of the numerous opportunities for mix-ups, losses, or pilferage.

Teachers need to be good models of appropriate attire for physical activities. An active teaching role is certainly enhanced by appropriate dress, and students are strongly influenced by the behavior of their teachers. It is difficult to defend teaching in blue jeans when students are not allowed to participate in similar attire.

Attendance and Participation Policies

If students enjoy physical education, there will be fewer problems with attendance and participation. The overall curriculum and instructional procedures will have more of an effect on students than policies and procedures on attendance and participation. Some teachers spend so much time and energy on these latter concerns that they lose sight of the importance of curriculum and instruction. Students are more enthusiastic about physical education if a qual-

ity curriculum and an effective instructional program exists.

Nevertheless, there do need to be policies for attendance, participation, and excuses from class. A system that allows students to earn reinforcers (such as points, activity time, privileges) for attending and participating is an effective strategy. Too often, a negative or "chop" system by which students lose points or privileges or receive lower grades for inappropriate behavior is used. This approach creates a negative environment, while the positive approach has the opposite effect. Students can be awarded 1 point per day for attendance, 1 point for dressing, and points for participating, rather than subtracting or cutting points for not attending and participating.

All medical excuses and notes from parents should be presented to the school nurse at the beginning of the school day rather than during class time. The nurse is more qualified than the physical educator to make decisions about medical problems requiring special attention. The nurse should make the final decision on participation and should communicate with the physical education teacher both verbally and in writing. A form can be developed to facilitate this communication (Figure 6.4). If students cannot participate for 3 consecutive days, most schools recommend they visit a physician. A physician's report form (Figure 6.5) can be sent to the stu-

---

School Nurse Excuse Form

Student _____   Date _____

Please excuse the above named student from physical education class for the following day(s):

_____

The reason the student is excused is: _____

_____

_____

_____

Thank you,

_____

School Nurse

FIGURE 6.4   School nurse excuse form

Physician's Report Form

Date _____

Dear Dr. _____

The following student, _____ , has requested that he/she be excused
from physical education activities. We would like your help in designing a program that is appropriate for this
student's physical condition. Our program offers a wide variety of physical activities. Please complete the
following information to enable us to develop a personalized program.

Thank you for your time.

Sincerely,

_____
Physical Education Department Head

- -

1. Type of illness, injury, or handicap _____

   _____

2. Restrictions _____

3. Activities to be avoided _____

4. Duration of restriction _____

5. Other important information _____

   _____

6. Physician's name _____

   Address _____   Phone _____

7. Signature _____   Date _____

Please send form to: Person   _____

                        School   _____

                        Address   _____

FIGURE 6.5   Physician's report form

---

dent's doctor. This type of form helps improve communication between the school nurse, the physician, and the physical educator. Students need to understand that credit for physical education is not awarded to people who cannot participate in the class sessions.

Students who have minor problems such as being tired or having a sore throat, headache, or cramps should be handled on an individual basis. Some students can participate with these problems, whereas others cannot. Teachers must become knowledgeable about the backgrounds and personalities of their students. A policy that treats all students the same is usually misdirected. Religious beliefs relative to participating on various holidays or holy days often result in students' asking to be excused. This should be handled individually through the school administration. If confusion arises about excuses due to minor illness or religious beliefs, students should be allowed to see the school nurse for illnesses and a guidance counselor or administrator about preferences and beliefs.

Students also have bad days, headaches, cramps, family problems, and other concerns that affect their daily performance. Sometimes students need a little extra encouragement to participate, and at other times they may need a day off. Effective teachers get to know their students so they have some basis for judging individual situations. In contrast, some teachers believe that students are "cheating" if the student does not want to participate on a given day. Initially, students should be given the benefit of the doubt, because they may indeed have a problem. If the same student continues to have participation problems, the teacher will have to contact the parents or apply some alternative procedures.

Develop a policy for tardiness. Start each class at a precise time. Students need to know exactly what time the class begins. Excessive tardiness should be integrated into the make-up policies and procedures for grades.

Class Make-Up Policies and Procedures

All students have the right to make up missed classes because of excused absences. Try to focus the make-up work on activities that were missed. Attending another physical education class or an extra class on the same activities is useful. Possibilities for make-up work can focus on knowledge activities, performance activities, or spectator activities. Depending on the objectives of the lessons missed, some activities will be more valuable than others. The following are examples that could be used in each area.

Make-Up Work—Knowledge Activities

The following alternatives might be offered to students who missed a knowledge activity. Students complete one of the following assignments and turn it in to the instructor:

1. Read an article in the sports section of the newspaper and write a 1-page analysis (form provided).
2. Read an article in any sports magazine and write a 1-page analysis (form provided).
3. Read a short biographical sketch about a noted sports figure and write a 1-page analysis (form provided).
4. List and define 15 terms from any of the following activities: basketball, field hockey, flag football, lacrosse, orienteering, physical conditioning, recreational games, running techniques, soccer, swimming, team handball, and volleyball.
5. List and explain 10 rules from any sport.
6. Diagram the playing area of any of the activities listed in activity number 4.
7. Read a book related to a sport and write a 1-page analysis (form provided).
8. Student choice (with teacher approval).

The form reproduced in Figure 6.6 can be used for student reports on these knowledge activities.

Article Report

Name _____

Date _____

Publication _____

Author _____

Major idea of article:

Your opinion of the material:

What are the benefits of this material to you?

Parent or guardian signature _____

FIGURE 6.6 Knowledge analysis sheet

Make-Up Work—Performance Activities

Students who have missed performance activities might be told to participate in any of the following activities and to write a 1-page analysis (form provided):

1. Run a mile for time.
2. Run a parcourse.
3. Ride a bike for 30 minutes.
4. Attend an aerobics class.
5. Lift weights for 30 minutes.
6. Play 18 holes of disc golf.
7. Play 1 set of tennis.
8. Play 2 games of racquetball.
9. Play 18 holes of regular golf.
10. Engage in a workout at a health spa.
11. Student choice (approved by instructor).

The form in Figure 6.7 can be used for reports in the performance area.

Make-Up Work—Spectator Activities

Students observe one of the following events and write a 1-page analysis (form provided). Events can take place at the middle or senior high school, community college, college, or professional level. Any of the following event activities is acceptable: football, soccer, cross-country running, tennis, volleyball, bas-ketball, softball, baseball, wrestling, track and field, swimming, and student choice (approved by instructor). Figure 6.8 is a form that can be used for reporting on spectator activities.

Showers and Towels

Students should be encouraged to shower after all vigorous activity sessions. Spend time discussing hygiene and why showering is necessary. Students need to understand the importance of developing lifetime health habits. Showering, like the uniform issue, should not evolve into a polarizing conflict. Many physical educators have developed avoidance behaviors in students because of inflexible or poorly managed showering policies. For example, a teacher required students to shower after every class including golf, archery, riflery, and discussion sessions. Showering is surely not necessary after every physical education class. Others give students only 5 to 7 minutes to shower and change clothes. This is not enough time for students to dry their hair, change clothes, and return to the classroom. Appearance is an important aspect of personal development. Physical education teachers who overlook this fact often alienate students.

Analyze the nature of each lesson and the allotted time schedule. Swimming, for example, requires

---

Performance Analysis

Name _____

Activity _____

Date _____

Explain the activity you participated in.

Explain the physical benefits of this activity.

What were your scores, time repetitions, and so forth?

Parent or guardian signature _____

FIGURE 6.7   Performance analysis sheet

Spectator Analysis

Name _____

Event _____

Date, place _____

Opponents _____

Final score _____

Type of offense and defense of each team:

How the scoring occurred:

Strengths and weaknesses of each team:

Your reactions to the event:

Parent or guardian signature _____

FIGURE 6.8   Spectator analysis sheet

more preparation time at the end of class, whereas an archery activity does not necessitate showering. Showering policies should be flexible so teachers can make appropriate time adjustments in lessons. When students resist taking showers, teachers need to search for the underlying reason. Many students are uncomfortable showering in front of peers due to menstruation, underdeveloped bodies, acne problems, deformities, or various other problems. Private showers can help alleviate this concern. Teachers need to be sensitive to the fact that poorly planned and poorly administered showering and dressing procedures can turn students off to physical activity.

Students should have a say in matters of personal health and cleanliness. If teachers make all of the decisions for students, little is learned about making decisions in later life. If students complain about peers who possess strong body odor, the matter should be discussed with the student and, possibly, with his or her parents. Teachers should try to avoid incorporating showering and dressing behaviors in the grading system.

A policy on towels should also be determined. The simplest procedure is to have students bring tow-els from home along with their activity clothing. Students are then responsible for changing towels and uniforms on a regular basis. Mark names on the towels to minimize loss. Some districts provide students with towels for physical education class. The towels can be purchased by the school and laundered on a regular basis in school facilities. This arrangement helps reduce mildew and odor problems created by students leaving wet towels in their lockers. Towels need to be checked out and in each day, and a security system must be developed. This approach creates a number of additional problems for teachers.

Another approach is to use a towel service company that provides freshly laundered towels on a daily basis. This approach is usually more expensive but easier to manage. Funding for a towel service can come from the school's general budget, a student fee, a booster club project, or a physical education department project such as selling candy or sponsoring car washes. Each school district has fund-raising and budget procedures that need to be followed. The physical education staff can weigh the advantages and disadvantages of each towel supply procedure before making a decision.

Locks, Lockers, and the Locker Room

Most schools assign students a combination lock and a small wire basket or metal locker for their activity clothes. A longer, larger locker is usually available for street clothes during each activity period. Longer lockers commonly alternate with the shorter lockers throughout the locker room. This helps spread students around the entire area. Older students are usually assigned upper locker rows because they can reach them. A master list of which student occupies which locker should be maintained. This can be done with a student locker assignment sheet. Problems such as forgotten combinations or misplaced locks can be readily solved when the teacher has a master list of combinations and the locker assignment sheet.

Supervision procedures for the locker room can be arranged to ensure safety and theft prevention. The room should be locked during class time to prevent thefts. Teachers should walk through the locker room regularly to check for unlocked lockers and clothes and towels that are left out accidentally. This routine reduces loss due to theft. In some situations, teacher aides can be hired to supervise the locker room, distribute towels, and help maintain the management policies.

Equipment

Proper types of equipment in adequate amounts are a must for quality programs. Students cannot learn various physical skills without proper equipment. Physical education departments need basketballs, tennis racquets, and Frisbees, just as math and reading departments need books, paper, and pencils. Students cannot learn to play tennis without a racquet, tennis balls, and the opportunity to practice on courts. In many instances, physical education departments are asked to get along without proper amounts of equipment. A class of 35 students needs more than 5 basketballs, 6 volleyballs, or 10 tennis racquets. Many administrators need to be convinced that physical education is more than 1 or 2 games of a specific activity.

Purchase

Funds from the general school budget are used to purchase equipment for the physical education pro-

gram, and the physical education budget and student-teacher ratio should be equal to those of other academic areas of the school. The physical education budget needs to be separate from the athletic budget. Some equipment can be shared, but a definite distinction should be made between the two budgets.

Equipment priorities should be determined by student interest surveys and the number of students who will use the equipment. Certain activities are offered more frequently than others, and equipment for these should be a higher priority. Certain types of equipment may receive lower priority because students are able to bring their own from home. This is a policy that must be determined by the department.

Order equipment from local dealers if possible. They are an important part of the community and usually provide fast and efficient service for the local schools. In addition, they usually support schools and will provide the best possible prices on equipment. Regional or nationwide companies may be able to provide reasonable prices on some equipment. Service, however, is often slower, and an order may not be filled for 1 to 6 months. Check with other teachers and schools on the reputation and reliability of specific companies before placing a large order. State and regional physical education conventions are attended by the equipment dealers in each area. This is a good opportunity to meet the dealers and discuss prices and new equipment.

The quality and price of equipment should be studied carefully before making a purchase. Check with other schools to see what experiences they have had with specific equipment. The cheapest price is not always the best deal. Durability and longevity are especially important. Equipment dealers may not know how well certain equipment will hold up over a period of time. This is why talking with people who are currently using the equipment is important.

The concept of progression in buying equipment is useful in negotiating with budget committees or school boards when a large amount of capital is necessary for equipment. If several thousand dollars are needed to add equipment for a new activity, it may be possible to implement the activity in 3 phases over 3 years. The activity could be started with $800 to $1,000 for the first year, and more equipment could be added gradually over the next few years. A budget committee is usually receptive to this approach.

Student interest and willingness to bring in personal equipment for particular activities is also an effective strategy for gaining administrative support for an activity. Offering a cycling unit with each student bringing in his or her own bicycle, or offering a golf class in which students use their own clubs are effective for generating student and administrative interest in new activities.

Another source of equipment is to have it constructed by the physical education staff, the maintenance department, or the industrial arts classes. Starting blocks, relay batons, soccer goals, team handball goals, and jump ropes are examples of equipment that can be constructed. Take care to ensure that all safety specifications have been met. There are several books and articles that describe how to make homemade equipment (Pangrazi and Dauer, 1995).

Physical education equipment can also be purchased jointly with other schools, city parks and recreation departments, and the athletic department. Many districts, for example, jointly purchase free weights and weight machines for the use of athletes, physical education classes, and adult community education programs. Joint purchases are an excellent way to share costs and involve the entire community. This method can be used for purchasing tennis, racquetball, badminton, volleyball, softball, basketball, and aerobic dance equipment.

Storage, Distribution, and Maintenance

An accurate equipment inventory should be completed at the beginning and the end of each school year. Records kept year to year help determine the needs of the department and facilitate the purchasing process. Documenting the type and amount of equipment lost each year will also provide information for improving the security and distribution procedures.

A storage area that is easily accessible to both male and female teachers is desirable. The storage area should be close to the teaching stations (that is, the gym, fields, and courts). It is inconvenient to pick up and return equipment to an area far from the station. The storage area can contain labeled shelves, bins, and containers for all pieces of equipment. All teachers, student leaders, and students who have access to the area need to cooperate fully in keeping the area clean and orderly. It is easy to become disorganized when many different people are sharing equipment.

Teachers need adequate methods for transporting equipment to and from the teaching areas. Various types of ball bags, shopping-type carts, and portable ball carts are available. These will reduce the amount of class management time expended on equipment transport. Students can be given responsibilities for the movement of equipment if they are trained properly.

Develop a system for using equipment that is not designated on the yearly curriculum. A sign-up and check-out list can be posted in the storage area along with the yearly sequence of activities. The department head or equipment coordinator is notified if any changes are made in the schedule with regard to equipment. This prevents problems with teachers not having necessary equipment for their classes. Equipment should not be loaned to outside groups without following designated procedures. If equipment is shared or loaned to other groups, it must be marked or identified with some regulation code to prevent losses or mix-ups with equipment from other sources.

Procedures should also be developed for repairing and maintaining equipment. Decisions on which equipment to repair and who will repair it must be made. If the repair work is minor and can be completed at school, who will do the work and where will it be done? If equipment must be sent out for repair, where and how will it be sent?

These decisions are all part of the ongoing process of implementing a quality physical education curriculum. Equipment is part of a program's lifeblood. Without adequate equipment, the effectiveness of the teaching-learning environment is greatly reduced, because students without equipment will become bored, unmotivated, and troublesome for the teacher. How can students learn to dribble, pass, and shoot a basketball when they must stand in line and take turns sharing a ball with 5 or 6 other students? The goal of a program should be to provide every student with a piece of equipment. The productive learning time can thus be greatly enhanced.

Grading Procedures

Grading is an important part of the policies and procedures described in the department handbook, and should be determined and discussed with students during the first week of classes. Parents should also be made fully aware of this area. Evaluation and grading recommendations are discussed in detail in Chapter 10.

EXPECTED OUTCOMES

After reading this chapter, you should be able to

- Identify various ways to listen and communicate with students in a physical education learning environment.

- Understand procedures needed to develop effective instructional cues.

- Cite various ways to enhance the clarity of communication between the teacher and the learner.

- Describe demonstration and modeling skills that facilitate an environment conducive to learning.

- Articulate strategies and techniques used to supply students with meaningful feedback regarding performance.

- Arrange a safe class environment characterized by active supervision and instructional involvement.

- Develop effective policies and procedures to guide the operation of the physical education program.

REFERENCES AND SUGGESTED READINGS

Fronske, H. 1996. *Teaching Cues for Sport Skills*. Boston: Allyn & Bacon.

Harrison, J. M. 1987. A review of the research on teacher effectiveness and its implications for current practice. *Quest* 39: 36–55.

Harrison, J. M., Blakemore, C. L., Buck, M. M., and Pellett, T. M. 1996. *Instructional Strategies for Secondary Physical Education*. 4th. ed. Dubuque, IA: Wm. C. Brown.

Pangrazi, R. P., and Dauer, V. P. 1995. *Dynamic Physical Education for Elementary School Children*. 11th ed. Boston: Allyn & Bacon.

Parker, J. 1995. Secondary teachers' views of effective teaching in physical education. *Journal of Teaching in Physical Education* 14(2): 127–139.

Sariscsany, M. J., Darst, P., and van der Mars, H. 1995. The effects of three teacher supervision patterns on student on-task and skill performance in secondary physical education. *Journal of Teaching in Physical Education* 14(2): 179–197.

Siedentop, D. 1991. *Developing Teaching Skills in Physical Education*. 3rd ed. Palo Alto, CA: Mayfield Publishing Co.

van der Mars, H., Vogler, W., Darst, P., and Cusimano, B. 1994. Active supervision patterns of physical education teachers and their relationship with student behavior. *Journal of Teaching in Physical Education* 14(1): 99–112.

Wuest, D., and Lombardo, B. 1994. *Curriculum and Instruction, The Secondary School Physical Education Experience*. St. Louis: Mosby.

7 Management and Discipline

PURPOSE

To provide information and techniques to help teachers direct students toward personal behavior management and self-discipline using a systematic approach.

KEY CONCEPTS

- Teaching many students is somewhat easy, but making marked gains in performance among low-aptitude and indifferent students is the mark of an excellent teacher.
- A basic requisite for teachers is to model the behavior they want from students.
- Class management skills are prerequisites to successful instruction.
- Management skills are practiced consistently throughout the school year.
- Students classified as deviants or learning disabled often are identified as behavior problems.
- Teachers' reactions to appropriate and inappropriate behavior are effective in altering the occurrence of such behavior.
- The focus of a discipline program should be positive, constructive, and designed to teach students to be responsible for their behavior.
- Praise is usually more effective in changing behavior when it refers to positive specific behavior exhibited by the student.
- Behavior games can be an effective strategy for changing student behavior.

Successful teachers efficiently manage students. Skills may vary among teachers in emphasis and focus, but the result is always a well-managed class. Effective teachers take guidance from the following assumptions: that teaching is a profession, that students are in school to learn, and that the teacher's challenge is to promote learning. These assumptions imply a responsibility to a range of students, both those who accept instruction and those who do not. Teachers who make a difference believe that students who have not yet found success will eventually do so. Instructing quality students is relatively easy, but making appreciable gains among low-aptitude and indifferent students identifies an effective teacher.

THE EFFECT OF A TEACHER'S BEHAVIOR ON STUDENTS

The basic responsibility of the teacher is to direct learning toward target goals. How teachers teach, more than their teaching style, determines what students learn. No matter what the methodology or style, a diagnostic-prescriptive approach is superimposed on all teaching processes. Effective class management and organizational skills create a relaxed environment that offers students freedom of choice in harmony with class order and efficient teaching procedures. Management techniques include the mechanics of organizing a class, planning meaningful activities, and enhancing the personal growth of students. Because skillful instructors have the ability to prevent problems before they occur, they spend less time dealing with deviant behavior. In short, teachers who fail to plan, plan to fail.

How teachers behave has an impact on the behavior of students. In many ways, teaching reflects the personality, outlook, ideals, and background of the teacher. A successful teacher provides high-quality learning experiences and communicates a zest for movement that is contagious. Knowing what personal habits and attitudes affect students negatively increases rapport. Proper dress, a sound fitness level, and the willingness to participate with students reveal clearly how a teacher regards the profession and the subject. A basic requisite for teachers is to model the behavior that they desire from students. This implies moving quickly if they demand that students hustle. It includes listening carefully to students or demonstrating a willingness to perform fitness activities. Modeling desired behavior has a strong impact on students. The phrase "actions speak louder than words" is a truism in the area of personal behavior.

Successful teachers communicate a belief that the students are capable, important, and self-sufficient. Stressing a positive self-concept and offering experiences to promote success are invaluable aids to learning. Students are motivated when a teacher responds to their effort to achieve. They will appreciate the teacher's concern and usually respond with increased efforts.

Effective teaching can be done without sarcasm, ridicule, or threats. Teachers and students may become angry with one another in class. If so, it is a teacher's responsibility to tell students quietly (and privately) that the misbehavior is unacceptable and must stop. At the same time, students must sense they are acceptable persons who are cared for and appreciated.

PREVENTING BEHAVIOR PROBLEMS

Many class management and discipline problems can be prevented through anticipation and planning. A sense of confidence is developed when discipline problems are anticipated and dealt with effectively. Most beginning teachers worry that a problem will occur and they will not know how to deal with it. Starting the school year properly is impor-

tant. Many experienced teachers admit they did not have a plan to prevent problems during their first year of teaching. After a rocky start, they had to do a midyear reevaluation of their management and discipline techniques. A better approach is to have a prevention plan designed before starting the school year.

Determine Rules and Procedures for the School Year

Teachers usually agree on a common set of rules. They want students to be respectful to them and to other students. It is not unreasonable to expect students to behave. In fact, if teachers can't manage students, they can't teach them anything. Most school administrators judge a teachers' effectiveness by how well they manage students. Managing students is a necessary and important part of teaching and may be more important (or a requisite) than delivery of content. When developing rules, try to select general categories rather than specific behavior. For example, "respect your neighbor" could mean many things, from not pushing to not swearing at another student. Rules should be posted where all students can easily read them. The following are examples of general rules:

- *Stop on signal.* This implies freezing on signal, looking at the instructor, and listening for instructions.
- *Take care of equipment.* This could include caring for the equipment, distributing and gathering it, and using it properly.
- *Respect the rights of others.* Usually this means not pushing others, leaving their equipment alone, not fighting and arguing.

The number of rules should be minimized. Try not to exceed 3 to 5 rules; more than this number makes it difficult for students to remember all the details and makes the teacher appear overly strict. Rules should be guidelines to desired behavior rather than negative statements telling students what they can't do. The following list summarizes points to consider when designing rules:

1. Select major categories of behavior rather than a multitude of specific rules.
2. Identify observable behavior. This makes it easy to determine whether a person is following the rule and does not involve teacher judgment.

3. Make rules reasonable for the developmental level of students.
4. Use no more than 3 to 5 rules.
5. State rules briefly and positively. It is impossible to write a rule that covers all situations and conditions. Make the rule brief and broad.

Establish Consequences for Breaking Rules

When rules are broken, students should reap the consequences of their misbehavior. Consequences should be listed and posted within the teaching area and discussed with the class. If students are going to make conscious decisions about their behavior, they must know clearly what the consequences are. Rules and consequences should be applied consistently to all students. A primary reason for listing rules and consequences is to avoid punishing students excessively or unfairly. For example, a teacher may like one student more than another and may punish them differently for the same misbehavior. This leads students to believe the teacher is unfair.

Meet with students and explain the rules and consequences. Take time to discuss the rules and consequences with students. Where appropriate, involve students in the process and attempt to arrive at a consensus set of behavior guidelines. When rules and consequences are mutually agreed upon, teachers assume the role of administering predetermined consequences in an unemotional and concerned manner.

Develop Routines for Students

Students feel comfortable when they know what is expected of them. Students expect to follow routines. These routines should be discussed so students understand why the chosen procedures are used. Examples of routines that teachers often use are the following:

1. How students are supposed to enter the teaching area.
2. Where and how they should meet—in squads sitting, moving and freezing on a spot, in a semicircle, and so on.
3. What they should do if equipment is located in the area.
4. What signal the teacher uses to freeze a class.

5. How they procure and put away equipment.
6. How the teacher will group them for instruction.

Once these routines are established and practiced, both teacher and students can work together comfortably. Using the routines consistently will contribute to efficient class management.

Be a Leader, Not a Friend

Students want a teacher who is knowledgeable, personable, and a leader. They are not looking for a new friend; in fact, most students will feel uncomfortable if they perceive the teacher wants to be "one of them." Let students know that they will learn during the semester and that it is exciting to be teaching them. Don't look to be a part of their personal discussions. There must be a comfortable distance between teacher and students. This is not to say that teachers shouldn't be friendly and caring. It is important to be concerned about students as long as it is expressed in a professional manner. Being a leader means knowing where to direct a class. The teacher is responsible for what will be learned and how it will be presented. Student input is important, but ultimately, it is the teacher's responsibility to lead the class to desired objectives.

Use Activities that Involve the Entire Class

To minimize class management problems when first meeting a class, select instructional activities that involve the entire group in activity. As rapport with the class is developed, different styles of teaching and class organization can be used. Most often the direct style of teaching is used in the first few weeks. This allows the teacher to view the entire class and see how students respond to the educational setting. Less directed teaching styles and different organizational schemes can be implemented after class management skills have been developed. Station teaching, peer teaching, and other approaches are most effective when the teacher and students have developed a feeling of mutual respect.

Communicate High Standards

Students perform to teacher's expectations. If a teacher expresses the need for students to perform at a high level, the majority of them will strive to do so.

A common expression is, "You get what you ask for." If you ask and expect students to perform to the best of their ability, they probably will do so. On the other hand, if you act like you don't care whether they try, some students will do as little as possible.

Give Positive Group Feedback

Positive feedback delivered to the class will help develop group morale. A class must see itself as a unit that works together and is rewarded when it meets group goals. Students will need to work with others in the workplace, so learning now about group cooperation and pride in accomplishment prepares them for adulthood.

Discipline Individually and Avoid Negative Group Feedback

When negative feedback is delivered, it should be done privately and personally to individual students. Few people want to have negative comments delivered globally for others to hear. All students should not be punished for the behavior of a few misbehaving youngsters. Group negative feedback can have contrary results. Teachers who criticize the group usually lose the respect and admiration of students who were behaving properly.

CLASS MANAGEMENT SKILLS

Class management skills are a prerequisite to instruction. Moving and organizing students quickly and efficiently requires the teacher's comprehension of various techniques and the students' effective acceptance of those techniques. Observers of the teaching process agree that if a class is unmanageable, it is unteachable. Instructing students in management areas should not be viewed as a negative or punishing proposition. Most students and teachers enjoy a learning environment that is organized, efficient, and allows for a maximum amount of class time to practice an activity.

Effective teachers are efficient managers of students. Teachers should strive to help students develop the ability to manage themselves. Management policies need to be planned carefully for every aspect of the learning environment. As defined here, the term *management time* refers to the class time when instruction or practice is not taking place. The following are examples of management time activities:

1. Students dressing for class.
2. Teachers taking class roll.
3. Teachers explaining and directing the rotation format for skill work.
4. Students rotating from station to station.
5. Students picking up equipment and moving to a practice area.
6. Students forming a circle or an open formation for exercises.
7. Students returning equipment and returning to the locker room.

Management time usually has 2 phases that involve both the teacher and students. The first is the time it takes a teacher to explain management procedures and give students the signal to begin. An example would be when the teacher tells each of 6 squads to move to a designated spot and begin practicing. The second phase of management time refers to response latency, or the time it takes students to respond and begin the appropriate activity. An illustration of response latency is the time elapsed while students pick up equipment and before they begin practicing their skills. Total management time is a combination of teacher talk and the response latency. Excessive management time reduces the time available for instruction and practice. Totally eliminating management time is impossible, but through effective planning, management time can be held to a minimum. Teacher talk can be efficiently planned and response latency can be minimized through practice.

Manage Students Efficiently

Verbalizing management strategies should take a minimum amount of time yet be clear to students. Students need to know the what, when, and where of activity sessions. Teachers should plan what they are going to say in order to move students efficiently. Give directions slowly and succinctly, using a limited amount of information. When necessary, enhance directions with a diagram or a graphic display of the organizational scheme. Post the diagram in the locker room to be used concurrently with the explanation. The adage that a picture is worth a thousand words is appropriate in many situations.

Reduce Response Latency

Many variables affect a class's rate and speed of response. The nature of the activity, the students' motivational level, their feelings about the teacher, the time of day, and the weather are a few examples. Teachers control some of these variables, while others are fixed. A positive, success-oriented atmosphere helps decrease response time. Positive teacher reactions focused on appropriate student managerial behaviors are effective. Examples of such responses include:

1. "Way to go class, everyone dressed and ready in 4 minutes."
2. "Jim, great hustle back to your squad."
3. "Thank you for getting quiet so quickly."
4. "Look at squad 1 line up quickly."
5. "Hey, I'm impressed how quickly you all got in position."
6. "Way to stop on the whistle, thank you."

Another effective strategy is setting goals for management time (Darst and Pangrazi, 1981) and posting the results. Reinforcing contingencies can be tied to the accomplishment of these goals (Siedentop, Rife, and Boehm, 1974). Activities like playing games, free time, or novelty activities are effective rewards for responsible management behaviors. The section on behavior games in this chapter can also be used to improve special management problems (Hamilton, 1974).

Integrate Roll Call

A common scenario in secondary schools occurs as students trail out of the locker room and loiter while waiting for roll call. During this time, they talk, get involved in horseplay, and generally get the class off to a noisy and disorganized start. An effective method for taking roll each day helps reduce management and behavior problems. One useful approach is to use squads and squad leaders. Each squad leader reports any absentees to the teacher orally or by filling out an attendance sheet. Another approach is to paint numbers on the floor and assign each student a number. The teacher or a student leader glances quickly through the numbers and records the absentees while the students are exercising. Some teachers post a sign-in sheet for attendance, which students quickly initial. Yet another approach is to check attendance while students are beginning the first class activity. Regardless of the method used, the technique should save time and foster self-management qualities in students.

Minimize Instructional Time Episodes

Teachers want all students listening before they give instructions. Following a few simple principles can increase attentiveness. Instructions should be as specific and clear as possible and usually not last more than 1 minute. A teacher who talks longer during any single instructional episode will begin to lose student attention. If extensive directions are required, alternate instructional episodes with periods of activity. Too often, teachers sit students down and explain a number of technical points of skill performance. In a series of directions, most people remember the first and last. Understand the importance of giving students only 1 or 2 key focal points when performing a skill. The length of instructional episodes will be minimized and student frustration reduced.

Establish a Consistent Signal to Stop the Class

A consistent signal should be established for stopping the class. It does not matter what the signal is, as long as it always means the same thing. Often, having both an audio signal (such as a whistle blast) and a visual signal (raising the hand overhead) is effective, since some students may not hear the audio signal if they are engrossed in activity. Regardless of the signal used to indicate a stop, it is usually best to select a signal different from the one used to start the class. To evaluate class effectiveness in responding to the stop signal, the teacher can time the latency of the response to the signal (see Chapter 9).

Teachers must have 100% cooperation when students are asked to stop. If some students stop and listen to directions and others do not, class morale soon degenerates. The teacher can easily scan the class to see if all students are stopped and ready to comprehend the next set of directions. If the teacher settles for less than full attention, students will fulfill those expectations.

Organize Students into Groups and Formations

Instructors should be able to quickly divide their classes into teachable groups. The drill toe-to-toe can be used to teach students to find partners. The goal of the activity is to get toe-to-toe with a partner as fast as possible. Other challenges can be to get back-to-back or shoulder-to-shoulder or to look into the eyes of a partner. Students without a partner move quickly to the center of the teaching area and find someone else without a partner. Emphasis should be placed on rapid selection of the nearest classmate to prevent students from looking for a favorite friend or telling someone that he or she is not wanted as a partner.

Another effective activity for arranging small groups is to alert students with an audio or visual signal (whistle or fingers held high). When the whistle is blown a certain number of times, students form groups corresponding to the number of whistles and sit down to signify that they have the correct number in their group. Students who are not part of a group go to the center of the area and find the needed number of group members. Mastering this activity allows teachers to quickly move students into proper-sized groups depending on the number of whistle signals.

To divide a class into 2 equal groups, signal students to get toe-to-toe with a partner. One partner goes to one side of the area while the other moves to the opposite side.

An effective technique for moving a class into a single-file line is to have students run randomly throughout the area until a signal is given. On signal, while continuing to move, they fall in line behind someone until a single line is formed. This exercise can be done while students are running, jogging, or walking. As long as students continue to move behind another person, the line will form automatically. The teacher or a student leader then leads the line into a desired formation or position.

Use Squads to Reduce Management Time

Squads can be an effective means for arranging students for various class functions. Squads may meet at a designated spot in the gymnasium, at the pool, or on the playing field. Boundary cones are useful markers for assembling squads. Teachers can assign the squads and squad leaders and post the assignments in the locker rooms. Squad leaders should have specific opportunities to lead. The position carries extra responsibilities such as leading fitness activities, helping with equipment, taking attendance, setting up station work, or organizing team strategies. All students should get the chance to be a squad leader at some time throughout the year (Figure 7.1).

FIGURE 7.1 Students in squads

Teachers can help develop a certain esprit de corps within each squad by letting students select a squad name and by rewarding squads for good management behaviors. The best behaved squads might be allowed to select equipment first, receive extra play time, or participate in novelty activities. When employed properly, squad formation can be an effective means of arranging students. The following are guidelines for using squad formations to maximize teaching effectiveness.

1. Selection of squads or groups must never embarrass a student who might be chosen last. In no case should this be a "slave market" approach, in which the leaders look over the group and visibly pick those whom they favor.

2. A designated location should be used for assembling students in squad formation. When the teacher wants students in squads, students move to the pre-designated area, with squad leaders in front and the rest behind.

3. Squads can provide opportunities for peers to learn leadership and how to follow. Make use of squad leaders so that students regard being a leader as a privilege entailing certain responsibilities. Examples of leadership activities are moving squads to a specified location, leading squads through exercises or various introductory activities, and appointing squad members to certain positions in sport activities.

4. Squad leaders and the compositions of squads should be altered regularly. All students should have an opportunity to lead.

5. In most cases, an even number of squads should be formed. This allows the class to be broken quickly into halves for games. Having a class of 30 students divided into 6 squads of only 5 members each means a small number of students per piece of apparatus (and less waiting in line) in group activities.

6. A creative teacher makes the use of squads an exciting, worthwhile activity, not an approach that restricts movement and creativity. For example, cones can be numbered and placed in different locations around the activity area. When students enter the gym, they are instructed to find their squad number and assemble. This is an efficient way of moving students in position for circuit training or station teaching.

Distribute Equipment Effectively

Equipment should be distributed to students as rapidly as possible. When students wait for a piece of equipment, time is wasted. Often, teachers assign student leaders to get the equipment for a squad. This results in leaders being active while others sit and wait (and may become discipline problems). The easiest and fastest method is to have leaders place the equipment around the perimeter of the area. Students then move on signal to a piece of equipment and begin practicing immediately. The reverse procedure can be used for putting equipment away. This contrasts with the practice of placing the equipment in a bag and telling students to "run and get a ball." This approach usually results in youngsters being knocked down or pushed, and an argument could ensue.

INCREASE DESIRABLE BEHAVIOR

A class is a group of individuals all of whom need to be treated and understood for their uniqueness. Most students cooperate and participate in the educational setting. In fact, the learner is largely responsible for allowing the teacher to teach. No one can be taught if they choose not to cooperate. Effective management of behavior means maintaining an environment where all students can learn. It is the teacher's responsibility to fashion a learning environment where all students can learn and feel comfortable. Students who are disruptive and off task infringe on the rights of others. If a teacher has to spend a great deal of energy working with youngsters who are disorderly, students who want to learn are short-changed.

The focus of this section is to help teachers develop an action plan for modifying and maintaining desirable behavior. It is a constructive and positive approach to behavior. There are 3 phases to such a program: (1) reinforcing behavior, (2) prompting desirable behavior, and (3) shaping behavior. Such an approach teaches students the importance of responsible behavior.

Select Effective Reinforcement

A common question among teachers is, "How do I know what is reinforcing to students?" It is impossible to know what will reinforce a student until it is tried. However, there are many things that most secondary students will respond to (for example, praise, attention, games, free time, and special privileges). An easy way to identify effective activity reinforcers is to observe students and see the things they enjoy doing during free time. Another approach is to observe the things they do to gain attention. Attention seeking is an attempt to gain social reinforcement from peers.

Try Social Reinforcement First

Social reinforcers are most commonly used by teachers. Teachers apply social reinforcement when desirable behavior occurs. Most students are familiar with social reinforcers. Parents use praise, physical contact, and facial expressions to acknowledge desired behavior in their children. The following are examples of reinforcers that are typically used by teachers in a physical education setting:

Words of Praise
"Great job."	"That's the best one
"Way to go."	yet."
"I really like that job."	"Perfect arm
"Exactly right."	placement."
"Show the class	"Nice going, Mike."
your jump."	"Nice hustle."

Physical Expressions
Smiling	Clenched fist overhead
Winking	Thumbs up
Nodding	Clapping

Physical Contact
High 5	Shaking hands

Social reinforcement is characterized by praise, positive statement, and nonverbal feedback. Praise is most effective when it refers to specific behavior exhibited by the adolescent. This contrasts with general statements such as "Good job" or "You are an excellent performer." General and nonspecific statements do not delineate what was done well (see Chapter 6). It requires that the student try and identify what the teacher has in mind. If the student's guess does not align with the teacher's intent, the wrong behavior is reinforced. Describe the specific behavior to be reinforced. For example, compare the following:

Describing: "Way to go, James; you tucked your head on that roll."

Judging: "That's a good forward roll."

In the first example, the student is identified, and the specific behavior performed is reinforced. In the second situation, it is impossible to identify what was good or to whom the feedback was directed. If the feedback needs a follow-up question for clarity (such as what was good about it or why was it a poor performance?), the reinforcement is nonspecific and open to misinterpretation. To increase desired behavior, verbally or physically describe what makes the performance effective, good, or noteworthy. This reinforces the student and communicates to the rest of the class the type of behavior expected by the instructor.

Some teachers feel uncomfortable when learning to administer positive reinforcement to adolescents because it makes them feel inauthentic. A common complaint when learning how to reinforce is, "This isn't me; students will think I don't mean it." Any change in communication patterns causes discomfort. New patterns of communication require a period of adjustment. When learning new ways to praise and reinforce, the feedback may, at first, seem contrived and insincere. Instructors who are unwilling to experience the uneasiness of learning will remain unchanged. If practiced regularly, new behavioral patterns eventually become a natural part of a teacher's repertoire.

Use Activity as Reinforcement

Beyond social reinforcers, free time for physical activity can be used as reinforcement. Free time always ranks high among middle and senior high school students' preferences. Some examples of activities that might be used to reinforce a class are free time to practice a skill, the opportunity to play a game, act as a teacher's aid, be a teacher in a cross-aged tutoring situation, or be a team captain. Prudent use of free time as a reinforcer can get students to participate in a self-selected activity.

Access to novelty activities, competitive games, and class tournaments can be used as activity reinforcers. Frisbee games such as golf, baseball, Guts, and Ultimate are different and may be well-received by classes. By analyzing the likes and dislikes of students, teachers can develop a set of activity reinforcers that work.

Apply Extrinsic Reinforcement Sparingly

To increase desired behavior, some physical educators feel a need to offer some type of extrinsic reinforcer. Commonly, a system is used where students are given points when they are in uniform, on time, and so on. If points are given to students to encourage desirable behavior, it is possible that students will choose to perform in the desired fashion primarily to earn points. When they find themselves in a setting where points are not assigned, they may be less motivated to behave in a desirable manner. Self-discipline skills may be undermined. In addition, evidence shows that such extrinsic rewards may actually decrease a student's intrinsic motivation (Greene and Lepper, 1975; Whitehead and Corbin, 1991). In most cases, it is best to use extrinsic reinforcers only when it appears social reinforcers are ineffective.

Take Advantage of the Premack Principle

The Premack principle (Premack, 1965) is often used unknowingly by teachers. The principle states that when a high-frequency behavior (preferred) is contingent on completion of a lower-frequency behavior (less desirable), it is likely to increase the occurrence of the lower-frequency behavior. This implies that when the less desirable behavior is completed, a more desirable behavior is allowed. An activity that students enjoy is used to increase the occurrence of an activity that students are reticent to perform.

Learning activities can be planned utilizing the Premack principle. The Premack principle is sometimes referred to as "Grandma's law," or "Eat your spinach, then you may have dessert." Teachers can arrange the environment so that students must spend a certain amount of time completing a certain number of attempts at a less popular activity before they can gain access to a preferred activity. For example, 7th grade students would have to complete the skill objectives shown in Figure 7.2 before being allowed to participate in a 3-on-3 class tournament. The skill objectives demand practice and are less favorable activities, while the 3-on-3 tournament is the favorable activity.

Another example allows students to participate in basketball for 10 minutes after they have completed fitness activities. Whenever possible, select reinforcing activities that are within the realm of physical education. In some situations, when student motivation and interest are very low, teachers may choose to use reinforcements outside the physical education area. These might include free time, talking with peers, or going to a sporting event. Such rewards are harder to defend educationally but may be necessary in extreme situations.

The following skills must be completed before you are eligible to play 3 on 3.

Dribbling

1. Bounce (dribble) the ball 15 times consecutively with control.
2. Walk forward 25 feet while dribbling the ball with control.
3. Run forward 50 feet while dribbling the ball with control.

Passing (with a Partner)

4. Make 8 of 10 chest passes to a partner standing 10 feet away.
5. Make 8 of 10 bounce passes to a partner standing 15 feet away.
6. Make 6 of 10 overhead passes to a partner 15 feet away.

Shooting

7. Make 7 of 10 lay-ups from the preferred side.
8. Make 5 of 8 set shots from inside the key.
9. Make 4 of 8 set shots from the perimeter of the key.

FIGURE 7.2 Basketball skill objectives

Prompt Desired Behaviors

Prompts are used to remind students to perform desired behavior and to encourage the development of new patterns of behavior. There are many ways to prompt students in the physical education setting. The most common are:

1. *Verbal cues.* The most common method of prompting in secondary school classes is verbal cues; using words such as "Hustle" and "Keep going." The purpose is to remind students to maintain the desired behavior. Usually, they are used to maintain the pace of the lesson, increase the intensity of the performance, or motivate students to stay on task.

2. *Nonverbal cues.* Teachers can give many physical cues with their hands and related body language that communicate concepts such as "Hustle," "Move over here," "Great performance," or "Quiet down." In addition, when learning skills, youngsters can be physically prompted if moved into proper position, directed through the correct pattern, or have body parts properly aligned.

3. *Modeling.* Performing desired behavior in an attempt to prompt students to respond in similar fashion is called modeling. For example, placing equipment on the floor when stopping the class reminds students to do likewise. Modeling is an effective prompt because students often mimic the teacher without thinking.

Prompts should not be used to the point where students will not perform unless they are prompted. In fact, the goal is to remove the prompt so that behavior will be self-motivated. This process is called **fading** and implies a gradual removal of the prompts. The major use of prompts is to implement new behavior patterns and increase the occurrence of desired behavior. Use the weakest (least intrusive) prompt possible to stimulate the behavior. For example, it is possible to give students a long lecture about the importance of practicing the skill and staying on task. However, this approach is time consuming and overreactionary. It is not suited to multiple use and would be ineffective in the long run. Select a cue that is short and concise.

In addition to these points, be sure that the prompt identifies the task being prompted. For example, if the teacher prompts the class to "hustle" and has not tied it to desired behavior, there may be confusion. Some students may think it means to perform the skill as fast as possible; others may see it meaning to stop what they are doing and hustle to

the teacher. Tie the prompt to the desired behavior in a consistent manner and make sure students clearly understand the meaning of your prompt.

Shape Desired Behaviors

Shaping techniques can be used to build new behavior. Shaping is used when the behavior does not exist in the student's repertoire. This technique involves the use of extinction and reinforcement. Shaping is slow and inefficient and should be used when prompting is not possible. Two principles are followed when shaping behavior.

1. *Use differential reinforcement to increase the incidence of desired behavior.* Reinforce responses that reach a predetermined criterion, and ignore those that do not meet the criterion (extinction). Extinction refers to the technique of ignoring certain inappropriate behaviors that are not seriously disruptive to the learning environment.

2. *Increase the criterion that needs to be met for reinforcement to occur.* Shift the criteria toward the desired goal. For example, if the desire is to get a class to become quiet within 5 seconds after a signal has been given, it might be necessary to start with a 12-second interval. Why the longer interval? In all likelihood, it is not reasonable to expect that an inattentive class will be able to quiet down quickly. If the 5-second interval is selected initially, there is a good possibility that both teacher and students will be frustrated by the lack of success. In addition, in the beginning this behavior will not be achieved often, resulting in few opportunities to praise the class. The end result may be a negative situation where both teacher and youngsters feel they have failed. This is the basis for gradually shifting the criteria toward the desired objective. In this case, start with 12 seconds until the class performs as desired. Then, shift to a 10-second interval and ask the class to perform to this new standard. The process is gradually repeated until the terminal behavior is reached.

DISCIPLINE: DECREASING UNDESIRABLE BEHAVIOR

Society is based on personal freedom hinged to self-discipline. Americans have tremendous freedom as long as they do not encroach on the rights of others. In similar fashion, students can enjoy freedom as long as their behavior is consistent with educational objectives and does not prevent other students from learning. Discipline teaches students what behaviors are appropriate in the teaching-learning situation. Discipline is used when attempts to increase desirable behavior have failed.

Design a Behavioral Response Plan

Appropriate behaviors are defined as those that contribute positively to the learning environment. In contrast, inappropriate behaviors detract from learning. These behaviors can be related either to physical skill development or to the development of social-emotional skills. Appropriate behaviors include attending class, being on time, following directions, participating, cooperating with peers and teachers, and showing emotional control. Inappropriate, disruptive-type behaviors include tardiness, profanity, obscene actions, defiance of authority, talking out of turn, and interfering with the rights of others.

An important step in behavior control is to decide exactly which behaviors are acceptable and which are unacceptable. These can be listed in a handout and discussed with students at the beginning of the year. The list should be posted in the locker room and in the gymnasium and sent to parents and administrators. A common understanding of appropriate and inappropriate responses is the start of the process of students learning to behave properly.

Teachers know what behaviors are appropriate and inappropriate to them. Teacher reactions play a powerful role in controlling student behavior and establishing an effective, positive learning environment. Make a careful plan for responding to different types of misbehavior. Determine specific student behaviors that will be praised, scolded, or ignored. A list of specific student behaviors and accompanying reactions should be developed by each teacher. An instructor's list might look like this:

Praise	*Reprimand*	*Ignore*
Listening	Fighting	Talking out
Following directions	Pushing	Raising a hand
Hustling	Disrupting others	Snapping fingers
Being on time	Cursing	Showing off
Proper dress	Obscene gestures	Constantly asking questions

Student behavior can be maintained by the attention of the teacher and the peer group. For example, a student will misbehave, and the teacher will publicly reprimand the behavior. The friends of the student will laugh at the situation. Unfortunately, peer laughter is reinforcing to this student, and the behavior occurs more often. If the behavior is not seriously distracting, then ignoring it and showing a positive reaction to an appropriate behavior occurring later may be more effective. It could be explained to the class that they, too, should ignore the student's inappropriate behavior. In this way, the misbehaving student loses the attention of both teacher and peers.

Use Behavior Correction Techniques

Behavior correction techniques can be used to decrease undesirable behavior after positive reinforcement has failed. Using positive reinforcement to increase desired behavior is done with the hope that it will replace negative behavior. For example, if a skilled athlete is always criticizing less able students, it might be effective to ask that student to help others and serve as a student assistant. The intent is to teach students to deliver positive and constructive feedback rather than criticism. A rule of thumb to follow before using negative consequences is to reinforce the desired behavior twice. For example, assume a youngster is slow to stop talking, but the majority of other students are listening properly. Reinforce correctly behaving students. Often, the misbehaving student will emulate those being reinforced in order to receive similar positive feedback. If not, the use of negative consequences is warranted. When correcting behavior, consider the following points:

• Consequences should be clear and specific. Students should know exactly what will occur if they misbehave. Negative consequences have to be enforceable. This means that the teacher must be able to carry out such consequences. For example, keeping a bus student after school may not be possible. "Kicking" a student out of class may not be possible (or desirable). Be sure the negative consequence can be used in the school setting and is approved by the appropriate administrator.

• Apply the correction as near to the misbehavior as possible. Just as positive reinforcement should be delivered immediately following the desired behavior, so should negative consequences.

• Negative consequences can be anything the student does not want or need as long as there is no violation of the rights or dignity of the student. Just as teachers need to know what reinforces students, they need to know what is a negative experience for students who misbehave.

• Remind yourself behavior correction is used to teach youngsters how to behave properly rather than to punish them. There should be no punitive measures involved. Focus on natural consequences that occur when students behave improperly.

Behavior correction techniques include reprimands, removal of positive consequences, behavior contracts, behavior games, and time out.

Reprimands

A common approach is used to decrease undesirable behavior. If done in a caring and constructive manner, reprimands serve as effective reminders to behave.

• Identify unacceptable behavior, state briefly why it is unacceptable, and communicate to students what behavior is desired. For example, "You were talking while I was speaking. It bothers other students, so please listen to me."

• Don't do it in front of other students. Not only does it embarrass students, it can diminish their self-esteem. When students feel belittled, they may lash out and react in a manner more severe than the original behavior.

• Reprimands should speak about behavior, not the person. Ask that the behavior stop rather than tell the student, "You are always causing problems in this class." General statements related to the personality of the student should be avoided.

• After reprimanding and asking for acceptable behavior, reinforce it when it occurs. Be vigilant in looking for the desired behavior since reinforcing such behavior will cause it to occur more often in the future.

Removal of Positive Consequences

This is a common approach used by parents, so students are familiar with it. The basic approach is to remove something positive from the student when misbehavior occurs. For example, students give up

some of their free time due to misbehavior. They lose points related to a grade. They are not allowed to participate in an activity that is exciting to them. For removal of positive consequences to be effective, teachers must be sure that the students really want to participate in the removal activity. It wouldn't work to keep a student out of a game if the student didn't like the game. A few key principles should be followed when using this technique:

• Be sure the magnitude of the removal fits the crime. In other words, students who commit a minor infraction shouldn't have to go to the office.

• Be consistent with all students and with the same student. Students think teachers are unfair if they are more severe with one student than another. In addition, a student penalized for a specific misbehavior should receive the same penalty for a later repetition.

• Explain to students the consequences of their misbehavior before misbehavior occurs. This prevents applying penalties in an emotional, unthinking manner. If students know what the consequences are, they are choosing to accept the consequences when they misbehave.

• At times, it is helpful to chart a student's misbehavior to see if the frequency is decreasing. If the behavior does not decrease or increases, change methods until a decrease in frequency occurs.

Time-Out

In "time-out," students are removed from a positive or enjoyable situation (Martin and Pear, 1983). It is similar to the penalty box in an ice hockey game. If a student is behaving inappropriately, he or she is asked privately to go to the time-out area. The area should be far enough away from the class to avoid the ridicule of peers, but close enough to be within the supervision of the teacher. The area can be specifically designated in the gymnasium, or it can be an area in an outside field such as under a tree, on a bench, or in a baseball dugout.

Being placed in time-out should communicate to students that they have disrupted the class and must be removed so that the rest of the class can participate as desired. Students can also use the time-out area as a "cooling-off" spot that they can move to voluntarily if they are angry, embarrassed, or frustrated. If students have been placed in the time-out area for fighting or arguing, they should be placed at opposite ends of the area so the behavior does not escalate. In addition, it can be mandated that they stay in their own half of the gymnasium until the next meeting of the class. This prevents the possibility of continued animosity.

Time-out does not stifle misbehavior if the student receives reinforcement. Time-out means receiving *No* reinforcement. If class is a negative experience for a student, taking them out of class is not a punishment and may be a reward. The class must be an enjoyable experience and be reinforcing to students. Too often, sitting a student out results in an experience that is reinforcing. For example, the student who is sent to the office gets to avoid activity while visiting with friends who come into the office. Notoriety can be achieved among peers for surviving the office experience and being able to tell others, "It doesn't matter one bit what that teacher does to me." Sitting on the side of the gymnasium and watching peers participate may be more reinforcing than participating in class activities. Time-out is effective only when class participation is an enjoyable experience. A possible set of consequences for unacceptable behavior might be as follows:

First misbehavior: To avoid embarrassment, the student is warned quietly on a personal basis. This could be a peer or teacher warning. At times, students are not aware that they are bothering others, and a gentle reminder by a peer or teacher will refocus the youngster.

Second misbehavior: The student is quietly asked to go to the time-out area for a predetermined time. The duration of the stay is usually 5 to 10 minutes.

Third misbehavior: The student goes to time-out for the remainder of the period and loses free-time privileges. This can be enforced by serving time in detention. Detention is served during the student's free time in a study hall atmosphere supervised by teachers on a rotating basis.

If these consequences are ineffective, the last alternative is to call the parents for a conference with the principal and teacher. Participating in educational endeavors is a privilege, and people who choose to disrupt society ultimately lose their privileges (for example, incarceration in reform school, prison, and so on).

Behavior Contracts

A behavior contract is a written statement specifying certain student behaviors that must occur in order to earn certain rewards or privileges. The contract is usually signed by the student and the teacher involved and is drawn up after a private conference to decide on the appropriate behaviors and rewards. Letting the student make some decisions dealing with the contract is often useful.

The behavior contract may be a successful strategy for students with severe behavior problems. Make every attempt to use rewards that occur naturally in physical education class (such as Frisbee play, jump rope games, aerobics, basketball). In some cases, however, different types of rewards may have to be used. For example, a student who is interested only in rock music and motorcycles could be allowed to spend some time reading, writing about, or discussing one of these topics. As behavior improves and the student's attitude becomes more positive, the rewards should be switched to physical education activities. The contract is gradually phased out over a period of time as students gain control of their behavior and can participate in normal class environments.

Contracts can be written for a small group of students or for an entire class with similar problems, but teachers must be careful about setting up a reward system for too many students. The system can become too complex or time consuming to supervise properly. The contract is best used with a limited number of students in several problem situations. An example of a behavior contract that can be used with an individual, a small group, or an entire class of students is shown in Figure 7.3.

Behavior Games

Behavior games are an effective strategy for quickly changing student behaviors in the areas of management, motivation, or discipline. If a teacher is having severe disruptive problems in any of these areas, a well-conceived behavior game may quickly turn the situation around. These games can be packaged for a group of students to compete against each other or against an established criterion level. The goal of the game is to use group contingencies to develop behaviors that enhance the learning environment and eliminate behaviors that detract from it.

Various forms of behavior games have been used successfully by physical educators and athletic

---

Behavior Contract

		Points
I.	Class Preparation	
	A. Attendance	1
	B. On time	1
	C. Properly dressed	1
II.	Social Behavior	
	A. Showering	1
	B. Lack of inappropriate behaviors	5
	Cursing	
	Fighting	9 points per day
	Disruption	(36 points per week)

During Friday's class, points may be exchanged for time in aerobics, weight training, Frisbee, or basketball.

I agree to these conditions.

_____

Student

_____

Teacher

FIGURE 7.3   Group behavior contract

---

coaches (Darst and Whitehead, 1975; McKenzie and Rushall, 1973; Paese, 1982). Behavior games are effective with certain types of inappropriate behaviors: nonattendance, tardiness, nondressing, cursing, talking out, low practice rates, and high rates of management time. The following is an example of a behavior game that was used successfully with 7th graders in an effort to improve management behaviors:

1. The class is divided into 4 squads. Each squad has a designated color for identification. Four boundary cones with appropriate colors are set up as a starting area.
2. The rules of the game are as follows:
   a. Each squad member has to be dressed and in the proper place at a designated starting time. Reward: 2 points.
   b. Each squad member has to move from one activity to another activity within the specified time (10, 20, or 30 seconds) and begin the appropriate behavior. Reward: 1 point for each instance.
   c. Each point earned is rewarded with 1 minute of free activity time on Friday. Free activity time includes basketball, Frisbee, jump ropes, flag football, or any other activity popular with students.

   d. The squad with the most points for the week earns a bonus of 5 points.
3. The teacher explains the allotted time for each management episode (10, 20, or 30 seconds) and gives a "go" signal. At the end of the allowed time, the teacher gives a "stop" signal and awards points for appropriate behavior.
4. Squads that are successful are praised by the teacher, and the points are recorded on a small card. The unsuccessful squads are not hassled or criticized, just reminded that they did not earn a point.
5. On Fridays, the appropriate squads are awarded the special free-time activities, while the others continue work on the regularly scheduled class activities.
6. The game is slowly phased out as students begin to manage themselves better.

The results of the game were as follows:

1. The use of group contingencies and free-time activities reduced the overall class management time.
2. The free-time activities were within the physical education curriculum objectives and created a break from regular activities.

3. The free-time activities gave the teacher an opportunity to interact with students on a personal level.
4. The students enjoyed the competition and the success they experienced when they performed appropriate behaviors.
5. Students enjoyed the free time with novelty activities.
6. The positive approach of the game seemed to improve the overall teaching-learning atmosphere. The students were more attentive and cooperative.
7. The teachers felt that more time was available for instruction because of the reduction in management time.

Behavior games should enable all students or squads to "win." Games do not have to have a winner and a loser. Sometimes 1 or 2 students may find it reinforcing to cause their team to lose the behavior game. They will try to break every rule to force their team to lose consistently. In these cases, a special team discussion may be held with the opportunity to vote to eliminate those students from the team and the game. The disruptive students can be sent to a time-out area or channeled into some special, alternative activity. They can be asked to sit out an entire day's activities.

A variation of the behavior game can be used to help students persist at learning activities in a station-type approach. Assume there are 4 or 5 learning stations for activities such as basketball, volleyball, soccer, or football. Performance objectives or learning tasks are posted at each station with skills for students to practice. Some of the students, however, are not motivated and do not use their time productively until the teacher rotates to their station. The teacher then prods the group, hassles a few students, and praises a few others. The overall environment is not productive, and the teacher is tired of hassling unmotivated students. A possible solution is the following game:

1. Divide the class into 4 or 5 squads. Let the students pick a name for their squad.
2. Set up learning stations with the activities to be practiced. An equal number of squads and learning stations is necessary.
3. Program a cassette tape with popular music. The tape should have short gaps of silence for the duration.
4. Inform students that if everyone in their squad is properly engaged in practicing the appropriate tasks, a point will be awarded to their squad at each gap in the music. If 1 or more persons is not engaged, no point will be awarded.
5. Points earned can be exchanged for minutes of free time for reinforcing motor activities such as Frisbee or jump rope. Fridays could be designated as reward time.
6. Music should be changed regularly. Time intervals between gaps are gradually lengthened until the gaps are eliminated. The music then serves as a discriminative cue for future practice time.

Students enjoy exercising and practicing skills while listening to music. The music seems to increase motivation. Students can bring in their own music as a special reward for productive behavior. The music should be screened to assure it is not offensive to others because of sexual, ethnic, or religious connotations.

Another use of behavior games is to offer challenge or change of pace to an activity. The teacher may not have serious behavior problems in class but simply wants to add an enjoyable learning activity. An example of this is the "burnout" game. It can be used in the following manner:

1. Fridays can be designated as "burnout" days. The last 5 to 10 minutes of the period can be used for the game.
2. To qualify for the "burnout" award, a student must have attended, been on time, dressed properly, and worked diligently all week.
3. On a rainy or nonparticipation day, each student submits a piece of paper with a written explanation of a "burnout" challenge activity that she or he would enjoy. Examples might include a storkstand on one foot, one-arm push-ups, pull-ups, hanging on a rope for time, doing a headstand, or juggling without dropping an object. Students should be encouraged to select activities in which they excel. These challenge suggestions can be kept in a jar or hat for future choices.
4. A "burnout" award is made up and hung on a locker, posted on a bulletin board, announced over the morning news, or put in any similar, visible medium. A photograph of the "burnout" winner might be posted each week in the hall of fame.
5. On Friday, the teacher and the entire class try the burnout challenge to determine a winner. The winner might also receive several privileges like selecting the next activity from the jar or hat. The activity could be selected on Monday so students can practice during the week.

Develop a Plan for Dealing with Severe Misbehavior

At times, corrective behavior techniques don't work. Many strategies may have been tried with a student with little success. At this time, teachers must go beyond their own resources. A note of caution: all the previous techniques have assumed that a teacher is working individually to solve the problem. This is the first and best approach. It is easier to send the student to the office and ask someone else to solve the problem. Unfortunately, this does not solve the problem between the student and the teacher. Also, administrators may feel that the teacher is incapable of dealing effectively with students. The steps listed here assume that all other avenues have been tried and have failed.

Most secondary schools have some type of disciplinary referral form for severe problems. The form is used to keep an accurate record of behavioral problems and is a part of the communication process between students, teachers, parents, administrators, and counselors. The referral form is an effective tool for documenting student behavior. A disadvantage is that the approach is time consuming, and some teachers are unwilling to use it. However, there are few shortcuts to a well-disciplined class. The following is a 4-step approach for dealing with behavior that is difficult and continuous.

Step 1. An informal, private conference between the teacher and student focusing on the behavioral aberration. An agreement should be reached regarding the consequences of future behavior.

Step 2. A telephone call to the parents to discuss the problem and possible solutions.

Step 3. A conference with the teacher, parent, student, and principal or counselor to discuss the problem and develop a plan for changing the behavior. A written copy of the plan should be distributed to all people involved.

Step 4. Severe disciplinary actions
a. *Loss of privileges:* Privilege losses could include access to the library, cafeteria, clubs, athletics, or dances. Parents are notified in writing about the procedures used.
b. *In-school suspension:* Students are sent to a designated area with a supervisor who enforces strict rules and guidelines for school work.

c. *Short- and long-term suspensions from school:* The student is suspended from school for 3 to 10 days, depending on the severity of the behavior and the student's history. Strict policies and procedures are arranged and followed carefully to assure due process. Parents must be notified in writing as to the steps that have been followed.
d. *Expulsion:* The final step used in extremely severe instances is expulsion. The principal initiates the action with a letter to the student and parents. An official action from the board of education may be required to expel a student. Due process and appeal procedures must be used and made available to the student.

USE OF PUNISHMENT AND CRITICISM

Criticism is used by teachers with the belief that it will improve the performance of students. Teachers find criticism and sarcasm to be their behavior control tools of choice because they give the impression results are effective and quick acting. Usually, the misbehavior is stopped immediately and the teacher assumes that the situation has been rectified. Unfortunately, this is not always the case, as will be described later. Criticism and punishment lend a negative air to the instructional environment, and that has a negative impact on both student and teacher. In most cases the person who is most affected by criticism or punishment is the teacher. The old saying, "It hurts me more than you," is often the case. The majority of teachers feel badly when they have to criticize or punish students. It makes them feel as though they cannot handle students and that the class is incorrigible. This feeling of incompetence can lead to a negative cycle in which the students feel negative about the instructor and the instructor negative about the class. The net result is that both parties finish the lesson feeling incompetent. In the long run, this may be one of the most debilitating effects of criticism and punishment.

As mentioned, another problem with criticism is that it does not offer a sure solution. In a study by Thomas, Becker, and Armstrong (1968), a teacher was asked to stop praising a class. Off-task behavior increased from 8.7% to nearly 26%. When the teacher was asked to increase criticism from 5 times in 20 minutes to 16 times in 20 minutes, more off-task behavior was demonstrated. On some days the percentage of off-task behavior increased to more than 50%. The point is that when attention is given to off-task behavior and no praise is offered for on-task accomplishment, the amount of off-task behavior increases dramatically. What happens is that the teacher who primarily criticizes is reinforced by the students (they respond to the request of the criticism), but they do not change. In fact, the students are reinforced (they receive attention from the teacher) for their off-task behavior. In addition, since their on-task behavior is not praised, it decreases. The net result is exactly the opposite of what was desired.

Punishment is another matter. It is a difficult decision to decide when to use punishment. Contrary to what many teachers think, punishment does work and is effective at stopping undesirable behavior. In fact, just as reinforcement increases the occurrence of behavior, punishment will decrease undesirable behavior. The principles of reinforcement can be transferred to the use of punishment. The question is whether or not punishment should be used in an educational setting. A consideration should be made about the long-term effects of the punishment. If the long-term effects of using punishment are more beneficial than not using it, it would be unethical not to use punishment. In other words, if the student is going to be in a worse situation from not being punished, it would be wrong not to use it. It may be necessary to punish a student for protection from self-inflicted harm (such as using certain apparatus without supervision). It may be necessary to punish students so that they learn not to hurt others. Punishment in these situations may cause discomfort to teacher and student in the short run but may allow the student to participate successfully in society later.

Most situations in the educational setting do not require punishment since they are not as severe as those described above. A major reason for avoiding punishment is that it can have undesirable side effects. When students are punished, they learn to avoid the source of punishment. It forces them to be more covert in their actions. They spend time finding ways to be devious without being caught. Instead of encouraging students to discuss problems with teachers and parents, punishment teaches them to avoid these individuals for fear of being punished. Punishment also teaches students how to be aggressive toward others. Students who have been physically or emotionally punished by parents act in a similar fashion with others. The result is a student who is secretive and aggressive with others, certainly a less than desirable trait. Finally, if punishment is used to stop certain behavior, as soon as the punishment stops the behavior will return. Little has been learned; the punishment has just caused short-term change. If it becomes necessary to use punishment, consider the following.

1. *Be consistent and make the "punishment fit the crime."* Students will quickly lose their respect for a teacher who treats others with favoritism. They will view the teacher as unfair if the punishment is extreme. In addition, peers will quickly side with the student who is treated unfairly causing a class morale problem for the instructor.

2. *Offer a warning signal.* This may prevent excessive use of punishment since students will often behave after receiving a warning. In addition, they will probably view the teacher as caring and fair.

3. *Do not threaten students.* Offer only one warning. Threats have little impact on students and cause them to feel that the teacher cannot handle the class. One warning gives students the feeling that you are not looking to punish them and are fair in your dealings. Follow through; do not challenge or threaten students and then ignore the same or similar behavior.

4. *Punishment should immediately follow the misbehavior.* It is much less effective and more often viewed as unfair when punishment is delayed.

5. *Punish softly and calmly.* Do not seek revenge or be vindictive. If responsible behavior is expected from students, teachers must reprimand and punish in a responsible manner. Studies (O'Leary and Becker, 1968) have demonstrated that soft reprimands are more effective than loud ones.

Try to avoid having negative feelings about the student and internalizing the student's misbehavior. Sometimes teachers become punitive in handling deviant behavior, which destroys any chance for a worthwhile relationship. Misbehavior should be handled in a manner that contributes to the development of a responsible, confident student who understands that all individuals who function effectively in society must adjust to certain limits. Try to forget about past bouts of deviant behavior and to approach the student in a positive fashion at the start of each class. If this is not done, the student soon becomes labeled, making behavioral change difficult to accomplish and causing the student to live up to the teacher's negative expectations.

Assure that only those students who misbehave are punished. Punishing an entire class for the deviant behavior of a few youngsters is not only unfair but may trigger undesirable side effects. Students become hostile toward those who caused the loss of privileges, and this peer hostility lowers the level of positive social interaction. If the group as a whole is misbehaving, punishing the entire group is appropriate.

EXPULSION: LEGAL CONSIDERATIONS

If serious problems occur, expulsion may be necessary. Many times, deviant behavior is part of a larger, more severe problem that is troubling a student. A cooperative approach may provide an effective solution. A group meeting involving parents, principal, counselor, and physical education specialist can open avenues that encourage understanding and increase productive behavior.

Legal concerns involving the student's rights in disciplinary areas are an essential consideration. While minor infractions may be handled routinely, expulsion and other substantial punishments can be imposed on students only after due process. The issue of student rights is complicated, and most school systems have established guidelines and procedures for dealing with students who have been removed from the class or school setting. Youngsters should be removed from class only if they are disruptive to the point of interfering with the learning experiences of other students and all other means of altering behavior have failed. Sending a student out of class is a last resort and means that both teacher and student have failed.

EXPECTED OUTCOMES

After reading this chapter, you should be able to

- Describe the role of the physical education teacher as it pertains to managing students in a physical activity setting.
- Understand the skills of effective class management.

- Identify techniques used to start and stop a class, organize the class into groups and formations, employ squads, and prepare students for activity.
- Cite acceptable and recommended procedures for dealing with inappropriate behavior.
- Describe techniques to increase or decrease specific behaviors.
- Explain the role of a teacher's reaction in shaping and controlling student behavior.
- Design or modify activities that are effective in changing the behavior of students.
- Understand the legal ramifications associated with expelling a student from school.

REFERENCES AND SUGGESTED READINGS

AAHPERD. 1976. *Personalized Learning in Physical Education.* Reston, VA: AAHPERD.

Boehm, J. 1974. The effects of competency-based teaching programs on junior high school physical education student teachers and their pupils. Doctoral dissertation, Ohio State University.

Canter, L., and Canter, M. 1976. *Assertive Discipline.* Santa Monica, CA: Canter and Associates.

Charles, C. M. 1981. *Building Classroom Discipline.* New York: Longman.

Cruickshank, D. R. 1980. *Teaching Is Tough.* Englewood Cliffs, NJ: Prentice-Hall.

Curwin, R. L., and Mendler, A. N. 1988. *Discipline with Dignity.* Washington, D.C.: Association for Supervision and Curriculum Development.

Darst, P. 1976. The effects of a competency-based intervention on student teaching and pupil behavior. *Research Quarterly* 47(3): 336–345.

Darst, P., and Pangrazi, R. 1981. Analysis of starting and stopping management activity for elementary physical education teachers. *Arizona JOHPERD* 25(1): 14–17.

Darst, P. W., and Whitehead, S. 1975. Developing a contingency management system for controlling student behavior. *Pennsylvania JOPER* 46(3): 11–12.

Glasser, W. 1986. *Control Theory in the Classroom.* New York: Harper & Row.

Greene, D., and Lepper, M. R. 1975. Turning play into work: Effects of adult surveillance and extrinsic rewards on children's internal motivation. *Journal of Personality and Social Psychology* 31: 479–486.

Hamilton, K. 1974. The application of a competency-based model to physical education student teaching in high school. Doctoral dissertation, Ohio State University.

Martin, G., and Pear, J. 1983. *Behavior Modification—What It Is and How to Do It.* Englewood Cliffs, NJ: Prentice-Hall.

McKenzie, T., and Rushall, B. 1973. Effects of various reinforcing contingencies on improving performance in a competitive swimming environment. Unpublished paper, Dalhousie University.

Nelson, J. 1987. *Positive Discipline.* New York: Ballantine.

O'Leary, K. D., and Becker, W. C. 1968. The effects of intensity of a teacher's reprimands on children's behavior. *Journal of School Psychology* 7: 8–11.

Paese, P. 1982. Effects of interdependent group contingencies in a secondary physical education setting. *Journal of Teaching in Physical Education* 2(1): 29–37.

Premack, D. 1965. Reinforcement theory. In D. Levine (ed.). *Nebraska Symposium on Motivation.* Lincoln, NE: University of Nebraska Press.

Siedentop, D. 1991. *Developing Teaching Skills in Physical Education.* 3rd ed. Palo Alto, CA: Mayfield Publishing Co.

Siedentop, D., Rife, F., and Boehm, J. 1974. Modifying the managerial effectiveness of student teachers in physical education. Unpublished paper, Ohio State University.

Thomas, D. R., Becker, W. C., and Armstrong, B. 1968. Production and elimination of disruptive classroom behavior by systematically varying teacher's behavior. *Journal of Applied Behavior Analysis* 1: 35–45.

Whitehead, J. R., and Corbin, C. B. 1991. Effects of fitness test type, teacher, and gender on exercise intrinsic motivation and physical self-worth. *Journal of School Health* 61: 11–16.

Wolfgang, C. H., and Glickman, C. D. 1980. *Solving Discipline Problems.* Boston: Allyn & Bacon.

8

Teaching Styles

PURPOSE

To establish that a variety of instructional styles exist and that secondary school physical education teachers will be able to use a variety of these styles. There is no one best style for all situations. Each style has advantages that can be more effective depending on the type of students, specific activities, desired objectives, and various conditions.

KEY CONCEPTS

- An instructional style is a scheme for organizing all aspects and elements in the educational environment.
- Secondary school physical education teachers should develop a repertoire of instructional styles that can be used with many different situations.
- There is mounting evidence from teacher effectiveness research indicating that many teaching styles can be effective if certain characteristics are present in the teaching situation.
- Direct instruction is probably the most common approach to teaching in the secondary schools. It can be an effective style depending on how it is implemented.
- The task style of instruction involves selecting and arranging tasks for students to practice in specific learning areas called stations. The students usually rotate through each learning area and work on the tasks.
- Mastery learning style takes terminal target skills and divides them into progressive subskills.
- Individualized styles of teaching use learning packets, resource centers, and self-paced learning.
- Cooperative learning places students in groups with common goals. Students are interdependent in order to achieve group goals.
- The inquiry style of instruction focuses on the process of instruction rather than the product of instruction. Students are placed in situations where they have to inquire, speculate, reflect, analyze, and discover.
- Guided discovery is an inquiry style of instruction where the teacher leads students to discover one planned solution to a given problem.
- Problem solving is another inquiry style where students are led to the discovery of multiple correct answers to a problem.

Different teaching styles have been used successfully in various secondary school physical education classes (Mosston and Ashworth, 1994; Zakrajsek, Carnes, and Pettigrew, 1994; Rink, 1993; Harrison, Blakemore, Buck, and Pellet 1996; Siedentop, 1991). Professionals present, label, and categorize styles in many ways. Many of the labels overlap and can be confusing to the beginning teacher. A teaching style is an overall scheme for organizing the educational environment. The style of teaching provides direction for presenting information, organizing practice, providing feedback, keeping students engaged in appropriate behavior, and monitoring progress toward goals or objectives. Teaching styles are defined in terms of the teacher's planning and setup of the environment, the teacher's approach during the lesson, the student's responsibilities during the lesson, and expected student outcomes.

There is no single "best" or universal teaching style. Even though educators endorse their favorite approach, evidence does not suggest that one style is more effective than another. There is no one best way of doing anything in education. A repertoire of styles that can be used with different objectives, students, activities, facilities, and equipment is the mark of a master teacher. Many variables have to be considered before an appropriate style can be selected. These variables include:

1. The objectives of the lesson such as physical skills, physical fitness, knowledge, and social behaviors.
2. The nature of the activities involved such as tennis, volleyball, swimming, or fencing.
3. The nature of students, including individual characteristics, interests, developmental level, socioeconomic status, motivation, and background.
4. The total number of students in the class.
5. The equipment and facilities available, such as tennis racquets and courts.
6. The abilities, skills, and comfort zone of the teacher.

A conscious effort to maintain professional interest and enthusiasm will maintain instructional effectiveness. Too often, a favorite teaching style can become the norm. Perhaps the use of a different teaching style in an appropriate setting would improve the environment for students and teachers. A new or modified teaching style is not a panacea for all the ills of every school environment or setting, and a teaching style is not selected without considering all variables. Different styles do, however, offer advantages in certain situations. A teacher who has developed a quality instructional program can keep the program exciting by implementing various teaching styles. Teachers can use combinations of styles in a lesson or unit plan; they do not have to adopt just one style at a time. Mosston's continuum of styles (Mosston and Ashworth, 1994) move from a teacher-centered approach at one extreme to a student-centered approach at the other. A continuum of teaching styles based on the degree of teacher control exercised in a lesson is shown in Figure 8.1.

DIRECT STYLE

The direct teaching style has been disliked by some teachers because they identified it with Mosston and Ashworth's (1994) command style. The direct teaching style has more flexibility and variations than the command style. The direct style, like any other type of instruction, can be effective or ineffective depending on how it is used and administered. The direct style can be an effective strategy for teaching physical skills, especially when activities present an inherent hazard or danger with inexperienced students. Activities such as fencing, riflery, and rock climbing need to be tightly organized and supervised with a teacher-directed format. Students are given little freedom until they understand the hazards of activity and demonstrate responsibility. The direct style may also be necessary in situations where discipline is a problem because it allows a tighter rein on class management. Beginning teachers with new students, large classes, or high rates of inappropriate student behavior will probably do best with the direct style.

When using this teaching style, the teacher provides instruction to either the entire class or small groups in the class. The teacher is the central figure and guides the pace and direction of the class. Direct instruction is followed by guided practice so errors

Direct	Task (Station)	Mastery Learning (Outcomes)	Individualized	Cooperative (Reciprocal)	Inquiry (Guided Discovery and Problem Solving)

Teacher-Centered   Student-Centered

FIGURE 8.1 Continuum of teaching styles

can be corrected. Guided practice is then followed by independent practice that is supervised by an actively involved teacher. Students spend most of class time engaged in appropriate subject matter. Goals are clearly presented to students, and much time is devoted to practice. Students practice while the teacher actively supervises and provides frequent feedback. A positive, supportive atmosphere is set for students.

A common model of direct teaching begins with the teacher explaining and demonstrating skills to be developed. Students are organized into partners, small groups, or squads for practice. As students practice, the teacher moves around the area correcting errors, praising, scolding, encouraging, and asking questions. On a signal to stop, students gather around the teacher for evaluative comments and a refocus toward another skill. The teacher serves as the major demonstrator, lecturer, motivator, organizer, disciplinarian, director, and error corrector.

The direct teaching style emphasizes instruction in a controlled class environment that is safe for students. Emphasis is placed on minimizing time passively watching, listening to a lecture-demonstration, or waiting in line. When using this style, it is important to offer activities that meet the needs of all students. Higher skilled and lower skilled students are hindered when learning activities are too easy and unchallenging, or too difficult and cause repeated failure. Enough options must be offered for the various ability levels.

TASK (STATION) STYLE

The task style of teaching focuses on arranging and presenting learning tasks at several **learning areas** or **stations**. Students rotate between learning stations and work on assigned tasks. At each station, students have a number of tasks to practice. They start and stop working on the tasks without specific teacher directions. For example, students may be given 5 minutes to work at stations that have 4 or 5 tasks. A cue or signal to rotate to a new station is given after the time has elapsed. There is more freedom with this style as compared to the direct approach because students work individually on the tasks.

Some teachers are not comfortable with the task style because there is less order and control compared to direct instruction. With proper planning, organization, and supervision, however, teachers can

effectively order and manage the environment. The task style is motivating to students because of the variety and levels of learning tasks. Students often need time to adjust to the increased freedom, flexibility, and opportunities to make decisions, but the end result is better self-management skills.

This instructional style allows teachers to move off center stage and away from being the central figure in the instructional process. Teachers become agents of feedback by visiting various learning stations and interacting with students who need help on tasks. Less time is spent directing and managing the entire group. This approach requires more preparation time for planning and designing tasks. Adequate facilities, equipment, and instructional devices are necessary to keep students productive and working on appropriate tasks. The following guidelines should be considered when selecting, writing, and presenting tasks for secondary school physical education classes:

1. Select tasks that cover all the basic skills of an activity.

2. Select tasks that provide students with success and challenge. The tasks should be within the appropriate ability range of the students. The highest skilled student should be challenged, and the lowest skilled student should be successful.

3. Avoid tasks that demand excessive risk and could cause injury.

4. Tape task cards on the wall, strap them to boundary cones, or place them on the floor if students can avoid stepping on them. Another alternative is to give students a copy of the tasks on a sheet of paper that they carry station to station. The task sheets can be maintained by students and taken home for practice after school.

5. Write the tasks so they are easy to comprehend. Use key words or phrases that students have learned previously. Effective task descriptions explain what to do and how to do it (see the examples in Figure 8.2). Check to see if students understand the tasks and are able to practice when unsupervised.

6. Incorporate a combination of instructional devices that add feedback, variety, and a challenge to the environment. Examples of such devices include targets, cones, hoops, ropes, and stopwatches.

The task style of instruction can be used with a variety of grouping patterns. Students can work

---

Basketball Tasks

Dribbling Tasks   *(What to do)*

1. Standing—right and left hand—25 times
2. Half speed—right and left hand—baseline to midcourt
3. Full speed—right and left hand—baseline to midcourt
4. Around the cones—25 sec

Ball Handling   *(What to do)*

1. Around head—left and right—5 times each
2. Around waist—left and right—5 times each
3. Around each leg—left and right—5 times each
4. Figure 8 around legs—10 times
5. Hand switch between legs—10 times
6. Bounce between legs and switch—10 times

Jump Shots   *(What to do)*

1. 3 ft away—right angle, center, left angle
2. 9 ft away—right angle, center, left angle
3. 15 ft away—right angle, center, left angle
4. 20 ft away—right angle, center, left angle

Passing Skills   *(What to do)*

Strike the target from 8 ft, 10 ft, 12 ft, 15 ft
1. Chest—10 times
2. Bounce—10 times
3. Overhead—10 times
4. One hand overhead (baseball)—10 times

Dribbling Cues   *(How to do)*

1. Fingertips
2. Lower center of gravity
3. Opposite hand in front
4. Eyes on opponents

Jump Shot Cues   *(How to do)*

1. Straight-up jump
2. Wrist position
3. Elbow position
4. Slight backspin on ball
5. Follow-through

Passing Cues   *(How to do)*

1. Use your peripheral vision—do not telegraph.
2. Step toward target.
3. Transfer your weight to the front foot.
4. Aim for the numbers.

FIGURE 8.2   Basketball tasks

---

alone, with a partner, or in a small group. The partner or reciprocal grouping pattern is useful with large classes, limited amounts of equipment, and with skills where a partner can time, count, record, or analyze the skill work. For example, 1 student can dribble through a set of cones while the other is timing and recording. In a group of 3 students, 1 student bumps a volleyball against the wall, another analyzes the form with a checklist, and the third counts and records. The social aspect of being able to work on tasks with a partner or friend is a form of cooperative learning discussed later. Arrange tasks so all students find success and challenge by offering a progressive arrangement of experiences from simple to complex

with small steps along the way. Allow students to progress at their own speed through the activities. As they build a backlog of success, learning activities become more challenging.

An effective instructional approach for soccer using learning stations could be organized as follows: The soccer field practice area is arranged with 4 learning stations and performance objectives written on a card at each station. Students spend 3 to 5 minutes working on the objectives at each station and rotate to the next station. Objectives are arranged so students can experience success quickly and frequently at first and then are challenged by later objectives. Objectives can be changed daily or repeated depending on the progression of the class. Points earned through completion of the objectives can be used to signal competency in the area

Breakdown - Simple → Complex

MASTERY LEARNING (OUTCOMES-BASED) STYLE

Mastery learning is an instructional strategy that takes terminal target skills and divides them into progressive subskills. Each of the subskills becomes the focus of learning. The subskills are usually written as objectives that must be mastered to achieve the target outcome. The continuum of subskills must be mastered at a high level (usually 80 to 90 percent correct) before students attempt more complicated tasks. The number of subskills depends on the complexity of the skill. If mastery is not achieved, corrective activities are offered so that the student has the opportunity to learn from alternative materials, peer tutoring, or any type of learning activity that meets personal preferences. For an in-depth discussion of mastery learning, see Guskey (1985).

Mastery learning as a strategy is useful in a number of ways. First, students can move at an individualized pace and master preliminaries needed for the target skill. The style is well suited for students who are low-skilled or have disabilities. It also provides homework when necessary, enabling youngsters to work during their spare time on areas needing improvement. The process of the style can be outlined as follows:

1. The target skill or movement competency is divided into sequenced, progressive units.
2. Prerequisite competency is evaluated.
3. Performance objectives for each of the successive learning units is established.
4. Informal progress testing can be done by the performer to determine readiness for more formal testing by the teacher or a peer.
5. When a student is ready, testing by the teacher determines pass or fail for a particular subskill. A youngster who passes moves to the next learning unit.
6. Should the student fail, practice continues, incorporating any alternatives or corrective measures provided.

A mastery learning breakdown for soccer skills is outlined here. The target outcome is soccer profi-

ciency and the ability to play soccer. Accomplishing the following outcomes would assure that students have a basic level of competency in dribbling, trapping, kicking, heading, and throw-ins.

Dribbling Tasks

1. Dribble the soccer ball a distance of 20 yards 3 consecutive times, making each kick no more than 5 yards.
2. Dribble the soccer ball through an obstacle course of 6 pylons over a distance of 30 yards in 25 seconds or less.
3. With a partner, pass the soccer ball back and forth 5 times while in a running motion for a distance of 50 yards 2 consecutive times.

Trapping Tasks

4. When the ball is rolled to you by a partner 10 yards away, trap it 4 of 5 times, using the instep method with the right and then the left foot.
5. Same as Task 4 using the sole of the foot.
6. With a partner tossing the ball, trap 4 of 5 shots using the chest method.

Kicking Tasks

7. Kick the ball to a partner, who is standing 10 yards away, 5 consecutive times with the right and left inside of the foot push pass.
8. Same as Task 7 using the instep kick. Loft the ball to your partner.
9. Kick 4 of 5 shots that enter the goal in the air from a distance of 20 yards.

Heading and Throw-In Tasks

10. Head 3 consecutive balls in the air at a height of at least 10 feet.
11. Head 6 consecutive balls back and forth with a partner.
12. Make 4 of 5 throw-ins from out of bounds into a hula hoop placed 15 yards away.

Designing Mastery Learning Units of Instruction

Another way to use mastery learning is to develop units of instruction. Such instructional units have been used successfully in secondary schools with many activities, including badminton, volleyball, soccer, tennis, racquetball, skin diving, and gymnastics. Middle and high school students are gradually given opportunities to make decisions and control their practice behaviors. This type of instruction is ef-

- What if students can't master skill in first step? - Change skill

fective with physical activities that require the development of individual skills (for example, bumps, sets, forehands, backhands).

The following steps for developing instructional units for mastery learning define the process:

1. Define the specific tasks or behaviors in observable, measurable terms (such as volleyball bumps, badminton clears, tennis serves, and soccer kicks) rather than vague, hypothetical terms (such as positive attitudes, physical fitness, or self-concept).

2. Specify clearly the final performance for the end of the unit. Knowing the specific final goal will increase student motivation. Final goals, such as bump 10 consecutive shots, serve 3 of 4 into a target area, or successfully kick 3 of 4 goals, can serve as personal challenges for students.

3. Develop a monitoring and measuring system. This enables students to see daily improvement and set goals that progress toward the final, terminal objective. In addition to teacher assessment, peer assessment and self-assessment should be encouraged.

4. Develop meaningful outcomes that consider the many parameters of successful performance. These include speed, strength, endurance, accuracy, and consistency. For example, volleyball serves require a combination of speed and accuracy. An objective should include both parameters. Students could hit serves between the net and a rope strung 10 feet higher than the net. The serves must land inbounds and 10 feet or less from the backline. This ensures both speed and accuracy. Many other physical skills, such as dribbling in soccer, pitching in baseball, or dribbling in basketball, require similar combinations.

5. Arrange performances in a progressive sequence so students can experience success quickly and frequently. As students build a backlog of success, the tasks should become more difficult and challenging.

Figure 8.3 is a volleyball mastery learning unit that is appropriate for high school students. The core objectives are required, but students can choose from optional objectives. Figure 8.4 is a flag football unit that can be used with middle school students. It follows the same format as the volleyball unit with core and optional performance objectives.

In Chapters 19 through 22, a number of mastery learning units are provided. The units are general units, and objectives can be modified depending on the particular situation. They may be too difficult for certain students and too easy for others. It is important that all students find success and challenge with some of the objectives.

Performance objectives that are listed focus primarily on physical skills rather than on cognitive activities. Teachers may want a specific combination of cognitive and physical skills to be built into the unit. For example, the unit could provide a balance of objectives related to attendance, participation, physical skills, and cognitive activities. The mastery learning approach allows teachers to be flexible in the choice of objectives, and allows students the flexibility to select objectives and levels of performance.

Using Mastery Learning Units of Instruction

When using mastery learning units, it is requisite that students understand the objectives, learning activities, and importance of self-direction. Units are given to students so they can explain them to their parents, work on the objectives at home in their free time, or keep records of their performance at school. Students have to understand how involvement in this strategy is different from other strategies. Some students take longer to adapt and become comfortable with this instructional format. Explain and demonstrate the performance objectives to students in the learning areas where they will be practicing. Introduce various instructional devices and targets. Arrange the gymnasium or playing field with learning areas for specific objectives, such as the dribbling area, passing area, shooting area, or ball-handling area.

A rotational scheme utilizing small groups can be incorporated. Students can be placed in small groups at learning stations. After an adequate amount of time, they rotate to a new station. Another alternative is to allow students to rotate to any learning area they need to practice. A variety of grouping patterns (individually, with a partner, or with a small group) can be used depending on available facilities, equipment, objectives, and student choice. Consider the amount of freedom, flexibility, and choice students can handle and yet be productive. It is best to start with small amounts of freedom and gradually expand the options as students get used to the system.

Successful completion of objectives can be monitored by the teacher or peers. If class size is small and the number of objectives is small, the teacher may be able to do all of the monitoring. Otherwise, a combination of procedures is recommended. Student in-

---

Volleyball

Core Objectives

Forearm Pass (Bump)
1. Bump 12 consecutive forearm passes against the wall at a height of at least 10 ft.
2. Bump 12 consecutive forearm passes into the air at a height of at least 10 ft.
3. Bump 10 consecutive forearm passes over the net with the instructor or a classmate.

Overhead Set Pass
4. Hit 15 consecutive set passes against wall at a height of at least 10 ft.
5. Hit 15 consecutive set passes into the air at a height of at least 10 ft.
6. Hit 12 consecutive set passes over the net with the instructor or a classmate.

Serves
7. Hit 3 consecutive underhand serves into the right half of the court.
8. Hit 3 of 4 underhand serves into the left half of the court.
9. Hit 3 consecutive overhand serves inbounds.

Attendance and Participation
10. Be dressed and ready to participate at 8:00 A.M.
11. Participate in 15 games.
12. Score 90% or better on a rules, strategies, and techniques test (2 attempts only).

Optional Objectives

1. Standing 2 ft from the backline, bump 3 of 5 forearm passes into an 8-ft circle surrounding the setter's position. The height must be at least 10 ft, and the ball must be thrown by the instructor or a classmate.
2. Bump 3 of 5 forearm passes over the net at a height of at least 12 ft that land inbounds and not more than 8 ft from the backline.
3. Standing in the setter's position (CF), hit 3 consecutive overhead sets at least 10 ft high that land in a 5-ft circle where the spiker would be located. The ball will be thrown by the instructor or a classmate.
4. Hit 3 of 5 overhead passes over the net at least 12 ft high that land inbounds and not more than 8 ft from the backline.
5. Standing in the setter's position (CF), hit 3 of 5 back sets at least 10 ft high that land in a 5-ft circle where the spiker would be located. The ball will be thrown by the instructor or a classmate.
6. Volley 12 consecutive times over the net with the instructor or a classmate by alternating forearm passes and overhead passes.
7. Alternate forearm passes and overhead passes in the air at a height of 10 ft or more for 12 consecutive times.
8. Spike 3 of 4 sets inbounds from an on-hand position (3-step approach, jump, extended arm, hand contact).
9. Spike 3 of 5 sets inbounds from an off-hand position.
10. Recover 3 consecutive balls from the net. Recoveries must be playable (8 ft high in the playing area).
11. Hit 3 consecutive overhand serves into the right half of the court.
12. Hit 3 of 4 overhand serves into the left half of the court.
13. Hit 3 of 5 overhand serves under a rope 15 ft high that land in the back half of the court.
14. Officiate at least 3 games, using proper calls and signals.
15. Coach a team for the class tournament. Plan strategy, substitution, and scheduling.
16. Devise and carry out a research project that deals with volleyball. Check with the instructor for ideas.

FIGURE 8.3   Volleyball mastery learning example

volvement in the monitoring process enhances their understanding of the objectives and increases the level of responsibility. Monitors can use a performance chart to monitor objectives at each learning station or carry a master list from station to station. Another approach is to develop a performance sheet for each student that combines teacher and peer monitoring (Figure 8.5). Peers monitor some objec-

Flag Football

Core Objectives

Passing Tasks
1. Throw 10 passes to the chest area of a partner standing 10 yd away.
2. Throw 3 of 4 consecutive passes beyond a target distance of 20 yd.
3. Throwing 5 passes, knock over 3 targets from a distance of 10 yd.
4. Throw 4 of 6 passes through a tire from a distance of 10 yd.

Centering Tasks
5. With a partner 5 yd away, execute 10 over-the-head snaps to the chest area, using correct holding, proper rotation, and follow-through techniques.
6. Facing the opposite direction from a partner, 5 yd away, execute a proper center stance with feet well spread and toes pointed straight ahead, knees bent, and two hands on the ball. Snap the ball back through the legs for 10 consecutive times.
7. Same as task 6 but move back 10 yd.
8. Center snap 4 of 6 times through a tire a distance of 5 yd away.

Punting Tasks
9. With a partner centering the ball, from a distance of 10 yd away punt the football using proper technique to another set of partners 15 yd away 3 consecutive times.
10. Same as task 9 but at a distance of 20 yd.
11. Punt the ball 3 consecutive times within the boundary lines of the field and beyond a distance of 20 yd.
12. Punt the ball 3 consecutive times for a hang time of 2.5 sec or better (use stopwatch).

Catching Tasks
13. With a partner run a "quick" pass pattern and catch the ball 2 of 3 times (5–7-yd pattern).
14. With a partner run a 10–15-yd "down and in" pass pattern and catch the ball 2 of 3 times.
15. With a partner run a 10–15-yd "down and out" pass pattern and catch the ball 2 of 3 times.
16. With a partner run a 5–7-yd "hook" pattern and catch the ball 2 of 3 times.

Attendance and Participation

1. Be ready to participate in football activities 5 min after the last bell rings each day.
2. Use proper locker room behavior (will be discussed or posted) at all times.
3. Score at least 90% on a written test (2 attempts only).

Optional Objectives

1. Attend two football games (flag or regular) during the grading period.
2. Throw 3 of 4 passes through a tire from a distance of 10 yd.
3. Throw 3 of 4 passes through a tire from a distance of 15 yd.
4. Throw 3 of 4 passes through a moving tire from a distance of 10 yd.
5. Throw 3 of 4 passes through a moving tire from a distance of 15 yd.
6. Catch 2 passes in a game.
7. Intercept a pass in a game.
8. Write a 1-page report on a fiction or nonfiction book related to the topic of football.

FIGURE 8.4 Flag football mastery learning example

tives while the teacher monitors more difficult objectives. A third method allows students to privately monitor themselves on the performance objectives (Figure 8.6). Teachers can experiment with several monitoring approaches depending on the activity, the number of objectives, the students' abilities, the size of the class, and the available equipment and facilities.

Performance Objectives: Beginning Handball

Name _____

Instructor Checked	Class Member Checked	
_____	_____	1. Stand approximately 6 ft from the back wall and in the center of the court. Bounce the ball against the side wall and hit 3 of 4 shots below the white line with preferred hand.
_____	_____	2. Same as objective 1 but 3 of 5 with the nonpreferred hand.
_____	_____	3. Hit 3 of 5 power serves that land within 2 ft of the side wall and are otherwise legal.
_____	_____	4. Hit 3 of 4 lob serves within approximately 3 ft of the side wall that do not bounce out from the back wall more than 8 ft.
_____	_____	5. Stand approximately 6 ft from the back wall, bounce the ball against the back wall, and hit 3 of 4 shots below the white line on the front wall with the preferred hand.
_____	_____	6. Same as objective 5 but 3 of 5 with the nonpreferred hand.
_____	_____	7. Hit 3 of 4 diagonal or "Z" serves that hit the front, side, floor, opposite side, in that order. The ball may hit, but need not hit the back wall for the serve to be effective.)
_____	_____	8. Hit 3 of 4 Scotch serves or "Scotch toss" serves that hit the front, side, floor, back, side, in that order. This is similar to the "Z" serve in execution, except that the ball hits the back wall after bouncing on the floor.
_____	_____	9. Return 3 of 4 serves hit to you by the instructor. (One of each of the following will be used: power, lob, diagonal, and Scotch.)
_____	_____	10. Execute 3 of 4 attempts at "3-hit drill." (Instructor will explain in detail.)
_____	_____	11. Execute 3 of 4 attempts at "4-hit drill." (Instructor will explain.)
_____		12. Hit 3 of 5 ceiling shots with preferred hand. The ball will be thrown or hit by instructor and must be returned to the ceiling, front wall, and floor, in that order.

Note: Entry into ladder tournament is contingent on completion of any 8 of the 12 objectives. To receive a grade of <u>A</u> for the class, you must exhibit proficiency in all 12 objectives.

Objectives 1–8 may be checked by a class member; however, the instructor may spot-check any objectives at his or her discretion.

Objectives 9–12 will be checked by instructor. Performance objectives may be tested in courts 1 and 4.

FIGURE 8.5 Performance objectives—handball

Skin Diving—Number 1

Use of FACE MASK

Mark the date that each performance objective is met.

_____ 1. Adjust face mask strap to your head size.

_____ 2. Apply saliva to face mask—rub all around face plate; <u>do not rinse</u> (fog preventive).

_____ 3. Vertical tilt: Fill mask with water and hold to face without strap. In chest-deep water, go under in vertical position and by tilting head backward, away from chest, push against upper edge of mask and exhale gently. Completely clear mask 3 of 5 attempts.

_____ 4. Horizontal roll: Fill mask with water and hold to face without strap. While in a horizontal position, roll onto left shoulder, push gently with right hand against side of mask, and exhale gently. Completely clear mask 3 of 5 attempts.

_____ 5. Repeat objective 3 with strap around back of head.

_____ 6. Repeat objective 4 with strap around back of head.

_____ 7. In 6 ft of water, submerge to bottom of pool by pinching nostrils and gently exhaling into mask until you feel your ears equalize. Successfully equalize pressure in 4 of 5 attempts.

_____ 8. In 9 ft of water repeat objective 7.

_____ 9. Repeat objective 3 in deep water.

_____ 10. Repeat objective 4 in deep water.

_____ 11. Throw mask into shallow water, submerge, and put mask on. Complete vertical tilt clear in one breath, 4 of 5 attempts.

_____ 12. Throw mask into shallow water, submerge, and put mask on. Complete horizontal roll clear in one breath, 4 of 5 attempts.

_____ 13. Same as objective 11 in 6 ft of water.

_____ 14. Same as objective 11 in 9 ft of water.

_____ 15. Same as objective 12 in 6 ft of water.

_____ 16. Same as objective 12 in 9 ft of water.

FIGURE 8.6 Skin diving mastery learning example

INDIVIDUALIZED STYLE

Learning packages that incorporate a learning laboratory-resource center are used in the individualized style. An example of a learning center is shown in Figure 8.7. The individualized style is based on student-centered learning through an individualized curriculum. Students select the level of proficiency they want to pursue and proceed at their own rate of learning. Learning packets with objectives, study guides, learning activities, and assessment procedures are developed as independent study guides. Students work independently on objectives, view videotapes and slides, work on computer software, look at overhead materials, read books and articles, and prepare for the assessment procedure. Assessment usually progresses from self, to peers, and finally to the teacher. This approach requires that teachers develop learning materials and procedures for supervising the distribution and return of those materials.

The individualized style of teaching follows 5 steps:

1. *Diagnosis*. Pre-assessment is done to determine the student's current level of cognitive knowledge and psychomotor skill.
2. *Prescription*. Each student begins at a level related to their performance on the initial assessment.

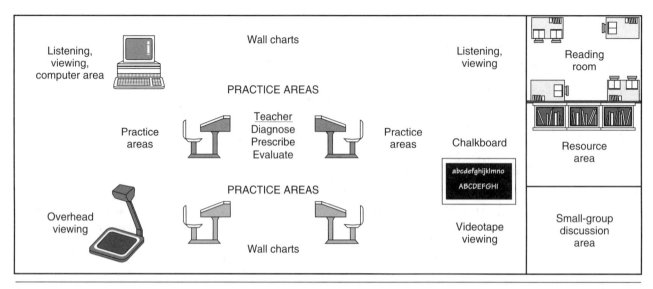

FIGURE 8.7 Organization of a learning center

From R. Pangrazi and V. Dauer. 1995. *Dynamic Physical Education for Elementary School Children.* 11th ed. Boston: Allyn & Bacon. p. 84.

3. *Development.* Each student is given a learning package that guides them toward successful completion of the predetermined criterion level. Students proceed to the next learning level after completing a level.

4. *Evaluation.* The student is given a final evaluation by a peer or the teacher after completing the steps in the learning package. Evaluation includes both cognitive and psychomotor skills.

5. *Reinforcement.* As students complete the learning packages, accomplishments are recorded. New packages are prescribed, and teaching is given for key points of the material.

Individualized instruction offers the following advantages:

1. Students, parents, and administrators know exactly what is expected and accomplished by students.
2. Self-direction enhances the motivational level of most students.
3. Students at most competency levels find success and challenge with objectives.
4. Students progress through the objectives at their own rate.
5. Students can choose and sequence learning activities.
6. Students have some choice concerning the grouping arrangement of skill practice (such as alone, with a partner, or in a small group).

7. Students accept a large degree of responsibility for learning.
8. Teachers have more freedom to give individual attention and offer feedback.

Problems that may need to be solved when using the individualized approach include the following:

1. Performance objectives are time consuming to write and require constant revision.
2. A monitoring system needs to be developed that does not take up too much time.
3. Instructional devices are necessary to provide variety and feedback. These increase the set-up and take-down time for the teacher.
4. Many teachers and students need time to get used to the format. Students and teachers are often more comfortable with the direct approach. Changing to an individualized format will require time for adjustment.

COOPERATIVE LEARNING STYLE

Cooperative learning places students in groups to work together toward common goals. In cooperative learning activities, individuals seek outcomes that are beneficial to themselves and the group. Student work is arranged so there is an interdependence in the achievement of group goals but also an accountability procedure for all individual members of the group (Johnson, Johnson, and Holubec, 1990). Cooperative learning strategies have a strong research base (Slavin, 1990) and have become a national trend in academic classrooms. When these strategies are used appropriately, social gains occur across racial groups as well as across skill levels. Higher-skilled students develop a better understanding of lower-skilled students. Lower-skilled students get a better view of the proper mechanics of the skills. Learning is solidified for all students because they fulfill different roles such as performer, observer, recorder, or evaluator (Dunn and Wilson, 1991). Physical educators can impact students in a positive way in the social, cognitive, and psychomotor areas by using cooperative learning formats.

Teachers who want to foster constructive relationships among students and improve skills and knowledge utilize cooperative learning strategies. Emphasis is placed on group outcomes rather than on individual outcomes. Students are placed in groups or teams and are given an opportunity to work together to foster the success of all team members. The groups are usually heterogeneous (that is, a mix of skill level, knowledge, socioeconomic level, race, and gender). The groups are set up with 2 to 5 students per team. The focus is on helping peers rather than competing against peers and hoping that peers fail. Students must perceive that they cannot complete the task alone. All members of the group must reach established goals. Success occurs when groups have completed the assignments through cooperation and participation of all members of the team. A number of roles can be assigned to group members including:

- A performer who does the skills or tasks.
- A recorder who keeps track of statistics, trials, or key points made by the group.
- A coach who provides feedback to the performer or times practice trials.
- A presenter who communicates key points to the rest of the class.
- A motivator who encourages and provides positive feedback to all group members.

Students switch roles often, and stated group tasks proceed from simple to complex in order to ensure success. Teachers monitor the groups to ensure all members contribute. Selected activities should require the knowledge and efforts of all members of the group. If students feel like cooperation is not necessary to complete the task, the style will not work. It must be clear that all members of the team are needed, even if in varying amounts of involvement. The tasks can be cognitive or psychomotor skills. The following are examples of class activities that might be used with the cooperative learning style:

1. Teams could be responsible for developing a warm-up or physical fitness routine. Each member of the team would focus on a different component of fitness (such as upper-body flexibility, abdominal strength, cardiovascular efficiency, upper-body strength, or lower-back flexibility).

2. Each member of a team could be responsible for teaching others a skill that is a part of a sport unit. For example, in basketball, students could teach dribbling, passing, free throws, lay-ups, rebounding, defense footwork.

3. In a dance unit, teams could develop a dance that includes a variety of dance steps or skills. Each member of the team could be responsible for incorporating the specific skills into the routine. The team would perform the dance before the rest of the class.

4. Teams could be set up for a class tournament in a sport unit such as volleyball. Each member of the team could be responsible for some aspect of the unit, such as a warm-up procedure, a team strategy for offense or defense, keeping statistics for the tournament, providing a scorekeeper, or setting up a substitution rotation. Students could switch roles each day or week.

5. In a tumbling or gymnastics unit, students could be assigned to develop a small group or partners stunt or routine and then be responsible for teaching another team the same stunt. Another example is to have an "expert" from each team get together with "experts" from other teams for a short clinic on a particular stunt. These experts then return to their team and teach the stunt.

6. Team members could be asked to modify or redesign a sport or activity to make it more inclusive or success oriented. The goal would be to allow more participation and success for all team members. For example, a different-sized ball, more bounces, a lower net, or a larger goal could be used for game modifications.

7. Teams could work with a study sheet that focuses on 3 to 5 key elements of a skill like serving in volleyball or tennis. Teams design several drills that emphasize each of the key points of the skill. Student

roles could be drill planner, director of the drill, coach for the skill points, recorder of the attempts and successful trials, and so on.

Reciprocal Teaching Style

Mosston and Ashworth (1994) describe a similar style they label reciprocal. Reciprocal teaching is a form of cooperative learning because several students are involved with different roles, such as doer, retriever, and observers. Figures 8.8 and 8.9 are examples of reciprocal style sheets that can be used with badminton and soccer. The doers are the performers, and the observers are watching and providing feedback to the doers. The retriever is returning the balls for more trials. The tosser is helping with the set-up of the drill.

Guided Discovery

INQUIRY STYLE

The inquiry style is process oriented, rather than product oriented. A student's experience during the process is considered more important than the final product or solution. Students experience learning sit-

---

Name _____   Style   B   (C)   D

Class _____

Date _____

Partner _____

Badminton—forehand overhead clear

To the students:	This task is performed in groups of three: doer, tosser, and observer.
The tosser:	Throw a high, clear service to the doer.
The doer:	Practice the forehand overhead clear 10 times.
The observer:	Analyze the doer's form by comparing the performance to the criteria listed below. Offer feedback about what is done well and what needs to be corrected.
	Rotate roles after each inning of 10.

Center line

Task—Criteria:
1. Backswing taken with racket, as if to throw it.   _____
2. Left side of the body turned to the net as weight shifts to back leg.   _____
3. Shuttle struck overhead but in front of body, with arm fully extended.
   Racket head contacts bird form below.   _____
4. Body weight put into shot, as weight shifts onto front leg. Strong wrist
   action.   _____
5. Follow through in direction of intended flight of bird.   _____

FIGURE 8.8 Badminton forehand overhead clear

From M. Mosston and S. Ashworth. 1994. *Teaching Physical Education.* 4th ed. New York: MacMillan. p. 83.

Name _____ Style   B   Ⓒ   D

Class _____

Date _____

Partner _____

Soccer—long throw-in

Work in groups of three—doer, retriever, and observer. Doer executes the task 10 times to a distance of approximately 15 yards. The retriever returns the ball, while the observer offers feedback to the doer by comparing the performance to the criteria listed below.

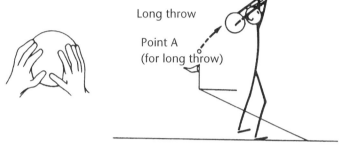

Long throw

Point A
(for long throw)

Criteria:

1. Both hands are used as ball is swung to point A behind the head.
2. Player takes one or two quick steps forward to gain momentum.
3. Body is bent backward, with a slight bend at the knees.
4. A whipping action of the body and a forceful straightening of legs develops thrust.

Note: Both feet must stay on the ground until ball is released and it must be thrown in the direction the thrower is facing.

FIGURE 8.9   Soccer long throw-in

From M. Mosston and S. Ashworth. 1994. *Teaching Physical Education.* 4th ed. New York: MacMillan. p. 95.

uations that require them to inquire, speculate, reflect, analyze, and discover. They are cognitively active in this type of instruction. The teacher guides and directs students, rather than commanding or telling. Students discover their own answers and solutions.

The teacher is responsible for stimulating student curiosity about the subject matter. A combination of questions, problems, examples, and learning activities lead students toward one or more final solutions. The steps follow a sequence and are arranged logically so students can move from one step to the next after a certain amount of thinking. The steps should not be too large or small to keep students from becoming frustrated or bored. The instructional environment is one of open communication; students must feel comfortable experimenting and inquiring without fear of failure.

Some educators believe inquiry methods of instruction should have a more prominent place in educational methodology (Mosston and Ashworth, 1994). Students need opportunities to inquire, solve problems, and discover, instead of primarily experiencing approaches that emphasize listening, absorbing, and complying. Arguments have been made to expand the focus of physical education methodology to include the inquiry style. Proponents of this style believe that it enhances students' ability to think, improves creativity, creates a better understanding of the subject matter, enhances self-concept, and develops lifelong learning patterns. Some educators argue that students who do not experience inquiry methods are dormant, unchallenged, and unused. These are broad and dramatic claims that are not supported by research findings.

Critics of the inquiry method point out the following problems with the approach: Too much time is spent on one subject or topic, a focus is on trivial or nonessential learning, most motor skills have one best solution that should be quickly explained, secondary students already know the answers, and the instruction is difficult to plan because each class has a wide range of knowledge and ability. Depending on the situation, these methods offer advantages when learning about cognitive issues. The inquiry style offers teachers another teaching tool in their repertoire of skills.

Guided Discovery (Convergent) Style

The inquiry method in physical education is generally characterized by two approaches called guided discovery or convergent styles and problem-solving or divergent styles (Mosston and Ashworth, 1994). Teachers using the guided discovery style lead students through a series of experiences in the hope that students will discover the pre-planned solution. The teacher has a best, specific answer that she or he wants students to discover. Guided discovery could be used to help students discover knowledge about some of the following:

1. Court coverage strategies in tennis, badminton, racquetball, and handball.
2. Angles of release for distance throwing with the shot put, discus, football, and softball.
3. Batting stance and foot pattern alterations for hitting the baseball or softball to various fields.
4. Ready position for basketball, baseball, football, and tennis.
5. Specific passes in basketball for various situations depending on the defenders and the type of defense.
6. Dribbling techniques in soccer used to fake a defender and move the ball up field.
7. The need for a specific type of pass or hand off in certain situations to advance the ball in a game of team handball.
8. The role of a person's center of gravity and momentum in performing activities in gymnastics such as the balance beam or the side horse.

Teachers can arrange the learning environment for these activities in many different ways. Students are asked a series of questions and given several learning activities to perform. After performing the activity, a brief discussion is held to see if students have discovered the proper solution. Examples of learning activities might be:

• In basketball, students could analyze and determine the best offensive solution when a defender is playing very tight defense. The best solution probably is to fake a shot and then drive to the basket. If the defender is playing loose defense, then the offensive player should probably take a shot. Students should have the opportunity to practice playing tight and loose defense as well as the opportunity to try the offensive position with a tight and loose defender on them. This gives them a chance to discover the best solution.

• In soccer, students could experiment with long and short passes with defenders in certain positions. Long, high passes are necessary to get the ball over a defender, whereas quick, short passes that stay on the ground are necessary to keep the defender from intercepting, and the quick passes are easier for a teammate to receive and trap.

• In the shot put and discus throws, students could experiment with various release angles to see how they affect the flight and distance of the throws. Students should discover the best angle of release for maximum distance.

Problem-Solving (Divergent) Style

The problem-solving method involves a divergent approach, rather than converging on one solution. Students move through a series of experiences and devise as many acceptable solutions to the problem as possible. The teacher encourages students to be creative and to develop unique solutions. Students analyze the pros and cons of each solution. This style is useful for discussions and assignments dealing with values, social issues, wellness concepts, and controversial topics related to sport and physical education. Honesty in sports, cooperation with teammates, competition, violence in sports, amateur versus professional sports, athletes taking drugs to improve performance, arguing with officials, women participating in sports, and masculine and feminine roles are examples of topics that could be researched, explored, discussed, and debated in a physical education class.

Wellness is an area that lends itself to the problem-solving approach. Many different approaches and methods can be used for maintaining good health. Students can learn to solve their personal fitness problems with physical activity programs that are personalized to meet their needs. Problem-solving approaches are also useful in resolving the issues of proper diet and weight control. Stress reduction, alcohol and drug abuse, and tobacco use are areas that can be addressed effectively with problem-solving techniques.

When using this style, the teacher is responsible for creating an open environment where students can explore all aspects of these controversial topics. Books, articles, movies, interviews, questions, and discussions are possibilities for accumulating and sharing information. Students are encouraged to gather information and weigh all alternatives before making a decision. The teacher's opinion does not carry more weight or emphasis than student opinion. An effective strategy for starting the problem solving involves using a "trigger story." The following are examples:

• You and your partner are involved in a tightly contested golf match with another twosome. Your partner hits his drive into the woods. While you are getting ready for your second shot, you turn and see your partner kick his ball out of the woods into an area where there is a clear shot to the green. His kick was not visible to either of your opponents. What would you do in this situation?

• You are playing a Pop Warner football team. During the game, you make an aggressive, yet legal, tackle on your opponent's best running back. The running back receives a leg injury as a result and has to be carried off the field. Your teammates cheer and praise you for injuring the star player. Your coach also praises you when you come off the field. What should you do?

• At a bicycle motocross race, you hear the father of a 5-year-old criticizing his daughter for losing the championship race. The daughter is crying. You hear the father say to the mother, "She has to learn to compete. That's what life's all about." How do you react?

• You are coaching a freshman girls volleyball team. The game is close and everyone is excited. The mother of a member of your team is being obnox-

ious. She yells mean things at players on both teams, at the coaches, and at the officials. During a time-out, the referee comes over and says, "Can't you do something about her?" What would you do?

• Your team is warming up when the referee walks in. Everybody recognizes him. He refereed your last game that you lost because he called a foul every time you moved. A member of your team loudly says, "Not him again!" What would you say?

• Right after the fourth game of the season, which your team just lost by 4 points, you are walking out of the locker room when you hear a parent say to a player on your team, "Boy, did you embarrass me tonight. You were terrible!" How would you react in this situation?

The problem-solving approach can be useful for some physical skill areas, particularly when skills can be performed or developed in more than one way. Teachers can allow students to experiment briefly with these skills to determine which approach would be most effective for them. In many cases a skill can be adapted for certain situations. Some examples are the batting stance in baseball, golf grips and swing, putting grip and stroke, starts for sprints, high jumping technique, and training methods for distance running. A problem-solving style can also be used to develop routines for gymnastics including the many different ways to correctly perform on pieces of apparatus. Students can experiment with many ways to mount the equipment, to make various turns, to make various swings, to travel across the equipment, and to perform various dismounts. In team sports, students design several offenses that work against a particular defense and several defenses that will work against a specific offensive strategy. In basketball, a defender can experiment with options against a taller or quicker player. Students can also determine their options against opponents in various individual sports. In racquetball, there are several serves that counter an opponent's strong forehand or extreme quickness. If a lob serve does not work, maybe a power serve, or a Z serve will be more effective.

DYNAMIC INSTRUCTION: ELEMENTS COMMON TO ALL STYLES

Regardless of the teaching style used, an effective learning environment can be identified by a set of instructional behaviors that occur regularly. These behaviors do not describe a specific method or style and provide significant room for individual approaches to teaching content. The focus is less on what the teacher does and more on what students are doing. For example, any style of teaching that produces high rates of student engaged time and positive attitudes toward the subject matter is considered an effective learning environment. Evidence from teacher effectiveness research (Evertson, 1989; Brophy and Good, 1986; and Siedentop, 1991) indicates that, regardless of the teacher's instructional style, an educational environment is most effective when the following elements are present:

1. *Students are engaged in appropriate learning activities for a large percentage of class time.* Effective teachers use class time wisely. Little time is wasted on noninstructional activities such as taking attendance, dressing, lunch tickets, or yearbook photos. Teachers plan carefully and insist on appropriate learning activities that deal with the subject matter. Students need time to learn; effective teachers assure that students use class time to receive information and practice skills. Learning activities are matched to students' abilities and contribute to overall class objectives.

2. *The learning atmosphere is success oriented, with a positive, caring climate.* Evidence clearly shows that teachers who develop a positive and supportive atmosphere are more effective in terms of student learning and student attitudes toward school The old idea of creating a harsh, negative, "tough guy" climate has proved not to be the best way to foster learning and positive attitudes toward physical activity. Appropriate social and organizational behavior needs to be supported by teachers. Students and teachers should feel positive about working and learning in the physical education environment.

3. *Students are given clear objectives and receive high rates of information feedback from the teacher and the environment.* Students need to know what they are going to be held accountable for in the physical education class. Class activities should be arranged so students spend large amounts of time on the required objectives. Activities should be meaningful with a clear-cut tie to the class objectives. Positive and corrective feedback should be available from the teacher. The environment is designed so students can receive feedback on learning attempts even when the teacher is not available. Peers and instructional devices are used to provide feedback.

4. *Student progress is monitored regularly, and students are held accountable for learning in physical education.* Students are expected to make progress toward class objectives. Records are kept relative to various objectives. Students know exactly what is expected of them and how the expectations are tied to the accountability system. Reward students for small steps of progress toward larger goals. If progress is not monitored regularly, students cannot be held accountable, and the environment will be less effective.

5. *Low rates of management time and smooth transitions from one activity to another characterize the environment.* Effective teachers are efficient managers of students. Students move from one learning activity to another smoothly and without wasting time. Time-saving procedures are planned and implemented efficiently. Students spend little time waiting during class transitions. Equipment is organized to facilitate smooth transitions. Attendance procedures, starting and stopping procedures, and instructional procedures are all tightly organized with little wasted time.

6. *Students spend a limited amount of time waiting in line or in other unproductive behaviors.* Effective environments are characterized by high rates of time engaged in subject matter. In physical education, this means high rates of time spent practicing, drilling, and playing. Physical education is activity based, and students need to spend class time doing the activity, not waiting for an opportunity.

7. *Teachers are organized with high but realistic expectations for student achievement.* Structure learning activities to challenge students. The activities must not be too easy or too difficult. Students need success and challenge from learning activities. Expect students to learn, and hold them accountable for their progress.

8. *Teachers are enthusiastic about what they are doing and are actively involved in the instructional process.* Students need an enthusiastic model—someone who has incorporated physical activity into his or her lifestyle. Active involvement means active supervision, enthusiasm, and high interaction rates with students. These characteristics enhance learning regardless of the teaching style used; they are important for assuring student achievement and positive attitudes.

EXPECTED OUTCOMES

After reading the chapter, you should be able to

- Discuss the specific areas where an instructional style provides direction for the teacher.

- Explain in detail the characteristics of an effective educational environment as indicated by current teacher effectiveness research.

- Plan and teach an appropriate secondary school physical education lesson using each teaching style discussed.

- Describe the advantages and disadvantages of each teaching style.

- Give examples that illustrate when a particular teaching style should be used.

- Discuss the reasons why a physical education teacher should be able to use a variety of instructional strategies.

REFERENCES AND SUGGESTED READINGS

Brophy, J., and Good, T. 1986. Teacher behavior and student achievement. In M. Wittrock (ed.). *Handbook of Research on Teaching*. New York: Macmillan.

Darst, P., and Model, R. 1983. Racquetball contracting—A way to structure your learning environment. *Journal of Physical Education, Recreation, and Dance* 54(7): 65–67.

Dunn, S. E., and Wilson, R. 1991. Cooperative learning in the physical education classroom. *Journal of Physical Education, Recreation, and Dance* 62(6): 22–28.

Evertson, C. 1989. Classroom organization and management. In M. Reynolds (ed.). *Knowledge Base for the Beginning Teacher*. Washington, D.C.: American Association of Colleges for Teacher Education.

Guskey, T. R. 1985. *Implementing Mastery Learning*. Belmont, CA: Wadsworth.

Harrison, J. M., Blakemore, C. L., Buck, M. M., and Pellett, T. M. 1996. *Instructional Strategies for Secondary Physical Education*. 4th. ed. Dubuque, IA: Wm. C. Brown.

Johnson, D. W., Johnson, R. T., and Holubec, E. J. 1990. *Circles of Learning: Cooperation in the Classroom*. 3rd ed. Edina, MN: Interaction.

Melograno, V. J. 1996. *Designing the Physical Education Curriculum*. Champaign, IL: Human Kinetics Publishers.

Mosston, M., and Ashworth, S. 1994. *Teaching Physical Education*. 4th ed. New York: Macmillan Publishing.

Pangrazi, R. P., and Dauer, V. P. 1995. *Dynamic Physical Education for Elementary School Children*. 11th ed. Boston: Allyn & Bacon.

Rink, J. E. 1993. *Teaching Physical Education for Learning*. 3rd ed. St. Louis: Mosby College Publishing.

Siedentop, D. 1991. *Developing Teaching Skills in Physical Education*. 3rd ed. Palo Alto, CA: Mayfield Publishing Co.

Slavin, R. 1990. Research on cooperative learning: Consensus and controversy. *Educational Leadership* 47(4): 52–55.

Zakrajsek, D., Carnes, L., and Pettigrew, F. 1994. *Quality Lesson Plans for Secondary Physical Education*. Champaign, IL: Human Kinetics Publishers.

9 Improving Instruction Systematically

PURPOSE

To establish that teaching can be improved by using a systematic, data-based approach in an on-going manner. Teachers can identify areas that need to be modified and improved and develop a system of self-evaluation to improve the instructional process.

KEY CONCEPTS

- Effective instruction is best measured by what students learn through their contact with a teacher.
- Teaching is a skill that can be improved by practice that is structured around goals and feedback.
- Systematic evaluation of instruction follows a data-based approach that quantifies the components of the teaching process.
- The methods of systematic observation include event recording, duration recording, interval recording, and placheck sampling.
- Self-evaluation is a key to improving the instructional process.
- Evaluation is kept simple by focusing on one specific area at a time. Attempting to record and change too many behaviors frustrates and confuses teachers.
- Areas teachers can evaluate include the following: practice time, instruction time, class management, response latency, student performance, instructional feedback, student contacts, and active supervision.
- After mastering the simple single-behavior systems in this book, teachers may want to use 1 of 3 combination systems for looking at multiple teaching and student behaviors.

Few professionals question the need for trying to improve instructional effectiveness. Most teachers want to be respected for their ability to impart knowledge and change behavior patterns of their students. University classes in teacher education strive to impart teaching skills to students. Those students who become effective instructors have one thing in common: They are motivated to improve and excel. It is not enough, however, to be motivated. Motivation without proper teaching skills leaves teachers in a predicament. They want to change and grow but do not know what needs to be changed and learned.

Therefore, a systematic approach for evaluating instruction is advocated so teachers can assess when they are improving or need to improve.

DEFINING EFFECTIVE INSTRUCTION

Effective instruction is a broad and general term that can be defined many ways. Simply put, it is probably best characterized by what students learn through contact with a teacher. The goal of an instructor is to teach new skills, refine previously learned skills, change attitudes, and leave students with a positive feeling about what they have learned. If students do not learn, instruction has not occurred. Some teachers feel they are successful if they teach students all the key points of skill performance. If, in spite of the presentation of key points, students do not perform differently than they did prior to the skill analysis, instruction was ineffective.

A common saying in education is "students learn when teachers teach." This is probably true if teachers are effective in their teaching methods. On the other hand, learning is not guaranteed. Teaching effectively demands that positive changes in behavior occur. The changes may be attitudinal, skill oriented, or knowledge based. Regardless of the learning domain affected, learning occurs and teaching is effective only when observable changes result. Think about it: If noticeable changes in students do not occur, how can teachers say they have taught effectively? This speaks to the need for systematic evaluation of instruction.

IMPROVING TEACHING SKILLS

Teaching is learned just like any other skill. If you want to learn to play racquetball, you practice racquetball. Most people who have learned sport skills have followed the process of setting goals, diagnosing their problems, prescribing methods for improving, and evaluating their progress. This approach is needed to improve teaching skills as well. To learn to teach, a cyclical process must occur; teach, analyze the results, prescribe changes, and evaluate progress made. It is not enough to listen, read, and observe. Active participation in teaching is necessary.

The second part of improving teaching skills requires that teachers do more than teach. Many teachers have taught the same thing for years without changing. They have not incorporated new skills and ideas into their teaching methods. This results in a teacher who is stagnant and unchanging. What if athletes never tried to change or use newly discovered techniques? Quite likely they would not remain competitive. When teachers fail to update their techniques, the public may believe they do not care about being effective.

Practice and improvement goes hand in hand. Teachers need to evaluate their performances so they know whether they are improving or becoming stag-

nant. Ask teachers you know whether they are better teachers this year as compared to last year. If they say yes, ask them to prove it. If they can't give you anything more than a belief that they are better, you probably have found teachers who have never utilized the process of systematic instructional improvement.

NEED FOR GOALS AND FEEDBACK

Teachers need goals aimed at improving their teaching effectiveness. Establishing goals and not evaluating them is like driving down a highway without a map. How can you know when you have reached your goals if you do not establish some method of evaluation? Goals and feedback need to be developed concurrently. It is necessary to have an objective way of evaluating whether they have improved. This is feedback: information gathered for the purpose of modifying future responses.

Feedback about teaching can be used to guide improvement in instructional methods. Assume you have a goal of improving volleyball skills. For comparative purposes, you want to try teaching the volleyball set using a reciprocal teaching method for instruction. You allow half the class to teach a friend the set while you teach the other half using a teacher-centered, direct style of instruction. After a week of practice, you evaluate the performance level of the volleyball set. Comparing the reciprocal style versus the direct style generates feedback about the effectiveness of the method.

This example illustrates goal setting and data gathering related to instructional outcomes. Later in the chapter, systematic approaches for improving instruction will be offered. All the approaches involve setting goals and establishing a data base of information to see if the goals were accomplished. Learning to collect meaningful data about teaching is necessary for improvement.

NEED FOR SYSTEMATIC EVALUATION

Instruction has most often been evaluated using inexact and insensitive methods such as intuition, checklists, rating scales, and observation. Over time, these methods have proven to be relatively ineffective for improving the quality of instruction. The use of intuition relies on the expertise of a supervisor, who observes the instructor, recommends changes, and reinforces the result. Improvement is difficult to identify because the evaluation process offers little or no quantification. It is possible the supervisor will forget what the quality of the first lesson was compared with the present teaching episode. In this situation, evaluating whether or not improvement has occurred is next to impossible.

Checklists and rating scales are used as evaluation tools and give the appearance of an objective, quantified method (Figure 9.1). However, rating scales are unreliable and become more so when the number of rating points is increased. Scales and checklists are open to a wide spread of interpretation depending on who is performing the evaluation. Most evaluation done using checklists and rating scales is subject to the impressions and opinions of the evaluator.

This lack of objectiveness indicates the need for a systematic method of observing teaching effectiveness. Siedentop (1991) has developed a number of systematic methods for teacher evaluation and re-

Student _____ Activity _____ Grade _____

	5	4	3	2	1	*Comments*
1. Use of language						
2. Quality of voice						
3. Personal appearance						
4. Class management						
5. Presentation and teaching techniques						
6. Professional poise						
7. Enthusiasm, interest						
8. Adaptability, foresight						
9. Adequate activity						
10. Knowledge of subject						
11. Appropriate use of student help						
12. Demonstration (if any)						
13. Progression (if applicable)						
14. General organization						

General evaluation
    5–Superior
    4–Above average
    3–Average
    2–Below average
    1–Poor

Evaluating Teacher

_____

Date _____

FIGURE 9.1   Example of a rating scale

search. These techniques have led to increased educational research in the area of pedagogy. This chapter discusses methods that are systematic in nature and feasible for self-evaluation of instructional effectiveness.

Methods described here use systematic observation for self-improvement. If the reader chooses to conduct research projects and to study this area indepth, the Siedentop text *Developing Teaching Skills in Physical Education* (1991) is an excellent resource. Another useful text for learning about observation instruments and evaluation techniques is *Analyzing Physical Education and Sport Instruction* (Darst, Zakrajsek, and Mancini, 1989). This chapter shows how systematic evaluation can be implemented in a typical school setting.

EVALUATING EFFECTIVE TEACHING

What should be evaluated in the teaching process? There are 3 major areas that can be observed and evaluated. The first is teacher behavior. This includes evaluation of areas such as teacher movement, giving instructions, the praise-to-criticism ratio, use of first names, and the length of instructional episodes. Focus is on the performance of skills that are managed by the teacher. The responsibility for performing behaviors in this category rests solely with the teacher.

The second category of observable behavior is student behavior. Examples of student behavior are the rate of deviant behavior, the amount of time students stay on task, the number of students on task, and the number of practice trials students receive. These variables can be evaluated through direct observation; they link more closely to student learning than teacher behavior variables. Note that these behaviors are process oriented. Emphasis is placed on increasing or decreasing the occurrence of student behavior rather than measuring the actual performance of a skill.

The best indication of learning is the evaluation of student skill performance, fitness levels, knowledge levels, and attitudes toward physical education. Chapter 10 provides ideas and examples for evaluating these areas. This third category focuses on the product of learning. How students learned is not the issue—if they learned is the concern. On the surface, this seems to many teachers to be the only important evaluative area. Either students learn the skill or they don't. If they learn the skill, teachers have taught.

However, things are not always so simple. It may be that students have learned the skills but leave physical education with a negative attitude toward activity. What would be gained if students learned skills they never wanted to use again? What about unskilled students? Can they ever find success in physical education classes?

The best evaluation system includes behavior from all 3 categories. It is important to look at teaching behavior. It is also necessary to evaluate how students respond in a class setting. If both teachers and students are demonstrating effective behavior patterns, the evaluation of skill performance is appropriate. All 3 areas are interrelated, and all 3 need to be evaluated.

METHODS FOR SYSTEMATICALLY OBSERVING INSTRUCTION

Instruction can be systematically observed using a variety of methods to gather information. The instruments are easy to use. A key is to clearly define the area to be evaluated. Definitions should be written and followed to make the data meaningful. The methods require little more than pencil, paper, tape recorder, and stopwatch. A videotape recorder can add another dimension but is not a necessity.

Event Recording

In simplest terms, event recording involves noting how many times an event occurs during a specified time period. Event recording identifies the frequency with which certain behavior occurs. It measures the quantity of events, not the quality. For example, event recording might be defined as the number of times a teacher interacts with students or the number of times a positive statement is made. A teacher might tally the number of practice attempts students receive after a skill has been introduced or the number of times the class is asked to stop and come to attention. Event recording results are usually divided by the number of minutes in the evaluation session to give an event rate per minute. This enables the teacher to compare lessons that involve different content or teaching styles.

To lessen the time needed for analysis, use a sampling technique. For example, if the lesson is 30 minutes long, 4 bouts of recording, each lasting 2 minutes at evenly distributed points in the lesson, reduces the burden of recording and yields representative results. Any observable behavior of teachers, students, or between teachers and students can be recorded when the behavior has been clearly defined.

Duration Recording

While event recording offers insight into the frequency of certain behavior, duration recording reveals how long behavior occurs in terms of minutes and seconds. Time is the measure used in this type of recording. As with event recording, duration recording does not have to be done for an entire lesson. Representative sampling of 3 or 4 bouts of observation, 3 minutes per bout, can be used to generalize about the entire session.

These data are usually converted to percentages so comparisons can be made from lesson to lesson. This is done by dividing the entire observation time into the amount of time devoted to the specific observed behavior. For example, if 20 minutes of observation was done and the student was in activity for 10 of the 20 minutes, the result would be 50%. This would be expressed as "50% of the total time was spent in activity." This approach is used to identify the duration of certain behaviors, such as practice, managerial, or instructional behaviors.

Interval Recording

Interval recording analyzes behavior patterns for short periods of time. When interval recording, intervals should be 6 to 12 seconds, with one interval for observing and the other for recording. If a teacher used 6-second intervals during a 1-minute session, 5 intervals would be for observing and 5 for recording the results. According to Siedentop (1991), it is important to have at least 90 data points (observe-record = 1 point) to establish the validity of the technique. This would generate 100 data points in 20 minutes using 6-second intervals.

Data generated from this technique are usually converted to a percentage of the data points in which the behavior occurred. If, for example, the behavior occurred in 40 of 100 data points, the figure is 40%. Percentages can be compared lesson to lesson. A simple way to keep track of intervals is to wear a recorder headset that "beeps" every 6 seconds. The observer can alternate observing and recording with each signal. This technique is reliable, particularly when the intervals are short, and can be used to record instructional time, managerial time, academic learning time, and other types of observable behavior.

Placheck Recording

Scan of the room

Placheck (planned activity check) recording is similar to interval recording in that behavior is observed at different intervals. This technique is used to observe group behavior. At regular intervals during a lesson, the observer scans the group for 10 seconds. The scan begins at the left side of the instructional area and moves to the right side, taking note of which students are not on task. The observer makes 1 observation per student, and does not go back or change the decision, even if the student changes behavior during the 10-second interval.

The technique is used to identify student effort, productive activity, and participation. It is usually best to record the less-frequently occurring behavior to speed counting. For example, if the teacher is interested in identifying the percentage of students involved in the assigned activity, recording the number of students who are not participating is easier. Intervals should last 10 seconds and be spaced randomly throughout the lesson. There should be 8 to 10 observation intervals. Again, signals to observe can be recorded on a tape recorder at random intervals to cue the observer. This technique will yield information concerning the behavior of the group.

SYSTEMATIC OBSERVATION FOR SELF-IMPROVEMENT

Each teacher has different strengths and weaknesses and different concerns for improvement. The approach used for systematic observation directed at self-improvement varys greatly from teacher to teacher. Instructors decide which variables they want to evaluate and determine the best possible way to record and monitor the data. Evaluating 1 area at a time is usually best. Trying to record more than 1 variable at a time may frustrate and confuse. It may also confound the picture by making it difficult to decide how to change the teaching behavior in question.

After deciding which behavior needs to be changed, a plan for meaningful evaluation is developed. Identifying the behavior that affects the desired educational outcome and deciding which method of observation is necessary. A coding form is developed to facilitate recording the data. Coding sheets should be specific to each situation and suited to the teacher. Areas on the sheet can provide for recording the teacher, the date, the focus and con-

Why systematic observation? - to see what you need to improve on

tent of the lesson, the grade level and competency of the students, the duration of the lesson, and a short description of the evaluation procedure. The sheets should be consistent for each type of behavior so the instructor can compare progress throughout the year.

Deciding what behavior will be recorded depends on the instructor's situation. For example, can the data be gathered by students who are not participating? Can another teacher easily gather the data? Can the data be gathered from an audiotape or is a videotape necessary? Is the instructor willing to let others gather the information, or does the teacher believe that it is important to keep the data confidential? These and other questions determine what areas the teacher is willing to evaluate. In most cases the teacher is least threatened by self-evaluation techniques and more willing to change when it is not required by outside authorities. Another advantage of self-evaluation is that teaching behavior changes least when outside observers are not present. Self-evaluation techniques can better reveal actual patterns exhibited in day-to-day teaching.

IMPROVING THE QUALITY OF INSTRUCTION

Quality instruction results when an effective teacher implements a well-planned lesson. Successful teachers have learned how to do this over a period of years through a somewhat inefficient method of trial and error. Sheer experience does not, unfortunately, guarantee an outstanding teacher. Witness the fact that there are many experienced yet mediocre teachers. A key to improving teaching ability is experience coupled with meaningful feedback about the teacher's performance.

Teachers may find it difficult to find someone capable of offering evaluative feedback. Principals and curriculum supervisors may be too busy or may not possess skills necessary for systematically observing teaching behavior. This accentuates the importance of learning to self-evaluate. Teachers have long been told to talk less, move more, praise more, learn more names, and increase student practice time—primarily without documented methods of measurement. This section shows a number of teacher behaviors that are observable and measurable. The data can be gathered by the teacher, by teaching peers, or by selected students.

Take a do-it-yourself approach to evaluation. Feedback gained in the privacy of one's office is eas-

ier to digest and less threatening. Teachers can make personal goals and chart their performance without others knowing. When teachers evaluate their own teaching procedures, they are usually willing to change. This attitude contrasts with a resistant attitude when principals or department heads impose external evaluation.

Instructional Time

The educational process requires that teachers instruct. The throw-out-the-ball approach is nothing more than leisure time activity in a school setting. Instructors need to know the amount of instruction they offer students. Instructional time refers to initial demonstrations, cues, and explanations to get students started on an activity. This time deals directly with physical education content.

Find a meaningful balance between instruction and practice. An observer can tally the number of instructional episodes and the length of each episode occurring in a daily class. At a later time, the average length of instruction can then be evaluated, as well as the proportion of the lesson that was used for instruction. Instructional episodes should be short and frequent, with an attempt made to limit episodes to 45 seconds or less.

How to Do It
1. Design a form for duration recording.
2. Have a colleague or a nonparticipating student turn on the stopwatch every time an instructional episode begins, and stop the watch when instruction ends. Record the episode on the form, clear the watch, and be ready to time the next instructional episode. An alternative method is to record the lesson using a videotape recorder and rerun the tape at the end of the day. Establish a criterion for identifying the difference between instructional and management episodes. (For a description of management episodes, see Chapter 7.)
3. Total the amount of time spent on instruction.
4. Convert the amount of time to the percentage of lesson time devoted to instruction by dividing the length of the lesson into the time spent on instruction. The average length of an instructional episode can be determined by dividing the total instructional time by the number of instructional episodes. Figure 9.2 shows an example of a form used for recording instructional time.

[handwritten: Teach → analyze results → prescribe changes → evaluate progress]

Instructional Time

Teacher _Charlene Darst_   Observer _B. Pangrazi_

Class _1st period_   Grade _10_   Date and time _3/22 – 9:05_

Lesson focus _Golf_   Comments _1st class meeting of unit_

Starting time _9:15_   End time _10:00_   Length of lesson _45 min_

15	10	8	35	17	1:03	31	9	8
14	21	10	21	43	7	3:19	25	

Total instructional time _8 min 56 sec_

Percent of class time devoted to instruction _19%_

Number of episodes _17_   Average length of episodes _31.5 sec_

FIGURE 9.2   Sample form for instructional time

Class Management Episodes

Effective teachers efficiently manage students. Management time is when no instruction or practice is taking place. Management occurs when students are moved into various formations, when equipment is gathered or put away, and when directions are given about these areas. It also includes taking roll, keeping records, recording fitness scores, and changing clothes (see Chapter 7 for a description of management skills). Figure 9.3 is an example of a form for duration recording using a stopwatch.

Understanding the amount of time being used for class management, and the length and number of episodes, is useful. The number of episodes and the length of each can be recorded by an observer. These data are useful for analyzing how much lesson time is devoted to the area of management. A high percent-age of management time can indicate an inefficient organizational scheme or students' slow response to explanations.

How to Do It
1. Design a form that gathers the data desired (Figure 9.3).
2. Record the lesson with a videotape recorder. Time the length of each management episode, and record each episode in a box on the form.
3. Total the amount of management time and divide it by the length of the period to compute the percent of management time during the lesson.
4. Total the number of episodes and divide this number into the amount of time devoted to management to find the average length of a management episode.

Management Time

Teacher _Don Hicks_   Observer _Connie Pangrazi_

Class _5th period_   Grade _7_   Date and time _11/7 – 2:05_

Lesson focus _Frisbee_   Comments _____

Starting time _2:13_   End time _2:50_   Length of lesson _37 min_

55	10	21	1:15	19	18	55	33	16
43								

Total management time _5 min 45 sec_

Percent of class time devoted to management _15%_

Number of episodes _10_   Average length of episodes _34.5 sec_

FIGURE 9.3   Sample form for management time

Response Latency

Response latency is the amount of time it takes a class to respond to commands or signals. It occurs when instructions are given to begin practicing an activity or to stop an activity. An observer can evaluate the amount of time that elapses from the moment a command is given to start or stop an activity to the moment when the students actually begin or stop. The amount of time that elapses is response latency. An accompanying criterion needs to be set for the percentage of students who are expected to be on task. It is not unreasonable to expect 100% of the students to respond to the command. If less than 100% of the class is expected to respond, a gradual loss of class control can occur. The average amount of response latency can be calculated so the instructor can set a goal for improving student behavior. A certain amount of response latency should be expected.

Few groups of students stop or start immediately, and most instructors have a strong feeling about the amount of latency that they are willing to tolerate. After more than a 5-second response latency, teachers usually become uneasy and expect the class to stop or start.

How to Do It
1. Develop a form for gathering the data (Figure 9.4).
2. Have a nonparticipating student or colleague time the response latency each time the class is asked to stop (or start). The clock should run from the time the command to stop is given until the next command is given, or until the class is involved in productive behavior. For example, the teacher gives the command to stop the activity and return to squads (watch is started). Students stop the game and slowly re-

Response Latency

Teacher __Paul Darst__   Observer __Reid Wilcox__

Class __5th period__   Grade __9__   Date and time __2/5 – 12:45__

Lesson focus __Team Handball__   Comments _____

Starting time __12:50__   End time __1:33__   Length of lesson __43 min__

Starting Response Latency

3	12	17	5	5	11	18	9	7
11	3	5	6	14				

Stopping Response Latency

12	13	8	18	5	5	14	12	11
3	10	19	18	17				

Total amount of starting response latency __2 min 6 sec__

Percent of class time devoted to response latency __4%__

Number of episodes __14__   Average length of episode __9 sec__

Total amount of stopping response latency __2 min 45 sec__

Percent of class time devoted to stopping response latency __6%__

Number of episodes __14__   Average length of episode __11.8 sec__

FIGURE 9.4   Sample form for response latency

turn to squads. The teacher waits until all students are sitting quietly before giving the next direction (watch is stopped). Starting and stopping response latency are 2 separate behaviors and should be recorded separately.

3. Identify the number of response latency episodes and divide this number into the total amount of time logged for response latency to calculate the average.

Active Learning Time—Physical Education

To learn physical skills students must be involved in meaningful physical activity. Physical education programs deal with a finite amount of scheduled time per week. High-success, engaged time with motor activities is defined as academic learning time—physical education (ALT-PE). ALT-PE is defined as activity where students are practicing skills in a setting that enables them to experience success. Learning is related to the amount of time students are involved in productive, on-task activity. In a well-regarded school district, the average amount of activity time per 50-minute period was only 9 to 12 minutes. Evidence shows that teachers can significantly increase the amount of ALT-PE for students (Randall and Imwold, 1989).

To evaluate ALT-PE, duration recording is most effective. A student or fellow teacher can observe a lesson and time the intervals when students are involved in practicing skills. The chart in Figure 9.5 is an example of the results of a duration recording for ALT-PE. The goal is to increase the amount of successful time students receive for meaningful practice. A teacher could increase the amount of practice time by using more equipment, selecting drills that require a minimum of standing in line, or streamlining the amount of verbal instruction.

How to Do It
1. Design a form for collecting the data (Figure 9.6).

Parts of the Lesson	Practicing	Inactive, Off Task, Listening
Introductory activity	2.5 min	1.0 min
Fitness development	11.5 min	2.5 min
Lesson focus	15.0 min	7.5 min
Total	29.0 min	11.0 min

Teacher: Debbie Massoney
School: Jason Junior High

FIGURE 9.5 Results of duration recording for practice time

2. Have a nonparticipating student or colleague identify students who will be used for the evaluation. These are the students the evaluator will observe when they are involved in practice and for how long.

Practice Time

Teacher _Eugene Petersen_ Observer _P. W. Darst_

Class _2nd period_ Grade _8_ Date and time _11/15 – 9:15_

Lesson focus _Basketball_ Comments _week two_

Starting time _9:25_ End time _10:00_ Length of lesson _35 min_

35	10	2:04	25	29	1:39	17	55	34
43	1:55	1:01	33	10	10	18	1:17	4:50
24	39	31	34					

Total practice time _20 min 13 sec_

Percent of class time devoted to practice _57.8%_

Number of episodes _22_ Average length of episodes _55.1 sec_

FIGURE 9.6 Sample form for collecting data on practice time

3. Turn on the stopwatch when the students are engaged in practice activity, and record the interval of practice.

4. Total the amount of time for student practice (in minutes) and divide it by the length of the lesson. This will compute the percent of practice time in a given lesson.

Student Performance

Some classes have a greater percentage of students performing at optimum levels than others. Reasons for this vary. A class may be poorly motivated, have difficulty understanding instructions, or be out of control. In any case, instructors can evaluate the percentage of students who are performing in a desired manner. This can be accomplished by using the placheck observation technique. Examples of areas that can be evaluated are students performing the stipulated activity, productive behavior, effort, and interest in the activity. Once baseline data are gathered, teachers can strive to increase the percentage of students involved in the desired observable behavior.

How to Do It

1. Design a form for recording the desired data. Figure 9.7 is an example of a form that can be used for placheck observation. The example can be used to identify 3 different areas of student performance.

Student Performance

Teacher ___Bob Pangrazi___   Observer ___Norma Pike___

Class ___2nd period___   Grade ___12___   Date and time ___1/26 – 9:20___

Lesson focus ___Weight Lifting___   Comments _____

Starting time ___9:28___   End time ___10:12___   Length of lesson ___44 min___

Active/inactive

5	4	12	7	8	5
9	2	1	8		

On task/off task

Effort/noneffort

Number of plachecks ___10___

Total number of students in class ___33___

Average number of students not on desired behavior ___6.1___

Percentage of students not on desired behavior ___18%___

FIGURE 9.7   Placheck observation of student performance

2. Place 8 to 10 audio signals (whistle) at random intervals on a tape recorder to signal when a placheck should be conducted.

3. Scan the area in a specified and consistent direction from left to right every time the taperecorded signal sounds. The class is scanned for 7 to 10 seconds while the number of students who are not engaged in the desired behavior is recorded.

4. Convert the data to a percentage by dividing the total number of students into the average number of unproductive students and multiplying the result by 100. Eight to 10 plachecks spaced randomly throughout a class period will yield valid information about the conduct of the class.

Instructional Feedback

Feedback teachers offer to students influences instructional effectiveness. It is possible for instructors to analyze their interaction patterns and set meaningful goals for improvement. Few teachers enter the profession with the ability to communicate with clarity. The process of changing communication behaviors can create discomfort and concern but will ultimately pay rewarding dividends. Evaluation in the following areas can create improvement in feedback delivery.

Praise and Criticism

When students are involved in activity, teachers deliver feedback dealing with student performance. This feedback can be positive and constructive, or negative and critical. It is easy to measure the occurrences of praise and criticism. The occurrences can be tallied and evaluated at the end of the day. Calculate the number of instances and the ratio of positive to negative comments. Using these data, begin to set goals for increasing the number of comments per minute and modifying the ratio of positive to negative comments. A teacher can expect to average 1 to 2 comments per minute with a positive to negative ratio of 3 or 4 to 1.

General versus Specific

Feedback given to students can be specific or general. Comments like "Good job," "Way to go," and "Cut that out" are general in nature. General feedback can be either negative or positive and does not specify the behavior being reinforced. In contrast, specific feedback identifies the student by name, mentions the behavior being reinforced, and can be accompanied by a valuing statement. An example is, "Michelle, that's the way to keep your head tucked! I really like that forward roll!"

To evaluate this area, teachers can tally the number of general and specific feedback instances. Since both types of feedback can be negative or positive, this can also be counted. Using first names personalizes the feedback and directs it to the right individual. Total the number of times first names are used. The number of valuing statements can also be monitored. Divide the totals in all of the categories by the length of the lesson (in minutes) to render a rate per minute. Figure 9.8 is an example of a form that can be used to tally the feedback behaviors described in this section.

Positive feedback should be specific whenever possible so students know exactly what it was they did well. An instructor might say, "Your throw to second base was exactly where it should have been!" This type of feedback creates a positive feeling in a class. Sometimes, however, teachers use this type of feedback to such an extent that it becomes a habitual form of communication (that is, "good job, nice serve"). These comments do not identify specific desirable behavior and may be ignored by students. It is also possible that an undesirable behavior may be reinforced when feedback is general.

Corrective Instructional Feedback

Effective teachers coach students to higher levels of performance. This involves giving performers meaningful corrective feedback. Corrective feedback focuses on improving the performance of the participant. Teachers should ignore poor performances if students are already aware of them. Corrective instructional feedback is specific whenever possible, so performers know what it is they must correct. An example of corrective instructional feedback might be, "Your throw to second base was too far to the left of the base! Try to throw the ball directly over the base." This type of feedback tells the student what was incorrect about the skill attempt and how the skill should be performed.

Nonverbal Feedback

Much performance feedback can be given nonverbally. This is certainly meaningful to students and may be equal to or more effective than verbal forms of communication. Examples of nonverbal feedback that could occur after a desired performance are a pat on the back, a wink, a smile, a nod of the head, the thumbs-up sign, and clapping the hands. Nonverbal feedback can also be negative: a frown, shaking the

---

Instructional Feedback

Teacher _____   Observer _____

Class _____   Grade _____   Date and time _____

Lesson focus _____   Comments _____

Starting time _____   End time _____   Length of lesson _____

Interactions unrelated to skill performance	+							
	−							
General instructional feedback	+							
	−							
Specific positive instructional feedback								
Corrective instructional feedback								
First names								
Nonverbal feedback	+							
	−							

Ratio + to −/nonskill related   _____

Ratio + to −/skill related   _____

FIGURE 9.8   Sample form for tallying feedback behaviors

---

head in disapproval, walking away from a student, or laughing at a poor performance.

It is possible to tally the number of positive and negative nonverbal behaviors exhibited by a teacher. A student or another instructor can do the tallying. Students may be better at evaluating the instructor in this domain, because they are aware of what each of the instructor's mannerisms means.

How to Do It

1. Design a form to collect the data. Figure 9.8 is an example of a form that can be used.
2. Videotape a lesson for playback and evaluation at a later time.
3. Record the data to be analyzed. Analyze 1 category at a time when beginning. For example, analyze the use of first names during the first playback, and then play the tape again to evaluate corrective feedback.
4. Convert the data to a form that can be generalized from lesson to lesson (such as rate per minute, rate per lesson, or ratio of positive to negative interactions).

Active Supervision and Student Contact

Contact and active supervision are important in maintaining students' involvement with learning tasks (van der Mars, Vogler, Darst, and Cusimano, 1994). Contact means moving among and offering personalized feedback to the students. To evaluate student contact, count the number of times an instructor becomes involved with a student. This type of feedback differs from total class interaction and demands that the instructor have keen insight into each student's behavior and particular needs.

Related to this area is teacher movement and supervision. Instructors often have a particular area in the gymnasium from which they feel comfortable teaching. Before instruction begins, the teacher moves back to this area. The teacher's movement pattern causes students to drift to different areas, depending on their feeling about the activity or the instructor. Students who like the instructor will move closer, whereas students who dislike the teacher or are uneasy about the activity may move away. This results in a configuration where competent performers are near the instructor and students who are deviant or less competent move away and become difficult to observe.

These problems can be decreased by moving throughout the teaching area. Teacher movement can be evaluated by dividing the area into quadrants and tallying the number of times the instructor moves from section to section. A tally is made only if the teacher speaks to a student or to the class as a whole. Do not tally when the teacher merely passes through a quadrant.

A more precise measure is the amount of time a teacher stays in a quadrant. The length of time can be recorded on the form in relationship to where the teacher stands. At the end of the lesson, analyze the amount of time spent in each quadrant. Another technique is to code the type of teacher behavior that occurs each time the instructor moves into a new quadrant. For example, an "M" might signify management activity, an "I" instructional activity, and a "P" practice time. This tally reveals the amount of time the instructor spent in each area and also where the teacher moved to conduct different types of class activities.

How to Do It

1. Develop a coding form similar to the one in Figure 9.9.

Teacher Movement

Teacher ___Danny Marcello___   Observer ___Ellen Colleary___

Class ___5th period___   Grade ___9___   Date and time ___3/17 – 1:05___

Lesson focus ___Volleyball___   Comments _____

Starting time ___1:15___   End time ___2:01___   Length of lesson ___46 min___

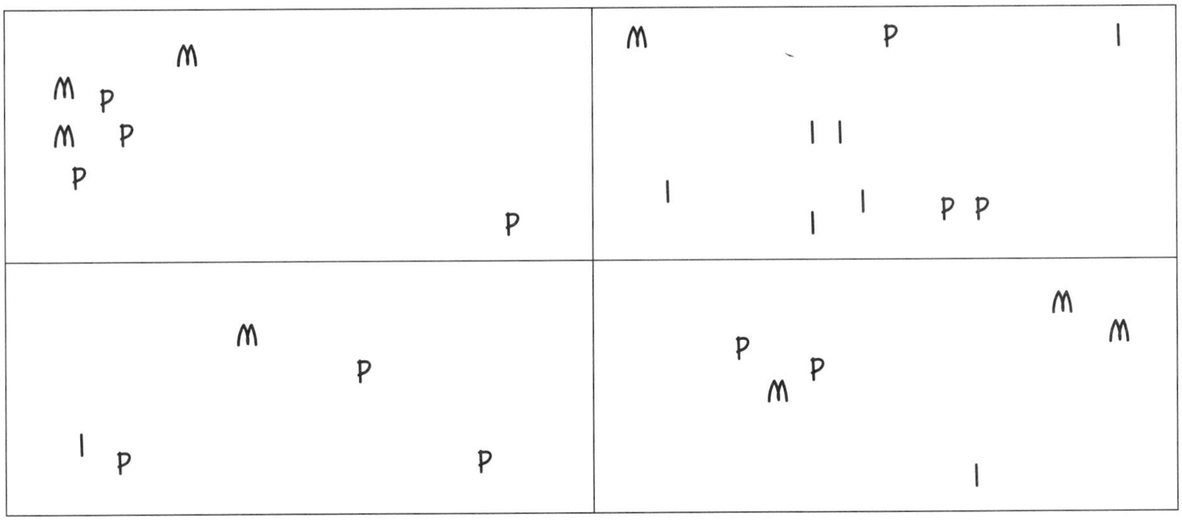

Total number of moves ___28___

Number of moves (I) ___8___   (M) ___8___   (P) ___12___

Average number of moves per min ___.6___

FIGURE 9.9 Sample form for recording active supervision and student contact (M = management activity, I = instructional activity, P = practice time)

2. Ask a nonparticipating student or a colleague to record the desired data on teacher movement. A better alternative is to videotape the lesson and evaluate it later.

3. Evaluate the data by calculating the number of moves per lesson and the number of moves during instruction, management, and practice.

COMBINATION SYSTEMS FOR OBSERVING TEACHERS AND STUDENTS

After practicing these observation systems that focus on 1 or 2 teaching behaviors, a more sophisticated system that focuses on multiple teaching or multiple student behaviors can be used. These systems include the simultaneous observation of teacher and student behaviors. Many instruments have been field-tested in middle and senior high school settings for research purposes. The more sophisticated systems require more practice time in order to code data that are valid and reliable.

Flow of Teacher Organizational Patterns (FOTOP)

FOTOP is an instrument that describes the way a teacher uses organizational patterns while teaching physical education (Johnson, 1989). This system focuses on the sequential behavior patterns of the teacher, not the student. It uses a 15-second interval recording technique. Organizational behavior patterns are divided into teaching and nonteaching categories. The 5 teaching categories include the following:

1. *Cognitive structuring.* The teacher speaks directly to the entire class such as in lecturing, demonstrating, or asking questions. The students are passively standing or sitting while listening.

2. *Mass activity instruction.* The entire class is involved in activity that is controlled by the teacher. The teacher directs instruction toward the entire class such as drills, scrimmage, or controlled game situations.

3. *Small group instruction.* The teacher instructs a small group of 2 or more students but not the entire class as in station teaching or circuit training.

4. *Individual instruction.* The teacher works with 1 specific student.

5. *Testing.* Any formal evaluation procedure such as written tests or skill tests.

The 5 nonteaching categories involve the following:

1. *Managerial functions.* Administrative duties such as taking attendance, passing out equipment, moving the class to various teaching areas, or giving management directions.

2. *Supervision functions.* Observing the class without giving any instruction. Students are playing or practicing on their skills.

3. *Officiating.* Performing the role of an official or referee.

4. *Participating.* Participating in the activity but not for instructional purposes.

5. *Other.* Any other behavior or function that does not fit into any other category.

The FOTOP recording sheet (Figure 9.10) has 5 2-minute intervals across the top of the form and the specific behavior categories down the left side. The observer enters the number 1 in the appropriate category slot after observing the first 15 seconds. Then, the number 2 is entered after the next 15 seconds and the number 3 after the next 15 seconds and so forth until number 8 is entered after the last 15 seconds of the 2-minute interval. Each 2-minute column will have numbers 1 to 8 entered. If more than one behavior pattern occurs during the 15-second interval, the observer must decide which behavior dominated the interval.

After all 5 2-minute segments are recorded, the time is converted to minutes and seconds for each category. Each number entered on the form represents 15 seconds. This time can be converted to a percentage of total observed time as shown in Figure 9.10. Using this data from the FOTOP instrument, teachers make decisions and set goals for changing their behavior patterns.

Arizona State University Observation Instrument (ASUOI)

The ASUOI is an observation system that focuses on 14 categories of teacher behavior (Lacy and Darst, 1989). The system has been expanded and modified several times to create an instrument that is sensitive

Instructor ____Instructor A_____   Date ____10/14_____

Observer ____Observer A_____   Activity ____Volleyball_____   Teaching station ____Gym 203_____

Class beginning time ____10:00_____   Ending time ____10:50_____

Coding beginning time ____10:00_____   Ending time ____10:10_____

Teaching	2 min 1	2 min 2	2 min 3	2 min 4	2 min 5	Total time min:sec	% of total time
Cognitive structure	5, 6, 7, 8	1, 2, 3				1:45	17.5
Mass activity instruction		4, 5, 6, 7, 8				1:15	12.5
Group instruction							
Individual instruction				(5, 6)	1, 2	1:00	10
Testing							
Nonteaching							
Managerial functions	1, 2, 3, 4					1:00	10
Supervising				7, 8	3, 4	1:00	10
Officiating			1, 2, 3, 4, 5, 6, 7, 8	1, 2, 3, 4		3:00	30
Participating					5, 6, 7, 8	1:00	10
Other							

Instructions: Record by placing numbers 1–8 in the appropriate category and time module every 15 sec. To find percentage, convert time to seconds and divide by 600.

Comments: (Use back of sheet if necessary.)

FIGURE 9.10 Completed FOTOP recording sheet

From P. Darst, D. Zakrajsek, and V. Mancini (eds.). 1989. *Analyzing Physical Education and Sport Instruction.* 2nd ed. Champaign, IL: Human Kinetics Publishers. Copyright 1989 by P. Darst, D. Zakrajsek, and V. Mancini. Reprinted by permission of Human Kinetics Publishers.

to the instructional category of behavior. The system can be used with event or interval recording.

The teacher behaviors include the following:

1. *Use of first name.* Using a student's first name or nickname.

2. *Preinstruction.* Information that is given to students prior to participation, such as explaining a skill, drill, or strategy.

3. *Concurrent instruction.* Specific instructional cues or prompts given during practice or playing time.

4. **Postinstruction.** Information or feedback that is given to students after a skill attempt.
5. **Questioning.** Questions that are asked about skills, strategies, or assignments.
6. **Physical assistance.** Manually moving a student's arms or legs to get them into the proper position or to move through the proper range of motion.
7. **Positive modeling.** The teacher demonstrates the correct way to perform a skill.
8. **Negative modeling.** The teacher demonstrates the incorrect way to perform a skill.
9. **Hustle.** Teacher statements that are intended to intensify the efforts of the students.
10. **Praise.** Verbal or nonverbal compliments or statements of acceptance.
11. **Scold.** Teacher behaviors that express displeasure with the students. These can be verbal or nonverbal.
12. **Management.** Teacher behaviors that focus on organizational aspects of a class such as lining up, taking attendance, rotating from stations, and so on.
13. **Uncodable.** Behavior that does not fit into the remaining categories.
14. **Silence.** Used with interval recording and focusing on periods of time where the teacher is monitoring without any verbal interactions.

The event recording procedure involves placing a tally within a behavior category as the behavior occurs. Figure 9.11 is an example of a completed event

---

Arizona State University Observation Instrument (ASUOI)

Date *11-15*   Coach *Darst*   Sport *Basketball*   Observer *Lacy*

Categories	Time _____	Time _____	Total	RPM	Percentage
Use of first name	~~HHT HHT~~ IIII	~~HHT HHT HHT~~ I	30	1.5	15.5
Preinstruction	~~HHT~~	II	7	.35	3.6
Concurrent instruction	III	I	4	.2	2.1
Postinstruction	~~HHT HHT HHT HHT~~ ~~HHT HHT HHT~~ II	~~HHT HHT HHT HHT~~ ~~HHT HHT HHT HHT~~ IIII	81	4.05	41.2
Questioning	IIII	II	6	.3	3.1
Physical assistance	II		2	.1	1.0
Positive modeling	III	IIII	7	.35	3.6
Negative modeling	II	I	3	.15	1.5
Hustle	~~HHT HHT~~	~~HHT~~ III	18	.9	9.3
Praise	IIII	~~HHT~~ I	10	.5	5.2
Scold	III	IIII	7	.35	3.6
Management	~~HHT HHT HHT HHT~~ ~~HHT~~ II	~~HHT HHT HHT~~ IIII	46	2.3	23.7
Uncodable	II	I	3	.15	1.5
Total	102	92	194	9.7	

Comments   *Preseason Practice—20 minutes total observation*

FIGURE 9.11 Completed ASUOI event recording sheet

From P. Darst, D. Zakrajsek, and V. Mancini (eds.). 1989. *Analyzing Physical Education and Sport Instruction.* 2nd ed. Champaign, IL: Human Kinetics Publishers. Copyright 1989 by P. Darst, D. Zakrajsek, and V. Mancini. Reprinted by permission of Human Kinetics Publishers.

Arizona State University Observation Instrument (ASUOI)

12	14	14	7	4	13	4	14	10	1/12	4	3	14	5	14	5	14	14		
12	14	14	12	4	13	10	14	1/10	11	4	14	14	14	14	14	14	14		
12	14	14	12	6	12	14	14	14	9	6	14	14	14	14	4	11	14		
13	14	14	11	4	12	14	14	14	2	4	1/3	14	4	13	4	4			
12	14	1/3	1/3	7	12	1/10	14	14	2	5	4	14	4	14	10	4			
12	3	5	4	14	12	9	14	14	14	14	4	12	14	14	4	4			
1/5	4	14	6	14	2	9	14	14	14	14	5	12	14	14	14	14			
2	4	14	4	14	2	6	14	Rest	14	5	14	12	1/9	14	14	14			
2	14	4	4	14	2	7	14	1/10	14	14	14	12	14	1/2	14	10			
2	14	4	14	14	14	7	14	14	14	10	9	14	14	2	14	4			
7	14	4	14	14	14	3	1/3	14	14	14	4	1/4	14	14	14	4			
2	1/10	9	14	14	14	4	14	12	14	14	7	4	1/6	3	14	14			
7	9	7	14	14	1/11	4	14	12	1/4	14	14	8	4	14	1/10	14			
1/5	10	8	14	14	4	14	14	12	1/4	14	14	7	4	4	14	14			

Coach ___Claxton___   Date ___4–15___   Observer ___Lacy___

School ___Grand Canyon H. S.___   Sport ___Tennis (varsity boys)___

Comments ___Record (10 min.) – Rest (2 min.) – Record (10 min.)___

___Mid-Season – Day after match.___

Behavior Codes

1. Use of first name	5. Questioning	10. Praise
2. Preinstruction	6. Physical assistance	11. Scold
3. Concurrent instruction	7. Positive modeling	12. Management
	8. Negative modeling	13. Uncodable
4. Postinstruction	9. Hustle	14. Silence

FIGURE 9.12 Completed ASUOI interval recording sheet

recording sheet for a basketball session. The behaviors can be totaled, a rate per minute established, and a specific percentage for each behavior calculated. Figure 9.12 is an example of an ASUOI interval recording sheet. A 5-second interval is used, and the appropriate number assigned to the behavior is entered in the block. If a student's first name is used with a behavior, then a 1 is entered with the number of the other behavior; for example, 1/10 to show a

first name with a praise. The number of intervals for each behavior is tallied and a percentage determined (see Figure 9.13).

Teachers use feedback from this instrument to analyze and set goals for their teaching behaviors in the various categories. Examples of behavior that teachers analyze include the use of the various instructional categories, praise to scold ratios, management procedures, or hustle behaviors.

Arizona State University Observation Instrument (ASUOI)		
Categories	Number of intervals	Percentage of intervals
1. Use of first name	18	7.5
2. Preinstruction	11	4.6
3. Concurrent instruction	8	3.3
4. Postinstruction	34	14.2
5. Questioning	8	3.3
6. Physical assistance	4	1.7
7. Positive modeling	8	3.3
8. Negative modeling	2	0.8
9. Hustle	8	3.3
10. Praise	12	5.0
11. Scold	8	3.3
12. Management	19	7.9
13. Uncodable	4	1.7
14. Silence	114	47.5
Total	240	100

FIGURE 9.13   Completed ASUOI recording worksheet

From P. Darst, D. Zakrajsek, and V. Mancini (eds.). 1989. *Analyzing Physical Education and Sport Instruction.* 2nd ed. Champaign, IL: Human Kinetics Publishers. Copyright 1989 by P. Darst, D. Zakrajsek, and V. Mancini. Reprinted by permission of Human Kinetics Publishers.

Self-Assessment Feedback Instrument (SAFI)

SAFI was designed for use as a simple self-assessment system for teachers and coaches (Mancini and Wuest, 1989). It focuses on how feedback is given during instruction. The categories developed are a modification of the Cheffers' Adaptation of Flanders' Interaction Analysis System (CAFIAS). SAFI gives teachers an event recording system that is easy to learn for recognizing various sequences of teaching behavior. This system is best used with an audiotape or videotape of a class.

The system focuses on the following 11 behaviors:

1. *Praise.* Teacher praise or encouragement directed toward student efforts, such as "Way to hustle, Seth."

2. *Praise/Reinstruct.* Teacher praise followed by useful information for future behavior, such as "Good hit, try to extend your arms for more power."
3. *Acceptance.* Teacher accepts and builds on student ideas.
4. *Questions.* Teacher asks questions about skills and class materials and requires students to answer.
5. *Instruction during performance.* Teacher provides information while students are practicing skills, drill, or scrimmage; for example, "Don't forget to block out for rebounding."
6. *Directions.* Teacher gives directions for students to follow, such as "Set up the figure 8 drill."
7. *Hustle.* Intense directions or orders that increase the enthusiasm or motivation of the students.
8. *Criticism.* Teacher expresses displeasure with students by using criticism, anger, or sarcasm; for example, "That's not good enough."

9. *Constructive criticism.* Teacher displeasure that is aimed at improving students' skills or behaviors; for example, "Almost, but it still is not quite correct."

10. *Criticism/Reinstruct.* Criticism that is followed by information for improvement; for example, "You dingbat, keep your weight back or you will never have any power."

11. *Constructive criticism/reinstruct.* Constructive criticism with additional information; for example, "Almost correct, but you still need to shorten the length of your stride another 3 to 5 inches."

As the observer watches the videotape, a tally is made in the proper behavior category during the 10-minute segment that is under observation (see Figure 9.14). The tallies are totalled and converted to a percentage of the total and a rate per minute. These data provide the teacher or coach with objective informa-

---

Self-Assessment Feedback Instrument (SAFI)

Directions: Classes or practices are divided into 10-minute segments for ease of observation. During each 10-minute segment, place a tally next to the appropriate behavior category each time this behavior occurs. The use of various behaviors may be calculated in terms of percentage of total behaviors or as rate per minute.

Name _____   Date _____

Class/practice no. _____   Length _____

Category	0–10	11–20	21–30	31–40	41–50	Total	Percent or Rate
Praise (2)							
Praise/reinstruct (2-5)							
Acceptance (3)							
Questions (4)							
Insruction during performance (8–5, 8\–5 or 9–5)							
Gives directions (6)							
Hustle behavior (6H)							
Criticism (7)							
Constructive criticism (7–2)							
Criticism/reinstruct (7–5)							
Constructive criticism/ reinstruct (7–2–5)							
Other behavior of interest							
Total							

FIGURE 9.14   SAFI recording sheet

From P. Darst, D. Zakrajsek, and V. Mancini (eds.). 1989. *Analyzing Physical Education and Sport Instruction.* 2nd ed. Champaign, IL: Human Kinetics Publishers. Copyright 1989 by P. Darst, D. Zakrajsek, and V. Mancini. Reprinted by permission of Human Kinetics Publishers.

tion about the type and frequency of feedback provided to the students. After a teacher establishes a normal pattern of behavior, decisions for changes and specific goals are established for future lessons. Goals are usually expressed as target percentages or rates per minute.

EXPECTED OUTCOMES

After reading this chapter, you should be able to

- Discuss the problems of evaluating instruction by using checklists and rating scales.

- Explain the advantages of self-evaluation concerning instruction in physical education.

- Describe the use of the specific systematic observation methods.

- Define specific teacher and student behaviors that are part of an on-going evaluation scheme.

- Set up a systematic observation plan for analyzing a specific teaching or student behavior.

- Complete a self-evaluation and set future goals for instructional improvement.

- Complete an evaluation of a taped or live lesson and make recommendations for improvement.

REFERENCES AND SUGGESTED READINGS

Darst, P. W., Zakrajsek, D. B., and Mancini, V. H. (eds.). 1989. *Analyzing Physical Education and Sport Instruction.* 2nd ed. Champaign, IL: Human Kinetics Publishers.

Johnson, T. W. H. 1989. Flow of teacher organizational patterns (FOTOP). In P. W. Darst, D. B. Zakrajsek, and V. H. Mancini (eds.). *Analyzing Physical Education and Sport Instruction.* 2nd ed. Champaign, IL: Human Kinetics Publishers. 173–177.

Lacy, A., and Darst, P. 1989. The Arizona State University Observation Instrument (ASUOI). In P. W. Darst, D. B. Zakrajsek, and V. H. Mancini (eds.). *Analyzing Physical Education and Sport Instruction.* 2nd ed. Champaign, IL: Human Kinetics Publishers. 369–377.

Mancini, V., and Wuest, D. 1989. Self-assessment feedback instrument (SAFI). In P. W. Darst, D. B. Zakrajsek, and V. H. Mancini (eds.). *Analyzing Physical Education and Sport Instruction.* 2nd ed. Champaign, IL: Human Kinetics Publishers. 143–147.

Randall, L., and Imwold, C. 1989. The effect of an intervention on academic learning time provided by preservice physical education teachers. *Journal of Teaching in Physical Education* 8(4): 271–279.

Siedentop, D. 1991. *Developing Teaching Skills in Physical Education.* 3rd ed. Palo Alto, CA: Mayfield Publishing Co.

van der Mars, H., Vogler, W., Darst, P., and Cusimano, B. 1994. Active supervision patterns of physical education teachers and their relationship with student behavior. *Journal of Teaching in Physical Education* 14(1): 99–112.

10 Evaluation and Grading

PURPOSE

To establish the difference between evaluation and grading. Teachers need to carefully consider what they want to accomplish before decisions are made on a specific evaluation and grading plan. Many ideas should be considered before deciding on the best procedure for a given situation.

KEY CONCEPTS

- Evaluation instruments can be used for grading, motivation, diagnosis, placement and equalization, program evaluation, and program support.
- Sport skill tests can be used to objectively assess students' skill levels in many sport areas. There are tests for general and specific components of skill.
- A wellness evaluation can be used as an on-going segment of the physical education program.
- Physical fitness testing can be part of a wellness program. The most popular test is the Prudential Fitnessgram System.
- Subjective methods of evaluation of skills include checklists, anecdotal records, personal interviews, and self-evaluation.
- Knowledge tests assess students' understanding of rules, strategy, etiquette, and history of sports and physical activities.
- Attitudes and values can be evaluated formally and informally.
- There are pros and cons to using a grading system in physical education.
- There are many different views on the best way to grade students. Some of the important issues are educational objectives versus administrative tasks, process versus product, improvement and potential, negative versus positive systems, and pass-fail versus letter grades.
- All grading systems have strengths and weaknesses. Teachers need to understand the various options.
- Evaluation and grading are used to enhance the educational process and contribute to the accomplishment of intended program objectives.

Evaluation and grading are 2 areas teachers are expected to integrate into the teaching process. Regardless of how evaluation is managed, the emphasis on accountability continues to place more importance on this area. No longer are school boards willing to support a program that does not document its impact on students. Similarly, students are much less willing to accept a grade in physical education if it is not grounded on principles similar to those in other academic areas. Evaluation and grading are two different entities. *Evaluation* is defined as the measurement of skills, knowledges, and attitudes taught in physical education classes. *Grading* is a composite score that incorporates the information and data gathered through the evaluation process. Evaluation offers students a view of how they are performing in different areas under the physical education umbrella. For example, a student might earn high marks in volleyball and basketball skills but lower in soccer and team handball. A grade is assigned as a composite score for all the areas measured in physical education; to some degree it is an average report of all data gathered through the process of evaluation.

EVALUATING STUDENT PERFORMANCE

Many components are evaluated in physical education. A major part of evaluation is examining the skill learning and development that occurs through the instructional process. Even though skill development is the primary focus of physical education, it is not enough; students need to learn about strategy, skill performance techniques, and sport etiquette. Written exams can evaluate whether students have requisite knowledge for successful participation. Finally, the area of attitudes and values is important to the program. Students will choose not to participate if their attitudes and values have not developed concurrently with skills and knowledge. The focus of this section is to discuss each of the 3 areas of learning and offer examples of evaluative instruments.

Using evaluative instruments can serve a number of purposes (Strand and Wilson, 1993). Some of the more common reasons for evaluation include the following:

Grading. Performance on physical skill instruments offer objective data for grading. Communicating with students and parents is more effective when an objective and systematic tool has been used for evaluation. Parents and students can see how they compare to others and are given a realistic view of their performance in relation to other students. Grades based on objective data carry more credibility and respect both inside and outside the profession.

Motivation. Nothing motivates individuals more than improvement. When improvement can be documented through evaluation, it can be clear evidence that effort has been rewarded. It is difficult to know the extent of improvement (or lack of) if evaluation is not a part of the program. Another factor that motivates students is the setting of reachable goals. It is difficult to know what is reasonable and reachable if students are unaware of their performance level and ability.

Diagnosis. Evaluation will often reveal problems or deficiencies. When teaching an entire class, it is difficult to sense the ability and progress of each student. Often more energy is placed on monitoring student behavior than student performance. Evaluation will focus energy on progress of individual students and reveal those students who are deficient or performing skills incorrectly.

Placement and equalization. At times, it is effective to group students homogeneously, that is, students with equal ability are placed in groups. On the other hand, using a peer tutoring method can be done if evaluation reveals skilled performances and students having problems. Student evaluation will help teachers place students with helpers and equalize small groups when it enhances learning.

Program evaluation. Evaluation of students can reveal the effectiveness of the program and the relevancy of objectives. If all students pass the evaluation, it may mean that the goals of the program are too low. If many fail, the quality of instruction may be inadequate or the standard of performance may be out of reach. Over time, evaluation of students can give direction to the program as objectives and instructional strategies are modified to increase student success.

Program support. Results of regular evaluation can be used to validate and support the program. The data gained through evaluation is objective and can reveal what students are expected to learn and how effectively they are learning. Accountability is a buzz word among educators as schools try to document what students are learning in order to gain public support. When administrators need to make cutbacks in programs, they usually ask faculty members to justify continuation of their program. Data gained through consistent evaluation of students is a strong and effective way to defend the program.

OBJECTIVE EVALUATION OF PHYSICAL SKILLS

Physical skill development is the primary purpose of physical education. Knowledge and attitude development can be developed in other areas of the curriculum, but skill development only occurs through an effective physical education program. Physical skills can be divided into 2 subsets: The first set contains the general components of skill such as agility, balance, coordination, power, reaction time, and speed. These components are often referred to as skill-related fitness. The second set of skills relates to the ability to perform specific sport skills, such as basketball, tennis, or team handball.

General Components of Skill

Individuals who are skilled usually display ability in a number of skill components. The more a person excels in each of the components, the greater the possibility they will perform well in sport skills. The following discussion identifies each of the components of skill and offers an example of a test commonly used to measure the component.

Agility

Agility is the ability of the body to change position rapidly and accurately while moving in space. Most sports require agility and the ability to move in different directions quickly.

Sample Test.   Shuttle run (AAHPER, 1976). Two blocks of wood are placed side by side on a line 30 feet from the starting line. On command to start, the student runs from behind the starting line to retrieve one of the blocks. After placing it behind the starting line, the student runs to pick up the second block and carries it back across the starting line. Two trials are given, with rest allowed between them. The score is recorded as the number of seconds required to retrieve both blocks.

Balance

Balance is usually classified into 2 types: static and dynamic. Static balance occurs when the person is in a fixed position, such as doing a hand stand or balancing on a balance beam. Dynamic balance is the ability to move in a stable manner without falling and is used in activities such as skating, gymnastics, and most locomotor sports.

Sample Tests.   Stork stand for static balance (Safrit, 1990). The student stands erect on the dominant foot placing the opposite foot flat on the medial part of the supporting knee, with the hands on hips. The score is the amount of time the balance position can be held.

Balance beam walk for dynamic balance (Jensen and Hirst, 1980). The student is instructed to stand at one end of a 4-inch wide balance beam. When ready, the student begins to slowly walk (1 foot in front of the other) the full length of the beam, pausing at the end for 5 seconds, turning 180 degrees, and returning to the starting point. Three trials are given. The test is a scored as pass-fail.

Coordination

Coordination is the ability to smoothly integrate a number of motor patterns together to produce a complete and effective skill. Coordination is most often required for complex skills such as throwing, catching, striking, and kicking.

Sample Test.   Stick test of coordination (Corbin and Lindsey, 1994). The stick test of coordination requires juggling 3 wooden wands. One wand is held in each hand and the third wand rests across the other 2. The resting wand is flipped a half turn (1 point) or full turn (2 points) and caught using the wands in each hand. Five attempts are allowed for a half turn and 5 attempts for a full turn. The test is scored by adding the points earned for the number of successful flips (15 points possible).

Speed and Reaction Time

Speed and reaction time are closely related components. Speed is the ability to move quickly in the shortest time possible. Reaction time is the amount of time necessary to respond to a signal. Even though both can be measured separately, it is most common to group them and measure them singly in a dash. Running a sprint for time requires rapid reaction time and speed.

Sample Test.   Fifty-yard dash (AAHPER, 1976). The student is timed while running the 50-yard distance as fast as possible.

Power

Power is the ability to exert maximum muscular force in a minimum amount of time.

Sample Test. Standing long jump (AAHPER, 1976). The student assumes a starting position behind the take-off line. The student takes off of both feet simultaneously and jumps as far as possible. The long jump is scored on the best of 3 trials to the nearest inch.

Specific Sport Skills

A wide number of tests have been designed to objectively evaluate sport skills. These tests are usually carefully designed and have been designed for high validity and reliability. Norms are usually available for the tests so teachers can compare the performance of their students with a larger number of students who have been tested. This section is not meant to be comprehensive but to give a few examples of the types of objective tests that are available to teachers. Two excellent textbooks that contain a wide variety of tests are Hastad and Lacy (1994) and Strand and Wilson (1993).

Bear in mind that tests evaluate components of a sport only and can never completely evaluate actual performance under competitive pressure. Skill tests can also become so complex that the teacher may find them unacceptable in the instructional setting. Some tests require a large number of trained personnel for administration, which may not be feasible. Regardless of these restrictions, however, an instructor should arrange to conduct some skill evaluations. It is important that students know they are responsible for learning specific skills.

Cornish Handball Test

The test (Cornish, 1949) consists of 5 test items: the 30-second volley, the frontwall placement, the backwall placement, the service placement, and the power test. When the tests were analyzed for validity, however, the power test and the 30-second volley alone predicted handball performance almost as effectively as all 5 items together. To conserve time, it is therefore recommended that only the 2 items be used.

Equipment. Several handballs are required. The service line is the only marking necessary for the volley test. For the power test, a line is drawn on the front wall at a height of 6 feet. Lines are also drawn on the floor as follows: the first line is 18 feet from the front wall; the second line is 5 feet behind the first; the third, fourth, and fifth lines are each 5¾ feet apart. These lines form 6 scoring zones. The area from the front wall to the first line scores 1 point, as does the first of the 5 zones behind. The 2, 3, 4, and 5 zones score 2, 3, 4, and 5 points, respectively. A stopwatch is needed for the volley test.

Power Test Directions. The subject stands in the service zone and throws the ball against the front wall. Subject lets the ball hit the floor on the rebound before striking it. The subject then hits the ball as hard as possible, making sure that it strikes the front wall below the 6-foot line. Subjects must throw the ball against the wall before each power stroke. Five trials are given with each hand. A retrial is allowed for an attempt in which the subject steps into the front court or fails to hit the wall below the 6-foot line. Scoring: The value of the scoring zone in which each trial first touches the floor is recorded. The subject's score is the total points for the 10 trials.

Thirty-Second Volley. The subject stands behind the service line, drops the ball, and begins volleying it against the front wall for 30 seconds. The subject should hit all strokes from behind the service line. If the ball does not return past this line, the subject is allowed to step into the front court to hit the ball, but must then get back behind the line for the succeeding stroke. If the subject misses the ball, the instructor hands over another ball and volleying continues.

Scoring. The score is the total number of times the ball hits the front wall in 30 seconds.

Kemp-Vincent Tennis Rally Test

This test (Kemp and Vincent, 1968) evaluates rallying ability in tennis under game conditions. Two students of similar ability assume ready positions on opposite sides of the net on a singles tennis court. Each player has 2 tennis balls on his or her side of the court. On signal, 1 student bounces a ball behind the baseline and with a courtesy stroke puts the ball into play. The 2 students rally the ball as long as possible. When a ball is hit into the net or out of bounds, either player starts another ball into play with a courtesy stroke from behind the baseline. Any type of stroke may be used during a rally. If all 4 balls are hit out of play, the testing students are responsible for retrieving them to continue the test. One 3-minute trial is allowed.

Scoring. For a 3-minute rally, the combined number of hits for the 2 players are counted including any erroneous hits. The courtesy stroke to put a ball in play counts as a hit. Errors committed by each player are counted. From the combined number of hits for both players, each individual player subtracts the number of his or her errors to arrive at a final rally score.

AAHPERD Basketball Test

This comprehensive test battery (AAHPERD, 1984) evaluates a number of basketball skills including dribbling, passing, shooting, and defensive ability. Each of the areas is briefly described.

Speed Spot Shooting. Five spots are laid out around the key. The shooter must shoot, retrieve the ball, dribble to another spot, and shoot again. The student must attempt at least 1 shot from each spot. All students get 3 trials of 60 seconds each.

Passing. Six targets are placed on a wall with a restraining line 8 feet away from the wall. On signal, the student performs a chest pass to the first target, recovers the ball, and moves to the second target. This action continues until they reach the last target. While at the last target, they throw two chest passes, then repeat the sequence moving to the left. This pattern continues until time runs out (30 seconds). Three trials are given.

Control Dribble. Five cones are placed in the key, one in each corner and the fifth in the middle. On signal, the student weaves in and out of the cones and completes the course as fast as possible. The score is recorded in the number of seconds required to complete the course. Three trials are given.

Defensive Ability. The student slides in defensive position from marker to marker without crossing the feet. Each time a marker is reached, the student must touch the floor. The score is recorded in number of seconds required to complete the course.

Johnson Soccer Test

The purpose of the test (Johnson, 1963) is to evaluate general ability in soccer. A wall marked with the same dimensions as a soccer goal and a supply of soc-

cer balls are needed. The student starts behind a restraining line that is 15 feet from the wall. On signal, the student kicks a ball against the wall so that it rebounds back on the fly or after bouncing. The objective is to return the ball against the backboard as many times as possible during a 30-second timed interval. All kicks must be initiated from behind the restraining line. If a ball goes out of control, the student can retrieve another from the supply. Three 30-second trials are given. The score is the number of legal kicks made during the 3 trials.

Wellness

A wellness evaluation can be undertaken annually to identify and assess factors that, if untreated, might result in later health problems. The data can be gathered at different places in the school setting by school nurses and physical education teachers. The information is collated and made available to teachers, students, and parents. The wellness profile needs to contain a section that interprets data for students and parents. The wellness profile does not diagnose disease but offers information about basic health-related areas. If results of the measurements give cause for concern, parents can decide if the student should see a doctor.

The example of a wellness profile shown in Figure 10.1 consists of 2 parts. The first is a listing of the data gathered, and the second is a description of what each item measures and why it is important to sound health. When a battery of professionals is brought together, the profile information can be gathered quickly. With the help of school nurses, physical education instructors, and clerical aides, it is usually possible to gather all the data in 1 period. Data other than those shown in Figure 10.1 can also be included in the wellness profile (for example, visual screening, auditory screening, posture checks, and immunization and medical examinations).

Health-Related Fitness

Physical fitness testing has occurred for decades in physical education. Some experts make an argument for placing less emphasis on fitness testing and more on activity evaluation (Corbin, Pangrazi, and Welk 1994). There is much to be said, however, for using a standardized test that is administered to many students. Currently the Prudential Fitnessgram System

Wellness Profile

It is important to understand your personal health. As an ongoing component of the physical education program, you recently participated in the health screening. Listed below are the results and corresponding percentile scores for a person in your age group. An explanation of the items included in this screening is listed below.

Health Component	Score	Acceptable/ Unacceptable
Skinfold	_____ % body fat	_____
Sit and reach test	_____ centimeters	_____
Sit-ups (1 min)	_____ repetitions	_____
Aerobic field test (run-walk 1 mi)	_____ minutes: seconds	_____
Height	_____ inches	_____
Weight	_____ pounds	_____
Blood pressure		
Systolic	_____ mm Hg	_____
Diastolic	_____ mm Hg	_____

Dental and oral inspection _____

The profile is not meant to diagnose disease, but to indicate basic measurements of health. If you are concerned or uncertain, please take this form to your doctor or clinic. Please feel free to contact the school nurse if you have any questions.

Explanation of Wellness Profile Items

Skinfold:	This measurement relates to the amount of fat a person carries. People who have too much fat are more likely to have problems such as diabetes (excessive sugar in the blood) and high blood pressure.
Sit and reach:	The sit and reach test measures flexibility of the lower back and hamstring (back of thigh) muscle group. A lack of flexibility often contributes to low back pain.
Sit-ups:	Sit-ups measure the strength and endurance of the abdominal muscle group. Strength in this area is important for proper posture and to prevent low back pain.
Aerobic field test:	The aerobic field test consists of running or walking a mile in the least amount of time possible. This test is the best single indicator of cardiorespiratory endurance, which is important in preventing heart disease.
Height and weight:	These are general measurements of a child's growth. It is important that children's growth be observed regularly to ensure that the body is developing normally.
Blood pressure:	Blood pressure is recorded using two values. The top number (systolic) represents the pressure in the arteries when the heart is pumping blood. The bottom number (diastolic) is the pressure in the arteries when the heart is at rest. High blood pressure increases the risk of heart disease.
Dental and oral inspection:	An inspection of the gums and teeth is conducted to visualize noticeable inflammation, sores, and cavities.

Interpreting the Results:

Results are in two categories. The first is the raw score, which is your actual performance. The second column checks whether your scores are acceptable or unacceptable for a minimum fitness level needed for a healthy lifestyle.

FIGURE 10.1   Wellness profile

FIGURE 10.2   Self-testing health-related fitness

(1992) is the most popular test being used to measure health-related physical fitness and is the recommended test for the AAHPERD. The test items have been validated for validity and reliability. The test items are described in detail in Chapter 16.

SUBJECTIVE EVALUATION OF PHYSICAL SKILLS

Most teachers use subjective evaluation at different times by observing students and making a judgment about their performance. One of the drawbacks of the observation system is that it is less reliable; 2 different teachers may differ dramatically in their assessment of the same student. On the other hand, observation can be done with a minimum of effort, it requires little time, and gives students immediate feedback.

Checklists

Subjective evaluation can be improved by using a check sheet or scorecard. Criteria are listed and ranked on a scale of points. Even though using the checklist will increase the reliability of the data, the overall approach is still subjective. A score sheet can be used to evaluate skill development. For example, teachers select the types of skills they believe a student should learn in a basketball unit. While the unit is in progress, the teacher observes students and as-

signs a score. Grades are awarded on the basis of various areas evaluated, with students who accumulate the most points receiving the highest grade.

Checklists are useful for reporting progress to students and parents and to identify youngsters who are in need of special help. A class list with skills listed across the top of the sheet is a common method used for recording class progress. If grading is based on the number of activities students master, the checklist can deliver this information. Checklists are usually most effective when skills are listed in the sequence in which they should be learned. In this way, the teacher can gear the teaching process to diagnosed needs. To avoid disrupting the learning process, teachers can record student progress informally while students are practicing. Figure 10.3 is a sample checklist for rope-jumping skills.

Anecdotal Record Sheets

A record sheet that contains student names and has room for comments about student performance can be used to assess student progress. Anecdotal records of student progress can be reinforcing to both student and teacher as it is often difficult to remember how much progress has been made over a period of time. With anecdotal records, teachers can inform students of their initial skill level compared with their present performance. When making anecdotal records, record the performance as soon as possible and with accuracy. If background information is needed to put the performance in proper context, it should be included.

A tape recorder is useful for recording anecdotal information. The teacher may record comments during observation and transcribe them later. This process helps teachers learn the names and behavior patterns of students and leads to an increased understanding of student performance. Observations should be recorded at the start of the unit and compared with observations made at a later date as instruction proceeds.

Personal Interviews

The interview system is used to monitor students. In this approach, teachers question individual students about their knowledge and monitor their skill levels. The strength of the approach lies in the relationship teachers develop with students. The personal interview can make students feel wanted and cared for,

Rope-Jumping Checklist

Student	Jump in Place	Jump, Turn Both Ends	Jump, Pendulum Swing	Slow Time	Fast Time	Alternate-Foot Step	Swing Step Forward	Rocker Step	Spread Legs, Forward	Toe-and-Heel Touch	Shuffle Step	Cross Arms	Cross Arms, Backward	Double Jump

FIGURE 10.3 Example of a checklist for rope-jumping skills

From R. Pangrazi and V. Dauer. 1995. *Dynamic Physical Education for Elementary School Children.* 11th ed. Boston: Allyn & Bacon. p. 201.

since few students have the opportunity to share with an instructor how much they have learned in a class. The weaknesses of the approach are in the areas of time and objectivity. A teacher who comes in contact with a large number of students finds it impossible to talk individually with each one. The approach is highly subjective and may result in a grade being assigned on the quality of the interview rather than on the knowledge and performance of the student. The interview system can be made less subjective if checklists of questions and skill evaluations are developed and followed with each student.

Even if this approach cannot be used on a broad scale, interviewing can be a useful tool for evaluating the effectiveness of the program and the instruction. Teachers can select key students to interview to see how well they are learning, how they feel about the instructional approach, and what they might like to have added to the program. Seldom do teachers sit down and discuss the wants and concerns of students. This approach can enhance this important phase of instruction.

Self-Evaluation

Since an important phase of evaluation is to teach students how to personally assess their performances, a self-evaluation scheme can be a useful component of a grading system. The most common approach is to teach students to set goals, develop strategies for reaching the goals, and self-evaluate their performance. When student self-evaluation is used, the instructional approach must teach students how to evaluate. Less instructional time is available for teaching skills because time must be allowed to teach students to set meaningful goals and strategies and to apply evaluation techniques. In most cases, teachers who use this approach also evaluate students, with the final grade being a composite of student and teacher evaluations.

Another variation of the self-evaluation approach is to allow the class to develop goals they want to achieve. The class decides democratically what they wish to accomplish, and together they decide how to best accomplish the goals. At the end of the instructional session, both students and teacher evaluate the progress made and the final grade.

Some teachers add a third phase to the evaluation process by having students evaluate students. This results in a 3-pronged evaluation scheme: teacher, student, and self-evaluation. One of the strongest reasons given for using this approach is that it makes students feel more involved in the educational process. Students are more likely to believe that the grading system is fair when it manifests itself through teacher, peer, and self-evaluation.

EVALUATION OF KNOWLEDGE

Evaluating cognitive achievement is an area of physical education that can be controversial. Students often feel that it is enough to learn skills and that they should not have to take written exams in physical education. Some parents resent it when their youngsters receive a lower grade because of poor performance on written tests. Teachers have often been unwilling to administer written tests in physical education because of the amount of time it takes from skill practice. Regardless of feelings, it is apparent that knowledge is involved in the application of all motor skills. An individual must know rules, regulations, and proper etiquette to participate fairly and enjoyably with others. The "how to" of proper skill performance is knowledge based, and personal skill improvement does not occur if the individual does not know proper skill techniques. Most likely, to minimize concern, teachers need to explain to students and parents why cognitive achievement is as important in physical education as in any other academic area.

Evaluating the cognitive domain should be done efficiently and only when necessary. The goal of physical education should always be focused on maximizing activity and assuring that students learn physical skills. When physical education instruction becomes a classroom endeavor, other teachers in academic areas can deliver and measure requisite knowledge as effectively as a physical educator. Including the cognitive element as a part of instruction will indicate that effective skill learning requires knowledge.

Knowledge tests can be given to assess understanding of the rules, strategy, and history of a sport or activity. The tests should be developed according to the ages of the students involved at the different grade levels. Test questions can be multiple choice,

true-false, completion, or essay. To minimize the amount of time necessary to complete the test, avoid essay questions. This will also reduce the amount of grading time. Figure 10.4 is an example of a test that might be administered to junior high school students at the completion of a unit on racquetball.

When designing written tests, observing a few key points can make the examinations more effective.

1. Group different types of questions by format. True-false, multiple-choice, and matching questions should be in separate sections.
2. Place all instructions on the test. Particular instructions for different types of questions should precede each section.
3. Place the test items in increasing order of difficulty. Students may give up on the exam if the first question or two is high in difficulty.
4. Assure that there is not an obvious pattern to the exam such as alternating true and false items or key words that tip off the answer (for example, using *always* or *never* in true-false questions).
5. Carefully monitor the exam. Students feel the instructor is unfair if it is easy to cheat or share answers. Also, when monitoring the exam, teachers can listen to student questions. Similar questions about similar items often tip off an instructor to a poorly designed or written item.

Sometimes an acceptable alternative is to give students a crossword puzzle or a word search in place of a written test. (See units on archery, badminton, and bowling in Chapters 20 and 21 for examples of puzzles and word searches.) Teachers can check students' knowledge using both of these approaches, and the students seem to enjoy the activities more than a conventional test.

Sources of Knowledge Test Questions

A few sources are available that contain test questions. "Canned" questions are seldom adequate for most teachers because they do not cover all desired areas. Most teachers have favorite areas of emphasis and know what students need to know. However, these sources can give direction to test writing and offer an indication of what others deem important in the way of knowledge. Such questions can also be modified to meet the specific needs of teachers. The text by McGee and Farrow (1987) includes 250 to 400

Racquetball Exam

I. In the blanks below, fill in the name of the area of the court designated by each letter. (10 points)

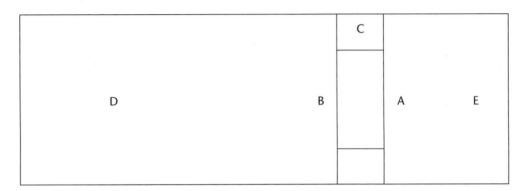

A _____ Line

B _____ Line

C _____

D _____ Court

E _____ Court

II. In the following diagrams, draw an arrow to indicate the path that the ball is most likely to follow. None of these shots has hit the floor. The (X) indicates the point of origin of the shot. (6 points)

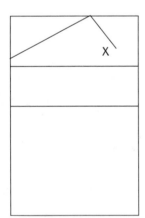 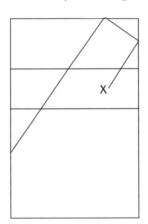 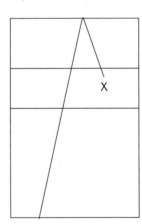

III. In the spaces at the left, place a (+) if the statement is *True;* place a (0) if the statement is *False.* (60 points)

_____ 1. A game consists of 15 points.

_____ 2. Only the server may score a point.

_____ 3. The server may either bounce the ball before serving, or hit it straight out of her hand.

_____ 4. Only one foot need be in the service zone when serving.

_____ 5. In doubles, the partner with the better left hand usually plays the left side.

FIGURE 10.4   Knowledge test for racquetball

_____ 6. The choice for the right to serve is decided by the toss of a coin, and the side winning the toss starts the first and third games.

_____ 7. If a player swings and misses on the serve, he is given only one more chance.

_____ 8. A legal serve must bounce in the back court on a fly or after touching one side wall.

_____ 9. In doubles, only one person serves in the first and second service. After that, both players on each team serve.

_____ 10. A player is out if he is hit with his own shot on the fly, but it is a hinder if his own shot hits him on one bounce.

_____ 11. It is common courtesy to alternate serves to each court, but in tournament play there is no such rule.

_____ 12. The more walls that a shot hits, the deader the rebound will be.

_____ 13. When playing a "lane shot," it is usually best to hit the ball underhand.

_____ 14. It is good to use the side wall when using the "lob serve."

_____ 15. The "kill shot" should be attempted when the ball is chest high.

_____ 16. The most advantageous court position is just behind the short line.

_____ 17. It is often wise to let a waist-high shot bounce off the back wall so that it can be returned from a lower height.

_____ 18. In doubles, a player may call a hinder when she is obstructed from hitting the ball by her partner.

_____ 19. In doubles, the server's partner must lean against the side wall until the ball passes the service line.

_____ 20. The ball should be contacted at the junction between the fingers and the palm.

IV. In the spaces at the left, place the letter of the answer that best completes the statement. (24 points)

_____ 1. Which of the following is _not_ a serve?
A. Scotch toss serve
B. Ceiling serve
C. Power serve
D. Z serve

_____ 2. All of the following concerning body position for hitting the "kill shot" are correct _except:_
A. Bend the knees and waist.
B. Weight transfer is from the front foot to the rear foot.
C. Contact should be at shin level or lower.
D. The forearm should be parallel to the floor.

_____ 3. All of the following are "shorts" _except:_
A. Hitting the side wall and then the front wall.
B. Hitting the front wall and then having the ball bounce in front of the short line.
C. Hitting the front wall and then the two side wails.
D. Hitting the front wall and then the ceiling.

_____ 4. All of the following statements concerning receiving the serve are true _except:_
A. The receiver must be behind the short line while the ball is being served.
B. The receiver may return the service on either the volley or the first bounce.
C. A short may be returned if so desired.
D. The receiver does not have the option of returning the service on a foot fault.

_____ 5. How many bounces are permitted on the serve?
A. 2
B. 3
C. 4
D. unlimited amount

FIGURE 10.4 Continued

multiple-choice questions for each of 15 different physical education activities. Questions range from beginning to advanced performance level and are appropriate for junior and senior high schools students.

EVALUATION OF ATTITUDES AND VALUES

A common claim among physical educators is that they build character and help students become better human beings. Few educators measure the impact their program and instruction have on this important area. Usually, teachers agree about what to do for students in the affective learning domain. Most teachers want to

1. Develop positive attitudes toward physical activity. If students learn physical skills but develop a negative feeling about activity, it is quite likely they will not participate when left on their own. Feeling positive about one's ability and competency in physical activities will increase the possibility of participation.

2. Enhance a positive self-concept. If students learn physical skills and are able to perform them adequately, they will be viewed positively by peers. The self-concept is reinforced through feedback from others. When teachers and peers respond positively, individuals learn that they are worthy individuals.

3. Develop proper social skills. Students need to learn to play fair and with proper respect for others. The opportunity to cooperate and compete with peers offers students a chance to learn what personal behavior is acceptable or unacceptable. Since most behavior in physical education is visible to others, feedback about proper social behavior is effective and immediate.

Behavioral attitudes can informally be monitored with a checklist similar to the one in Figure 10.5. This instrument is informal and relates specific behaviors to attitude. Teachers often view a "good attitude" as one where the student does what the teacher tells them to do. This approach deals more with behavior than attitude toward physical education. If such a tool is used, it offers the advantage of listing specific criteria. At times, teachers will tell a student they have a "bad attitude" but not define why they are being chastised. A checklist defines what behavior is expected and helps prevent making snap judgments about attitudes.

A number of instruments are available for measuring attitudes and values. A few examples are of-

---

Attitude Check Sheet

Assign 0 to 5 points during each observation with 5 being the highest score. A number of observations should be made during the semester in order to reveal consistency and improvement.

Student _____ Date _____ Lesson focus _____

		0	1	2	3	4	5
1.	Tries all activities	0	1	2	3	4	5
2.	Is on time	0	1	2	3	4	5
3.	Consistently gives a maximum effort	0	1	2	3	4	5
4.	Shows concern for others	0	1	2	3	4	5
5.	Listens to and applies criticism	0	1	2	3	4	5
6.	Shows enthusiasm	0	1	2	3	4	5
7.	Participates with all students	0	1	2	3	4	5
8.	Shares ideas with teacher and class	0	1	2	3	4	5
9.	Demonstrates leadership	0	1	2	3	4	5
10.	Volunteers to help others	0	1	2	3	4	5

FIGURE 10.5   Student attitude check sheet

fered here. For a review of a wide variety of instruments, see the text by Hastad and Lacy (1994). Such instruments have been evaluated over time and are somewhat more accurate in evaluating long-term attitudes and values. Regardless of the instrument used, teachers should use caution; personality traits change and are difficult to measure.

Edgington Attitude Scale

This scale (Edgington, 1968) measures the attitude of high school students toward physical education. The inventory consists of 66 statements about physical education class. Students are asked to place a mark next to the response option that best reflects their feelings about the statement. A Likert scale is used and students can respond with 6 options, from very strongly agree to very strongly disagree.

Adams Physical Education Attitude Scale

On this scale (Adams, 1963), attitudes toward physical education are measured using statements about physical education. The student reads the statement and then indicates agreement or disagreement; for example, "I suppose physical education is all right, but I don't much care for it.

TO GRADE OR NOT TO GRADE?

Another issue related to grading is whether physical education should be graded. Some feel that the most important purpose of a physical education program is to offer students the opportunity to recreate and exercise. Others feel that education should be a primary focus and a grade is needed to reflect how much students have learned. Arguments are offered on each side of the issue, to grade or not to grade, to help teachers better understand and defend the approach they choose. For an in-depth review of grading, the text by Hastad and Lacy (1994) is recommended.

Arguments against Using a Grading System

• Grades are difficult to interpret. A grade means one thing to one teacher and another to a different teacher. When moving to a different school, the meaning of the grade does not transfer, and teachers at the new school may view the grade differently.

• Physical education does not place emphasis on content and product. Rather, it judges success by improvement of skills. Grades in academic areas reflect achievement and accomplishment; because grades in physical education reflect improvement and effort, they may be interpreted incorrectly.

• Often, time is limited in physical education, and classes only meet a few days a week. Testing for the purpose of assigning a grade is time consuming and takes away from learning opportunities. Physical educators try to squeeze as much learning as possible into a minimal amount of time, and grading will dramatically reduce their instructional time.

• Physical education is diverse and broad by definition. Instruction covers all 3 learning domains, that is, skill development, attitude formation, and content knowledge. Trying to grade all 3 of these areas is difficult and demands a great deal of time. In addition, which of these 3 domains is most important, and can any of them be overlooked?

• Grading is done only in areas where standardized instruments have been developed. Fitness testing is the major area in physical education where a variety of standardized tests have been developed. Due to the dearth of standardized tests in other areas, excessive attention is given to fitness testing.

• Physical education places emphasis on physical fitness and skill performance. Performance in these areas is strongly controlled by genetics, making it difficult for all students to achieve, even when they "give it their best effort." In addition, when grades are given for physical fitness performance, some youngsters feel discouraged because they train and still do not reach standards of high performance (see Chapter 16).

Arguments for Using a Grading System

• Giving grades makes physical education similar to other academic areas in the school curriculum. This gives physical education credibility and gains respect from parents, teachers, and administrators.

• Grades communicate the performance of students to parents. Parents have a right to know how their youngsters perform in physical education. Grades are used by teachers in other areas and are easily understood and interpreted by parents; therefore, they should be used in physical education.

• When grades are not given, academic respect is lost. Physical education already suffers from the misguided perception that physical educators don't teach anything, they just "roll out the ball." Lack of a grading system may make it appear to others that little learning is occurring.

• A grading system gives accountability. When grades are given, administrators and parents often assume that teaching and student accomplishment have occurred.

• A grading system rewards skilled students. Students are rewarded in academic areas for their intelligence and performance and should be similarly rewarded for accomplishment in physical education settings.

GRADING—DIFFERING VIEWPOINTS

Many approaches are used for grading students. Grading methods vary depending on the philosophies of teachers and district-wide school regulations. This section examines different viewpoints, offers insight into each, and challenges readers to defend the grading procedure they choose.

Educational Objectives versus Administrative Tasks

There is general agreement that physical education should help students achieve in 4 areas: skill development, physical fitness, personal values, and cognitive development. Some grading systems assign weight to each of the areas when compiling a grade. Regardless of the amount of emphasis given to each area, the final grade depends on accomplishment of educational objectives. This contrasts with grading on completion of administrative tasks where students earn a part or all of their grade by showering, attendance, participation, promptness, and wearing the proper uniform. This latter approach grades students on tasks that have little to do with accomplishment of physical education objectives.

Consider the conflicts arising when students are graded on achievement of educational objectives versus accomplishment of administrative tasks. Assume a student in a math class regularly forgets to bring a pencil and is tardy but earns an A grade on all math exams. Does this student earn a final grade of A, or is the student penalized for doing poorly on administrative tasks (tardiness, and so on) and given a C grade. Reverse the situation and assume the student has an outstanding attitude, is never tardy, and always brings the proper supplies to class. At the end of the semester, the student has earned a C grade on exams yet performed all administrative tasks at a high level. Does this student receive a final grade of A? If grades in other curricular areas of the school are earned through accomplishment of educational objectives or performance of administrative tasks, it is probably wise to follow suit in the physical education area.

Administrative tasks are usually enforced through school or district-wide regulations. For example, most districts have procedures for dealing with excessive absences or tardiness. Usually, teachers need not further penalize students through a grade reductions. Sometimes students are graded on participation, which is similar to receiving a grade just because one is physically present in class. On the other hand, students should be able to choose not to participate in class only when they are excused by the administration or by the school nurse (for sickness or injury). Participation alone should not be used as a factor in assigning grades. Rather, all students should be expected to participate unless excused by administrative edict.

If a student does not attend class, it is defensible to ask the student to repeat the class. This is usually done by assigning a failing grade. Because instructors do this in other academic areas, excessive absences are usually an acceptable criterion for failing the student. The major theme to remember is that grading systems in physical education should be in line with the grading systems in other subject-matter areas. If physical educators choose to grade otherwise, the grade may be meaningless to other teachers, parents, and students. Differences in grading approaches have caused some school districts to not calculate physical education grades in the overall grade point average nor include them in graduation requirements. When grades earned in physical education become unimportant to school requirements, it makes it easy to say that physical education should no longer be required of all students since the grade is meaningless. The bottom line is to grade in a manner that is compatible with other subject-matter areas.

Process versus Product

Another area of concern when evaluating is whether the process or the product of education is more important. Those who emphasize the process of education stress the importance of students leaving school with warm and positive feelings toward physical activity. These educators state their beliefs in the following manner: "I am not concerned about how many skills my students learn, I just want them to walk out of my class with positive feelings about physical activity." The assumption is that students who feel positive about physical activity will be willing to be active throughout their lifetime. These teachers assign grades based on the process of trying rather than the product of performance. Students who receive higher grades may not be the most skilled but have shown improvement and effort throughout the semester.

Teachers who reside in the product camp focus primarily on student accomplishment and see effort as something that is laudable but not part of the grading process. Their philosophy might be stated as follows: "I don't really care whether students like me or physical education. What is ultimately important is their performance. After all, the students who are best in math earn the highest grades, so why should it be any different in physical education?" Teachers who focus on product give the highest grade to the best performer, regardless of other factors. Less-skilled students, no matter how hard they try, will not receive an above-average grade.

This is a difficult problem to resolve in physical education and is always hotly debated. One point of view is that students should learn how society works from the grading system. People are not rewarded in life based on how hard they try, but rather, on their performance. For example, if real estate agents try hard but never sell a house, they will not make any money. The payoff is for selling houses, not for trying hard to sell houses. An opposing viewpoint is that many people in society are rewarded for effort, and "doing your best" should be rewarded.

The need to develop competency in various physical skills offers support for the product point of view. Research shows (AAHPER, 1954) that 78% of all hobby interests are established before the age of 12. Interests are established based on competency in different areas. A relatively low percentage of adults select new hobbies in areas where they feel incompetent. To assure lifetime activity, school physical education programs need to graduate students whose skill competencies allow them to feel comfortable in public view. A grading system that focuses on skill development and performance will encourage the quest toward competency.

A solution to consider is to grade on performance while teaching in a manner that focuses on the process of learning. Much is to be said for teaching in a manner that helps students develop a positive attitude toward activity. Attitude development depends largely on how teachers present the material rather than on actual performance. Help students understand that they perform differently from each other in math or science and receive a respectively higher or lower grade. This would make physical education similar to other academic areas in that those who perform best would receive the highest grade.

Relative Improvement

Some physical educators believe that effort, or "just doing the best that you can," should be the most important factor in assigning grades. To reward effort, these teachers base student grades on the amount a student improves. This involves pretesting and posttesting to determine the amount of progress made throughout the grading period. This approach contrasts with basing the grade on absolute performance; it is quite possible that the best performer in the class will not receive the highest grade because of lack of improvement.

Grading on improvement is time-consuming and requires that the same test be given at the beginning and end of the semester or unit. The test may or may not be a valid reflection of what has been learned in the class and may not be sensitive enough to reflect improvement made by both poor and outstanding performers. Testing at the beginning of a unit can be discouraging and demoralizing if a student performs poorly in front of peers. It can also be hazardous in some activities, such as gymnastics or archery, which require intensive instruction to prevent accident or injury.

Another factor to consider is the issue of performing for a grade. Students learn quickly that if they perform too well on the pretest, they will be penalized at posttest time. It is thus important to perform at a low level in order to demonstrate a higher degree of improvement on the posttest. A related problem is that improvement is sometimes easier at beginning levels of skill than at high levels of performance. Most teachers are aware of the rapid improvement beginners make before reaching a learning plateau. A skilled performer may be at a level where improvement is difficult to achieve. Lack of improvement in this situation would result in a skilled performer receiving a lower grade than a beginner.

Grading on Potential

Some teachers choose to grade on potential. These teachers may lower a student's grade because the student did not reach their potential. On the other hand, a grade may be raised because the teacher felt that student didn't have much ability but did reach their potential. In other words, the teacher decides what a student's potential performance level should be and then assigns a grade based on whether they reached this level. The grade a student receives depends on the teacher's subjective perception of that student's genetic limitations. How can any teacher really know the absolute potential of any student? This approach results in students being assigned a grade based on an unknown factor: potential.

This approach depends on the teacher's feelings about the student in question. It is based on intangibles, and may result in a grade being assigned because the student is "just like her brothers or sisters." When grades are based on the teacher's subjective beliefs rather than on criteria that can be measured and evaluated, grades become difficult to defend. How would a parent react to a teacher's statement that, "Your youngster received a failing grade because he just didn't live up to his potential." To be defensible, grading systems need to be based on tangible data gleaned from observable behavior and performance.

Negative versus Positive Grading

To make the grading system defensible and concrete, some teachers have used point systems. In most point systems, both performance objectives and administrative factors are listed as grade components. A student earns a grade through performance, attitude, and knowledge. Point systems can become a negative influence if handled incorrectly. For example, some teachers give students 100 points at the start of the semester and then "chip off" points for various unsatisfactory levels of performance. A student may lose points for not trying, not performing, or not knowing answers on a test. Students soon realize that

energy should be spent on concentrating on negative behaviors that lose points rather than educational objectives.

This contrasts with a system that rewards positive behavior. When the student performs well, points are assigned and the student can earn their grade through self-direction. In a negative system, teachers make all the judgments about points lost and receive in turn the negative feelings of the student. In a positive system, students can behave in a positive manner to earn points. Teachers are constantly rewarding their behavior, which fosters positive feelings toward physical education and teachers. Rewarding positive behavior makes students feel that the teacher cares about their welfare and growth.

A negative system tends to make teachers focus on what students cannot do, rather than on what they should or can do. Energy is spent on "policing" students and threatening to take away points if they do not behave. Students do not respond well to this approach, since a loss of points does not require an immediate change in behavior and a redirection. The loss of points results in a reduction of the final grade, a consequence that is usually 6 to 9 weeks away. Few students respond positively to grade leverage through a negative system. Students who care about their grades are performing well in the first place. Threatening to lower the grade of a student who does not like physical education or school in general only further alienates the student and is based on a system of negative reinforcement. The grading system should positively encourage students to perform.

Pass-Fail versus Letter Grades

Another approach to grading involves assigning a pass-fail grade instead of a letter grade. Pass-fail has become more common today because of the push to avoid having physical education grades count in the academic grade point average. This approach prevents students from receiving a low grade in physical education while earning high grades in subject matter areas.

When using a pass-fail grading system, no method is available for rewarding outstanding performers. A student who earns a grade of C or D receives the same final grade as the top performer in the class. This approach reinforces making a minimal effort to accomplish goals, because differing levels of performance are not rewarded. The pass-fail system also does little to show students that they have improved. For example, if a student is performing at the

C level and earns a B by the end of the next quarter, the pass grade reflects no change in performance. Grading systems are most effective when they reward improved standards of performance.

Some teachers endorse pass-fail grading because it eases the burden of evaluation. They no longer have to worry about bookkeeping chores, because the grade is only grossly indicative of student progress. Recording anything more than the minimum performance required for passing the class becomes unnecessary. Some teachers therefore support this grading system because of ease of implementation.

Once again, when the grading system in physical education differs from those in other subject matter areas, defending the program in the school setting becomes difficult. If physical education does not require grading integrity, the subject probably should not be counted in the grade point average. The problem lies in the final outcome. If the physical education department chooses to operate autonomously from the rest of the school system, it then becomes vulnerable to nonsupport and abandonment. Physical education should be considered an integral part of the school system and should be graded in a manner consistent with other subject matter areas.

EXPECTED OUTCOMES

After reading this chapter, you should be able to

- Explain the difference between evaluation and grading.

- Administer a sport skills test to a class of secondary school students in physical education.

- Develop and defend a wellness profile for secondary school students in physical education.

- Devise a knowledge test for secondary school students on specific sports units.

- Discuss controversial issues regarding evaluation and grading. These issues should include: educational objectives versus administrative tasks, process versus product, improvement and potential, negative versus positive, and pass-fail versus letter grades.

- Explain the pros and cons of specific methods of grading in physical education.

- Develop a grading scheme that is in line with stated objectives for secondary school physical education.

REFERENCES AND SUGGESTED READINGS

AAHPER. 1954. *Children in Focus*. Reston, VA: AAHPERD.

AAHPER. 1976. *Youth Fitness Test Manual*. Reston, VA: AAHPERD

AAHPERD. 1984. *AAHPERD Skills Test Manual: Basketball for Boys and Girls*. Reston, VA: AAHPERD.

Adams, R. S. 1963. Two scales for measuring attitude toward physical education. *Research Quarterly* 34: 91–94.

Cooper Institute for Aerobic Research. 1992. *The Prudential Fitnessgram Test Administration Manual*. Dallas: Cooper Institute for Aerobics Research.

Corbin, C. B., and Lindsey, R. 1994. *Concepts of Physical Fitness*. 8th ed. Dubuque, IA: Brown & Benchmark.

Corbin, C. B., Pangrazi, R. P., and Welk, G. J. 1994. Toward an understanding of appropriate physical activity levels for youth. *Physical Activity and Fitness Research Digest* 1(8): 1–8.

Cornish, C. 1949. A study of measurement of ability in handball. *Research Quarterly* 20: 215–222.

Edgington, C. W. 1968. Development of an attitude scale to measure attitudes of high school freshman boys toward physical education. *Research Quarterly* 39: 505–512.

Hastad, D. N., and Lacy, A. C. 1994. *Measurement and Evaluation in Physical Education and Exercise Science*. Scottsdale, AZ: Gorsuch Scarisbrick.

Jensen, C. R., and Hirst, C. C. 1980. *Measurement in Physical Education and Athletics*. New York: Macmillan.

Johnson, J. R. 1963. *The Development of a Single-Item Test as a Measure of Soccer Skill*. Masters thesis, University of California, Los Angeles.

Kemp, J., and Vincent, M. F. 1968. Kemp-Vincent rally test of tennis skill. *Research Quarterly* 39: 1000–1004.

McGee, R., and Farrow, A. 1987. *Test Questions for Physical Education Activities*. Champaign, IL: Human Kinetics Publishers.

Safrit, M. J. 1990. *Introduction to Measurement in Physical Education and Exercise Science*. 2nd ed. St. Louis: Times Mirror/Mosby.

Strand, B. N., and Wilson, R. 1993. *Assessing Sport Skills*. Champaign, IL: Human Kinetics Publishers.

11 Students with Disabilities

PURPOSE

To understand the most common types of disabilities and cite ways to modify activities and determine categories of placement for students with disabilities.

KEY CONCEPTS

- Every state is required by federal law to develop a plan for identifying, locating, and evaluating all students with disabilities.
- Due process for students and parents is an important requisite when conducting formal assessment procedures.
- Assessment plays a vital part in determining proper placement of the disabled student into physical education.
- Moving a student to a less restrictive learning environment should be based on achievement of specified competencies that are necessary in the new environment.
- Mainstreaming involves the practice of placing students with disabilities into classes with able peers.
- An individualized learning environment increases opportunities for successful mainstreaming.
- The special student should not be permitted to use a disability as a crutch or as an excuse for substandard work.

The Education for All Handicapped Children Act (Public Law 94-142) was passed by Congress in 1975. It was the 142nd act of legislation passed by the 94th Congress. This legislation introduced new requirements, vocabulary, and concepts into physical education programs across the United States. These concepts include individual education programs (IEP), mainstreaming, least restrictive environments, zero reject, and progressive inclusion. The purpose of the law is clear and concise:

It is the purpose of this act to assure that all handicapped children* have available to them a free

*The term *handicapped* is used in P.L. 94-142 to include youngsters who are mentally retarded, hard of hearing,

appropriate public education which emphasizes special education and related services designed to meet their unique needs, to assure that the rights of handicapped children and their parents or guardians are protected, to assist States and localities to provide for the education of all handicapped children, and to assess and assure the effectiveness of efforts to educate handicapped children.

deaf, speech impaired, visually handicapped, seriously emotionally disturbed, orthopedically impaired, other health impaired, deaf, blind, multihandicapped, or specific learning disabled. More appropriate wording is *students with disabilities,* which will be used throughout this chapter.

In short, the law requires that all students with disabilities, ages 3 to 21, receive a free and appropriate education that meets their particular needs. The law includes students with disabilities in public and private care facilities and schools. Students with disabilities who can learn in regular classes with the use of supplementary aides and services must be educated with students who are able. Physical education is the only specific subject area mentioned in P.L. 94-142. In the law, the term *special education* "means specially designed instruction, instruction in physical education, home instruction, and instruction in hospitals and institutions."

To comply with P.L. 94-142, secondary schools must locate, identify, and evaluate all students who might have a disability. A screening process must be followed by a formal assessment procedure. An assessment must be made and an IEP developed for each student before placement into a special program can be made. The law states who will be responsible for developing the IEP and what the contents of the IEP will include.

The passage of P.L. 94-142 shows that a strong commitment has been made to equality and education for all Americans. Prior to 1970, these students had limited access to schools. They certainly did not have an equal opportunity to participate in school programs. The government also assured that funding would be made available to assure quality instruction. The law authorizes a payment to each state of 40% of the average per-pupil expenditure in U.S. elementary and secondary schools, multiplied by the number of youngsters with disabilities who are receiving special education and related services. The federal mandate reveals the concern of the public for comprehensive education programs for all students regardless of disability.

LEAST RESTRICTIVE ENVIRONMENT

P.L. 94-142 uses the term **least restrictive environment** to help determine the best placement arrangement of students with disabilities. This concept refers to the idea that not all individuals can do all of the same activities in the same environment. However, the concept of **zero reject** entitles everyone of school age to some aspect of the school program. No one can be totally rejected because of a disability. The focus should be on placing students into settings that offer the best opportunity for educa-

1. Regular physical education classes
2. Regular physical education classes with restricted class size (e.g., 15 able students per 1 child with disability).
3. Regular physical education classes with an aide or classroom teacher support.
4. Regular physical education classes plus part-time special education classes (e.g., 3 days regular, 2 days special per week).
5. Full-time special education class.
6. Full-time physical education in school for special education students only.

FIGURE 11.1 Physical education options, least to most restrictive environments

tional advancement. It is inappropriate to place a youngster in an environment where success is impossible. However, it would be debilitating to put a student in a setting that is more restrictive than necessary. Special educators speak about many experiences that offer a variety of opportunities from participation in regular physical education classes to physical education in a full-time special school. Figure 11.1 shows a series of options that might be available for physical education.

The least restrictive environment also varies depending on the unit of instruction and the teaching style. For example, for a student in a wheelchair, a soccer or football unit might be very restrictive, whereas in a basketball or Frisbee unit, the environment would not be as restrictive. For a student with emotional disabilities, the direct style of instruction might be the least restrictive environment, while a problem-solving method with group cooperation may be too difficult and would be more restrictive. Consistent and regular judgments need to be made since curriculum content and teaching styles change the type of environment the student enters. It is shortsighted to place students into a situation and then forget about them. Evaluation and modification of environments need to be ongoing. The concept of "progressive inclusion" focuses on the idea that students make progress as a result of educational experiences. Thus, students with disabilities should have the opportunity to progress to the least restrictive environments and experience more and more of the mainstream of our schools and their programs.

MAINSTREAMING

Physical educators usually speak in terms of mainstreaming rather than least restrictive environments. **Mainstreaming** means that students with disabilities must have opportunities to integrate with other students in public schools. Prudent placement in a least restricted educational environment means that the setting must be as normal as possible (normalization), while ensuring that the student can fit in and achieve success in that placement. The placement may be mainstreaming but is not confined to this approach. There are several categories of placement relative to physical education classes.

1. *Full mainstreaming.* Students with disabilities function as full-time members of a regular school routine. They go to all classes with able students. Within the limitations of their disability, they participate in physical education with able peers. An example may be auditory-impaired students who with a minimal amount of assistance are able to participate fully.

2. *Mainstreaming for physical education only.* Students with disabilities are not members of the regular academic classes in the secondary schools but can still participate in physical education with able peers. This setting may include students with emotional disabilities who are grouped in the classroom and are separated into regular physical education classes.

3. *Partial mainstreaming.* Students participate in selected physical education experiences but do not attend on a full-time basis because they can be successful in only a few of the offerings. Their developmental needs are usually met in special classes.

4. *Special developmental classes.* Students with disabilities are in segregated special education classes.

5. *Reverse mainstreaming.* Able students are brought into a special physical education class to promote intergroup peer relationships. The PEOPEL (Physical Education Opportunity Program for Exceptional Learners) program is an example of this approach.

Segregation can be maintained only when it is in the best interests of the student. The purpose of segregated programs is to establish a level of skill and social proficiency that will eventually enable the special student to be transferred to a less-restricted learning environment. The goal of the process is to place students in the least restrictive environment, where they can benefit most. Students with disabilities, working on their own, have often been denied opportunities to interact with peers and to become a part of the social and academic classroom network.

Students with disabilities need contact with support personnel during mainstreaming. Even though the physical education teacher is responsible for the mainstreamed students during class time, these students may still require access to special education teachers, school psychologists, and speech therapists. Support personnel may view physical education as a time to get rid of their students"; however, they are a source of information and support for the physical education teacher in charge.

SCREENING AND ASSESSMENT

Every state is required to develop a plan for identifying, locating, and evaluating all students with disabilities. Generally, screening involves all students district-wide and is usually conducted at the start of the school year. Screening tests include commonly used test batteries such as the Prudential Fitnessgram (1992). In most situations, screening tests may be administered without parental permission. They are used to make initial identification of students who may need special services.

Assessment is conducted after screening evaluations have been made and appropriate students are referred to special education directors. Assessment is performed by a team of experts, which may include the physical education specialist. **Due process** for students and parents is important during formal assessment procedures. Due process assures that parents and students are informed of their rights and have the opportunity to challenge educational decisions they feel are unfair or incorrect.

Due Process Guidelines

To assure that due process is offered to parents and students, the following guidelines must be followed:

1. *Written permission.* A written notice must be sent to parents stating that their child has been referred for assessment. The notice explains that the

district requests permission to conduct an evaluation to determine if special education services are required for the child. Also included in the permission letter must be reasons for testing and the tests to be used. Before assessment can begin, the letter has to be signed by the parents and returned to the district.

2. *Interpretation of the assessment.* Results of the assessment must be interpreted in a meeting with the parents. Persons who are knowledgeable of the test procedures need to be present to answer questions parents may ask. At the meeting, parents are told whether their child has any disabilities and what services will be provided.

3. *External evaluation.* If parents are not satisfied with the results of the assessment, an evaluation outside of school can be requested. The district must provide a list of agencies that can perform such assessments. If the results differ from the school district evaluation, the district must pay for the external evaluation. If the results are similar, parents have to pay for the external testing.

4. *Negotiation and hearings.* If parents and the school district disagree on the results of the assessment, the district is required to negotiate the differences. When negotiations fail, an impartial hearing officer listens to both parties and renders an official decision. This is usually the final review; however, both parties do have the right to appeal to the state department of education, which renders a binding and final decision. Civil action through the legal system can be pursued should the district or parents still disagree. However, very few cases ever reach this level of long-term disagreement, and educators should not hesitate to serve the needs of youngsters with disabilities based on this concern.

5. *Confidentiality.* As is the case with other student records, only parents of the child or authorized school personnel can review the student's evaluation. Review by other parties can be done only after written permission has been given by the student's parents.

Procedures for Assuring Assessment Standards

P.L. 94-142 assures that assessment will be held to certain standards to assure fair and objective results. The following areas are specifically delineated in the law.

Selection of Test Instruments

The test instruments used must be a valid examination of what they purport to measure. When selecting instruments, it must be clear to all parties how the tests were developed and how they will measure the area of disability. More than one test procedure must be used to determine the student's status. Both formal and informal assessment techniques should be used to assure that the results measure the student's impairment rather than simply reflect the student's shortcomings.

Unfortunately, youngsters must be labeled as disabled in order to reap the benefits of a special education program. The stigmatizing effect of labels and the fallibility of various means of testing students is a dilemma that must be faced. Although current pedagogical practices discourage labeling, in this case it is necessary because school districts have to certify the disability to receive funding.

Administration Procedures

Many disabilities interfere with standard test procedures. For example, many students have communication problems and must be tested in a manner that assures testing of motor ability rather than communication skills. Many students have visual and hearing disabilities that prevent using tests that rely on these faculties.

A possibility of misdiagnosis and incorrectly classifying students as mentally retarded can occur with certain ethnic groups, such as Native Americans, blacks, and Spanish-speaking students. These youngsters, often victims of poor and impoverished living, may be only environmentally retarded and in need of cultural enrichment. It is subtle discrimination, but it must be replaced with understanding that students differ because of culture, poverty, migrancy, and language. Many of the tests are based on white, middle-class standards. Minority students need to be carefully assessed to determine the validity of the testing procedure.

Team Evaluation

A number of experts are used for assessment to help assure that all facets of the student will be reviewed and evaluated. Evaluation professionals who are well trained and qualified administer the various tests. It is the responsibility of the school district to assure that this will occur.

DEVELOPMENT OF THE IEP

P.L. 94-142 requires that an **individualized educational program** (IEP) be developed for each student with disabilities receiving special education and related service. The IEP must be developed by a committee as stipulated by the law. Included on the committee are the following members: a local education association representative who is qualified to provide and supervise the administration of special education, the student's parents, the teachers who have direct responsibility for implementing the IEP, and, when appropriate, the student. Other individuals, such as an independent evaluator, may be included at the discretion of the parents or school district. This program identifies the student's unique qualities and determines educationally relevant strengths and weaknesses. A plan is then devised based on the diagnosis. The IEP needs to contain the following material:

1. Current status of the student's level of educational performance.
2. A statement of long-term goals and short-term instructional objectives.
3. A statement of special education and related services that will be provided to the youngster. Also, a report as to what extent the student will be able to participate in regular educational programs.
4. The dates for initiation of services and anticipated duration of the services.
5. Appropriate objective criteria for determining on an annual basis whether the short-term objectives are being reached.

Figure 11.2 is an example of a comprehensive IEP form.

Developing and sequencing objectives for the student is the first step in formulating the IEP. Short-range and long-range goals are delineated, and data collection procedures and testing schedules are established to monitor the student's progress. Materials and strategies to be used in implementing the IEP are established followed by a determination of the methods of evaluation to be used in order to monitor the student's progress and effectiveness of the program. Movement to a less-restrictive environment is based on achievement of specified competencies that are necessary in the new environment.

The IEP must contain a section determining whether specially designed physical education is needed. If not, the student is held to the same expectations as his or her peer group. A student who needs special physical education might have an IEP with specified goals and objectives and still be mainstreamed in regular physical education with goals that do not resemble those of classmates.

Continued and periodic follow-up of the student is necessary. Effective communication between special and regular teachers is essential because the student's progress needs careful monitoring. At the completion of the designated time period or school year, a written progress report is filed along with recommendations for action during the coming year or time period. A summer program is often an excellent prescription to ensure that school year improvement is maintained. Comprehensive records are maintained so that information about the youngster's problem and the effects of long-term treatment are always available.

CRITERIA FOR PLACEMENT OF STUDENTS

Standards to be used for placing students into special programs are necessary so parents feel that well-defined criteria have been used. Several states have adopted criteria for determining eligibility of students for adapted physical education classes. State guidelines differ but should be followed closely if they exist. Often, standards are based on the administration of standardized tests for which norms or percentiles have been developed. This procedure helps assure that objective guidelines are used and avoids subjective judgment that may be open to disagreement and controversy. The following are examples of criteria used by the state of Alabama:

1. Perform below the thirtieth percentile on standardized tests of
   a. Motor development
   b. Motor proficiency
   c. Fundamental motor skills and patterns
   d. Physical fitness
   e. Game/sport skills
   f. Perceptual motor functioning
   g. Posture screening
2. Exhibit a developmental delay of 2 or more years based on appropriate assessment instruments.
3. Function within the severe or profound range as determined by special education eligibility standards.

Individualized Education Program

☐ Initial Placement
☐ Re-evaluation
☐ Change of Placement
☐ Review

A. STUDENT INFORMATION:

Student Name _____ Student No. _____ Home School _____
 Last   First   Middle

Date of Birth _____ Chronological Age _____ (M ____ or F ____) Present Placement/Grade _____

Parent/Guardian Name(s) _____ Receiving School _____

Home Address _____ Program Recommended _____
 Street   City/State   Zip

Home Phone _____ Work Phone _____ Starting Date _____

Emergency Phone _____ Three (3) Year Re-evaluation Due Date _____ / _____ / _____

Primary Language (Home) _____ (Child) _____ Interpreter Needed: Yes ____ No ____

B. VISION SCREENING RESULTS: Pass ____ Fail ____   **HEARING SCREENING RESULTS:** Pass ____ Fail ____

Date: _____ Comments: _____   Date: _____ Comments: _____

_____   _____

C. REQUIRED OBSERVATION(S): (All categories other than regular teacher)

_____ By: _____   _____ By: _____   _____ By: _____
 Date(s)   Name(s)   *Date(s)   Name(s)*   *Date(s)   Name(s)*

D. SUMMARY OF PRESENT LEVELS OF PERFORMANCE:

Educational: _____

_____

_____

_____

_____

_____

_____

_____

_____

_____

Behavioral: _____

_____

_____

_____

_____

_____

_____

_____

_____

_____

_____

E. Additional justification. See comments _____ See addendum _____
 Initial   *Initial*

F. PLACEMENT RECOMMENDATION INDICATING LEAST RESTRICTIVE ENVIRONMENT:

Related services needed: Yes ____ No ____ (*List below.)

Placement Recommendation	Person Responsible	Amount of Time (Range)	Entry Date On/About	Review Reports On/About	Projected Ending Date	IEP Review Date
Primary:						
*Related Services:						

Transportation Needed? Yes ____ No ____ (If Yes, submit MPS Special Education Transportation Request Form.)

Describe extent student will participate in regular program. _____

_____

Page 1 of ____

FIGURE 11.2 Example of an individualized educational plan

INDIVIDUALIZED EDUCATION PROGRAM   **REPORT OF MULTIDISCIPLINARY CONFERENCE**

Date Held _____

Student Name _____   Student No. _____

G. PROGRAM PLANNING:

Long-Term Goals: Short-Term Objectives (Goals):

H. EVALUATION:

Evaluation criteria are described in the Individual Implementation Plan (IIP) which is available in the classroom file.

I. PLACEMENT COMMITTEE:

The following have been consulted or have participated in the placement and IEP decisions:

Names of Members	Position	Present (Initial)	Oral Report	Written Report	Signatures
	Parents/Guardian				
	Parents/Guardian				
	School Administrator				
	Special Ed Administrator				
	School Psychologist				
	Nurse				
	Teacher(s) Receiving				
	Teacher(s) Referring				
	Interpreter				

Dissenting Opinion: Yes _____   No _____   If Yes, see comments _____   See addendum _____
                                                                    Initial   *Initial*

J. PARENT (OR GUARDIAN) STATEMENT:

We agree to the placement recommended in this IEP.   Yes _____   No _____

We give our permission to have our child counseled by the professional staff, it necessary.   Yes ____   No ____

We understand that placement will be on a continuing trial basis and we will be contacted it any placement changes are contemplated. We are aware that such placement does not guarantee success; however, in order to help our child, we accept the responsibility to cooperate in every way with the school program. We acknowledge that we have been notified of and have received a copy of our due process rights pertaining to Special Education placement and have a basic understanding of these rights. We acknowledge that we have received a copy of the completed IEP Form.

_____   _____
Parent or Guardian Signature   Date

Comments: _____
_____
_____
_____

Page 2 of ____

FIGURE 11.2   Continued

4. Possess social, emotional, or physical capabilities that would render it unlikely for the student to reach his or her physical education goals without significant modification or exclusion from the regular physical education class.

If a student is determined not to be eligible for special education services, it may be beneficial to refer the student to programs for secondary students with special needs. These programs deal with areas that are not delineated by P.L. 94-142, such as obesity, physical fitness, and motor deficiencies. Unfortunately, few secondary schools offer such programs, and eligible students must survive in the regular programs. Physical educators need to show concern for helping students with these problems since obesity and physical fitness are areas of strong concern among parents.

GUIDELINES FOR SUCCESSFUL MAINSTREAMING EXPERIENCES

Mainstreaming is a moral issue. Educators have the responsibility to see that all students have the opportunity to experience activity and related social experiences. All parents desire the maximum of experiences for their youngsters, and the goal of teachers should be to meet this need. The issue is not whether to mainstream but how to mainstream effectively. The physical educator has to teach a number of students, some with disabilities and diverse impairments. Learning strategies that the instructor is familiar with and has been using successfully may not be appropriate for students with disabilities. Attitudinal change is important since the teacher must accept the student as a full-fledged participant and assume the responsibilities that go along with special education. Few disagree that mainstreaming increases the difficulty of offering instruction for all students; however, teachers who support it show their concern for the human spirit regardless of condition.

An important consideration when planning the IEP is whether the student is ready for mainstreaming. Many students with disabilities have severe developmental lags that become insurmountable factors working against successful integration in normal classes. The student must be physically able to accomplish a portion of the program without much, if any, assistance. Placement may need to be limited to certain activities where success can be achieved.

When a student is deemed ready for placement, consultation between the physical education teacher and the special education supervisor is of prime importance. In a setting where emotions and feelings run high, it is important to assure that communication and planning occur on a regular basis. The reception and acceptance of special students cannot be left to chance. A scheduled plan has to be instituted before the student is mainstreamed. Special and physical education professionals can discuss the needs of the student and develop realistic expectations. It is quite possible that the special education teacher may have to participate in the physical education class to assure a smooth transition. The thrust should center on what students can do rather than on what they cannot do. Any approach that treats students with disabilities as cripples is dehumanizing. Full information about the needs of the student is due the physical education teacher before the student participates. This procedure should also be implemented when the student moves from one mainstreaming situation to another. Both able students and students with disabilities need opportunities to make appropriate progress. The educational needs of students with disabilities must be met without jeopardizing the progress of other students. This does not rule out activity modifications so that those with disabilities can be included. Some adapted equipment may also be necessary.

The teacher is advised to help all students understand the problems related to being disabled. A goal should be to have students understand, accept, and live comfortably with persons with disabilities. They should recognize that students with disabilities are functional and worthwhile individuals who have innate abilities and can make significant contributions to society. The concept of understanding and appreciating individual differences is one that merits positive development and should concentrate on 3 aspects:

1. Recognizing the similarities among all people: their hopes, rights, aspirations, and goals.
2. Understanding human differences and focusing on the concept that all people are disabled. For some, disabilities are of such nature and severity that they interfere with normal living.
3. Exploring ways to deal with those who differ without overhelping, and stressing the acceptance of all students as worthwhile individuals. People with disabilities deserve consideration and understanding, based on empathy, not sympathy.

Once the mainstreamed student, able students, and teacher have undergone preliminary preparation, consideration can be given to integrating the disabled youngster into the learning environment. When correctly implemented, mainstreaming allows the student to make educational progress, achieve in those areas outlined in the IEP, learn to accept limitations, observe and model appropriate behavior, and become socially accepted by others. Some guidelines for successful integration of students with disabilities into physical education follow.

1. It is important for students with disabilities to meet target goals specified in the IEP in addition to participating in the regular program of activities. This can involve resources beyond the physical education class, including special work and homework.
2. Build ego strength; stress abilities. Eliminate established practices that unwittingly contribute to embarrassment and failure.
3. Foster peer acceptance, which begins when the teacher accepts the student as a functioning, participating member of the class.
4. Concentrate on the student's physical education needs and not on the disability. Give strong attention to fundamental skills and physical fitness qualities.
5. Provide continual monitoring and assess periodically the student's target goals. Anecdotal and periodic record keeping are implicit in this guideline.
6. Be constantly aware of students' feelings and anxiety concerning their progress and integration. Provide positive feedback as a basic practice.
7. Modify the regular program to meet the unique capacities, physical needs, and social needs of youngsters with disabilities.
8. Provide individual assistance and keep youngsters active. Peer or paraprofessional help may be needed. On-task time is important.
9. Consult regularly with the special education professional.
10. Give consideration to more individualization within the program so that youngsters with disabilities are smoothly integrated. The individualized approach must be based on the target goals of the IEP.
11. Consider using computer programs for recording data and generating meaningful reports.

TEACHER BEHAVIOR AND THE MAINSTREAMING PROCESS

The success or failure of the mainstreaming process depends largely on the interaction between the teacher and the student with a disability. There is no foolproof, teacher-proof system. Purposes and derived goals are perhaps more important to students with disabilities than to so-called normal peers. Proper levels of organic fitness and skill are vital for healthful living. Such levels enable them to compete with peers. It is important to accept responsibility for meeting the needs of students, including those with disabilities that permit some degree of mainstreaming. Teachers need to be able to judge when referral for special assistance or additional services is in order. Physical education teachers must be able to do the following: (1) analyze and diagnose motor behavior of the students with disabilities, (2) provide appropriate experiences for remediation of motor conditions needing attention, and (3) register data as needed on the student's personal record. Record keeping is important. A short period, perhaps 5 minutes between classes, could be set aside to accomplish the task promptly. When time between classes is short, the teacher may want to use a portable tape recorder for recording evaluative comments during class time.

To work successfully with students with disabilities, teachers have to understand specific impairments and how they affect learning. Also, it is necessary to know how to assess motor and fitness needs and how to structure remediation to meet those needs. Teachers should have alternative strategies in reserve in case the original method fails. Referral to the special education teacher then becomes a last resort. When giving explanations and directions, couch them in terms that all students, including those with disabilities, can understand. Be sure that students with disabilities understand what is to be accomplished before the learning experiences begin, especially when working with the hearing impaired. Concentrate on finding activities where students can excel. Avoid placing students with disabilities in situations where they could easily fail. Give them opportunities that make the best use of their talents. Stress the special objectives of those with disabilities. Obvious increments of improvement toward terminal objectives are excellent motivators for both students and teachers. Let youngsters know that you as a teacher are vitally interested in their progress.

Additional sources of information can aid teachers in dealing effectively with students with disabilities. Books about disabilities and suggested guidelines for dealing with special students are available. Workshops can be organized featuring knowledgeable individuals with successful programs who can help solve specific problems. Larger school systems may organize in-service education for physical education teachers.

FITNESS AND POSTURE FOR STUDENTS WITH DISABILITIES

The normalization process has directed attention to posture as a factor in peer acceptance. Since many secondary students with disabilities have low physical fitness levels, posture problems occur in this group. One aim of mainstreaming is to make special students less visible, hence the need to help them achieve acceptable posture. Values received from an attractive appearance include better acceptance by peers and more employment opportunities later.

Physical fitness is also important for these students. To compete with and gain respect from peers, the goal of fitness is a justified thrust of the physical education program. Adequate physical fitness helps the student move through the school day, which may be complicated by a sensory deficit, a mobility problem, or a mental deficiency.

Special care must be given to students who have been excluded from physical education programs. Wheelchair students need special attention given to their cardiovascular development through activities that stimulate deep breathing. Arm development is important so that they can move in and out of the wheelchair easily.

An idiosyncratic gait or an appearance that gives the impression of abnormality are often problems for mentally retarded youngsters. Early identification of a problem and inclusion of a posture correction program are important. The physical educator is often best qualified to initiate and supervise this program. Informal screening includes several tasks: walking, sitting, and stair climbing. Obesity may need to be considered in amelioration. Once identification is made, a more detailed analysis of the subject's posture can follow. The degree of postural abnormality governs whether referral is indicated. Videotaping can provide baseline data from which to monitor corrections. Achieving acceptable posture is both a short-term (progress) and long-term (achievement) goal to be included in the student's IEP. Referral for severe conditions or for postural conditions that are difficult to correct usually involves the support services of a physician or an orthopedic specialist.

The psychosocial aspects of posture should be considered, with attention focused on the establishment of a good self-concept and effective social relations. Behavior management can focus on motivation toward better postural habits when standing, walking, sitting, lifting, and general movement. Proper posture should become a habit.

MODIFYING PARTICIPATION

Special education students may need additional consideration when participating in group activities, particularly when the activity is competitive. Much depends on the physical condition of the student and the type of disability. Students like to win in a competitive situation, and resentment can be created if a team loss is attributed to the presence of a student with a disability. Equalization helps reduce this source of friction. Rules can be changed for everyone so that the student with a disability has a chance to contribute to group success. On the other hand, students need to recognize that everyone, including the disabled and the inept, has a right to play.

Be aware of situations that might devalue the student socially. Avoid using the degrading method of having captains choose from a group of waiting students. Elimination games should be changed so that points are scored instead of players being eliminated (this is an important consideration for all youngsters). Determine the most desirable involvement for students with disabilities by analyzing participants' roles in game and sport activities. Assign a role or position that will make the experience as natural or normal as possible.

Offer a variety of individual and dual activities. Students with disabilities have to build confidence in their skills before they want to participate with others. Individual activities give them a greater amount of practice time without the pressure of failing in front of peers. The aim of these techniques is to make students with disabilities less visible and not set apart from able classmates. Using students with disabilities as umpires or scorekeepers is a last resort. Overprotectiveness benefits no one and prevents the special student from experiencing challenge and personal accomplishment. Avoid the tendency to underestimate students' abilities. The following sections offer ideas for modifying activities to facilitate integration of students with disabilities.

Modifications for Students Lacking Strength and Endurance

1. Lower or enlarge the size of the goal. In basketball, the goal can be lowered; in soccer the goal might be enlarged.
2. Modify the tempo of the game. For example, games might be performed using a brisk walk rather than running. Another way to modify tempo is to stop the game regularly for substitution. Auto-substitutions can be an excellent method for allowing students to determine when they are fatigued; they ask a predetermined substitute to take their place.
3. Reduce the weight and/or modify the size of the projectile. A lighter object will move more slowly and inflict less damage upon impact. A larger object will move more slowly and be easier for students to track visually and catch.
4. Reduce the distance that a ball must be thrown or served. Options are to reduce the dimensions of the playing area or add more players to the game. In serving, others can help make the serve playable. For example, in volleyball, other teammates can bat the serve over the net as long as it does not touch the floor.
5. In games that are played to a certain number of points, reduce the number required for a win. For example, volleyball games could be played to 7 or 11, depending on the skill and intensity of the players.
6. Modify striking implements by shortening and reducing their weight. Racquets are much easier to control when they are shortened. Softball bats are easier to control when the player "chokes up" and selects a lighter bat.
7. If possible, slow the ball by letting out some air. This will reduce the speed of rebound and make the ball easier to control in a restricted area. It will also keep the ball from rolling away from players when it is not under control.
8. Play the games in a different position. Some games may be played in a sitting or lying position, which is easier and less demanding than standing or running.
9. Provide matching or substitution. Match another student on borrowed crutches with a student on braces. Two players can be combined to play 1 position. A student in a desk chair with wheels can be matched against a wheelchair student. Permit substitute courtesy runners.
10. Allow students to substitute skills. For example, a student may be able to strike an object but may lack the mobility to run. Another student can be selected to run.

Modifications for Students Lacking Coordination

1. Increase the size of the goal or target. Increasing the size of a basketball goal will increase the opportunity for success. Another alternative might be to offer points for hitting the backboard near a goal. Since scoring is self-motivating, modification should occur until success is assured.
2. Offer protection when appropriate. The lack of coordination will make the student more susceptible to injury from a projectile. Use various types of protectors (such as glasses, chest protectors, or face masks).
3. When teaching throwing, allow students the opportunity to throw at maximum velocity without concern for accuracy. Use small balls that can be grasped easily. Fleece balls and beanbags are easy to hold and release.
4. Use a stationary object when teaching striking or hitting. The use of a batting tee or tennis ball fastened to a string can offer the student an opportunity for success. In addition, a larger racquet or bat and "choking up" on the grip can be used.
5. Make projectiles easily retrievable. If a great deal of time is spent on recovering the projectile, students will receive few practice trials and feel frustrated. Place them near a backstop or use a goal that rebounds the projectile to the shooter.
6. When teaching catching, use a soft, lightweight, and slow moving object. Beach balls and balloons are excellent for beginning catching skills since they allow the student to track their movement visually. In addition, foam rubber balls eliminate the fear of being hurt by a thrown or batted projectile.

Modifications for Students Lacking Balance and Agility

1. Increase the width of rails, lines, and beam when practicing balance. Carrying a long pole will help minimize rapid shifts of balance and is a useful leadup activity.

2. Increase the width of the base of support. Students should be taught to keep the feet spread at least to shoulder width.

3. Emphasize use of many body parts when teaching balance. The more body parts in contact with the floor, the easier it is to balance the body. Beginning balance practice should emphasize controlled movement using as many body parts as possible.

4. Increase the surface area of the body parts in contact with the floor or beam. For example, walking flat-footed is easier than walking on tiptoes.

5. Lower the center of gravity. This offers more stability and greater balance to the youngster. Place emphasis on bending the knees and slightly leaning forward.

6. Assure that surfaces offer good friction. Floors and shoes should not be slick or students will fall. Carpets or tumbling mats will increase traction.

7. Provide balance assistance. A barre, cane, or chair can be used to keep the student from falling.

8. Teach students how to fall. Students with balance problems will inevitably fall. Practice in learning how to fall should be offered so that they gradually learn how to absorb the force.

SPECIFIC TYPES OF DISABILITIES

To assist students, an understanding of the disability and what it means to the student is essential. Basic information is provided here, and additional materials can be secured from special education consultants. The information provided here is a starting point; students do not always fit into neat categories. These students need to develop strength and endurance as well as leisure and sport skills just like any able-bodied student. National associations offer information about various disabilities and suggest ways of helping these students.

Mental Retardation

The capacity of the mentally retarded student is deficient and does not allow the student to be served by the standard program. Deficient mental functioning is a question of degree, usually measured in terms of intelligence quotient (IQ). Mildly retarded students (with IQs ranging roughly from 50 to 75 or 80) are most often mainstreamed in both physical education

and the regular classroom. Students with IQs below 50 usually cannot function in a regular classroom environment; they need special classes. These students are generally not mainstreamed and therefore are excluded from the following discussion.

Academically, mildly retarded students (also termed "educable mentally retarded") are slower to understand directions, to follow directions, to complete tasks, and to make progress. Conceptually, they have difficulty pulling facts together and drawing conclusions. Their motivation to stay on task is generally lower. Academic success may have eluded them. These realities must be considered in the physical education setting. Improvement in these areas is a goal to be achieved.

Do retarded students differ physically from other students? In a study by Ulrich (1983), a comparison was made of the developmental levels of 117 disabled and 96 educable mentally retarded youngsters with respect to criterion-referenced testing of 12 fundamental motor skills and 4 physical fitness skills. The investigation supports the findings of the previous study in that the educable mentally retarded students lagged 3.5 years behind normal students in motor skill development, as based on the researcher's selected criterion reference point. The investigator attributes this lag to a lack of opportunity for movement experiences at an early age. The students with disabilities were from special education classes, not from a mainstreaming situation.

Instructional Procedures

Studies of mildly retarded students support the assumption that they can learn but at a slower rate and not to the depth of normal mentally functioning students. To help the mildly retarded develop their capacities so that they can become participating members of society, the learning process should concentrate on fundamental skills and fitness qualities. Unless this base is established, the retarded student faces considerable difficulty later in learning specialized skills. Minimizing skill and fitness lags can help ease the student into mainstream living.

The fitness approach involves motivation, acquisition of developmental techniques, and application of these to a personalized fitness program. The retarded student reacts well to goal setting, provided that the goals are challenging yet attainable. The pace of learning depends on the degree of retardation. Before a retarded student can learn, the student needs to know what is expected and how it is to be accomplished. Common sense governs the determination of progress increments. These should be challenging but within the performer's grasp. Often, past experiences have made retarded students the victims of a failure syndrome. The satisfaction of accomplishment must supplant this poor self-image.

Place emphasis on gross motor movement that is progressive in nature. Teach activities that are presented through demonstration rather than verbalization. Many of the skills may have to be accompanied by manual assistance to help the student get the "feel" of the skill. To avoid boredom and frustration, practice periods should be short. Allow ample opportunity for youngsters to "show off" skills they have learned so that they can enjoy the feeling of accomplishment. Shaping behavior by accepting approximation of the skill will encourage the student to keep trying. Progress arrives in small increments and teachers must be sensitive to improvement and accomplishment, no matter how small.

Effort should be rewarded. Many of these youngsters are reticent to try a new activity. Instructions should be repeated a number of times. Safety rules must be followed since these students may not understand the risk of injury involved.

Epilepsy

Epilepsy is a dysfunction of the electrical impulses emitted by the brain. It is not an organic disease. It can happen at any period of life but generally shows up during early childhood. With proper care and medication, many people overcome this condition and live normal lives. Epilepsy is a hidden problem. A student with epilepsy looks, acts, and is like other students except for unpredictable seizures. Unfortunately, epilepsy carries an unwarranted social stigma. Students with epilepsy meet with a lack of acceptance, even when adequate explanations are made to those around them. A major seizure can be frightening—or even revolting—to observers.

Gaining control of seizures is often a long process, involving experimentation with appropriate anticonvulsive medication in proper doses. Fortunately, most epilepsy can be controlled or minimized with proper medication. One factor in control is to be sure that the student is taking the medication as prescribed.

Sometimes a student can recognize signs of seizure onset. If this occurs in a physical education class, the student should have the privilege of moving to the sideline without permission. A seizure may, however, occur without warning. The instructor should know the signs of a seizure and react accordingly. The teacher may be the first (even before the student) to recognize that a seizure is imminent.

Three kinds of seizures are identified. A petit mal seizure involves a brief period (a few seconds) of blackout. No one is aware of the problem, including the student. Sometimes it is labeled inattention and thus is difficult to identify. A psychomotor epileptic seizure is longer lasting (perhaps a few minutes) and is characterized by involuntary movements and twitching. The student acts like a sleepwalker and cannot be stopped or helped. The affected youngster does not respond when addressed and is unaware of the seizure. A grand mal seizure is characterized by complete neurological involvement. The student may become unconscious and lose control of the bladder or bowels, resulting in loss of urine, stool, or both. Rigidity and tremors can appear. The seizure must run its course.

Two points are important. First, throughout any seizure or incident, preserve a matter-of-fact attitude and try not to exhibit pity. Second, educate the other students to understand and empathize with the problem. Stress what the condition is and, later, what it is not. Explain that the behavior during a seizure is a response to an unusual output of electrical discharges from the brain. Everyone needs these discharges to function in normal living, but the person with epilepsy is subject to an unusual amount of the discharges, which results in unusual activity. The condition involves a natural phenomenon that gets out of control.

Students need to understand that the seizure must run its course. When the seizure is over, everyone can resume normal activity, including the involved student, although the student may be disoriented and uncoordinated for a brief period of time. Offer the student the option of resting or returning to activity. Proper emotional climate of the class is established when the teacher maintains an accepting and relaxed attitude.

Information about epilepsy should be a part of the standard health curriculum in the school rather than a reaction to an epileptic seizure or to the presence of a student who may have seizures. Epilepsy can be discussed as a topic relevant to understanding the central nervous system. Certain risks are involved if the lessons have as their focus the problems of a particular student because this may heighten the student's feelings of exclusion and place disproportionate attention on what might have been a relatively inconsequential aspect of the student's life. (This caution does not rule out helpful information being given to peers when a seizure has taken place.)

In the event of a grand mal seizure, some routine procedures should be followed. Have available a blanket, a pillow, and towels to clean up as necessary. Make the student comfortable if there is time. Do not try to restrain or place something in their mouth. Support the head on the pillow, turning it to one side to allow the saliva to drain. Remove from the area any hard or sharp objects that might cause harm. Get help from a doctor or nurse if the seizure continues more than 3 or 4 minutes, or if seizures occur 3 or more times during a school day. Always notify the school nurse and the parents that a seizure occurred. Assure the class that the seizure will pass and that the involved student will not be harmed or affected.

Instructional Procedures

Recommendations regarding special modes of conduct and guidelines governing participation in school activities must come from the student's physician, since most epileptic students are under medical supervision. Today's approach is to bring epilepsy into the open. A concerted effort should be made to educate students so that traditional attitudes toward the condition can be altered. Emphasize inclusion of the student rather than exclusion. If there is some doubt about control of the seizures, climbing and elevated activities should be eliminated. Perhaps tomorrow's adults will then possess a better understanding. The student with epilepsy is a normal, functioning person except at the time of a seizure. Epilepsy is not a form of mental illness, and most people with epilepsy are not mentally retarded.

Visual Impairment

Mainstreaming for the visually impaired must be handled carefully and with common sense. The visually impaired designation includes those who are partially sighted as well as those who are legally blind. One has only to move about in a strange dark room to realize the mobility problems faced by a visually impaired student. This disability poses movement problems and puts limits on participation in certain types of physical activity. Total mainstreaming may not be a feasible solution.

There is a need to bring the student in contact with classmates, however, and to focus on the student's unique qualities and strengths. Empathy for

and acceptance of the visually impaired student are most important. The task of monitoring movement and helping this student should be considered a privilege to be rotated among class members. If participation in the class activity selected is contraindicated, the monitor can help provide an alternate activity.

Instructional Procedures

Visually impaired students have to develop confidence in their ability to move freely and surely within the limits of their disability. Since limited mobility often leads to reduced activity, this inclination can be countered with a specialized physical fitness and movement program in which the lack of sight does not prove insurmountable. The student can participate in group fitness activities with assistance as needed. Exercises pose few problems. Rope jumping is an excellent activity. Individual movement activities, stunts and tumbling, rhythms and dances (particularly partner dances), and selected apparatus activities are appropriate. Low balance beams, bench activities, climbing apparatus, and climbing ropes may be within the student's capacity. Manipulative activities involving tactile senses are not always appropriate. If the student has some vision, brightly colored balls against a contrasting background in good light can permit controlled throwing, tracking, and catching.

The visually impaired student usually cannot take visual cues from other students or the teacher, so explanations must be precise and clear. Use a whistle or loud verbal cue to signal the class. For some situations, an assigned peer can monitor activity, helping as needed or requested. In running situations, the helper can hold hands with the visually impaired student. Another way to aid the student is with physical guidance until the feel of a movement pattern is established. This is the last choice, however, occurring only after the student has had a chance to interpret the verbal instructions and still cannot meet the challenge. Touching a part of the student's body to establish correct sequencing in a movement pattern also can be of help.

Auditory Impairment

Auditory impaired students are those who are deaf or who must wear hearing aids. In physical education classes, these students are capable of performing most, if not all, activities that able students can perform. Since most instruction is verbal, a deaf student is isolated and often frustrated in a mainstreaming situation unless other means of communication are established. Accomplishing this while keeping the class functioning normally is a serious problem.

Teaching the deaf is a specialized process, requiring different communication techniques. Many deaf students have poor or unintelligible speech and inevitably develop a language gap with the hearing world. Sign language, lip reading, and speech training are all important facets of communicative ability for the deaf. Integrating deaf students in the regular physical education class setting is a process that must be handled with common sense. The experience should be satisfying to the deaf student or it is a failure.

Instructional Procedures

Certainly, hearing-impaired students can perform physically and at the same level as students with normal hearing when given the opportunity. One successful approach to teaching both the hearing impaired and normal youngsters is to use contract or task card techniques. Written instructions can be read loudly by the teacher or monitor. Pairing students with severe hearing loss with other students can be a frustrating experience for both, but meaningful possibilities also exist. Such a pairing necessitates lip reading, the use of verbal cues, or strong amplification on a hearing aid. Visual cues, featuring a "do as I do" approach, can stimulate certain types of activity.

The deaf student should be near the teacher to increase the opportunities to read lips and receive facial cues. Keep the class physically active. Avoid long delays for explanations or question-and-answer periods. This becomes a blank time for the hearing impaired and may lead to frustration and aggressive action. For rhythmics, some devices can be of benefit. Keep stereo speakers on the floor to provide vibration. Use a metronome or blinking light. For controlling movement patterns, hand signals should be developed for starting, stopping, moving to an area, assembling near the teacher, sitting down, and so on.

Static and dynamic balance problems are prevalent among hearing-impaired students. Focus on activities that challenge balance and insist on proper procedures. Have the student maintain the position or movement for 10 to 15 seconds and recover to the original position, all in good balance.

Orthopedic Disabilities

Orthopedic disabilities in students encompass a wide range of physical ailments, some of which may involve external support items such as splints, braces, crutches, and wheelchairs. A few post-polio cases may be encountered. Generalizing procedures for such a wide range of physical abnormalities is difficult. Students with orthopedic problems usually function on an academic level with other students and are regular members of a classroom. As such, they appear with the class for physical education.

Instructional Procedures

Instructional focus must be on what the student can do and on the physical needs that are to be met. Mobility is a problem for most, and modification is needed if the class activity demands running or agility. Students with temporary conditions (fractures, sprains, strains) are handled on an individual basis, according to physician recommendations. Individualized programs are made to order for this group, because the achievement goals can be set within the student's capacity to perform.

Although volleyball and basketball are popular team sports, there will be few leisure opportunities for these individuals because of the difficulty of getting enough participants together for team play. Strong emphasis should be placed on individual and dual sports such as tennis, track and field, road racing, table tennis, badminton, and swimming. This allows the orthopedically impaired individual to play a dual sport with an opponent or to participate individually in activities such as road racing and swimming.

For wheelchair students, certain measures are implicit. Special work is needed to develop general musculature to improve conditions for coping with the disability and to prevent muscle atrophy. In particular, students in wheelchairs need strong arm and shoulder musculature to transfer in and out of the wheelchair without assistance. Flexibility training to prevent and relieve permanent muscle shortening (contracture) should be instituted. Cardiorespiratory training is needed to maintain or improve aerobic capacity, since immobility in the chair decreases activity. From these experiences, students in wheelchairs should derive personal, functioning programs of activity that they can carry over into daily living.

Time devoted to special health care after class must be considered for students with either braces or in wheelchairs. Students with braces should inspect skin contact areas to look for irritation. If the student has perspired, a washcloth and towel will help him freshen up and remove irritants. Students in wheelchairs can transfer to a sturdy chair that is rigid and stabilized to allow the wheelchair to dry out. Provide adequate cushioning for any surface to which an orthopedically impaired person transfers, such as chairs, weight machines, and pool decks, to prevent pressure sores and skin abrasions. Adjust schedules so that time for this care is available. Scheduling the class during the last period before lunch or recess (or at the end of the day) allows this time.

Emotional Disorders

Students with emotional disorders represent an enigma for mainstreaming. They have been removed from the regular classroom situation because they may cause a disruption and because they need psychological services. Physical education seems to be one area in which they can find success. Each case is different, however, and generalization is difficult. Some students may be withdrawn, loud, aggressive, mute, or rebellious.

Instructional Procedures

An important key when working with students with emotional disorders is to establish a learning environment that is fair and consistent. The students need to know exactly what is expected and accepted in the instructional setting. In addition, rules must be clearly defined and nonpunitive in nature. Explanation of reasons for rules should be a regular topic of discussion since these youngsters often feel that someone is making rules that are meant to punish them personally. Students with emotional disorders need a stable and organized environment that focuses on individual progress. They will become easily frustrated and quit if the activities are too difficult or cause embarrassment. Expect occasional outbursts, even when instructional procedures have been correct. If the unexpected is anticipated, teachers will not feel as threatened or hurt by the student's behavior.

Students with emotional disorders need to know their limits of behavior. Set the limits and enforce them consistently. Students must know who is in charge and what that person will accept. It may take a long time to develop confidence in the student,

and vice versa. During this time it is important to build a sense of trust. Plan on problems and be ready to deal with them before they occur. A teacher who is patient and understanding can have a positive effect on students with this disability. Loving and forgiving teachers are most effective with the youngster who is emotionally disturbed

Other Disabilities

A range of other disabilities may arise. These include cardiac problems, cerebral palsy, asthma, and diabetes. Students with cardiac problems are generally under the guidance of a physician. Limitations and restrictions should be followed to the letter. The student should, however, be encouraged to work to the limits of the prescription.

An asthmatic student has restricted breathing capacity. The condition carries a warning against activities that can cause breathing distress. Students should be the judge of their physical capacity and stop when rest is indicated.

Cerebral palsy, like epilepsy, has strong negative social implications. Peer education and guidance are necessary. The signs of cerebral palsy are quite visible and, in severe cases, result in odd, uncoordinated movements and a characteristic gait. Medical supervision indicates the limits of the student's activities. Students with cerebral palsy are usually of normal intelligence; their chief problem is control of movement. An important goal is ensuring that they can achieve competency in performing simple movements. The excitability threshold is critical and must not be exceeded. Many need support services for special training in both neural and movement control.

Occasionally, a diabetic student may be found in a physical education class. Diabetes is an inability to metabolize carbohydrates, which results from the body's failure to supply insulin. Insulin is taken either orally or by injection to control serious cases. If the student is overweight, a program of weight reduction and exercise prescription may be useful solutions. Diabetics are usually under medical supervision. Knowing that a diabetic student is in a physical education class is important because the student must be monitored to detect the possibility of hypoglycemia (abnormally low blood sugar level). The condition can be accompanied by trembling, weakness, hunger, incoherence, and even by coma or convulsions. The solution is to raise the blood sugar level immediately through oral consumption of simple sugar (such as skim milk or orange juice) or some other easily converted carbohydrate. The diabetic usually carries carbohydrates, but a supply should be available to the instructor. Immediate action is needed because low blood sugar level can be dangerous—even life-threatening. The diabetic probably has enough control to participate in almost any activity. This is evidenced by the number of diabetic professional athletes who meet the demands of high activity without difficulty.

USING COMPUTERS

Computers are becoming increasingly available in schools all over the country. The computer is a time-saving device that can take over record-keeping chores required by the provisions of P.L. 94-142. Printouts of present and past status reports can be made available on demand. The computer can also provide comparisons with established norms, especially in physical fitness areas, and it can record progress toward the target goals set by the IEP. The computer minimizes the time necessary for recording student progress. In addition, computerized graphic compilations facilitate quick comprehension of progress reports. Several computer programs are available for writing and updating the IEP.

Another significant computer service is related to informational printouts. The due process regulations of P.L. 94-142 might be one such topic. Information concerning specific disabilities could be made readily available. Guidelines for formulating the IEP are another possibility. Long- and short-term objectives can be retrieved from a growing data bank.

Making relevant progress information available to students can be excellent motivation and stimulates a systematic approach to the attainment of specific achievements. The same information can also be the basis for reports to parents and other adults who are interested in the student. These reports can enhance parental cooperation.

PARENTAL SUPPORT

Having parents on the IEP committee spurs their involvement and establishes a line of communication between home and school. Home training or homework may be recommended for many students.

If home training is indicated, parents must be committed in terms of time and effort. Their work need not be burdensome but must be done regularly in accordance with the sequenced learning patterns. Also, the school must supply printed and sequenced learning activities for a systematic approach to the homework. Materials should be understandable and goals clear. Parents should see obvious progress in their youngsters as assignments unfold.

Older students with disabilities may accept some responsibility for home training, relegating the parent to the role of an interested, encouraging spectator. Even if homework is not feasible, parental interest and support are positive factors. The parents can help their youngster realize what skills have been learned and what progress has been made.

RECRUITING AND TRAINING AIDES

The use of aides can be an effective way of increasing the amount of instruction and practice for students who are disabled. Volunteers are quite easy to find among various community organizations, such as parent-teacher associations, foster grandparents, and community colleges. High school students who volunteer have proven effective with middle school students. An effective program, the PEOPEL project (discussed in the next section), was developed using trained student peers to teach students with disabilities in small classes.

An initial meeting with volunteer aides should explain the type of youngsters with whom they will work and clarify their responsibilities. Aides must learn how to be most effective in assisting the instructor. Training could include learning how to work effectively with individuals, recording data, and developing special materials and instructional supplies. In addition, the potential aides should receive experience in working with youngsters to see if they are capable and enjoy such work. Physical education specialists must also learn how to work with aides. In some cases, physical educators often find the task of organizing and supervising aides to be burdensome if they have not learned to supervise and organize.

Aides can assume many roles that increase the effectiveness of the instructional situation. For example, the aide may gather and locate equipment and supplies prior to the lesson. They may officiate games and assure that they run smoothly. Seasoned aides enjoy and are capable of offering one-on-one or small group instruction to youngsters. Aides should not reduce the need for involvement of the physical education instructor since they only implement instruction strategies that have been organized and developed by the professional educator. In addition, the physical educator must monitor the quality of the presentations made by the aide.

NATIONALLY VALIDATED PROGRAMS

For several years, nationally validated programs of proven practices in special education have been available. Portions of many of these programs are in or related to physical education. These programs are funded and endorsed by the U.S. Office of Education. Some deal with screening, assessment, and curriculum for students with special needs. Others feature management practices associated with special students. A number deal with early recognition and intervention so that the student can be fitted more successfully into the mainstreaming situation. Information pertaining to these programs can be secured from state departments of education or from the U.S. Office of Education. Four programs that have been recognized for outstanding contributions and have been identified as demonstration projects are described below.

Project ACTIVE (All Children Totally Involved Exercising)

Project ACTIVE provides direct service delivery to students with psychomotor problems through a competency-based teaching and individualized learning approach. A second component involves in-service training. Materials include a battery of tests and 7 program manuals. Conditions addressed are low motor ability, low physical vitality, postural abnormalities, nutritional deficiencies, breathing problems, motor disabilities or limitations, and communication disorders.

Project Unique

Project Unique is a fitness assessment project designed to determine the best tests for measuring fitness in students with sensory (visual or auditory) or

orthopedic impairments. Tests include AAHPERD Best items and others that can be administered in a mainstream setting.

Project I CAN (Individualize Instruction, Create Social Leisure Competence, Associate All Learnings, Narrow the Gap Between Theory and Practice)

Three separate programmatic systems make up Project I CAN, including preprimary skills, primary skills, and sport, leisure, and recreation skills. Each system includes an observational assessment approach, illustrative goals, objectives, instructional strategies, and program evaluation materials. Emphasis is placed on an achievement-based curriculum model.

Project PEOPEL (Physical Education Opportunity Program For Exceptional Learners)

Project PEOPEL is a peer-teaching model that pairs trained student aides with students with disabilities in small mainstream high school classes. Aides must complete a 1-semester training course. This model has been extensively field-tested and offers many advantages for students such as a high rate of feedback, individual attention, and additional instruction.

EXPECTED OUTCOMES

After reading this chapter, you should be able to

- Understand the implications of P.L. 94-142 on physical education.
- Develop a plan for identifying, locating, and evaluating all students with disabilities.
- Cite standards associated with assessment procedures for special students.
- Identify essential elements of an individualized educational program and list the stages of development.

- List guidelines for successful mainstreaming experiences.
- Describe characteristics of specific impairments and ways to modify learning experiences in physical education to accommodate students with disabilities.
- Identify and interpret nationally validated programs to assist in the screening, assessment, and curriculum development for students with special needs.

REFERENCES AND SUGGESTED READINGS

Arnheim, D. D., and Sinclair, W. A. 1985. *Physical Education for Special Populations: A Developmental, Adapted, and Remedial Approach.* Englewood Cliffs, NJ: Prentice-Hall.

Cooper Institute for Aerobics Research. 1992. *The Prudential Fitnessgram Test Administration Manual.* Dallas: Cooper Institute for Aerobics Research.

Dobbins, D. A., Garron, R., and Rarick, G. L. 1981. The motor performance of educable mentally retarded and intellectually normal boys after covariate control for differences in body size. *Research Quarterly* 52(1): 6–7.

Dunn, J., and Fait, H. 1989. *Special Physical Education: Adapted, Individualized, Developmental.* 6th ed. Dubuque, IA: Brown & Benchmark.

Rimmer, J.H. 1994. *Fitness and Rehabilitation Programs for Special Populations.* Dubuque, IA: Brown & Benchmark.

Seaman, J. A., and DePauw, K. P. 1982. *The New Adapted Physical Education.* Palo Alto, CA: Mayfield Publishing Co.

Sherrill, C. 1993. *Adapted Physical Activity, Recreation, and Sport: Cross-disciplinary and Lifespan.* 4th ed. Dubuque, IA: Brown & Benchmark.

Ulrich, D. A. 1983. A comparison of the qualitative motor performance of normal, educable, and trainable mentally retarded students. In R. L. Eason, T. L. Smith, and F. Caron (eds.). *Adapted Physical Activity.* Champaign, IL: Human Kinetics Publishers.

12 Legal Liability and Proper Care of Students

PURPOSE

To develop an understanding of liability and negligence and how each area affects methods of instruction. The practice of safety involves preventing accidents. Teachers need to understand the health status of students and have a plan for emergency care when an accident occurs. A safety and liability checklist is a preventive approach to avoiding the possibility of lawsuit.

KEY CONCEPTS

- Liability is a responsibility to perform a duty to a particular group, namely students in an educational setting.
- Tort liability is a lawsuit for breach of duty. Money is given to the offended individual when the breach of duty was flagrant.
- Negligence involves 4 major areas: (a) Duty to the individual, (b) breach of duty or failure to carry out the required duty, (c) injury to the student, and (d) proximate cause (was the accident due to the teacher not carrying out the duty?).
- There are many types of negligence: malfeasance, misfeasance, nonfeasance, contributory negligence, and comparative or shared negligence.
- The major areas of neglect that often lead to lawsuits are supervision of students, instruction of students, equipment and facilities, and athletic participation. Written policies and guidelines in these areas need to be developed and integrated into the educational process.
- Safety primarily involves preventing accidents before they occur. Written procedures need to be developed in the area of safety and continuously updated and reviewed.
- A written plan for emergency care should be established, approved by the school district, and followed to the letter by teachers. The administration of first aid should be undertaken by the physical education instructor only for saving a life.
- Accident reports should be filled out immediately while the results of the accident are fresh.
- A safety and liability checklist can be used to monitor the physical education environment.

School district personnel, including teaching and nonteaching members, are obligated to exercise ordinary care for the safety of students. This duty is manifested as the ability to anticipate reasonably foreseeable dangers and the responsibility to take necessary precautions to prevent problems from occurring. Failure to do so may cause the district to be the target of lawsuits.

Compared with other subject-matter areas, physical education is particularly vulnerable to accidents and resultant injuries. More than 50 percent of all accidents in the school setting occur on the playground and in the gymnasium. Even though schools cannot be held financially accountable for costs associated with treatment of injuries, they can be forced to pay these expenses if the injured party sues and wins judgment. Legal suits are conducted under respective state statutes. Principles underlying legal action are similar, but certain regulations and procedures vary among states. Teachers should acquire a copy of the legal liability policy in their district. Districts usually have a written definition of situations in which teachers can be held liable.

All students have the right to freedom from injury caused by others or due to participation in a program. Courts have ruled that teachers owe their students a duty of care to protect them from harm. Teachers must offer a standard of care that any reasonable and prudent professional with similar training would apply under the given circumstances. A teacher is required to exercise the teaching skill, discretion, and knowledge that members of the profession in good standing normally possess in similar situations. Lawsuits usually occur when citizens believe that this standard of care was not exercised.

Liability is the responsibility to perform a duty for a particular group. It is an obligation to perform in a particular way that is required by law and enforced by court action. Teachers are bound by contract to carry out their duties in a reasonable and prudent manner. Liability is always a legal matter. It must be proved in a court of law that negligence occurred before one can be held liable.

TORTS

In education, a **tort** is concerned with the teacher-student relationship and is a legal wrong that results in direct or indirect injury to another individual or to property. The following legal definition is from *Black's Law Dictionary* (1990):

> [A tort is] a private or civil wrong or injury, other than breach of contract, for which the court will provide a remedy in the form of an action for damages. Three elements of every tort action are: existence of legal duty from defendant to plaintiff, breach of duty, and damage as proximate result.

As the result of a tort, the court can give a monetary reward for damages that occurred. The court can also give a monetary reward for punitive damages if a breach of duty can be established. Usually, the court rewards the offended individual for damages that occurred due to the negligence of the instructor or other responsible individual. Punitive damages are much less common.

NEGLIGENCE AND LIABILITY

Liability is usually concerned with a breach of duty through negligence. Lawyers examine the situation that gave rise to the injury to establish if liability can be determined. Four major points must be established to determine if a teacher was negligent.

Duty. The first point considered is that of duty owed to the participants. Did the school or teacher owe students a duty of care that implies conforming to certain standards of conduct? When examining duty or breach of duty, the court looks at reasonable care that a member of the profession in good standing would provide. In other words, to determine a reasonable standard, the court uses the conduct of other teachers as a standard for comparison.

Breach of Duty. The teacher must commit a breach of duty by failing to conform to the required duty. After it is established that a duty was required, it must be proved that the teacher did not perform that duty. Two situations are possible: (a) the teacher did something that was not supposed to be done (such as putting boxing gloves on students to resolve their differences), or (b) the teacher did not do something that should have been done (such as failing to teach an activity using proper progressions).

Injury. An injury must occur if liability is to be established. If no injury or harm occurs, there is no liability. Further, it must be proved that the injured party is entitled to compensatory damages for financial loss or physical discomfort.

Proximate Cause. The failure of the teacher to conform to the required standard must be the proximate cause of the resulting injury. It must be proved that the injury was caused by the teacher's breach of duty. It is not enough to prove simply that a breach of duty occurred. It must simultaneously be shown that the injury was a direct result of the teacher's failure to provide a reasonable standard of care.

Foreseeability

A key to the issue of negligence is **foreseeability**. Courts expect that a trained professional is able to foresee potentially harmful situations. Was it possible for the teacher to predict and anticipate the danger of the harmful act or situation and to take appropriate measures to prevent it from occurring? If the injured party can prove that the teacher should have foreseen the danger involved in an activity or situation (even in part), the teacher will be found negligent for failing to act in a reasonable and prudent manner.

This points out the necessity of examining all activities, equipment, and facilities for possible hazards and sources of accident. As an example, a common game (unfortunately) in many school settings is bombardment, or dodge ball. During the game, a student is hit in the eye by a ball and loses vision in that eye. Was this a foreseeable accident that could have been prevented? Were the balls being used capable of inflicting severe injury? Were students aware of rules that might have prevented this injury? Were the abilities of the students somewhat equal, or were some capable of throwing with such velocity that injury was predictable? Were all students forced to play the game? These questions would likely be considered in court in an attempt to prove that the teacher should have been able to predict the overly dangerous situation.

TYPES OF NEGLIGENCE

Negligence is defined by the court as conduct that falls below a standard of care established to protect others from unreasonable risk or harm. Several types of negligence can be categorized.

Malfeasance

Malfeasance occurs when the teacher does something improper by committing an act that is unlawful and wrongful, with no legal basis (often referred to as an act of commission). Malfeasance can be illustrated by the following incident. A male student misbehaved on numerous occasions. In desperation, the teacher gave the student a choice of punishment—a severe spanking in front of the class or running many laps around the field. The student chose the former and suffered physical and emotional damage. Even though the teacher gave the student a choice whereby he could have avoided the paddling, the teacher is still liable for any physical or emotional harm caused.

Misfeasance

Misfeasance occurs when the teacher follows the proper procedures but does not perform according to the required standard of conduct. Misfeasance is based on performance of the proper action but not up to the required standard. It is usually the subpar performance of an act that might have been otherwise lawfully done. An example would be the teacher's offering to spot a student during a tumbling routine and then not doing the spotting properly. If the student is injured due to a faulty spot, the teacher can be held liable.

Nonfeasance

Nonfeasance is based on lack of action in carrying out a duty. This is usually an act of omission: The teacher knew the proper procedures but failed to follow them. Teachers can be found negligent if they act or fail to act. Understanding and carrying out proper procedures and duties in a manner befitting members of the profession is essential. In contrast to the misfeasance example, nonfeasance occurs when a teacher knows that it is necessary to spot certain gymnastic routines but fails to do so. Courts expect teachers to behave with more skill and insight than parents (Strickland, Phillip, and Phillips, 1976). Teachers are expected to behave with greater competency because they have been educated to give students a higher standard of professional care than parents.

Contributory Negligence

The situation is different when the injured student is partially or wholly at fault. Students are expected to exercise sensible care and to follow directions or regulations designed to protect them from injury. Improper behavior by the injured party that causes the accident is usually ruled to be **contributory negligence**, because the injured party contributed to the resulting harm. This responsibility is directly related to the maturity, ability, and experience of the youngster. For example, most states have laws specifying that a child under 7 years of age is incapable of contributory negligence (Baley and Matthews, 1984). To illustrate contributory negligence, assume that a teacher has thoroughly explained the shot put and all related safety rules. As students begin to practice, one of them runs through a restricted area that is well marked and is hit by a shot put. In this case, the possibility is strong that the student would be held liable for such action.

Comparative or Shared Negligence

Under the doctrine of **comparative negligence**, the injured party can recover only if found to be less negligent than the defendant (the teacher). Where statutes apply, the amount of recovery is generally reduced in proportion to the injured party's participation in the circumstances leading to the injury.

COMMON DEFENSES AGAINST NEGLIGENCE

Negligence must be proved in a court of law. Many times, teachers are negligent in carrying out their duties, yet the injured party does not take the case to court. If a teacher is sued, some of the following defenses are used in an attempt to show that the teacher's action was not the primary cause of the accident.

Act of God

The **act of God** defense places the cause of injury on forces beyond the control of the teacher or the school. The defense is made that it was impossible to predict an unsafe condition, but through an act of God, the injury occurred. Typical acts would be a gust of wind that blew over a volleyball standard or a cloudburst of rain that made a surface slick. The act of God defense can be used only in cases in which the injury still would have occurred even though reasonable and prudent action had been taken.

Proximate Cause

The defense of **proximate cause** attempts to prove that the accident was not caused by the negligence of the teacher. There must be a close relationship be-

tween the breach of duty by the teacher and the injury. This is a common defense in cases dealing with proper supervision. The student is participating in an activity supervised by the teacher. When the teacher leaves the playing area to get a cup of coffee, the student is injured. The defense lawyer will try to show that the accident would have occurred regardless of whether or not the teacher was there.

Assumption of Risk

Clearly, physical education is a high-risk activity when compared with most other curriculum areas. **Assumption of risk** implies the participant assumes the risk of an activity when choosing to be part of that activity. The assumption of risk defense is seldom used by physical education teachers because students are not often allowed to choose to participate or not participate. An instructor for an elective program that allows students to choose desired units of instruction might find this a better defense than one who teaches a totally required program. Athletic and sport club participation is by choice, and players must assume a greater risk in activities such as football and gymnastics.

Contributory Negligence

Contributory negligence is often used by the defense in an attempt to convince the court that the injured party acted in a manner that was abnormal. In other words, the injured individual did not act in a manner that was typical of students of similar age and maturity. The defense attempts to demonstrate that the activity or equipment in question was used for years with no record of accident. A case is made based on the manner of presentation—how students were taught to act in a safe manner—and that the injured student acted outside the parameters of safe conduct. A key point in this defense is whether the activity was suitable for the age and maturity level of the participants.

AREAS OF RESPONSIBILITY

A 2-tiered approach for analyzing injuries is useful for determining responsibility. The first tier includes the duties that the administration must assume in support of the program. The second tier defines the duties of the instructor or staff member charged with teaching or supervising students. Each party has a role to fill, but some overlap occurs. The following example illustrates the differences.

A student is hurt while performing a tumbling stunt. A lawsuit ensues charging the teacher with negligence for not following safe procedures. The administration is usually included in the suit, being charged with negligence for hiring an incompetent (not qualified) instructor and not implementing proper safety factors. The 2 levels of responsibility should be considered when delegating responsibility because:

1. They identify different functions and responsibilities of the teaching staff and administration.
2. They provide a framework for reducing injuries and improving safety procedures.
3. They provide perspective for following legal precedents.

For the responsibilities that are described in the following sections, both administrative and instructional duties are presented.

Supervision

All activities in a school setting must be supervised, including recess, lunch times, and field trips. The responsibilities of the school are critical if supervision is to function properly.

Administration

Two levels are identified in supervision: general and specific. General supervision (study hall, lunch room, and so on) refers to broad coverage, when students are not under direct control of a teacher or a designated individual. A plan of supervision should be made, designating the areas to be covered and including where and how the supervisor should rotate. This plan, kept in the principal's office, should cover rules of conduct governing student behavior. Rules should be posted prominently on bulletin boards, especially in classrooms. In addition to the plan, administrators must select qualified personnel, provide necessary training, and monitor the plan properly.

The general supervisor must be concerned primarily with student behavior, focusing on the student's right to a safe and unthreatening experience. Supervisors should observe the area, looking for breaches of discipline, particularly when an individual or group "picks on" another youngster. If it becomes necessary to leave the area, a qualified substitute must be found to prevent the area from going unsupervised.

Staff

General supervision is necessary during times when students congregate but are not involved in instruction. The supervisor should know the school's plan for supervision and emergency care procedures to follow in case of an accident. Supervision is a positive act that requires the supervisor to be actively involved and moving throughout the area. The number of supervisors should be determined by the type of activity, the size of the area, and the number and age of the students.

Specific supervision requires that the instructor be with a certain group of students (that is, a class). An example is spotting students who are performing challenging gymnastic activities. If certain pieces of apparatus require special care and proper use, rules and regulations must be posted near the apparatus. Students should be made aware of the rules and should receive appropriate instruction and guidance in applying the rules. When rules are modified, they should be rewritten in proper form. There is no substitute for documentation when the need to defend policies and approaches arises.

When teaching, arrange and teach the class so that all students are always in view. This implies supervising from the perimeter of the area. Teachers who are at the center of the student group with many students behind them will find it impossible to supervise a class safely and effectively. Equipment and apparatus should not go unsupervised at any time when left accessible to students in the area. An example would be equipment that is left on the playing field between classes. If other students in the area have easy access to the equipment, they may use it in an unsafe manner, and the teacher can be found liable if an injury occurs.

Teachers should not agree to supervise activities in which they are unqualified to anticipate possible hazards. If this situation arises, a written memo should be sent to the department head or principal stating such lack of insight and qualification. Teachers should maintain a copy for their files.

Merriman (1993) offers 5 recommendations to assure that adequate supervision occurs:

1. The supervisor must be in the immediate vicinity (within sight and hearing).

2. If required to leave, the supervisor must have an adequate replacement in place before departing. Adequate replacements do not include paraprofessionals, student teachers, custodial help, or untrained teachers.
3. Supervision procedures must be preplanned and incorporated into daily lessons.
4. Supervision procedures should include what to observe, listen for, where to stand for the most effective view, and what to do if a problem arises.
5. Supervision requires that age, maturity, and skill ability of participants must always be considered, as must be the inherent risk of the activity.

Instruction

Instructional responsibility rests primarily with the teacher, but administrative personnel have certain defined functions.

Administration

The administration should review and approve the curricular plan. The curriculum should be reviewed regularly to assure that it is current and updated. Activities included in the curriculum should be based on contributions they make to the growth and development of youngsters. It makes little sense in a court of law to say that an activity was included "for the fun of it" or "because students liked it." Instead, include activities in the curriculum because they meet program objectives. Administrators are obligated to support the program with adequate finances. The principal and higher administrators should visit the program periodically. Unfamiliarity with program content and operation obviates the possibility that practices were occurring without adequate administrative supervision.

Instructional Staff

With regard to instruction, the teacher has a duty to protect students from unreasonable physical or mental harm. This includes avoiding any acts or omissions that might cause such harm. The teacher is educated, experienced, and skilled in physical education and must be able to foresee situations that could be harmful.

The major area of concern involving instruction is whether the student received adequate instruction before or during activity participation. Adequate instruction means (a) teaching students how to perform activities correctly and use equipment and apparatus properly, and (b) teaching youngsters necessary safety precautions. If instructions are given, they must be correct, understandable, and include proper technique, or the instructor can be held liable. The risk involved in an activity must be communicated to the learner.

The age and maturity level of students play an important role in the selection of activities. Younger students require more care, instructions that are easy to comprehend, and clear restrictions in the name of safety. Some students have a lack of appropriate fear in activities, and the teacher must be aware of this when discussing safety factors. A dare devil may have little concern about performing a high-risk activity even if an instructor is nearby. This places much responsibility on the instructor to give adequate instruction and supervision.

Careful planning is a necessity. Written curriculum guides and lesson plans should offer a well-prepared approach that can withstand scrutiny and examination by other teachers and administrators. Written lesson plans should include proper sequence and progression of skill. Teachers are on defensible grounds if they can show that the progression of activities was based on presentations designed by experts and was followed carefully during the teaching act. District and state guidelines enforcing instructional sequences and restricted activities should be checked closely.

Proper instruction demands that students not be forced to participate. If a youngster is required to perform an activity unwillingly, the teacher may be open to a lawsuit. In a lawsuit dealing with stunts and tumbling (Appenzeller, 1970), the court held the teacher liable when a student claimed that she was not given adequate instruction in how to perform a stunt called "roll over 2." The teacher was held liable because the student claimed she was forced to try the stunt before adequate instruction was offered. Gymnastics and tumbling are areas in which lawsuits are prevalent due to a lack of adequate instruction. Posting the proper sequence of skills and lead-up activities may be useful to ensure that they have been presented properly. Teachers need to tread the line carefully between helpful encouragement and forcing students to try new activities.

For teachers who incorporate punishment as a part of the instructional process, the consequences of its use should be examined carefully before implementation. Physical punishment that brings about permanent or long-lasting damage is certainly indefensible. Using some type of physical activity (push-ups or running) is an unacceptable practice that increases the risk of being sued. Any punishment used must be in line with the physical maturity and health of the student involved. A teacher's practice of having students perform laps when they have misbehaved might go unchallenged for years. However, what if an asthmatic student or a youngster with congenital heart disease is asked to run and suffers injury or illness? What if the student is running unsupervised and is injured from a fall or suffers heat exhaustion? In these examples, defending such punitive practices would be difficult. Making students perform physical activity for misbehavior is indefensible under any circumstance. If a student is injured while performing physical punishment, teachers are usually found liable and held responsible for the injury.

The following points can help teachers plan for meaningful and safe instruction:

1. Sequence all activities in units of instruction and develop written lesson plans. Many problems occur when snap judgments are made under the daily pressure and strain of teaching.
2. Scrutinize high-risk activities to assure that all safety procedures have been implemented. If in doubt, discuss the activities with other experienced teachers and administrators.
3. Activities used in the curriculum must be within the developmental limits of the students. Since the range of maturity and development of youngsters in a class is usually wide, activities may be beyond the ability level of some students.
4. If students' grades are based on the number of activities in which they participate, some students may feel forced to try all activities. Teachers should make it clear to students that the choice to participate belongs to them. When they are afraid of getting hurt, they can elect not to perform an activity.
5. Include in written lesson plans necessary safety equipment. The lesson plan should detail how equipment should be arranged, the placement of mats, and where the instructor will carry out supervision.
6. If a student claims injury or brings a note from parents requesting that the student not participate in physical activity, the teacher must honor the communication. Excuses are almost always given at the start of the period when the teacher is busy with many other duties (such as getting equipment ready, taking roll, and opening lockers). It is difficult to make a thoughtful judgment at this time. The school nurse is qualified to make these judgments when they relate to health and should be used in that capacity. If the excuses continue over a long period of time, the teacher or nurse should have a conference with the parents to rectify the situation.
7. Make sure that activities included in the instructional process are in line with the available equipment and facilities. An example is the amount of space available. If a soccer lead-up activity is brought indoors because of inclement weather, it may no longer be a safe and appropriate activity.
8. If spotting is required for safe completion of activities, it should always be done by the instructor or by trained students. Teaching students how to spot is as important as teaching them physical skills. Safe conduct must be learned.
9. If students are working independently at stations, carefully constructed and written task cards can help eliminate unsafe practices.
10. Have a written emergency care plan posted in the gymnasium. This plan should be approved by health care professionals and should be followed to the letter when an injury occurs.

EQUIPMENT AND FACILITIES

School responsibility for equipment and facilities is required for both noninstructional and class use.

Administration

The principal and the custodian should oversee the fields and playground equipment that are used for recess and outside activities. Students should be instructed to report broken and unsafe equipment, as well as hazards (glass, cans, rocks), to the principal's office. If equipment is faulty, it should be removed from the area. A regular inspection of equipment and facilities, preferably by the physical education specialist, should be instituted, perhaps weekly. If a specialist is not employed, the inspection will have to be performed by the principal or the custodian. Results of the inspection should be filed with the school district safety committee. Replacement of sawdust, sand, or other shock-absorbing material must be done regularly.

Administrators should develop a written checklist of equipment and apparatus for the purpose of recording scheduled safety inspections. The date of inspection should be noted to show that inspection occurs at regular intervals. If a potentially dangerous situation exists, rules or warnings should be posted so that students and teachers are made aware of the risk before participation is allowed.

Proper installation of equipment is critical. Climbing equipment and other equipment that must be anchored should be installed by a reputable firm that guarantees its work. When examining apparatus, inspection of the installation is important. Maintenance of facilities is also important. Grass should be kept short and the grounds inspected for debris. Holes in the ground should be filled and loose gravel removed. A proper finish that prevents excessive slipping should be used on indoor floors. Shower rooms should have a roughened floor finish applied to prevent falls when the floors are wet.

Equipment and facilities used in the physical education program must allow safe participation in activity. The choice of apparatus and equipment should be based on the growth and developmental levels of the students. For example, allowing middle school students to use climbing equipment that was designed for high school students may result in a fall that causes injury. Hazards found on playing fields need to be repaired and eliminated. The legal concept of an attractive nuisance should be understood. This implies that some piece of equipment or apparatus, usually left unsupervised, was so attractive to youngsters that they could not be expected to avoid it. When an injury occurs, even though students may have been using the apparatus incorrectly, teachers and school administrators are often held liable because the attractive nuisance should have been removed from the area when unsupervised.

Instructional Staff

Indoor facilities are of primary concern to physical education instructors. While the administration is charged with overall responsibility for facilities and equipment, including periodic inspection, the instructor should make a regular safety inspection of the instructional area. If corrective action is needed, the principal or other designated administrator should be notified in writing. Verbal notification is not enough, since it offers little legal protection to the instructor.

Facilities should be used in a safe manner. Often, the side and end lines of playing fields for sports such as football, soccer, and field hockey are placed too close to walls, curbings, or fences. The boundaries should be moved to allow adequate room for deceleration, even though the size of the playing area may be reduced. In the gymnasium, students should not be asked to run to a line that is close to a wall. Another common hazard is baskets positioned too close to the playing area. The poles that support the baskets must be padded.

Proper use of equipment and apparatus is important. Regardless of the state of equipment repair, if it is misused, it may result in an injury. Students must receive instruction in the proper use of equipment and apparatus before they are issued to the students and used. Safety instruction should be included in the written lesson plan to ensure that all points are covered.

Equipment should be purchased on the basis of quality and safety as well as potential use. Many lawsuits occur because of unsafe equipment and apparatus. The liability for such equipment may rest with the manufacturer, but this has to be proved, which means that the teacher must state, in writing, the exact specifications of the desired equipment. The process of bidding for lower-priced items may result in the purchase of less-safe equipment. If teachers have specified proper equipment in writing, however, the possibility of their being held liable for injury is reduced.

SPORTS PROGRAMS

A common problem for administrators of school sports programs is providing qualified coaches. The administration should set minimum requirements for coaches and assure that incompetent individuals are removed from coaching duties (see Chapter 13). When students are involved in extracurricular activity, teachers (coaches) are responsible for the safe conduct of activities. The following areas often give rise to lawsuits if they are not handled carefully.

Mismatching Opponents

A common error that gives rise to lawsuits is the mismatching of students on the basis of size and ability. Just because the competitors are the same sex and choose to participate does not absolve the instructor of liability if an injury occurs. The question that courts examine is whether an effort was made to match students according to height, weight, and ability. Courts are less understanding about mismatching in the physical education setting compared with an athletic contest, but mismatching is a factor that should be avoided in any situation.

Waiver Forms

Participants in extracurricular activities should be required to sign a responsibility waiver form. The form should explain the risks involved in voluntary participation and discuss briefly the types of injuries that have occurred in the past during practice and competition. Signed waiver slips do not waive the rights of participants; teachers and coaches still can be found liable if injuries occur. However, the waiver form does communicate clearly the risks involved and may be a strong "assumption of risk" defense.

Medical Examinations

Participants must have a medical examination before participating. Records of the examination should be kept on file and should be identified prominently when physical restrictions or limitations exist. It is common to "red dot" the folders of students who have a history of medical problems. Students must not be allowed to participate unless they purchase or show proof of medical insurance. Evidence of such coverage should be kept in the folders of athletic participants.

Preseason Conditioning

Preseason conditioning should be undertaken in a systematic and progressive fashion. Starting the season with a mile run for time makes little sense if students have not been preconditioned. Coaches should be aware of guidelines dealing with heat and humidity (see pp. 34–35). For example, in Arizona, guidelines are to avoid strenuous activity when the temperature exceeds 85 degrees F and the humidity exceeds 40 percent (Stone, 1977). When these conditions are exceeded, running is curtailed to 10 minutes and active games to 30 minutes. Drinking water should be available and given to students on demand.

Transportation of Students

Whenever students are transported, teachers are responsible for their safety both enroute and during the activity. Transportation liability can be avoided by not providing transportation but instead requiring participants to meet at the site of the event (Pittman, 1993). If the school must provide transportation, licensed drivers and school-approved vehicles should always be used. Travel plans should include official approval from the appropriate school administrator. One special note: If the driver receives pay or reimbursement for the trip, the possibility of being held liable for injury increases dramatically. To make the matter worse, many insurance policies do not cover drivers who receive compensation for transporting students. If teachers are transporting students and receiving reimbursement, a special insurance rider that provides liability coverage for this situation should be purchased.

SAFETY

The major thrust of safety should be to prevent situations that cause accidents. It is estimated that over 70 percent of injuries that occur in sport and related activities could be prevented through proper safety procedures. On the other hand, some accidents occur despite precautions, and proper emergency procedures should be established to cope with any situation. A comprehensive study of injuries received in sport and related activities was conducted by the U.S. Consumer Product Safety Commission (1992). This study involved a network of computers in 119 hospital emergency rooms that channeled injury data to a central point. The sports and activities that produced the most injuries were, in order, football, touch football, baseball, basketball, gymnastics, and skiing. The facility that produced the most disabling injuries was the swimming pool.

Learning to recognize potential high-risk situations is an important factor in preventing accidents. Teachers must possess a clear understanding of the hazards and potential dangers of an activity before they can establish controls. Instructors must not assume that participants are aware of the dangers and risks involved in various activities. Students must be told of all dangers and risks before participation.

Guidelines for Safety

1. Inservice sessions in safety should be administered by experienced and knowledgeable teachers. Department heads may be responsible for the training, or outside experts can be employed to undertake the responsibility. Giving in-district credit to participating teachers offers strong indication that the district is concerned about using proper safety techniques.

2. Medical records should be reviewed at the start of the school year. Atypical students should be identified and noted within each class listing before the first instructional day. If necessary, the teacher or school nurse can call the doctor of a student with disabilities or activity restrictions to inquire about the situation and discuss special needs. Physical education teachers should be notified by the classroom teacher or school nurse about youngsters who have special problems (such as epilepsy) or temporary problems (such as medication).

3. Throughout the school year, safety orientations should be conducted with students. Discussions should include potentially dangerous situations, class conduct, and rules for proper use of equipment and apparatus. Teachers should urge students to report any conditions that might cause an accident.

4. Safety rules for specific units of instruction should be discussed at the onset of each unit. Rules should be posted and brought to the attention of students regularly. Posters and bulletin boards can promote safety in an enjoyable and stimulating manner.

5. If students are to serve as instructional aides, they should be trained. Aides must understand the techniques of spotting, for example, and must receive proper instruction if they are to be a part of the educational process. Caution must be used when using student aides because teachers are still responsible even if an aide performed a duty incorrectly.

6. Instructional practices need to be monitored for possible hazards. For example, students in competitive situations should be matched by size, maturity, and ability. Proper instruction necessary for safe participation should occur prior to activity. Instructors should receive a competence check to ensure that they are adequately trained to give instruction in various activities. The instructional area should be properly prepared for safe participation; if the area is lacking necessary apparatus and safety devices, instruction should be modified to meet safety standards.

7. An inventory of equipment and apparatus should include a safety checklist. Whenever necessary, equipment in need of repair should be sent to proper agents. If the cost of repair is greater than 40 percent of the replacement cost, discarding the equipment or apparatus is usually a more economical choice.

8. When an injury occurs, it should be recorded and a report placed in the student's file. An injury should also be filed by type of injury, such as ankle sprain or broken arm. The report should list the activity and the conditions to facilitate analysis at regular intervals. The analysis may show that injuries are occurring regularly during a specific activity or on a certain piece of equipment. This process can give direction for creating a safer environment or for defending the safety record of a sport, activity, or piece of equipment.

9. Teachers need to maintain up-to-date first-aid and CPR certification. Administrators should ensure that teachers meet these standards and should provide training sessions when necessary.

Safety Committee

Safety should be publicized regularly throughout the school, and a mechanism should exist that allows students, parents, and teachers to voice concerns about unsafe conditions. A safety committee can meet at regular intervals to establish safety policies, rule on requests for allowing high-risk activities, and analyze serious injuries that have occurred in the school district. This committee should develop safety rules that apply districtwide to all teachers. It may determine that certain activities involve too high a risk for the return in student benefit. Acceptable criteria for sport equipment and apparatus may be established by the committee.

The safety committee should include 1 or more high-level administrators, physical education teachers, health officers (nurse), parents, and students. School administrators are usually indicted when lawsuits occur, because they are held responsible for program content and curriculum. Their representation on the safety committee is therefore important. Students on the committee may be aware of possible hazards, and parents may often voice concerns overlooked by teachers.

Emergency Care Plan

Before any emergency arises, teachers should prepare themselves by learning about special health and physical conditions of students (Gray, 1993). Most schools have a method for identifying students with special health problems. If a student has a problem that may require treatment, a consent-to-treat form should be on file in case the parent or guardian is unavailable. Necessary first-aid materials and supplies should be available in a kit and be readily accessible.

Establishing procedures for emergency care and notification of parents in case of injury is of utmost importance in providing a high standard of care for students. To plan properly for emergency care, all physical education teachers should have first-aid training. First aid is the immediate and temporary care given at an emergency before a physician is available. Its purpose is to save life, prevent aggravation of injuries, and alleviate severe suffering. If there is evidence of life-threatening bleeding or if the victim is unconscious or has stopped breathing, the teacher must administer first aid. When already injured persons may be further injured if they are not moved, then moving them is permissible. As a general rule, however, an injured person should not be moved unless absolutely necessary. If there is indication of back or neck injury, the head must be immobilized and should not be moved without the use of a spine board. The purpose of first aid is to save life. The emergency care plan consists of the following steps:

1. Administration of first aid to the injured student is the number 1 priority. Treat only life-threatening injuries. The school nurse should be called to the scene of the accident immediately. Emergency care procedures should indicate whether the student can be moved and in what fashion. It is critical that the individual applying first aid avoid aggravating the injury.

2. Notify parents as soon as possible when emergency care is required. Each student's file should list home and emergency telephone numbers where parents can be reached. If possible, the school should have an arrangement with local emergency facilities so that a paramedic unit can be called immediately to the scene of a serious accident.

3. In most cases, the student should be released to a parent or a designated representative. Policies for transportation of injured students should be established and documented.

4. A student accident report should be completed promptly while the details of the accident are clear. Figure 12.1 is an example of an accident form that covers the necessary details. The teacher and principal should both retain copies and additional copies should be sent to the administrative office.

PERSONAL PROTECTION: MINIMIZING THE EFFECTS OF A LAWSUIT

In spite of proper care, injuries do occur, and lawsuits may be initiated. Two courses of action are necessary to counteract the effects of a suit.

Liability Insurance

Teachers may be protected by school district liability insurance. Usually, however, teachers must purchase their own policy. Most policies provide for legal services to contest a suit and will pay indemnity up to the limits of the policy (liability coverage of $500,000 is most common). Most policies give the insurance company the right to settle out of court. Unfortunately, when this occurs, some may infer that the teacher was guilty even though the circumstances indicate otherwise. Insurance companies usually settle out of court to avoid the excessive legal fees required to try to win the case in court.

Recordkeeping

The second course of action is to keep complete records of accidents. Many lawsuits occur months or even years after the accident, when memory of the situation is fuzzy. Accident reports should be filled out immediately after an injury. The teacher should take care to provide no evidence, oral or written, that others could use in a court of law. Do not attempt to make a diagnosis or to specify the supposed cause of the accident in the report.

If newspaper reporters probe for details, the teacher should avoid describing the accident beyond the basic facts. When discussing the accident with administrators, only the facts recorded on the accident report should be discussed. School records can be subpoenaed in court proceedings. The point here is not to dissemble, but to be cautious and avoid self-incrimination.

Student Accident Report

_____ School

In all cases, this form should be filed through the school nurse and signed by the principal of the school. The original will be forwarded to the superintendent's office, where it will be initialed and sent to the head nurse. The second copy will be retained by the principal or the nurse. The third copy should be given to the physical education teacher if accident is related.

Name of Injured _____ Address _____

Phone _____ Grade _____ Home Room _____ Age _____

Parents of Injured _____

Place of Accident _____ Date of Accident _____

Hour _____ A.M. P.M. Date Reported _____ By Whom _____

Parent Contact Attempted at _____ A.M. P.M. Parent Contacted at _____ A.M. P.M.

DESCRIBE ACCIDENT, GIVING SPECIFIC LOCATION AND CONDITION OF PREMISES _____

_____

NATURE OF INJURY _____
(Describe in detail)

CARE GIVEN OR ACTION TAKEN BY NURSE OR OTHERS _____

_____

REASON INJURED PERSON WAS ON PREMISES _____
(Activity at time—i.e., lunch, physical education, etc.)

STAFF MEMBER RESPONSIBLE FOR STUDENT SUPERVISION AT TIME OF ACCIDENT _____

IS STUDENT COVERED BY SCHOOL-SPONSORED ACCIDENT INSURANCE?   ____ YES   ____ NO

MEDICAL CARE RECOMMENDED   ____ YES   ____ NO

WHERE TAKEN AFTER ACCIDENT _____
(Specify home, physician, or hospital, giving name and address)

BY WHOM _____ AT WHAT TIME _____ A.M. P.M.

FOLLOW-UP BY NURSE TO BE SENT TO CENTRAL HEALTH OFFICE

REMEDIATIVE MEASURES TAKEN _____
(Attach individual remarks if necessary)

School _____ Principal _____

Date _____ Nurse _____

On the back of this sheet, list all persons familiar with the circumstances of the accident, giving name, address, telephone number, age, and location with respect to the accident.

FIGURE 12.1   Sample student accident report form

Safety and Liability Checklist

The following checklist can be used to monitor the physical education environment. Any situations that deviate from safe and legally sound practices should be rectified immediately.

Supervision and Instruction

1. Are teachers adequately trained in all of the activities that they are teaching?
2. Do all teachers have evidence of a necessary level of first-aid training?
3. When supervising, do personnel have access to a written plan of areas to be observed and responsibilities to be carried out?
4. Have students been warned of potential dangers and risks and advised of rules and the reasons for the rules?
5. Are safety rules posted near areas of increased risk?
6. Are lesson plans written? Do they include provisions for proper instruction, sequence of activities, and safety? Are all activities taught listed in the district curriculum guide?
7. When a new activity is introduced, are safety precautions and instructions for correct skill performance always communicated to the class?
8. Are the activities taught in the program based on sound curriculum principles? Could the activities and units of instruction be defended on the basis of their educational contributions?
9. Do the methods of instruction recognize individual differences among students, and are the necessary steps taken to meet the needs of all students, regardless of sex, ability, or disability?
10. Are substitute teachers given clear and comprehensive lesson plans so that they can maintain the scope and sequence of instruction?
11. Is the student evaluation plan based on actual performance and objective data rather than on favoritism or arbitrary and capricious standards?
12. Is appropriate dress required for students? This does not imply uniforms, only dress (including shoes) that ensures the safety of the student.
13. When necessary for safety, are students grouped according to ability level, size, or age?
14. Is the class left unsupervised for teacher visits to the office, lounge, or bathroom? Is one teacher ever asked to supervise 2 or more classes at the same time?
15. If students are used as teacher aides or to spot others, are they given proper instruction and training?

Equipment and Facilities

1. Is all equipment inspected regularly, and are the inspection results recorded on a form and sent to the proper administrators?
2. Is a log maintained recording the regular occurrence of an inspection, the equipment in need of repair, and when repairs were made?
3. Are "attractive nuisances" eliminated from the gymnasium and playing field?
4. Are specific safety rules posted on facilities and near equipment?
5. Are the following inspected periodically:
   a. Playing field for presence of glass, rocks, and metal objects?
   b. Fasteners holding equipment, such as climbing ropes, horizontal bars, or baskets?
   c. Goals for games, such as football, soccer, and field hockey, to be sure that they are fastened securely?
   d. Padded areas, such as goal supports?
6. Are mats placed under apparatus from which a fall is possible?
7. Are playing fields arranged so participants will not run into each other or be hit by a ball from another game?
8. Are landing pits filled and maintained properly?

Emergency Care

1. Is there a written procedure for emergency care?
2. Is a person properly trained in first aid available immediately following an accident?
3. Are emergency telephone numbers readily accessible?
4. Are telephone numbers of parents available?
5. Is an up-to-date first-aid kit available? Is ice immediately available?
6. Are health folders maintained that list restrictions, allergies, and health problems of students?
7. Are health folders reviewed by instructors on a regular basis?
8. Are students participating in extracurricular activities required to have insurance? Is the policy number recorded?
9. Is there a plan for treating injuries that involves the local paramedics?
10. Are accident reports filed promptly and analyzed regularly?

Transportation of Students

1. Have parents been informed that their students will be transported off campus?

2. Are detailed travel plans approved by the site administrator and kept on file?
3. Are school vehicles used whenever possible?
4. Are drivers properly licensed and vehicles insured?
5. If teachers or parents use their vehicles to transport students, are the students, driver, and car owner covered by an insurance rider purchased by the school district?

EXPECTED OUTCOMES

After reading the chapter, you should be able to

- Clearly delineate the different types of negligence and give an example of how each situation might occur in the physical education setting.

- Identify the different types of defense arguments that are made to prove that the instructor was not negligent. Allied to this is understanding why each defense leaves the teacher at the mercy of the court.

- Explain why careful planning is a prelude to adequate instruction.

- List several guidelines a teacher should incorporate when planning for meaningful and safe instruction.

- Describe the features of athletic participation that make it a high-risk activity. Define a set of guidelines that will help minimize the chance of a lawsuit.

- Develop a working definition of safety that represents the risks inherent in physical education.

- Write a plan for emergency care when an accident occurs in a physical education class.

- Dictate the need for effective record keeping of accidents and purchasing liability insurance.

- Write a safety checklist for a physical education-athletic program that is comprehensive in scope.

REFERENCES AND SUGGESTED READINGS

Appenzeller, H. 1970. *From the Gym to the Jury*. Charlottesville, VA: Michie Company Law Publishing.

Arnold, D. E. 1983. *Legal Considerations in the Administration of Public School Physical Education and Athletic Programs*. Springfield, IL: Charles C. Thomas.

Baley, J. A., and Matthews, D. L. 1984. *Law and Liability in Athletics, Physical Education, and Recreation*. Boston: Allyn & Bacon.

Black, H. C. 1990. *Black's Law Dictionary*. 6th ed. St. Paul, MN: West.

Blucker, J. A., and Pell, S. W. 1986. Legal and ethical issues. *Journal of Physical Education, Recreation, and Dance* 57: 19–21.

Carpenter, L. J. 1995. *Legal Concepts in Sport: A Primer*. Reston, VA: AAHPERD.

Clement, A. 1988. *Law in Sport and Physical Activity*. Dubuque, IA: Brown & Benchmark.

Dougherty, N. J. (ed.). 1987. *Principles of safety in physical education and sport*. Reston, VA: AAHPERD.

Gray, G. R. 1993. Providing adequate medical care to program participants. *Journal of Physical Education, Recreation, and Dance* 64(2): 56–57.

Institute for the Study of Educational Policy, Law Division. 1986. *School Athletics and the Law*. Seattle: University of Washington Press.

Kaiser, R. A. 1984. *Liability and Law in Recreation, Parks, and Sports*. Englewood Cliffs, NJ: Prentice-Hall.

Maloy, B. P. 1988. *Law in Sport: Liability Cases in Management and Administration*. Dubuque, IA: Brown & Benchmark.

Merriman, J. 1993. Supervision in sport and physical activity. *Journal of Physical Education, Recreation, and Dance* 64(2): 20–23.

Pittman, A. J. 1993. Safe transportation—A driving concern. *Journal of Physical Education, Recreation, and Dance* 64(2): 53–55.

Stone, W. J. 1977. Running and running tests for Arizona school children. *Arizona JOHPERD*, 21: 15–17.

Strickland, R., Phillip, J. F., and Phillips, W. R. 1976. *Avoiding Teacher Malpractice*. New York: Hawthorn.

U.S. Consumer Product Safety Commission. 1992. *Handbook for Public Playground Safety*. Washington, D.C.: U.S. Government Printing Office.

van der Smissen, B. 1990. *Legal Liability and Risk Management of Public and Private Entities*. Cincinnati, OH: Anderson.

13 Intramurals, Sport Clubs, and Athletics

PURPOSE

To develop an understanding of the role of intramurals, sport clubs, and athletics in the total school program. These programs should be available for all students and conducted in a manner that contributes to educational objectives.

KEY CONCEPTS

- The intramural program is a voluntary laboratory situation that enables students to develop interest and competence in a wide range of physical activities.
- Intramurals offer something of interest to all students in the school.
- The programs offer a balance of competitive and recreational activities.
- Student interest surveys give direction to activity offerings in intramural and sport club programs.
- Leadership of the program is a joint arrangement that includes students and faculty.
- Many motivational devices can be used to encourage and reward students' participation in intramurals.
- Facilities, equipment, officials, and equating competition are critical elements in developing a successful intramural program.
- Types of tournaments include round robin, ladder pyramid, and elimination. Properly organized tournaments are important to a successful program.
- Sport clubs include students that have a common interest in a particular sport or physical activity. These clubs are usually organized and funded by students.
- Important matters for a sport club to consider are membership rules, funding procedures, use of equipment and facilities, supervision, legal liability, and transportation.
- The school athletic program should contribute to educational goals.
- How an athletic program is conducted determines whether a program is a positive or negative experience for students.
- The recruitment of qualified coaches is the cornerstone of a high-quality athletic program.
- The ability to perform well as a physical educator and as an athletic coach are difficult challenges.

Cocurricular programs sponsored by schools that focus on sports, games, and physical activities are especially important to students. Valuable lessons are learned that enhance and shape physical skills, knowledge, social skills, and attitudes. Physical educators should be involved in the overall planning and delivery of these programs to ensure that the educational value of these programs is enhanced. Many

241

school districts that have cut back offerings in these areas are reconsidering their previous position and planning to reinstitute after-school programs (Wright, 1995; Hall, 1995). These programs serve a valuable function for students. They provide adolescents with positive alternatives to youth crimes, gangs, violence, drop-out problems, discipline problems, and drug experimentation. The activities are important for middle school students who are exploring and searching for programs where they can be involved.

Intramural programs and sport clubs are rarely priority items in middle and senior high schools. In school districts, the athletic program is the number 1 after-school activity and gets most of the facilities, money, and qualified personnel. Even in districts where athletics are strong at the high school level, many middle school athletic programs are inadequate or nonexistent. Quality programs should be offered in all 3 areas. A well-developed model for athletics, intramurals, and sport clubs can serve the needs of many students, while offering activity and recreation in a school-sanctioned setting.

Studies have revealed that a high percentage of students who participate in athletics in elementary school drop out or are eliminated during the secondary school years. This would not be such an alarming figure (considering that athletic programs are for the elite) if there were other avenues for students to enjoy sports and physical activities. One of the best and most economical approaches is the intramural and sport club program. If, however, the school district does not hire qualified personnel to administer them, these programs soon become second-rate and fail to attract participants. The ensuing discussion offers direction for developing quality intramurals, sport club programs, and athletic programs based on student interest and conducted through student input and energy.

INTRAMURALS

What, Who, and Why of Intramural Programs

An **intramural program** is an organized activity for students that is an extension of the physical education program. Student attendance and participation are voluntary, and the program is limited to the boundaries of a specific school. The intramural program can be a laboratory for using the skills and knowledge gained in the physical education program. In terms of supervisory personnel, equipment, and facilities, the intramural program should be funded by the school district. In some cases, fees are required if the activity involves private facilities such as bowling alleys, skating rinks, and horseback riding stables.

When a broad variety of activities are offered in the intramural program, physical education teachers can delegate more class time to instruction because opportunity to play sport can occur in the intramural setting. The intramural program is a social meeting ground for students. Youngsters participate in activities they may enjoy and use throughout their lives.

Who participates in an intramural program? Hopefully, every student in the school. The program should offer something of interest to all students and provide appropriate competitive experiences for students of all sizes, shapes, and skill levels. All students need to have ample opportunity to find success and enjoyment in the program, regardless of their physical stature or ability level.

Why have an intramural program? An intramural program offers students an opportunity to develop interest and competence in a wide range of recreational activities. The program also gives students an opportunity to develop and maintain a reasonable level of fitness. Evidence has shown that if people do not develop competence and confidence during their school years in their ability to participate in recreational activities, they seldom participate in later life. In the intramural program, students learn to compete against and cooperate with each other in an environment that has little at stake in terms of winning and losing. The program can be a setting for developing lifelong friendships.

The intramural program can also be a place to learn leadership and followership skills. Students learn to compromise and assert themselves. Through these programs, students, parents, and teachers become closer friends. Finally, the program offers students a place to spend some of their out-of-school time in a supervised setting, rather than walking the streets with nothing to do. Few programs for youth offer so many benefits at such a low cost to society.

Recreation versus Competition

Since a successful intramural program should attract all types of students, the question arises as to whether competition or recreation should be featured. If competition is the overriding concern, then tournaments that identify champions and reinforce winners are featured. Competition emphasizes practicing as much as possible, only playing participants who are the best, and avoiding mistakes as much as possible.

If recreation is featured, emphasis is placed on participation and playing all teams an equal number of times. Tournament and league standings are avoided or not posted, and students play each game as an entity in itself. Rewarding recreation emphasizes attendance and participation, and all students are expected to play the same amount. Awards and trophies are not offered, but in some cases, certificates of participation are given.

Which direction should the intramural program take? As usual, no easy answer exists, but several points need to be considered. Because many students may have been cut from an athletic program, they may still want to compete. However, many of the participants may not have participated on an athletic team after the elementary school years, and they may simply desire a positive experience. In a survey by Fagan (1979), 581 students in a public high school were asked if they would like to have a competitive program, a recreation-oriented program, or a mixture of both. The results indicated that 9% preferred a competition-oriented program, 9% wanted a recreation program only, and 82% desired a combination of recreation and competition. This is not surprising, since one of the elements of a game is the opportunity to match skill and wits with an opponent in a competitive setting. The survey result points out that students want to have an opportunity to relax, play, and communicate with peers. The best programs probably offer students a balance of competition and recreation.

Types of Activities

The types and varieties of activities offered to students are the heart of the intramural program. There should be activities to meet the desires of all students. In some cases, the intramural program has been an outgrowth of the athletic program rather than of the physical education program and has been directed by athletic coaches. The result is probably a program that is conducted in a manner similar to the athletic program. In most cases, this type of program may be inappropriate. The scope of intramural activities should be unlimited and dictated by students. If students are expected to participate in the program during their free time, it must cater to their desires and wants. The intramural program should not be re-

garded as "minor" league for athletes who might make the varsity team at a later date.

A student survey is a good idea to determine student interests and to establish the magnitude of those interests. Surveys can be conducted by homeroom teachers and returned when they are completed. Compilation of results should then be posted so students can clearly see that the activities offered are a result of their expressed interests. The survey is a strong tool when bargaining with the administration for program facilities and equipment. When principals understand that many students desire certain activities, the physical educator then has some leverage to gain program support. Figure 13.1 is a sample of the type of survey that could be administered. The survey will also indicate to students the number and variety of activities that can be offered. After a survey has been administered and compiled, information about desired activities, times to offer the program, and qualified supervisors are identified. A program that matches student interests is easier to develop if a diagnostic instrument similar to the one in Figure 13.1 is administered.

Leadership

Leadership of an intramural program is a joint obligation. School districts should fund personnel to supervise the program and to minimize liability programs. However, students also have a responsibility to organize committees and to implement a successful program. They should develop the policies, rules, and procedures that guide the program. An effective way to ensure student input and energy for implementing the intramural program is to develop an intramural council. The council consists of 6 to 10 students and is balanced by gender and grade level. This group makes the final decisions about the wide-ranging aspects of the program. Committees that report to the council are developed and maintained with productive students. Some of the following committees might be organized to serve the intramural council.

Activity Development.   The activity development committee is responsible for selecting intramural activities as well as facilities, equipment, and personnel necessary for implementation.

Rules and Regulations.   The rules and regulations committee develops guidelines for administering the program. This committee is also the enforcement body when rule infractions occur.

Humerus High School Intramural Survey

Student name _____ Class standing _____

1. Would you participate in the intramural program if activities were offered that interest you?

   Yes _____ No _____ If no, why not?

2. What do you like most about the present intramural program?

3. What do you like least about the present intramural program?

4. If you choose not to participate, would you be willing to help out in the program in other roles? Check those ways in which you could offer your aid.

   Officiating _____ Publicity _____ Secretarial _____ Scorekeeping _____ Other (identify) _____

5. It is possible to develop a program that emphasizes competition, recreation, or a combination of both. Which would you desire?

   Competition _____ Recreation _____ Both _____

6. What days and what time of the day would be best for your participation?

Day		Time
Monday	_____	_____
Tuesday	_____	_____
Wednesday	_____	_____
Thursday	_____	_____
Friday	_____	_____
Saturday	_____	_____

7. Should awards be given to winning participants?

   Yes _____ No _____ Please justify your answer.

8. Please list any other points that would make the program better suit your needs.

9. The following is a list of activities that might be offered. Please circle 5 that you would most like offered in the intramural program. If an activity that you want is not offered, please write it in the blank at the end of the form.

Archery	Chess	Golf	Paddle tennis	Swimming
Badminton	Cooperative games	Driving	Relays	Table tennis
Bait and fly casting	Croquet	Putting	Riflery	Tennis
Basketball	Cross country	Gymnastics	Roller hockey	Tetherball
One on one	Darts	Handball	Roller skating	Track and field
Two on two	Decathlon	Horseshoes	Shuffleboard	Tumbling
Other	Deck tennis	Ice hockey	Skiing	Volleyball
Free-throw	Fencing	Judo	Soccer	Two player
shooting	Field hockey	Kite Flying	Softball	Volley tennis
Billiards	Figure skating	Lacrosse	Fast pitch	Water basketball
Bowling	Flag football	Lawn bowling	Slow pitch	Water polo
Box hockey	Flickerball	Marbles	One pitch	Weight lifting
Cards	Floor hockey	New games	Speed-a-way	Wrestling
Checkers	Frisbee golf	Orienteering	Steeplechase	
Others _____				

10. Do you know of any experts who could teach and help organize any of the activities designated above? If so, please describe how they can be contacted.

FIGURE 13.1 Sample high school intramural survey

Scheduling and Statistics. The scheduling and statistics committee schedules games and contests, maintains school intramural records and league standings, and oversees other related matters.

Referees. The officiating committee recruits referees, trains them, and interprets and makes rulings dealing with protests.

Public Relations. The public relations committee develops all materials for promoting the program; seeks funding from private organizations; and sponsors car washes, raffles, and other fund-raising activities.

Safety. The safety committee develops an approved list of procedures for first aid and emergency situations and provides a trained student capable of administering first aid and able to be present at activities.

The formation of the student intramural council should not supersede the need for qualified adult personnel, and the school district should be willing to hire adequate help. Without district funding, there is usually little administrative commitment to the program, and a lack of administrative commitment leads ultimately to program failure.

Motivating Students to Participate

Many methods are available for promoting intramural programs and encouraging participation. Regardless of the method used, to have the program work students must see the benefits of participating. The program must exude a spirit and be an "in" thing to do. Some of the following suggestions have been used with success in varying situations and can be modified to meet the needs of a particular school.

Intramural Bulletin Board. Bulletin boards, located throughout the school, display schedules, standings, and future activities. Pictures of champions can also be posted and labeled.

Patches. Winners are awarded arm patches with a school designation, the year, and activity. Some successful programs have awarded patches for participating in a certain number of activities regardless of winning or losing.

T-shirts. T-shirts can be given to winners or participants. The school can hold a T-shirt day on which teachers and participants wear their shirts to school.

Point-Total Chart. Points are given for winning first, second, third, or fourth place in an activity, or points can be awarded simply for participation. The points may be awarded to homeroom teams or on an individual basis. The point-total chart keeps a running tally throughout the year.

Trophies. Trophies are awarded to homerooms based on point totals at the end of the school year. An excellent idea is to award an "outstanding participant trophy" to those who earned the most participant points.

Newspaper Reports. These articles are written by students and are placed in the school or local newspaper. They motivate best when they explicitly name students.

Field Trips. Field trips are awarded to all participants at the end of the activity. For instance, at the end of the basketball tournament, all participants might attend a college or professional game together.

Extramural Competition. A playday activity can be organized between one or more schools that have similar activities. The participants meet at one school on a Saturday and compete against each other. These students are nonathletes; the playday provides an opportunity for them to compete in a setting similar to athletic competition.

Two schools of thought are involved in promoting intramural programs. One awards notoriety and trophies to winners, while the other offers awards and equal publicity to all participants. A case can be made for both approaches. A consideration is that winners already receive reinforcement, but others of lesser accomplishment may need additional positive strokes to assure equal publicity for all students in the program.

Facilities and Equipment

Without proper facilities and equipment, an intramural program has little chance for success. A major problem is the conflict between athletics and intramurals. Much time and money has been poured into athletic programs, and athletics can be expected to take priority in terms of facility use. At best, the programs should compromise on the use of facilities at opportune times, such as during the final game of the intramural tournament.

Another way to work through the facility problem is to schedule program activities out of season. For example, scheduling intramural basketball programs in the fall or spring would alleviate the conflict. Or, schedule intramural activities during low-demand times such as before school, during noon hour, and later in the evening. Community facilities such as churches, the YMCA or YWCA, and city park and recreation areas can be used at times to increase the number of participants who can be accommodated. Scheduling becomes paramount in assuring that facilities will be available. The scheduling committee should work with the athletic director and staging director to avoid conflicts.

Equipment should be provided by the district. Some successful programs have been funded by student activities such as car washes or raffles, but in general, when the district chooses not to give funding, the program is held in low esteem. If the program involves private facilities (such as bowling alleys, golf courses, or skating rinks), club members will usually receive reduced rates. Having an equipment committee to determine how and when money will be spent is effective. The committee is responsible for maintaining and repairing equipment. The school provides a storage area for intramural equipment that is used solely by intramurals. It usually creates conflict when physical education program equipment is used for the intramural program. When equipment is lost or damaged, hard feelings or loss of program support may occur.

Officials

Critical to the success of any athletic endeavor is the quality of the officiating. The intramural program should be officiated by students. It is unrealistic to think teachers will be willing to work ball games. A sound approach is to develop an officiating committee with the responsibility for acquiring and training officials. Many students who do not play competitively are willing to officiate and enjoy being an integral part of an event.

Students should be recruited as soon as possible so they can acquire experience and work confidently with experienced officials. They should be trained in rules and game mechanics prior to a tournament and be allowed to practice with as little pressure as possible. The word of the officials is absolute. If a disagreement arises, it is filed and resolved through proper protest channels.

Scheduling officials and being sure that they make their assignments is crucial. Turner (1978) pro-

poses a plan that is easy to implement. Figure 13.2 is a chart showing who is assigned to officiate. The initials to the left of the typed name indicate the individual has read and accepted the assignment. Blank lines are provided for names of people who are willing to officiate, if needed. If an official has accepted an assignment but cannot carry it out, he or she must contact the first person who has signed up for that day. When a replacement has been found, the person who cannot make the appointment notifies the intramural office.

Officials can be given points for the number of games they work; they can also be awarded patches, T-shirts, and trophies for their accomplishments in a fashion similar to participants. Without some recognition, students will have little motivation for carrying out the thankless obligations of officiating.

Equating Competition

All participants need to know that they have an opportunity to succeed in the intramural setting. Students fail to participate if they foresee a constant diet of losing or other negative experiences. Grouping by ability has both advantages and disadvantages. It can be awkward to have skilled and unskilled players together when the activity demands a great deal of progression and skill performance. In those cases, having similarly skilled students play together and compete against teams of similar ability is probably better. However, placing less-skilled athletes with skilled athletes may improve the performance level of the unskilled students and enhance their confidence. It also provides opportunities for skilled persons to aid the less skilled.

When grouping for teams, try the following methods. Homerooms can compete against homerooms. This is the most heterogeneous method of grouping. Students of varying skill levels will then play on the same team. Grouping by homeroom may be effective if students are randomly placed there. Another method is to use divisions of competition. Depending on the activity, students are grouped by ability, size, or age. Homerooms could sponsor 2 or more teams of different ability that play in different leagues. The advantage of homeroom sponsorship lies in the camaraderie developed among students and the possibility of enhancing the classroom relationships. Probably the best solution is to equalize the competition regardless of homeroom assignments or other segregating factors. Choosing teams that are somewhat equal can be done in the following ways:

Intramural Department
Flag Football Officiating Assignments
(For Week of October 1–5)

FIELD	Oct. 1 MONDAY	Oct. 2 TUESDAY	Oct. 3 WEDNESDAY	Oct. 4 THURSDAY	Oct. 5 FRIDAY
1	___ Williams	_TK_ Kelley	_AB_ Bell	_TT_ Tucker	_FG_ Gordon
	___ Robbins	_CM_ Morton	_JG_ Goodall	_MN_ Nagel	___ Jackson
2	___ Nagel	_SG_ Geltman	_MG_ Gallagher	_DA_ Andrews	_jh_ Houle
	___ Horton	_EC_ Chapin	___ Jackson	_AK_ Keene	___ Turner
3	___ Andrews	_jh_ Houle	_FG_ Gordon	___ Bent	_SG_ Geltman
	___ Sullivan	___ Stinson	_SK_ Kenton	___ Chapin	_BR_ Robbins
	___ ___	___ Bert	_AW_ Williams	_FG_ Gordon	_EC_ Chapin
	___ ___	___ Bell	___ Houle	_SG_ Geltman	_CM_ Morton
	___ ___	___ Williams	___ Andrews	___ ___	___ Bert
	___ ___	___ ___	___ Jackson	___ ___	___ Bell

FIGURE 13.2 Chart of officials' assignments

Reprinted with permission from *Journal of Physical Education, Recreation, and Dance,* February 1978, p. 42.

1. Leaders are elected by the students. The leaders then choose teams in a private session held away from the rest of the participants.
2. Students are arranged by height or weight. The names of students within a certain range are put in one box, and a different range of heights in another box. Teams are then selected by drawing the names of an equal number of students of similar size for each team.

Whatever method is used to form teams, be sensitive to maintaining a balance of competition and preventing embarrassing situations. Teams should never be selected in such a fashion that the poorest player is chosen last. The intramural experience should be a positive experience that all students anticipate with enthusiasm. If the program is to succeed, participants are needed, and should be treated as important and meaningful people.

Tournaments

A variety of tournaments can be organized to carry out the intramural program. The type will depend on the number of entries, the number of sessions or how many days the tournament will continue, the facilities and equipment available, and the number of officials, scorers, and other helpers on hand. The following types of tournaments are often used with success.

Round Robin Tournament

The round robin tournament is a good choice when adequate time is available for play. In this type of tournament, every team or individual plays every other team or individual once. Final standings are based on win-loss percentages. To determine the amount of time the tournament will take, the following formula can be used:

$$TI(TI - 1)/2$$

where TI = number of teams or individuals. For example, if there are 5 teams in a softball unit, $5(5 - 1)/2 = 10$ games are to be scheduled.

To arrange a tournament for an odd number of teams, each team should be assigned a number (number the teams down the right column and up the left column). All numbers rotate, and the last number each time draws a bye. An example using 7 teams follows:

Round 1
7—1 (bye)
6—1
5—2
4—3

Round 2
6—1 (bye)
5—7
4—1
3—2

Round 3
5—1 (bye)
4—6
3—7
2—1

Round 4
4—1 (bye)
3—5
2—6
1—7

Round 5
3—1 (bye)
2—4
1—5
7—6

Round 6
2—1 (bye)
1—3
7—4
6—5

Round 7
1—1 (bye)
7—2
6—3
5—4

To arrange a tournament for an even number of teams, the plan is similar, except that the position of Team 1 remains stationary and the other teams revolve around it until the combinations are completed. An example of an 8-team tournament follows.

Round 1
1—2
8—3
7—4
6—5

Round 2
1—8
7—2
6—3
5—4

Round 3
1—7
6—8
5—2
4—3

Round 4
1—6
5—7
4—8
3—2

Round 5
1—5
4—6
3—7
2—8

Round 6
1—4
3—5
2—6
8—7

Round 7
1—3
2—4
8—5
7—6

Ladder Tournament

A ladder format is used for an ongoing tournament that is administered by a teacher or informally by students. Competition occurs by challenge and is supervised minimally. Various arrangements are possible, but participants usually challenge only those opponents who are 2 steps above a participant's present ranking. If the challenger wins, that person changes places with the loser. The teacher can establish an initial ranking, or positions can be drawn out of a hat. Figure 13.3 shows an example of a ladder.

Pyramid Tournament

A pyramid tournament is similar to a ladder tournament, but more challenge and variety are possible because there is a wider choice of opponents (Figure 13.4). In the pyramid tournament, players challenge any opponent one level above their present ranking. In another variation, players challenge someone at their level and beat that person before they can challenge a person at a higher level.

Elimination Tournament

The disadvantage of the elimination tournament is that poorer teams are eliminated first and do not get to play as many games as more proficient teams. The skilled thus get better, and less-skilled students sit out without an opportunity to improve. The advantage of the elimination tournament is that it can be completed in a shorter amount of time than, for ex-

---

**Shuffleboard
Tournament**

1. _____

2. _____

3. _____

4. _____

5. _____

6. _____

7. _____

FIGURE 13.3   Ladder tournament chart

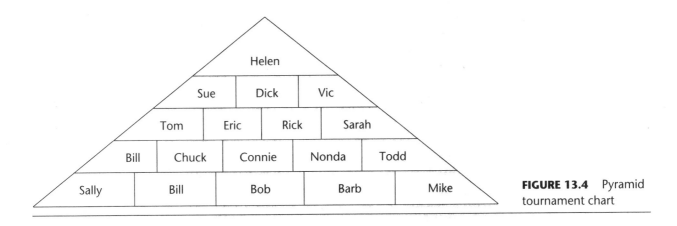

FIGURE 13.4 Pyramid tournament chart

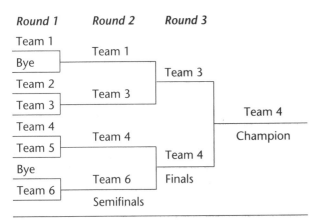

FIGURE 13.5 Elimination tournament chart

ample, the round robin tournament. Double-elimination tournaments are somewhat better than single elimination because 2 losses are required before a team is relegated to the sidelines. Students come to intramurals to play rather than sit on the side and watch others play. Figure 13.5 is an example of a simple single-elimination tournament with 6 teams.

SPORT CLUBS

Sport clubs are filled with students who are bonded by their common interest in some sport or activity. The concept originated in Europe and has become more common in the United States, largely because of the inability of school districts to fund a wide variety of activities. The clubs are for students, are run by students, and are often funded by the students. They offer young people the chance to orga-

nize a club that meets the specific needs of a group and the opportunity to socialize with friends.

Sport clubs are often administered by guidelines set by the intramural director in a school district. The clubs can be an outgrowth of either the intramural or athletic program. The types of sport clubs to be developed are usually dictated by students. The following steps are typical of a system for developing a sport club network in the school setting.

1. *Determine the interests of students.* A survey instrument (see Figure 13.1) is used to determine student interests in and concerns for sport clubs. It is usually best to develop 1 or 2 clubs first to demonstrate the effectiveness of this approach to the district administrators.

2. *Meet with interested students.* Before the meeting with students, find a faculty member or some other person to serve as the club's advisor. The advisor should have a keen interest in the area and a minimal amount of expertise. For example, it is foolish to appoint someone as an advisor to the backpacking club if they have never backpacked. During the first meeting, dues necessary for conducting club activities should be discussed. If the cost is prohibitive, many students may choose not to participate. Students should also discuss the joys and dangers of participating in the activity. Discuss school guidelines for clubs so students understand the parameters involved.

3. *Develop a constitution.* After the initial meeting, students who are interested meet again to develop a constitution. This document delineates membership requirements, the function and selection of officers, and meeting dates. An outline form can be used to aid in the development of similar club constitutions.

4. *Establish rules and regulations.* Clubs need to determine the scope of their organization and the requirements of club members to retain active membership. If competition with other clubs is involved, travel funding and housing requirements are explicitly outlined. The need for adult chaperons and drivers and the need for a waiver of responsibility signed by parents are vital parts of the rules. The basic premise of rules is to eliminate misunderstandings and to encourage a safe, liability-free club setting.

5. *Seek funding, facilities, and equipment.* With the help of the advisor, students should determine what facilities and equipment are available and when they can be scheduled. Seeking outside funding from private organizations and service clubs is important. In some cases, school time may be given for clubs to conduct meeting and planning sessions. Appropriate facilities such as bowling alleys or swimming pools need to be contacted to see if 1 or 2 hours per week can be reserved for club activities.

6. *Conduct a periodic evaluation.* Clubs should be evaluated on a regular basis to see if interest is waning, whether the needs of students are being met, and whether the manner of club conduct needs to be modified. Sometimes when clubs are developed based on the interests of students, that interest can decrease to such an extent that the club should be discontinued. New student interests may also develop and result in new clubs. A periodic evaluation can result in a new club advisor, better ways to facilitate club goals, or an attempt to stimulate renewed interest in the club.

Implementing a Club Sport

The following areas should be considered when developing a club sport. They are considerations that school district personnel need to be aware of if a successful program is to be implemented.

Liability

Students who participate in the club should have liability insurance. Depending on the activity, regular school insurance may cover the student during participation. However, if the activity is exceptionally risky (such as skiing or rugby), supplementary insurance is usually needed. Parents must certify that the student is covered by their insurance policy if students choose not to purchase insurance offered by the district's carrier.

A signed parental responsibility waiver form is necessary for participation in club activities. Even though the form does not waive the student's right to sue and seek redress, a signed form communicates to the school district that the parents approve and are aware of their student's participation in the program.

Instructors and advisors to the program must be competent to administer the activity. If the school district advisor lacks proper training, experts outside the school should be secured. These may be parents or interested community volunteers. In most cases, the responsibility for supplying a safe environment falls on the school district.

Procedures for handling injuries are important and may involve having a physician on call. Written procedures should be available and understood by all club members in case an accident occurs. For example, what steps will be taken if someone is injured on a backpacking trip? Accidents do happen, and there is much less trouble if proper emergency procedures have been planned for such an occurrence.

Budget

It is ideal when the school district funds sport clubs. In some cases, student fees are assessed at the start of the school year and distributed on an equal basis to all clubs. This provides a financial foundation, but almost all clubs require additional funding. The most common methods used are cake sales, car washes, rummage sales, sales of old and outdated equipment, candy sales, and donations. When travel and lodging are necessary, students are usually expected to absorb the cost. School districts will often provide a bus if the activity is scheduled when buses are available. Travel by private car is the least acceptable method of transport due to the possibility of an accident and subsequent liability problems.

Many clubs have an equipment bank where equipment is stored for use year after year. The club develops an adequate source of equipment over a period of years. Used equipment from local colleges and high school athletic programs can sometimes be secured to augment the equipment bank.

Coaching

Qualified coaches and other school-affiliated advisors are usually involved in administration of the athletic and intramural programs. This means club advisors and coaches may have to be selected from the community. Some type of screening should be undertaken by the school district to see that the advisors are properly qualified. The club programs have to be conducted at a time when these people are available since many potential advisors are employed during the school day. If the activity is recreational in nature, interested parents may carry out the supervisory responsibilities. All adults involved should be approved by the school district and required to sign a form agreeing to abide by district policies.

Facilities

Facilities usually have to be scheduled at low-use times. Sport clubs are often last in line for facilities, after the athletic and intramural programs. Facilities need to be found in the community if the clubs involve sports that are offered interscholastically. For example, city parks have softball fields that can be used. Some school districts choose not to approve clubs dealing with sports that are offered at the intramural and interscholastic level. The philosophy behind this ruling is that club sports should offer opportunities that are not available through other avenues. If that is the case, then most sport club programs will be conducted in private facilities such as bowling alleys, swimming pools, ski areas, skating rinks, riflery and archery ranges, and racquetball clubs.

Achievement Clubs

Many of the activities suggested in the intramurals section for motivating students can be used with sport club activities. In addition, some clubs can be formed for which students are eligible only after they have met predetermined standards of achievement. Examples might be a jogging club, bike-riding club, distance swimming club, and a weight-lifting club. In each case, students join the club and are a part of the group only after they have met the minimum standards.

INTERSCHOLASTIC ATHLETICS

The interscholastic athletic program usually stands at the top of the pyramid in terms of attention, time, and money focused on the program. Sports in the school setting should contribute to the educational purposes of the institution. Arguments

abound as to whether the athletic program is a negative or positive influence on students. Athletics are not inherently good or bad. How the athletic program is conducted makes it a positive or negative experience for participants. It is possible to create a positive experience for students through a competitive sports program.

Values of an Athletic Program

A strong athletic program can develop a sense of belonging among the participants. Students like to see what they can accomplish by themselves and with the help of peers. Team sports teach them that goals can be reached only if teammates are willing to cooperate. It quickly becomes apparent that cooperation precedes competition. Conducting a competitive game is impossible when teammates do not cooperate and follow the established rules.

Athletics teach students that the journey is more important than the destination. The work done to reach a goal is the essence of an athletic experience, and students learn that after the victory, continued hard work is still necessary. This lesson may carry over to adult life and help the participant continue to succeed.

Athletics give students something to talk about and something to do. Many of the problems of youth arise because of boredom and little to do when the school day is over. Athletics give status to participants and make them feel important. The program allows students to share their positive accomplishments with others and appreciate the accomplishments of friends.

The athletic program serves as a laboratory for gifted students. It offers students a chance to perfect their skills to a high level with the aid of a knowledgeable coach. Students who are athletically gifted are appreciated and rewarded for their accomplishments. The athletic program brings a community of people together for a common cause. Parents and business people begin to develop pride in their community and find a common ground for communication. The athletic team can be a unifying factor that brings together people of all backgrounds.

Participation in athletics can teach students how to maintain a level of physical fitness and to care for their bodies. They learn about the need for self-discipline when one desires to reach a goal. The importance of sacrifice, following training rules, and practicing regularly become an attitudinal set of participants. Sportsmanship and self-control must be practiced if students are to find success. Rules and regulations become an integral part of sport participation and illustrate to students the importance of following predetermined rules. Students learn they are penalized when rules are broken, and those unwilling to cooperate are seldom welcome to participate. Finally, the athletic program shows students how highly regarded and important excellence is to people. Athletics should try to embody excellence and the Olympic ideal. Students set goals and make sacrifices in an attempt to achieve excellence without any guarantee of success.

Detrimental Effects of an Athletic Program

The athletic program mobilizes large amounts of time, energy, and money to aid a relatively small number of participants. This sometimes leads to neglect of less-skilled performers. In contrast, an athlete who receives special attention can develop the attitude that athletes are better than others and are eligible for personal favors and special attention. This can lead to a situation whereby student athletes develop a value set that is detrimental when their playing days are over.

Participation in athletic programs often interrupts the educational environment. Athletes leave school to go on trips or receive released time to practice. The athlete may begin to believe that it is more important to be a successful athlete than a competent student. Another possible effect of the athletic program is a loss of personal identity. Athletes are told when to eat, when to practice, when they can have free time, and when to study. They may soon begin to wonder if they can make any important decisions for themselves and whether they have the right to live their own lives.

The pressures of coaching are apparent to all who have filled a head coaching position in a major sport. This pressure is often unjust and can lead to unacceptable coaching behavior. Athletic coaching is a good example of holding an individual accountable for the end result (winning) regardless of how that individual reaches the goal. When this occurs, students may suffer from the coach's lack of concern and caring about personal problems and injuries. Until an equal emphasis is placed on the process of coaching as well as on the product, the athletic setting will be less than a positive and developmental experience.

At times, parents and community members can become so deeply involved in the athletic program that they apply pressure on students to win at all costs. Student athletes begin to feel that if they do not win, they will not be accepted as an integral part of the community. The athletic program then becomes an incessant effort on the part of students to achieve the adults' goals. In these situations, adults forget that the athletic program was developed for students in an effort to contribute to the youngsters' personal growth. When the program becomes instead an adult program with adult goals, students cannot separate what is important from what is not.

Another concern for athletes is injury. All participants assume the risk of injury through involvement. If the desire to win exceeds the desire to provide a safe environment, then some students may be ordered to play with an injury or may receive injuries due to lack of proper care and treatment. Concern for the health of participants is the paramount program goal.

Developing a Quality Athletic Program

Depending on how it is organized and presented, an athletic program can be a positive or negative experience for students. The following guidelines, if heeded, help ensure meaningful experiences for participants. All districts have to interpret the guidelines based on their specific situation, but it is difficult to imagine that a worthwhile program will result if the guidelines are deviated from to a large degree.

1. The athletic program should be voluntary. All students who choose to participate should have an opportunity to compete. All athletes should have the opportunity to play if they have practiced and disciplined themselves. Cutting players from a squad is an accepted practice, but there should be another arena in which players can compete. This may mean a junior varsity, C squad, or strong intramural or sport club program. If athletics is regarded as an educational experience, all students have the right to receive that experience.

2. The program should be based on the maturation level of participants. This is particularly important at the middle school level, because these students exhibit a wide range of development. Grouping by age, ability, or size may be necessary if the program is to be meaningful.

3. The athletic program should be an after-school program. The practice of giving a period of school time for practice is discriminatory and runs counter to the established rule that an academic education is the school's priority. Along the same lines, excusing athletes from physical education is difficult to justify. If the program is educational, then all students, regardless of background, should benefit from it.

4. The athletic program should offer a broad spectrum of activities for participants; the fewer activities offered, the fewer participants. The program should also be balanced in offering activities to all groups—skilled and unskilled, boys and girls, able-bodied and students with disabilities.

5. Organization of the athletic program should meet the needs of students. The concerns of the spectators should be met only after the program has been developed. Many sports are dropped because they do not draw large numbers of spectators and make money. If this trend continues, football and basketball might represent the total athletic program.

6. All participants should be certified medically healthy by a physician. The program should be evaluated regularly in terms of safety practices to ensure that proper procedures are being conducted.

7. Procedures to be followed should an accident occur must be written, posted, and sent to parents. Most districts ask that parents sign a waiver of responsibility form before a student can participate. This is an opportune time to explain the safety and first-aid procedures being followed. Insurance for all participants is a must.

8. As idealistic as it may sound to many coaches, the program should emphasize enjoyment and participation. Skill development and a positive experience are a heritage that students can take with them after graduation. One might well question what has been gained if students win most of their games but lose the desire to participate in sports once they leave school.

9. Physical conditioning should be an important phase of the program. Preconditioning is essential to the safety and welfare of players and should precede intense, early-season practice sessions.

10. Facilities should be shared by all facets of the athletic, intramural, and sport club programs. It is understandable that athletics expect to take priority, but someone needs to direct the situation so that all programs are given acceptable use of the facilities and equipment.

11. Awards, trophies, and other incentives used to identify outstanding achievement should be minimized. This is not to avoid rewarding excellence but to encourage proper discretion. If awards are given in excess, they become meaningless.

12. The athletic program should be constantly evaluated. In some cases, the program is seldom scrutinized until an infraction occurs. Periodic evaluations by the athletic director, principal, and coaching staff can aid in preventing problems. Evaluation can serve to improve offerings for both boys and girls, upgrade scheduling efficiency, and show the need for in-service training.

The Athletic Council

To help assure that a quality athletic program is maintained, many school districts organize an athletic council. The council is a district-wide body composed of the superintendent (or a representative), principals, the athletic director for the district, coaches from each of the schools, and student representatives from each school. All schools, sports, and genders should be equally represented.

The athletic council plans and evaluates the total district program and deals with problems such as finance, facilities, and personnel. The council promotes the athletic program and serves as a screening body when outside parties become involved with the program. This body is responsible for evaluating coaches and hearing grievances. Sometimes, for example, parents have a concern but are hesitant to approach the coach involved. The council hears such cases confidentially without revealing the plaintiff's identity. The council can enhance the image of the coaching community. It can be a place where coaches work together to achieve the highest ideals and to reach common goals. In summary, the council should be a valuable asset for coaches, administrators, and athletes.

Securing Qualified Coaches

Qualified coaches are the cornerstone of a sound athletic program. Most coaches are highly motivated and dedicated. In most cases, they have to be motivated by their enjoyment of sport rather than by the financial remuneration, for coaching is one of the lowest paid professions. An athletic director recently calculated that assistant coaches were receiving about 50 cents per hour. Most coaches enter the profession because they were successful athletes and found positive experiences in the athletic program. Being an outstanding athlete seldom guarantees success in coaching, however. Coaches need to have a wide range of abilities. The following attributes are representative of the characteristics of successful coaches:

Strong Character. The coach should be a model for athletes to emulate. How the coach relates to others, the individual's physical appearance, honesty, integrity, and other personal qualities often teach students more about athletics than the actual participation experience. Many administrators find cause for concern when coaches swear, drink, or smoke excessively, and most students cannot deal with the double standard of a coach who advocates team fitness but does not practice fitness, who tells them to be respectful but yells when a mistake is made, who preaches honesty but shows them how to foul without being caught. Many athletes remember their coach much longer than they remember the actual playing experience.

Knowledge of Growth and Development Patterns. The coach must have a strong background in motor development and motor learning. Understanding the physical limits of athletes is as important as understanding their capabilities under pressure. The coach should also have some knowledge of psychology and the emotional development of secondary-level students. Knowing when to reinforce, when to scold, and when to praise are key components of a successful coaching career.

Knowledge of the Activity. Coaches should know the fundamentals of the sport that they are coaching and the best ways to present and teach the basic skills. A good coach understands strategy and knows when to use various types of game plans. The coach must be an excellent teacher, and in many cases, the best coaches are also regarded as the best teachers. Concurrent with a knowledge of the sport is the ability to plan carefully. Both teaching and coaching demand a high degree of planning to succeed. Effective coaches always attempt to account for every minute of practice time so that idle or wasted time is minimized.

Coaching Certification

The need for certification in the coaching profession is great. The belief is still widely held that anyone can coach—regardless of background or training. Unfortunately, almost anyone can find the opportunity to coach due to the lack of certification requirements and standards. Each state sets the specific requirements for coaches within the schools in that state. Some states have an age requirement only, whereas others require a teaching certificate or a specific coaching education program, such as the *American Sport Education Program* (available through Human Kinetics Publishers.

Training in many areas is necessary for coaches to be productive and motivating. A NASPE task force of AAHPERD has developed the publication *National Standards for Athletic Coaches* (1995). The task force identified 37 standards in the following 8 domains:

1. Injuries: prevention, care, and management
2. Risk management
3. Growth, development, and learning
4. Training, conditioning, and nutrition
5. Social/psychological aspects of coaching
6. Skills, tactics, and strategies
7. Teaching and administrative aspects
8. Professional preparation and development

Coaching is an impressive responsibility, and regardless of certification, coaches should make an attempt to seek the best possible training.

The Teaching-Coaching Conflict

A personal conflict often occurs when teachers choose to coach. Particularly in physical education, a teacher who is required to coach long hours has a difficult task. Many physical education instructors are not hired for their expertise in teaching, but rather for their ability to coach more than 1 sport. This policy can result in a situation where teaching takes second place to coaching, and most of the teacher's planning and energy are dedicated to the coaching assignment.

Teachers who also coach often end up working 10- to 12-hour days. The pay is low, but the rewards can be great. Coaching ability is scrutinized regularly in terms of the winning and losing record, and teachers may become caught up in the pressure of trying to be a winning coach for fear of losing their position. In this situation, it takes a strong and gifted person to place equal emphasis on teaching and coaching. Physical educators should not lose sight of the fact that about 90% of their salary comes from teaching and the remaining 10% from coaching. Many more students are affected by the outstanding teacher than by the effective coach. The ability to perform well in both roles is a difficult challenge, particularly when the majority of contingencies apply to the coaching role.

EXPECTED OUTCOMES

After reading this chapter, you should be able to

- Explain the relationship and the differences between intramurals, sport clubs, and athletics.
- Set up a student interest survey that could be used for determining the activities to be offered in an intramural program.
- Discuss the issues regarding intramural programs such as: leadership, motivation, facilities, officials, competition, and tournament construction.
- Discuss the issues regarding sport clubs such as: objectives, regulations, facilities, liability, budget, coaching, and transportation.
- Defend the values of a properly organized and conducted athletic program.
- Explain many possible detrimental effects of an athletic program.
- Identify procedures for developing a high quality athletic program.
- Defend the implementation of intramural, sport club, and athletic programs in an educational setting.

REFERENCES AND SUGGESTED READINGS

Fagan, K. 1979. Intramural survey, Arcadia High School. Unpublished report.

Hall, M. 1995. Interscholastic sports on way this year, insiders predict. *Albuquerque Journal*, September 3, 1, 8–9.

Martens, Rainer. 1991. *Successful Coaching*. Champaign, IL: Human Kinetics Publishers.

NASPE. 1995. *National Standards for Athletic Coaches*. Reston, VA: AAHPERD.

Turner, M. 1978. Scheduling student officials. *JOPERD* 49(2): 42.

Wright, R. 1995. Plotting a comeback at APS. *Albuquerque Journal*, September 3, 1, 8–9.

14 Public Relations

PURPOSE

To establish that public relations are important if teachers expect parents and the community to understand and support the physical education program. Teachers must become involved in improving the image of physical education teachers and programs.

KEY CONCEPTS

- Public relations activities are vital to the future of the physical education profession.
- Physical educators are hesitant to advertise and promote their programs.
- Many people have little idea of what constitutes a high quality physical education program.
- Most people in the community still equate physical education with the athletic program.
- A strong, well-developed program is the first step before developing a public relations program.
- Students who are excited about physical education are excellent public relations agents.
- The program and its objectives need to be communicated to students, administrators, parents, and community members.
- The day-to-day behavior of physical education teachers has a powerful public relations impact.
- Public relations are an on-going process that should continue as long as there is a physical education program.
- Promotional ideas for physical education include bulletin boards, displays, posters, outstanding student awards, assembly presentations, half-time presentations, and the school newspaper.
- Promotional ideas for parents are parent participation nights, parent observation nights, a physical fitness booklet for students and parents, and a parent information newsletter.
- The local newspaper is an effective way to inform the community about the physical education program. Slide programs and videotapes are also excellent ways to communicate with the public.
- The public needs to know how the physical education program impacts all students. Areas of importance include health-related fitness, wellness, lifetime physical skills, and the development of a positive self-concept.
- A physical education advisory council composed of many different members from the school and community can be an effective public relations strategy.
- Professional physical education associations offer many public relations services for physical educators. AAHPERD is an excellent source for information.

Public relations activities are vital to the future of the physical education profession. The public's current interest in physical fitness, health, wellness, and nutrition offers the profession unique opportunities. The increasing concern for preventive medicine and the emphasis on maintaining wellness make this time an opportunity for significant growth within the physical education profession. Nothing is more important than the health and vitality of an individual. Unfortunately, most people do not associate physical education with learning how to make the most of one's health. In the past, the emphasis in physical education was on participation in team sports. Little information was presented on why and how certain activities could be healthful.

Physical educators have been hesitant to advertise and promote their programs. For many years, it was considered unprofessional to advertise and tell others about the merits of using the services of doctors, lawyers, or teachers. Today, however, all professional fields are using promotion. Witness the advertisements on television and in newspapers for various hospitals, doctors, and lawyers. Even churches are erecting billboards in an attempt to increase the size of their congregations, but seldom does one see an advertisement promoting physical education as a profession.

For years, people have associated physical education with athletics. When physical education teachers tell the public in what area they teach, many will ask which sport they coach. No one can question the exposure athletics receive through parental support and the media. The critical point is that few parents and community members understand that physical education emphasizes preparation for a lifetime of involvement in activity.

When the public does not understand the educational value of a profession, they find it easy to eliminate. For example, driver training is taught in most schools, and statistics have shown that such training reduces the number of accidents and deaths. Lower insurance rates are given to those who have participated in driver education. If the public looks to physical education and sees little payoff in terms of lifestyle and the quality of life, they may become advocates of making the program elective or doing away with it altogether. When money is in short supply, which areas are scrutinized first? Physical education is usually at the head of the line. Why? Because the public has decided that it is of little value. This is the bottom line of public relations. A program must offer something of lifetime value to participants, and the public must come to understand that. Nothing sells physical education like a sound program.

Another point of concern is trying to reach the public. Teachers often do an adequate job of reaching parents and telling them about the program, but many people who pay taxes and help support education never receive any information about the schools. It is not enough to reach the parents. Colleagues, people without children in school, and other students should receive attention and concern. This large group of people will not support physical education programs if physical education professionals have not kept them informed.

GUIDELINES FOR EFFECTIVE PUBLIC RELATIONS

The public relations program should be based on a number of points because many factors are involved in developing a strong program of publicity and exposure. The following points should be considered:

1. Explain to students why they are in physical education. If you are attempting to influence their lives, they have a right to know why you are asking them to do various activities. In most cases, understanding why one is doing something is more important than actually performing an activity.

2. Encourage students to explain to their parents why they are experiencing various activities and learning episodes. An effective public relations agent is an excited student telling Mom and Dad all about a unit in physical education.

3. Share your program with colleagues and administrators. It is important they understand innovations and the new activities presented. Many times, physical educators need the support of colleagues to reach goals, and administrators are seldom informed about physical education programs. What do they tell complaining parents, and how do they defend a program if they are not aware of it?

4. Inform the community media of newsworthy happenings. For example, when a new unit of instruction is being presented, send a note to the television, radio, and newspaper organizations. Over a period of time, they have a need for material and may make contact. Maintaining an ongoing program of news releases is important. Large public relations firms often send out news releases with the expectation that not many will be used. They operate on the law of averages, that sooner or later the media will need some of the material.

5. Find friends of physical education. Many people who are not associated with the profession are strong advocates. They can speak forcefully for physical education in the schools without having a vested interest. Develop a physical education booster group that is invited to visit the program regularly. They need to know what is going on if they are expected to share the program with others. Another way to communicate with the group is through a "friends of physical education" newsletter that describes the various aspects of the program. The athletic program has used booster groups to strong advantage for years. There is no reason why the physical education program cannot be as successful.

6. How one acts and communicates with others has a great impact on the profession. Some teachers become disenchanted with teaching and start to communicate these feelings to students, parents, and the public. Teachers are walking billboards for their chosen professions. Students respect teachers who are enthusiastic and positive about the work they perform. Examining carefully why one chose to enter the teaching profession and explaining those reasons to others is important.

7. Communicate to others how the program influences the lives of participants. Parents and students have a right to know the benefits of a sound physical education program. Send home brochures or newsletters that explain the impact of physical education on youth, and tell parents how they can help their children become more proficient in physical activity.

8. Become actively involved in professional organizations such as the state, local, and national associations of health, physical education, recreation, and dance. Professionals sometimes forget the old adage, "United we stand, divided we fall." A professional organization is for teachers and gives them a chance to pursue and establish professional goals. Physical education has suffered from teachers deciding to get along without paying dues to an organization. Certainly one can get along without an organization, but who listens to one lonely voice? Unfortunately, physical educators who are only interested in coaching weaken these organizations by their lack of interest. They become so involved in coaching they believe there is not enough time to participate. Some of the most dynamic and respected teachers are coaches; these people add a great deal to a professional organization. The best-known professional organization for physical education is the American Alliance for Health, Physical Education, Recreation, and Dance (AAHPERD). Its membership consists of teachers and professors from all levels and professional backgrounds throughout the United States. Each state has an AAHPERD organization related to the national organization. Both organizations have political advocacy groups that work for bettering the standing of the physical education profession.

9. Reach out to experts in other physical activity areas. For example, there are many capable people in specialized areas such as yoga, fencing, martial arts, and gymnastics who could conduct special workshops or help students begin a unit. They add new and exciting curriculum activities that might not be strong competency areas for the physical educator. When these people are used, all prosper. Students receive sound instruction, and teachers make good friends and advocates for their program.

10. Teach and emphasize lifetime skills and activities. When students and parents can see that the skills they learn will be used throughout their lives, they are more likely to become strong advocates of a program. Few people participate in team sports after age 25, yet most want to participate in some type of activity. If competency in lifetime sport skills is not developed, few people will have the desire to participate in later life. Those who can look back and give credit to physical education will become forceful believers and backers of physical education programs in the schools.

11. Expressing appreciation to those who have participated and supported the program is important. Students often elect to cooperate and participate in a program. Giving them credit for their support is important. Administrators make a quality program possible through their support for equipment, facilities, scheduling, and so on. They need to be shown appreciation regularly. When a demonstration program is sponsored, thank parents for their support. Working with students becomes difficult if parents tell them that the program or the teachers are poor. Cooperative students usually have supportive parents. Thank them.

IDENTIFY PUBLIC RELATIONS INFORMATION

An important step in designing the public relations program is to determine what information should be shared with the public. It is a procedure similar to planning a lesson or drawing up a game plan in that it gives direction and goals to the public relations program. Information can then be released to the public in a meaningful progression and through different media. Some of the following points are useful in sharing the philosophy and workings of the physical education program with the public. They are areas that are sure to stimulate interest in the program.

1. Discuss the impact of the program on the physical growth and development of students. Exercise has many beneficial effects that contribute to the wellness of an individual. Parents and the public should hear about the effect of regular aerobic exercise on the cardiovascular system, the impact of weight lifting on the development of the skeletal system, and how conditioning programs improve various fitness attributes.

2. Emphasize the importance of physical education and of regular activity in developing a strong, positive self-concept (Pangrazi, 1982). Physical fitness and the performance of motor skills affect how one feels personally. This can lead to renewed confidence in one's self.

3. Explain how the program is organized to help all students improve and develop, not just skilled athletes. The majority of students are not skilled athletes, but the program must meet their needs. Parents are concerned about whether the program is designed to aid their child.

4. Share the rationale, aims, and objectives of the program with the public. When most people are asked about the goals of a physical education program, many think it is the same as an interscholastic athletic program. This misunderstanding is due largely to a lack of communication about the program.

5. The public should know that a sound physical education program provides an opportunity for all students to participate and compete. Explain that the program is allied with intramurals and sport clubs and that students are helped to find a place, become involved, and interact with others.

6. Convince others of the need to offer students organized leisure-time activities. Physical education is the only area in school where students are offered a chance to be physically active.

7. Reinforce the importance of health as a top priority. People seldom take time to maintain their health status. Physical education teaches students how to maintain wellness for a lifetime. When one's health is lost, working, playing, and sharing with others is difficult. Nothing is more important than good health. Sell this fact.

ESTABLISH AN ADVISORY COUNCIL

A public relations advisory council is helpful in disseminating information about the program. The advisory council consists of people such as a school board member, an administrator, teachers, interested parents, community media personnel, students, and any other key members of the community. The purpose of the committee is to determine how the program can be promoted, what program components should be shared, and how information can be disseminated. The committee is not involved in curriculum development but in analyzing the program and determining how it can be promoted. Develop a working policy for bringing information to the public. This usually consists of the following steps:

1. Survey a representative sample of the public to see what they know and do not know about the program. This prevents the sharing of information that is common knowledge. The survey can be a simple tool that is designed by the council to diagnose areas they deem important.

2. Develop a public relations policy to begin disseminating information to the public in areas they know little about.

3. Determine how the facts will be presented to make them interesting and informative.

4. Perform a cost analysis to see what needs to be acquired in terms of supplies, equipment, and related materials in order for the council to function.

5. Assign tasks such as fund-raising, writing copy, and disseminating information to different members of the council.

Search for people who are friends of physical education. The council composition should be balanced with people who have different abilities. For example, some people may have media contacts, other council members may know people who are willing to be benefactors, and still others may possess expertise in writing copy.

IMPLEMENT A PUBLIC RELATIONS PROGRAM

The public relations program can be implemented in different ways. All methods should help the public understand the operation of a program. Regardless of the method used, selling an inferior program is impossible. People will refuse to endorse and accept a program that does not benefit its participants. Therefore, begin with a quality program, for nothing sells like quality. When students tell parents about their accomplishments in the program, public relations benefits are accrued. Strong planning, excellent teaching, and concern for students are the cornerstones of a physical education program that is supported.

Monitor Personal Conduct

Many people still imagine physical educators as being slightly obese, carrying a bat in one hand, wearing a whistle around the neck, and being outfitted in baggy sweat pants. This stereotype yells at people to hustle, seldom exercises, and is often in poor physical condition. A teacher's dress and actions are scrutinized by the public and continue to be a point of reference long after the image has changed. Teachers must model the behavior they desire in others. They must stay fit, exercise regularly, and use up-to-date methods of dealing with people. A physical education teacher who behaves in a professional manner does more to sell physical education than any public relations ploy.

Develop a Positive School Setting

Developing a meaningful relationship with students is important. Students must understand why various activities are taught and how they benefit from participation. Students who dislike the program communicate their dislike to parents, and parents often know little about the program other than what their youngsters tell them. If most of the messages are negative, parents share negative comments with other parents. Students ultimately grow up to become school board members, teachers, and administrators. If their experience was negative, they may be unwilling as adults to support physical education.

Teachers in other areas need to know about the program. In too many cases, the physical educator stays in the gymnasium and seldom mingles with other teachers. This creates an atmosphere of animosity, particularly when physical educators are coaches and choose to miss faculty meetings and related social functions. Behaving in a manner consistent with the rest of the faculty members is politic.

Some physical educators have had excellent success with a faculty fitness program offered 1 day a week for faculty members. During this time, they demonstrate various skills and activities that can be performed during the week. Another related program is a faculty recreation program. Faculty members can gather after school or in the evening to participate in volleyball, badminton, basketball, and other desired activities. Administrators can be invited to participate too, which offers personal contact in an informal setting.

Another activity that develops goodwill toward the physical education program is a school playday. Students participate together in an activity that is lighthearted and enjoyable. Teachers become involved and participate with students in this recreational setting. An example of a playday is sponsoring "looney" contests such as a water balloon throw, trike ride, three-legged race, pie-eating contest, pit-spitting contest, and any other novel activities. The emphasis is on friendly competition and participation.

Announcements can be placed regularly in the school newspaper. Tell the school about upcoming units, about registering for the playday, when special speakers are scheduled, and about happenings in the intramural program. The school newspaper is a source of strong public relations with students. Along the same lines, the school district newsletter that is sent to parents should be used. For instance, the grading system could be explained or the results of fitness testing published.

Communicate with Parents

The more parents understand the educational nature of the program, the more willing they will be to support it. Many parents do not distinguish between an athletic program and a physical education program, the public relations thrust must be to help clarify the differences. Parents can be involved actively as program participants or passively as spectators. A parents' night can be scheduled when different activities are taught by instructors to both students and their parents. This gives parents a first-hand experience with the instructional nature of the program. If parents are not asked to participate, a wide variety of student demonstrations can be planned to show the broad spectrum of skills that are taught. In either case, demonstrations should illustrate the features and organization of the program.

The physical education booster group can be used to help interpret the program to parents. Discussions and panel representations at parent-teacher organizations can be conducted, and interpretive booklets distributed. Slides of program highlights might be shown to enhance the presentation. The use of outside experts is also effective in dealing with controversial issues. Parents should be given the opportunity to ask questions and resolve points of concern.

Another way to involve parents is to use them as teacher's aides. They can help with fitness testing projects and thus begin to understand how students function in the physical education setting. Projects should also be scheduled on Saturdays or evenings so parents working outside the home can be involved.

Brochures and handouts explaining the program can be sent home with students. Parents should be encouraged to follow up and help their students practice skills at home. Surprisingly, few parents receive calls from teachers at the junior and senior high school level unless something is wrong. Parents should also be called when their son or daughter has accomplished something positive and has performed well. Parents will begin to support a program when they hear positive messages about their youngsters.

A source of public relations with parents that sometimes goes unheeded is grade reporting. The wellness profile (see Chapter 17) is an excellent tool for communicating the status of student health to parents. The profile can forewarn parents of possible health problems that need medical attention. Programs are now available for students to enter their fitness test results in the computer. The data are analyzed and the computer prints out a personalized report for the student. Some districts now use these data to maintain files that follow students from kindergarten through high school. Comparative data that describe a youngster's growth and development can be sent to parents at regular intervals. When parents understand that the school is helping to maintain the wellness of their youngster, positive feelings result.

IDEAS FOR PUBLIC RELATIONS PROMOTIONS

The following ideas are possibilities for increasing the exposure of the physical education program. All of these suggestions can be modified and are offered simply to inspire other ideas.

Bulletin Boards, Displays, and Posters

In the school setting, visual displays serve to advertise and promote the program. They show the rest of the faculty that physical educators are active and proud of their accomplishments. The art teacher will sometimes help to develop posters that require special artistic ability, and students with artistic skills are often willing to work on the media products. The following are some suggestions:

1. A schedule bulletin board shows what will be done in the program 3 to 4 weeks in advance. On it are listed special events, activities to be taught, and testing days.
2. A special announcement board can be used to post special events such as intramural games, interscholastic games, guest speakers, and film screenings.
3. Visual displays at opportune times can reach a wide variety and large number of people. Examples of such times are open houses, just before school closes for the summer, prior to Christmas vacation or spring holidays, and before school opens in the fall. At these times, parents are visiting the school and forming their opinions of the program.

Hints for Making Bulletin Boards

First, select a bulletin board that is located where the largest number of people will see it. A bulletin board in the main hall of the school will remind students who are not involved in physical education of important and exciting happenings in the program. The bulletin board should attract and hold the attention of observers. The message should be apparent to viewers and should stimulate interest. Do not put too much detail on the bulletin board.

Print or write in large letters. Visibility from 20 to 25 feet is a good guideline. To attract attention, use catchy titles such as Quiz, Mystery Pictures, or Unusual Facts, or use humor. The bulletin board should give specific dates and times, who to contact, and the names of program directors. Clippings and photographs are always interesting to students. Brightly colored paper, colored yarn, cut-out letters, and three-dimensional designs are also eye catching.

Bulletin boards and posters should be changed often (at least every 4 to 6 weeks). If they go unchanged, they go unobserved after a while. Make sure that student accomplishments are displayed on the bulletin boards from time to time. In summary, make sure the bulletin boards list the 5 Ws: who, what, why, when, and where.

Parent Involvement

Invite parents to a physical education awards assembly or banquet. This is a good time to present physical activity achievement awards. Another award that can be issued is the improvement award. This award is within reach of all students and is based on percentage of improvement. For example, if activities are listed on a performamce basis, students are pretested to see which skills they performed at passing standards. Criteria are then set, such as "increase the number of skills you know by 25%." Awards are given to students meeting the criteria. Figure 14.1 is a letter sent to parents of students who earn the award.

Community Relations

Community organizations are interested in school instruction, and it is important that information about physical education be included in the programs and meetings of these organizations. Examples of such community organizations are coordinating councils, service clubs, youth clubs, and parent-teacher groups. These groups are always looking for speakers for luncheon meetings. The program chair should be contacted and given an explanation of the type of physical education curriculum offered. A short description of the program can then be forwarded, along with a form such as the one in Figure 14.2. After all arrangements have been made, it is most important to deliver a well-planned and well-executed presentation that focuses on the learning accomplished through the physical education curriculum.

Dursthill Junior High School
850 Fairview Avenue
Picante, AZ

Dear Dad and Mom,

It may surprise you to learn that I have won an achievement award. This award will be given to me during the awards banquet (assembly) on Friday, November 21, at 7:00 P. M. I hope you will be able to attend, as this historic occasion deserves your presence.

The cost for the banquet is $4.00 per person. This is a small amount to spend on such a fine daughter.

Come on, Dad and Mom! Jog out of the house and contribute to character development.

Your daughter,

FIGURE 14.1 Letter to parents announcing award winner

Physical Education Program Request

1. Name of organization _____

2. Location _____
   Place   Address   Room

3. Time: _____ From _____ To _____
   Day   Date   Time of Program

4. Topic preferred _____

5. Type or program desired (speaker, films, etc.) _____

6. Questions and answers, if desired: Yes ___   No ___   (Please check)

7. Background or interests of group _____

8. Chairperson introducing _____

9. Estimated size of audience (circle):   1–15, 16–20, 50–100, over 100

10. If film is involved: Can room be darkened? _____

    Is screen available? _____   Size and type of screen _____

    Type of projector _____   Microphone available _____

    Other facilities _____

11. Other factors, requests, suggestions _____

    _____

    _____

    _____

    _____

    _____

    Name of person making request _____

    Position in organization _____

    Address _____

    Telephone _____

    Please telephone in request and follow up by forwarding this form to:

    Name _____

    Address _____

    Phone _____

FIGURE 14.2   Request form for a physical education program

Program Description

The physical education program at Centennial is appropriately entitled "The Dynamic Physical Education for Middle School Students." We believe the program is dynamic because it places each individual student at the core of its driving force.

The skills are taught in order from simple to complex, in an environment to remove pressure and/or a fear of failure. This environment allows each student to experience success and progress at his or her own rate.

Instructional Format

Briefly, the 4 instructional parts of the lesson and major purposes of each are as follows:

1. *Introductory Activity:* Occupies 2 or 3 minutes for the purpose of physically preparing students and ensuring that they immediately become involved in activity when entering the gym or activity area.
2. *Fitness Development Activity:* This part of the lesson takes 7 to 9 minutes. The purpose of this section is to develop physical fitness. The activities are demanding and progressive in nature, and exercise all parts of the body.
3. *Lesson Focus Activity:* The purpose of the lesson focus is to help students attain major program objectives such as hand-eye coordination, body management, and basic and specialized skills. The lesson focus uses 15 to 20 minutes of the daily lesson.
4. *Game Activity:* This part of the lesson takes place at the closing of the lesson, using the last 5 to 6 minutes of the period. The game is the culminating activity for practicing skills, with enjoyment the overriding consideration.

Physical Education Climate

As the physical education teachers at Centennial, our goal is to establish the following attitudes and climate in our classes:

The students will:

- Incorporate physical activity into their lifestyle.
- Display a positive attitude toward physical activity.
- Maintain an appropriate level of health-related physical fitness.
- Develop their physical skill level.
- Acquire knowledge about sports, games, dance, exercise, and fitness.
- Develop social skills that will enable them to be responsible citizens.
- Feel good about their physical self.

Sabercats Get Ready for Action . . .

Centennial Middle School

- Everyone is a winner. Everyone counts. Everyone is important.
- Class activities and games are not designed to produce a group of winners and a group of losers.
- Winning is always related to doing one's best, acquiring and improving skills, and enjoying oneself during physical activity.
- Fitness can be exciting. Not everyone can be a gymnast or run the fastest, but everyone can be physically fit through hard work.
- P.E. is fun!

FIGURE 14.3   Centennial Middle School demonstration program

Newspapers

The local newspaper can be the physical education program's best friend. The types of skills performed in the program are visual and will create an impact in the newspaper. Local newspapers are often looking for articles that will fill in pages and stimulate interest. The following are guidelines to help make the news release more acceptable to the news editor.

Type all articles double-spaced on white paper with wide margins. Some room should also be left at the top of the page for editing. Be sure to include a name and telephone number so the editor can easily reach the contributor if a question arises. Keep paragraphs to 5 or fewer typewritten lines, 1 to 3 sentences per paragraph, and 10 to 20 words per sentence.

Report facts, and if you are unsure about any facts, verify the information. Begin the article with a lead sentence or paragraph that gives the who, what, why, when, where, and how of the story. Place the single most important point of the article in the lead paragraph, and arrange the rest of the facts in descending order of importance. Make the last few paragraphs short so they can be cut without affecting the story significantly. Try always to make the story emphasize the educational value of the physical education program.

When possible, include photographs with the news release. The pictures should be close-ups that show faces and emotion. Photographs should also be action-oriented and illustrate phases of the program. Type captions and attach them to the photos. Indicate who is to receive credit for the photo (for example, "Photograph by . . .").

Demonstration Programs

Demonstration programs can attract a large number of parents. The activities should illustrate the attainment of the program objectives and also be typical of the experiences that occur regularly. If rehearsal is going to take place, it should only be to keep the program moving smoothly. A demonstration program need not offer perfect performances. In fact, the spontaneous and natural appearance of a program will usually stimulate more response and appreciation from parents.

As many students as possible should be included in the program. Parents will usually not attend if their youngster is not included. Specialty numbers can be integrated in the program to show off outstanding performances. A printed program that includes all of the names of participants is desirable and makes all of the students feel important. If possible, ask someone unrelated to the program, such as the principal, to open the demonstration and welcome parents. The program should be fast moving and take 45 to 60 minutes. Parents are interested primarily in seeing their youngster perform and will not sit for much longer than 1 hour.

It is usually wise to omit competitive contests that cause some to be declared losers. Focus instead on educational performances that show skill development. Since all students can perform physical fitness activities, including this type of activity in the program is meaningful. Different students could perform the 4 parts to the lesson that have been suggested: introductory activity, physical fitness activity, lesson focus, and modified games. Figure 14.3 is an example of a program for a middle school demonstration night.

EXPECTED OUTCOMES

After reading this chapter, you should be able to

- Explain the importance of public relations.
- Discuss various public relations strategies that are effective with students, faculty, administrators, parents, and community members.
- Describe many misconceptions that people have regarding physical education programs.
- Devise and carry out several public relations strategies in a school setting.
- Give a presentation on how a physical education program will affect the lives of students in the school.
- List several ways for changing the negative image of a physical education teacher.
- Discuss the various physical education associations that provide public relations services.
- Write a short article for a school newspaper on the importance of physical education.
- Organize and implement a demonstration program for parents and community members.

REFERENCES AND SUGGESTED READINGS

Nelson, J. E. 1986. Communication: the key to public relations. *JOPERD* 57(4): 64–67.

Pangrazi, R. P. 1982. Physical education, self-concept, and achievement. *JOPERD* 53(9): 16–18.

Rolloff, B. D. 1985. Public relations: Objectives for physical education. *JOPERD* 56(3): 69–71.

Schneider, R. D. 1992. Don't just promote your profession—market it! *JOPERD* 63(5): 70–71.

15 Introductory Activities

PURPOSE

To establish a justification for introductory activities in the daily lesson plan for secondary school physical education. In addition, this chapter will provide teachers with a variety of activity ideas that can be used with students as introductory activities.

KEY CONCEPTS

- Introductory activities are vigorous in nature, consist primarily of gross locomotor movement, are not rigidly structured, and allow for considerable freedom of movement.
- Introductory activities serve as a psychological and physiological warm-up for the ensuing physical fitness portion of the lesson.
- Introductory activities are characterized by a minimum of instruction and a maximum of movement.
- Introductory activities should be selected with the interests, development levels, and physical abilities of the students in mind.
- Introductory activities can be novel and challenging. They can also allow students to be somewhat creative.
- The introductory activity period should last only 2 to 3 minutes and should be somewhat relaxed, with an emphasis on enthusiasm and motivation.
- Students should learn to develop introductory activities that will be useful to them as a lead-up for activities that they intend to pursue for a lifetime. As long as the activities are vigorous and emphasize large muscle movement, they can be used in this part of the lesson.

Introductory activities are used during the first part of the lesson as preparatory exercises. They require minimal instruction and allow for a maximum amount of movement. Starting a lesson is difficult, but the task is eased when instructors can begin with activity and little verbal interaction. Most students desire immediate activity when they arrive for class. The introductory activities can meet this need.

Introductory activities are vigorous in nature and revolve around large muscle activity. An objective of introductory activities is to develop a high level of skill in movements basic to sport and leisure pursuits. Students should understand how the activities can be applied to their personal activity interests.

Involvement in introductory activities helps prepare students for strenuous activity. They serve as a psychological and physiological warm-up for the fitness portion of the lesson. During the introductory activity, teachers can work on reaction drills in which students freeze in response to a signal. This helps refocus class management skills and reinforces the need for stopping on signal.

Introductory activities should be selected with the interests and developmental levels of the students in mind. Junior high school students, because of their rapid growth spurt, need activities that emphasize body control, coordination, and agility. Senior high school students need to understand how introductory activities will affect sport and dance performance and other activities in which they have developed competency and interest.

Use vocabulary and jargon appropriate to the maturity level of the students when introducing activities. Effective teachers possess some acting skills when presenting introductory activities. Capitalize on popular movies and television series, and on famous people and news items. This adds enthusiasm and motivation to the learning environment.

To minimize unproductive time, use students as leaders. They need opportunities to lead and to learn not to always depend on teachers to make decisions. Inform the class of the goal and the desired accomplishment. Students can perform signals that are necessary for some of the day's lesson activities.

Students should learn to develop introductory activities suited to their needs. As long as the activities are vigorous and emphasize large muscle movement, they can be used in this part of the lesson. It is also entirely possible that the introductory activity may place demands on the cardiovascular system and can be used for this purpose after the fitness portion of the lesson. As usual, a large variety of introductory activities should be taught and presented to show students that there are many acceptable methods for preparing for activity.

AGILITY ACTIVITIES

Seat Roll

Students are on all fours with head up, looking at the instructor. When the teacher gives a left- or right-hand signal, students respond quickly by rolling in that direction on their seat. Seat rolls can be alternated with running in place or with rope jumping to increase the challenge.

Arkansas Flip

Begin in the same position as the seat roll. Students flip over to the left or right, without touching their seats to the floor, so they are in a crab position (half

flip). The flip should be a quick, continuous movement. Students can wait for the next signal in the crab position or, if the teacher designates, can continue over to all-fours position with the head up (full flip).

Quarter Eagle

Students are in a ready position with the head up, arms flexed in front of the body, knees slightly bent, feet straight ahead and shoulder width apart. The instructor gives a hand signal left or right. The class responds by making a quarter turn in that direction and returning to the starting position as quickly as possible.

A variation involves having participants move on a verbal signal such as "go." The students then make a quarter turn to the left or right and wait for the next signal. They continue to make quarter turns on each signal.

Wave Drill

In the wave drill, students are in ready position. They shuffle (without a crossover step) left, right, backward, or forward on signal. A useful variation is to place an obstacle (boundary cone) for students to shuffle over.

Variation 1. Same as original, except use a crossover step.

Variation 2. Same as original, except that students are on all fours.

Variation 3. Students stand between 2 cones or bags stuttering the feet (rapid running in place). On a hand signal to the left or right, the performer steps over the obstacle in the corresponding direction and moves the feet in place while waiting for the next signal.

Variation 4. Same as variation 3 except that students move left or right with both feet together (ski hop). Emphasis is on watching the signal and moving quickly.

Log Roll (3-Person Roll)

Students are in groups of 3 and on all fours to start the log roll. The instructor gives a signal left or right. The middle person rolls in that direction, while the person on that side rolls up and over the top of the middle person. The drill continues with each person rolling several times. The objective is to roll straight, get up quickly, and not touch anybody while rolling over them.

Square Drill

The class forms several 10-yard squares with boundary cones. Students stand in the middle of each side of the square and face the center. On signal, they shuffle around the square to the left or right, depending on the signal of the teacher. A student can be in the center of the square to give a direction signal.

Lateral Shuffle

Place 2 cones about 5 yards apart. A student stands in the middle and shuffles quickly back and forth between the cones, touching the cone each time. Students try to touch as many cones as possible in 15 seconds. Set up enough pairs of cones so all students can participate simultaneously.

Rooster Hop Drill

Students hop 10 yards on 1 leg in the following sequence: (1) left hand touching the right toe, which is on the ground, (2) right hand touching the left toe on the ground, (3) right hand touching the right toe on the ground, (4) left hand touching the left toe on the ground. Students can be challenged to develop different combinations and tasks.

Weave Drill

The weave drill is similar to the wave drill, except that students shuffle in and out of a series of obstacles such as cones, blocking dummies, or boards. A shuffling step is used rather than a crossover step.

Running Weave Drill

Students run through the maze with a regular running stride. A stopwatch can challenge students to improve their time, and the maze can be arranged in many different ways. Let students set up the maze and time each other. A variation could be done using the carioca (or grapevine) step.

Leaping Lena with a Forward Roll

Students stand in a ready position stuttering the feet quickly. On the first command, students leap forward as far as possible and begin moving the feet again. Two more leaps are repeated and then a forward roll is performed. Students return to the end of the line when finished.

Burpee-Flip Drill

The burpee-flip can be done in small groups or in unison with the entire class. The teacher calls out the number, and students yell the number while performing the movement. The sequence is as follows:

1. Standing position
2. Bend the knees, hands on the floor or ground
3. Legs kick back into an all-fours position, head up
4. Half flip right to a crab position
5. Half flip right to an all-fours position

This drill can also be done with a left flip or with 2 flips, 1 left and 1 right, and so forth. Let students try this drill with a small group. Challenge them to stay together and to continue enlarging the group. Participants must call the numbers for their group.

Another variation is to put a push-up in before the flip. Step 4 would be the down motion and Step 5 would be the up motion. Use caution to ensure that students are far enough apart in case 1 student flips the wrong way.

All-Fours Circle

Students lie on their stomachs with heads close together and legs extended outward like the spokes of a wheel. One person starts by placing the hands in the center and moving around the circle over the other students without touching anyone. The last person who is passed is the next participant. The drill can be done with 4 to 12 people.

Coffee Grinder Square

With the coffee grinder square, students start at 1 corner of the square, run to the next corner, and perform a coffee grinder on the right arm (arm extended on the ground, supporting the body weight, while the feet walk 360 degrees around the arm). At the next corner, they put their left arm down and do another coffee grinder. This continues through the 4 corners. The square should be made with something flat, such as beanbags or bases. Students should move in the same direction around the square.

Flash Drill

Students stand in a ready position facing the teacher. The teacher exclaims "feet," and students stutter the feet quickly. The teacher then "flashes" the following hand signals:

1. Hands up: Students jump up and return to stuttering feet.
2. Hands down: Students move to the floor and return to stuttering feet.
3. Hands right: Students shuffle right.
4. Hands left: Students shuffle left.
5. Hands make a circle: Students do a forward roll and get up stuttering.

SPORT MOVEMENT CHALLENGES

The following activities can be done with sport movements such as sliding, leaping, running, and jumping. The locomotor movement is then combined with a challenging activity that is used in sport such as a pivot, stop, or change of direction.

Move and Change Direction

Students run in any direction, and change direction on signal. The change in direction can be specified or student selected. If specified, the commands might be to reverse, right angle, 45 degrees, or left turn. The change in direction should be made quickly in pivotlike fashion.

Move and Change Speed or Level

Students move throughout the area. On signal, they are challenged to move close to the floor or as elongated as possible. They can be challenged to touch the floor or give a "high five" while moving. Combinations of changing the level (as well as changing the speed of the movement) can be developed.

Move and Change the Type of Locomotion

Students move using a specified locomotor movement. On signal, they change to another type of movement. Challenges can be given to do the movements forward, backward, sideways, or diagonally.

Change Move and Quickly Stop

Students move throughout the area and quickly stop under control. Emphasis should be placed on stopping using proper technique. Students should lower the center of gravity, widen the base of support, and place 1 foot in front of the other to absorb the force.

Move and Perform Athletic Movement

Students move and stop on signal. They then perform an athletic skill move, such as a basketball jump shot, leaping football pass catch, volleyball spike, or soccer kick. Students should place emphasis on correct form and timing. A variation of the activity is for students to move with a partner and throw a pass on signal, punt a ball, or shoot a basket. The partner catches the ball or rebounds the shot.

Move, Stop, and Pivot

Students move under control throughout the area. On signal, they stop, pivot, and resume moving. Emphasis should be placed on making a sharp pivot and a rapid acceleration. The skill is similar to running a pass pattern in football.

Move and Perform a Fitness Task

The class moves throughout the area. When a signal is given, students perform a predesignated fitness task. Examples of tasks are push-ups, sit-ups, squat thrusts, and crab kicks. The fitness tasks can be written on a card and flashed to the class to signal the next challenge.

Move and Perform a Stretch

The class is challenged to run throughout the area. On signal, they stop and perform a designated stretching activity. (See Chapter 16 for a comprehensive list of stretching exercises.) A list of stretches that covers all body parts can be posted, and students can perform a different stretch after each signal.

INDIVIDUAL ACTIVITIES

Number Challenges

Students are challenged to move and perform to a set of 3 to 4 numbers. For example, the given set of numbers might be 25, 10, 30. The first number would signify some type of locomotor movement, the second number a set of stretching exercises, and the last an activity with equipment. Implemented, this challenge might be 25 running steps, 10 repetitions of a stretching activity, and 30 rope-jumping turns.

Four Corners

A square is marked using 4 boundary cones. Students spread out around the perimeter of the square. On signal, they move in the same direction around the square. As they pass a corner, they change the locomotor movement they are doing. Other challenges would be to move on all fours, in crab position, or using a frog jump.

Gauntlet Run

Students line up at 1 end of a football field or area of similar size. Challenges are placed every 10 yards. Examples of challenges might be to jump over benches, crawl through hoops, run through tires, long-jump a certain distance, hop backwards, high-jump over a bar, do a forward roll, or perform an animal walk. Students can begin at different challenges so the activity does not become a race. Emphasis should be placed on warming up and achieving quality movement.

Rubber Band

Students begin from a central point with the instructor. On signal, the students move away from the instructor using a designated movement such as a jump, run, hop, slide, carioca, or walk. On the second signal, students sprint back to the instructor's position where the activity originated. The cycle is repeated with different movements. As a variation,

students can perform 1 or 2 stretching activities when they return to the teacher.

Rope Jumping

Each student has a jump rope. On the first signal, they begin jumping rope. On the second signal, they drop the rope and perform a stretching activity. A third signal can be used to designate performing a light, easy run. Emphasis should be placed on preparing students for fitness activity rather than offering a severe workout.

Milk Carton Kicking

Half-gallon paper milk cartons filled with newspaper, or gallon-size plastic milk containers can be used for this introductory activity. Each student has a carton and dribbles or kicks it throughout the area. Students can also work with a partner and dribble the container back and forth. The carton is a medium for encouraging movement. All kicking and dribbling should be done on the move.

Ball Activities

Each student has a ball and dribbles it throughout the area while moving. On signal, students stop and move the ball behind the back, around each leg, and overhead. Emphasis is on learning to handle the ball as well as on moving. A variation is to drop 1 ball on signal and play catch with a partner until the signal to resume dribbling is given.

Beanbag Touch and Go

Spread different colored beanbags throughout the area. On signal, students run to a beanbag, touch it, and resume running. To increase the challenge, the color of the beanbag can be specified and the touch must be made with a designated body part. An example might be, "Touch 6 yellow beanbags with your left hip." Students can also move to a beanbag, perform a pivot, and resume running.

Vanishing Beanbags

Spread beanbags throughout the area to allow 1 per student. Students move around the area until a signal is given. On the signal, they find a beanbag and sit on it. The instructor then signals for the class to move again, and 1 or more beanbags are removed during this interval. Now when students are signaled to find a beanbag, some will be left without one. A challenge is offered to not be left out more than 5 times. Locomotor movements and different body parts can be specified to add challenge and variety.

Rolling Hoops

Each student has a hula hoop and rolls it alongside while running. On signal, the hoops are dropped, and students are challenged to move in and out of 15 hoops. The number and color of hoops to move in and out of can be specified, as well as the type of activity to perform. When the task is completed, the student picks up the hoop and resumes rolling it.

Animal Walks

Two parallel lines marked with boundary cones are placed 10 to 20 yards apart. Half of the class lines up on 1 line and the other half on the opposite line. On signal, students animal-walk from 1 line to the other. Examples of walks that can be done are the dog walk, seal walk, crab walk, rabbit jumps, bear walk, and walrus walk.

PARTNER AND SMALL-GROUP ACTIVITIES

Marking

Marking is an excellent activity for learning to elude an opponent and also for learning to stay defensively near someone. Partners are selected, and one elects to chase the other. On the first signal, the challenge is to stay as close as possible to the partner who is attempting to get away. When a second signal is given, both partners must immediately freeze. If the chaser can reach out and "mark" the partner, the chaser scores a point. Roles are reversed each time a signal is given.

Pentabridge Hustle

To start the Pentabridge hustle, students form groups of 5. They spread out as far as possible in the playing area and form individual bridges that another person

can move under. On signal, the first person in the group of 5 moves under the other 4 bridging students and runs ahead and forms a bridge. The next person in sequence moves under the 4 bridges. This becomes a continuous movement activity. Activity success depends on making sure that students form bridges that are quite a distance apart so that enough running occurs to ensure warm-up.

Over, Under, and Around

Students find a partner. One person gets in position on all fours while the other stands alongside, ready to begin the movement challenge. The challenge is given to move over, go under, and run around the partner a certain number of times. For example, move over your partner 5 times, go under 8 times, and run around 13 times. When the task is completed, partners change positions and the challenge is repeated. To increase motivation, the challenge can be made to move over, under, and around different students. For a more difficult challenge, the persons on all fours can move slowly throughout the area.

New Leader

Students work in small groups. The task is to continuously move in a productive fashion that will warm up the group. One person begins as the leader. When a signal is given, a new leader steps up and leads the next activity.

Pyramid Power

Students move throughout the area. On signal, they find a partner and build a simple pyramid or partner stand. Examples are the hip-shoulder stand, double-crab stand, double-dog stand, and shoulder stand. Students should be cautioned to select a partner of similar size and to stand on the proper points of support.

Leapfrog

Students work in groups of 4 or 5. All students in the group move into the leapfrog base position with the exception of the last person in line. On signal, the last person leapfrogs over the others and moves into a base position. The next person now leapfrogs over the others, and the activity becomes one of continuous movement. Activity success depends on maintaining a large distance between each of the leapfrog bases.

Tag Games

A variety of tag games can be used to motivate students to move. They are excellent for teaching students to elude and chase each other. Examples of tag games are:

1. *Balance tag.* To be safe, balance in a stipulated position.
2. *Push-up tag.* Assume the push-up or other designated position to avoid being tagged.
3. *Snowball tag.* Two people begin by being "it." When they tag someone, they hold hands. As a number of people are tagged, the chain of people becomes long, and only those at the end of the chain are eligible to tag.
4. *Frozen tag.* When tagged, the person must freeze with the feet in straddle position. To be able to resume play, 3 people must move under and through a "frozen" person's legs.
5. *Spider tag.* Students stand back-to-back with a partner with the elbows hooked. A pair of people are "it" and chase the other pairs. If a pair is tagged (or becomes unhooked), they are "it."
6. *Triangle plus 1 tag.* Three students hold hands to form a triangle. One person in the triangle is the leader. The fourth person outside the triangle tries to tag the leader. The triangle moves around to avoid getting the leader tagged. Leader and tagger are changed often.
7. *Fugitive tag.* One person is the fugitive and is given a head start. The partner is a police person trying to tag the fugitive. Flag belts can be used by the fugitive.

Follow the Leader

Students are grouped by pairs. On signal, the leader performs all types of movements to elude his or her partner. Zigzags, rolls, 360-degree turns, and jumps are encouraged. Partners switch after 30 seconds. The same drill can be done with 1 leader and 2 or more followers.

Hoops on the Ground

Students run around the area where hoops are spread. When the teacher calls a number, students must get that number of students inside 1 hoop in 5 seconds or less.

Mirror Drill in Place

Each student faces a partner. One person is the leader and makes a quick movement with the hands, head, legs, or body. The partner tries to be a mirror and perform the exact movement. The leader must pause briefly between movements. Leader and partner exchange places after 30 seconds.

Formation Rhythmic Running

The class begins in circular formation. Students move to a drumbeat or other steady beat. They attempt to run rhythmically to the beat, lifting the knees and maintaining a formation or line with even spacing between students. Challenges can be added, such as clapping hands on the first beat, stamping the feet on the third beat, and thrusting a hand into the air on the fourth beat of a 4-count rhythm.

As students become experienced at maintaining the formation and rhythm of the activity, they can be led into different formations such as a rectangle, square, triangle, or line. Students can also "wind up" and "unwind" the line, and can learn to cross in front of each other to "break a line."

EXPECTED OUTCOMES

After reading this chapter, you should be able to

- Discuss the objectives of introductory activities for secondary school physical education.
- Select appropriate introductory activities for a specific grade level of students taking a specific unit of activity.
- Characterize the various features of the introductory phase of the lesson.
- Develop a new or modified introductory activity.

16 Physical Fitness

PURPOSE

To explain the importance of including physical fitness activities in the lesson plan and identify novel strategies and techniques that could be used to implement fitness into the lesson structure. A variety of exercises and techniques that can be used to develop physical fitness are discussed.

KEY CONCEPTS

- Fitness is defined into 2 different categories: health-related and skill-related. Health-related fitness is the most important outcome for the majority of people.

- People mistakenly believe that American youth are unfit.

- Fitness performance is strongly controlled by genetic factors including trainability.

- The relationship between activity and fitness performance is weak and leads to misconceptions about the importance of training and passing fitness tests.

- Newer fitness tests evaluate the amount of fitness necessary for good health. Instead of percentile rankings, criterion-referenced health standards are used to measure good health.

- Secondary school students need the opportunity to experience and select fitness routines that are useful and motivating to them personally.

- Physical fitness activities should be offered as a positive contribution to total wellness. These activities should not be used as punishment.

- Novel routines using a variety of equipment and activities can help to motivate students toward a lifetime of fitness activities.

- The school physical education program should help students make the transition into community-based physical activity programs.

- Instruction and participation relative to physical fitness should be done in a positive atmosphere.

All students want to be fit and active. Physical education programs that do not make time for fitness development indirectly teach students that fitness is not important for a healthy lifestyle. At the secondary school level, students should have the opportunity to experience and select fitness routines that are useful and motivating to them personally. Physical fitness activity should be offered as a positive contribution to total wellness. It should be something that benefits those who participate, and not something to be used as punishment for misbehavior.

THE BROAD PROGRAM OF PHYSICAL FITNESS

Offering students a broad and comprehensive physical fitness program is more than just providing physical fitness routines. The following are several components included in a quality program:

1. Teaching students to assume responsibility for their personal fitness development. This includes helping students set personal goals that have meaning. It implies an extension of fitness development beyond free time in school, as well as application to the home and community environment.

2. Providing an understanding of how fitness is developed. An explanation of the value of the procedures followed in class sessions helps students understand the purpose of all fitness developmental tasks. In addition, it includes teaching students basic components of a personal fitness program.

3. Developing cognition about the place of fitness in a healthy lifestyle. Students should understand how to perform fitness activities and why these activities should be performed. They need to know the values derived from maintaining an adequate fitness level.

4. Offering the opportunity to participate in a range of fitness activities. Knowledge and understanding are not enough. Fitness is experiential and must be participatory. A program of activity makes the fitness approach a total package.

WHAT IS PHYSICAL FITNESS?

Although it is generally agreed that physical fitness is an important part of normal growth and development, a general definition of its precise nature has not been universally accepted. Through research and scholarly inquiry it is becoming increasingly clear that the multidimensional characteristics of physical fitness can be divided into 2 areas: health-related physical fitness and skill-related physical fitness. Classifying fitness into 2 categories should not lessen the importance of either in the total growth and development of youngsters. Understanding the distinctive features of health-related physical fitness and skill-related physical fitness should help educators develop a program that facilitates all students.

Health-Related Physical Fitness

Teaching health-related fitness should be a top priority in physical education. The beauty of health-related fitness is that all students can improve their performance through regular and progressive exercise. This is one of the few areas in physical activity where a teacher can say with confidence and integrity, "If you are willing to exercise, you will improve." This contrasts with skill-related fitness, which is driven by genetic traits and abilities. The other reason it is important to teach health-related fitness is to develop exercise patterns that leave students with tools for lifetime activity.

Health-related physical fitness includes those aspects of physiological function that offer protection from diseases resulting from a sedentary lifestyle. It can be improved and/or maintained through regular physical activity. Specific components include cardiovascular fitness, body composition (ratio of leanness to fatness), abdominal strength and endurance, and flexibility.

Cardiovascular Fitness

Aerobic fitness is important for a healthy lifestyle and may be the most important element of fitness. Cardiovascular endurance is the ability of the heart, the blood vessels, and the respiratory system to deliver oxygen efficiently over an extended period of time. To develop cardiovascular endurance, activity must be aerobic in nature. Activities that are continuous and rhythmic require that a continuous supply of oxygen be delivered to the muscle cells. Activities that stimulate development in this area are paced walking, jogging, biking, rope jumping, aerobic dance, swimming, and continuous movement sports such as basketball or soccer.

Body Composition

Body composition is an integral part of health-related fitness. Body composition is the proportion of body fat to lean body mass. After the thickness of selected skinfolds has been measured, the percentage of body fat can be extrapolated from tables. The conversion of skinfold thickness to percent body fat can be a less accurate measure, but it is easier to communicate to parents than skinfold thickness. Since the wellness status of individuals is dependent on body composition, students must learn about concepts and consequences in this area.

Flexibility

Flexibility is the range of movement through which a joint or sequence of joints can move. Inactive individuals lose flexibility, whereas frequent movement helps retain the range of movement. Through stretching activities, the length of muscles, tendons, and ligaments is increased. The ligaments and tendons retain their elasticity through constant use. People who are flexible are less subject to injury in sport, usually possess sound posture, and have less lower back pain.

Muscular Strength and Endurance

Strength is the ability of muscles to exert force; it is an important fitness component for learning motor skills (Rarick and Dobbins, 1975). Most activities in physical education do not build strength in the areas where it is most needed: the arm-shoulder girdle and the abdominal region. Muscular endurance is the ability to exert force over an extended period. Endurance postpones the onset of fatigue so that activity can be performed for lengthy periods. Most sport activities require that muscular skills, such as throwing, kicking, and striking, be performed many times without fatigue.

Skill-Related Physical Fitness

Skill-related fitness includes those physical qualities that enable a person to perform in sport activities. For years, the primary fitness test for teachers was the AAHPERD Youth Fitness Test (1987). This test was also known as the President's Council on Physical Fitness and Sports Youth Fitness Test. Because skill-related fitness is closely allied to one's natural or inherited traits, it is difficult for most students to achieve. Skill-related fitness is closely related to athletic ability. The traits of speed, agility, coordination, and so on form the basis of the ability to excel in sports.

Skill-related fitness components are useful for performing motor tasks related to sport and athletics. The ability to perform well depends largely on the genetic endowment of the individual. Where it is possible for all students to perform adequately in health-related fitness activities, it is difficult, if not impossible, for a large number of youngsters to excel in this area of fitness. Asking students to "try harder" only adds to their frustration if they lack native ability, because they see their more skilled friends perform well without effort. When skill-related fitness is taught, it should be accompanied by an explanation of why some students can perform well with a minimum of effort, whereas others, no matter how hard they try, never excel. There are many examples that can be used to illustrate the situation such as the differences in speed, jumping ability, strength, and physical size in individuals. Specific components of skill-related fitness are described in the following sections.

Agility

Agility is the ability of the body to change position rapidly and accurately while moving. Wrestling and football are examples of sports that require agility.

Balance

Balance refers to the body's ability to maintain a state of equilibrium while remaining stationary or moving. Maintaining balance is essential to all sports but is especially important in the performance of gymnastic activities.

Coordination

Coordination is the ability of the body to perform smoothly and successfully more than 1 motor task at the same time. Needed for football, baseball, tennis, soccer, and other sports that require hand-eye and foot-eye skills, coordination can be developed by practicing repeatedly the skill to be learned.

Power

Power is the ability to transfer energy explosively into force. To develop power, a person must practice activities that are required to improve strength but at a faster rate involving sudden bursts of energy. Skills requiring power include high jumping, long jumping, shot putting, throwing, and kicking.

Speed

Speed is the ability of the body to perform movement in a short period of time. Usually associated with running forward, speed is essential for the successful performance of most sports and general locomotor movement skills.

THE FITNESS OF AMERICA'S YOUTH

A popular point of view among physical education teachers is that children and youth today are less fit than they were in the past. This opinion is often used as a justification for more physical education time in the schools. Recent research (Corbin and Pangrazi, 1992) suggests that the fitness of today's youngsters has not degenerated and that they do quite well when compared to past students. When data from the last 4 national surveys (1957 to 1985) of youth fitness conducted by AAHPERD and/or the President's Council on Physical Fitness and Sports were compared, it was found that children and youth today are just as fit as they were in the past. The only items used in all 4 surveys were pull-ups and the flexed-arm hang. Youngsters, both boys and girls, showed an increase in performance when these 2 items were compared over 4 decades. The only area where teenagers have shown a minor decrease in fitness is body composition (Centers for Disease Control and Prevention, 1994; Gortmaker, Dietz, Sobol, and Wehler, 1987); today's teens are 6% fatter than they were about 12 years ago.

Why the Opinion That Youth Are Unfit?

It is quite likely that many physical education teachers want to believe that youngsters are unfit. If it can be demonstrated that youngsters are not fit, a strong case can be made for employing physical education teachers. Interestingly, physical educators have been teaching fitness for years and fitness levels of youth have not substantially changed (Corbin and Pangrazi, 1992). An explanation for why people believe youngsters are unfit may be the arbitrary manner in which fitness was measured and standards set. For years, the common fitness test for teachers was the AAHPERD Youth Fitness Test. The test was a skill-related test that offered the Presidential Fitness Award to youngsters performing at the 85th percentile or better in all test items. Results of the National School Population Fitness Survey (Reiff et al., 1987) funded by the President's Council on Physical Fitness and Sports showed that only one-tenth of 1% of boys and three-tenths of 1% of girls could pass a battery of 6 tests at the 85th percentile, the standard used for earning the Presidential Fitness Award over the years. Why was the standard set at the 85th percentile? The

best explanation is that this was comparable to academic standards, and test developers felt that physical education needed to accomplish at the same level. Since many physical educators and parents felt the 85th percentile standard was unrealistically high, a new award was created—the National Fitness Award. To earn this award, youngsters have to pass the same battery of test items at the 50th percentile or better. Unfortunately, when using a battery of tests, the majority of students usually fail at least 1 item, causing them to lose the award and be identified as unfit. Only 15% of boys and 19% of girls were able to score above the 50th percentile. Using a battery of tests to define fitness and setting arbitrary standards are sure ways for the majority of youth to fail. Even at this lowered standard, over 80% of youngsters are failures.

Another reason people continue to believe that youngsters are unfit is due to changing definitions of fitness. Fitness testing has evolved from skill-related fitness to health-related fitness and its relationship to good health and feelings of well-being. We now know that high performance on fitness test items is not necessary for good health, especially when the performance is based on skill-related items such as the 50-yard dash and the shuttle run. Evidence shows that moderate amounts of health-related physical fitness are enough to contribute to good health (Blair et al., 1989). When health-related fitness test items are compared, today's students perform as well (and better) than students in years past.

Genetic Endowment and Fitness Performance

A significant amount of fitness test performance is explained by heredity (Bouchard, 1990; Bouchard, Dionne, Simoneau, and Boulay, 1992). Various factors such as environment, nutrition, heredity, and maturation affect fitness performance as reflected in physical fitness test scores. Research clearly shows that heredity and maturation strongly impact fitness scores (Bouchard et al., 1992; Pangrazi and Corbin, 1990). In fact, these factors may have more to do with youth fitness scores than activity level. Lifestyle and environmental factors can also make a difference. For example, nutrition is a lifestyle factor that can influence test scores, and environmental conditions (heat, humidity, and pollution) strongly modify test performances. Fitness performance is only partially determined by activity and training.

Some youngsters have a definite advantage on tests because of the types of muscle fibers they inherit (see Chapter 2). Others inherit a predisposition to perform well on tests. In other words, even in an untrained state, some students score better because of heredity. On the other hand, some youngsters who train will not score as well as others who are untrained because of their genetic predisposition. Beyond heredity lies another factor that predisposes some youngsters to high performance. Recent research has shown that **trainability** is inherited (Bouchard et al., 1992) which means some people receive more benefit from training (regular physical activity) than others. As an example, assume that 2 students perform the same amount of activity throughout a semester. Student A shows dramatic improvement immediately while student B does not. Student A simply responds more favorably to training than student B. Student A inherited a system that is responsive to exercise. Student A not only gets fit and scores well on the test but gets feedback that says, "The activity works—it makes me fit." The less responsive student scores poorly, receives no feedback, and concludes that, "Activity doesn't improve my fitness, so why try?" The unfortunate thing is that student B will improve in fitness but to a lesser degree than student A and will take longer to show improvement. Student B will probably never achieve the fitness level attained by student A. Trainability and genetic endowment differences limit performance making it important to have different expectations for students.

Should teachers assume from this point of view that there is little use in helping students become more fit and active? Certainly not. Whereas heredity plays an important role in fitness and in trainability of fitness, all youngsters benefit from regular activity. Accept the fact it takes some students longer to benefit from regular physical activity and show fitness gains. Less-gifted students will need more encouragement and positive feedback since their improvement will be in smaller increments and of a lesser magnitude.

The Relationship Between Fitness Results and Activity

Teachers and parents want to believe that fitness in youngsters is primarily a reflection of how active they are. A common belief is that because students excessively watch television and play video games, they score poorly on fitness tests. A low relationship exists between activity and fitness test performance (Morrow and Freedson, 1994) among adolescents. The mistaken belief that activity builds fitness may lead teachers to the conclusion that youngsters who score high on fitness tests are active and those who don't score well are inactive. Physical activity is an important variable in fitness development for adults, but for youth other factors can be of equal or greater importance. If teachers make the mistake of assuming that a student is inactive because of scores on a fitness test, problems can result.

Problems can occur when teachers mistakenly assume that fitness and activity are highly related. If youngsters are encouraged to do regular exercise to improve their fitness scores, many will take the challenge seriously. When fitness tests are given, students will expect to do well on the tests if they have been exercising regularly, and, of course, teachers will also expect them to do well. If, however, they receive scores that are lower than expected, they will be disappointed. They will be especially discouraged if the teacher concludes that their low fitness status is a reflection of inactivity. Such a conclusion as, "You are not as fit as you should be compared to other students, therefore you have not been active," is most likely untrue. It may cause a loss of self-esteem and a loss of respect between student and teacher.

The other side of this issue is assuming that youngsters who make high scores on fitness tests are active. Youngsters who are genetically gifted may be inactive, yet may perform well on fitness tests. Students are always aware of peers who don't train, aren't active, and maintain poor health habits yet still perform well on fitness tests. If teachers do not teach otherwise, these youngsters learn that it is possible to be fit and healthy without being active. Neither of these scenarios is accurate, and it is necessary to correct such misconceptions.

PHYSICAL ACTIVITY AND HEALTH

For years physical and health educators, coaches, and fitness and recreation leaders have been secure in their recommendations concerning how much physical activity is enough. A recent recommendation about physical activity offers new direction. The new recommendation is concisely stated: "**Every U.S. adult should accumulate 30 or more minutes of moderate-intensity activity on most, preferably all, days of the week**" (Pate et al., 1995). This recommendation was issued from the Centers for Disease

Control and Prevention (CDC) and the American College of Sports Medicine (ACSM) (Pate et al., 1995). It is just one of many statements that point in the same direction. In 1990, health goals for the nation were outlined in the document *Healthy People 2000* (Public Health Service, 1991). The first chapter of this document outlined the need to increase physical activity levels of Americans. Physical activity was included as the first chapter of the national health goals because changing physical activity can do more than any other change in lifestyle to improve the health of the country (McGinnis, 1992). These health goals were based on the same evidence as the new CDC/ACSM recommendation. The American Heart Association (1992) issued a statement that sedentary living had been elevated from a secondary to a primary risk factor along with high blood pressure, high blood fat levels, and smoking. Again, the same collective medical and public health evidence was used.

What is moderate-intensity activity? Experts generally agree on what constitutes light, moderate, and vigorous physical activity. METS (resting metabolic rate) are used to quantify activity. One MET equals calories expended at rest (resting metabolism). Two METS is activity that is twice as intense. Three METS requires 3 times as much energy, and so on. Activities of 3 METS or less are considered to be light activities. Examples are strolling (slow walking), slow stationary cycling, stretching, golf with a motorized cart, fishing (sitting), bowling, carpet sweeping, and riding a mower (Pate et al., 1995). Activity that expends 4 to 6 times the energy expended at rest (4 to 6 METS) is considered to be moderate in nature. Examples of activity at this level are brisk walking, racquet sports, and mowing the lawn with a power mower. To meet the new recommendation, a person should do 30 minutes of activity equivalent in intensity to brisk walking most, or all, days of the week.

How Much Activity Is Necessary for Adolescents?

A consensus statement developed by a board of experts is available to teachers. This statement delineates the amount of activity adolescents need (ages 11 to 21) and contains 2 basic guidelines (Sallis and Patrick, 1994). **Guideline 1** states that "All adolescents should be physically active daily, or nearly every day, as part of play, games, sports, work, transportation, recreation, physical education, or planned exercise, in the context of family, school, and community activities." Adolescents who participate in

the 30 minutes of activity discussed earlier in this chapter meet the first guideline. **Guideline 2** states that "Adolescents should engage in 3 or more sessions per week of activities that last 20 minutes or more and require moderate to vigorous levels of exertion."

Meeting guideline 1 should be a priority and a minimum. Participation in 30 minutes of daily activity is a reasonable goal, even for sedentary youth. Beyond this, guideline 2 is a desirable goal. The consensus statement includes brisk walking, jogging, stair climbing, basketball, racquet sports, soccer, dance, swimming laps, skating, strength (resistance training), lawn mowing, and cycling as some examples of activities that meet guideline 2. Maintaining the heart rate at a pre-selected target heart rate for the full 20 minutes is not necessary to meet guideline 2, and many of the activities listed do not produce such a result.

Role of Vigorous Activity

The new recommendation does not discourage or downplay the value of vigorous activity. Activities done at 7 METS or higher are considered vigorous in nature. They include very brisk walking, walking uphill, jogging, relatively fast cycling, active involvement in many sports, mowing the lawn with a hand mower, and doing exercise routines such as aerobic dance. For years, students have been told that aerobic activity must be continuous to be beneficial. A major implication of the new recommendation is that activity can be beneficial even if accumulated in several shorter bouts of activity throughout the day. In a recent review, Haskell recommended that until more scientific data are available, it is best to consider only bouts of activity that ". . . last for 5 minutes or longer" when accumulating total activity (Haskell, 1995). In other words, six 5-minute bouts of brisk activity meet the recommendation. Other examples of activity that meet the recommendation are 15 minutes of walking and 15 minutes of aerobic dance done at different times of the day, or three 10-minute intervals of continuous cycling done at different times of the day.

This new recommendation is not meant to replace the **FIT formula** (Frequency, Intensity, and amount of Time) to prescribe exercise: exercise should be done at least 3 days per week (frequency), at a heart rate of 60 to 90% of maximum heart rate or 50 to 85% of maximal aerobic power (intensity), and for at least 20 to 60 minutes per exercise bout (ACSM,

1991). These are the guidelines most teachers have used for developing cardiovascular fitness or aerobic fitness. Higher intensity exercise using the FIT formula certainly satisfies the new recommendation. On the other hand, expending calories in activity that equals 30 minutes of walking briskly most days (1000 to 2000 kcal per week) achieves health benefits. There is more than 1 way to prescribe physical activity for good health. Different forms of activity have different benefits; it is appropriate to use 1 set of guidelines or recommendations to achieve certain purposes while using the other guidelines to meet other objectives.

The FIT formula is best for individuals interested in cardiovascular or aerobic fitness improvement. Among those for whom these guidelines are particularly good are athletes and those in jobs requiring great physical demands such as law enforcement or fire safety. They are also effective for those who have little time to exercise. For example, a busy person can improve fitness in 3 relatively short but quite vigorous exercise sessions a week.

The new activity recommendations include a broad range of less-intense activities including those that can be done as part of work or normal daily routines as well as during free time. These recommendations are useful for students who do not like vigorous physical activity (Pollock, 1988). These people may remain sedentary or drop out of activity because they believe that exercise is only beneficial when it is vigorous, high heart-rate activity. The new recommendations make it easier for sedentary people to see value in participation in moderate activity.

Importance of Total Fitness

Much of the discussion to this point has centered on aerobic performance. However, a balanced approach to fitness is important for proper adolescent development. Total fitness is important because when a certain part or component of the body is exercised, only that part develops. For example, if jogging for aerobic fitness, the cardiovascular system will be developed. However, flexibility will decrease in the lower back and hamstrings and abdominal strength will decrease. Muscular power, as revealed by the vertical jump, will decrease also. A balanced approach to total fitness includes flexibility, strength development, and cardiovascular endurance activity in an exercise regimen. Aerobic activity is important but not enough for adolescents. Youngsters need activity

for the development of all parts of health-related fitness including muscle strength and endurance, flexibility, and a desirable level of body fat. Physical activity programs should promote total fitness and teach appropriate exercise that develops all components of fitness.

HEALTH-RELATED FITNESS EVALUATION

Health-related fitness evaluation can be an important part of the physical education program. A number of issues need to be considered before implementing the evaluation program. An overriding consideration should be to assure that the experience is positive and educational. Students should have the opportunity to learn about personal fitness and develop a lifestyle for good health. Students should not lose self-esteem because of the evaluation experience; imagine the number of youth who have been embarrassed when their fitness test results were announced to the class. Fitness testing can be done in a manner that creates a positive and meaningful experience.

Prudential Fitnessgram System

The Prudential Fitnessgram system of the Cooper Institute for Aerobic Fitness (1992) consists of a flexible test battery, software for reporting results, and an awards system for rewarding participation and performance in fitness activities. In addition, an instructor's package filled with information and educational activities for students is available to teachers. The Fitnessgram offers a variety of fitness test items so teachers can develop a customized test battery. The focus of the Fitnessgram is on teaching students about the importance of activity for good health. Students are not compared to one another but are given feedback about their fitness and whether it meets the minimum standard for good health.

The Fitnessgram test has an accompanying recognition program. This recognition system is based primarily on exercise behaviors rather than students' attempts to demonstrate that they are the "best." The Fitnessgram recognition program acknowledges and commends performance; however, it places its highest priority on the development and reinforcement of health-related behaviors that are attainable by all students. These behavior recognition programs are used to recognize participants for any of the following activities: completion of exercise logs, achievement of specific and personalized goals, and fulfillment of a contractual agreement (with a responsible adult). A text that is helpful for developing health-related teaching strategies is *Teaching Strategies for Improving Youth Fitness*, 2nd ed. (Pangrazi & Corbin, 1994).

Fitnessgram Test Items

The suggested test items in the Fitnessgram are briefly described. Other items are included in the manual to give teachers a choice of designing a different test battery. A comprehensive test manual, related materials, and software can be ordered from The Prudential Fitnessgram, The Cooper Institute for Aerobics Research, 12330 Preston Road, Dallas, TX 75230.

Aerobic Capacity

One-mile run/walk or the PACER (Progressive Aerobic Cardiovascular Endurance Run). The PACER is an excellent alternative to the mile—it involves a 20-meter shuttle run and can be performed indoors. The test is progressive and starts out at a level that all youngsters can be successful in and gradually increases in difficulty. The objective of the PACER is to run back and forth across the 20-meter distance within a specified time that gradually decreases. The 20-meter distance is not intimidating to youngsters (compared to the mile) and avoids the problem of trying to teach young students to pace themselves rather than running all-out and fatiguing rapidly.

Body Composition

Body composition is evaluated using percent body fat, which is calculated by measuring the triceps and calf skinfolds (Figure 16.1 and Figure 16.2) or body mass index (calculated using height and weight).

Abdominal Strength

Curl-up test. This item uses a cadence (1 curl-up every 3 seconds). The maximum limit is 75. Students lie in a supine position with the knees bent at a 140-degree angle. The hands are placed flat on the mat

FIGURE 16.1 Measuring the triceps skinfold

FIGURE 16.2 Measuring the calf skinfold

alongside the hips. The objective is to gradually sit up and move the fingers down the mat a specified distance.

Upper-Body Strength

Push-up. This test is done to a cadence (1 every 3 seconds) and is an excellent substitute for the pull-up. A successful push-up is counted when the arms are bent to a 90-degree angle. This item allows many more students to experience success as compared to the pull-up and flexed-arm hang. Other alternative test items are the modified pull-up, the pull-up, and the flexed-arm hang.

Trunk Extensor Strength and Flexibility

Trunk lift. From a face-down position, this test involves lifting the upper body 6 to 12 inches off the floor using the muscles of the back. The position must be held until the measurement can be made.

Flexibility

The back-saver sit and reach is similar to the traditional sit-and-reach test except that it is performed with 1 leg flexed to avoid encouraging students to hyperextend. Measurement is made on both the right and left legs.

Criterion-Referenced Health Standards

A major reason for doing health-related fitness evaluation is to provide students, teachers, and parents with information about good health. The Prudential Fitnessgram (1992) uses **criterion-referenced health standards** that represent good health instead of traditional percentile rankings. These standards represent a level of fitness that offers some degree of protection against diseases resulting from sedentary living. The Fitnessgram uses an approach that classifies fitness performance into 2 areas: needs improvement and healthy fitness zone (HFZ). All students are encouraged to score in the HFZ; however, there is little advantage to scoring beyond the healthy fitness zone. Criterion-referenced health standards do not compare students against each other as do percentile rankings. Instead, youngsters should score within the healthy fitness zone to minimize possible health problems.

Criterion-referenced health standards for aerobic fitness are based on a study by Blair et al. (1989). A significant decrease in risk of all-cause mortality occurred when people were active enough to avoid classification in the bottom 20% of the population. The risk level continues to decrease as fitness levels increase, but not significantly when compared to moving out of the least active group. The aerobic performance minimums (mile run or PACER) for the Fitnessgram HFZ require achieving a fitness level that is above the least active portion (bottom 20%) of the population.

Criterion-referenced health standards for percent of fat are calculated from equations reported by Slaughter et al. (1988). Detailed information on the development of these equations and other issues related to the measurement and interpretation of body composition information is available in Lohman (1992). Williams et al. (1992) reported that students with body fat levels above 25% for boys and 30 to 35% for girls are more likely to exhibit elevated cholesterol levels and hypertension. The lower limit for the Fitnessgram HFZ corresponds to these levels of body fat. In other words, students who are fatter may be at risk for future health problems.

Criterion-referenced health standards have not been established for abdominal strength, upper-body strength, and flexibility. For example, it is difficult to determine whether a lack of upper-body strength is important for quality health. Instead, criterion-referenced training standards are used for these areas of fitness. The lower limit represents a performance level that youngsters should be able to accomplish if they are reasonably active and exercise. These standards reflect how many push-ups active students should be able to perform. Stated another way, these standards reflect a reasonable expectation for students who are sufficiently active.

Effective Uses of Fitness Tests

Fitness tests are designed to evaluate and educate youngsters about the status of their physical fitness. In spite of continued research and improvement, fitness tests have limitations and usually show low validity (that is, they do not measure what they purport to measure). It is important to bear in mind that the results of fitness evaluation are often flawed or inaccurate. Therefore, how the tests are used becomes an important issue. The 3 major ways to use fitness tests are: (a) to teach personal self-testing, (b) to establish personal best fitness performances, and (c) to evaluate institutional fitness goals. The personal self-testing program is most strongly advocated in the physical education program. It can be done in the least amount of time, is educational, and can be done frequently. In addition, little instructional time is lost, and students learn how to evaluate their fitness, a skill that will serve them for a lifetime.

Personal Self-Testing

The **personal self-testing** program is an approach that is student centered, concerned with the process of fitness testing, and places emphasis on learning to self-evaluate. When using this technique, students can work individually or find a friend with whom they would like to self-test. With a partner they evaluate each other and develop their own fitness profiles. The goal is to learn the process of fitness testing so students will be able to evaluate their health status during adulthood. Students are asked to do their best, but the teacher does not interfere in the process. The results are the property of the student and are not posted or shared with other students. The personal self-testing program is an educational endeavor; it also allows for more frequent evaluation because it can be done quickly, privately, and informally.

Figure 16.3 is an example of a self-testing form that can be used by students. It allows for 2 testing trials so progress can be monitored. In addition, it contains a column to check off whether the minimum criterion-referenced health standard for each test item has been met. Students can store the forms, or they can be collected by the teacher and returned to the students later for the second test trial. The purpose of recording the data is to help students learn to self-evaluate themselves without the stigma of others having to view or know about it. A final note: it is acceptable for some students to choose not to be tested on a certain item because they fear embarrassment (skinfolds) or failure (mile run). It is worse to be tested and embarrassed than to not be tested at all.

Personal Best Testing

The **personal best testing** approach appeals to gifted performers and to students who are motivated by achieving a maximum performance. The objective is to achieve a maximum score in each of the test items. This approach has been used for years with most fitness tests. In addition, several awards (presidential, national, and others) are issued to high-level performers. This is a formal testing program as compared to the self-testing approach discussed previously. Test items must be performed correctly, following test protocol to the letter. It requires a considerable amount of time to administer.

Personal best testing is an elective program. It requires maximal performance and usually is not motivating to less-capable students. Some students are threatened and fear the embarrassment of failing to perform well in front of peers. A way to avoid embarrassing students who are less capable is to administer the test outside of class time. Testing opportunities can be offered after or before school and on a weekend when school is not in session. Some city recreation departments can offer fitness testing opportunities outside the physical education program as another elective option. This approach is much less threatening; students can choose to participate in the personal best testing session or decide to entirely avoid such situations.

Institutional Evaluation

The **institutional evaluation** program involves examining the fitness levels of students to see if the institution (school) is reaching its desired objectives. Institutional objectives are closely tied to the physical education curriculum. If the curriculum being taught to students is adequate and the goals meaningful, the majority of students should be able to reach institutional goals. A common approach for institutional goal setting is to establish a percentage of the student body that must meet or exceed criterion-referenced health standards for a fitness test. If the percentage is below established institutional standards, it may indicate that the curriculum needs to be modified in order to meet the objective.

Since this type of testing impacts teachers and curriculum offerings, it is done in a formal and standardized manner. A common approach is to train a team of parents to administer tests throughout the system. This ensures accuracy and consistency across all schools in the district. Each test item is reviewed separately, since it is possible that objectives are reached for some but not all of the items. To avoid testing all students every year, some districts evaluate students at regular intervals during their school career, such as at the 5th, 8th, and 10th grades. This minimizes the amount of formal testing youngsters have to endure during their school career.

My Personal Fitness Record
(Fitnessgram Items)

Name _____ Age _____ School _____ Grade _____ Room _____

	Trial 1		Trial 2	
	Score	HFZ*	Score	HFZ*

Body Composition
- Calf (leg) Skinfold
- Triceps (arm) Skinfold
- Total (leg + arm)

Cardiovascular Endurance
- PACER

Abdominal Strength
- Curl-ups

Upper Body Strength
- Push-ups

The following items are pass-fail.

Back Strength
- Trunk Lift

Lower Back Flexibility
- Sit & Reach   L R   L R

Upper Body Flexibility
- Shoulder Stretch   L R   L R

*HFZ means you have scored in the Healthy Fitness Zone. This means that you have achieved or passed the minimum fitness standard required for good health and minimal health risk. Regardless of whether you passed all the tests, you must maintain an active lifestyle for good health. Try to accomplish at least 30 minutes of activity every day.

You do not have to share the results of your personal fitness record. It is for your information and should help you determine your health status. Ask your teacher if you need ideas for increasing your physical activity level.

FIGURE 16.3 Example of a self-testing form

GUIDELINES FOR EXERCISE PRESCRIPTION

As discussed earlier, one of the guidelines for adolescent activity recommended 3 or more sessions per week of activities that last 20 minutes or more and require moderate to vigorous activity. Students have the option of training to improve their fitness level. For aerobic activity, this implies monitoring the Frequency, Intensity, and amount of Time in activity. The application of these 3 factors is often referred to as the FIT principle. Students should leave the physical education program with an understanding of these principles and be able to apply them to a personal fitness program.

FIT Formula

To increase one's level of physical fitness, a gradual increase in activity must occur over time. This gradual increase in workload requires an understanding of frequency, duration, and intensity. The FIT formula is an effective method of promoting cardiovascular or aerobic fitness levels needed for high-level performance. Therefore, FIT formula exercise that requires a continuous heart rate in a target range is appropriate for teenagers who seek high-level fitness requisite for activities such as school sports.

Frequency is the number of exercise sessions an individual performs per week. In cardiovascular endurance exercise, a strenuous and demanding workout is usually followed the next day by mild exercise. Strength training demands a day of complete rest between workouts. To maintain an acceptable level of fitness, a minimum of 3 workouts per week is usually required.

To measure **intensity** in aerobic activity, the heart rate is monitored. If training and improvement is the goal, the heart rate should reach the training state, which is 60 to 80% of the maximum rate possible. Time and intensity can be monitored in strength development. The amount of weight regulates intensity, and the number of sets or repetitions regulates the time factor.

Time is the length of each exercise bout. When developing cardiovascular endurance, the minimum amount of aerobic exercise should be 20 to 30 minutes. The intensity of the exercise will have an impact on the duration of the fitness session.

Progression is important to maintain motivation and reduce the chance of injury. Work loads should be compounded gradually by increasing the intensity and duration of exercise. Students can sometimes be overly enthusiastic about developing fitness in a short amount of time. Achieving fitness is an ongoing process that occurs throughout a lifetime. The important point is to stimulate and then maintain the students' desire to exercise. A reasonable progression helps insure that the desire to exercise is maintained.

Training Heart Rate

Heart rate can be used to determine the intensity of exercise. It gives an indication of whether the workload should be increased or decreased. To monitor heart rate, palpate at the wrist or carotid artery. When palpating the pulse at the wrist, place the index and middle finger near the joint on the thumb side. If the pulse is to be found at the carotid artery, first find the Adam's apple, then slide the index and middle finger to either side. Apply only slight pressure at either site to allow blood flow to continue.

To count the heart rate, begin the count within 5 seconds after stopping exercise. The count should start at 0, be taken for 10 seconds, and multiplied by 6 to give the heart rate per minute. The heart rate should decrease to less than 120 beats per minute after exercise has been terminated for 5 minutes. This is called the recovery heart rate and gives a rough indication of fitness level. For exercise to enhance the level of cardiovascular endurance, the heart rate must be elevated to the **training zone.** Using the following formula, the heartbeat range that should be maintained during exercise can be calculated.

1. Determine the estimated maximum heart rate by taking 220 minus the individual's age.
2. Multiply the difference by 60% and 80%.

The 2 results give the range of heart rates per minute that should be maintained while exercising. For example, assume that a student is age 16. Subtract 16 from 220, which equals 204. Multiply 204 by 60% and 80%. According to these results, a heart rate between 122 and 163 beats per minute should be maintained during exercise to reach the training state. Once the training heart rate has been determined, the exercise routine can be undertaken. At the conclusion of the workout, monitor the heart rate. If it is above the beats per minute allowed by the formula, reduce the intensity of the workout. However, if the heart rate is too low, increase the intensity of the aerobic exercise.

CREATING A POSITIVE FITNESS EXPERIENCE

How the fitness program is taught will increase the possibility of students being "turned on" to activity. Fitness activity in and of itself is neither good nor bad. Instead, how fitness activities are taught influences what youngsters feel about making fitness a part of their lifestyle. Consider the following strategies to make activity a positive learning experience.

Individualize Fitness Workloads

Students who are expected to participate in fitness activities and find themselves unable to perform exercises are not likely to develop a positive attitude toward physical activity. Students should be allowed to determine personal workloads and capabilities. Use time (instead of repetitions and distance) as the workload variable and ask youngsters to do the best they can within the time limit. People dislike and fear experiences of failure they perceive to be forced upon them from an external source. Voluntary long-term exercise is more probable when individuals are internally driven to do their best. Fitness experiences that give control to students offer better opportunity for development of positive attitudes toward activity.

Present a Variety of Physical Fitness Routines and Exercises

Teaching a variety of fitness opportunities decreases the monotony of doing the same routines week after week and increases the likelihood that students will experience fitness activities that are enjoyable. Most youngsters are willing to accept activities they dislike if they know there will be a chance to experience routines they enjoy in the near future. A year-long routine of "calisthenics and running a mile" forces students, regardless of ability and interest, to participate in the same routine whether they like it or not. When youngsters know a new and exciting routine is on the horizon their tolerance for routines they dislike will increase. Avoiding potential boredom by systematically changing fitness activities is a significant way to help students perceive fitness in a positive way.

Give Students Meaningful Feedback About Their Performance

Teacher feedback contributes to the way students view fitness activities. Immediate, accurate, and specific feedback regarding performance encourages continued participation. Provided in a positive manner, this feedback can stimulate youth to extend their participation habits outside the confines of the gymnasium. Reinforce everybody, not just those who perform at high levels. All youngsters need feedback and reinforcement even if they are incapable of performing at an elite level.

Teach Physical Skills and Fitness

Physical education programs teach skill development and fitness. Some states mandate fitness testing, which may make teachers worry that their students "will not pass." This concern can lead to the skill development portion of physical education being sacrificed in order to increase the emphasis on teaching fitness. Physical education programs develop 2 major objectives: fitness and skill development. Skills are the tools that most adults use to attain fitness. The majority of individuals maintain fitness through various skill-based activities such as tennis, badminton, swimming, golf, basketball, aerobics, bicycling, and the like. People have a much greater propensity to participate as adults if they feel competent in an activity. Skills and physical activity go hand in hand for an active lifestyle.

Be a Positive Role Model

Appearance, attitude, and actions speak loudly about teachers and their values regarding fitness. Teachers who display physical vitality, take pride in being active, participate in fitness activities with students, and are physically fit positively influence youngsters to maintain an active lifestyle. It is unreasonable to expect teachers to complete a fitness routine each period and 5 days a week. However, teachers must exercise with a class periodically to assure students they are willing to do what they ask others to do.

Consider the Attitudes of Students

Attitudes dictate whether youth choose to participate in activity. Teachers and parents sometimes take the approach of forcing fitness on students in order to "make them all fit." This can lead to resentment and insensitivity to the feelings of students. Training does not equate to lifetime fitness. When youngsters are trained without concern for their feelings, it is possible the result will be fit students who dislike physical activity. Once a negative attitude is developed, it is difficult to change. This does not mean that youngsters should avoid fitness activity. It means that fitness participation must be a positive success-based experience. Avoid funneling youngsters into 1 type of fitness activity. For example, running may be an inappropriate activity for obese youth, and lean, uncoordinated students may not enjoy contact activities. The fitness experience must be a challenge rather than a threat. A challenge is an experience that participants feel they can accomplish. In contrast, a threat appears to be an impossible undertaking; one where there is no use trying. Fitness goals should be designed to be challenging. A final note: whether activity is a challenge or a threat depends on the perceptions of the learner not the instructor. Listen to students express their concerns rather than telling them "Do it for your own good."

Start Easy and Progress Slowly

Fitness development is a journey not a destination. No teacher wants students to become fit in school and become inactive adults. A rule of thumb is to allow students to start at a level they can accomplish. This means offering the option of self-directed workloads within a specified time frame. Don't force students into heavy workloads too soon. It is impossible to start a fitness program at a level that is too easy. Start with success and gradually increase the workload to avoid the discouragement of failure and excessive muscle soreness. When students successfully accomplish activities, they learn a system of self-talk that expresses exercise behavior in a positive light. This avoids the common practice of self-criticism when students fail to live up to their own or others' standards.

Encourage Lifetime Activity

Teachers want students to exercise throughout adulthood. Certain activities may be more likely to stimulate exercise outside of school. Some evidence (Glasser, 1976) shows that if the following activity conditions are met, exercise will become positively addicting and a necessary part of one's life. These steps imply that many individual activities like walking, jogging, hiking, biking, and the like are activities that students might regularly use for fitness during adulthood.

1. The activity must be noncompetitive; the student chooses and wants to do it.
2. It must not require a great deal of mental effort.
3. The activity can be done alone, without a partner or teammates.
4. Students must believe in the value of the exercise for improving health and general welfare.
5. Participants must believe that the activity will become easier and more meaningful if they persist. To become addicting, the activity must be done for at least 6 months.
6. The activity should be accomplished in such a manner that the participant is not self-critical.

EXERCISES FOR DEVELOPING PHYSICAL FITNESS

Exercises discussed in this section are divided into 4 groups. The first group consists of warm-up and flexibility activities. These groups of exercises primarily develop muscular strength and endurance in the upper body, midsection, and lower body. When exercise routines are planned, they should contain a balance of activities from all groups. The following instructional procedures (and exercises to avoid) should be considered carefully when developing exercise routines.

Instructional Procedures

Fitness instruction is exclusively dedicated to the presentation of a variety of fitness activities. The following are suggestions to aid in the successful implementation of the fitness module.

1. Fitness instruction should be preceded by a 2- to 3-minute warm-up period. The introductory activity is useful for this purpose because it allows youngsters the opportunity to "loosen up" and prepare for strenuous activity.

2. The fitness portion of the daily lesson, including warm-up, should not extend beyond 15 to 20 minutes. Some argue that more time is needed to develop adequate fitness. However, there is a limited amount of time for fitness and skill instruction. Since skill instruction is part of a balanced physical education program, compromise is necessary to assure that all phases of the program are covered.

3. Activities should be vigorous in nature, exercise all body parts, and cover the major components of fitness.

4. A variety of fitness routines comprising sequential exercises for total body development is a recommended alternative to a yearlong program of regimented calisthenics and running. Since different people like different forms of exercise, a diverse array of routines should replace the traditional approach of doing the same routine day in and day out.

5. The fitness routine should be conducted during the first part of the lesson. Relegating fitness to the end of the lesson does little to enhance the image of exercise. Further, by having the exercise phase of the lesson precede skill instruction, the concept of get-

ting fit to play sport, instead of playing sport to get fit is reinforced.

6. Teachers should assume an active role in fitness instruction. Students respond positively to role modeling. This does not imply doing all exercises with all classes; however, students must see an instructor's willingness to exercise.

7. When determining workloads for exercise, the available alternatives are time or repetitions. It is best to base the workload on time rather than on a specified number of repetitions so youngsters can adjust their workload within personal limits. Having students perform as many repetitions as they are capable of in a given amount of time will result in successful and positive feelings about activity.

8. Use audiotapes to time fitness activity segments so they are free to move throughout the area and offer individualized instruction. Participation and instruction should be enthusiastic and focus on positive outcomes. If the instructor does not enjoy physical fitness participation, such an attitude will be apparent to students.

9. Fitness activities should never be assigned as punishment. Such a practice teaches students that "push-ups and running are things you do when you misbehave." The opportunity to exercise should be a privilege as well as an enjoyable experience. Think of the money adults spend to exercise. Take a positive approach and offer students a chance to jog with a friend when they do something well. This not only allows them the opportunity to visit with the friend but to exercise on a positive note. Be an effective salesperson; sell the joy of activity and benefits of physical fitness to students.

10. When a new exercise is introduced, it should be demonstrated, broken into components, and its value explained. It should be practiced at a slower-than-normal pace and then speeded up. Emphasize proper form.

11. Proper form is important when performing exercises. For instance, in exercises requiring the arms to be held in front of the body or overhead, the abdominal wall needs to be contracted to maintain proper positioning of the pelvis. The feet should be pointed reasonably straight ahead, the chest should be up, and the head and shoulders in good postural alignment.

12. Exercises in this section are not adequate for developing cardiovascular endurance. Additional aero-bic activity is necessary to enhance this important fitness component. Furthermore, vary the aerobic activity. Too often, such activity consists of everybody running a lap. This practice is not only boring, but does little to meet the personal needs of all students. Exercise substitutes for running might be interval training, rope jumping, obstacle courses, grass drills, astronaut drills, brisk walking, rhythmic aerobic exercise, and parachute movements.

Avoid Harmful Practices and Exercises

The following points contraindicate certain exercise practices and should be considered when offering fitness instruction. For in-depth coverage of contraindicated exercises, see Lindsey and Corbin (1989) and Corbin and Lindsey (1994).

1. The following techniques (Macfarlane, 1993) should be avoided when performing abdominal exercises that lift the head and trunk off the floor:
   - Avoid placing the hands behind the head or high on the neck. This may cause hyperflexion and injury to the discs when the elbows swing forward to help pull the body up.
   - Keep the knees bent. Straight legs cause the hip flexor muscles to be used earlier and more forcefully, making it difficult to maintain proper pelvic tilt.
   - Don't hold the feet on the floor. Having another student secure the feet places more force on the lumbar vertebrae and may lead to lumbar hyperextension.
   - Don't lift the buttocks and lumbar region off the floor. This also causes the hip flexor muscles to contract vigorously.

2. Two types of stretching activity have been used to develop flexibility. **Ballistic stretching** (strong bouncing movements) formerly was the most common stretching used but has been discouraged for many years because it was thought to increase delayed-onset muscle soreness. The other approach to flexibility, **static stretching**, involves increasing the stretch to the point of discomfort, backing off slightly to where the position can be held comfortably, and maintaining the stretch for an extended time. Static stretching has been advocated because it was thought to reduce muscle soreness and prevent injury. However, a recent study (Smith et al., 1993), has disputed the muscle soreness and tissue damage

theory with findings that showed ballistic and static stretching both produced increases in muscle soreness. In fact, the static stretching actually induced significantly more soreness than did ballistic stretching. Until findings show otherwise, it is probably acceptable to use either type of stretching to improve flexibility.

3. If forward flexion is done from a sitting position in an effort to touch the toes, the bend should be from the hips, not from the waist, and should be done with 1 leg flexed. To conform with this concern, the new Fitnessgram sit-and-reach test item is now performed with 1 leg flexed to reduce stress on the lower back.

4. Straight-leg raises from a supine position should be avoided because they may strain the lower back. The problem can be somewhat alleviated by placing the hands under the small of the back, but it is probably best to avoid such exercises.

5. Deep knee bends (full squats) and the duck walk should be avoided. They may cause damage to the knee joints and have little developmental value. Much more beneficial is flexing the knee joint to 90 degrees and returning to a standing position.

6. When doing stretching exercises from a standing position, the knees should not be hyperextended. The knee joint should be relaxed rather than locked. It is often effective to have students do their stretching with bent knees; this will remind them not to hyperextend the joint. In all stretching activities, participants should be allowed to judge their range of motion. Expecting all students to be able to touch their toes is an unrealistic goal. If concerned about touching the toes from this position, do so from a sitting position with 1 leg flexed.

7. Activities that place stress on the neck should be avoided. Examples of activities in which caution should be used are the inverted bicycle, wrestler's bridge, and abdominal exercises with the hands behind the head.

8. Avoid the hurdler's stretch. This activity is done in the sitting position with 1 leg forward and the other leg bent and to the rear. Using this stretch places undue pressure on the knee joint of the bent leg. Substitute a stretch using a similar position with 1 leg straight forward and the other leg bent with the foot placed in the crotch area.

9. Avoid stretches that demand excessive back arching. For example, while lying in prone position, the student reaches back and grabs the ankles. By pulling and arching, the exerciser can hyperextend the lower back. This places stress on the discs and stretches the abdominal muscles (not needed by most people).

Flexibility and Warm-Up Exercises

The exercises in this section increase the range of motion at various joints. They also prepare the body for more strenuous activity that may follow. In the beginning, the stretching positions should be held for approximately 10 seconds. As flexibility increases, the stretches can be held for up to 30 seconds.

Lower Leg Stretches

Lower Leg Stretch. Stand facing a wall with the feet about shoulder-width apart. Place the palms of the hands on the wall at eye level. Walk away from the wall, keeping the body straight, until the stretch is felt in the lower portion of the calf. The feet should remain flat on the floor during the stretch.

Achilles Tendon Stretch. Stand facing a wall with the forearms on it. Place the forehead on the back of the hands. Back 2 to 3 feet away from the wall, bend, and move 1 leg closer to the wall. Flex the bent leg with the foot on the floor until the stretch is felt in the Achilles tendon area. The feet should remain flat on the floor as the leg closest to the wall is flexed. Repeat, flexing the other leg.

Balance Beam Stretch. Place 1 foot in front of the other, about 3 feet apart. The feet should be in line as though one were walking a balance beam. Bend the forward leg at the knee, lean forward, and keep the rear foot flat on the floor. Repeat with the opposite leg forward. The calf of the rear leg should be stretched.

Upper Leg Stretches

Bear Hug. Stand with 1 leg forward and the other to the rear. Bend the forward knee as much as possible while keeping the rear foot flat on the floor. Repeat the exercise with the other foot forward. Variation: Different muscles can be stretched by turning the hips slightly in either direction. To increase the stretching motion, look over the shoulder and toward the rear foot.

Leg Pick-Up.   Sit on the floor with the legs spread. Reach forward and grab the outside of the ankle with 1 hand and the outside of the knee with the other. Pick the leg up and pull the ankle toward the chin. The back of the upper leg should be stretched. Repeat the stretch, lifting the other leg.

Side Leg Stretch.   Lie on the floor on the left side. Reach down with the right hand and grab the ankle. Pull the ankle and upper leg toward the rear of the body. Pull the ankle as near to the buttocks as possible and hold, stretching the front of the thigh. Repeat with the other side of the body.

Hurdler's Stretch.   Sit on the floor with one leg forward and the other leg bent at the knee with the foot tucked into the crotch. Lean gradually forward, bending at the hips and tucking the head. Allow the forward leg to flex at the knee. This stretches the back of the thigh. Next, lean backward, away from the forward leg, to stretch the top of the thigh. Repeat, reversing leg positions.

Groin Stretch.   Sit on the floor with the legs spread as far apart and kept as straight as possible. Slowly lean forward from the hips and reach with the hands. Do not bend at the neck and shoulders, because that puts pressure on the lower back. Stretch and hold in 3 positions: left, right, and directly ahead.

Lower Back Stretches

Back Bender.   Stand with the feet about shoulder width apart. Bend the knees slightly and gradually bend the lower back starting at the hips. Relax the arms and neck and let the upper body hang. If more stretch is desired, gradually straighten the legs.

Ankle Hold.   From a standing position with the knees bent, reach down and hold both ankles with the hands. Gradually straighten the legs, applying stretch to the lower back.

Sitting Toe Touch.   Sit on the floor with the legs straight and together. Reach forward and grab the lower legs. Gradually walk the hands down the legs toward the ankles; continue to walk the hands down and touch the toes. Bend from the hips, not the upper back.

Feet Together Stretch.   Sit with the knees bent and the soles of the feet touching. Reach forward with the hands and grasp the ankles. Gently bend forward from the hips, applying stretch to the inside

FIGURE 16.4   Body twist

of the legs and lower back. To increase the stretching effect, place the elbows on or near the knees and press them toward the floor.

Cross-Legged Stretch.   Sit on the floor with the legs crossed and tucked toward the buttocks. Lean forward with the elbows in front of the knees. To stretch the sides of the lower back, lean forward to the left and then the right.

Body Twist.   Figure 16.4 shows the body twist. Sit on the floor with the right leg straight. Lift the left leg over the right leg and place it on the floor outside the right knee. Move the right elbow outside the upper left thigh and use it to maintain pressure on the leg. Lean back and support the upper body with the left hand. Rotate the upper body toward the left hand and arm. Reverse the position and stretch the other side of the body.

Table Stretch.   Stand facing a table, chair, or similar platform. Place 1 leg on the table while maintaining the weight on the other leg. Lean forward from the hips to apply stretch to the hamstrings and lower back. Repeat with the other leg on the table. Variation: Stand with the side of the body facing the table. Place 1 leg on the table and bend toward the table to stretch the inside of the leg. Repeat with the other side of the body facing the table.

Back Stretches

Back Roller Stretch.   Curl up by holding the lower legs with the arms. Tuck the head gently on the knees. Tip backward and then roll back and forth gently. The rolling action should be slow and should stretch the length of the back. Variation: Perform the same stretch but cross the legs and tuck them close to the buttocks.

Straight-Leg Roller.   In a sitting position, roll backward and allow the legs to move overhead. Support the hips with the hands to control the stretch. The legs can be straightened and moved to different positions to vary the intensity and location of the stretch.

Squat Stretch.   Begin in a standing position with the legs shoulder width apart and the feet pointed outward. Gradually move to a squatting position, keeping the feet flat on the floor if possible. If balance is a problem, the stretch can be done while leaning against a wall.

Side of the Body Stretches

Wall Stretch.   Stand with 1 side toward the wall. Lean toward the wall and support the body with the hand. Walk away until the feet are 2 to 3 feet from the wall. While supporting the weight in the leaning position, bend the body toward the wall, stretching the side. Reverse and stretch the other side.

Elbow Grab Stretch.   In a standing position with the feet spread, raise the hands above the head. Grab the elbows with the hands. Lean to the side and pull the elbow in that direction. Reverse and pull to the opposite side.

Standing Hip Bend.   Stand with 1 hand on the hip and the other arm overhead. Bend to the side with the hand resting on the hip. The arm overhead should point and move in the direction of the stretch with a slight bend at the elbow. Reverse and stretch the opposite side.

Sitting Side Stretch.   Sit on the floor with the legs spread as far apart as possible. Lift the arms overhead and reach toward 1 foot. Reverse and stretch in the opposite direction. Try to maintain an erect upper body.

Arm and Shoulder Girdle Stretches

Arm and Shoulder Stretch.   Standing, extend the arms and place the palms of the hands together. Move the arms upward and overhead. Lift the arms as high as possible over the head.

Elbow Puller.   Bend the right arm and place it behind the head. Reach to the right elbow with the left hand. Pull the elbow to the left to stretch the triceps and the top of the shoulders. Reverse the positions of the arms and repeat.

Elbow Pusher.   Place the right arm over the left shoulder. Push the right elbow toward the body with the left hand and hold. Repeat in the opposite direction.

Wishbone Stretch.   Move the arms behind the back and clasp hands. Keep the arms straight and raise the hands toward the ceiling to stretch the shoulder girdle. Variation: Stand near a wall (back toward the wall) and place the hands on it. Gently bend at the knees and lower the body while keeping the hands at the same level.

Exercises for Upper-Body Development

Push-Ups.   The basic push-up is done from the front leaning rest position. Only the hands and toes are on the floor, and the body is kept as straight as possible. The exercise is a 2-count movement as the body is lowered by bending only at the elbows and then returned to the starting position.

As the body is lowered, only the chest touches the floor before the return to starting position. The push-up should be done with controlled movement. The arms can be adjusted together or apart, depending on the desired muscles to be exercised. As the arms are moved closer together, greater demands are placed on the triceps. Spreading the arms beyond shoulder width increases the work load on the muscles across the chest (pectorals). Variation: If it is difficult to perform a full push-up, the half (knee) push-up is excellent. Movement is the same as the push-up, but the body is supported by the hands and knees.

Inclined Wall Push-Ups.   This exercise can be done with either the feet or the hands on the wall. The hands version is easier and should precede the push-up with feet on the wall. In the hands version, the hands are placed on the wall while the feet walk as far from the wall as possible. The farther the performer's feet move from the wall, the more inclined and difficult the push-up will be.

When the student is able to do the inclined push-up with the hands on the wall, the feet-on-the-wall version can be attempted. This exercise is similar to doing a push-up in the handstand position and demands a great deal of strength. As the hands are walked closer to the wall, the incline becomes less, and a greater demand is placed on the shoulder girdle muscles.

Reclining Partner Pull-Ups.   Students find a partner of similar strength. One partner assumes a supine position on the floor while the other stands in a straddle position at chest level. Partners use a wrist-lock grip with both hands. The standing partner stands erect while the partner in supine position attempts to do a reclining pull-up (Figure 16.5). The upward pull is done completely by the person in supine position bending at the elbows. The standing person's task is to remain rigid and erect.

It is helpful for the person in supine position to start this exercise with the feet against a wall. This will prevent the person from sliding and will keep the focus of the activity on upper-body development.

Rocking Chair.   The exerciser moves to prone position on the floor. With the arms out to the sides of the body, the back is arched in an attempt to raise the upper body off the floor. While the upper body is

elevated, different activities and arm positions can be attempted. For example, arm circling, waving, clapping hands, or placing the hands behind the head can add challenge to this upper-back and shoulder development activity. Variation: The lower body can be elevated instead of the upper. Various movements can then be done with the legs. In either exercise, a partner may be required to hold the half of the body not being moved.

Crab Walk.   This activity can be modified in several ways to develop trunk and upper-body strength. The crab position is an inverted walk on all fours. The stomach faces the ceiling with the weight supported on the hands and feet. Crab walking can be done in all directions and should be performed with the trunk as straight as possible. Variations: The crab kick can be executed from this position by alternating forward kicks of the left and right leg. The double crab kick is done by kicking both feet forward and then backward simultaneously.

Midsection Exercises

Reverse Curl.   Lie on back with the hands on the floor to the sides of the body. Curl the knees to the chest. The upper body remains on the floor. Try to lift the buttocks and lower back off the floor. To increase the challenge, do not return the feet to the floor after each repetition, lowering them to within 1 or 2 inches off the floor. This activity requires greater abdominal strength as there is no resting period (feet on floor).

Pelvis Tilter.   Lie on the back with feet flat on the floor, knees bent, arms out in wing position, and palms up. Flatten the lower back, bringing it closer to the floor by tensing the lower abdominals and lifting up on the pelvis. Hold for 8 to 12 counts. Tense slowly and release slowly.

Knee Touch Curl-Up.   Lie on the back, with feet flat and knees bent, and with hands flat on top of thighs. Leading with the chin, slide the hands forward until the fingers touch the kneecaps and gradually curl the head and shoulders until the shoulder blades are lifted off the floor. Hold for 8 counts and return to position. To avoid stress on the lower back, the performer should not curl up to the sitting position.

Curl-Up.   Lie on the back with feet flat, knees bent, and arms on the floor at the side of the body with

FIGURE 16.5   Reclining partner pull-ups

palms down. Lift the head and shoulders to a 45-degree angle and then back in a 2-count pattern. The hands should slide forward on the floor 3 to 4 inches. The curl-up can also be done as an 8-count exercise, moving up on 1 count, holding for 6 counts, and moving down on the last count.

Curl-Up with Twist.   Lie on the back with feet flat and knees bent. Arms are folded and placed across the chest with hands on shoulders. Do a partial curl-up and twist the chest to the left. Repeat, turning the chest to the right.

Leg Extension.   Sit on the floor with legs extended and hands on hips. With a quick, vigorous action, raise the knees and bring both heels as close to the seat as possible (Figure 16.6). The movement is a drag with the toes touching lightly. Return to position.

Abdominal Cruncher.   Lie in supine position with feet flat, knees bent, and palms of hands cupped over the ears (not behind the head). An alternate position is to fold the arms across the chest and place the

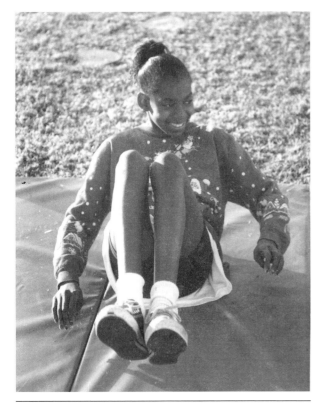

FIGURE 16.6   Leg extension

hands on the shoulders. Tuck the chin and curl upward until the shoulder blades leave the floor. Return to the floor with a slow uncurling.

Lower Body Exercises

Squat Jumps.   Begin in squatting position with 1 foot slightly ahead of the other. Assume part of the weight with the hands in front of the body. Jump as high as possible and return to the squatting position. Taking some of the body weight with the hands is important to avoid stressing the knee joints.

Treadmill.   Begin on all fours with 1 foot forward and 1 behind. Rapidly alternate foot positions while taking the weight of the body on the arms. The movement of the feet can be varied by moving both feet forward and back simultaneously or by moving the feet apart and together.

Jumping Jacks.   Begin in standing position with the arms at the sides and feet together. Simultaneously lift the arms overhead and spread the legs on the first count. On the second count, return arms and legs to the starting position. Variations: Feet and arm movements can be varied. The arms can be moved in front of the body, behind the body, and in different patterns. The legs can be split forward and backward, crossed in front of each other, and swung to the front of the body.

Running in Place.   Running in place is most beneficial when the upper leg is lifted parallel to the floor. The thighs can touch the hands held slightly above the parallel line to encourage the high lift.

Side Leg Flex.   Lie on your side on the floor. Rest the head in the right hand and place the left hand along the side of the body. On the first count, lift the left leg and arm and point them toward the ceiling. Return to the starting position on the second count. Rotate to the other side of the body after performing the desired number of repetitions. Variation: The double side leg flex is an exercise that demands more effort. Both legs are lifted simultaneously as far off the floor as possible.

Front Leg Kick.   From standing position, alternately kick each leg forward and as high as possible. This exercise should be done rhythmically so that all movement occurs on the toes. When the leg is kicked upward, the arm on the same side should be moved forward in an attempt to touch the toe of the lifted leg.

ACTIVITIES AND ROUTINES FOR DEVELOPING FITNESS

The following are methods of organizing exercises and aerobic activities to develop total body fitness. All of the routines should enhance muscular strength and endurance, as well as cardiovascular endurance.

Teacher and Student Leader Exercise Routines

During the first part of the school year, teachers should lead and teach all exercises to ensure that they are learned correctly. It is also important that teachers stay involved in fitness activities throughout the year to demonstrate their willingness to do the activities that they are asking students to perform. In some cases, teachers ask students to exercise and maintain fitness while they choose not to do either. Pushing others to be fit is difficult if the teacher does not make a similar personal commitment.

When a wide repertoire of exercises has been learned, students can begin to lead the exercise routines. Leading not only means starting and stopping the exercises but includes designing well-balanced routines that offer total body development. Students can be guided in the desirable number of repetitions and how to count exercises as they are being performed. In any case, students should not be forced to lead the exercises; leading should be a personal choice.

More than 1 student leader can be used at a time. For example, if 4 leaders are selected, they can be thinking of the exercises to choose when it is their turn. Leaders can be placed on 4 sides of the class, with the class rotating one-quarter turn to face a new leader after each exercise. If a leader cannot think of an appropriate exercise, the class can be asked to volunteer one. In any case, emphasis should be placed on learning to weave together a set of exercises that offers total body development. Continuous movement activity should also be added to the exercise routines to assure cardiovascular endurance development.

Squad Leader Exercises

Squad leader exercises offer students the opportunity to develop fitness routines without teacher intervention. Squad leaders take their squad to a designated area and put the squad through a fitness routine. It is helpful if a blank exercise card is given to each squad leader a few days before the student will lead. The leader can develop a routine and write down the exercises and repetitions or duration of each.

Squad leaders can also assign members of the group to lead or to offer certain activities. A number of exercises can be specified to develop a particular area of the body. For example, ask leaders to develop a routine that has 2 exercises for the arm-shoulder girdle area, 2 for the abdominal region, 1 for the legs, 3 for flexibility, and 2 minutes of continuous movement. The responsibility for planning a fitness routine that is balanced and developmental should shift gradually from the teacher to the students.

Exercises to Music

Without question, music increases the motivational level of students during exercise. While many commercial exercise-to-music records are available, they all suffer from 1 major problem. They seldom meet the specific work-load requirements of different groups of students, and they cannot provide the necessary systematic overload. Teachers therefore need to develop their own homemade exercise-to-music tapes that can be tailored to meet the needs of a specific class or grade.

Homemade exercise tapes can be developed using a record player and a tape recorder. Music that is currently popular can be combined with exercises that students have already learned. Avoid music that might affront some members of the community. Either the teacher or a group of students can make the tapes. When students do the taping, they have control over the selection, sequence, and number of exercises and repetitions. The routines can be adapted to particular needs and characteristics of the group. Procedures for starting and stopping exercises can be incorporated easily in the taping.

Continuous Movement Activities

Jogging

Jogging is running at a slow pace. It is faster than walking, but slower than sprinting. Jogging is an excellent conditioner for the cardiovascular system and can be done by virtually all students. It does not require specialized equipment or specialized skill.

Any 1 of 3 approaches can be used to develop a jogging program. The first is the jog-walk approach, which emphasizes the amount of time that one is involved in continuous movement. Students determine how far they can jog before they need to slow down and walk. Walking is continued until the exerciser is again ready to jog. The goal is to decrease the length and time of the walking episodes and to increase the jogging.

A second approach to increasing endurance through jogging is to set up definite and measured intervals. An example would be setting up cones to mark jogging intervals of 110 yards and walking intervals of 55 yards. As the fitness level increases, the length of the jogging interval is increased and the walking interval decreased.

Finally, the work load can be increased by increasing either the duration or the pace of the jogging. The goal is either to maintain a constant pace and to increase the distance run or to run the same distance at an increased pace. Increasing the speed is usually the less desirable alternative because the intensity of the exercise may discourage students.

Jogging is performed in an erect body position with a minimal amount of leaning. Excessive leaning is less efficient and demands a greater amount of energy. The elbows should be bent and the arms carried in a relaxed manner. Most joggers strike the ground with a flat foot. This allows the force of impact to be absorbed over a larger surface area, which seems to be more desirable. Some joggers land on the heel and then rotate to the toe. In either case, trying to change a jogger's foot action is often ineffective.

Jogging should be a noncompetitive activity. Students should be encouraged to look for self-improvement instead of comparing their performance with others. An enjoyable technique is to ask students to jog with a partner who has similar ability. They should be encouraged to talk and visit while they jog. Suggest that if they find it difficult to talk while jogging, they are probably running too fast.

Endurance and continuous activity should be rewarded. Teachers sometimes have a tendency to ask students to run a certain distance and then they reward those students who complete the distance first. This is discouraging to the majority of the joggers. Students should be permitted to run in any direction they desire until a certain amount of time has elapsed. This prevents the situation in which a few gifted runners finish first and have to sit and wait for the rest of the class to complete a given distance.

A general rule of thumb for beginning a jogging program is to ask students to walk and jog continuously for 5 minutes. Increase the amount of time 1 minute per week up to 15 minutes. Individuals can increase the total amount of time while they also try to reduce the amount of walking. Ideas for an instructional unit on jogging can be found in Chapter 20.

Walking

Walking is an activity that almost all people can do. The disadvantage of walking compared with jogging is that it must be done for a longer period of time to receive similar cardiovascular benefits. Walking has the advantages, however, of not requiring any special equipment and of having a low injury rate. Walking, probably more than any other activity, will be done by students when they reach adulthood.

Rope Jumping

Rope jumping is a demanding activity that requires little equipment. For some participants it can be a valuable approach to cardiovascular fitness. The energy demands of rope jumping are similar to jogging. Rope jumping can be performed for a specified amount of time or for a specified number of jumps.

A variety of activities can be done with a jump rope to help avoid the monotony and excessive fatigue of continuous jumping. The rope can be turned at fast or slow speeds while different foot steps are performed. If rope jumping is used for the fitness portion of the lesson, it should be alternated with stretching activities to give students an opportunity to recover from aerobic demands. See Chapter 20 for ideas on developing a unit of instruction on rope jumping.

Four Corners

A large rectangle is formed using 4 cones as markers. Students move continually around the perimeter of the rectangle. At each corner, a different movement is performed. Examples of activity alternatives that can be performed on the long sides of the rectangle are jogging, skipping, sliding, jumping, and hopping. On the short sides of the rectangle, movements on all fours (for example, bear walk, crab walk, seal crawl) can be performed. Another interesting variation is to use tumbling activities, or use tires and challenge students to go over, around, and through them. The need for continuous movement should be emphasized, and the rectangle should be large enough to provide a challenging work load for the cardiovascular system.

Interval Training

Interval training involves carefully controlling the work and rest intervals of the participant. Intervals of work (exercise) and rest can be measured in distance, repetitions, or time. Interval training is done by monitoring the heart rate. The student first needs to get the heart rate up to 120 to 140 beats per minute by warming up. Strenuous activity is then performed to push the heart rate into the 170 to 180 beats-per-minute range. At this point, the runner begins the rest interval (usually walking) until the heart rate returns to 120 to 140 beats per minute. Theoretically, the amount of time it takes for the heart rate to return to 120 to 140 beats per minute should not exceed 90 seconds. The major advantage of interval training is that endurance can be increased markedly in a short period of time.

Interval training can be used with various locomotor movements. For example, the following work and rest activities can be alternated. Intervals can be measured in either distance or time.

Work Activities	Rest Activities
Brisk walking	Slow walking
Jogging	Walking
Sprinting	Jogging
Rope jumping	Walking
Jumping in place	Walking

Rhythmic Aerobic Exercise

At present, this type of activity is popular throughout the United States. Aerobic dance is the basis for many variations of rhythmic exercise now implemented. These routines develop a high level of cardiorespiratory fitness, as well as strength and flexibility. Popular music is used to increase the activity enjoyment. Rhythmic aerobic exercise consists of a mixture of fundamental movements—dance steps, swinging movements, and stretching exercises. Routines are developed to music that has a definite and obvious beat.

The activities and routines should ease the burden of learning. If the movement patterns are too difficult, students become self-conscious and discouraged. Use the following points as guidelines when teaching new aerobic exercise routines.

1. Alternate the intensity of the activities. This allows interval training to be built into the routines. Stretching movements can be alternated with demanding locomotor movements.

2. Routines motivate more students when they appear not to be dance activities. The challenge is to develop demanding routines that will increase the endurance level of all participants. All students should feel comfortable performing the routines.

3. Follow-the-leader activities work well with students after they have developed a repertoire of movements. Each student can be responsible for leading one activity.

4. Energetic and positive teachers strongly influence the success of the presentations. Students need to see teachers enjoying fitness activities.

Basic Steps

The basic steps and movements can be used to develop a wide variety of routines. The majority are performed to 4 counts, although this can be varied, depending on the skill level of the students.

Running and Walking Steps

1. Directional runs can be done forward, backward, diagonally, sideways, or turning.
2. Rhythmic runs integrate a specific movement (knee lift, clap, jump, jump-turn) on the fourth beat.
3. Runs with stunts are performed while lifting the knees, kicking up the heels, or slapping the thighs or heels. Runs can also be done with the legs extended, such as the goose step.
4. Runs with the arms in various positions can include the arms on the head, straight up or down, or on the hips.

Movements on the Floor

1. Sit-ups or curl-ups can be used in many ways. For example, use 4 counts: (1) up to the knees, (2) touch the floor, (3) back to the knees, (4) return to the floor. A V-seat can be held for 2 counts and rested for 2 counts.
2. Side leg raises can be done with a straight leg on the side or with bent knees on the back extending the lower leg.
3. Alternate leg raises are performed in supine position with 1 leg raised to meet the opposite hand. Repeat using the opposite leg or both legs.
4. Push-ups can be done in 2- or 4-count movements. A 4 count would be: (1) halfway down, (2) touch chest to floor, (3) halfway up, (4) arms fully extended.
5. Crab kicks and treadmill can be performed to 4-count movements.

Standing Movements

1. *Lunge variations.* To perform a lunge, step forward onto the right foot while bending at the knees and extending arms into the air (counts 1 and 2). Return to starting position by bringing the right foot back and pulling arms into a jogging position (counts 3 and 4). Vary the exercise by changing the direction of the move or the depth and speed of the lunge.
2. *Side bends.* Begin with the feet apart. Reach overhead while bending to the side. This movement is usually done to four beats: (1) bend, (2) and, (3) hold, and (4) return.
3. *Reaches.* Alternate reaching upward with the right and left arms. Reaches can be done sideways also and are usually 2-count movements.
4. *Arm and shoulder circles.* Make arm circles with 1 or both arms. Vary the size and speed of the circles. Shoulder shrugs can be done in similar fashion.

Jumping Jacks Variations

1. *Arms alternately extended.* Jump with the arms alternately extended upward and pulled into the chest.
2. *Side jumping jacks.* Use regular arm action while the feet are kept together for jumping forward, backward, and sideways.
3. *Variations with feet.* Try forward stride alternating, forward and side stride alternating, kicks or knee lifts, crossing the feet, and a heel-toe step.

Bounce Steps

1. *Bounce and clap.* The step is similar to the slow-time jump rope step. Clap on every other bounce.
2. *Bounce, turn, and clap.* Make a quarter- or half-turn with each jump.
3. *Three bounces and clap.* Bounce 3 times and then clap and bounce on the fourth beat. Turns can be performed using the 4 counts.
4. *Bounce and rock side to side.* Transfer weight from side to side and forward and backward. Add clapping or arm swinging.
5. *Bounce with body twist.* Hold the arms at shoulder level and twist the lower body back and forth on each bounce.
6. *Bounce with floor patterns.* Bounce and make different floor patterns such as a box, diagonal, or triangle.
7. *Bounce with kick variations.* Perform different kick variations such as knee lift, kick, knee lift, and kick; double kicks, knee lift, and slap knees; kick and clap under the knees. Combine the kicks with 2- or 4-count turns.

Activities with Manipulative Equipment

1. *Jump ropes.* Using the jump rope, perform basic steps such as forward, backward, slow, and fast time. Jump on 1 foot, cross arms, and jump while jogging. Swing the rope from side to side with the handles in 1 hand and jump over it.
2. *Beanbags.* Toss and catch while performing various locomotor movements. Challenge students using different tosses.
3. *Hoops.* Rhythmically swing the hoop around different body parts. Perform different locomotor movements around and over hoops.
4. *Balls.* Bounce, toss, dribble, and add locomotor movements while performing tasks.

Sample Routine

1. March, moving arms in large circles.
2. Hold side lunge position and circle right arm. Reverse circling with left arm.
3. Bounce forward twice, slapping thighs; then bounce backward twice, thrusting arms in the air.
4. Bounce and clap turn. Perform a quarter-turn on every second bounce. Perform clockwise counterclockwise.
5. Grapevine step with clap on fourth beat. Repeat to the left.
6. Jumping jack variation extending arms up and out.
7. Bounce and twist.
8. Side jumping jacks, 2-count version.
9. Bounce, bounce, bounce, clap—4-count movement.
10. Rhythmic running with clap on fourth beat. While running, move into a circle formation.
11. Bounce and twist.
12. Side leg raises. Perform with each leg.
13. Rhythmic running with a clap on every fourth beat.

Resistance Training

Most coaches use strength development through resistance training. Physical education programs should instruct students in the use of weights and weight machines for proper development with an emphasis on safety. Using resistance training as an instructional unit is often difficult because of lack of equipment and facilities.

Resistance training routines should develop all major body parts. This prevents the excessive development of specific body parts, which can lead to postural or joint problems. Exercises should be performed through the full range of motion. If training is being done for a specific sport, it may be important to analyze the sport and develop exercises that replicate the range of motion it utilizes.

Resistance exercises should be performed at a speed similar to the movements performed in various physical activities. If a student is involved in an activity requiring speed, then the exercises should be performed at a similar speed. Similarly, if a student is training for activities demanding high levels of endurance, the exercises should be designed to increase this attribute. When the sport or activity demands strength, the training program can be geared to develop muscular strength. In each case, students should understand program differences and be able to develop a personal program.

Safety

Students must know and practice necessary safety precautions. The following points should be clear and reinforced regularly. It is wise to post safety rules as a further reminder and to avoid the consequences of possible lawsuits.

1. Perform warm-up exercises before intense lifting. These may be a set of calisthenics or a set of resistance exercises at a lower level.
2. Correct form is necessary to prevent injury as well as to develop strength. When a heavy weight is lifted from the floor, the lift should be done with bent knees, straight back, and head up.
3. Spotters are absolutely necessary when near-maximum weight is being lifted. Exercises such as the bench press, squats, and declined presses should always have 2 students present to spot.
4. Weights should be checked by the instructor before each period and by students each time they use them. Collars should be tightly fastened, cables checked, and bolts on machines periodically tightened.
5. Wide leather practice belts should be used when heavy lifting is performed. This prevents injury to the lower back and abdominal wall.
6. All exercises should be explained in class before implementation. This implies that proper form, points of safety, and necessary spotting be discussed before students participate.

Repetitions and Sets

There are many theories about the proper number of repetitions and sets that need to be performed to achieve optimum results. Repetitions are the number of times a participant performs an exercise to make a set. Each set, in turn, consists of a specified number of repetitions of the same exercise. Determining the proper number of repetitions or sets is difficult. Literally dozens of experts have researched this area without agreement. For physical education classes, a middle-of-the-road approach is probably best. Three sets of 10 repetitions should be performed for each exercise.

Strength or Endurance?

Muscular strength and endurance are developed using different methods. If maximum strength is desired, the exercise program should emphasize heavy resistance and fewer repetitions. If endurance is the desired outcome, the program should emphasize a high number of repetitions with less resistance. Some strength and endurance will be developed regardless of the type of program, but major gains will depend on the selected emphasis.

Frequency and Rest Intervals

Frequency is the number of workouts per week. The most common pattern is lifting every other day, 3 days per week. The day-long rest between workouts allows muscle tissues to recover and waste products to dissipate. Some participants alternate by exercising the upper body and the lower body on different days. This results in a 6-day program while retaining the day of rest between workouts.

The rest interval between repetitions and sets can be timed carefully to increase the intensity of the workout. By organizing the exercises in a circuit stressing different muscle groups, the amount of time needed for a total workout can be reduced. In other words, less recovery time is needed between sets if the next exercise places demands on a different group of muscles.

Planning a Unit

Chapter 20 contains several ideas and activities for a unit on resistance training that can be modified or augmented to meet the needs of the instructor, the students, and the physical education program.

Circuit Training

Exercise stations are organized into a circuit for the sake of fitness development. Each of the stations contributes, in part, to the total fitness of the participant. The components of fitness—flexibility, muscular strength and endurance, and cardiovascular endurance—are represented in the circuit.

Developing a Circuit

1. If the circuit is to be used as a group activity, all class members must be capable of performing each of the exercises.
2. Organize the stations so different muscle groups or fitness components are exercised. In other words, consecutive stations should not place demands on the same area of the body.
3. Students should know how to perform all of the activities correctly. Proper form is important. Instruction can be done verbally, or descriptive posters can be placed at each station.
4. Distribute students evenly among the stations at the beginning of the exercise bout. A rotation plan ensures that students move to the correct station.
5. Measure dosage in time or repetitions. Students can move on their own to the next station if they have completed the required number of repetitions. If a time criterion is used, the class moves as a whole when students have exercised for a specified amount of time.
6. To increase the demands on the cardiovascular system, one or two of the stations can include rope jumping or running in place. Another alternative is to have students run around the perimeter of the entire circuit a certain number of times before moving to the next station.
7. The circuit should contain no fewer than 10 stations. The result of participation in the circuit is a total body workout.

Timing and Dosage

Work load at each station should be based on time and each student asked to do their best within that time. Signals to start exercising, stop exercising, and to rotate to the next stations are given. This allows accurate timing of intervals. A reasonable expectation for beginning circuit training is 40 seconds per station. The amount of rest between stations can also be monitored to increase or decrease the work load. An effective way of timing the circuit is to use a tape

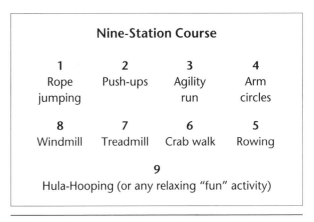

FIGURE 16.7 Circuit-training stations

recording of popular music that students enjoy, with signals to stop and start activities interspersed at proper intervals.

Figure 16.7 is an example of a circuit that might be developed for middle school students.

Astronaut Drills

Astronaut drills are continuous movement activities that combine exercises with walking and jogging. Students move randomly throughout the area or follow each other in a circle formation. The drills begin with brisk walking. On signal, the teacher or selected students lead the class in exercises or stunt activities. If a movement is not developed immediately, the class runs or walks in place. Combinations of the following activities can be arranged to develop a demanding routine:

1. Various locomotor movements such as hopping, running, jumping, leaping, skipping, and running on the toes.
2. Moving throughout the area on all fours in the crab position, and using various animal walks such as the seal walk, dog walk, and rabbit walk.
3. Performing exercises, such as arm circles, body twists, and trunk and upper-body stretches, while moving around the area.
4. Performing stationary exercises, such as push-ups, sit-ups, and jumping jacks, to stress development of the upper body and abdominal wall.

Students move throughout the area and perform as many exercises as possible. They can also develop individual routines that control the amounts of time allotted for movement activity and stationary activity. The following is an example of an astronaut drill that might be implemented. The duration of the movements is timed, and students are encouraged to do the best they can within the specified time.

1. Walk throughout the area.
2. Run and leap.
3. Stop, perform push-ups.
4. Walk and do arm circles.
5. Crab-walk.
6. Stop, find a friend, and perform partner resistance exercises.
7. Hop for a period of time on each foot.
8. Walk on all fours.
9. Run, with the knees lifted as high as possible.
10. Stop, perform treadmill.
11. Repeat the above steps.

Continuity Exercises

Continuity exercises can be done in squad formation or scatter formation. Since each student has a jump rope, students must have plenty of room to avoid hitting each other. Performers alternate between rope jumping and exercises. Rope jumping is done for timed episodes with music to help maintain the rhythm. At the signal to stop rope jumping, students quickly drop the rope and move into position for the exercise. Selected exercises should be performed in a down position with a leader who says "Ready" and the students respond "One-two," while performing the exercise. For each repetition, students wait until the command "Ready" is given. Students are allowed to monitor their own speed and intensity. The following is an example of a routine:

First signal. Begin rope jumping.

Second signal. Stop jumping, drop ropes, and move to the push-up position. On each command of "Ready," do 1 push-up.

Third signal. Resume rope jumping.

Fourth signal. Drop ropes and move into supine position on the floor with the arms overhead, preparatory to doing the rowing exercise. On the command "Ready," perform the exercise.

Fifth signal. Resume rope jumping.

Sixth signal. Drop the ropes, and move into crab position. Prepare to do the double crab kick. On the signal "Ready," both feet are extended forward and back.

Seventh signal. Resume rope jumping.

Eighth signal. Move into position for the side leg flex exercise. On the command "Ready," lift the upper leg and return it to starting position.

Ninth signal. Resume rope jumping.

Tenth signal. Move into position for the reclining partner pull-up. On signal, pull the body up on count 1, and return to the floor on count 2. Switch positions with partner after the proper number of repetitions has been performed.

The number of repetitions and the duration of the rope-jumping episodes should be determined by the fitness levels of the students. More exercises can be added to the routine. Instructors can use a tape recorder to signal the start and finish of the rope-jumping episodes. Continuity exercises are an example of interval training. The rope jumping stresses the cardiovascular system, while the exercises develop strength and allow the performer to recover.

Grass Drills with Partner Resistance Exercises

Grass drills require performers to move alternately from a rapid running-in-place position to a down position on the grass or floor. The activities are strenuous and are performed in quick succession at top speed. Work load progression is developed by increasing the duration of the bouts. Since grass drills are quite demanding, they are alternated with partner resistance exercises. This type of interval training allows participants to rest the cardiovascular system while developing strength in the partner resistance exercises.

Grass Drills

Basic grass drills involve moving rapidly from 1 of 3 basic positions to another on the commands "Go," "Front," and "Back." "Go" tells students to run in place at a rapid pace on the toes, raising the knees, and pumping the arms. "Front" signals students to drop quickly to the floor in prone position with the hands in push-up position. The head should point toward the center of the circle or the front of the room. When "Back" is stated, students move into a supine position with the arms alongside the body and palms down. The head-to-leg position is opposite that of the "Front" position. Grass drills can be done in 2 ways:

1. *Continuous motion.* When "Front" or "Back" commands are given, the student moves to the corresponding position and immediately returns to the "Go" phase without the command being issued.
2. *Interrupted motion.* The performer stays in position until the "Go" command is given. This allows a number of variations to be built into the drills. For example, push-ups, sit-ups, crab-kicks, and various movements on all fours can be executed prior to issuing the "Go" command.

Partner Resistance Exercises

Partner resistance exercises are enjoyable for students because they offer variable work loads and a chance to work with a partner. Partners must be matched in size and strength so they can challenge each other. The exercises should be performed throughout the full range of motion at each joint and take 8 to 12 seconds each to complete. The partner providing the resistance gives the "Begin" command and counts the duration of the exercise. Three sets of each exercise are done by each student as they alternate the exercise and resistance roles.

The following are examples of exercises that can be performed. Challenge students to invent their own partner resistance exercises and to develop a set of exercises that strengthens all body parts.

Arm Curl-Ups.   The exerciser keeps the upper arms against the sides of the body, bends the elbows, and turns palms up. The partner puts fists in the exerciser's palms. The exerciser then attempts to curl the forearms upward to the shoulders. To develop the opposite set of muscles, push down in the opposite direction, starting with palms at shoulder level.

Forearm Flex.   The exerciser places the hands, palms down, on the partner's shoulders. The exerciser attempts to push the partner into the floor. The partner may slowly lower the body to allow the exerciser to move through the full range of motion. Try the exercise with the palms up.

Fist Pull-Apart.   The exerciser places the fists together in front of the body at shoulder level. The exerciser attempts to pull the hands apart while partner forces them together with pressure on the elbows. Reverse this exercise and begin with the fists apart. Partner tries to push them together by grasping the wrists.

Butterfly.   The exerciser holds the arms straight, forming a right angle with the side of the body (Figure 16.8). The partner attempts to hold the arms down, while the exerciser lifts with straight arms to the sides. Try the activity with the arms above the head; move them down to the sides against partner's effort to hold them up.

Camelback.   The exerciser is on all fours with the head up. The partner sits or pushes on the exerciser's back while the exerciser attempts to hump the back like a camel.

Back Builder.   The exerciser spreads the legs and bends forward at the waist with the head up. The

FIGURE 16.8   Butterfly

partner faces the exerciser and clasps the hands together behind the exerciser's neck. The exerciser then attempts to stand upright while the partner pulls downward.

Scissors.   The exerciser lies on one side while partner straddles him or her and holds the upper leg down. The exerciser attempts to raise the top leg. The exercise is reversed and performed with the other leg.

Bear Trap.   Perform as in the scissors, but spread the legs first and attempt to move them together while partner holds them apart.

Knee Bender.   The exerciser lies in prone position with legs straight, arms ahead on the floor. The partner places the hands on the back of exerciser's ankle. The exerciser attempts to flex the knee while the partner applies pressure. Reverse legs. Try this exercise in the opposite direction with the knee joint at a 90-degree angle.

Resistance Push-Up.   The exerciser is in push-up position with arms bent so that the body is halfway up from the floor. The partner straddles or stands alongside the exerciser's head and puts pressure on the top of the shoulders by pushing down. The partner must judge the amount of pressure to apply in order to prevent the exerciser from collapsing.

Isometric Exercises

Isometric exercises are done without movement. The primary purpose of isometrics is to develop strength. The amount of time needed to exercise the major muscle groups in this way is minimal. A complete isometric exercise can usually be done in 5 minutes or less. These exercises do not require equipment, do not cause a high level of fatigue, and can be performed easily in a small space or office.

The disadvantage of isometric exercise is that it appears to raise the blood pressure of the individual. This may be a problem for someone who has heart disease. Other disadvantages are that isometric exercise does not benefit cardiovascular endurance and builds strength only at the joint angle at which the exercise is performed. Finally, many individuals receive little feedback from their isometric performance in terms of perspiration, increased muscle size, or healthy fatigue. They therefore see little point in continuing the activity.

To achieve results, the contractions must be maximal in nature. They should be held for 8 to 12 seconds and performed at various joint angles to develop strength throughout the total range of motion. An isometric routine is performed a minimum of 3 days a week and should contain 10 to 15 exercises. The following is a sample routine that might be used to develop overall body strength. All of the exercises should be held at maximum contraction for 8 to 12 seconds.

Handhold.   The exerciser makes a fist of 1 hand and holds it with the other hand. The hand holding the fist attempts to squeeze the fist as hard as possible.

Pull and Push Hands.   The exerciser locks both hands together and attempts to pull them apart. To push, the palms are placed together and pressure is applied.

Neck Developer.   To develop muscles in the back of the neck, the hands are clasped and placed behind the head. The head attempts to move backward while the hands pull forward. For the front of the neck, place the palms on the forehead and push backward while the head pushes forward. This exercise can be modified by placing a hand on the side of the head and applying force.

Arm Curl.   Hold the forearm at waist level in front of the body. Place the palm of the other hand into the hand of the flexed arm. Attempt to curl the flexed arm upward while applying downward pressure with the other hand. Switch hand positions.

Knee Hold.   Sitting on the floor, spread the knees approximately 12 inches apart. Put the hands on the inside of the knees and apply outward pressure, while simultaneously applying inward pressure with the knees. Switch the hand position to the outside of the knees and reverse the force application.

Knee Lift.   Sit on the floor with 1 leg extended and the other flexed. Place the palms of the hands on top of the flexed knee. Lift the knee upward while applying downward pressure to the knee. Switch to the other knee.

Body Tightener.   In a standing position, contract and hold the following muscle groups: shoulders forward, shoulders back, shoulders upward, abdominals toward the spine, lower back muscles, lower leg muscles by standing on tiptoe, lift toes as high as possible, and turn the upper body as far as possible and hold, then reverse the direction of body twist.

Ankle Hold. Sitting on the floor, cross the legs at the ankles. Lift the lower leg while applying downward pressure with the leg on top. Reverse the positions.

Leg Squeeze. Sit on the floor with the knees bent and near the chest. Reach around the legs with both arms and clasp hands. Attempt to pull the lower legs toward the seat while applying outward pressure with the legs.

Many isometric exercises can be developed with a partner or by using jump ropes or cut inner tubes to make large rubber bands. The partner resistance exercises described earlier can be performed as isometric exercises.

Obstacle Courses

Obstacle courses, or parcourses, are popular throughout the country. Different stations are developed and the participants move from station to station as they cover the course. The type of movement done between stations can also place demands on the participants' body systems. Courses can be run for time, or repetitions can be increased to ensure balanced fitness development. Courses should be developed to exercise all parts of the body. A variety of activities, such as stretching, vaulting, agility runs, climbing, hanging and chinning, and crawling, can be included to place demands on all aspects of fitness. Figure 16.9 represents an indoor obstacle course that might be constructed for students.

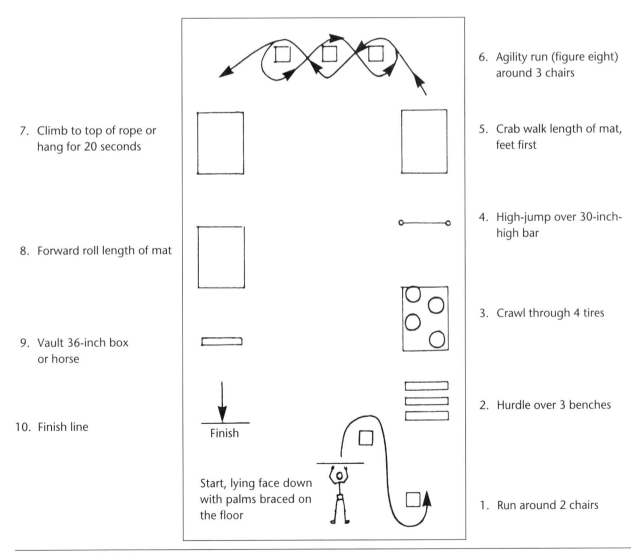

7. Climb to top of rope or hang for 20 seconds

8. Forward roll length of mat

9. Vault 36-inch box or horse

10. Finish line

6. Agility run (figure eight) around 3 chairs

5. Crab walk length of mat, feet first

4. High-jump over 30-inch-high bar

3. Crawl through 4 tires

2. Hurdle over 3 benches

1. Run around 2 chairs

Finish

Start, lying face down with palms braced on the floor

FIGURE 16.9   Obstacle course

Parachute Exercises

The parachute can be used to develop fitness activities that are exciting and challenging. Through these activities, students work together to enhance their fitness level. They should be encouraged to develop personalized group activities. The following are examples of exercises that use the parachute.

Toe Toucher.   Sit with the feet extended under the parachute and hold the chute taut with a 2-hand grip, drawing it to the chin. Bend forward and touch the grip to the toes. Return the chute to the stretched position.

Curl-Up.   Extend the body under the parachute in curl-up position, so the chute comes up to the chin when held taut. Do curl-ups, returning each time to the stretched position. Encourage students to work together and snap the chute tight each time they recline.

Dorsal Lift.   In prone position, lie with the head toward the chute. Grasp the chute with the arms extended overhead. On signal, raise the chute off the floor while simultaneously raising the head and chest. Encourage students to lift the chute high enough so they can "see a friend" across the way.

Sitting Leg Lift.   In a sitting position with the legs under the chute, lift the legs on signal while holding the chute taut, and lift the chute off the floor. Hold the position for 6 to 10 seconds. Try to keep the legs straight. As a variation, start in a supine position with the legs under the chute and do a V-seat.

Sitting Pulls.   Sit with the back to the parachute. Grasp the chute and raise it overhead. On signal, try to pull the chute down to the knees. Other variations are done facing the chute and raising it above the head, lowering it to eye level and to waist level. Emphasis should be placed on using the arms and shoulder girdle to apply force rather than leaning.

All-Fours Pulls.   Get on the floor in a crab-, bear-, or seal-walk position. Grasp the chute with 1 hand. On signal, pull and hold the contraction for 6 to 10 seconds. Repeat using the other hand and different positions.

Isometric Exercises.   A wide variety of isometric exercises can be done using the parachute. Various body parts can be exercised by applying pressure to the chute. The exercises should be held for 6 to 10 seconds. Encourage students to develop new isometric techniques.

Rhythmic Aerobic Activity.   The parachute is excellent for stimulating aerobic activity. For example, students can do various locomotor movements while holding onto the chute. A sample routine with the chute follows:

1. Skip clockwise.
2. Skip counterclockwise.
3. Jump to the center of the parachute.
4. Hop backward and tighten the chute.
5. Slowly lift the parachute overhead.
6. Slowly lower the parachute to toes.
7. Quickly lift the parachute overhead.
8. Quickly lower the parachute to toes.
9. Repeat steps 5 through 8.
10. Run clockwise with the chute held overhead.
11. Run backward with the chute held at waist level.
12. Make a dome.
13. Repeat steps 10 through 12.
14. Finish with a parachute lift and release the chute.

Running Activities and Drills

A number of running drills and activities can be used to improve running techniques, agility, and fitness levels, depending on how they are administered. Aerobic ability varies widely in classes, and many students may not be able to do much running because of obesity and other disabilities. Offer other options, or allow them to perform the drill while walking.

Form Running

This drill works well on a football field using the yard lines as markers. A squad of students lines up on the boundary line at the goal line, 10-yard line, 20-yard line, 30-yard line, and so forth. The teacher stands on the hash mark closest to the students, on about the 25-yard line. On signal, the first student in each line runs across the field on the respective yard line. The teacher continues to give a starting signal for each wave of students until all of the students are on the opposite boundary line. The teacher then moves to the opposite hash mark and starts the students running back across the field. Each time the students run across the field, they should be told to concentrate on 1 aspect of their running form. The following aspects can be emphasized:

1. Keep the head still—no lateral or turning movements. Eyes should be focused straight ahead. Keep the chin down.
2. Relax the hands. Place thumb on the first pad of the index finger. Put hands in the front pocket as they move backward.
3. Bend elbows approximately 90 degrees, and move the arms straight forward and back with no lateral movement across the chest. Arms gently brush the sides of the body.
4. Align feet straight ahead. Knees drive straight ahead rather than upward. High knee action can be used as another variation, although it is not necessary for good running form. The heel of the foot should come close to the buttocks.
5. Align the foot, knee, and hip. The body tilts forward about 5 degrees from the feet, not from the hips.
6. The length of the stride is usually shorter for longer runs (that is, a longer stride for sprinting and a shorter stride for distance running).

Give students only 1 aspect of running form to concentrate on during each trip across the field so that they can emphasize and overlearn each point. Beginning slowly and increasing the speed gradually works best. Start the drill at half-speed, then proceed to three-quarter speed, and finally, full speed.

This same drill format can also be used with other running activities.

1. *Backwards running.* Stay on the line. Roll the shoulders forward and keep them forward while running. Emphasize the arm movement forward and back. Pull that arm through with each step.

2. *Crossover step backward.* The teacher stands on the boundary line and the first wave of students moves 5 yards out on their respective yard lines facing the teacher. The teacher gives a left- or right-hand signal. The students start backward with a crossover step. When the teacher changes the direction signal, students rotate their hips and crossover step on the opposite side. Students must keep their eyes on the teacher and concentrate on rotating their hips and staying on the line.

3. *Crossover step forward.* As students run forward, they concentrate on stepping across the line with each step. It is important to start slowly and to increase the speed gradually.

4. *Carioca.* Students stand sideways on the line with their arms held out, parallel to the ground. On a signal, the students move sideways down the line by using a crossover step in front and a return step, a crossover step in back, and finally another step. This process is repeated for the length of the field. Students should make sure that they lead with both the right and left shoulder.

5. *Shuffle sideways.* Students stand sideways on the line in a ready position (feet shoulder width, knees bent, head up, arms flexed in front of the body). On signal, students shuffle down the line without a crossover step. Students should also lead with both the left and right sides. A variation is to have students spread out down the line and face the teacher, who is standing in front of the entire group. The teacher gives a left- or right-hand signal to start the group moving.

Form running drills can be done without lines if necessary. Use boundary cones to mark the beginning and end of each running section. Another variation is to place cones at one-third and two-thirds of the distance and ask students to vary their speed in each third. For example, students could jog the first third, sprint the second, and ease to three-quarter speed during the last third. Or change the type of running during each third. The following combinations might be used:

1. Jog, shuffle right, and shuffle left.
2. Carioca, shuffle, and sprint.
3. Backward run, crossover left, and crossover right.
4. Form run, crossover front, and form run.
5. Carioca left, carioca right, and sprint.

File Running

Divide the class into 2 or 3 groups according to cardiovascular fitness level: high, medium, and low. Each group lines up single file and begins to jog around a given distance, such as a quarter-mile track, a field, or a set of boundary cones. Students should keep a 2- to 3-yard distance between each person. The last person in line sprints past the file and becomes the leader. When the new leader is in place, the new last person begins to sprint past the file. This procedure continues for a given distance or a given number of minutes. The high fitness group will cover more distance in a given time.

Walk-Jog-Sprint

This is a continuous movement activity in which the teacher controls the speed of movement with a whistle signal. Three whistles mean sprint, 2 mean jog, and 1 means walk. The students start by walking around a given area (track, field, or boundary cone). The teacher then alternates the periods of jogging, sprinting, and walking for a number of minutes or for a given distance. It is important to progressively build up the time or distance.

Pace Work

Students need to practice running at an even pace for a given distance, such as a 6-, 8-, or 10-minute mile. Pacing can be practiced by running shorter segments of the distance at the correct speed. Figures 16.10 and 16.11 show the required time for covering certain distances in order to maintain correct pacing. It is easiest to use a marked track, but a workable track can be developed through placement of boundary cones. Using a rectangle is helpful for ease of measurement. Students are divided into groups and challenged to run distances at a given time. For example, the fast group might work on a 6-minute-mile pace: 110 yards in 22.5 seconds, 220 yards in 45 seconds, and 440 yards in 90 seconds. The medium group could work on an 8-minute pace, and the slow group could focus on a 10-minute-mile pace. It is interesting to have students calculate a world record pace for

Times for 40- and 100-Yard Dashes

To run 1 mi in:	You would have to run the 40-yard dash 44 times, with each dash run in:	Or run the 100-yard dash 17.6 times, with each dash run in:
3:48 min (world record time)	5.18 sec	12.95 sec
5:00 min	6.81 sec	17.04 sec
6:00 min	8.18 sec	20.45 sec
7:00 min	9.55 sec	23.87 sec
8:00 min	10.90 sec	27.25 sec
10:00 min	13.62 sec	34.08 sec

FIGURE 16.10   Pace chart—1

a given distance and then try to run a small segment of that distance at the record pace. For instance, have them run 50 yards at a 4-minute-mile pace, or 440 yards at a 2.5-hour-marathon pace.

Another strategy for teaching students about pace is to set up a square, 50 yards on a side. Place a cone at every corner and in the middle of each side. Put an equal number of students at each cone. Calculate the 25-yard time for various speeds (such as 6-, 8-, or 10-minute mile). Have students try to run at a given speed, and blow a whistle each time they should have completed a 25-yard run. The students should be at a cone each time the whistle sounds. They can tell if they are going too fast or too slow.

Interval	To run 1 mi (1760 yd) in:								
	4:00	5:00	6:00	7:00	8:00	9:00	10:00	11:00	12:00
³/₄ (1320 yd)	3:00	3:45	4:30	5:15	6:00	6:45	7:30	8:15	9:00
¹/₂ (880 yd)	2:00	2:30	3:00	3:30	4:00	4:30	5:00	5:30	6:00
¹/₄ (440 yd)	1:00	1:15	1:30	1:45	2:00	2:15	2:30	2:45	3:00
¹/₈ (220 yd)	:30	:37½	:45	:52½	1:00	1:07½	1:15	1:22½	1:30
¹/₁₆ (110 yd)	:15	:18¾	:22½	:26¼	:30	:33¾	:37½	:41¼	:45

FIGURE 16.11   Pace chart for a 1-mile run—2

Random Running

Random running is a simple and effective way to improve cardiovascular fitness (Pangrazi and Wilcox, 1979). The emphasis is on long, slow distance (LSD) running. Students are allowed to run randomly throughout the area at a pace that is comfortable for them. They are encouraged to find a partner and to talk while jogging.

Students who need to walk because of their subpar level of fitness can do so without experiencing the stigma of finishing last during a run. The distance each student runs is not charted. Effort is acknowledged rather than speed or distance-running ability. Emphasis is placed on being active, involved, and moving during the entire episode rather than on seeing how far one can run or jog.

Students can begin with a 10-minute random running episode 3 times per week. The duration of the run can be increased 1 minute per week until a maximum 20-minute episode is achieved. This allows the majority of students to increase their work load in a gradual and palatable manner.

Fartlek

Fartlek is a form of training that was developed in Sweden in the 1930s and 1940s. (The term *Fartlek* means "speed play.") The training is aerobic in nature and entails hard, but untimed, long-distance efforts over topographic challenges. The hilly terrain is run at varied tempos. Fartlek is usually done on soft surfaces. A typical workout for an athlete in training might be as follows:

1. Five to 10 minutes of easy jogging.
2. Steady, intense speed for 1 to 2 kilometers.
3. Five minutes of rapid walking.
4. Easy running broken by 50 to 60 meters of accelerated runs that cause moderate fatigue.
5. Easy running with 2 to 5 intermittent swift strides every 100 meters to moderate fatigue.
6. Full uphill effort for 150 to 200 meters.
7. One minute of fast-paced running on level ground.
8. Easy running for 5 to 10 meters.

This workout illustrates the variation involved in Fartlek. Students can be given a workout that might last 10 to 20 minutes and encompasses the many different tempos and geographic features described. The run challenges can be written on cards, and students select runs of varying difficulty (easy, moderate, difficult, strenuous).

Novel Routines for Middle School Students

A middle school program should include a variety of physical fitness routines in order for students to explore and experience many activities. Novel fitness routines can add variety to exercise. The following (Darst, Pangrazi, and Stillwell, 1995) are some examples of fitness routines that can be used with middle school students.

Fitness Scavenger Hunt

Students can work together in teams or small groups. The teams stay together and "hunt" for the exercise area of the gym or field space. The teams are given a laminated sheet or card that lists the area to find and the activities to perform at the designated area. The sheets could have 8 to 12 activities depending on how long the fitness segment of the lesson is going to last. Each group can be assigned a different starting point to ensure that students are spread across all areas and that a backup of students does not occur at one of the fitness areas. Examples of entries on the exercise sheet or card could be the following:

1. Run to each corner of the gym and perform 25 curl-ups. All team members should work together.
2. Run to the open set of bleachers and perform 25 step-ups on the first row. The count should be "up, up, down, down," with your steps.
3. Carioca to each of the other groups and tell them that they are doing a good job.
4. Jog to the tumbling mats and perform 2 sitting stretches and hold each for an 8 count.
5. Run and find the short jump ropes. Complete 25 jumps at a "fast time" pace.
6. Jog and touch 5 walls, 2 different red lines, and 3 different black lines. Stay together with your group.
7. Jog to the "jumping jacks" sign and perform 25 jumping jacks with at least 4 different variations in arm or foot patterns.

Students can complete all 7 activities and then return to their squad and wait for the next activity.

Fitness Cookie Jar Exchange

A variation of the fitness scavenger hunt is called the "fitness cookie jar." A variety of fitness activities are written on different index cards and then placed in a "cookie jar" (shoe box). The shoe box can then be placed at the center of the gym or at another convenient place for students to pick up and return the cards. Students can work alone or with a partner. Partners take turns selecting the fitness card from the box. The activities can be similar to the scavenger hunt activities or could also include ball handling skills with a specific area designated for the use of equipment. Examples could include the following:

1. Dribble the basketball down and back the length of the gym.
2. Crab walk the width of the gym.
3. Jog and shake hands with 8 different people. Tell them to have a good day.
4. Perform 2 lay-up shots at 3 different baskets.
5. Slide to the drinking fountain and get a drink.
6. Carioca around the basketball court 2 times.
7. Perform a "mirror drill" with a partner for 30 seconds.
8. Jog over and tell your teacher that physical education is a fun activity.
9. Perform 3 partner resistance exercises with a different partner.

Music can be programmed on a tape for 30-second intervals to structure the transitions for students. A 10-second interval without music could be used for getting a new card. Students could then perform as many repetitions as possible while the music is playing. This allows more individualization for students with varying fitness and skill abilities. Students should be challenged to do as many as possible and try to improve as the units continue.

Partner Racetrack Fitness

Students begin work with a partner at 1 of 5 or 6 stations in the gym or on a field outside. The stations are arranged in a circle or rectangle around the area. Each station has a sign with 5 or 6 exercises or stretches to perform. On the start signal, 1 partner begins the first exercise or stretch on the card while the other partner jogs around the perimeter of the stations. Upon returning, the partners switch roles and then move down the list of activities on the

cards. The teacher can also change the locomotor movement for the students going around the cones. For example, in addition to jogging, students could carioca, slide, run backwards, skip, or hurdle around the stations. The signs at the stations could include stretches, jumping jacks, crab kicks, treadmills, sit-ups, push-ups, body twists, and other variations. Continuous music could be used to motivate students.

The 12 Ways of Fitness

This is an add-on fitness game using 12 student leaders. It follows the same format as the song "The Twelve Days of Christmas." Students could be in groups of 12, or a large group could be used with the student leaders. Each student adds on the next number of exercises. Here is an example:

1 push-up (first student leader)
2 sit-ups (Second leader adds on)
3 coffee-grinders (third leader adds on)
4 crab kicks (fourth leader adds on)
5 golden rests (fifth leader adds on)
6 leaping leaps (sixth leader adds on)
7 jumping jacks (seventh leader adds on)
8 forward lunges (eighth leader adds on)
9 carioca steps (ninth leader adds on)
10 skipping skips (tenth leader adds on)
11 rooster hops (eleventh leader adds on)
12 running steps (last student leader adds on)

EXPECTED OUTCOMES

After reading this chapter, you should be able to

- Differentiate between skill-related and health-related physical fitness.
- Know how to effectively use newer fitness tests with health-related criterion standards.
- Describe why activity is more important than fitness in assuring health.
- Identify the various components of physical fitness and how they can be measured and evaluated.
- Be able to explain when and how to use the 3 methods of fitness testing

- Describe the impact that physical fitness can have upon the overall wellness of a person.

- Cite strategies and techniques to motivate students to develop and maintain physical fitness.

- Demonstrate the instructional procedures associated with established exercise routines included in this chapter.

- Develop new and different physical fitness routines that will accomplish fitness objectives and motivate students to continue to be active for a lifetime.

REFERENCES AND SUGGESTED READINGS

AAHPERD. 1987. *Youth Fitness Test Manual*. Reston, VA: AAHPERD.

American College of Sports Medicine (ACSM). 1991. *Guidelines for Exercise Testing and Prescription*. 4th ed. Philadelphia: Lea & Febiger.

American Heart Association. 1992. Medical/scientific statement on exercise: Benefits and recommendations for physical activity for all Americans. *Circulation* 85(1): 2726–2730.

Blair, S. N., Kohl, H. W., Paffenbarger, R. S., Clark, D. G., Cooper, K. H., and Gibbons, L. W. 1989. Physical fitness and all-cause mortality: A prospective study of healthy men and women. *Journal of the American Medical Association* 17: 2395–2401.

Bouchard, C. 1990. Discussion: Heredity, fitness and health. In C. Bouchard, R. J. Shepard, T. Stephens, J. R. Sutton, and B. D. McPherson (eds.). *Exercise, Fitness, and Health.* 147–153. Champaign, IL: Human Kinetics Publishers.

Bouchard, C., Dionne, F. T., Simoneau, J., and Boulay, M. 1992. Genetics of aerobic and anaerobic performances. *Exercise and Sport Sciences Reviews* 20: 27–58.

Centers for Disease Control and Prevention. 1994. Prevalence of overweight among adolescents—United States, 1988–1991. *Journal of the American Medical Association* 272: 1737.

Cooper Institute for Aerobics Research. 1992. *The Prudential Fitnessgram Test Administration Manual*. Dallas: Cooper Institute for Aerobics Research.

Corbin, C. B., and Lindsey, R. 1994. *Concepts of Physical Fitness with Laboratories*. 8th ed. Dubuque, IA: Wm. C. Brown.

Corbin, C. B., and Pangrazi, R. P. 1992. Are American children and youth fit? *Research Quarterly for Exercise and Sport* 63(2): 96–106.

Darst, P. W., Pangrazi, R. P., and Stillwell, B. 1995. Middle school physical education—Make it more exciting. *Journal of Physical Education, Recreation, and Dance* 66(8): 8–9.

Glasser, W. 1976. *Positive Addiction*. New York: Harper & Row.

Gortmaker, S. L., Dietz, W. H., Sobol, A. N., and Wehler, C. A. 1987. Increasing pediatric obesity in the United States. *American Journal of Diseases in Children*, 14: 535–540.

Haskell, W. L. 1995. Physical activity in the prevention and management of coronary heart disease. *Physical Activity and Fitness Research Digest* 2(1): 1–8.

Lindsey, R., and Corbin, C. 1989. Questionable exercises—Some safer alternatives. *Journal of Physical Education, Recreation, and Dance* 60(8): 26–32.

Lohman, T. G. 1992. *Advances in Body Composition*. Champaign, IL: Human Kinetics Publishers.

Macfarlane, P. A. 1993. Out with the sit-up, in with the curl-up. *Journal of Physical Education, Recreation, and Dance* 64(6): 62–66.

McGinnis, J. M. 1992. The public health burden of a sedentary lifestyle. *Medicine and Science in Sport and Exercise* 24: S196–S200.

Morrow, J. R., Jr., and Freedson, P. W. 1994. Relationship between habitual physical activity and aerobic fitness in adolescents. *Pediatric Exercise Science* 6(4): 315–329.

Pangrazi, R. P. 1994. Teaching fitness in physical education. In R. R. Pate, and Hohn, R.C. (eds). *Health and Fitness through Physical Education*, p. 75–80. Champaign, IL: Human Kinetics Publishers.

Pangrazi, R. P., and Corbin, C. B. 1990. Age as a factor relating to physical fitness test performance. *Research Quarterly for Exercise and Sport* 61(4): 410–414.

Pangrazi, R. P., and Corbin, C. B. 1994. *Teaching Strategies for Improving Youth Fitness*. 2nd ed. Reston, VA: AAHPERD.

Pangrazi, R. P., and Wilcox, R. 1979. RRP: An effective approach to cardiovascular fitness for children. *Arizona JOHPERD* 22(2): 15–16.

Pate, R. R. 1995. Recent statements and initiatives on physical activity and health. *Quest* 47(3): 304–310.

Pate, R. R. et al. 1995. Physical activity and public health. *Journal of the American Medical Association* 273(5): 402–407.

Pollock, M. L. 1988. Prescribing exercise for fitness and adherence. In Dishman, R. K. (ed.), *Exercise Adherence*. Champaign, IL: Human Kinetics Publishers.

Public Health Service. 1991. *Healthy People 2000*. Washington, D.C.: U.S. Government Printing Office.

Rarick, L. G., and Dobbins, D. A. 1975. Basic components in the motor performances of children six to nine years of age. *Medicine and Science in Sports* 7(2): 105–110.

Reiff, G. G., Dixon, W. R., Jacoby, D., Ye, X. Y., Spain, C. G., and Hunsicker, P. A. 1987. *The President's Council on Physical Fitness and Sports, 1985 National School Population Fitness Survey*. Washington, D.C.: U.S. Department of Health and Human Services.

Sallis, J. F., and Kevin Patrick. 1994. Physical activity guidelines for adolescents: Consensus statement. *Pediatric Exercise Science* 6(4): 302–314.

Slaughter, M. H., Lohman, T. G., Boileau, R. A., Horswill, C. A., Stillman, R. J., Van Loan, M. D., and Benben, D. A. 1988. Skinfold equations for estimation of body fatness in children and youth. *Human Biology* 60: 709–723.

Smith, L. L., Brunetz, M. H., Chenier, T. C., McCammon, M. R., Hourmard, J. A., Franklin, M. E., and Israel, R. G. 1993. The effects of static and ballistic stretching on delayed onset muscle soreness and creatine kinase. *Research Quarterly for Exercise and Sport* 64(1): 103–107.

Williams, D. P., Going, S. B., Lohman, T. G., Harsha, D. W., Webber, L. S., and Bereson, G. S. 1992. Body fatness and the risk of elevated blood pressure, total cholesterol and serum lipoprotein rations in children and youth. *American Journal of Public Health* 82: 358–363.

17 Wellness Instruction

PURPOSE

To develop an understanding of human wellness and components that can be enhanced within the physical education setting. To offer methodology for holding discussions to develop an understanding and insight into behavior necessary to maintain an optimum level of wellness.

KEY CONCEPTS

- Human wellness is a state of general health and personal functioning that helps determine the quality of life.
- Discussion sessions must include the opportunity for students to have the psychological freedom to explore alternatives.
- A difficult skill for students to learn is independent decision making based upon careful consideration of alternatives and consequences rather than peer pressure.
- Teachers can help students understand the requisites to wellness by offering a discussion session that is structured so students can feel comfortable.
- Focus setting, clarifying, acknowledging, and silence are behaviors teachers need to learn to use when conducting discussion sessions.
- To ensure total body development, exercises must follow principles of exercise.
- Stress affects performance and is not unique to any age group.
- Obesity is associated with various degenerative diseases and can be curtailed through a reduction of caloric consumption and increased activity.
- Substance abuse among students is common and serves to stimulate the onset of emotional problems and degenerative diseases.

The need for teaching students how to maintain personal wellness for a lifetime becomes apparent when one examines the skyrocketing costs of minimal health care. Health insurance policies cost 5 to 10% of an individual's gross income. A short stay in the hospital may incur a bill for thousands of dollars, yet in spite of runaway costs, Americans continue to pay and put little or no effort into maintaining a healthy lifestyle.

Human wellness is a state of health that allows an individual to participate fully in life. Having the energy and enthusiasm to undertake activities of all types after a full day's work is characteristic of people who are well. An individual who is well is not only free of sickness or other malady but is happy, vibrant, and able to solve personal problems.

Teaching students how to achieve a lasting state of wellness lends credibility to the physical education profession. For many years, physical educators were seen solely as teachers of physical skills who had little concern for the knowledge and comprehension involved in physical performance. The various personalities and unique needs of the student participants were often ignored by teachers who appeared to be concerned only about the product (that is, "Learn the skill or else!"). The age-old argument of product versus process can be moderated by teaching the process of developing physical wellness, for wellness is a process. There are no trophies or other extrinsic rewards for achieving it. Wellness is personal. When it is achieved, the individual is directly rewarded by an enhanced lifestyle. Teachers can no longer ignore the importance of teaching students the what, why, and how of maintaining a healthy profile. Maintaining wellness must be considered a primary objective of secondary school physical education.

Why teach wellness in the physical education setting? Teachers are often skeptical about teaching material other than physical skill activities, yet the ability to develop and maintain personal wellness will remain with an individual for a lifetime. This is one of the few long-lasting gifts teachers can offer to students. Achieving wellness is unique and personal. What is useful to one person may be superfluous to another. Teachers must therefore teach students how to search for wellness and then maintain it once found.

At present, the credibility of the physical education profession is strained. Teachers often offer students skills and activities that they will never use again. For example, students may spend 9 weeks each year from junior high through the sophomore year of high school involved in football. This is equivalent to 36 weeks of football or an entire school year. The possibility is strong that few of these individuals will play football after graduation from high school. Few people play football after age 25, yet 1 year of physical education was spent playing and learning a sport that becomes literally useless in maintaining a healthy lifestyle in adulthood. Small wonder that many adults believe that they learned little in physical education to help them after graduation. The point here is not to belittle football or to ask for its elimination; rather, it is to suggest that physical education programs have often shown an inadequate concern for teaching students the skills that are useful after they leave school.

Teaching students how to maintain a state of wellness makes activity purposeful. Students begin to understand why certain activities and games are selected in place of others. Selection of activities for a lifetime of physical involvement can only occur after students have been exposed to a wide range of instructional units. A systematic approach to curriculum development is critical in assuring that students know the many alternatives and pathways to personal fitness and health.

INTEGRATE WELLNESS INTO INSTRUCTION

Paramount to all instruction dealing with wellness is an emphasis on self-responsibility for maintaining a healthy lifestyle. Regardless of what students are taught, if an emphasis is not placed on teaching students how to make personal decisions, little will have been gained. Most students will do what is asked of them when they are in school. The critical point is teaching students the problem-solving skills that will enable them to make meaningful decisions throughout life, when teachers are no longer present.

At the secondary school level, teachers should take a multifaceted approach to developing units of instruction dealing with wellness. The first step is to ensure that students understand how the body functions. This involves understanding the anatomy of the body, the physiological functioning of the body during exercise, and the mechanical principles involved in movement. It is beyond the scope of this text to list all the information that students should digest and comprehend. An outline and an instructional unit in each of these areas will be offered. References are listed at the end of the chapter for instruction in greater depth.

Students may receive instruction about the systems of the body in health education classes. In most cases, however, material covered in those classes does not deal with exercise and the impact it has on the body. Learning how the body reacts and adapts to exercise is of utmost importance, and students probably will not receive this information anywhere else.

The second step in presenting units of instruction dealing with wellness is to delineate which concepts students need to understand. This provides direction for both teacher and students. The concepts should give students a general idea of what is important and what areas must be understood to achieve proper functioning. The concepts should help the instructor organize the material to be presented. Students should be given an outline that they can follow. The concepts, when taken as a whole, offer a framework to help students make personal decisions about health maintenance. This approach contrasts with giving students a set of objectives that must be learned and that leave little room for student input and inquiry.

The third step in organizing units of instruction in this area is to present mini-laboratory experiences that apply the concepts and bring them to life. These learning activities can be used to add substance to the instructional concepts. The laboratory experiences are simple, yet they illustrate clearly how the body functions in different settings. Many of these experiences can be done in 5 or 10 minutes by a whole class. They are excellent rainy-day activities, or students can do them as homework. Students should be encouraged to develop a notebook of activities and lab experiences that they can use for a lifetime.

The authors have discussed curriculum models in Chapter 3. Most models contain a unit of instruction on wellness and self-testing. This approach should be analyzed carefully and considered when developing a comprehensive physical education curriculum. It is strongly recommended that instruction be offered at each grade level in this important area. The instruction should be clearly devoted to developing wellness for a lifetime and should receive instructional emphasis on a par with other units in the physical education curriculum.

INSTRUCTIONAL STRATEGIES FOR TEACHING WELLNESS

Physical education enhances fitness and skill levels of students, allowing them opportunities for developing an active lifestyle. A program goal should be to help young people make responsible decisions about wellness and its impact on their lives. Throughout life, people are faced with many decisions that may have a positive or negative impact on their level of wellness. The ability to make responsible choices depends on a wide range of factors: understanding one's feelings and personal values, the ability to cope with stress and with problems in general, the impact of various factors on health, and practice in using decision-making skills.

DEVELOP AWARENESS AND DECISION-MAKING SKILLS

The focus should be on helping students to view themselves as total beings. Stability occurs when all parts fit together in a smooth and consistent fashion. When a problem occurs, the balance of physiology, thinking, and function is disrupted. Individuals must then use their knowledge, coping ability, and decision-making skills to restore the equilibrium associated with personal stability. Teachers can try to help students understand their feelings, values, and attitudes, and the impact that all of these have on coping and decision-making ability. Each of these areas will be discussed.

Self-Concept

Self-concept is defined as the total perception an individual has of self. Self-concept is enhanced when the individual has a strong, positive feeling of belonging and a sense of worth. These attitudes can be fostered by providing activities that focus on themes that help a person to

1. Recognize that there are many individuals, yet each of us is unique.
2. Feel loved and able to love.
3. Be able to recognize and cope with feelings and emotions.
4. Function in a group, yet also be comfortable alone.
5. Like to and be able to do many things.
6. Relate successfully to others.

A student who has a healthy self-image will be better able to make a decision in the presence of peer pressure. Individuals who feel positive about themselves are less influenced by peer pressure than those with poor self-concepts. Through the process of education, each student should be made to feel important and worthwhile. Youngsters will realize that they are not perfect and that change is desirable. The identification of personal strengths and weaknesses can offer direction for self-growth and for understanding personal limitations. When dealing with areas of self-concept and personal worth, students should be comfortable to express feelings. They should feel free to ask questions without fear of ridicule or embarrassment. Discussions should be positive and criticism constructive. As students develop more positive feelings about themselves, their ability to make responsible decisions will improve. They will be prepared to make decisions in everyone's interests, including their own.

Coping Skills

Coping is the ability to deal with problems successfully. Learning to cope with life's problems is dependent on and interrelated to knowledge of self, decision-making skills, and the ability to relate to others. Specific skills that deal with coping include the following:

1. Admit that a problem exists and face it. It is impossible to cope with a problem if the problem is not recognized.
2. Define the problem and who "owns" it. Individuals must identify what needs to be faced and decide if the problem is theirs or belongs to others.
3. List alternative solutions to the problem. A basic step in decision making, problem solving, and coping is to identify the alternatives in a given situation.
4. Predict consequences for oneself and others. After the alternatives are identified, weigh the potential consequences of each, and then rank them in order of preference.
5. Identify and consult sources of help. All sources should be considered. In order to do this, teachers should introduce students to some of the resources available and explain how to locate helpful sources.
6. Experiment with a solution and evaluate the results. If the decision did not produce satisfactory results, another alternative can often be tried. Evaluation of results also allows people to keep track of their ability to discover satisfying solutions.

Decision-Making Skills

Youngsters are faced with many situations that require decisions. Making decisions is something everyone does every day, often without thinking. Because it is a common process, it receives little attention until a person is faced with an important decision that has long-term consequences. Although the schools attempt to help students learn how to make personally satisfying decisions, a major portion of a teacher's time involves developing information or

supplying it to students. Obtaining information, although extremely important, is only one segment of the decision-making process. A question that should be asked is, "If you are going to provide information to others, what do you want them to do with that information?" Students should be given the opportunities to put information to use.

Decision making is defined as a process in which a person selects from 2 or more possible choices. A decision does not occur unless there is more than 1 course of action, alternative, or possibility to consider. If a choice exists, the process of deciding may then be used. Decision making enables the individual to reason through life situations, to solve problems, and, to some extent, to direct behavior.

Often there are no "right" answers or outcomes of the decision-making process. The decision is instead judged on the effective use of a process that results in satisfying consequences. This distinguishes decision making from problem solving. Problem solving usually identifies 1 best or correct solution for everyone involved.

When making decisions, it is important for students to consider each of the following steps:

1. Gather information. If meaningful choices are going to be made, gathering all the available information is important. Information should be gathered from as many sources as possible. Students generally consider information valid when they see that it comes from many different sources and they are allowed to view both sides of an issue. Teachers too often present students with information that supports only 1 point of view.

2. Consider the available choices. The next step is to consider all the available choices. This is an important step if students are to realize that they have many different possibilities from which to choose and that their choices will influence the direction of their lives. It does not make sense to consider possibilities that students have no chance of selecting. Many choices have been made for students in the school setting, and they sometimes come to believe that others will make all the decisions for them and that they, in turn, bear no responsibility for their successes or failures.

3. Analyze the consequences of the choices. When the various choices are delineated, students must consider their consequences. If the consequences are ignored, an unwise choice may be made that is detrimental to one's health. Making wise decisions about wellness demands that students be made aware of consequences. They should understand some of the reasons why people may choose to smoke or drink, even though the consequences are negative. The most important role of the teacher is helping students understand positive and negative consequences without moralizing or telling students how to think.

4. *Make a decision and implement it.* When all of the information has been gathered, students must make decisions and implement them in their lifestyles. The decisions will be personal to each student and need not be revealed to others.

Skillful decision makers have greater control over their lives because they can reduce the amount of uncertainty surrounding their choices and limit the degree to which chance or their peers determine their future.

Two individuals may face a similar decision, but because each person is different and places differing values on the outcomes, each decision will be unique. Learning decision-making skills increases the possibility that each person will achieve what he or she most values.

Decisions also have limits. Each decision is necessarily limited by what a person is capable of doing, by what a person is willing to do, and by the environment in which the decision is being made. Important to the development of these skills is the environment in which they are practiced. A nonjudgmental atmosphere is most productive. Since there is no "right" answer, the person making a decision should be free to select from any of the available choices and be willing to accept the probable consequences and results.

HOW TO LEAD DISCUSSION SESSIONS

The success of discussions depends on how effectively the teacher is able to establish and maintain the integrity and structure of the lesson and the students' psychological freedom. Integrity and structure mean that all students are dealing with the same issue in a thoughtful and responsible way. Psychological freedom means that individual students participate to the degree that is most comfortable for them, such as choosing to comment or to refrain, responding to directed questions or choosing to pass, agreeing or disagreeing with what has been said, or

deciding what data is needed and requesting that data. This demands certain teacher behavior to establish a meaningful environment. A brief description of necessary teaching behaviors follows.

Structuring

Structuring is used to create a climate that is conducive to open communication by all parties. This is accomplished by outlining expectations and role relationships for both teacher and student. **Structuring** includes any of the following:

1. Establish a climate at the beginning of the lesson by explaining what the student and teacher will be doing and how they will work together.
2. Maintain the established lesson structure by forbidding students to be pressured to respond or to be put down for their ideas.
3. Add to or modify the lesson structure established at the beginning of the lesson. For example, this may involve changing to small-group sessions rather than a total class discussion.

Focus Setting

The purpose of **focus setting** is to establish an explicit and common topic or issue for discussion. Because this teaching behavior is used in different circumstances, the behavior can be formulated by the following methods:

1. Present a topic, usually in the form of a question, to the group for discussion.
2. Use focus setting to restate the original question or to shift to a new discussion topic when students have finished discussing the original question.
3. Use focus setting to bring the discussion back to the topic when a student unknowingly shifts to a new topic.
4. Use focus setting to label a discussion question presented by a student as a new topic and to allow discussion of it.

Clarifying

Clarifying teaching behavior is used to invite a student to help the teacher better understand the substance or content of the student's comment. Whenever possible, the clarifying teaching behavior should give the student some indication of what it is that the teacher does not understand. In addition, the behavior should be formulated in a way that puts the burden on the teacher for not being able to understand, rather than implying that the student was unclear or inadequate in any way. Clarifying is used only when the teacher does not understand. The teacher does not assume the responsibility of clarifying for the students.

Acknowledging

Acknowledging teaching behavior is used to let a student who is talking to the teacher know that the teacher understands what has been said and that the student has made a contribution to the discussion. Unlike most other teaching behaviors, this one can be implemented through nonverbal as well as verbal means.

How an acknowledging teaching behavior is worded and when it is and is not used must be considered carefully. This behavior is intended to be a nonjudgmental way of saying, "I understand." To use acknowledging only when the teacher understands and agrees, but to do something else when the teacher understands and disagrees, is a serious misinterpretation of the purpose and function of this teaching behavior.

Teacher Silence

The purpose of **teacher silence** is to communicate to students through nonverbal means that they are responsible for initiating and perpetuating the discussion. Teacher silence is used only in response to student silence. It protects the students' rights and responsibility to make their own decisions about the topic being discussed. In one sense, this teaching behavior is a nonbehavior.

UNDERSTAND MAJOR SYSTEMS OF THE BODY

A basic understanding of how the body functions is important if students are to learn how to maintain a healthy organism. The 3 major systems discussed here are the skeletal, muscular, and cardiorespiratory system. A brief discussion of each is provided with concepts and suggested learning activities offered to enhance student understanding.

Skeletal System

The skeletal system is the framework of the body. The bones act as a system of levers and are linked together at various points called joints. The joints are held together by ligaments, which are tough and unable to stretch. In a joint injury when the bones are moved beyond the normal limits, it is the ligaments that are most often injured.

Joints that are freely movable are called synovial joints. Synovial fluid is secreted to lubricate the joint and reduce friction. A thin layer of cartilage also reduces friction at the ends of the bones. A disk, or meniscus, forms a pad between many of the weight-bearing joints and absorbs shock. When the cartilage is damaged, the joint becomes less able to move easily, and arthritis often occurs.

Muscular activity increases the stress placed on bones. The bones respond to this added stress by increasing in diameter, becoming more dense (and more resistant to breakage), and by reorganizing their internal structure, which offers more bone strength (Rarick, 1973). The bones act as a mineral reserve for the body and can become deformed as a result of dietary deficiency. The bones also can change shape due to regular stress. This may give athletes, whose skeletal systems are conditioned, a mechanical advantage in performing certain skills. The skeletal system is not a static system but changes and adapts in response to the demands placed on it.

The bones are connected to make 3 different types of levers, with the joint acting as the fulcrum (Figure 17.1). The muscles apply force to the joints, while the body weight or an external object provides the resistance. The levers are classified as first-, second-, or third-class levers. Examples of third-class lever actions are the movement of the biceps muscle to flex the forearm at the elbow joint, the sideways movement of the upper arm at the shoulder joint by the deltoid muscle, and the flexion of the lower leg at the knee joint by the hamstring muscles. A second-class lever occurs where the gastrocnemius muscle raises the weight of the body onto the toes. The forearm is an example of a first-class lever when it is being extended at the elbow joint (fulcrum) by the triceps muscle.

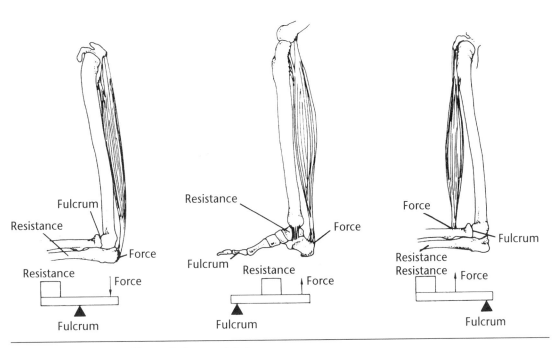

FIGURE 17.1 Types of levers in human joints

Basic Concepts

1. The skeletal system consists of 206 bones and determines the external appearance of the body. This network of bones is somewhat malleable and can be reshaped, made denser, and stronger.

2. Joints are where 2 or more bones are fastened together by ligaments to allow movement that is restricted by the range of motion. The range of motion at various joints can be increased by regularly performing flexibility exercises. The most flexible people have the greatest range of motion at a combination of joints.

3. Bones are held together by ligaments and muscle tissue. The stronger the muscles become, the stronger the ligaments and tendons become in response. This makes a stronger joint, which is more resistant to injury.

4. Attractive posture occurs when the bones are in good alignment. Alignment depends on the muscular system to hold the bones in correct position. Poor posture occurs when the muscles are weak, and increased stress is placed on the joints.

5. The bones meet at joints to establish levers. Movement occurs when muscles apply force (by contraction only) to the bones.

6. The attachment of the muscle to the bone determines the mechanical advantage that can be gained at the joint. Generally, those muscles that attach farther from the joint can generate more force. There is, however, a trade-off. When the attachment is farther from the joint, the amount of speed that can be generated is less, and vice versa.

7. The human body has 3 types of lever arrangements. These are classified by the fulcrum, force, and resistance. The majority of levers in the body are third-class levers in which the point of force (produced by the muscles) lies between the fulcrum (joint) and the point of resistance (the weight of the object to be moved).

Suggested Learning Activities

1. Identify and locate the bones of major significance in movement. (Approximately 167 bones are capable of moving.) Some that can be assigned are:
   a. Arm-shoulder girdle—radius, ulna, humerus, scapula, and clavicle
   b. Back-pelvis—spinal column, pelvis, coccyx
   c. Thigh-leg—femur, tibia, fibula, patella
   d. Chest—sternum, ribs

2. Identify the type of movement possible at selected joints. Use various terms to identify the movements (such as extension, flexion, adduc-

tion, abduction, pronation, supination, and plantar flexion).

3. Diagram and list the types of levers found in the body. Illustrate the force, fulcrum, and resistance points. Identify muscle attachments and the impact of such in terms of generating force or speed in movement.

4. Obtain animal bones and analyze the various parts of the bone. Identify the bone marrow, growth plates, epiphyses, ligaments, tendons, muscle origins and attachments, and cartilage.

5. Study outdated X-ray films of children to see the different rates of ossification. Note differences in bone shape and structure between individuals.

Muscular System

The muscular system (Figure 17.2) is complex. Muscles apply force to the bones to create movement and always create movement through contraction. When 1 set of muscles contracts, the other set relaxes. Muscles are always paired. The muscle (or group of muscles) that relaxes while another set contracts is called the antagonistic muscle. The muscles located on the anterior side of the body are flexors and reduce the angle of a joint while the body is standing. Muscles on the posterior side of the body produce extension and a return from flexion.

People are born with 2 types of muscle fiber. These are commonly referred to as slow-twitch and fast-twitch fibers. Slow-twitch fibers respond efficiently to aerobic activity, while fast-twitch fibers are suited to highly demanding anaerobic activity. This explains, in part, why people perform physical activities at varying levels. People are born with a set ratio of fast- and slow-twitch fibers. Those with a higher ratio of slow-twitch fibers are better able to perform in endurance activities; those with a greater percentage of fast-twitch fibers might excel in activities of high intensity and short duration.

Strength gains are made when muscles are overloaded, and overload occurs when people do more work than they performed previously. This means that more weight must be lifted on a regular basis if gains are to occur. Exercises should overload as many muscle groups as possible in order to ensure total body development. Both the flexors and extensors should receive equal amounts of overload exercise so a proper balance between the 2 muscle groups is maintained. Muscular strength appears to be an important factor in performing motor skills.

Muscular exercises should apply resistance through the full range of motion in order to maintain maximum flexibility. Strenuous exercise such as weight lifting should be done every other day so that the muscles have an opportunity to heal and regenerate. Maintaining muscular strength throughout life is important. If exercises are not done to maintain strength, atrophy will occur rapidly. It has been shown that the average American will gain 1 pound of additional weight per year after age 25. This can result in 30 pounds of excess weight by age 55. During the same period, the bone and muscle mass decreases by approximately 0.5 pounds per year, which results in a total gain of 45 pounds of fat (Wilmore, 1977).

Basic Concepts

1. Muscles contract and apply force by pulling only. They never push. When movement in the opposite direction is desired, the antagonistic muscles must contract.

2. A reduction in joint angle is called flexion; an increase in the joint angle is extension. Generally, the flexor muscles are on the anterior side of the body, and the extensors are on the posterior side.

3. Exercises should focus on developing the flexors and extensors equally if proper posture and joint integrity are to be maintained.

4. Muscles can be attached directly to the bone. A tendon, such as the Achilles, can also be the source of attachment. The origin of the muscle is the fixed portion of the muscle; the insertion is the moving part of the muscle.

5. Progression involving gradual overloading of the muscles is necessary to increase muscular strength and endurance. Males find that regular exercise can cause an increase in the girth of a muscle. Females rarely attain similar results from strenuous exercise. This is because the male hormone testosterone is responsible for the increase in muscle size and is present in greater quantity in males.

6. Different types of training are necessary for developing muscular strength and muscular endurance. Larger amounts of weight and fewer repetitions will cause a greater increase in strength; less weight and more repetitions will enhance muscular endurance.

7. There are different types of muscular contractions: isometric (without movement), isotonic

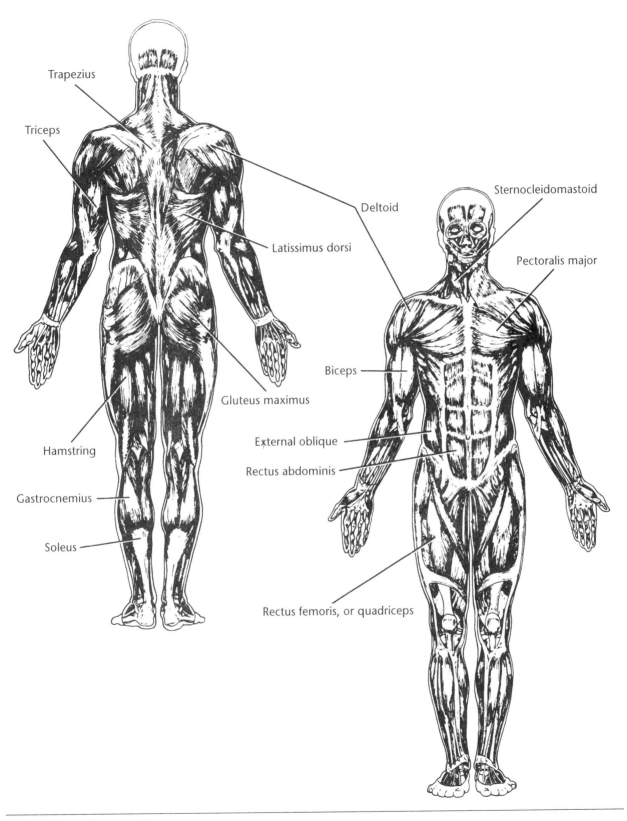

FIGURE 17.2 The muscular system

(with movement), and eccentric (movement that lengthens the muscle from a contracted state). The contraction most commonly used for developing strength and endurance is the isotonic.

8. Static stretching can increase flexibility. Flexibility (the range of motion at a joint) increases due to a lengthening of connective tissue that surrounds the muscle fibers.

9. Muscle soreness occurs when the work load is applied too intensely. The soreness probably results from muscle tissue damage. Static stretching will alleviate the pain somewhat and will help prepare the body for continued activity.

10. The principle of specificity is important in developing muscular strength. Only those muscles that are exercised will develop. If the goal is stronger leg muscles, they must be exercised. There is no carry-over from other muscle groups (that is, strengthening the arms will not cause an increase in leg strength).

Suggested Learning Activities

1. Identify major muscle groups and their functions at the joints. Discuss the origins and insertions of the muscles.

2. Study muscles from animals under a microscope. Show stained biopsies of human muscle fiber that reveal fast- and slow-twitch muscle fibers.

3. Perform some skill-related activities that might reveal which individuals appear to be endowed with more fast-twitch than slow-twitch fibers. Examples might be the standing long jump, vertical jump, and an endurance activity such as the mile run.

4. Develop a personal strength profile for students. Measure the strength of various muscle groups using a dynamometer, and set goals for well-rounded strength development.

5. Perform an action research project. As an example, pretest students for strength and divide them into equal groups. Have 1 group train for 12 weeks using muscular endurance techniques while the other trains for 12 weeks using muscular strength techniques. Retest and compare the results of the 2 groups after training.

6. Identify various sports and games, and determine what type of training will achieve maximum results.

7. Discuss certain exercises that should be avoided, such as straight-leg sit-ups and deep knee bends.

8. Have students identify why backache occurs in over 70% of Americans. Prescribe a program of exercise that could remedy the majority of these back problems.

Cardiorespiratory System

The cardiorespiratory system consists of the heart (Figure 17.3), lungs, arteries, capillaries, and veins. The heart is a muscle that pumps blood throughout the circulatory system—arteries, capillaries, and veins. The coronary arteries bring the heart a rich supply of blood. Heart disease occurs when fatty deposits block or seriously impede the flow of blood to the heart.

The heart has 2 chambers and is, in effect, divided in half with each side providing different functions. The left side of the heart pumps blood carrying nutrients and oxygen to the body through the arteries to the capillaries, where the nutrients and oxygen are exchanged for waste products and carbon dioxide. The waste-carrying blood is returned through the veins to the right side of the heart, from which the blood is routed through the lungs to discharge the carbon dioxide and pick up oxygen. This oxygen-renewed blood returns to the left side of the heart to complete the circuit.

Each time the heart beats, it pumps blood through both chambers. The beat is called the pulse; its impact travels through the body. Pulse is measured in number of beats per minute. A pulse rate of 75 means that the heart is beating 75 times each minute. The cardiac output is determined by the pulse rate and the stroke volume, which is the amount of blood discharged by each beat.

The pulse is measured by placing the 2 middle fingers of the right hand on the thumb side of the subject's wrist while the subject is seated. Taking the pulse at the wrist is usually preferable to using the carotid artery because pressure on the carotid can decrease blood flow to the brain.

The respiratory system includes the entryways (nose and mouth), the trachea (or windpipe), the primary bronchi, and the lungs. Figure 17.4 shows the components of the respiratory system.

Breathing consists of inhaling and exhaling air. Air contains 21% oxygen, which is necessary for life. Inspiration is assisted by muscular contraction, and expiration is accomplished by a relaxing of the muscles. Inspiration occurs when the intercostal muscles and the diaphragm contract. This increases the size

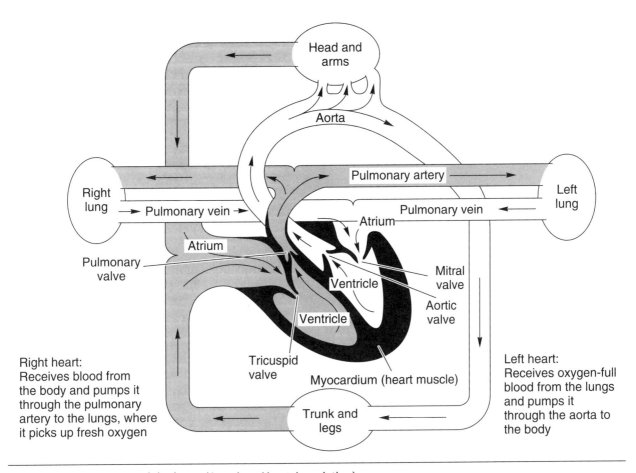

FIGURE 17.3   Structure of the heart (American Heart Association)

of the chest cavity, and expansion of the lungs causes air to flow in as a result of reduced air pressure. When the muscles are relaxed, the size of the chest cavity is reduced, the pressure is increased, and air flows from the lungs.

The primary function of the lungs is to provide oxygen to the cells on demand. The amount of oxygen needed will vary depending on activity level. When an individual exercises strenuously, the rate of respiration increases in order to bring more oxygen to tissues. If the amount of oxygen carried to the cells is adequate to maintain the level of activity, the activity is termed **aerobic**, or endurance exercise. Examples are walking, jogging, and bicycling for distance. If, because of high-intensity activity, the body is not capable of bringing enough oxygen to the cells, the body will continue to operate for a short time without oxygen. This results in an oxygen debt, which must be repaid later. In this case, the activity is termed **anaerobic** exercise.

The respiratory rate will return to normal after exercise. The recovery rate will be faster if the oxygen debt incurred during exercise was small. An individual has recovered from the exertion of exercise when blood pressure, heart rate, and ventilation rate have returned to preexercise levels.

Basic Concepts

1. The heart is a muscular organ that must be exercised like other muscles to maintain maximum efficiency. The most effective heart exercise is activity of low intensity and long duration, which is aerobic in nature.
2. Pulse rate varies among individuals. It does slow down at rest, however, as a result of aerobic training. Resting pulse rate is sometimes used as an indicator of the state of training.
3. Cardiorespiratory training appears to decrease the susceptibility of individuals to heart disease.

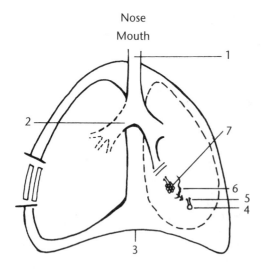

Nose
Mouth

1. Trachea
2. Bronchus
3. Diaphragm
4. Alveolus

5. Respiratory bronchiole
6. Alveolar sacs
7. Terminal bronchiole

FIGURE 17.4 The respiratory system

The younger one begins maintaining fitness, the better the opportunity to retard the onset of cardiovascular disease.

4. Aerobic endurance activities (jogging, brisk walking, bicycling) appear to change the chemistry of the blood and lower the cholesterol level. There are 2 types of lipoproteins, high density (HDL) and low density (LDL), and exercise appears to increase the ratio of HDL to LDL. This is important because HDL seems to prevent harmful plaque from building up in the arteries.

5. Hypokinetic diseases are somewhat influenced by gender, heredity, race, and age. Many of these diseases can be prevented, however, by controlling factors such as smoking, obesity, inactivity, improper diet, and high blood pressure.

6. The heart rate must reach the training state if cardiorespiratory benefits are to be realized. (See item 7 in the following Suggested Learning Activities for calculating the training zone.)

7. The heart grows stronger and larger when the body is involved in aerobic activity (30 minutes or more). A larger and stronger heart results in a greater stroke volume per beat.

8. If weight control is a concern, maintaining muscle mass is important. Severe dieting often results not only in a loss of fat cells, but in a loss of muscle tissue as well. Since muscle tissue burns twice

as many calories as fat tissue, it is important in weight control as well as for cosmetic and performance reasons.

9. The vital capacity of the lungs can be increased through regular aerobic exercise. This makes the oxygen exchange system more efficient.

Suggested Learning Activities

1. Discuss the acronym DANGER in regard to cardiovascular disease.

   Don't smoke.

   Avoid foods high in fat and cholesterol.

   Now control high blood pressure and diabetes.

   Get medical examinations at least every other year.

   Exercise moderately each day.

   Reduce and lose weight if carrying excess fat.

2. Compare resting pulse rates among students. Look for differences between sexes, ages, and states of training. Try taking the resting pulse rate in different positions.

3. Examine the impact that exercise has on heart rate. Record the resting heart rate. Have each person run in place for 1 minute. Take the pulse rate immediately and record it. Continue taking the pulse rate at 2-minute intervals 3 to 5 times to demonstrate recovery rate. Discuss individual differences in maximum heart rate and recovery heart rate.

4. Teach students how to take blood pressure. Exercise for 1 minute as described above and monitor the effect that exercise has on blood pressure.

5. Demonstrate the effects on the cardiovascular system of carrying excess weight. Identify 2 students who weigh the same, are of the same sex, are in similar training states, and who do not carry excess weight. Monitor their resting heart rate before starting. Ask 1 person to perform the upcoming task while carrying 2 10-pound weights. Set 2 markers 20 yards apart, and have both students run back and forth between the cones 10 times. Immediately after they finish, monitor their heart rate and recovery rate as described above. Discuss the fact that excessive body fat is merely dead weight that must be moved, and note how the excess weight decreases physical performance.

6. Compare heart rates after 2- or 3-minute bouts of different types of exercise. Experiment with walking, jogging, sprinting, rope jumping, bicycling, and calisthenics. Discuss the differences.

7. Calculate the heart rate training zone that should be maintained to achieve the training effect and to ensure that the individual is not under- or over-exercising. To do this, first determine the estimated maximum heart rate by taking 220 minus the student's age, then multiply the difference by 60% and 80%. An example for a student who is 15 follows:

220 – 15 = 205

60% of 205 = 123

80% of 205 = 164

The heart rate training zone for this student would be a heartbeat (or pulse rate) between 123 and 164. Have the class try different modes of exercise and see if they raise their heart rates into the training zone.

8. Identify resting respiratory rates. Have students try different types of exercise and compare the effects each has on the respiratory rate.

AVOID ROADBLOCKS TO WELLNESS

Wellness involves knowing what activities to avoid as well as what to do. Teaching about these activities should not be done by preaching and telling students what they should or should not do. Emphasis is placed instead on showing students the pros and cons of various practices and the consequences of making certain decisions. The ultimate decision and responsibility rest with the student, not the teacher.

This section includes stress, nutrition and weight control, substance abuse, and personal safety. All are areas where behavior can be modified to enhance the quality of life. Students can make decisions in these areas that affect how they live and, sometimes, whether they will live.

Stress

Stress is the body's reaction to certain situations in life. Everyone experiences some stress. Stress, by itself, is probably not harmful, but handling stress is critical in determining the impact it will have on one's life. Many students are affected by stress. Often, students are seen as carefree and without worries. Quite the opposite is usually the case. Students live under the stress of other's expectations, peer pressure, sexual mores, and the necessity of becoming an independent being. If teachers appreciate that stu-dents are subject to stress, they can begin to deal with them in ways that alleviate possible stressors and allow for stress release. In this way, teachers can have an impact on the students' self-concept and their world view.

Psychologically, stress may take the form of excitement, fear, or anger. Physical changes also accompany psychological stress. For example, heart rate increases, blood pressure rises, ventilation rate increases, perspiration increases, body temperature may rise, and the pupils may dilate. This response to stress once aided human beings in survival and is labeled the "fight or flight" syndrome. When a situation arises that may cause one harm, the body's endocrine system prepares it to fight or to flee the situation. People often speak of the "adrenaline flowing" when they are scared or worried about upcoming situations.

Unfortunately, our society and schools offer few opportunities to relieve tension through activity, and few individuals find the motivation to do so. The resulting tension and stress that build up cause individuals to expend a great deal of energy in unproductive ways. People often feel fatigued when they are unable to release stress. Many nervous habits, such as constant movement while sitting, playing with an item in the hands, and various facial twitches, are the body's attempts to relieve tension.

The ultimate question when dealing with stress might be: "What does it matter if I'm under stress? All people are." It matters because excessive stress has many detrimental effects on the body. It increases the risk of heart disease and can lead to insomnia and hypertension. Indigestion is common in stressed individuals, as is constipation. Many backaches and general body aches originate through stress. Doctors are diagnosing more and more "psychosomatic" diseases that have no physical prognosis and appear to be caused by stress. Another serious problem associated with unrelieved stress is the tendency of individuals to try to cope by using substances such as alcohol, tobacco, and drugs.

Individuals who exhibit Type A behavior (Friedman and Rosenman, 1974) are much more likely to suffer from the ill effects of stress. Type A behavior is characterized by some of the following patterns:

1. Moving everywhere rapidly, even when it is unnecessary.
2. Feeling bored and impatient with classes and how things are being done by others.
3. Trying to do 2 or more things simultaneously. (This is referred to as polyphasic thought or action.)

4. Having to always feel busy and feeling uneasy when time is taken to do nothing or to do something relaxing.

5. Needing to do everything faster and more efficiently than everyone else.

6. Exhibiting many strong gestures such as clenching the fists, banging a hand on the table, or dramatically waving the arms.

Students need to learn to identify Type A behavior and to understand various methods of modifying it to achieve more productive patterns.

Learning to cope with stressful situations is important. The first step involves developing an awareness of what types of situations cause stress. Sharing situations with others often releases the tension and allows students to feel that they are "normal" and are maturing properly. In the physical education setting, emphasis should be placed on the role that activity can play in stress reduction. Involvement in enjoyable and success-oriented physical activities can decrease tension. This involvement has a side effect because the required concentration will provide a diversion from worries and stressors. Note, however, that if the activity is not enjoyable and if the student consistently fails to find success, the level of stress may actually increase.

Some experts believe that exercise applies stress to the body in a systematic fashion and thus prepares the individual to deal with other stressful situations. One goal of teachers should be to provide a variety of activities and to help students select activities that will be productive and meaningful ways of relieving tension.

Another beneficial strategy is to teach various relaxation techniques that help relieve general body stress. These are discussed in a later section in this chapter.

Basic Concepts

1. Stress affects all individuals to varying degrees. Some stress is necessary to stimulate performance and increase motivation.

2. The amount of stress one is able to cope with depends on how it is perceived. Positive self-concepts help people accept threatening situations in a less stressful manner.

3. When people have difficulty dealing with stress through productive methods, such as exercise, relaxation activities, and talking with friends, they often attempt to relieve stress through un-

healthy and potentially dangerous means, such as alcohol, tobacco, and drug usage.

4. Stress causes changes in perceptible bodily functions. An awareness of these changes is necessary if students are to recognize when they are under stress and need to cope with its effects.

5. Stress appears to increase susceptibility to many diseases and causes psychosomatic illnesses.

6. Exercise is an excellent way to relieve stress and tension when the activity is perceived as enjoyable and success-oriented.

7. Stress is a critical risk factor that influences the onset of heart disease. Type A behavior is accompanied by an increased risk of heart disease.

8. There are different ways of relieving stress, among them are exercise, expressing feelings to friends, developing problem-solving skills, and performing accepted relaxation techniques.

Suggested Learning Activities

1. Hold an isometric contraction at the elbow joint. With the other hand, feel the contraction in the biceps and triceps. Repeat the activity with other muscle groups. Discuss how stress causes generalized body tension that can result in tensed muscles and an increase in general body fatigue. Learning to recognize muscle tension is a desired outcome of this discussion.

2. Discuss the concept of "choking" under pressure. How does this relate to athletic performance? What happens when stress is greater than the individual's ability to cope with it? Discuss how some stress increases performance, while too much decreases it.

3. Discuss the importance of perception in stressful situations. How is stress perceived? Should students face up and admit it when they are worried or scared? Is it better to be "tough" and not tell anyone how they feel? Is it better to keep emotions inside or to share feelings with others?

4. Discuss the importance of finding activities in which students believe they are successful. How are positive self-concepts developed? Why are some people able to cope with failure and losing better than others?

5. Discuss situations in physical activity settings that give rise to increased stress, such as failing in front of others, not being selected for a team, being ridiculed for a poor performance, or losing a game that was personally important. How could these situations be handled differently?

6. Discuss the parameters of Type A behavior patterns. How can they be modified through activity and changes in behavior? Why do people develop Type A behavior? Are Type A behavior patterns productive?

7. Identify physical activities that seem to relieve tension and stress. Discuss the relationship between involvement in activity and the reduction of stress.

8. Identify and discuss unproductive attempts to relieve stress such as drinking, smoking, and drug abuse. Why are these methods chosen rather than exercise, discussions, or relaxation activities?

9. Discuss the many effects of stress on bodily health. Give students a stress inventory to see how much stress they are under, and discuss ways of reducing this pressure.

10. Teach relaxation techniques such as deep breathing, progressive muscle relaxation, and personal meditation. Emphasize the importance of taking time for these activities daily. Just as brushing the teeth is necessary for healthy dentition, relaxation is necessary for a healthy body and mind.

Nutrition and Weight Control

Proper nutrition is necessary if students are to expect a high level of physical performance from their body. An important area of concern deals with the balance between caloric intake and expenditure in order to maintain proper weight control. Students should understand the reasons and methods for maintaining an optimum level of body weight. Discuss the impact of empty calories through excessive ingestion of junk foods. Explain the importance of a balanced diet to help the body grow and develop. Point out that the role of exercise in weight control and muscle development is as important as a balanced diet.

Students should understand the elements of a balanced diet. The body needs fats, carbohydrates, proteins, minerals, and vitamins. A balanced diet draws from each of the 4 basic food groups: milk and milk products; meat, fish, and poultry with nuts and legumes as supplements; fruits and vegetables; and breads and cereals. The usual recommendation is that carbohydrates make up a little more than 50% of the daily diet, with fats contributing 30% and proteins about 12%. The impact of various vitamins and minerals on body functions should be understood, as well as which foods are sources of the specific nutrients.

Foods high in cholesterol and fat should be consumed moderately. Some cholesterol and fat are necessary for proper body function. When too much fat is ingested, however, cholesterol and triglyceride levels in the blood plasma increase. This increase is probably detrimental to the body, for many studies have shown a relationship between high cholesterol and triglyceride levels and coronary heart disease. To travel in the bloodstream, fats must combine with water-soluble protein molecules called lipoproteins, which have an important effect on cholesterol and triglyceride levels. Some of these compound molecules are of a type called high-density lipoproteins (HDL), which are associated with a decreased risk of cardiovascular disease. Because polyunsaturated fats appear to increase HDL levels, the general recommendation is to include some polyunsaturates in the diet. Students should know which foods are high in saturated and unsaturated fats, and should be encouraged to have their cholesterol levels monitored by a physician.

Depending on the criteria used, anywhere from 30 to 50% of students are overweight, meaning that their body weight is over the accepted limits for their age, sex, and body build. It is important for students to begin to develop an awareness of the caloric content of foods as well as the nutritional value. They can then begin to count calories and practice consistency in the amount of calories they ingest. Coupled with this awareness should be some comprehension of the number of calories expended through various types of physical activity (Figure 17.5). Students need to understand that when caloric intake exceeds caloric expenditure, obesity results. A well-documented and common cause of obesity is inactivity. Most experts believe that obese students do not eat more than normal weight students; rather, they exercise less.

Obesity is a roadblock to wellness. Life insurance companies view overweight people as poor risks because of their shorter life expectancy. Excessive body fat makes the heart work harder, increases the chance of having high blood pressure, and lowers the possibility of recovery from a heart attack. Even more detrimental to students is the psychological impact that obesity has on self-concept development. Students of normal weight find it much easier to perform physical tasks because strength in relationship to body weight is a critical performance factor. Overweight students are often punished more severely

Activity	Calories per Hour
Moderate activity	*200–350*
Bicycling (5½ mph)	210
Walking (2½ mph)	210
Gardening	220
Canoeing (2½ mph)	230
Golf	250
Lawn mowing (power mower)	250
Lawn mowing (hand mower)	270
Bowling	270
Fencing	300
Rowboating (2½ mph)	300
Swimming (¼ mph)	300
Walking (3¾ mph)	300
Badminton	350
Horseback riding (trotting)	350
Square dancing	350
Volleyball	350
Roller skating	350
Vigorous activity	*Over 350*
Table tennis	360
Ice skating (10 mph)	400
Tennis	420
Water skiing	480
Hill climbing (100 ft/hr)	490
Skiing (10 mph)	600
Squash and handball	600
Cycling (13 mph)	660
Scull rowing (race)	840
Running (10 mph)	900

FIGURE 17.5   Caloric expenditure

Adapted from material from the President's Council on Physical Fitness and Sports, Washington, D.C.

than normal weight students for the same type of deviance and may receive lower grades for a similar quality of work.

Basic Concepts

1. Diet should be balanced and contain foods from each of the 4 basic groups. This ensures that the body will receive essential nutrients.
2. Caloric expenditure (body functions plus exercise) and intake (eating) must be balanced to maintain a healthy weight. A weight-reducing program should include a reduction in caloric intake and an increase in daily exercise.
3. Activities vary in the energy they require. Individual needs must be considered in the selection of activities to promote weight control and physical fitness maintenance.
4. Junk foods add little if any nutritional value to the diet and are usually high in calories. Foods such as sugar, margarine and butter, oils, and alcohol are high in calories but make little or no contribution in terms of nutrition.
5. Excessive weight makes performing physical tasks difficult. This results in less success and in less motivation to be active, thus increasing the tendency toward obesity.
6. Obesity increases the risk of heart disease and other related diseases such as diabetes.
7. A majority of obesity cases are caused by inactivity or lack of sufficient activity. The majority of overweight students do not consume more calories than normal weight students; they are simply less active.
8. Vitamins are not nutrients but are catalysts that facilitate metabolic processes. Certain vitamin deficiencies can produce various diseases.
9. Various foods are excellent sources of specific nutrients. Students should be able to identify which foods to ingest to provide a balance of the needed nutrients, vitamins, and minerals.

Suggested Learning Concepts

1. Post a list of activities and their energy demands on the bulletin board. Discuss the need for selecting activities that will burn enough calories to balance caloric intake.
2. Maintain a food diary. Record all the foods eaten daily and the amount of calories in each. Compare the amount of calories ingested with the amount of calories expended.
3. Maintain a nutritious-food diary. Record all the foods eaten daily and categorize each by food group. Determine the percentage of carbohydrates, proteins, and fats in relation to all the food ingested during each day.
4. Develop a desirable and practical balanced diet that can be followed for 1 week. Arrange with parents to facilitate the diet within their budget restrictions.
5. Calculate the Recommended Daily Allowance (RDA) for various nutrients. Compare a daily intake with the recommendations for various minerals and vitamins.
6. Bring various foods to class that have labels offering nutrition information. Determine which foods are good buys for desired nutrients.

7. Develop an activity diary. For 1 week, record all activity over and above maintenance activities. Calculate the number of calories burned per day.
8. Discuss and analyze the ways in which society rewards physically fit individuals. Contrast these with the ways in which obese people are discriminated against in various situations.

Substance Abuse

Substance abuse is defined as the harmful use of alcohol, tobacco, or drugs. It is common in today's schools as students seek different ways to explore an expanding world. If students are expected to make wise and meaningful decisions in this area, they must understand the impact of various substances on their physical and psychological being. Facts, both pro and con, should be presented in a nonjudgmental environment, without moralizing and preaching. It is difficult for students to make personal decisions if most of the information they receive is from peers or moralizing adults.

Alcohol, tobacco, and drugs deter wellness and are usually detrimental to total health. The use and misuse of these substances should be discussed objectively with students because much of the information they receive is from biased sources, such as parents, peers, and various media formats. The physical education teacher can promote unbiased discussions and fact-seeking sessions that relate to wellness. Many times, the physical educator is the only person oriented to wellness promotion. As mentioned earlier, however, if the instructor feels strongly that an issue has only 1 acceptable point of view, then discussions should be avoided. Telling students only the reasons why not to do something can result in a strong polarization in the opposite direction.

Alcohol has both short-term and long-term effects. Short-term effects vary as a result of the depressant effect that alcohol has on the central nervous system. Some people become relaxed, others become aggressive, and some become active in differing degrees. Ultimately, a lack of coordination and confusion occur if a great deal of alcohol is ingested. The long-term effects of alcohol abuse may be liver damage, heart disease, and malnutrition. The greatest concern surrounding long-term drinking is the possibility of alcoholism. Most agree that alcoholism has the following components: loss of control of alcohol intake, presence of functional or structural damage (physical and psychological), and dependence on alcohol to maintain an acceptable level of functioning.

Students usually drink for any of the following reasons: curiosity, desire to celebrate with parents, peer pressure, to be like adults and appear more mature, to rebel against the adult world, because their models or admired adults drink, or because they are alcoholics. Students are often ambivalent about alcohol. They know its detrimental effects, and yet they see many of their friends and role models using it. The problem is a difficult one, and an understanding of both moderate use and abstinence is needed. An understanding of how to cope with peer pressure to drink alcohol is also needed and is discussed in the next section on basic concepts.

Tobacco use is common among junior and senior high students. Smoking increases significantly the possibility of heart attacks, strokes, and cancer. Chronic bronchitis and emphysema are diseases prevalent among smokers. A recent study revealed that the average life-span of long-term smokers is seven years shorter than that of nonsmokers.

Students need to understand the impact of smoking on a healthy body. Along with this knowledge, they should examine why so many people choose to smoke. Today, the fastest growing segment of the smoking population is young girls and women. Students will make the final decision for their individual behavior, but before they do so, they need to understand thoroughly the ramifications of smoking.

The use of marijuana and of hard-core drugs should also be discussed. Outside agencies are often most helpful in discussing substance abuse in an objective manner with students. The use of steroids, "pep pills," and pain relievers in athletics should also be debated. In each case, the intent should be to enhance students' awareness so they know the alternatives and consequences. Substance abuse is contrary to the whole concept of physical wellness. Physical educators need to accept the challenge of increasing student understanding and knowledge in these areas.

Basic Concepts

1. The earlier one begins to smoke, the greater the risk to functional health.
2. People smoke for psychological reasons.
3. Young people may choose substance abuse out of curiosity, for status reasons, or from peer pressure.
4. Choosing a lifestyle independently of peers requires great courage.
5. Decisions about substance abuse are poor decisions if they are based on a dearth of knowledge.

Wise and purposeful decisions can be made only when all of the alternatives and consequences are understood.

6. Substance abuse is often an attempt to cope with stress-related problems. Exercise and relaxation are much more productive, healthy methods of coping.

7. The use of alcohol, tobacco, and drugs always carries the risk of addiction. When people are addicted, they are no longer in charge of their lifestyles. All people, to some degree, are subject to addiction; no one is immune.

8. Spending time and effort on developing personal competencies is more productive than substance abuse. Personal competency in many areas reduces the need to "be like everyone else," and contributes to a positive self-concept.

9. The use of harmful substances frequently reduces the pleasure one can receive from experiencing the world. Physical performance is often reduced because of substance abuse.

10. A person can drink and smoke and still excel at athletics, but maximum performance levels may be reduced and the ultimate effect on the athlete will be harmful. Students see many professional athletes who smoke and drink. They need to be aware that this happens, but they should understand that the choice is undesirable from a wellness standpoint.

Suggested Learning Activities

1. Identify and discuss the reasons why people choose or choose not to become involved in substance abuse.

2. Discuss the importance of making personal decisions based on what is best for you. Why do we follow others and allow them to influence our decisions, even when those decisions are not in our best interest?

3. Develop a bulletin board that illustrates the many ways used by the tobacco, alcohol, and drug industries to try to get young people to buy their products. Reserve a spot for advertisements (if any can be found) that admonish and encourage students to abstain or moderate the use of various substances.

4. Students often see professional and college athletes smoking and drinking on television while hearing from teachers and coaches that these habits impair performance. Discuss why these athletes can perform at a high level even though they may drink or smoke.

5. Students often choose to be part of a peer group at any cost. Discuss how our society often respects and honors individuals who have the courage to go their own way. Examples might be Columbus, Helen Keller, Braille, and so forth.

6. Identify and discuss the ways in which people in our society choose to relieve and dissipate stress. Discuss productive releases of tension such as recreation, hobbies, and sports.

7. Bring in speakers who are knowledgeable about the effects and uses of alcohol, tobacco, and drugs. If necessary, bring in a pair of speakers who might debate both sides of an issue.

8. Develop visual aids that identify the various effects that alcohol, tobacco, and drugs have on the body.

Safety and First Aid

Safety and first aid have often been part of the physical education program because more accidents occur in physical education than in any other area of the school curriculum. Safety is an attitude and a concern for one's welfare and health. An accident is an unplanned event or act that may result in injury or death. Often, accidents occur when they could have been prevented. The following are the most common causes of accidents: lack of knowledge and understanding of risks; lack of skill and competence to perform tasks safely, such as riding a bike or driving a car; false sense of security that leads people to think that accidents happen only to others; fatigue or illness that affect physical and mental performance; drugs and alcohol; and strong emotional states (such as anger, fear, or worry) that cause people to do things they might not otherwise do.

Traffic accidents are an area in which many deaths could be prevented. Wearing seat belts reduces the risk of dying by 50%. Drinking alcohol while driving increases the risk of an accident 20-fold compared to not drinking. Another factor that has reduced the number of traffic deaths is the 55-mph speed limit. Since students are going to drive, driver education and an awareness of the possibility of serious injury should be a part of the wellness program.

Bicycles are another source of numerous accidents. Automobile drivers have difficulty seeing bicycles, and the resulting accidents are often serious. Students need to learn bicycle safety. The physical education setting is often the only place where this training occurs. Classes in bicycling for safety and fitness are usually well received by middle school and high school students.

Swimming-related accidents are the second leading cause of accidental death among young adults. More than 50% of all drownings occur when people unexpectedly find themselves in the water. Another major cause of death from drowning is alcohol ingestion. Swimming and drinking do not mix well. Physical education programs should encourage all students to learn to swim and to learn water safety rules at sometime during their school career.

Physical education and sports are sources of injury in the school setting. Proper safety procedures should be taught, as well as first-aid techniques. Students should know how to stop bleeding, treat shock, and administer mouth-to-mouth respiration and cardiopulmonary resuscitation (CPR). Many physical education programs now include a required unit of instruction dealing with these topics. It is estimated that 100,000 to 200,000 lives could be saved by bystanders if they knew CPR.

Basic Concepts

1. Accidents are unplanned events or acts that may result in injury or death. The majority of accidents could be avoided if people were adequately prepared and understood the necessary competencies and risks involved.
2. Wearing seat belts and not drinking alcohol while driving will dramatically decrease the risk of death by automobile accident.
3. Bicycles are often not seen by car drivers. Bicycling safety classes can help lower the number of bicycle accidents.
4. Swimming-related accidents are the second leading cause of accidental death among young people. Drownproofing programs and avoiding alcohol will dramatically decrease the risk of death by drowning.
5. Many thousands of lives could be saved if all people knew how to perform CPR.
6. All students should know how to stop bleeding and how to administer mouth-to-mouth respiration and CPR.
7. Basic first-aid procedures to prevent further injury to victims are competencies that all students should possess.

Suggested Learning Activities

1. Discuss the causes of different types of accidents and how many accidents could be avoided.
2. Identify the types of accidents that happen to different age groups and why this appears to be the case.

3. Identify the role of alcohol and drugs in causing accidents. Why are these substances used in recreational settings?
4. Develop a bulletin board that illustrates how to care for shock victims. Practice the steps in a mock procedure.
5. Have an "accident day" when various types of accidents are staged that demand such treatments as stopping bleeding, mouth-to-mouth respiration, and CPR.
6. Outline the steps to follow in case of a home fire. Discuss how many fires could be prevented.
7. Conduct a bicycle safety fair. Have students design bulletin boards and displays that explain and emphasize bicycle safety.

ENHANCE STUDENT WELLNESS

It is apparent that the wellness of students can be seriously impaired when safety issues are dealt with incorrectly. However, proper nutrition, avoiding substance abuse, and practicing proper safety when bicycling or driving a car can enhance the wellness of participants. The purpose of this section is to help students further advance their wellness status through positive action rather than by simply avoiding various foods, substances, and situations. This section takes a 3-pronged approach: (1) physical fitness and activity, (2) stress reduction, and (3) self-evaluation. None of the areas will be covered in its entirety since many in-depth sources are available. A highly recommended source for helping students develop lifetime fitness is the text by Corbin and Lindsey (1996a).

Physical Fitness and Activity

There are 2 types of physical fitness that are generally identified (Corbin and Lindsey, 1994). The first is skill-related physical fitness and the other is health-related fitness. Skill-related fitness contains many elements that deal with sport performance, among them are balance, coordination, reaction time, agility, power, and speed. Skill-related fitness has less impact on the wellness of an individual and will not be further discussed in this section.

Health-related fitness is directly related to the wellness of individuals and is generally defined as consisting of cardiovascular fitness, strength, muscular endurance, flexibility, and body fatness. *Cardiovascular fitness* is the most important phase of fitness for wellness. Cardiovascular fitness is a complex concept but, simply put, involves efficient functioning of the heart, blood, and blood vessels in order to supply oxygen to the body during aerobic activity. *Strength* refers to the ability of a muscle or muscle group to exert force. Without strength, a low standard of performance can be expected, because muscles will fatigue before an individual can perform well. *Muscular endurance* refers to the ability of a muscle or muscle group to exert effort over a period of time. Endurance utilizes strength and postpones fatigue so the effort can be expended for long periods. Cardiovascular fitness also plays a key role in how long people can perform an activity. *Flexibility* is a person's range of movement at the joints. It allows freedom of movement and ready adjustment of the body for various movements. *Body fatness* refers to the percentage of body weight that is fat. People who are physically fit generally have a lower percentage of body fat than those who are unfit. For males in secondary school, 11 to 15% fat is a reasonable range, while 20 to 25% is acceptable for females (Corbin and Lindsey, 1994).

It is important to help students develop a health-related fitness plan that they can use to monitor themselves throughout their lives. The basic steps for such a plan are as follows:

1. Identify present areas of fitness and weakness by pretesting. Many tests can be used to evaluate the 5 components of health-related fitness.

2. Identify the present activities that the students are performing by having them fill out a survey that lists a wide variety of activities. Post a chart that shows the components of health-related fitness enhanced by each activity. A good source for surveys and lists of activity benefits is *Fitness for Life* by Corbin and Lindsey (1996a).

3. Select some activities that will build the health-related fitness components that each student needs, as identified in step 1. Each student will begin to have a personalized plan that is meaningful only to him or her.

4. Plan a week-long activity program that contains activities that are enjoyable and help alleviate weaknesses in various component areas. Evaluate the week-long program and develop a month-long program in order to provide longer range goals. In the program, delineate the frequency of exercise, the intensity, and the amount of time to be spent exercising.

Stress Reduction

Many methods are recommended for learning to cope with stress. Only the most popular and acceptable in the school setting are covered here. An excellent text devoted entirely to this topic is *Human Stress: Its Nature and Control* (Allen, 1983).

In an earlier section, exercise was discussed as an excellent method of controlling stress. It appears to allow negative feelings to dissipate and positive feelings to replace them. The relaxed feeling that occurs after an exercise bout is championed by many as the best part of activity.

Many deep-breathing exercises are available. The relaxation response advocated by Benson (1975) is supposed to replicate the effects of Transcendental Meditation™. Individuals sit comfortably and quietly and breathe deeply through the nose. The word *one* is said each time the person exhales. Twenty-minute bouts, once or twice a day, are recommended.

Another popular method is progressive relaxation as developed by Jacobson (1968). In this technique, a muscle or muscle group is first tensed and then relaxed slowly and smoothly. All the major parts of the body are in turn relaxed as one works down from the head to the toes.

Regardless of the activity choice selected for relaxation, students should be taught the importance of taking time to relax. People are often told that they are wasting time if they are not busy scurrying here and there. It can be an important learning situation to take 4 or 5 minutes at the end of a class to sit down and relax. This communicates to students that relaxation is indeed important since the instructor allows time for the activity.

Self-Evaluation and Behavior Self-Control

Self-Evaluation

The final step in maintaining wellness is being able to evaluate oneself on a regular basis. Individuals ultimately answer to themselves, and thus students need not share the results of their evaluations. Many surveys can help people evaluate their level of wellness.

Many other inventories, such as drinking and smoking scales, are available from various governmental agencies. Students can begin to see the extent of a problem and whether they have a problem or are improving.

Finally, teach students to evaluate their own levels of physical fitness. Each of the health-related fitness items can be evaluated easily. If students are not given time in the physical education program to evaluate their own fitness levels, they will probably not take the time for evaluation once they leave school. One of the best techniques is to give each student a self-testing card that has room for recording 4 or 5 different testing episodes. Allow students to self-test themselves with a friend and record their performances. Instructors can file the cards and return them when it is time for another testing period. This system allows students to monitor their physical fitness gains or losses.

Behavior Self-Control

Students should be taught how to improve their self-control by altering their behavior. Attitudes can be changed by changing behavior patterns. Behavior self-control is a systematic approach to solving problems. It involves keeping records of behavior in order to understand the positive and negative variables that influence behavior. The following steps can be taught effectively to students to help them learn to manipulate their behavior.

1. *Maintain behavior records.* Students can learn to monitor their exercise patterns and record the performances on personal charts. They can then begin to observe their patterns of exercise, the duration of the exercise, and the intensity of effort. Such observation becomes self-reinforcing when, for example, students see clearly that they are exercising only 2 days per week and showing little gain, or when they observe rapid improvement after exercising 5 days per week for several weeks. Another advantage of recording behavior is that the routine act of recording reminds the performer that the behavior must be done. This routine reinforcement causes the behavior performance to improve.

2. *Develop a priority schedule.* If students want to exercise regularly, they must schedule the activity and make it a high-priority item. In other words, exercise must be done before other less important tasks are performed. Scheduling the activity for a certain number of days at a specified time is most effective.

3. *Analyze restrictive factors.* Even after behavior has been analyzed and priorities are set, students may find that desired behavior patterns are not being followed. The reasons for this must then be analyzed and other changes effected to increase the probability of carrying out the behavior. For example, the time of exercise may have to be changed or the length of the bout. Exercising for 2 shorter periods per day, instead of 1 long period, might be the answer. Exercising with a friend or changing the mode of exercise would be other possible solutions.

4. *Establish rewards.* To continue the activity over a long period of time, it can be helpful to establish personal contingencies that are available after performing the desired behavior. For example, students might relax and watch television immediately after exercise, or take a long, hot shower. Regardless of the reward, it must be meaningful and worthwhile to the individual. Verbalizing internally after each exercise routine is also effective as a contingency. One might say to oneself, "I feel better and look stronger after every bout of exercise." In any case, if students can identify something positive that occurs because of or after the exercise bout, they will have a tendency to continue on the path of wellness.

EXPECTED OUTCOMES

After reading this chapter, you should be able to

- Conduct a discussion session with students that successfully allows clarification and understanding of wellness concepts.

- Describe how wellness can be achieved through a properly structured instructional program of physical education.

- Understand the basic function of the skeletal, muscular, and cardiorespiratory systems.

- Explain how wellness can be integrated into the physical education setting at the middle and senior high school level.

- Delineate the type of teacher behavior that enhances the development of self-concept among students.

- Identify risk factors that are associated with degenerative diseases.

- Discuss factors that are roadblocks to wellness.

- Explain how stress reduction can be accomplished.

- Describe how students can learn to self-evaluate their levels of physical fitness.
- List a plan for improving self-control by altering behavior.

REFERENCES AND SUGGESTED READINGS

Allen, R. J. 1983. *Human Stress: Its Nature and Control*. Minneapolis, MN: Burgess Publishing Co.

Benson, H. 1975. *The Relaxation Response*. New York: William Morrow & Co.

Corbin, C., and Lindsey, R. 1994. *Concepts of Fitness and Wellness*. Dubuque, IA: Brown & Benchmark.

Corbin, C., and Lindsey, R. 1996a. *Fitness for Life*. 4th ed. Glenview, IL: Scott, Foresman & Company.

Corbin, C., and Lindsey, R. 1996b. *Fitness for Life Teacher's Resource Manual*. 4th ed. Glenview, IL: Scott, Foresman & Company.

Cottrell, R. R. 1992a. *Wellness: Stress Management*. Dubuque, IA: Brown & Benchmark.

Cottrell, R. R. 1992b. *Wellness: Weight Control*. Dubuque, IA: Brown & Benchmark.

Friedman, M., and Rosenman, R. H. 1974. *Type A Behavior and Your Heart*. New York: Alfred A. Knopf.

Hurley, J. S. 1992. *Wellness: Nutrition & Health*. Dubuque, IA: Brown & Benchmark.

Jackson, J. K. 1992. *Wellness: Aids, STD, & Other Communicable Diseases*. Dubuque, IA: Brown & Benchmark.

Jacobson, E. 1968. *Progressive Relaxation*. 2nd ed. Chicago: University of Chicago Press.

Kime, R. E. 1992. *Wellness: Environment & Health*. Dubuque, IA: Brown & Benchmark.

Klug, G., and Lettunich, J. 1992. *Wellness: Exercise & Physical Fitness*. Dubuque, IA: Brown & Benchmark.

Rarick, G. L. (ed.). 1973. *Physical Activity, Human Growth, and Development*. New York: Academic Press.

Schlaadt, R. G. 1992a. *Wellness: Alcohol Use & Abuse*. Dubuque, IA: Brown & Benchmark.

Schlaadt, R. G. 1992b. *Wellness: Drugs, Society, & Behavior*. Dubuque, IA: Brown & Benchmark.

Schlaadt, R. G. 1992c. *Wellness: Tobacco & Health*. Dubuque, IA: Brown & Benchmark.

Wilmore, J. H. 1977. *Athletic Training and Physical Fitness*. Boston: Allyn & Bacon.

18 Mini-Units of Instruction

The units in this chapter offer students and teachers a change of pace. The units are personally challenging and allow students to develop new skills and to work closely with classmates. Many are useful for rainy days, shortened period days, or for introductory activities. The units require equipment that is rarely used in typical physical education programs. They are novel tasks meant to be presented for 1 or 2 days in a noncompetitive setting. Since variation in student ability makes little difference in the presentation of these activities, they can be offered as challenges to students. For example, the proper progression of juggling activities can be taught. After the rudimentary skills are learned, some students may choose to progress to more challenging tasks, whereas others remain at a lower level.

An excellent way to implement mini-units is to present them on a Tuesday or Thursday to break up a longer unit of instruction. Students can be encouraged to help each other master the tasks, with emphasis placed on cooperation rather than competition. This creates a different environment that may be more meaningful for some students. The low-key instructional approach is also an inviting variation for instructors.

INDIVIDUAL AND DUAL UNITS OF INSTRUCTION

Units in this area include juggling, beanbags, wands, hoops, stunts, tumbling, and combatives. They focus on individual skill development and allow each student to progress at an optimum rate of development. Students can develop new and different challenges that the rest of the class can try.

Beanbags

The following are challenges that can be taken in any order. The best size beanbag is usually 6 inches · 6 inches, because it can be balanced on various body parts and used for many challenges. The advantage of the 4 inch · 4 inch beanbags is that they can be used for juggling activities as well as for many of the challenge activities listed here. Students should try to master the stunts with both the right and left hands.

1. Toss the beanbag overhead and catch it on the back of the hand. Try catching on different body parts such as shoulder, knee, and foot.
2. Toss the beanbag, make a half-turn, and catch it. Try making a different number of turns (full, double, and so forth).
3. Toss, clap the hands, and catch. Try clapping the hands a specified number of times. Clap the hands around different parts of the body.
4. Toss, touch various body parts or objects. For example, toss, touch the toes, shoulders, and hips before catching. Specify objects to touch, such as the wall, the floor, or a line.
5. Toss, move to various body positions, and catch the beanbag. Suggested positions are sitting, kneeling, supine or prone position, and on one's side.
6. Reverse task 5 by tossing the beanbag from some of the suggested positions and then resuming the standing position.
7. Toss and perform various stunts before catching the beanbag, such as heel clicks, heel slaps, jump and perform a full turn, and push-up.

8. Toss the beanbag from behind the back and catch it. Toss overhead and catch it behind the back.

9. Toss, move, and catch. Cover as much ground as possible between the toss and catch. Move forward, backward, and sideways, using different steps such as the carioca, shuffle, and slide.

10. Toss the beanbag with various body parts (feet, knees, shoulders) and catch it with the hands or other body parts. Try to develop as much height on the toss as possible.

11. Perform some of the stunts with a beanbag in each hand. Catch the bags simultaneously.

12. Play a balance tag game. Specify a body part that the bag must be balanced on while moving. Designate who is it. If the beanbag falls off or is touched with the hands, the player must freeze and is subject to being tagged.

13. Try partner activities. Play catch with a partner using 2 or 3 beanbags. Toss and catch the beanbags using various body parts.

Hoops

Hoops are useful for offering various challenges to students. A 42-inch-diameter hoop is usually the best size. This is a large enough hoop to move through and over and to use for hula-hoop activities. Students should try to master the activities with both sides of their body. Emphasis can be placed on creating new routines with the hoops. The following are suggested ideas:

1. Spin the hoop like a top and see how long the hoop will continue to spin. While the hoop is spinning, see how many times it can be jumped.

2. Hula hoop using various body parts (waist, knees, ankles, neck, wrist). Hula hoop from the neck to the knees and back up to the neck. Hula hoop on a wrist and then change to the other wrist. Pass the hoop to a partner while hula hooping.

3. Try many of the hula hooping challenges while using 2 or more hoops. Hula hoop with a hoop on 2 or more body parts.

4. Play catch with a partner while hula hooping. Catch more than one object and hula hoop with more than 1 hoop.

5. Jump or hop through a hoop held by a partner. Vary the challenge by altering the angle and height of the hoop. Try jumping through 2 or more parallel hoops without touching them.

6. Roll the hoop like a spare tire. Change direction on signal. Roll 2 or more hoops at the same time.

7. Use the hoop in place of a jump rope. Jump the hoop forward, backward, and sideways. Perform various foot stunts like toe-touching, rocker step, and heel-and-toe while jumping.

8. Roll the hoop forward with a reverse spin. The spin should cause it to return to the thrower. As the hoop returns, try some of the following challenges: jump the hoop, move through it, kick it up with the toe and catch it, and pick it up with the arm and begin hooping it.

9. Play catch with the hoop with a partner. Use 2 or more hoops and throw them alternately as well as simultaneously.

10. Employ the hoop relay. Break into equal-size groups. Join hands and place a hoop on a pair of joined hands. The object is to pass the hoop around the circle without releasing the hand grip. The first group to get the hoop around the circle is declared the winner.

Juggling

Juggling offers a challenge to secondary school students. If the majority of students have not mastered basic juggling skills, juggling scarves should be purchased. They are lightweight, sheer scarves that move slowly and allow students to master the proper arm and hand movements. Once the movement pattern is learned, beanbags, jugglebags (small round beanbags), and fleece balls can be used before proceeding to balls, rings, and clubs.

Juggling with scarves does teach students the correct patterns of object movement, however, it does not transfer automatically to juggling with faster-moving objects such as fleece balls, tennis balls, rings, and hoops. Therefore, 2 distinct sections for juggling are offered: a section on learning to juggle with scarves, and a section explaining juggling with balls. Juggling with scarves will bring success to a majority of the class, while youngsters who have mastered the scarves can move to balls and other objects.

Juggling with Scarves

Scarves are held by the fingertips near the center. To throw the scarf, it should be lifted and pulled into the air above eye level. Scarves are caught by clawing, a downward motion of the hand, and grabbing the scarf from above as it is falling. Scarf juggling should teach proper habits (such as tossing the scarves straight up in line with the body rather than forward or backward). Many instructors remind students to imagine that they are in a phone booth to emphasize tossing and catching without moving.

Cascading

Cascading is the easiest pattern for juggling 3 objects. The following sequence can be used to learn this basic technique.

1. *One scarf.* Hold the scarf in the center. Quickly move the arm across the chest and toss the scarf with the palm out. Reach out with the other hand and catch the scarf in a straight, downward motion (clawing). Toss the scarf with this hand using the motion and claw it with the opposite hand. Repeat the tossing and clawing sequence. The scarf should move in a figure-8 pattern as shown in Figure 18.1.

2. *Two scarves.* Hold a scarf with the fingertips in each hand. Toss the first one across the body as described in step 1. When it reaches its peak, look at it, and toss the second scarf across the body in the op-posite direction. The first scarf thrown is caught (clawed) by the hand throwing the second scarf and vice versa. Verbal cues such as toss, claw, toss, claw, are helpful.

3. *Three-scarf cascading.* Hold a scarf in each hand by the fingertips. Hold the third scarf with the ring and little finger against the palm of the hand. The first scarf to be thrown will be from the hand that is holding 2 scarves. Toss this scarf from the fingertips across the chest as learned earlier. When scarf 1 reaches its peak, throw scarf 2 from the other hand across the body. As this hand starts to come down, it catches scarf 1. When scarf 2 reaches its peak, throw scarf 3 in the same path as that of scarf 1. To complete the cycle, as the hand comes down from throwing scarf 3, it catches scarf 2. The cycle is started over by throwing scarf 1 with the opposite hand. Tosses are always alternated between left and right hands with a smooth, even rhythm.

Reverse Cascading

Reverse cascading involves tossing the scarves from waist level to the outside of the body and allowing the scarves to drop down the midline of the body (Figure 18.2).

FIGURE 18.1   Making a figure-8 motion with scarves

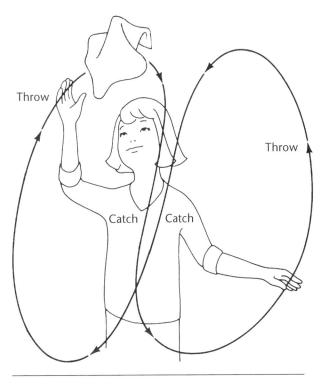

FIGURE 18.2   Reverse cascading

1. *One scarf.* Begin by holding the scarf as described in the Cascading section. The throw goes away from the midline of the body over the top, so the scarf is released and falls down the center of the body. Catch it with the opposite hand and toss it in similar fashion on the opposite side of the body.

2. *Two scarves.* Begin with a scarf in each hand. Toss the first as described in step 1. When it begins its descent, toss the second scarf. Catch the first scarf, then the second, and repeat the pattern in a toss, toss, catch, catch manner.

3. *Three scarves.* Think of a large funnel fixed at eye level directly in front of the juggler. The goal is to drop all scarves through this funnel so that they drop straight down the center of the body. Begin with 3 scarves as described earlier for 3-scarf cascading. Toss the first scarf from the hand holding 2 scarves.

Column Juggling

Column juggling is so-named because the scarves move straight up and down as though they were inside a large pipe or column and do not cross the body. To perform 3-scarf column juggling, begin with 2 scarves in 1 hand and 1 in the other hand. Begin with a scarf from the hand that has 2 scarves, and toss it straight up the midline of the body overhead. When this scarf reaches its peak, toss the other 2 scarves upward along the sides of the body (Figure 18.3). Catch the first scarf with either hand and toss it upward again. Catch the other 2 scarves and toss them upward continuing the pattern.

Showering

Showering is more difficult than cascading because of the rapid movement of the hands. There is less time allowed for catching and tossing. The scarves move in a circle following each other. It should be practiced in both directions for maximum challenge.

Start with 2 scarves in the right hand and 1 in the other. Begin by throwing the first 2 scarves from the right hand. Toss the scarves in a large circle away from the midline of the body and overhead as high as possible. As soon as the second scarf is released, toss the scarf across to the left hand and throw it in the same path with the right hand. All scarves are caught with the left hand and passed to the right hand.

Juggling Challenges
1. While cascading, toss a scarf under 1 leg.
2. While cascading, toss a scarf from behind the back.

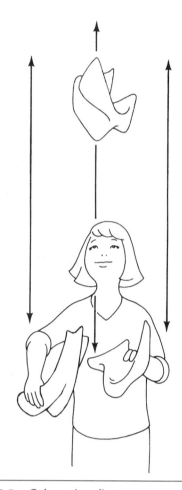

FIGURE 18.3   Column juggling

3. Instead of catching 1 of the scarves, blow it upward with a strong breath of air.
4. Begin cascading by tossing the first scarf into the air with a foot. Lay the scarf across the foot and kick it into the air.
5. Try juggling 3 scarves with 1 hand. Do not worry about establishing a pattern, just catch the lowest scarf each time. Try both regular and reverse cascading as well as column juggling.
6. While doing column juggling, toss up 1 scarf, hold the other 2 and make a full turn. Resume juggling.
7. Try juggling more than 3 scarves (up to 6) while facing a partner.
8. Juggle 3 scarves while standing side by side with inside arms around each other. This is easy to do since it is regular 3-scarf cascading.

Juggling with Balls

Juggling with balls requires accurate, consistent tossing, and this should be the first emphasis. The tosses should be thrown to the same height on both sides of the body, about 2 to 2.5 feet upward and across the body, since the ball is tossed from 1 hand to the other. Practice tossing the ball parallel to the body; the most common problem in juggling is that the balls are tossed forward and the juggler has to move forward to catch them.

The fingers, not the palms, should be used in tossing and catching. Stress relaxed wrist action. Encourage students to look upward to watch the balls at the peak of their flight, rather than watching the hands. Focus on where the ball peaks, not the hands. Two balls must be carried in the starting hand, and the art of releasing only 1 must be mastered. Progression should be working successively with 1 ball, then 2 balls, and finally 3 balls.

Recommended Progression for Cascading

1. Using 1 ball and 1 hand only, toss the ball upward (2 to 2½ feet), and catch it with the same hand. Begin with the dominant hand, and later practice with the other. Toss quickly, with wrist action. Then handle the ball alternately with right and left hands, tossing from 1 hand to the other.
2. Now, with 1 ball in each hand, alternate tossing a ball upward and catching it in the same hand so that 1 ball is always in the air. Begin again with a ball in each hand. Toss across the body to the other hand. To keep the balls from colliding, toss under the incoming ball. After some expertise has been acquired, alternate the 2 kinds of tosses by doing a set number (4 to 6) of each before shifting to the other.
3. Hold 2 balls in the starting hand and 1 in the other. Toss 1 of the balls in the starting hand, toss the ball from the other hand, and then toss the third ball. Keep the balls moving in a figure-8 pattern (Figure 18.4).

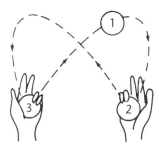

FIGURE 18.4 Cascading with 3 balls and 2 hands

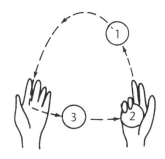

FIGURE 18.5 Showering with 3 balls and 2 hands

Recommended Progression for Showering

1. The showering motion is usually counterclockwise. Hold 1 ball in each hand. Begin by tossing with the right hand on an inward path and then immediately toss the other ball from the left directly across the body to the right hand. Continue this until the action is smooth.
2. Now, hold 2 balls in the right hand and 1 in the left. Toss the first ball from the right hand on an inward path and immediately toss the second on the same path. At about the same time, toss the ball from the left hand directly across the body to the right hand (Figure 18.5).
3. A few students may be able to change from cascading to showering and vice versa. This is a skill of considerable challenge.

Stunts and Combatives

This unit should emphasize personal challenge and brief competitive episodes. Students enjoy the chance to pit their strength and coordination skills against others. The combatives should be between opponents of approximately the same skill level and size. Partners should be switched often so there is little chance for animosity to develop. The contests start and stop by mutual agreement, with either party able to terminate the contest immediately. There is little point in running tournaments to see who is the class champion in a specific combative. Instead, emphasize enjoyment, learning one's strengths and weaknesses, and being able to contest a number of opponents.

Stunts, on the other hand, require that students work cooperatively to accomplish them successfully and are an excellent way to help students learn more about their peers.

Suggested Individual Stunts

Leg Dip.   Extend both hands and one leg forward while balancing on the other leg. Lower the body until the seat touches the heel and then return to the standing position. This must be done without the aid of the arms and without losing balance.

Behind the Back Touch.   Start in a standing position with the arms extended behind the back and hands clasped. Squat slowly and touch the floor with an extended finger, then return to the standing position.

Knee Jump.   Kneel on the floor with the seat on the heels and the toes pointing backward. In one continuous motion, swing the arms forward and jump to the feet. If accomplished, try to perform a half-turn during the jump.

Wall Climb.   Take a push-up position with the feet against the wall. Walk up the wall with the feet to a handstand position and then return to the push-up position.

Popover.   While in push-up position, propel the body upward and do a half turn to the inverted push-up position. Popover to the regular push-up position.

Double Heel Click.   Jump upward and click the heels twice. If accomplished, try to perform a triple heel click before landing.

Push-Up Inversion.   Begin in push-up position. Push strongly off the floor and bring the legs through the arms in 1 smooth motion—assuming the inverted push-up position. Return to the original position with a strong movement backward.

Jump Through.   Hold the left toe with the right hand. Jump the right foot through without losing the grip on the toe. Try the stunt with the other foot.

Sitting Lift-Off.   Sit on the floor with the legs extended forward. Place the hands on the floor somewhere between the hips and knees, depending on the balance point. Lift the entire body off the floor in a balanced position. The stunt can be learned in stages—first with the heels remaining on the floor, then with the heels held off the floor by a friend.

Jumping Toe Touch.   Begin in a standing position with the hands held in front of the body, shoulder-width apart, palms down. When ready, jump up and bring the feet quickly forward so the toe tips touch the hands in front of the body. The attempt should be to bring the hands to the feet, lifting the feet as high as possible.

Leg Circling.   In a squatting position with both hands on the floor, place the left knee between the arms and extend the right leg to the side. Swing the right leg forward and under the lifted right arm, under the left leg and arm, and back to starting position. Perform several circles in succession. Try circling with the other leg.

Suggested Partner and Group Stunts

Leapfrog.   One student forms the base by standing stiff-legged, bending over, and placing the hands on the knees. The other student runs and leaps over the base by performing a light push-off on the back of the base. A number of students can form bases to create a series of leaps for the moving student.

Wheelbarrow.   One partner is in push-up position with the legs spread. The other person walks between the legs and grasps and lifts the partner's lower legs. The partner in push-up position then walks the arms while the other person moves forward, backward, or sideways. A double or triple wheelbarrow can be performed with students extending their legs over the back of the student in push-up position and placing their hands on the floor.

Caterpillar.   One student is on hands and knees, acting as the support. Another student, facing the same direction, places the hands about 2 feet in front of the support's hands. The second student's legs are then placed on top of the support and locked together at the ankles. Five to 6 students can continue this process and then begin walking when everyone is in place.

Knee Stand.   The base student is in crab position. The other student stands on the knees of the base. A spotter may be necessary to help the second student come to a balanced position.

Cooperative Scooter.   Two students face each other and sit with toes under the seat of the other.

The arms are joined by holding the other student's arms at the wrist or above. Students scoot forward or backward by cooperatively lifting the feet when the other lifts the seat. Progress is made by alternately flexing and extending the knees and hips.

Spider Walk.   The base student is in a sitting position with the back against a wall. The next student backs up and sits lightly on the knees of the base. More students can be added in similar fashion. The hands should be placed around the waist of each person in front. Walking is done by moving the feet on the same side together.

Triple High Jump.   Students form groups of 3 and join hands. One of the students is designated as the performer and jumps over the joined arms of the other two. The performer is assisted in the jump by an upward lift from the others. The hands to be jumped over should be clasped lightly and released if the jumper does not gain enough height.

Octopus.   Eight to 12 students work together to develop this activity. Half of the students form a circle with hands joined, while each student in the other half finds a pair of joined hands to lean backward on, placing the weight on the heels. Each of the leaners then join hands behind the backs of the others, thus creating 2 separate groups with joined hands. The octopus begins moving slowly around the circle, taking small side steps. The stunt is brought to a climax by moving as fast as possible.

Double Bear Walk.   The base student is on hands and knees. The top student assumes the same position with the hands on the shoulders and the knees over the hips of the base. They move slowly throughout the area without losing balance.

Double Crab Walk.   The bottom student moves into crab position. The top performer straddles the base and also assumes the crab position with the hands on the shoulders and the feet on the knees of the base. They move slowly throughout the area.

Back Balance.   Students work with a partner. One partner lies in supine position and becomes the base. The base bends the knees, and the balancer places the small of the back on the soles of the base's feet. The balancer then lies back and balances in a layout position (Figure 18.6).

FIGURE 18.6   Spotting the back balance

Sitting Balance.   The base assumes a supine position on the floor. The balancer straddles the base so that they are looking at each other. The balancer sits on the soles of the base's feet while the base holds the ankles of the balancer. The legs of the balancer should be extended as much as possible.

Abdominal Balance.   The base assumes a supine position on the floor, then raises the legs and positions the feet so the soles are parallel to the floor. The balancer faces the base and places the abdomen on the soles of the base's feet. The base grasps the hands of the balancer and extends the legs to move the performer into a balanced position. The balancer should attempt to arch the back, raise the head, and extend the arms to the sides.

Seat Press.   The base lies on the floor with the knees bent and the feet flat on the floor. The balancer straddles the base facing the feet of the base. The two join hands, and the top partner sits on the joined hands supported by the base. The balancer's legs are placed on the knees of the base.

Mini-Pyramids.   Students can work in groups of 3 to 5 to develop various types of pyramids (Figure 18.7). Some examples are shown in the figure. Students should be encouraged to develop different types of pyramids and allowed time to share them with the rest of the class.

FIGURE 18.7   Mini-pyramids

Combatives

There are many types of combatives. This list should give insight into the many variations but is certainly not exhaustive.

Arm Wrestling.   This popular activity can be done lying on the floor or sitting at a table. The right hands are clasped, and the elbows are bent and rest on the floor or table. When ready, the goal is to force the opponent's hand down to the floor or table surface. The elbows cannot be lifted from the surface.

Leg Wrestling.   Opponents are side by side and supine on a mat with their heads in opposite directions. They lock the near elbows and prepare for action. On signal, they lift the inside leg vertically 2 times before hooking the legs on the third count. They then try to roll the opponent over backwards.

Standing Hand Wrestle.   Contestants place the toes of their right feet together and grasp right hands in a handshake grip. The left foot is moved to the rear for support. The goal is to force the opponent to move either foot.

Finger Wrestle.   Opponents stand on the right foot and hold the left foot with the left hand. The index fingers of the right hand are hooked, and opponents attempt to push each other off balance.

Flag Grab.   Contestants have a flag tucked in the belt and attempt to keep others from pulling it out. At the same time, opponents try to collect as many flags as possible.

Palm Wrestle.   Contestants face each other, standing 12 inches apart. The palms of the opponents are placed together and must remain so for the duration of the contest. The goal is to push the opponent off balance.

Push-Up Breakdown.   Opponents are in push-up position and attempt to break down the other's position. It is a fall when 1 of the opponents is brought down from the push-up position to the ground.

Crab Breakdown.   This is similar to the push-up breakdown, except that the opponents are in crab position. As a variation, try getting the opponent to touch the seat to the floor while keeping the hands and feet on the floor. The takedown must occur through jostling and pushing the opponent.

Toe Dance.   Contestants begin by placing their hands on the opponent's shoulders. The goal is to step on top of the toes of the opponent. A variation can be to see how many toe touches can be accumulated in a specified time.

Seat Pull-Up.   Opponents sit on the floor, facing each other, with the knees bent, and the soles of the contestants' shoes together. Players bend forward, grasp hands firmly, and attempt to pull their opponent's seat off the floor. The winner must be sitting upright in position when the opponent is lifted from the floor, or the contest is a draw.

Back-to-Back Takedown.   Contestants sit back to back and lock elbows. The feet are widely spread to form a broad base of support. Both players attempt to pull the other to the left and touch the opponent's shoulder (or elbow) to the floor. As a variation, attempt the contest by pulling in the opposite direction.

Tug-of-War Activities

Tug-of-war activities can be conducted in pairs. Partners should be changed often so students have a chance to compete with many others and are not subjected to constantly losing or to seldom being challenged. Tug-of-war ropes are easily made from 10 feet of 3/8-inch nylon rope and 2 sections of 5/8-inch garden hose 2 feet long. The rope is threaded through the garden hose, which serves as a handle, and tied with a bowline knot so there is a loop at each end of the rope.

Partner Pulls

Partners can have contests using some of the following suggested positions and activities.

Different Positions.   Facing, back to back, side to side, 1 handed, 2 handed, crab position with the rope hooked over the foot, push-up position, and on all fours are a few suggested variations.

Balance Pulls.   Students begin in a stationary position. The goal is to cause the opponent to move the feet or lose balance.

Pick-Up Contest.   Place Indian clubs or bowling pins behind the contestants. The goal is to pull and move backward in order to pick up the clubs.

Multiple Rope Pulls.   Ropes can be twisted together so 4 to 6 students can become involved in the contest.

Pick-Up and Pull.   The ropes are laid on the floor between 2 contestants. On signal, the 2 opponents run to the rope, pick it up, and the tug-of-war ensues.

Team Tug-of-War

Small groups and classes can have contests with the large commercially available tug-of-war ropes. Most are 50 feet in length and at least 1 inch in diameter. Many of the ropes have large loops on the end so students can stand inside of them. Caution must be used with the loops, however, because students cannot easily release the rope when the other team gains momentum.

A suggested manner for conducting team tugs-of-war is to tie a marker in the middle of the rope.

Two parallel lines are drawn 10 to 20 feet apart. The pull starts with the marker in the middle of the 2 lines. The goal is to pull the marker over your team's line. Variations for different types of pulls are to try pulling with the rope overhead, having opponents pull with their backs to each other, pulling with 1 hand on the ground or in the air, or pulling from a seated position.

Wands

Wands provide challenge through balance and flexibility activities, which can be performed individually. Wands are usually made from 5/8-inch or 3/4-inch dowels and should be 42 inches long. They can be painted, and rubber tips can be placed on the ends to soften the noise they make when falling on the floor.

Wand Whirl.   Stand a wand in front of the body, and balance it with 1 finger. Release the wand, perform a full turn, and catch the wand. Try the activity in both directions. Try catching with 1 finger on top of the wand.

Thread the Needle.   Hold the wand in both hands near the ankles. Without letting go of the wand, step over the wand and through the space between the arms. Return to the starting position. Try passing the wand under the feet side to side, 1 foot at a time, with the wand held in front and behind the body.

Thread the Needle (Jumping).   Virtually the same stunt as the previous activity, except that the stick is jumped over and passed under the feet simultaneously.

Wand Kickover.   Balance the wand in front of the body with 1 hand. Release the wand, kick a leg over, and catch the wand. Try kicking in both directions using both legs. Try catching the wand with 1 finger.

Walk Under.   Grasp the wand with the right hand. Twist under the right arm without letting go of the wand, without taking it off the floor, and without touching the knee to the floor. Try using the left arm also.

Broomstick Balance.   Balance the wand vertically in 1 hand. Begin by walking while balancing and then attempt to balance the wand in a stationary position. Try walking in different directions, using both hands, and balancing the wand on different body parts.

Wand Walkdown.   Start in a straddle stance, with legs straight. Hold a wand near 1 end, with the other end of the wand above the head and pointed toward the ceiling. Bend backward, place the wand on the floor behind, and walk the hands down the wand. Return to standing position. If the wands do not have rubber tips, a spotter may have to stabilize the wand end on the floor.

Partner Exchange.   Partners face each other, balancing a wand in front of them. On signal, each runs to the other's wand and catches it before it hits the floor. Challenge can be added by increasing the distance, using 2 wands, and performing stunts such as a full turn or heel click before catching the wand.

Reaction Time.   One partner holds the wand horizontally. The other partner places 1 hand directly above the wand, palm down. The wand is dropped and the person must try to catch the wand before it hits the floor. This can also be tried holding the wand vertically. The other person forms a "V" with the thumb and fingers and is challenged to catch the wand. Marks can be placed on the wand, and students challenged to catch the wand on certain marks.

Wand Wrestle.   A wand is held in the vertical position by 2 opponents. The goal is to move the wand to the horizontal plane. One person is designated to move the wand horizontally while the other resists the attempt. Roles are reversed after each bout.

Wand Release.   Players sit facing each other with the legs straight and the soles of the feet together. Together, they hold a wand horizontally at chest level. A win occurs when 1 person causes the other to release the grip on the wand. Neither player is allowed to leave or modify the starting position.

Isometric Exercises.   Wands are a useful instrument for performing isometric exercises. Examples are attempting to twist the wand, to stretch the wand, to compress the wand, or to pull against different body parts. Many stretching activities can also be done using the wands.

LOW-ORGANIZATION GAMES

The following activities are enjoyable for students because they demand few specialized skills yet require teamwork. The games help develop camaraderie among students, and teams can be reorganized periodically to equalize the competition. Rules listed are only starting points; students and teachers can modify any and all of the rules as they desire.

Cageball Games

Cageballs come in many different sizes. The most common size is 2 feet in diameter, which is an easy size to store and inflate. The next size is 4 feet in diameter, which makes the games more interesting at the high school level. Drawbacks to the larger size are storage, expense, and inflation time. The largest cageballs, often termed earth balls, are 5 or 6 feet in diameter. These can be kicked, batted, and tossed. Students should not be allowed to mount the ball and roll it, however, since falls in those circumstances are common.

Crab Cageball. Students are divided into 4 teams. Cones can be used to delineate the corners of a square. One team forms 1 side of the square, so a different team makes up each side. All players sit with hands behind them for support. Each team is numbered from right to left beginning with the number 1. The cageball is placed in the middle of the square. The instructor or another student calls out a number and 1 member from each team (with the number called) crab-walks to the center and attempts to kick the cageball over the other teams. A team has a point scored against it when: (1) the ball is kicked over or through the team, (2) a team member touches the ball with the arms or hands, or (3) a player stands to block or stop the ball. The team with the fewest points is declared the winner.

Long Team Cageball. Players are divided into 2 teams. The teams move into sitting position in 2 lines facing each other 10 to 15 feet apart. The teacher rolls or throws a cageball between the 2 lines. The object is for 1 team to kick the ball over the other team. A point is scored against a team when the ball goes over or through a line. The team with the fewer points wins. Again, a point is awarded if a player stands or touches the ball with the hands. More than 1 cageball can be used simultaneously.

Cageball Football. The game is played on a large playing field. The class is divided into 2 teams. The object of the game is to carry the cageball across the goal line. The only way the ball can be advanced, however, is when it is in the air. Whenever the ball is on the ground, it can only be moved backwards or sideways. This game is best played with a 4-foot or larger cageball.

Cageball Target Throw. The cageball is used as a target in this game. Divide the class into 2 teams and place them on opposite sides of the gym. A center line divides the area in half, and teams are restricted to movement in their half. Use cones to mark the goal line near the ends of the playing area. Center the cageball between the teams. Each team is given a number of playground balls or volleyballs for throwing at the cageball. The object is to move the cageball across the opponent's goal line by hitting the cageball with the volleyballs. The cageball cannot be touched by any player. If it is touched, regardless of intent, the point goes to the other team.

Scooter Cageball Soccer. Each player is given a scooter. The ball may be advanced by using the feet only. The object is to score a goal in a fashion similar to soccer. Penalty shots are awarded for rough play, touching the ball with the hands, and leaving the scooter.

RECREATIONAL ACTIVITIES

Many recreational activities can be used as mini-units. Rules and regulations usually accompany the activities and are specific to the situation. The authors have had success with some of the following activities:

Shuffleboard
Deck tennis
Tennis volleyball
Table tennis
Pillow polo
Sacket
Horseshoes
Tetherball
Lawn bowling
Global ball
Hocker
Pickleball

Frisbee, bowling, and orienteering are 3 excellent recreational activities that are covered in depth in later chapters. They can also be used as mini-activities.

RELAYS

When they are not overused, relays are enjoyable activities for students. To keep the atmosphere vibrant and the students motivated, the teams should be changed often to equalize the ability of various groups. If the same team wins every bout, the outcome is predetermined and the rest of the class will not be motivated. Another motivator is frequent changing of the relay. The relay can be run once to show students how it is to be conducted and then 1 to 3 times for competition. All relay teams should have the same number of persons on each squad. It is wise to change the order of the squads, so different people get a chance to run starting and finishing legs. Define the signals to start the relay, and tell students what position they must assume when finished (sitting, kneeling, or some alternative position).

Potato Relays. Potato relays have been played for years. A small box to hold the objects (potatoes) is placed in front of each squad. Four circles (hoops can be used) are placed 10 to 15 feet apart in front of each squad. The goal is for the first runner to pick up an object from the box and carry it to one of the hoops, come back, pick up another object, and place it in another hoop. This is done until all the hoops are filled. The next person picks up the objects one at a time from the hoops and places them back in the box. The pattern is repeated until all members of the squad have had a turn.

Wheelbarrow Relay. Use the wheelbarrow position described earlier in the chapter as the means of locomotion. All members of each squad must participate in both the carrying position and the down formation.

Bowling Pin Relay. Four bowling pins per squad are used. They are evenly spaced in front of each squad in a fashion similar to the potato relay. The first person in line lays all of the pins down, and the next person stands them up. Only 1 hand can be used.

Over and Under Ball Relay. Each team is spread out in open squad formation so players are 10 to 15 feet apart. The first person in line passes the ball backward overhead to the nearest teammate. That person throws it backward between the legs to another teammate, and the pattern repeats. When the ball gets to the end of the squad, that person runs to the front of the squad and passes the ball backward. The process is repeated until all players have had a turn at the end and front of the squad.

Stepping-Stone Relay. Two small carpet squares are used per squad. The first person in line is the mover and helps the next person in line move down and back. The only way to advance in this relay is by standing on a carpet square and moving to another. It is illegal to move or stand on the floor. The mover picks up the rear carpet square and moves it in front of the advancing player so the next step can be taken. All players must play both roles before the relay is completed.

Pass and Squat Relay. Players are spread out so they are 10 to 15 feet apart. The first person in line turns around, faces the rest of the squad, and throws a volleyball or soccer ball to the first person in line, who returns the throw and squats. The leader now throws the ball to the next person until all members have received a throw and have squatted. When the ball is thrown to the last player, that person dribbles the ball to the front of the squad and repeats the pattern.

Fetch Relay. Squads line up and place 1 member at the other end of the playing area, 10 to 20 yards away. This person runs back to the squad and fetches the next person. The person who has just been fetched in turn runs back and fetches the next person. The pattern continues until all members have been fetched to the opposite end of the playing area.

Snowball Relay. This relay is similar to the fetch relay, except that after 1 person has been fetched, both players run back and pick up another player. The pattern continues until the majority of squad members are running back and forth, picking up the remaining members. This relay can be exhausting for the first few people in line and should not be run too often.

Sport Skill Relays. Many sport skills can be used for relays. For example, dribble the basketball down the court, make a basket, and return. The problem with relays of this type is that success is predicated on the skill level of the participants. If some students are less skilled in basketball, the relay can be a source of embarrassment, causing these students to bear the brunt of losing the relay. An instructor who uses sport skill relays is wise to include a wide variety of skills and to develop many different types of relays.

Spread Eagle Relay. Break the class into groups of 8 to 10 students. They lie down on the floor and form a circle with their heads toward the center. They join hands and spread the legs. Participants in each squad are numbered, beginning with 1 through the number of squad members. When a number is called, that person stands up, runs around the circle, and then resumes the prone position on the floor. The runner must place both feet between each pair of legs. The first person to return to the starting position earns a point for that squad. The squad with the most points wins.

COOPERATIVE ACTIVITIES

Cooperative activities require students to work together. They can be used early in the year as mixers in an attempt to help students get to know one another. Emphasis is on enjoyment and accomplishment.

Group Games

Mass Stand Up. Start with 2 people sitting back to back. Lock elbows and try to stand up. Increase the number to 3 people, then 4, and so forth. See how many people can stand up simultaneously.

Butt Tug. Stand in 2 lines back to back. One line moves to the left 1 step. Bend over, cross the arms between the legs, and grasp the hand of 2 different people from the other team. Now begin tugging. Try forming 2 teams in the described position and have a race while maintaining the hand grips.

Circle Sit. Have students form a circle and hold hands. Close the circle so shoulders are touching. Move the right side of the body toward the center of the circle and move inward, eliminating gaps. Now sit on the knees of the person behind. Try walking in this position when everyone has assumed the sitting position. Put the left side toward the center and sit on a new partner's lap.

Animal Sounds. Students all close their eyes. Someone is designated to move throughout the group and assign animal names to the players. The number of animals assigned will determine the number of groups formed. This is a useful way to organize groups. When the command is given, the only noises that can be made are those that resemble the animals. Students must keep their eyes closed and move throughout the area in search of another person who has been assigned the same animal. For example, people assigned to be cows search for their counterparts by making a mooing sound and listening for others mooing.

Entanglement. Divide the class into 2 or more groups. Each group makes a tight circle with their arms pointing toward the middle. In each group, students hold someone's hand until everybody is holding hands. Each person must hold a hand of 2 different people. On signal, the 2 groups race to see which can untangle first without disjoining hands. The group may end up in either 1 large circle or in 2 smaller, connecting circles. People can be facing different directions when finished.

Bulldozer. Students lie in prone position side by side and as close as possible on the floor. The end person rolls on top of the next person and on down the line of people. When that person gets to the end of the line, the next person starts the roll. Two teams can be formed and a relay race conducted.

Zipper. Players make a single-file line. Each student bends over, reaches between the legs with the left hand, and grasps the right hand of the person to the rear. This continues on down the line until all hands are grasped. On signal, the last person in line lies down, the next person backs over the last person and lies down, and so forth until the last person lies down, and then immediately stands and reverses the procedure. The first team to zip and unzip the zipper is declared the winner.

Addition Tag. Two are selected to be "it." They must hold hands and can tag only with their outside hands. When they tag someone, that person must hook on. This continues and the tagging line becomes longer and longer. Regardless of the length of the line, only the hand on each end of the line is eligible to tag.

REFERENCES AND SUGGESTED READINGS

Darst, P., and Armstrong, G. 1991. *Outdoor Adventure Activities for School and Recreation Programs*. Prospect Heights, IL: Waveland Press.

Fluegelman, A. (ed.). 1976. *The New Games Book*. Garden City, NY: Doubleday and Co.

Orlick, T. 1982. *Cooperative Sports and Games Book*. New York: Pantheon Books.

Pangrazi, R. P., and Dauer, V. P. 1995. *Dynamic Physical Education for Elementary School Children*. 11th ed. Boston: Allyn & Bacon.

Rohnke, K. 1984. *Silver Bullets: A Guide to Initiative Problems, Adventure Games, and Trust Activities*. Dubuque, IA: Kendall/Hunt Publishing Company.

Rohnke, K. 1989. *Cowstails and Cobras II: A Guide to Games, Initiatives, Ropes Courses, and Adventure Curriculum*. Dubuque, IA: Kendall/Hunt Publishing Company.

Simpson, B. 1974. *Initiative Games*. Butler, PA: Encounter Four, Butler County Community College.

19

Team Sports

Chapters 19 to 22 offer beginning-level units in a wide variety of instructional activities. Rating scales, performance objectives for tasks, station work ideas, block plans, crossword puzzles, and rainy-day activities are some of the ideas presented in this section. It is important that teachers try new ideas to improve the instructional process. A variety of learning activities helps motivate both students and teachers. The various units serve as a framework for developing instructional units. These units are not all inclusive but starting points that stimulate and encourage a wide range of instructional approaches. The ideas can be adapted and shaped into a unit that is unique and meets the needs of students in different areas. This allows teachers to retain control in planning and developing instructional sequences.

Lead-up activities and skills are presented in detail for units where a dearth of resource materials exists. Some units are highly complex and demand in-depth, specialized instruction. In these cases, comprehensive resources have been listed. Such resources are listed for the areas of gymnastics, track and field, aquatics, and rhythms because of the complexity of the areas.

BASKETBALL

Basketball is a popular game played on schoolyards by many participants. It was invented in 1891 at Springfield College by Dr. Naismith, who used peach baskets and a soccer ball. The game offers reinforcement to participants when a basket is made, and is one of the few team sports requiring skills that can be practiced individually. The game demands great cardiorespiratory endurance and fine motor development.

Basketball instruction should focus on developing skills and competence so students leave school with the ability to participate in recreational games later in life. At the middle school level, emphasis should be on lead-up games that allow all students to find success and enjoyment. As students develop the skills necessary to play the game well, instruction during the high school years can concentrate on strategy and teamwork. Highly skilled and interested students should be offered additional opportunities to play through intramural programs, recreational leagues, or interscholastic competition.

Sequence of Skills

One of the attractive components of basketball is that little equipment is necessary for participation. Students should be required to wear a gym shoe made for the activity. Running shoes are a poor substitute for basketball shoes because they often leave black marks on the floor, do not offer adequate support, and wear out quickly.

The following skills are basic to the game of basketball. Students never learn these skills to perfection, so offer time for regular practice. For example, players can always make a better pass, develop more efficient dribbling skills, or shoot a higher percentage of baskets.

Passing

Regardless of the pass used, certain points should be emphasized. The ball should be handled with the fingertips. As the ball makes contact with the hands, the elbows should bend and the hands move toward the body in order to "give" with the ball and absorb the force. The passer should step forward in the direction of the receiver. The ball is released with a quick straightening of the elbows and a snap of the wrists. The arms and fingers are fully extended with the palms turned outward for the follow-through after the ball has been released. Passers should anticipate where their teammate is going to be when the ball reaches the receiver. Many of the passing drills should therefore focus on passing while moving.

Chest Pass

The chest pass is used frequently in basketball for passes up to 20 feet. The ball is held at chest level with the fingers spread on both sides of the ball. One foot is ahead of the other in stride position. The elbows remain close to the body, and the ball is propelled by extending the arms, snapping the wrists, and stepping toward the target.

Bounce Pass

The bounce pass is used to transfer the ball to a closely guarded teammate. It is directed to a spot on the floor that is closer to the receiver than the passer. The ball should rebound to waist level of the receiver. Passing form is similar to the chest pass.

Flip Pass

This pass is used for a close-range exchange. The ball is flipped somewhat upward to a teammate. It is used often as a pass to a player cutting to the basket for a lay-up shot.

Two-Handed Overhead Pass

This pass is used against a shorter opponent, usually in back court. The passer is in a short stride position with the ball held overhead. The momentum of the pass comes from a forceful wrist and finger snap. The upper arms remain relatively in place.

Catching

For effective catching, it is important to keep the eyes on the ball, follow the ball into the hands, and concentrate on the catch before beginning the next task. The receiver should move toward the ball and reach for it with the fingers spread. When the pass is at waist level or above, the thumbs should be pointed in and the fingers up. When the ball is to be caught below waist level, the thumbs are out and the fingers down. The hands should "give" and move toward the body to absorb the force of the throw and thus make the ball more catchable.

Dribbling

Dribbling requires bent knees and crouching. The forearm of the dribbling hand is parallel to the floor, and the ball should be pushed toward the roll, rather than slapped. The ball is controlled with the fingertips. Most of the force supplied to the ball should be from the wrist, so arm movement is minimized. Emphasis should be placed on controlling the ball.

Shooting

Certain points are common to all shooting. The body should be squared up with the basket whenever possible. The ball is held with the fingers spread, and the elbow of the shooting hand should always be directly behind the ball. The eyes are fixed on the rim, and the ball is shot with a slight backspin on it. The arm is extended on follow-through with the wrist flexed.

Lay-Up Shots

For a right-handed lay-up, the player approaches the basket from the right side at an angle of about 45 degrees. The ball is released with the right hand and the weight on the left foot. As the body is elevated off the floor by the left foot, the ball is released 12 to 18 inches above the basket on the backboard. For a left-handed shot, the sequence is the opposite. The shooter should always reach toward the spot on the backboard with the shooting hand, and students should practice shooting with each hand.

One-Hand Push Shots

The push shot is used primarily for shooting free throws. Few people shoot a 1-hand shot from a set position. The ball is held at shoulder level in the nonshooting hand. The shooting hand is behind the ball, the fingertips touching the ball, and the wrist is cocked. The legs are shoulder width apart and the knees slightly bent. To shoot, straighten the legs and push forward with the forearm and wrist. The wrist should be bent over on follow-through and the arm straight.

Jump Shots

The jump shot is the most popular shot in basketball because it is difficult to block. The hands are in the same position as described for the 1-hand push shot. After the shooter jumps, the ball is placed just above and in front of the head. The elbow must be kept under the ball so the shooting hand moves in a straight line toward the basket. The wrist snaps on release. The shot should be performed using a jump in an upward plane. Leaning forward, sideways, or backward will make the shot much less consistent. The jump shot is sometimes difficult for middle school students. They often learn the wrong motor pattern of throwing the ball instead of shooting it. If this is the case, use a smaller ball, a lower basket, or both to develop the correct pattern.

Ideas for Effective Instruction

Drills used in basketball should simulate game conditions as closely as possible. There are few situations in basketball where players are standing still. Passing drills should therefore include player movement, shooting drills should require movement and pressure, and drills for dribbling under control should include looking away from the ball.

Baskets can be lowered to 8.5 to 9 feet to increase the amount of success. This will also help develop better shooting patterns in the weaker, smaller players. Note that almost all students will select the lower basket when they have a choice of a basket at regulation height and another, lowered basket. Most people are motivated by being able to dunk the shot and thus shoot a higher percentage.

The program should concentrate on skill development and include many drills. Basketball offers endless drill possibilities, and using many drills gives variety and breadth to the instructional program. The drills should offer each student as much practice as possible in a stipulated amount of time. Lining up a squad of 8 players to take turns makes little sense. Use as many balls as possible. In some cases, students may be willing to bring one from home for class use. More baskets and balls mean that more students will have an opportunity to practice and learn skills.

There are many basketball drills to enhance passing, dribbling, and shooting, but the lead-up games that follow in the next section encourage skill practice while introducing competition and game play. When possible, therefore, isolate skills and practice them in lead-up games to maintain a high level of student motivation.

Lead-Up Games and Learning Activities

Keepaway

The essence of the game is to make as many consecutive passes as possible without losing control to the opposite team. Teams may consist of 5 to 10 players. Use colored vests so players can identify their teammates. The game is started with a jump ball, and the goal is to maintain control. Each defensive player must stay with a designated opponent, rather than the defensive team swarming in a zone defense. As soon as possession is lost, counting of passes is started by that team. The team that makes the most consecutive passes within a designated time is the winner.

Five Passes

This game is similar to keepaway, but the object is to make 5 consecutive passes. As soon as these have been made, the ball is turned over to the other team. Students are not allowed to travel with the ball. Two or 3 dribbles may be allowed between passes. Players may hold the ball for only 3 seconds.

Dribble Tag

Divide the playing area into 2 equal parts. All players begin dribbling in one-half of the area. The object of this game is to maintain a continuous dribble while avoiding being tagged by another player. If tagged or if control of the ball is lost, the player must move to the other half of the playing area and practice dribbling without the pressure of competition.

Dribble Keepaway

The area is divided into 2 equal parts. All players start in one-half of the area and begin dribbling. The goal is to maintain control of the dribble while trying to disrupt the dribble of an opponent. If control of the ball is lost, the player moves to the other side of the area and practices.

Around the World

Shooting spots are marked on the floor with tape. Players are in groups of 3. A player begins at the first spot and continues until a shot misses. The player can then wait for another turn or take a second "risk" shot. If the risk shot is made, the player continues "around the world." If the shot is missed, the player must start over on the next turn. The winner is the player who goes around the world first. A variation is to count the number of shots that players take to move around the world. The person who makes the circuit with the fewest shots is the winner.

Twenty-One

Players are in groups of 3 or 4. Each player receives a long shot (distance must be designated) and a follow-up shot. The long shot, if made, counts 2 points, and the follow-up shot 1 point. The follow-up shot must be taken from the spot where the ball was recovered. The first player to score 21 points is the winner. A variation is to play team 21 in which the first team of players to score 21 is declared the winner.

Horse

Players work in groups of 2 to 4 and shoot in a predetermined order. The first player shoots from any place on the court. If the shot is made, the next player must make the same type of shot from the same position. If the shot is missed by the next player, that player receives an "H," and the following player can shoot any shot desired. No penalty is assigned for a missed shot unless the previous player has made a shot. A player is disqualified if the letters spelling HORSE are accumulated. The winner is the last remaining player.

Sideline Basketball

The class is divided into 2 teams, each lined up along 1 side of the court, facing the other. The game is played by 3 or 4 active players from each team. The remainder of the players standing on the sideline can catch and pass the ball to the active players, but they may not shoot or enter the playing floor. They must keep 1 foot completely out-of-bounds at all times.

Active players play regular basketball with 1 variation, they may pass and receive the ball from sideline players. The game starts with the active players occupying their own half of the court. The ball is taken out-of-bounds under its own basket by the team that was scored upon. Play continues until one team scores or until a period of time (2 or 3 minutes) elapses. The active players then take places on the left side of their line, and 3 new active players come out from the right. All other players move down 3 places in the line.

No official out-of-bounds on the sides is called. The players on that side of the floor simply recover the ball and put it into play without delay by a pass to an active player. Out-of-bounds on the ends is the same as in regular basketball. If one of the sideline players enters the court and touches the ball, it is a violation, and the ball is awarded out-of-bounds on the other side to a sideline player. Free throws are awarded when a player is fouled. Sideline players may pass to each other and should be well spaced along the side.

Half-Court Basketball

Teams of 2 to 4 work best for this variation. The game is similar to regulation basketball with the following exceptions: When a defensive player recovers the ball, either from a rebound or an interception, the ball must be taken back to midcourt before offensive play can begin. After a basket is made, the ball must again be taken to midcourt. For out-of-bounds and ball-handling violations, the ball is awarded to the opponents out-of-bounds at a spot near the place where the violation occurred. The ball, in this case, does not have to be taken to midcourt. If a foul occurs, the ball is given to the offended team, or regulation foul shooting can be done.

Three on Three

There are many lead-up games in which the number of players on a team varies. The advantage of playing half-court basketball with only 2 or 3 players on a team is that each player gets to handle the ball more. Regulation rules are followed.

The game 3 on 3 can be played with 4 or 5 teams. An offensive team of 3 stands forward of the midcourt line while another team is on defense. The other teams wait behind midcourt for their turn. A scrimmage is over when 1 team scores. The defensive team then goes on offense, and a new team comes in to play defense. The old offensive team goes to the rear of the line of waiting players. The game can be varied so that the winning team stays on after a basket is scored. Caution must be used with the winner-stay-on approach as it sometimes means that the better players get much more practice than the less-skilled performers. Make the teams as equal as possible so all have a chance to win.

Suggested Performance Objectives

The following are examples of performance objectives that might be used in a beginning basketball class. The standards may have to be adjusted, depending on the skill level and age of the students.

Core Requirements

Dribbling Tasks

1. In a stationary position, execute a right-hand dribble 10 consecutive times.
2. Same as task 1 except use the left hand.
3. Using a reduced speed, dribble the ball with the right hand from the baseline to the midcourt line without losing control.
4. Using a reduced speed, dribble the ball with the left hand from the midcourt line to the baseline without losing the dribble.

Passing Tasks

5. Standing 10 feet away from the target on the wall, throw 10 consecutive 2-hand chest passes.
6. Standing 10 feet away from a partner, execute 8 of 10 consecutive 2-hand passes.
7. Standing 10 feet away from the target, throw 10 consecutive 2-hand bounce passes.
8. Standing 10 feet away from a partner, execute 8 of 10 consecutive bounce passes.
9. Standing 10 feet away from the target, throw 10 consecutive 2-hand overhead passes.
10. Standing 10 feet away from a partner, execute 8 of 10 consecutive 2-hand overhead passes.

Shooting Tasks

11. Starting from the right side about 20 feet from the basket, dribble the ball toward the basket and make 4 of 6 lay-ups using the backboard.
12. Same as task 11, but start from the left side.
13. Standing 6 feet from the basket (right side), make 4 of 6 bank shots.
14. Same as task 13, but use the left side.

15. Standing at the free-throw line, make 5 of 10 consecutive set shots.
16. Standing 10 feet from the basket, make 5 of 10 jump shots.

Rebounding Tasks

17. Standing with the feet shoulder-width apart and with both hands at shoulder level, jump up and touch the target on the wall 3 consecutive times using both hands.
18. Standing 2 to 3 feet away from the basket, toss the ball off the right side of the backboard and rebound with both hands 5 consecutive times.
19. Same as task 18, but use the left side.
20. Standing 2 to 3 feet from the basket, toss the ball off the right side of the backboard, rebound using both hands, and pivot right using the overhead pass or chest pass to a partner. Repeat 5 consecutive times.
21. Same as task 20, but use the left side and pivot left.

Optional Requirements

1. Officiate at least 1 regulation game during class time, using correct calls and signals.
2. Write a 1-page report on the game of basketball.
3. Make a list of 15 basketball terms and define them.
4. Write a one-page report on a basketball article or book.
5. Perform a figure-8 ball-handling technique by weaving the ball around 1 leg and then around the other leg—forming a figure 8—successfully for 10 seconds.
6. Make 8 of 10 bank shots from anywhere outside the foul lane.
7. Make 9 of 10 free throws.

FIELD HOCKEY

Field hockey is a popular team sport that has been played predominately by girls in the United States. Many clubs across the country are affiliated with the United States Field Hockey Association and offer playing experiences for participants ages 6 to 60 years old. In other countries, the game is also played by men and is a popular Olympic sport. Many high schools and colleges offer field hockey competition for girls and women.

The regulation game is played with 11 players on each team. The object of the game is to move a ball with a stick into the opponent's goal, which is 12 feet wide and 7 feet high. The game is started with a pass back in the center of the field. Besides the goalkeeper, a team usually has 3 forwards, 3 links, 3 backs, and 1 sweeper. The field is 60 yards by 100 yards with a 16-yard striking circle (Figure 19.1).

Hockey equipment includes the ball, sticks, shin guards, and the goalkeeper's helmet with mask, chest protector, gloves, full-length leg pads and kickers for the shoes. The ball is composed of cork and twine and is covered in leather. Sticks vary in length from 30 to 37 inches. Middle school students use sticks that are 30 to 34 inches long, and high school students use sticks that are 35 to 37 inches. All regulation sticks have a flat surface on 1 side and a rounded surface on the other. Only the flat side can be used for legal hits.

The game can be modified in several ways for secondary physical education units. The number of players and the field size can be reduced. Goals can be improvised by using boundary cones, high-jump standards, or even soccer goals. A whiffle ball or a rubber or plastic ball can be used, and plastic sticks that are flat on both sides are available. A flat plastic puck is recommended for play on the gymnasium floor. Goalies should wear a face mask, chest protector, and shin guards from softball or lacrosse equipment. If the goalie equipment is not available, then the game should be played without a goalie. Both boys and girls can enjoy the game in a coeducational unit. Field hockey can be played indoors, outdoors, or on a cement surface.

Sequence of Skills

Grip in is the basic grip. The left hand is placed on the top of the stick as though "shaking hands." The right hand is placed 6 to 8 inches below the left hand. The palms of the hands will face each other in most situations. The right hand can slide up the stick for a drive shot and for a reverse stick. The lower position is used for dribbling and for most passes.

Dribbling

Dribbling is propelling the ball downfield in a controlled manner. It can be done straight down the field or zigzagging to the left and right. In straight dribbling, the arms are kept in front of the body. The flat side of the stick faces forward. Short, controlled taps on the ball are used. The ball should remain in front of the body. The zigzag dribble moves the ball left and right by using a forehand tap to the left and a reverse stick tap to the right. In the reverse stick, the stick is turned over, with the toe of the stick pointing down. This type of dribble requires a lot of practice and stick control. The taps to the left and right should be short and controlled. Dribbling can also include dragging the ball with the flat side of the stick. The stick stays in contact with the ball as it is being dragged down field.

Passing and Shooting

The drive shot is the most forceful pass for longer distances and goal shots. The hands are together, and the stick comes back and forward in a manner similar to a shortened golf swing. The stick cannot be lifted higher than the shoulder in either the backswing or

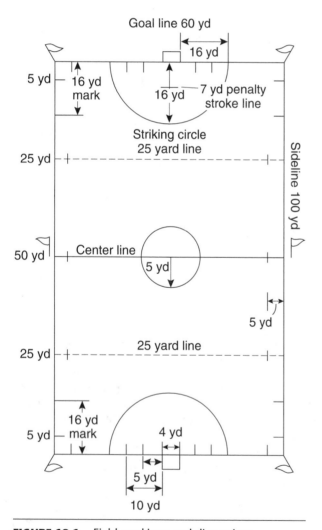

FIGURE 19.1 Field markings and dimensions

follow-through. Drive shots can be straight, to the left, or to the right.

The push pass is used for shorter, more accurate passes. The pass is usually executed quickly off the dribble. There is no backswing. The right hand is lower on the stick, and the ball is pushed or swept along the ground.

The scoop is a pass or shot that is lofted into the air using a shoveling motion for a shot or to get over an opponent's stick. The top of the stick must be tilted backward so the blade is behind and under the ball to give it loft as the force is applied. The flick pass or shot is the most popular aerial shot that gets off the ground about knee high and is an extension of the push pass. The flick is a popular shot on goal.

A slap hit is a modified drive shot or pass that uses a short backswing and does not require a change in the position of the hands. The pass can be used with the hands apart in the normal hand position for ball handling.

Fielding

Fielding refers to stopping and controlling a moving ball and must be practiced with balls coming from the right, left, and center. The face of the stick and the body position need to be adjusted according to the direction in which the ball is traveling. The front fielding position is similar to the straight dribbling position and is used for balls rolling straight toward a person. Balls coming from the left require a regular forehand position with the blade facing to the left. For balls coming from the right, the stick must intercept the ball before it reaches the body. The blade must be turned so that it is facing to the right. Fielding requires the ability to absorb the ball's momentum by "giving" with the stick, depending on the speed of the ball.

Tackling and Dodging

Tackling is attempting to take the ball away from an opponent. Tackles can be made straight on or from the left or the right side of an opponent. Timing is important, because the ball must be picked off while it is away from the opponent's stick. The stick is carried low, and the tackler must concentrate on the ball and on the opponent's stick. The speed of the opponent and of the ball must be considered. The tackle should not be a reckless striking of the stick.

Dodging is a skill for evading a tackler and maintaining control of the ball. A dodge can be executed to the left or right side of the tackler, and a scoop shot can also be used to go over an opponent's stick.

If a dodge is made to the left, the dodger should move the ball 90 degrees to the left just before the tackle. A dodger moving around to the left is on the stick side, which is the right, of the opponent. This maneuver is a stick-side dodge. A dodge to the right involves moving the ball to the right of the opponent, but the dodger's body must move around the other side of the tackler, that is, the ball goes to the right but the person goes to the left (nonstick-side dodge). A reverse stick technique can also be used for a nonstick-side dodge. The player uses the reverse stick to pull the ball across the body to the nonstick side of the defender and then step forward with the left foot and push the ball past the defender.

Bully or Face-Off

The bully is used only when simultaneous fouls occur. Two players face each other in the middle of the field with their respective sticks facing the direction of the goal where they can score. The bully starts with the two players striking the ground on their own side of the ball and then touching sticks above the ball. This is repeated 3 times, and then players attempt to control the ball or to pass it to a teammate.

Goalkeeping

The goalkeeper can kick the ball or block the ball with the body, hands, or stick. Most balls are blocked with the legs or feet, hence the padding on these areas. Most clears away from the goal are with a kick. The goalie cannot hold the ball or throw the ball away from the goal.

Ideas for Effective Instruction

Drills can be set up for partner work at several stations. Dribbling, passing, shooting, tackling, dodging, and goalkeeping can be specific stations with varying tasks to be practiced. Use the performance objectives detailed here for the tasks at each station. Set up boundary cones, stopwatches, targets, baskets, and other instructional devices for challenging skill work. Arrange classes so that students spend several minutes working at each of 4 stations. The station work can then be followed by several small group drills such as 3 on 3, keepaway, or 3-person weave. A modified or regulation game could follow the group work. This variety of learning activities helps to keep students active and motivated.

Remind students continually about the importance of safe stick handling. High sticking is extremely dangerous and rules must be enforced tightly. Body checking, tripping, and hooking with the stick should also be forbidden. A free hit or penalty corner can be used as a penalty for these violations depending on where the penalty occurs. The teacher must be clear about the rules, regulations, and penalties that are going to be enforced in the game.

Lead-Up Games and Learning Activities

Three-Person Weave

The ball is started by the center person and passed to either the person on the left or right. The person making the pass always runs behind the person who receives the pass. The person receiving the pass then becomes the middle person. This procedure continues downfield.

Partner Passing

Partners stand apart and try to hit as many passes as possible in 30 seconds. Each hit is counted. As variations, try the same activity with 3 people in a triangle, 4 in a square, or 5 in a circle.

Circle Keepaway

Students form a circle with 1 person in the middle. The people in the circle try to keep the ball away from the center person. This can also be played with only 3 people. The person in the middle is rotated after 1 minute.

Circle Dribble

A student dribbles the ball around the circle as fast as possible, concluding the dribble at the next person in the circle. All members of the circle go around quickly. Circles compete against each other or against the clock.

Star Drill

Five classmates make a star formation. Number 1 passes to 2, and 2 to 3, and so forth. After passing the ball, the passer runs and takes that person's spot. The passer always follows the pass, and more than 1 person can be in line. The game can also be played against another team or against the clock.

Defensive Squares Drill

Several squares are set up with boundary cones. The size of the squares can vary depending on the ability of the students. Smaller squares will make the drill more demanding for the offensive player. A defensive player is in the square and an offensive player tries to dribble through the square. The defensive player tries to keep the offensive player from dribbling through the square.

Dribble and Hit for Distance

Half of the class or group lines up 5 yards behind a drive line. A partner is downfield about 50 yards. On signal, the hitters dribble the 5 yards and hit a drive shot as far as possible. The partner stands over the ball, and a winner is determined. Partners change places after several hits.

No-Goalie Field Hockey

The game is played without a goalie. Person-to-person defense can be used. The goal size can also be modified if necessary.

End Zone Hockey

The entire end line of the field is the goal area. Each team designates a certain number of goalies and field players. The goalies must spread out over the entire goal line in order to cover it properly. Goalies and field players change places after a specified number of minutes.

Sideline Hockey

Part of each team lines up on 1 sideline, while the rest of each team is on the field. The sideline players keep the ball from going out-of-bounds, and they can also pass to the field players. A regulation goal and goalie are used in the game. The sideline and field players switch after 3 minutes of play. This game can be varied by putting members of each team on both sidelines, thus adding another challenge to the game.

Square Hockey

The game is played on a large square. Each team defends 2 sides of the square. Some team members are on the square sides as goalies, and others are on the field trying to hit the ball past either of the 2 end lines. At the start of the game, the teacher can have all students stand on the square and count off. Several numbers can then be called, and those students become the field players.

Half-Circle Hockey

This is similar to square hockey, but each team forms one-half of a circle. The half-circles connect, and the object is to push the ball through the opponent's half-circle. If the ball comes to rest inside the circle, it belongs to the team nearer the ball. That team can take a shot from the point where the ball stopped.

Modified Coed Field Hockey

This modified game is recommended for coeducational physical education classes. The rules and penalties are as follows:

1. A push back is used to start the game and after each goal.
2. A legal hit is used when the ball goes out-of-bounds.
3. A short corner shot is awarded to the offense when the ball goes past the end line within the striking circle last touching off a defender.
4. A long corner shot is awarded to the offense when the ball goes past the end line outside the striking circle last touching off a defender.
5. A defensive hit is awarded to the defensive team when the ball goes over the end line off an offensive player.
6. The striking circle is the 16-yard half-circle around the goal. A free shot is awarded for a foul occurring anywhere outside the striking circle. All players must be 5 yards away.
7. A penalty corner is awarded for a defensive foul inside the striking circle.
8. Off-sides occurs when an offensive player gains an advantage within the 25-yard line. A defensive hit is awarded at the top of the circle.
9. High sticking occurs when the stick is raised above the shoulder. The penalty is a free hit or a penalty corner if occurring in the striking circle.
10. Advancing is when a player uses any part of the body to advance the ball. The penalty is a free hit or a penalty corner.
11. Hooking, tripping, or dangerous stick use involves using the stick to slow down or trip an opponent. The penalty is a free hit or penalty corner.
12. Body checking is vigorous use of the body for blocking and other maneuvers. The penalty is a free hit or penalty corner.

Suggested Performance Objectives

These performance objectives can be used to structure the learning activities for station work. They can also be tied to a motivational scheme for earning grades or entry into a playing situation. Teachers might develop a contract from these objectives, which can be modified according to the ability levels of the students in a specific situation. If the objectives are too hard or too easy, they should be rewritten to provide a fair challenge and a successful experience for students.

1. Dribble the ball for 30 yards, 3 consecutive times, using proper technique at all times (straight dribble).
2. Dribble the ball through an obstacle course and back in 30 seconds or less (straight dribble).
3. Dribble the ball toward a target and execute a nonstick dodge in 3 of 5 attempts without losing control.
4. Dribble the ball toward a target and execute a stick-side dodge around the target in 3 of 5 attempts without losing control.
5. With a partner, push-pass the ball back and forth (jogging speed) for 30 yards, 2 consecutive times.
6. Push-pass the ball to a target 3 of 5 times from a distance of 10 yards.
7. Shoot 3 of 5 drive shots into the goal from 10 yards (no goalie).
8. Scoop the ball over an obstacle into a basket 3 consecutive times from within a stick-length distance.
9. Dribble the ball from the center of the field toward the goal, and hit 3 drive shots 3 consecutive times without a goalie.
10. Execute proper fielding of the ball from the front, right, and left side, passed by a partner from 10 to 15 yards away (5 times from each side).
11. Dribble the ball for 30 yards, 3 consecutive times, using proper technique at all times (zigzag dribble).
12. Dribble the ball through an obstacle course and back in 30 seconds or less (zigzag dribble).
13. Dribble the ball toward a goal and score 2 of 5 drive shots past a goalie from 10 yards.

14. Execute a 3-person weave passing drill from a distance of 15 to 30 yards, 2 consecutive times.
15. Hit 2 of 5 penalty shots past a goalie.
16. Execute a proper tackle from the left, right, and center.
17. Scoop and run with the ball for 25 yards.
18. Dribble 5 yards, then execute a scoop shot. Repeat 5 consecutive times.
19. Flick 3 of 5 balls into the left and right corners of the goal.

Rainy-Day Activities

Many of the drills and modified games can be played indoors with a flat plastic puck and an indoor stick. Teachers can set up station activities for working on performance tasks. Modified games, such as sideline hockey, end zone hockey, and square hockey, can be played indoors with large numbers of students. Strategies, terminology, and penalties can be discussed at indoor sessions.

FLAG FOOTBALL

Football is America's favorite spectator sport. Professional football players are held in high esteem by students. The shape of the football makes throwing and catching more difficult and challenging than similar maneuvers in other sports. Flag and touch football are variations of the game of football, modified so the game can be played without the padding and equipment necessary for tackle football. Flag football is usually the more enjoyable, because it eliminates the arguments about whether someone was touched or not.

Sequence of Skills

Passing

Passing is used to advance the ball downfield to a teammate. The passer looks at the receiver and points the shoulder opposite the throwing arm toward the receiver. The ball is brought up to the throwing shoulder with both hands. The fingers of the throwing hand are placed across the laces of the ball. The weight is transferred to the rear leg in preparation for the throw. On throwing, the weight is transferred forward, and a step is taken with the front foot in the direction of the receiver. The throwing arm is extended and the wrist flicked upon release of the ball. The longer the throw to be made, the higher the angle of release needs to be.

Lateral Pass

Lateral passing is pitching the ball underhand to a teammate. The ball must be tossed sideways or backwards to be a legal lateral that can then be passed again. There is no attempt to make the ball spiral as it does in a pass.

Catching

Since the football is a large and heavy object and can be thrown with great velocity, the catcher must "give" and bring the ball in toward the body. In a stationary position, the catcher faces the thrower and plants the feet about shoulder width apart. To catch a ball on the run, the catcher observes the ball by looking over the shoulder. The fingers should be spread and the arms extended to meet the ball. This allows giving with the ball and bringing the ball in toward the body in an attempt to absorb the force of the throw. Students should develop the habit of tucking the ball in close to the body after each catch.

Carrying the Ball

The ball is carried with the arm on the outside and the end of the ball tucked into the notch formed by the elbow and arm. The fingers cradle the forward part of the ball.

Centering

The center moves into position with the feet well spread and the toes pointed straight ahead. The knees are bent in preparation for forward movement. The dominant hand reaches forward slightly and is placed across the laces. The other hand is on the side near the back and guides the ball. The head is between the legs; the center's eyes are on the receiver. The arms are extended, and the ball is propelled by pulling both arms backward and upward. The ball should spiral on its way to the quarterback.

When centering in T formation, only 1 hand is used. The quarterback places the throwing hand in the crotch of the center and the other hand below with the hands touching at the base of the palms. The ball is given a one-quarter turn as it is centered and placed sideways in the quarterback's hands.

Stance

The 2-point stance is used by ends and backs so they can see downfield. The feet are spread shoulder width and the knees are bent slightly. The hands can be placed just above the knees.

The 3-point stance is used as a down position in order to move quickly forward or sideways. The feet are spread shoulder width apart with the toes pointing straight ahead. The player leans forward and places the desired hand on the ground while keeping the back parallel to the playing surface. The weight is on the balls of the feet; the head is up. Little weight is placed on the down hand.

The 4-point stance is used to move forward quickly. Lateral movement is sacrificed with this stance. It is similar to the 3-point stance, but both hands are on the ground and more weight is placed on the hands.

Blocking

The purpose of blocking is to prevent the defensive player from getting the flag of the ball carrier. It is accomplished by keeping the body between the defensive player and the ball carrier. Knocking the defensive player down is not necessary to accomplish a successful block.

Shoulder Block

The shoulder block starts from a 3- or 4-point stance. The blocker moves forward and makes shoulder contact at chest level of the opponent. The head should be placed between the opponent and the ball carrier in order to move the defensive player away from the ball carrier. The elbows are out and the hands are held near the chest.

Pass Block

The pass block is used when the quarterback is dropping back to throw a pass. The block can begin from any of the described stances. The blocker moves slightly backward with the rear foot as the opponent charges. The blocker should attempt to stay between the quarterback and the rusher.

Exchanging the Ball

The hand-off is made with the inside hand (nearest the receiver). The ball is held with both hands until the ball carrier is about 6 feet away. It is then shifted to the hand nearer the receiver, with the elbow bent partially away from the body. The receiver comes toward the quarterback with the near arm bent and carried in front of the chest, the palm down. The other arm is carried about waist high, with the palm up. As the ball is exchanged, the receiver clamps down on the ball to secure it.

Punting

The punter starts in standing position with both arms fully extended to receive the ball. The kicking foot is placed slightly forward. After receiving the ball, the kicker takes 2 steps forward, beginning with the dominant foot. The ball is slightly turned in and held at waist height. The kicking leg is swung forward, and at impact the knee is straightened to provide maximum force. The toes are pointed and the long axis of the ball makes contact on the top of the instep. The ball should be dropped rather than tossed into the air. The drop needs to be mastered before effective punting can occur.

Ideas for Effective Instruction

Since many drills are available for flag football, the authors have devoted this section to delineating the rules and equipment necessary for it. Most of the prerequisites for developing a sound flag football program are listed and discussed.

Uniforms

Rubber-soled shoes should be worn. Metal cleats or spikes are not allowed nor is any hard surface padding or helmets.

Flags

Flags are available in 2 colors for team play. All flags should be similar in terms of pulling the flags loose from players. The flag belts have 2 flags attached, one at each hip. Either flag pulled downs the ball carrier.

Downed Ball

To down a ball carrier, either flag must be withdrawn from the waist by a tackler. The tackler must stop at the point of tackle and hold up the hand with the withdrawn flag. It is illegal for ball carriers to deliberately touch their own flags or to defend them in any manner. Penalty: 15 yards from the point of the foul and loss of a down.

Dead Ball

The ball is ruled dead on a fumble when it hits the ground, or on a wild center when it hits the ground. When a fumble rolls out-of-bounds, the ball is returned to the team that had last full possession of it.

Loss of Flags

If the flag is inadvertently lost, the player is ineligible to handle the ball. The ball then becomes dead if the player is behind the line of scrimmage or the pass is called incomplete. It is illegal for a player to deliberately withdraw an opponent's flag unless that opponent is in possession of the ball. Such conduct is penalized as unsportsmanlike. Penalty: 15 yards.

Charging and Tackling

The ball carrier may not run through a defensive player, but must attempt to evade the tackler. The tackler must not hold, push, or run through the ball carrier, but must play the flag rather than the person. The officials decide these judgment calls. Penalty: 15 yards and loss of a down offensively, and 15 yards defensively.

Tackling

Tackling is not permitted. The ball is declared dead when defensive play pulls one of the runner's flags. Action against the runner, other than pulling the flag, is unnecessary roughness. Penalty: 15 yards from the point of the foul and loss of a down offensively, and 15 yards from the point of the foul defensively.

Hacking

It is a foul for the ball carrier to hack, push, or straight-arm another player. Penalty: 15 yards from the point of the foul and loss of a down.

Blocking

Line blocking is the same as regulation football. In open-field (out-of-the-line) line blocking, no part of the blocker's body, except the feet, shall be in contact with the ground during the block. Blocking is a type of body checking with the blocker in an upright position and without the use of hands or extended arms. Any rough tactics, such as attempting to run over or batter down an opponent, must be penalized as unnecessary roughness. Unnecessary roughness may be declared if the blocker uses knees or elbows in blocking. Penalty: 15 yards and loss of a down offensively, and 15 yards and first down defensively.

Passing

A forward pass may be thrown from any point behind the line of scrimmage. The passer is declared down if a flag is withdrawn by a defensive player, or if a flag falls out on its own before passer's arm is engaged in the throwing motion. It is the responsibility of the officials to make this decision.

Downs

A team has 4 downs to advance the ball from wherever they take over to score. If the team fails to score in 4 downs, its opponents gain possession of the ball at the spot where the ball is declared dead on the fourth down. To obtain a first down, the offensive team must complete 3 forward passes out of 4 downs. A forward pass is a pass thrown from behind the line of scrimmage past the line of scrimmage.

Miscellaneous Penalties

Illegal use of flags	15 yards
Offensive use of hands	15 yards
Defensive illegal use of hands	15 yards
Off-side	5 yards
Pushing ball carrier out-of-bounds	15 yards
Ball carrier pushing the interference	15 yards
Ineligible person downfield	5 yards
Illegal procedure	5 yards

Lead-Up Games and Learning Activities

The following lead-up games can be enjoyable ways to broaden the variety of activities in a football unit. They also avoid 1 student dominating a skilled position while others simply go through the motions of blocking.

Five Passes

The game can be played on a football field, but the size of the field is not critical and any large area is satisfactory. Players scatter on the field. The object of the game is for 1 team (identified by pinnies) to make 5 consecutive passes to 5 different players without losing control of the ball. This scores 1 point. The defense may play the ball only and may not make personal contact. No player is allowed to take more than 3 steps when in possession of the ball, or the ball is given to the other team.

There is no penalty when the ball hits the ground. It remains in play, but this interrupts the 5-pass sequence, which starts over. Students should call the number of consecutive passes out loud.

Kick Over

The game is played on a football field with a 10-yard end zone. Teams are scattered at opposite ends of the field. The object is to punt the ball over the other team's goal line. If the ball is caught in the end zone, no score results. A ball kicked into the end zone and not caught scores a goal. If the ball is kicked beyond the end zone on the fly, a score is made regardless of whether the ball is caught.

Play is started by 1 team with a punt from a point 20 to 30 feet in front of their own goal line. On a punt, if the ball is not caught, the team must kick from the point of recovery. If the ball is caught, the team also kicks from the point of recovery. When the ball is caught, 3 long strides are allowed to advance the ball for a kick. It is a good idea to number students and to allow them to kick in rotation so all receive equal practice.

Fourth Down

Six to 8 players are on a team and play in an area roughly half the size of a football field. Every play is a fourth down, which means that the play must score or the team loses the ball. No kicking is permitted, and players may pass at any time from any spot in any direction. There can be a series of passes on any play, either from behind or beyond the line of scrimmage.

The teams start in the middle of the field with possession determined by a coin toss. The ball is put into play by centering. The back receiving the ball runs or passes to any teammate. The receiver has the same options. No blocking is permitted. After each touchdown, the ball is brought to the center of the field and the nonscoring team resumes play. The ball is downed when the player's flag is pulled. If a player makes an incomplete pass beyond the line of scrimmage, the ball is brought to the spot from which it was thrown.

Positions are rotated so everyone has a chance to be the quarterback. The rotation occurs after every down. The quarterback rotates to center, which ensures that everyone plays all positions.

Captain Football

The game is played on half of a football field. Five yards beyond each goal is a 6-foot by 6-foot square, which is the box. The teams must be identified with pinnies. The object of the game is to complete a pass to the captain in the box.

To begin, the players line up at opposite ends of the field. One team kicks off from its 10-yard line to the other team. The game then becomes keepaway, with 1 team trying to secure possession of the ball and the other team trying to retain possession until a successful pass can be made to the captain in the box. To score a touchdown, the captain must catch the ball on the fly and still keep both feet in the box.

A player may run sideways or backwards when in possession of the ball. Players may not run forward but are allowed momentum (2 steps) if receiving or intercepting a ball. More than 2 steps is penalized by loss of possession.

The captain is allowed 3 attempts to catch a pass or 1 successful goal before a new player is rotated into the box. A ball hitting the ground in bounds remains in play. Players may not bat or kick a free ball. Penalty is the awarding of the ball to the other team out-of-bounds.

Aerial Ball

Aerial ball is similar to flag football with the following differences. The ball may be passed at any time. It can be thrown at any time beyond the line of scrimmage: immediately after an interception, during a kickoff, or during a received kick. Players have 4 downs to score a touchdown. If the ball is thrown from behind the line of scrimmage and an incomplete pass results, the ball is returned to the previous spot on the line of scrimmage. If the pass originates otherwise and is incomplete, the ball is placed at the point from which the pass was thrown.

Because the ball can be passed at any time, no downfield blocking is permitted. A player may screen the ball carrier but cannot make a block. Screening is defined as running between the ball carrier and the defense.

Suggested Performance Objectives

Basic Objectives

1. Throw 10 overhand passes to the chest area of a partner who is standing 10 yards away. Practice correct holding, point of release, and follow-through techniques of passing.

2. Throw 3 or 4 consecutive passes beyond a target positioned 20 yards away.

3. Facing the opposite direction from a partner 5 yards away, execute a proper center stance with feet well spread and toes pointed straight ahead, knees bent, and 2 hands on the ball. Snap the ball back through the legs 10 consecutive times.

4. With a partner centering the ball, from a distance of 10 yards punt the ball using proper technique to another set of partners 15 yards away, 3 consecutive times.

5. Same as task 4, except at a distance of 20 yards.

6. Punt the ball 3 consecutive times within the boundary lines of the field and beyond a distance of 20 yards.

7. With a partner, run a "quick" pass pattern and catch the ball 2 of 3 times (5- to 7-yard pattern).

8. With a partner, run a 10- to 15-yard "down and in" pass pattern and catch the ball 2 of 3 times.

9. With a partner, run a 10- to 15-yard "down and out" pass pattern and catch the ball 2 of 3 times.

10. With a partner, run a 5- to 7-yard "hook" pattern and catch the ball 2 of 3 times.

Optional Objectives

1. With a partner centering the ball, from a distance of 10 yards, punt the football using proper technique to another set of partners 15 yards away, 3 consecutive times.

2. Same as task 1, but at a distance of 20 yards.

3. Center-snap 4 of 6 times through a tire positioned 5 yards away.

4. Throw 3 of 4 consecutive passes beyond a target positioned 20 yards away.

5. Throw 4 of 6 passes through a tire from a distance of 10 yards.

LACROSSE

Lacrosse is played in the United States, Australia, and England, and it is the national sport of Canada. In the United States, lacrosse is most popular in the Middle Atlantic States. The game was originated by American Indians as early as the sixteenth century. The Indians played each game with over 100 players and often with as many as 1000 players.

Lacrosse is a wide-open game that offers aerobic activity for players. The game can be easily modified to suit all skill and age levels. Examples of modified games are soft lacrosse, which is played in a gym or on a field with a lacrosse stick, ball, and goals; plastic lacrosse, which is played with modified plastic sticks and does not require as much skill as regulation lacrosse; box lacrosse, which is played in an arena or lacrosse box and requires the highest skill; and field lacrosse, which is played on a soccer-size field with playing area behind each goal.

Sequence of Skills

Gripping the Stick

Position the dominant hand at least halfway down the handle of the stick, palm up. The other hand grips the stick at the end with the palm down. The stick should be held close to the body with relaxed hands and wrists.

Throwing

Bring the head of the stick backwards while keeping the eyes focused on the target. Step with the opposite foot in the direction of the throw. Keep the elbows high and throw overhand to improve accuracy. The hands should be kept shoulder width apart (don't push the ball). Break the wrists on follow-through with the head of the stick pointing to the target at the end of the throw.

Catching

Reach to meet the ball and "give" with the arms when the ball makes contact with the stick. Move the feet and align the body with the path of the oncoming ball. When catching, allow the dominant hand to slide on the handle for better stick control. The following techniques are used for catching balls at various levels:

1. *Above the shoulders.* Extend the crosse in the path of the ball. When the ball is caught, rotate the dominant hand sharply inward to protect it from a defender.

2. *Between the shoulders and knees.* Extend the face of the stick directly toward the ball. When caught, move the head of the crosse upward.

3. *Below the knees.* Rotate the handle outward and upward following the reception.

4. *Head high.* Put the face of the crosse directly in the path of the ball with the head and shoulders

dropping to the left. Rotate the crosse inward with the dominant hand upon reception.

5. **Ball on the weak hand side of the body.** Bring the dominant hand across the body to put the crosse in the path of the ball. Cross the leg on the dominant side in front of the other leg while turning the body. After catch, move the head of the crosse upward.

Scooping

When fielding ground balls, bend the knees and the back. Keep the butt end of the stick away from the midline of the body. Scoop the ball up with a slight shovel motion. As soon as the ball enters the stick, the player needs to break to the right or left to elude the defender.

Dodging

There are 4 basic dodges used by an offensive player who has the ball in an attempt to evade the defender:

1. **Face dodge.** The player with the ball fakes throwing the ball. When the crosse is about even with the head, it is twisted to the nondominant side. The offensive player then drops the shoulders and head slightly to the nondominant side, brings the leg on the dominant side across the other leg, and runs around the defender.
2. **Change-of-pace dodge.** Run quickly in 1 direction, stop suddenly and reverse directions. Continue this pattern of movement until the opportunity to move past the defender arises.
3. **Toss dodge.** When the offensive player meets the defender, the ball is tossed on the ground or in the air past the defender. The player then moves past the defender and recovers the ball.
4. **Force dodge.** The offensive player approaches the defender with the back side of the body. This causes the defender to retreat. The offensive player fakes to the left and right until an opportunity to run past the defender occurs.

Goaltending

The main duties of the goalie are to stop the ball, direct the defense, and start the offense by passing the ball out to the side or down the field. The goalie should be positioned as follows: feet shoulder width apart with the knees bent. Decrease the shooting angle for the offensive player by moving in an arc about 3 feet from the goal mouth with short shuffle steps. When the ball is behind the goal, the goalie should operate in the same arc, favoring the ball side. If regulation equipment is lacking, it is highly recommended that the goalie wear a softball catcher's mask and chest protector during shooting drills and games.

Ideas for Effective Instruction

Equipment

The lacrosse ball is solid rubber and white or orange in color. It is slightly smaller than a baseball, but just as hard. When dropped from a height of 6 feet above a solid wooden floor, it must bounce 43 to 51 inches. The lacrosse stick may be 40 to 72 inches long with the exception of the goalie's stick, which may be any length. For physical education, plastic sticks and balls are recommended. The net of the stick is between 6½ and 10 inches. The net is made of gut, rawhide, or nylon. Players wear gloves and a helmet with a face mask in regulation lacrosse.

Game Play

Lacrosse is often played in a football stadium. In physical education classes, it can be played on any field, gym, or court with portable goals. The regulation field is 110 yards long with the goals 80 yards apart, leaving 15 yards behind each goal. The field is 60 yards wide, but current rules allow for the width to be reduced to 53⅓ yards, which is the width of a football field (Figure 19.2). A rectangular box, 35 by 40 yards surrounds each goal and is called the goal area. The goal consists of 2 vertical posts joined by a top crossbar. The posts are 6 feet apart and the top crossbar is 6 feet from the ground.

There are 10 players on a team including a goalie, 3 midfielders, 3 attackers, and 3 defenders. The goalie guards the goal and receives support from the defenders. The defenders must remain in their half of the field. The midfielders serve as "rovers" and roam the entire field operating as both offensive and defensive players. One of the midfielders handles each face-off and is called the center. The attackers remain in the offensive half of the field and attempt shots on goal. The attackers, defenders, and the goalies often play the entire game, but the midfielders are often substituted.

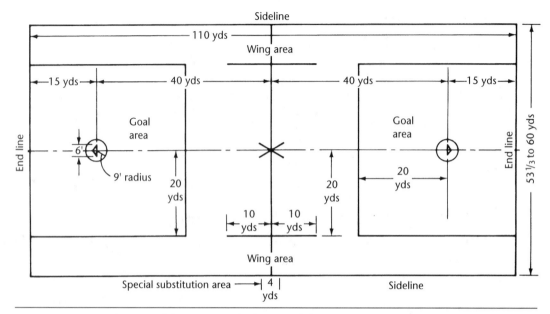

FIGURE 19.2   Markings and dimensions of a lacrosse field

Basic Rules

Face-Off.   Play begins with a faceoff (a draw) at the start of each quarter and after a goal is scored. The ball is placed between the back side of the opponents' sticks. All players must be in their assigned positions for the face-off. On signal, players in the wing areas are released, but all other players are confined until a player gains possession of the ball, the ball goes out-of-bounds, or the ball crosses either of the goal line areas.

Off-Side Rule.   Each team must have 3 players located on its attack half and 4 players on its defensive half of the field. This prevents piling up around the goal.

Out-of-Bounds.   When a player throws or carries the ball out-of-bounds, the opposing team gets possession. However, when a loose ball goes out-of-bounds as a result of a shot taken at the goal, it is awarded to the team whose player is closest to it at the exact time it rolls out-of-bounds.

Checking.   Body checking is allowed in regulation play in an attempt to dislodge the ball. Football blocks can be legally made on the player with the ball or on those who are going for a loose ball 5 yards away. Checking an opponent with the body or stick is a common practice and is used to dislodge the ball.

Penalty Box.   There are 2 types of fouls: personal and technical. Personal fouls are more serious than technical fouls and result in suspension for 1 to 3 minutes based on the severity and intention of the foul. Personal fouls are assigned for illegal personal contact, tripping, and unsportsmanlike conduct. Technical fouls usually result in a 30-second suspension from the game if the player does not have the ball. If the offending team has the ball, it loses possession of the ball. Technical fouls are assigned for the following infractions:

Interference with the opponent without the ball.

Holding any part of the opponent's body.

Pushing, particularly from the rear.

Illegal action with the stick or playing the game without the stick.

Withholding the ball from play by lying on it or trapping it longer than necessary to gain control.

Illegal procedure occurs when (1) an offensive player steps in the opponent's crease when the ball is in the attacking half of the field, or (2) a defending player with the ball runs through the crease.

Off-side occurs when a team has less than 3 players in its attack half or less than 4 players in the defensive half of the field.

Modified Rules

The regulation rules for lacrosse can be modified for use in a physical education setting where equipment and facilities are limited. The following are various modifications:

1. Reduce the number of players to less than 10 so players have more opportunity to handle the ball. Try assigning players to zones so all students have the opportunity to play the ball. This helps prevent the most dominant players from always "hogging" the ball.
2. No stick or body contact is allowed. Encourage students to play the ball rather than the opponent. If a violation occurs, a penalty shot is awarded at the spot of the infraction.
3. Players must keep both hands on their sticks at all times. A penalty shot is awarded at the spot of the infraction.
4. If a ball goes out of bounds, the team that did not touch it last may run it in or pass it in.
5. To steal the ball from an opponent, only stick-on-stick tactics may be used (no body contact).
6. To encourage teamwork and passing skills, two passes must be made before each shot on goal.
7. Play should be continuous without any stalling tactics. If problems develop in this area, add a time limit for holding the ball. For example, if the ball is held more than 5 seconds, it is turned over to the other team at the point of infraction.
8. The ball is a "free ball" when it is on the ground or in the air. Stick contact is allowed at these times without body contact.

Organization and Skill Work

A number of drills and lead-up games can be used to teach the fundamentals of lacrosse. See the units on basketball, soccer, and hockey for additional activities that can be modified for lacrosse.

Drills

Throwing and Catching
1. Practice throwing the ball against a wall.
2. With a partner, begin throwing and catching in close proximity. Gradually move apart until clearing passes are made.
3. Play keepaway in groups of 3.
4. Use the jack-in-the-box drill. The "jack" is located midway between the 2 other players, each with a ball. The "jack" receives a pass from one of the end players, who is about 10 yards away. The "jack" passes the ball back to that player, rotates 180 degrees, and receives a pass from the other end player. Change "jack" players frequently.
5. Use buddy passing for learning to pass on the move. Buddies jog around the area and pass back and forth to each other. Increase the challenge by giving each a ball.
6. Use the 3-person rush and 3-person weave similar to the common basketball drills.

Scooping.   Organize the class into groups of 3. Two students are positioned on 1 side with the third student across from them, 30 feet away. The ball is placed in the middle. One of the 2 students positioned on the same side runs to the ball, scoops it up, and carries it a few steps before dropping it. Continuing forward, the student runs behind the player on the opposite side. This player runs forward, scoops up the ball, carries it a few steps, drops it, and moves forward behind the remaining student. The pattern continues.

Shooting.   A line of 4 to 5 students face the goal. A "feeder" behind the goal passes the ball to a shooter who cuts toward the goal or moves to a different position. After the shot on goal, the shooter becomes the "feeder." Rotate goalies frequently.

Dodging.   Practice all types of dodges with a partner using 1 ball per 2 students.

Defense.   Three players form a circle with a 20-yard radius. Two offensive players try to keep the ball away from the defensive player while remaining in the circle.

Lead-Up Games

Three-Second No Steps.   Players cannot take any steps with the ball. In addition, the ball may be not be held longer than 3 seconds or it is turned over to the other team.

Half-Court Lacrosse.   The offensive team gets 5 attempts to score. Each shot on goal counts as an offensive attempt. Offense and defense switch roles after the 5 attempts.

Five Touch.   At least 5 members of a team must touch the ball before a goal can be scored.

SOCCER

Soccer, the most popular game in the world, is now rapidly gaining popularity among youth in the United States. Many sport clubs and programs run by organizations such as the YMCA, YWCA, Boys' Clubs, and municipal recreation departments now sponsor soccer teams, and many school districts are now including soccer in their intramural and athletic programs. Soccer is known throughout the rest of the world as "football." The game is said to have originated in England around the tenth century, but in fact, the Romans played a game similar to soccer. Soccer was brought to the United States about 1870 and was played by women in an organized fashion in 1919. From a physical education standpoint, one of the advantages of soccer is that it is one of the few sports that depends primarily on foot-eye coordination for success. Many kickers in American football are soccer-style kickers. The long hours of kicking practice have contributed to their success.

The object of the game is to move the ball down the field by foot, body, or head contact to score goals and to prevent the opposing team from scoring. Soccer demands teamwork and the coordination of individual skills into group goals. Position play becomes important as students become more skilled. It is an excellent game for cardiovascular development because it demands a great deal of running and body control.

Sequence of Skills

The skills of soccer are difficult to master, so instructors should teach the skills through short practice sessions. Many drills and lead-up games can be used to make the practice sessions interesting and novel.

Dribbling

The purpose of dribbling in soccer is similar to basketball, that is, to maintain control of the ball and advance it before passing off to a teammate or shooting on goal. The ball is advanced by pushing it with the inside or outside of the front of the foot. The player should keep the ball close during the dribble, rather than kicking it and then running after it. Practice should involve learning to run in different patterns such as weaving, dodging, and twisting or turning with the ball.

Kicking

The purpose of the kick is to pass the ball to a teammate or to take a shot on goal. When passing, the performer plants the nonkicking foot alongside the ball with the foot pointing in the desired direction of the kick. The ball is contacted with the inside portion of the instep of the foot. The body weight shifts forward after the kick. The pass can also be made with the outside of the foot, although this kick will not move the ball as great a distance or with as much velocity. It is an excellent kick for passing without breaking stride or for passing to the side.

In kicking for a shot on goal, the procedure is similar to the inside-of-the-foot kick. The nonkicking foot is planted alongside the ball with the toes pointing in the direction of the goal. The ball is contacted on the instep, followed by a snap of the lower leg and follow-through.

Trapping

The purpose of trapping is to deflect a moving ball and bring it under control so it may be advanced or passed. Any part of the body may contact the ball except the hands or arms. Effective trapping will result in the ball dropping in front of the body in position to be advanced. The sole-of-the-foot trap is most commonly used and is often called wedging. The ball is contacted between the foot and the ground just as the ball hits the ground. The ball is swept away under control immediately after the trap. The shin trap is done by moving to meet the ball just as it hits the ground in front of the lower legs. The ball is trapped between the inside of the lower leg and the ground. The chest trap is executed by arching the trunk of the body backwards and giving with the ball on contact. The giving occurs with the body collapsing, so the ball does not rebound and drops in front of the player.

Heading

Heading can be an effective way of propelling a ball in the air to a teammate or on goal. The player should strike the ball with the head, rather than waiting for the ball to hit the head. The player leans backward as the ball approaches. The head is up, with the eyes following the ball. On contact, the head moves forward and strikes the ball near the hairline on the forehead. The body also swings forward as the follow-through is completed.

Tackling

Tackling is used defensively to take the ball away from an offensive player who is dribbling or attempting to pass. The single-leg tackle is used when approaching an opponent directly, from behind, or from the side. Effective tackling depends, in large part, on being able to anticipate the opponent's next move with the foot. One leg reaches for the ball while the weight is supported on the other. The knees should be bent so good balance is maintained. Focus should be on a clean tackle rather than on body contact. The object is to reach out and bring the ball to the body, or to kick the ball away and then continue to pursue it.

Goalkeeping

Goalkeeping involves stopping shots by catching or otherwise stopping the ball. Goalkeepers should become adept at catching low, rolling balls, at diving on rolling balls, at catching airborne balls waist high and below, and at catching airborne balls waist high and above. The diving movements are the reason the goalie may choose to wear knee, elbow, and hip pads.

Students should get in the habit of catching low, rolling balls in much the same manner as a baseball outfielder: get down on one knee, with the body behind the ball to act as a backstop, and catch it with both hands, fingers pointing toward the ground. If diving for a ball is necessary, the goalie must throw the body behind it and cradle it with the hands. The body should always be between the goal and the ball.

The goalie may also punch the ball in order to deflect it if the ball is not catchable. The ball can be deflected off other body parts if it is not punchable.

After a ball is caught by the goalkeeper, it is thrown to a teammate. The ball can also be kicked, but this is less desirable because it is less accurate. Effective throws allow teammates to place the ball in action immediately.

Ideas for Effective Instruction

Soccer is played with 2 teams of 11 players each. For young players, however, decreasing the size of the teams is more effective. This results in each player's handling the ball more often and feeling an integral part of the soccer team.

Many of the drills, such as dribbling, kicking, and punting, can be learned individually. This means that 1 ball per player will ensure the maximum amount of practice time. Many types of balls can be used besides a regulation soccer ball. Playground balls (8½ inches) can be used if they are deflated slightly. Many students will play a more aggressive game of soccer if a foam-rubber training ball is used. They become less fearful of being hit by the ball and are willing to kick it with maximum velocity.

Field sizes can be reduced in order to increase the activity level of the game. The regulation game is played on a field with dimensions as illustrated in Figure 19.3. Soccer is meant to be played on grass. If a hard surface is used, deflate the ball so that it is not as live and will not bounce so readily.

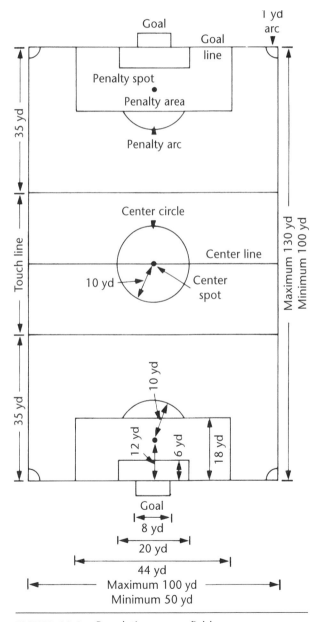

FIGURE 19.3   Regulation soccer field

The drills used for developing soccer skills should help all participants in achieving proper form. For example, if students are asked to pass and trap together, drills should focus on developing both skills, yet students are sometimes asked to kick with velocity, so the students trapping are fearful of getting hurt. Those students then develop an improper trapping style. An excellent source for many drills and activities to enhance the play of soccer is *Teaching Soccer* by Thomson (1980).

Lead-Up Games and Learning Activities

The following lead-up games are excellent for getting students involved in soccer activities. They emphasize participation and action. The lead-up activities are often more fun for the majority of students than an actual soccer game because these activities develop specific skills in which students may lack expertise.

Circle Kick Ball

Players are in circle formation. They kick the ball with the side of the foot back and forth inside the circle. The object is to kick the ball out of the circle beneath shoulder level. A point is scored against each of the players where the ball left the circle. If the lost ball is clearly the fault of a single player, however, then the point is scored against that player only. Players who kick the ball over the shoulders of the circle players have a point scored against them. Players with the fewest points scored against them are the winners. The game works well with a foam training ball because the ball can be kicked at someone from a short distance.

Soccer Croquet

The game is similar to croquet in that the object is for 1 ball to hit another. One player kicks a ball and tries to hit another ball lying ahead. Kickers alternate until a hit is made, which scores 1 point for the kicker. The game continues until a player scores a specified number of points.

Soccer Keepaway

Players are spaced evenly around a circle about 10 yards in diameter with 1 player in the center. The object of the game is to keep the player in the center from touching the ball. The ball is passed back and forth as in soccer. If the center player touches the ball with a foot, the person who kicked the ball goes in the center. If there is an error, the person responsible changes places with the person in the center.

Diagonal Soccer

Two corners are marked off with cones 5 feet from the corners on both sides, outlining triangular dead areas. Each team lines up as illustrated in and protects 2 adjacent sides of the square. The size of the area depends on the size of the class and must be adjusted accordingly. Dead areas on opposite corners mark the opposing team's goal line. To begin competition, 3 players from each team move into the playing area in their own half of the space. These are the active players. During play, they may roam anywhere in the square. The other players act as line guards.

To score, the active players must kick the ball through the opposing team's line (beneath shoulder height). When a score is made, active players rotate to the sidelines, and new players take their place. Players on the sidelines may block the ball with their bodies but cannot use their hands. The team against which the point was scored starts the ball for the next point. Only active players may score. A point is scored for the opponents whenever any of the following occurs:

1. A team allows the ball to go through its line below shoulder height.
2. A team touches the ball illegally.
3. A team kicks the ball over the other team's line above shoulder height.

Sideline Soccer

The teams line up on the sidelines of a large square with the end lines open. Three active players from each team are called from the end of the team line. These players remain active until a point is scored, and then they are rotated to the other end of the line.

The object is to kick the ball over the end line, which has no defenders, between cones that define the scoring area. The active players on each team compete against each other, aided by their teammates on the sidelines.

To start play, a referee drops the ball between 2 opposing players at the center of the field. To score, the ball must be kicked last by an active player and must go over the end line at or below shoulder height. Regular rules prevail with the restrictions of no pushing, holding, tripping, or other rough play. For out-of-bounds, the team on the side of the field where the ball went out-of-bounds is awarded a free kick near that spot. No score can result from a free kick. Violation of the touch rule also results in a free kick.

Line Soccer

Two goal lines are drawn 180 to 210 feet apart. A restraining line is drawn 15 feet in front of and parallel to each goal line. Field width can vary from 90 to 105 feet. Each team stands on 1 goal line, which it defends. The referee stands in the center of the field, holding a ball. At the whistle, 3 players (or more if the teams are large) run to the center from the right side of each line and become active players. The referee drops the ball to the ground, and the players try to kick it through the other team defending the goal line. The players in the field may advance by kicking only.

A score is made when an active player kicks the ball through the opposing team and over the end line, providing the kick was made from outside the restraining line. Place cones on the field corners to define the goal line. A player rotation system should be set up.

Line players act as goalies and are permitted to catch the ball. After being caught, the ball must be laid down immediately and either rolled or kicked. It cannot be punted or drop-kicked. One point is scored when the ball is kicked through the opponent's goal line below shoulder level. One point is also scored in cases of a personal foul involving pushing, kicking, tripping, or similar acts.

For illegal touching by the active players, a direct free kick is given from a point 12 yards in front of the penalized team's goal line. All active players on the defending team must be to 1 side until the ball is kicked. Only goalies may defend. A time limit of 2 minutes should be set for any group of active players. When no goal is scored during this time, a halt is called at the end of 2 minutes and players are changed.

An out-of-bounds ball is awarded to the opponents of the team last touching the ball. The regular soccer throw-in from out-of-bounds should be used. If the ball goes over the shoulders of the defenders at the end line, any end-line player may retrieve the ball and put it into play with a throw or kick.

Mini-Soccer

The playing area can be adjusted, depending on the size and skill of the players. A reasonable playing area is probably 150 by 225 feet. A goal, 24 feet wide, is on each end of the field, marked by jumping standards. A 12-foot semicircle on each end outlines the penalty area. The center of the semicircle is at the center of the goal.

The game follows the general rules of soccer, with 1 goalie for each side. The corner kick, not played in other lead-up games, needs to be introduced. This kick is used when the ball goes over the end line but not through the goal and was last touched by the defense. The ball is taken to the nearest corner for a direct free kick, and a goal can be scored from the kick. If the attacking team last touched the ball, the goalkeeper kick is awarded. The goalie puts the ball down and place-kicks it forward. The players are designated as center forward, outside right halfback, fullback, and goalie. Players should rotate positions at regular intervals. The forwards play in the front half of the field and the guards in the back half, but neither position is restricted to these areas entirely, and all may cross the center line without penalty.

A foul by the defense within its penalty area (semicircle) results in a penalty kick, taken from a point 12 yards distant, directly in front of the goal. Only the goalie is allowed to defend. The ball is in play, with others waiting outside the penalty area. Emphasize position play, and encourage the lines of 3 to spread out and hold their position.

Suggested Performance Objectives

The following objectives are designed for 3 skill levels: introductory, intermediate, and advanced. The objectives can be used in intermediate or advanced soccer classes or in a heterogeneously grouped class to challenge students of varying abilities.

Introductory Unit

Kicking
1. Execute a push pass, low drive, and lofted drive. Satisfy the instructor that these are understood and can be executed with the preferred foot.

Passing
(All objectives may be performed with the preferred foot.)
2. Push-pass 3 of 5 passes from 10 yards to partner.
3. Low-drive 3 of 5 passes from 15 yards to partner.
4. Loft-drive 3 of 5 passes from 20 yards to partner.

Dribbling

5. Dribble a distance of 20 yards twice with one or both feet. The ball must not be allowed to stray more than 5 yards.

Shooting

6. Shoot the ball with the preferred foot from 18 yards into an empty goal 8 of 10 times.

Heading

7. Head the ball back to serving partner 8 of 10 times over a distance of 5 yards. The partner must be able to catch the ball.

Control of the Ball

8. Control 3 of 5 passes on the ground using the feet only.
9. Control 3 of 5 passes in the air using the head, chest, or thigh.

Game Situation

10. Show an understanding of pass, run, and control in a mini-soccer game situation.

Rules of the Game

11. Score 80% on a rules-of-the-game test. One retake is permissible.

Introductory Unit: Optional Requirements

Goalkeeping

1. Save 6 of 10 shots from 18 yards. The shots must be on target.
2. Punt the ball 25 yards 4 of 5 times.

Juggling

3. Keep the ball in the air with at least 10 consecutive touches. Hands or arms may not be used.

Field Dimensions

4. Diagram a full-size soccer field and give dimensions.

Grading

Thirteen passes are required for a unit pass. The instructor reserves the right to lower the number of required passes for the unit as necessary.

Intermediate Unit

Kicking

1. Satisfy the instructor that the techniques of the push pass, low drive, and lofted drive are understood and can be executed with both feet.

Passing

2. Push pass: Complete 4 of 5 passes with the preferred foot from 10 yards. The passes must go between 2 cones placed 5 yards apart. Complete 3 of 5 passes with the nonpreferred foot.
3. Low drive: Complete 4 of 5 passes with the preferred foot from 10 yards. The passes must go between 2 cones placed 8 yards apart. Complete 3 of 5 passes with the nonpreferred foot.
4. Lofted drive: Complete 4 of 5 passes with the preferred foot from 10 yards. The passes must go over an obstacle 6 feet high. Complete 3 of 5 passes with the nonpreferred foot.

Dribbling

5. Dribble through 6 cones over 25 yards, 4 times with no misses. Both feet must be used.
6. Dribble around an advancing goalkeeper, and score a goal 3 of 5 times.

Shooting

7. Shoot the ball with the preferred foot from 18 yards into an empty goal 9 of 10 times.
8. Same as task 7, except with the nonpreferred foot, 7 of 10 times.

Heading

9. Head the ball to a serving partner 9 of 10 times over a distance of 10 yards. The partner must be able to catch the ball without its touching the ground.

Control of the Ball

10. Control 4 of 5 passes on the ground. Use the feet only.
11. Control 4 of 5 passes in the air. The head, chest, and thighs must be used.

Corner Kick

12. Propel 3 of 5 corner kicks inside the penalty area. The ball may not touch the ground between the corner and the penalty area.

Throw-In

13. Throw the ball with 2 hands to a partner 10 yards away 4 of 5 times. Partner must be able to catch the ball.

Juggle

14. Juggle the ball at least 10 consecutive times without allowing it to touch the ground.

Tackling

15. Successfully complete 3 of 5 front block tackles on a partner dribbling a ball at a walking pace.

Goalkeeping

16. Kick goal kicks at least 20 yards in the air 4 of 5 times.
17. Punt the ball 25 yards, 4 of 5 times.
18. Save at least 6 of 10 on-target shots from the 18-yard line.

Rules of the Game

19. Score 80% on a rules-of-the-game test. One retest is allowed.

Intermediate Unit: Optional Requirements

Officiating

1. Help officiate at least 2 games.
2. Know the roles of the referee and linesman.
3. Know the correct positioning of officials at corner kicks, goal kicks, and penalties.

Volleying

4. Volley 4 of 5 goals from outside the goal area with the preferred foot.

Swerving or Bending the Ball

5. Bend the ball into the goal from the goal line 3 of 5 times with the preferred foot.

Penalty Kicks

6. Score 7 of 10 penalty kicks against a recognized peer goalkeeper.

Power and Distance Kicking

7. Score 2 of 5 goals into an empty goal from the halfway line.

Grading

8. Twenty passes are required for a unit completion.

Advanced Unit: Basic Requirements

Passing

1. Push-pass 4 of 5 passes with the preferred foot from a distance of 10 yards between 2 cones, placed 5 yards apart, while running with the ball. Complete 3 of 5 passes with the nonpreferred foot.
2. Low-drive 4 of 5 passes with the preferred foot from a distance of 15 yards between 2 cones, placed 8 yards apart, while running with the ball. Complete 3 of 5 passes with the nonpreferred foot.

Dribbling

3. Dribble through 9 cones over a distance of 40 yards and back to the start in 30 seconds or less. Both feet must be used, and no cones may be omitted.
4. Dribble around an advancing goalkeeper and score 4 of 5 times. The goalkeeper must be beaten to the left and to the right at least once.

Shooting

5. Score 10 of 10 shots into an empty goal from outside the 18-yard line with the preferred foot, and 9 of 10 shots with the nonpreferred foot.
6. Score 8 of 10 penalty kicks against a recognized peer goalkeeper.
7. Volley 4 of 5 goals from a serving partner, from outside the goal area, with the preferred foot, and 3 of 5 with the nonpreferred foot.
8. Serve or bend the ball from the goal line into the goal 3 of 6 times with the preferred foot. The ball must be placed within 1 foot of the line any distance from the post.

Heading

9. Head the ball back to a serving partner 9 of 10 times over a distance of 10 yards. The partner must be able to catch the ball.
10. Head the ball back and forth with a partner a minimum of 10 times without touching the ground.
11. Head 9 of 10 serves from a partner into an empty goal from a distance of 10 yards.

Control of the Ball

12. Control 9 of 10 passes on the ground with the preferred foot.
13. Control 8 of 10 passes on the ground with the nonpreferred foot.
14. Control 9 of 10 passes from a partner with the head.
15. Control 9 of 10 serves from a partner with the chest.
16. Control 9 of 10 serves from a partner with the preferred thigh, and 8 of 10 with the nonpreferred thigh.

Corner Kick

17. Kick 9 of 10 corner kicks into the penalty area with the preferred foot from the preferred side. The ball may not touch the ground between the corner and the penalty area.
18. Kick 8 of 10 corner kicks into the penalty area from the nonpreferred side (same conditions as task 17).

Throw-In

19. Throw the ball with both hands to a partner 15 yards away, 9 of 10 times. The throw must be placed so partner is able to catch the ball.
20. Throw the ball to a moving partner at least 10 yards away. Partner must be able to catch the ball.

Juggling

21. Juggle the ball at least 20 times without its touching the ground. Head, foot, and thigh must be used. Start with the ball on the ground and get it into the air using the feet.
22. Juggle the ball with a partner. At least 10 passes must be made. No restrictions are placed on the number of touches by each player.

Tackling

23. Block tackle a partner jogging with the ball 8 of 10 times successfully.
24. Slide tackle a partner jogging with the ball 3 of 5 times successfully.
Goalkeeping
25. Kick 4 of 5 goal kicks at least 20 yards before hitting the ground.
26. Punt the ball at least 30 yards 4 of 5 times.
27. Save 7 of 10 shots on target from outside the 18-yard line.

Game Rules and Strategy

28. A thorough understanding of the rules of the game and principles of strategy must be demonstrated.
29. A score of 80% or higher must be achieved on a test covering the rules of the game. One retake is allowed.

Advanced Unit: Optional Requirements

Officiating

1. At least 3 games must be officiated.

Grading

2. To successfully complete the unit 26 passes must be obtained.

SOFTBALL

Softball raises controversy among physical education teachers. Some instructors believe that it is a game in which one only catches "varicose veins" from standing around. On the other hand, since it is a less-active game, softball is often played by adults for many years. When the skill level of the participants is developed, the game can be enjoyable. If skill is lacking, emphasis should be placed on developing skills and on individual practice.

Softball can be taught effectively by using stations. This gives students ample practice in many different skills and avoids the situation in which students play only 1 position and specialize in skills. Softball can be played coeducationally, and many of the lead-up games make the activity enjoyable and suited to students' ability levels.

Sequence of Skills

Equipment and Facilities

Softball is played on a diamond with the dimensions shown in Figure 19.4. Lines can be applied to the field with chalk or can be burned into the grass with a solvent that kills the grass and leaves a brown line.

Softball requires some specialized equipment. When ordering gloves, about 20% should be left-handed, and enough balls should be ordered so that each student has one. This allows many drills to be undertaken without waiting for the balls to be returned. Available equipment should include a set of bases for each diamond; bats of varying sizes (aluminum are the most durable); fielders' gloves; catcher's glove, protector, and face mask; and batting tees. For less experienced players, the soft softball is most desirable because it helps alleviate the fear that some players have of the ball. When a regulation softball is used, students often learn to dodge the ball, rather than catch it. Some teachers have had success with the large 16-inch ball. It moves slower, cannot be hit as far, and allows the game to be played in a smaller area. The drawback is that the large ball is difficult to throw because of its size.

Catching

Catching involves moving the body into the path of the ball. There are 2 ways to hold the hands for catching fly balls. For a low ball, the fielder keeps the fingers in and the thumbs turned outward. For a ball above waist level, the thumbs are turned inward and

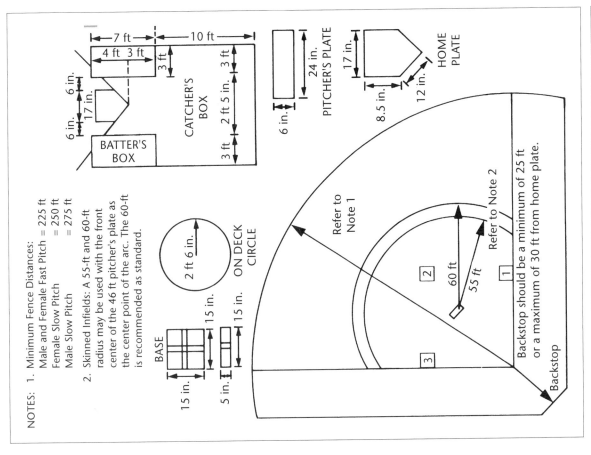

NOTES: 1. Minimum Fence Distances:
Male and Female Fast Pitch = 225 ft
Female Slow Pitch = 250 ft
Male Slow Pitch = 275 ft

2. Skinned Infields: A 55-ft and 60-ft radius may be used with the front center of the 46 ft pitcher's plate as the center point of the arc. The 60-ft is recommended as standard.

CATCHER'S BOX

BATTER'S BOX

PITCHER'S PLATE

HOME PLATE

ON DECK CIRCLE

BASE

Refer to Note 1

Refer to Note 2

Backstop should be a minimum of 25 ft or a maximum of 30 ft from home plate.

Backstop

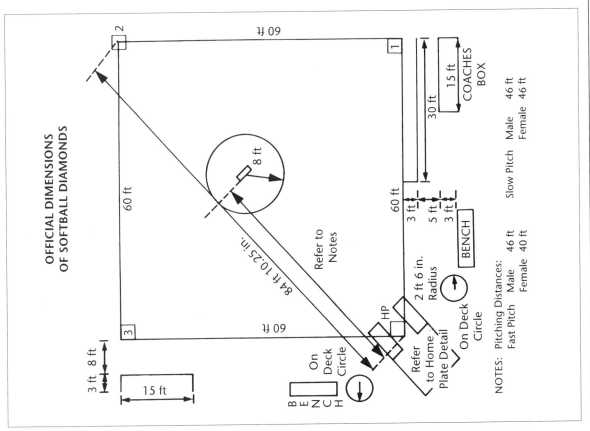

OFFICIAL DIMENSIONS OF SOFTBALL DIAMONDS

COACHES BOX

BENCH

On Deck Circle

Refer to Notes

Refer to Home Plate Detail

2 ft 6 in. Radius

HP

NOTES: Pitching Distances:
Fast Pitch Male 46 ft   Slow Pitch Male 46 ft
Female 40 ft   Female 46 ft

FIGURE 19.4 Softball diamonds

371

the fingers outward. The arms and hands extend and reach for the ball. As the ball comes into the glove, the arms, hands, and body give to create a soft home for the ball.

When catching grounders, move into the path of the ball, and then move toward the ball, and catch it on a "good" hop. Keep the eyes on the ball and follow it into the glove. The feet are spread, the seat is kept down, and the hands are carried low and in front. The weight is on the balls of the feet or on the toes, and the knees are bent to lower the body. As the ball is caught, the fielder straightens up, takes a step in the direction of the throw, and makes the throw.

Throwing

The ball is generally held with a 3- or 4-fingered grip. Smaller students usually have to use the 4-fingered grip. The fingers should be spaced evenly, and the ball held with the fingertips.

Because throwing is a complex motor pattern, it is difficult to break the skill into component parts. At best, throwing skills can be slowed down about 10% in an effort to teach proper throwing technique. If a mature pattern of throwing has not been developed, students should focus on throwing for velocity rather than accuracy. After proper form has been learned, accuracy becomes a prime objective.

Overhand Throw

The player stands with the side opposite the throwing arm facing the target. The hand with the ball is brought back, over the head, at just above shoulder height. The nonthrowing hand is raised in front of the body. The weight is on the rear foot (away from the target) with the front foot advanced toward the target. The arm comes forward with the elbow leading, and the ball is thrown with a downward snap of the wrist. The weight of the body is shifted simultaneously with the throw to the front foot. The rear foot rotates forward, and the throwing hand ends facing the ground during the follow-through. The eyes should be kept on the target throughout the throw.

Sidearm Throw

The sidearm throw is similar to the overhand throw, except that the entire motion is kept near a horizontal plane. The sidearm throw, which uses a quick, whiplike motion, is for shorter, quicker throws than the overhand. The sidearm throw should be used only for short infield throws, because the sideways motion causes a spin on the ball, which results in a curved path.

Underhand Throw

The underhand throw is used for short distances, such as throwing to the pitcher covering first base or the person on second base throwing to the shortstop covering second base. The player faces the target, and the hand is swung backward with the palm facing forward. The arm is then moved forward in a pendulum swing with the elbow slightly bent. The weight shifts to the front foot during the toss.

Pitching

The pitcher must begin with both feet touching the rubber. The ball is held in front of the body with the pitcher facing home plate. The pitching hand is brought backward in a pendulum swing, and the wrist is cocked at the back of the swing. The pitcher steps forward on the opposite foot and swings the arm forward. The wrist is snapped, and the ball is released from the fingertips as the arm finishes moving in an upward, lifting fashion. The follow-through should be accompanied by a forward step of the foot on the throwing side so the player is in a fielding position.

Fielding Position

Infielders should assume the ready position in a semicrouch, with the legs spread shoulder width apart, knees bent slightly, and hands on or in front of the knees. The weight is distributed evenly on both feet so the player can move easily to the left or right. To field a grounder, the fielder moves as quickly as possible into the path of the ball, then moves forward, and plays the ball on a good hop. The glove should be kept near the ground and raised only as the ball rises. (A common mistake is to not put the glove down soon enough.) The eyes follow the ball into the glove and the head is kept down. As the ball is caught, the fielder straightens up, takes a step in the direction of the throw, and releases the ball.

To catch a ground ball in the outfield, the player should employ the sure-stop method. This involves using the body as a barrier. The fielder drops to 1 knee in order to block the ball with the body if the catch is missed. This method should be used when runners are on base.

Batting

The bat is gripped with the dominant hand above and adjacent to the nondominant hand. The feet should be positioned comfortably apart, and the front of the body faces the plate. The knees are slightly bent and the weight is distributed equally on both feet. The hands and the bat are held shoulder high and slightly behind the rear foot. The elbows are away from the body, the wrists cocked, and the bat held in an upward position. The ball should be followed with the eyes as long as possible. The stride begins by stepping toward the ball with the front foot. The hips are rotated, followed by the trunk and forward shoulder. The arms are extended, wrists snapped, and contact is made with the ball in front of the forward hip. Different grips on the bat can be tried, including the choke and long grip.

Batters should avoid using poor techniques such as lifting the front foot high off the ground, stepping back with the rear foot, dropping the elbows, or crouching or bending forward.

Base Running

After a hit, the batter should run hard with the head up and eyes looking down the base path. The runner moves past the bag, tagging it in the process, and turns out into foul territory, unless it is an extra base hit. If it is an extra base hit, the runner swings 5 to 6 feet to the right of the base line, about two-thirds of the way down the base path, and makes the turn toward second.

Runners on base must stay in contact with the base until the pitcher releases the ball. The next base is faced, with 1 foot forward and the other foot touching the base in a push-off position. The knees are flexed, and the upper body leans toward the next base.

Ideas for Effective Instruction

Safety is important, and throwing the bat is a constant problem. The members of the batting team should stand behind the backstop or on the side opposite the batter. Techniques to make the batter think about the bat are carrying the bat to first base, changing ends of the bat before dropping it, or placing the bat in a circle before running. It is usually best not to allow sliding, because sliding can lead to injury if the proper equipment is not available. The catcher should always wear protective gear. In the early stages of practice, soft softballs can be used.

Many of the lead-up games were developed to increase the number of people who get to bat in each inning. One strategy for effective batting practice is to have a member of the batting team pitch so the ball is easy to hit. Players should rotate positions often. Another idea is to have players rotate to a new position each inning. This has the effect of making the players supportive of each other since the quality of the game depends on all of the participating players.

Station teaching is excellent for developing softball skills. It ensures that participants have the opportunity to practice a wide variety of activities. Players who are particularly skilled in an activity can help others. Teachers should position themselves at a different station each day to ensure that they have instructed all students at all stations over a 1- to 2-week period. The following stations can be used by placing task cards at each station so students know exactly what is expected of them.

Station 1. Catching Ground Balls

1. Roll the ball straight to the person.
2. Roll the ball to the left side. Increase the distance.
3. Roll the ball to the right side. Increase the distance.
4. Roll the ball in an unpredictable direction.
5. Bat the ball in different directions. Start at 5 yards and increase the distance up to 20 yards from the fielder.

Station 2. Batting

1. Work in groups of 3 with a batting tee. One person fields, 1 bats, and the other shags the ball. Hit 10 balls.
2. Same as item 1, except pitch the ball to the batter.
3. Try placing the ball. Call the direction where you are going to hit the ball, and then do so.

Station 3. Base Running

1. Run the bases using a circle technique. Have a partner time you.
2. Run the bases using a clover technique. Decide which you prefer and which allows you to run the bases faster.
3. Bunt and run to first. Have your partner time you.
4. Play "In a Pickle" in groups of 3.

Station 4. Throwing

1. One person stands at each base plus a catcher behind home plate. Practice throwing to each of the bases from each position. Rotate positions after each person has had 3 throws.

2. Throw the ball from the outfield. Throw the ball through a cutoff person. Make 5 throws and rotate to catcher position.
3. Those not throwing should back up the other positions and act as cutoff persons.

Station 5. Fly Balls
1. Throw fly balls back and forth.
2. Vary the height and direction of the throw so teammates have to move into the flight of the ball.
3. Make teammates move backward and forward to catch the ball.
4. Bat some flies and play the game "500".

Lead-Up Games and Learning Activities

Two-Pitch Softball

Two-pitch is played like regulation softball except that a member of the team at bat pitches. Every member of the team must have an opportunity to pitch. The batter receives only two pitched balls to hit, and the ball hit must be fair or it is an out. The pitcher does not field the ball, and no balls or strikes are called.

In a Pickle

A base runner is "in a pickle" when caught between 2 bases and in danger of being tagged out. To begin, both fielders are on a base with a runner in the middle. The goal is for the player in the middle to get to a base safely. If done, that person scores a point. In either case, rotation occurs.

Five Hundred

A batter hits balls to a group of fielders. The goal is to score 500 points. When the total is reached, that person becomes the new batter. Fielders earn 100 points for catching a fly ball, 75 points for catching a ball on 1 bounce, 50 points for catching a ball after 2 bounces, and 25 points for any other ball. The points must total exactly 500 or the total immediately earned is subtracted from the fielder's score. Points are also subtracted if an error is made.

Home Run

The critical players are a batter, a catcher, a pitcher, and 1 fielder. All other players are fielders and take positions throughout the area. The batter hits a pitch and on a fair ball must run to first base and back home before the ball can be returned to the catcher. The batter is out whenever any of the following occur: a fly ball is caught; a strike-out occurs; or, on a fair ball, the ball beats the batter back to home plate. The number of home runs per batter can be limited, and a rotation plan should be developed. The distance to first base may have to be varied, depending on the strength and skill of the players.

Work-Up

This is a game of rotating positions each time an out is made. The game is played using regulation softball rules. Three batters are up at bat. Each time there is an out, the players move up 1 position, and the player making the last out goes to right field. The pitcher moves up to catcher, the person on first base to pitcher, and all others move up 1 position. If a fly ball is caught, the batter and the person catching the ball exchange places.

Babe Ruth Ball

The outfield is divided into 3 sections: left, center, and right field. The batter calls the field to which the ball will be hit. The pitcher throws pitches that the batter can hit easily. The batter remains in position as long as the ball is hit to the designated field. Field choices are rotated. The batter gets only 1 swing but may let a pitch go by. There is no base running.

Speedy Baseball

Speedy baseball is played like regular softball with the following exceptions:

1. The pitcher is from the team at bat and must not interfere with or touch a batted ball on penalty of the batter being called out.
2. The team coming to bat does not wait for the fielding team to get set. Since it has its own pitcher, the pitcher gets the ball to the batter just as quickly as the batter can grab a bat and get ready. The fielding team has to hustle to get to their places.
3. Only 1 pitch is allowed per batter. Batters must hit a fair ball or they are out. The pitch is made from about two-thirds of the normal pitching distance.
4. No stealing is permitted.
5. No bunting is permitted. The batter must take a full swing.

Suggested Performance Objectives

The following are performance objectives that might be used in a softball unit.

Contract Requirements

Throwing Tasks

1. Standing 45 feet from a partner who is inside a hoop, complete 5 consecutive underhand pitches to that person without causing him or her to move outside of the hoop.
2. Standing 60 feet from a partner who is inside a hoop, complete 5 overhand throws to that person without forcing him or her to move more than 1 foot outside the hoop.
3. Be able to demonstrate the proper stance, wind-up, and delivery of the windmill pitch to the instructor.
4. From a designated area of the outfield, situated 150 feet (boys) or 100 feet (girls) away, throw the softball through the air directly to a 10-foot wide circle chalked in front of home plate. To count, the throw must bounce only once before landing or going through the circle. Student must make 3 of 5 throws to qualify for points.
5. Display pitching skills by striking out 3 or more batters or by allowing no more than 5 base hits in an actual game.
6. From an outfield or relay position, throw out a baserunner at any base in an actual game.

Fielding Tasks

1. Demonstrating correct fielding stance, cleanly field 5 consecutive ground or fly balls hit by partner.
2. Play a game of Pepper with a group of no more than 6 players, demonstrating good bat control, hand-eye coordination, and fielding skills.
3. Play a game of 500 with no more than 5 players and demonstrate skills in catching flies and line drives and in fielding ground balls.
4. In an actual game situation, participate in a successful double play.
5. Perform a diving or over-the-head catch in an actual game situation.

Hitting Tasks

1. Watch a film loop or read an article on hitting.
2. Using a batting tee, hit 5 consecutive softballs, on the fly or on the ground, past the 80-foot semicircle line marked off in chalk.
3. Execute proper bunting form and ability by dumping 3 of 5 attempts into designated bunting areas along the first or third base lines.
4. In an actual game, make 2 or more base hits.
5. Hit a triple or home run in an actual game.
6. During an actual game, observe an opponent or teammate's swing. Write down the strong and weak points of that particular swing and bring them to the instructor's attention. The instructor will then match observations with your critique.

Optional Requirements

1. Make a diagram of an official softball diamond on posterboard. Illustrate proper field dimensions.
2. On a piece of paper, show how batting average and earned run average are compiled.
3. Watch a college or fast-pitch softball game on TV or at the actual setting. Record the score, place, teams, and date of the contest. List the strengths and weaknesses of each team, and note how weaknesses could be corrected.
4. Umpire a game for 3 or more innings.
5. Keep accurate score in an official scorebook for 3 or more innings.

SPEED-A-WAY

The game of speed-a-way was originated in 1950 by Marjorie Larsen, but spent 10 years in experimental stages prior to its arrival on the field. It is a dynamic game that combines the challenges of soccer, basketball, speedball, fieldball, and field hockey. It was created in an effort to find a game that could serve as a lead-up for field hockey and bring enjoyment to participants without having to learn complicated rules and techniques.

Speed-a-way is intended for students from middle school through college. With the emphasis on student success, the game employs a great variety of fundamental movements such as running, throwing, catching, and kicking. This allows participants ample opportunities for vigorous activity, competition, and team cooperation.

The area in which speed-a-way is played is the same as for field hockey. The recommended size is 100 by 60 yards. This rectangle is divided into 4 parts with alleys and striking circles. There is an official speed-a-way ball, but a soccer or playground ball can be substituted. The game consists of 4 quarters of 8 minutes each, with a 2-minute rest period between quarters and a 10-minute rest period between halves. Substitutions can be made when the ball is dead.

Speed-a-way is played with 2 teams of 11 players. Each player wears a set of flags. They line up on their half of the field at the beginning of each quarter and after each score. The ball is put into play by a "push-kick" backwards from the center of the field. The object of the game is to advance the ball through the opponent's territory by means of kicking, dribbling, heading, or shouldering a ground ball by throwing an aerial ball or by running with an aerial ball. A field goal (3 points) is scored by kicking the ball between the opponent's goal posts from within the striking circle (if football or speedball goal posts are used, a dropkick over the bar scores 4 points). A touchdown (2 points) is scored by running across the goal line with the ball or by passing it to a teammate who is already over the goal line but not between the goal posts.

Rules

1. The defense can only pull offensive players' flags when they are carrying the ball.
2. If flags are pulled before the ball leaves the offensive player's hand, the defensive team gains possession. Everyone moves 5 yards away before play can be continued.
3. In order for a player to carry the ball in his or her hands, the player must first legally lift the ball up and catch it. This is usually done with the feet. A teammate can lift the ball to another teammate, or a player can lift the ball to his- or herself with the feet.
4. If the ball goes out-of-bounds over the goal line (not between the goal posts) and is last touched by the offense, the goalie gets possession. The goalie may punt, place kick, throw, or run the ball out. Once the goalie leaves the striking circle, the opposition can pull the goalie's flag. However, in the striking circle the goalie is "safe." Goalies may go anywhere on the field they desire, but can only use their hands inside the striking circle.
5. If the ball goes out-of-bounds over the goal line (not between the posts) and is last touched by the defense, the offense receives a corner kick on the side where the ball went out.
6. When a ball goes out-of-bounds over a sideline, a player from the opposing team uses a 2-handed overhead toss to put the ball in play.
7. A player holding the pivot foot in position cannot have their flag pulled for 3 seconds.
8. No contact is allowed during guarding. A player can be guarded by only 1 player.

Safety Precautions

Since the game of speed-a-way is fast-moving, the safety of the game depends on the instruction players receive and the quality of officiating. A player should be taught that good position play is an essential safety factor in speed-a-way. Good body control and skill in the fundamentals of running, starting, and stopping quickly should be encouraged to eliminate body contact. Players should be taught how to control the ball, to evade and dodge an opponent, to throw the ball, and to lift the ball to another teammate. The technique of guarding or tackling an opponent who is in possession of the ball is most important in the prevention of unnecessary body contact. Team play and its value in preventing injury should be emphasized. Players should be safety conscious and follow the rules at all times.

During the game, referees should be alert to the dangerous elements of the game. All harmful body contact such as obstruction, pushing, charging, tripping, and dangerous kicking (kicking an opponent or kicking the ball directly into an opponent) should be called immediately. Speed-a-way can be a low-risk and non-threatening game when taught and conducted with safety as a priority.

Lead-Up Games for Speed-A-Way

Circle Kick Ball

Ten to 20 players form a circle and use a speed-a-way, soccer, or playground ball. The skills used are kicking and trapping. Players kick the ball back and forth inside the circle. The object of the game is for a player to kick the ball out of the circle below the shoulder level of any other circle player. Each time a player achieves this, they collect a point. Any player who kicks the ball over the shoulders of a circle player will give back 1 of the points they have earned.

Croquet Ball

Students play in pairs or groups of 3. Each student has a ball. The object of this game is for 1 ball to hit another. Each hit scores a point. The first player kicks their ball out 10 to 15 yards ahead. The next player kicks their ball and tries to hit the ball lying ahead. Alternate kicking continues until a hit is made. The game continues until a player scores a designated number of points. If 3 play, turns are taken in sequence. If a successful hit is made on 1 ball, the kicker gets a try immediately at the other.

Touch Ball

Eight to 10 students form a circle with 1 player in the center. One ball is used. The students are spaced around a circle about 10 yards in diameter. The ball is thrown or passed back and forth. If the center player touches the ball, the circle player who last touched the ball moves into the center.

Pin Kick Ball

Two teams of 7 to 10 players face each other at 20 yards apart. Six or 7 pins and 2 balls are needed. The object is to knock down the pins. Each pin is worth 1 point. Kicks should be made from the line behind which the team is standing. Players should concentrate on controlled traps and accurate kicks. Feel free to vary the amount of players per team and the number of pins used.

TEAM HANDBALL

Team handball is an exciting and challenging game that combines skills from basketball, soccer, water polo, and hockey. It involves running, dribbling, jumping, passing, catching, throwing, and goal tending. The object of the game is to move a small soccer ball down the field by passing and dribbling and then to throw the ball into a goal area that is 3 meters wide and 2 meters high. The game is relatively simple to learn and can be enjoyed by both sexes. It is inexpensive to add to the curriculum and can be played indoors, outdoors, or on a tennis court. Virtually any space can be adapted or modified for team handball. The play is rapid and involves continuous running, making the sport a good cardiovascular activity. Because the game is relatively new to the United States, many students will be inexperienced. A unit on team handball can provide students with a fresh challenge and increased motivation, and teachers should enjoy introducing a new activity.

Basic Rules

In regulation play, each team has 6 court players and 1 goalie. The 6 court players cover the entire court. A player is allowed 3 steps before and after dribbling the ball. There is no limit on the number of dribbles. Dribbling is, however, discouraged because passing is more effective. A double dribble is a violation. A player can hold the ball for 3 seconds only before passing, dribbling, or shooting. No player except the goalie can kick the ball in any way.

The court is marked (Figure 19.5) with a 6-meter goal area, a 7-meter penalty line, and a 9-meter free-throw line. The goal is 2 by 3 meters. The goal area inside the 6-meter line is only for the goalie. Other players are not allowed in this area. The 7-meter line is used for a major penalty shot, and the 9-meter line is used for a minor penalty shot. A regulation court is 20 by 40 meters.

One point is awarded for a goal. Violations and penalties are similar to basketball. A free throw is taken from the point of the violation, and defense must remain 3 meters away while protecting the

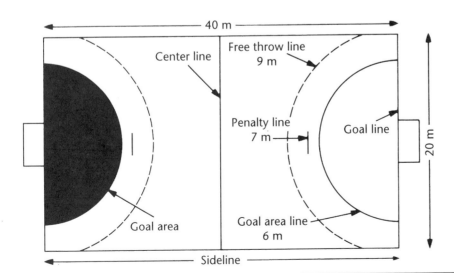

FIGURE 19.5 Team handball court markings

goal. A penalty throw is awarded from the 7-meter line for a major violation. A major violation occurs when an offensive player who is inside the 9-meter line in a good shooting position is fouled. During a penalty throw, all players must be behind the 9-meter line.*

The official team handball looks like a small soccer ball. The men's ball is 23 inches in circumference, and the women's ball is 21 inches. A smaller mini-handball is available for younger students. Handballs are carried by most sporting goods dealers. Playground balls and small volleyballs can be substituted if necessary. The goals can be improvised by using boundary cones, tape on the wall, rope through a chain-link fence, soccer goals, field hockey goals, or by building some regulation goals. The floor lines can be marked with floor tape or by putting boundary cones along the area where the lines should be. A basketball court can be easily modified for team handball by setting boundary cones along the goal area and by using the free-throw lane for the width of the goal.

Sequence of Skills

Team handball is a good unit to follow basketball, soccer, or water polo because it uses many of the same skills. The techniques and skill work are similar to those activities.

Passing

Team handball is a passing game, and many different passes can be used for short and medium ranges. The passing fundamentals are similar to those of basketball.

Chest, Bounce, and Overhead Passes. All 2-handed passes, similar to those in basketball.

One-Handed Shoulder or Baseball Pass. Similar to an overhand throw in baseball. If the student cannot grip the ball, the ball can rest on a flexed hand with the fingers spread.

Side-Arm Pass. Similar to the shoulder pass, except that the ball is released three-quarters to side arm to avoid a defender.

*Specific rules of team handball are available from the United States Team Handball Federation, 1750 E. Boulder, Colorado Springs, CO 80909.

Shovel Pass. A 1- or 2-handed underhand pass used for releasing the ball quickly and thus avoiding a defender.

Hand-Off Pass. Similar to a quarterback handing the ball off to a running back. The receiver forms a pocket for the ball.

Roller Pass. The ball is simply rolled along the floor to a teammate when all other passing lanes are blocked.

Hook Pass. Similar to the hook shot in basketball in which the passer hooks the ball over or around a defender. A jump may be added before the pass.

Jump Pass. Usually made with a shoulder pass. The passer jumps over or around a defender and throws the ball.

Behind-the-Back Pass. Similar to the basketball pass. Can be effective because the smaller ball is easier to control than a basketball.

Dribbling

Dribbling in handball is the same as the basketball skill, but the ball is harder to control because it is small and the ball surface is uneven. Players need to get used to the legal 3 steps before and after dribbling, as well as the 3-second holding rule. Dribbling should be practiced some but should in general be discouraged in team handball.

Goal Shooting

All of the aforementioned passes can also be used for shots on goal. The following shots are the most popular.

Jump Shot. Because the offensive player can jump outside the goal area and land in the goal area after a shot, the jump shot is the most popular shot. Shooters run 3 steps, jump, and shoot, using the 1-handed shoulder throw. This is the same as a 1-handed shoulder pass, except that it is a shot on goal. The shot can be used with or without a defender.

Dive Shot. The dive shot is a good shot on either wing, because the shooter can dive or fall away from an opponent.

Lob Shot. When a goalie comes out too far to defend, the shooter can lob the ball up and over the goalie's outstretched arms.

Penalty Shot. The penalty shot is the 1-on-1 free shot with only the goalie defending. The shooter must keep one foot stationary and cannot touch the 7-meter penalty line until the ball is thrown. The ball must be shot in 3 seconds. The goalie must be 3 meters or more away from the shooter. The shoulder or side-arm throw is usually most efficient for this shot.

Behind-the-Back. The shooter can fake a shot to the right and then bring the ball behind the back and the defender for a shot. The behind-the-back shot can be executed to either side.

Goal shooting involves the following general principles:

1. Attack the high or low corners on each shot.
2. Shoot primarily between the 6- and 9-meter line.
3. Find the open offensive player to take the shot.
4. Do not force a shot that is not open.
5. Do not shoot too far down on the wings because the angle is too extreme.
6. Use the floor or ground to bounce shots into the goal.
7. Jump shots toward the goal are effective. The ball must be released before the shooter lands in the goal area.
8. Develop a wide variety of goal shots.

Goal Tending

The position of goalie, the most important defender on the team, requires quick hands and feet and fast reaction time. All parts of the body can be used to deflect shots. The goalie also starts the offense after saving shots. The goalie needs to learn how to cut down shooting angles by moving out from the goal, depending on where the ball is located on the court. Goalies should practice saving shots in all 4 corners of the goal. They need to understand all of the rules governing the goalkeeper.

Defensive Strategy

The defensive strategy is similar to basketball in that person-to-person and zone defense are popular. Beginning players should start with the person-to-person defense and learn how to stay with an offensive

player. Zone defenses can be 6-0, 5-1, 4-2, and 3-3, with each person playing an area or zone. The back players in the zone are back against the goal line, while the front players are just inside the 9-meter line. The zone rotates with the ball as passes are made around the court.

Offensive Strategy

The offense starts the game with a throw-on from the center line. A throw-on also initiates play after each goal. All 6 offensive players line up at the center line, and 1 teammate throws the ball to another. The defense is in position, using either a zone or person-to-person defense. Offensive strategy is similar to basketball with picks, screens, rolls, and movement to open up shots on goal. With a zone defense, short, quick passes are made in an overloaded portion of the zone.

Ideas For Effective Instruction

Set up learning stations for passing, shooting, goal tending, dribbling, and defensive work. The performance objectives in this section, for example, are useful for structuring practice time at each station. Students can play with Nerf or comparable foam-rubber balls, playground balls, and volleyballs to get more practice attempts and to help beginning goalies perfect their skills. Group drills from basketball are applicable to team handball defense, offense, passing, and dribbling. Include various instructional devices for targets in passing, timing for dribbling through cones, or narrowing the goal area for shots to the corners. Penalty shots should be practiced daily. Competitive-type drills are enjoyable and motivating for most students.

Modified Games

No Bounce, No Steps, and No Contact

Students are forced to pass the ball rather than dribble. The walking or traveling rule from basketball is in effect, because students are usually comfortable with this rule. The no-contact rule gives the offense an advantage. The 3-second rule should remain in effect to force quick passes and deter holding of the ball.

Three Bounces, Three Steps, and No Contact

This game is closer to the regulation game and provides a gradual adjustment to the team handball rules. A variation would have the 3-bounce and 3-second rules, but with no steps allowed. Getting students used to the 3-step rule is difficult.

Sideline Team Handball

Sideline handball can be played when space is limited and the class is crowded. Extra team members spread out along each sideline. These sideline players can receive passes from teammates and can help pass the ball down the court. Sideline members can only pass the ball, however, and the 3-second rule applies to them. One sideline can be 1 team, and the other sideline the other team. A challenging variation is to have different team members on each sideline. This distribution forces the active players to sharpen their passing skills.

Suggested Performance Objectives

1. Dribble the ball with the right hand (standing position) for 10 consecutive times.
2. Same as task 1, but with the left hand.
3. Dribble the ball with the right hand (moving forward) from the center line to the goal line without losing the dribble.
4. Same as Task 3, but with the left hand.
5. Pass the ball to a partner standing 10 feet away with a 2-handed chest pass to the chest area (between chin and waist) 8 of 10 times.
6. Pass the ball to a partner standing 10 feet away with a 2-handed bounce pass to the waist area 8 of 10 times.
7. Pass the ball to a partner standing 10 feet away with a 2-handed overhead pass to the chest area 8 of 10 times.
8. Pass the ball to a partner standing 10 feet away with a 1-handed overhead pass to the chest area 8 of 10 times.
9. While running from the center line, pass alternately a 2-handed chest and bounce pass that can be caught by a partner running at a parallel distance of 12 feet with 3 of 4 passes hitting the partner.
10. While standing 7 meters from the goal, hit 3 of 5 goals.

11. Defend 3 of 5 attempted shots taken by a partner from a distance of 7 meters.
12. Dribble the ball with the right hand (moving forward) from the center line to the goal area without losing the dribble. Jump up and make a goal 3 of 5 times.
13. From 6 meters, hit a target 5 consecutive times with the following passes: roller, hook, jump, shovel, 1-handed shoulder, side-arm, and behind-the-back.
14. From 9 meters away, hit 2 of 5 goals.
15. From 9 meters away, defend 4 of 5 goal shots.
16. Dribble through a set of 6 cones in 25 seconds.

VOLLEYBALL

Since volleyball was adopted as an Olympic sport in 1964, it has gained a great deal of visibility through the media. The activity has grown in popularity throughout the world. In the United States, power volleyball has become a vigorous sport that many pursue in school and in recreational leagues. Volleyball is challenging, lends itself to coeducational participation, and can be modified in several ways to suit the abilities of many students.

Most states offer competitive volleyball for girls in the secondary schools. Many boys have had little interest in or experience with organized volleyball. Secondary physical education programs should offer coeducational volleyball classes to encourage both boys and girls. With the increased recreational volleyball offerings in YMCAs, community centers, and city recreational programs, students will be able to participate in and enjoy this activity for many years.

Sequence of Skills

Volleyball is difficult to play without a basic skills foundation. Help students to master these skills before beginning regulation games. Devising modified games for beginning-level students is important because they will not be able to play a regulation game (a few students would dominate, and the remaining students would become quickly frustrated). The type of ball, the height of the net, and the rules of the game can all be adjusted to ensure a successful experience for beginning students.

Serves

Underhand Serve. The underhand serve position starts with the left leg forward and both knees bent slightly. The ball is held in the left hand about waist height. The right arm starts with a long backswing and then comes forward, the right hand striking the ball just below the midline. The striking hand can be open or slightly closed, and the heel of the hand should contact the ball. The body weight is transferred from the rear foot to the front foot as the ball is contacted. The armswing follow-through should be in a straight line.

Overhand Serve. The overhand floater serve has no spin on the ball. The legs are staggered, with the left leg forward. The ball is held about shoulder height with the left hand under the ball and the right hand behind it. The ball is tossed 2 or 3 feet up above the right shoulder. The right arm is brought back, behind the ear, and then extended fully to hit the ball. The heel of the hand strikes the ball slightly below the midline. Little follow-through is used because the ball should float or wobble like a knuckle ball.

Students who lack the strength or ability to get the ball over the net can begin serving closer to the net, and the net can be lowered. As students develop skill, they should move back gradually to the regulation distance. Targets can be placed on the floor for work on accuracy as skill improves.

Passing and Setting

This skill involves moving the ball from 1 teammate to another. Forearm passes are used primarily for receiving a serve or a spike. Overhand set passes are used primarily for setting the ball into position for a spike. All passes require quick footwork while keeping a low center of gravity, which is necessary for getting under the ball.

Forearm Passes. In the forearm bump pass, the ball is hit off the forearms. The feet are about shoulder width apart, and 1 foot is ahead of the other. The knees are bent and the arms extended forward. The forearms are rolled outward to provide a flat, parallel surface for the ball. The elbows must be locked together on contact with the ball. The upward movement of the arms and legs depends on the speed of the ball and on the required distance of the pass. Passers must watch the ball carefully. Forearm passes can be made in different directions and also with 1 arm if necessary.

Overhand or Set Passes. In overhand passes, the body is set up under the ball, which is directly above the passer's nose. The hands are cupped to form a triangle-shaped window. The knees are bent and the legs are about shoulder width apart and in a stride position. The ball is contacted simultaneously with the fingers and thumbs of both hands. The legs, body, and arms uncoil into the ball in 1 smooth movement. Sets can be made from a front position facing the target and from a back position with the back to the target.

Spiking

Spiking is an offensive maneuver, which involves hitting the ball above the net and downward into the opponent's court. A spiker usually takes 3 or 4 steps toward the net. A final step with the right foot followed by a close step with the left foot precedes take-off. With both feet together, the spiker then jumps vertically straight up. The arms swing forward during the jump. As the arms come forward to about shoulder height, the back begins to arch, and the right arm is cocked behind the head. The left arm starts the forward motion downward, and the right arm uncoils and attacks the ball. The elbow leads the striking arm and shoulder. The striking hand is open and rigid, and the palm of the hand strikes the ball.

Blocking

Blocking is a defensive maneuver used to stop the ball from going over the net. Blocking can be done by any of the 3 players on the front line. Blockers can jump and reach over the net, as long as the ball has not been touched by the offensive player. Blockers should leave the floor slightly after the spiker. The takeoff starts with the legs bent at the knees. After the jump, the arms extend fully upward, as high as possible. The fingers are spread as wide as possible. The hands are held rigid and no wider apart than the width of the ball. As the blocker comes down, the arms are drawn back to the body, and the feet and legs absorb the landing.

Ideas for Effective Instruction

Volleyball lends itself to station work on forearm passes, sets, serves, and spiking. The performance objectives listed in the contract at the end of this unit can be posted on task cards at the various stations. A class period could include work on the performance objectives, group skill work, and a modified game. It is important to adjust the height of the net, the rules of the game, and the type of ball used so that inexperienced students can keep the ball in play. Foam-rubber balls and beach balls are excellent for beginners.

Many passing, setting, and serving activities can be done with partners. Having 1 partner toss the ball and the other partner pass or set is a good introductory drill. A smooth wall is useful for passing and setting practice, and small groups in a circle can also be effective for passing and setting. For serving practice, several players can line up along both base lines of a court and serve several balls at a time. Servers can practice anywhere along the base line. Beginning servers should always move closer to the net.

Setting and spiking drills can be arranged with a setter in the center forward position and a line of spikers in either the on-hand or off-hand position. The spiker tosses the ball to the setter and awaits a setup for a spike. Several ball chasers on the other side of the net can be useful. Net recovery shots can be practiced on a properly stretched net. One partner tosses the ball into the net, and the other player tries to recover the ball with a forearm pass.

Competitive situations are fun for drill work (for example, sets in a row, passes with a partner, serves to a target area, or spikes to an area). These competitive challenges can be individual, with partners, or among small groups. The contract included here offers many challenges that can be modified for students of different ability levels.

Lead-Up and Modified Games

Leader Ball

Organize students into several teams. The leader of each team stands about 5 yards away from teammates. The teammates can be in single file or standing side by side facing the leader. The leader uses a forearm pass or set and hits the ball to the first person in line. That person hits the ball back to the leader and goes quickly to the end of the line. The object is to hit the ball to all teammates quicker than the other teams.

Zigzag Relay

Half of the players on 1 team stand side by side about 2 to 3 yards apart, and face the other half of their team. The ball is started at 1 end and passed or set,

back and forth, down the line across a distance of 5 yards. The object is to control the ball and move it down the line quickly. The winning team is the fastest in getting the ball up and down the line to all team members. More than 1 ball can be added for variety.

Keep It Afloat

A group must keep the ball up in the air or against a wall for a specified amount of time. The group can be in a circle or arranged single file for the wall drill. Passes, sets, or alternating of the 2 can be used.

Beach Ball or Nerf Ball Volleyball

Regulation rules are followed, except that the server must move up close to the net. A beach ball or Nerf ball is easier to control than a regular volleyball.

One-Bounce Volleyball

Regular rules are followed, except that the ball can bounce 1 time on each side. The bounce can occur after the serve, pass, or set. A variation of this game is to allow 2 or 3 bounces.

Volley Tennis

The game can be played on a tennis court or on a volleyball court. The net is put on the ground, as in tennis, and the ball is put in play with a serve. It may bounce once or can be passed directly to a teammate. The ball should be hit 3 times before going over the net. Spiking is common because of the low net.

Sitting or Kneeling Volleyball

Sitting or kneeling volleyball is a good indoor game to play on a mat or in the gym. The net is lowered according to the general size and ability level of the group. An overhead pass starts the game. Court size and number of players can vary.

Serve and Catch

Serve and catch is started with a ball on each side of the net. Several balls are served at the same time, and all balls must be caught on the other side. Once the balls are caught, they can be served from the opposing serving area. The object is to catch the ball and quickly serve so that your opponent cannot catch the ball. A scorer from each side is necessary.

Rotation Under the Net

The game, played with 2, 3, or 4 people on a team, is started with 1 team on each side of the net and with 2 or 3 other teams waiting in line to enter the game. The teacher begins the game by tossing the ball up on either side of the net. The ball must be hit 3 times, with the third hit going over the net. No spiking is allowed. The winning team rotates under the net, a new team rotates into their place, and the losing team rotates off the court and becomes the last team in line. The teacher throws the ball up in the air quickly as the teams are rotating. All teams must move quickly to the proper court. The game is fast-moving and involves passing, setting, and court coverage. It is a good game for high school students who have developed passing and setting skills.

Three-Hit Volleyball

Three-hit volleyball is similar to regular volleyball, but the ball must be hit 3 times on a side with the third hit going over the net.

Mini-Volleyball

This is a modified game for students ages 9 to 12. The net is 6 feet 10 inches, and the court is 15 by 40 feet. Three students are on a team, with 2 front-line players and 1 back-line player. The rules are similar to regulation volleyball.

Blind-Man Volleyball

A cover is put over the net so that it is impossible to see what is happening on the other side. Regulation volleyball rules are followed. Teams must be ready, because they never know when the ball is coming over the net. A scorer is necessary for both sides of the net.

Regulation Volleyball—Serves Modified

Regulation rules are followed, but the server can have 2 attempts, or the service distance is shortened.

Suggested Performance Objectives

Performance objectives have been used successfully with volleyball units at both the middle and high school levels. The following list can help structure a learning envrionment for volleyball activities. These can be modified according to the abilities of the students and the facilities available.

Core Objectives

Forearm Pass

1. Bump 12 consecutive forearm passes against the wall at a height of at least 10 feet.
2. Bump 12 consecutive forearm passes into the air at a height of at least 10 feet.
3. Bump 10 consecutive forearm passes over the net with the instructor or a classmate.

Overhead Set Pass

4. Hit 15 consecutive set passes against the wall at a height of at least 10 feet.
5. Hit 15 consecutive set passes into the air at a height of at least 10 feet.
6. Hit 12 consecutive set passes over the net with the instructor or a classmate.

Serves

7. Hit 3 consecutive underhand serves into the right half of the court.
8. Hit 3 of 4 underhand serves into the left half of the court.
9. Hit 3 consecutive overhand serves inbounds.

Attendance and Participation

10. Be dressed and ready to participate at 8:00 A.M.
11. Participate in 15 games.
12. Score 90% or better on a rules, strategies, and techniques test.

Optional Objectives

1. Standing 2 feet from the backline, bump 3 of 5 forearm passes into an 8-foot circle surrounding the setter's position. The height must be at least 10 feet. The ball will be thrown by the instructor or a classmate.
2. Bump 3 of 5 forearm passes over the net at a height of at least 12 feet that land inbounds and not more than 8 feet from the backline.
3. Standing in the setter's position (center forward), hit 3 consecutive overhead sets at least 10 feet high that land in a 5-foot circle where the spiker would be located. The ball will be thrown by the instructor or a classmate.
4. Hit 3 of 5 overhead passes over the net at least 12 feet high that land inbounds and not more than 8 feet from the backline.

5. Standing in the setter's position (center forward), hit 3 of 5 back sets at least 10 feet high that land in a 5-foot circle where the spiker would be located. The ball will be thrown by the instructor or a classmate.

6. Volley 12 consecutive times over the net with the instructor or a classmate by alternating forearm passes and overhead passes.

7. Alternate forearm passes and overhead passes in the air at a height of 10 feet or more, 12 consecutive times.

8. Spike 3 of 4 sets inbounds from an on-hand position—3-step approach, jump, extend arm, hand contact.

9. Spike 3 of 5 sets inbounds from an off-hand position.

10. Recover 3 consecutive balls from the net. Recoveries must be playable, that is, 8 feet high in the playing area.

11. Hit 3 consecutive overhand serves into the right half of the court.

12. Hit 3 of 4 overhand serves into the left half of the court.

13. Hit 3 of 5 overhand serves under a rope 15 feet high that land in the back half of the court.

14. Officiate at least 3 games, using proper calls and signals.

15. Coach a team for the class tournament—planning strategy, substitution, and scheduling.

16. Devise and carry out a research project that deals with volleyball. Check with the instructor for ideas.

REFERENCES AND SUGGESTED READINGS

Basketball

Mood, D. P., Musker, F. F., and Rink, J. E. 1991. *Sports and Recreational Activities for Men and Women.* 10th ed. St. Louis: Mosby.

Moore, B., and White, J. 1980. *Basketball: Theory and Practice.* Dubuque, IA: Wm. C. Brown Group.

Summitt, P. H., and Jennings, D. 1991. *Basketball: Fundamentals and Team Play.* Dubuque, IA: Brown & Benchmark.

Wilkes, G. 1994. *Basketball.* 6th ed. Dubuque, IA: Brown & Benchmark.

Wissel, H. 1994. *Basketball: Steps to Success.* Champaign, IL: Human Kinetics Publishers.

Field Hockey

Fong, D. 1983. *The Coach's Collection of Field Hockey Drills.* West Point, NY: Leisure Press.

Marron, K. T. 1993. Field hockey. In N. Dougherty (ed.). *Physical Activity and Sport for the Secondary School Student.* Reston, VA: NASPE and AAHPERD.

Mood, D. P., Musker, F. F., and Rink, J. E. 1991. *Sports and Recreational Activities for Men and Women,* 10th ed. St. Louis: Mosby.

National Association for Girls and Women in Sport. 1980. *Field Hockey–Lacrosse Guide.* Reston, VA: AAHPERD.

Whitney, M. G. (ed.). *Eagle.* Official Publication of the United States Field Hockey Association Inc. Colorado Springs, CO: USFHA.

Flag Football

AAHPERD. 1980. *Rules for Coeducational Activities and Sports.* Reston, VA: AAHPERD.

Domitrovitz, M. 1993. Flagball. In N. Dougherty (ed.). *Physical Activity and Sport for the Secondary School Student.* Reston, VA: NASPE and AAHPERD.

Mood, D. P., Musker, F. F., and Rink, J. E. 1991. *Sports and Recreational Activities for Men and Women.* 10th ed. St. Louis: Mosby.

Seaton, D. C. et al. 1983. *Physical Education Handbook.* 7th ed. Englewood Cliffs, NJ: Prentice-Hall.

Lacrosse

Brackenridge, C. 1978. *Women's Lacrosse.* Woodbury, NY: Barrons.

Hinkman, J. 1975. *Box Lacrosse: The Fastest Game on Two Feet.* Radnor, PA: University Press.

Liebich, T. 1981. *Coach Lacrosse: Teaching the Fundamentals.* Vancouver, BC: British Columbia Lacrosse Association.

Mood, D. P., Musker, F. F., and Rink, J. E. 1991. *Sports and Recreational Activities for Men and Women.* 10th ed. St. Louis: Mosby.

Schrader, R., and Everden, S. 1977. *Team Sports: A Competency Based Approach.* Dubuque, IA: Kendall/Hunt Publishing Co.

Scott, R. 1976. *Lacrosse: Technique and Tradition.* Baltimore, MD: Johns Hopkins University Press.

Soccer

Fellenbaum, J. E. 1993. Soccer. In N. Dougherty (ed.). *Physical Activity and Sport for the Secondary School Student.* Reston, VA: NASPE and AAHPERD.

Luxbacher, J. 1990. *Teaching Soccer: Steps to Success.* Champaign, IL: Human Kinetics Publishers.

Mood, D. P., Musker, F. F., and Rink, J. E. 1991. *Sports and Recreational Activities for Men and Women.* 10th ed. St. Louis: Mosby.

Negroesco, S. 1993. *Soccer.* Dubuque, IA: Brown & Benchmark.

Thomson, W. 1980. *Teaching Soccer.* Minneapolis, MN: Burgess Publishing Co.

Softball

Kneer, M., and McCord, C. 1995. *Softball: Slow and Fast Pitch.* 6th ed. Dubuque, IA: Brown & Benchmark.

Mood, D. P., Musker, F. F., and Rink, J. E. 1991. *Sports and Recreational Activities for Men and Women.* 10th ed. St. Louis: Mosby.

Potter, D. L. 1989. *Softball: Steps to Success.* Champaign, IL: Human Kinetics Publishers.

Sisley, B. L. 1993. Softball. In N. Dougherty, (ed.). *Physical Activity and Sport for the Secondary School Student.* Reston, VA: NASPE and AAHPERD.

Team Handball

Cavanaugh, M. 1993. Team handball. In N. Dougherty (ed.). *Physical Activity and Sport for the Secondary School Student.* Reston, VA: NASPE and AAHPERD.

Cuesta, J. G. 1981. *Team Handball Techniques.* Colorado Springs, CO: United States Team Handball Federation.

Mood, D. P., Musker, F. F., and Rink, J. E. 1991. *Sports and Recreational Activities for Men and Women.* 10th ed. St. Louis: Mosby.

Team Handball—Official Rules of the Game. 1981. Colorado Springs, CO: United States Team Handball Federation.

Team Handball, Racquetball, Orienteering. 1979–1981. National Association for Girls and Women in Sport Guide. Reston, VA: AAHPERD.

Volleyball

Kluka, D. A., and Dunn, P. J. 1992. *Volleyball.* 2nd ed. Dubuque, IA: Brown & Benchmark.

Mood, D. P., Musker, F. F., and Rink, J. E. 1991. *Sports and Recreational Activities for Men and Women.* 10th ed. St. Louis: Mosby.

Slaymaker, T., and Brown, V. 1983. *Power Volleyball.* 3rd ed. Philadelphia, PA: W. B. Saunders Co.

Viera, B. L., and Ferguson, B. J. 1989. *Teaching Volleyball, Steps to Success.* Champaign, IL: Human Kinetics Publishers.

Viera, B. L. 1993. Volleyball. In N. Dougherty (ed.). *Physical Activity and Sport for the Secondary School Student.* Reston, VA.: NASPE and AAHPERD.

20 Individual Sports

Individual sports are excellent lifetime recreational activities because many of them require little equipment. The focus for instruction in these units should be on the benefits of participation.

AQUATICS

An aquatics instructional program in the secondary schools is an excellent addition to a balanced curriculum. Unfortunately, few school districts have the facilities necessary to implement swimming and related aquatics programs. It is, however, often possible to bus students to swimming pools outside the school. These may be municipal pools, YMCA and YWCA pools, or the facilities of various private organizations.

Swimming classes require teacher expertise in the area. Rotating teaching responsibilities is mandatory so that teachers with experience are used in the swimming instructional program. The swimming program can also have an aquatic games component, which focuses on learning to adjust to the water. The aquatic games can be taught by a less-qualified teacher. All aquatics teachers, regardless of assignment, should have the American Red Cross Water Safety Instruction certification.

The pool should be clean and warm. Nothing turns students off faster than having to swim in a pool that is inadequately heated. A pool with a uniform depth of 3 to 4 feet of water is often preferable for teaching nonswimmers because the students can stand up immediately if they have a problem. This offers beginning swimmers a measure of confidence. For intermediate and advanced swimmers, a standard pool, which can be used for diving as well as swimming, is preferable.

Keep lessons short in terms of time spent in the water. Students tire easily when learning new skills, and they can practice some skills out of the water. Since swimming is an important lifetime skill, it is most desirable that students leave the class with a positive feeling about the instruction. Introducing students to any new activity is difficult, and most students need extra encouragement and patience as they begin to overcome their fears of the water.

Sequence of Skills

A difficult aspect of teaching swimming to middle and high school students is the tremendous range of ability and experience that students bring to the class. Some students may not know how to swim, whereas others may have been swimming competitively since they were 3 years old. This necessitates homogeneous groupings according to ability. The skills to be taught may therefore range from drownproofing and survival skills to the American Red Cross Water Safety Instruction certification.

Because aquatics is a highly specialized activity involving specific skills that must be learned, it is difficult to develop meaningful lead-up activities. The authors recommend texts listed at the end of this section to teachers who are interested in creating a meaningful instructional program. They include chapters on developing a successful instructional program, teaching essential aquatic skills, springboard diving skills, and life-saving skills. Chapters are also offered on the evaluation of swimming skills. Of particular aid to the less-experienced teacher is a series of performance analysis sheets to help in evaluating various strokes and dives.

ARCHERY

Archery has long been recognized as an appealing activity for students of both sexes, of all ages, and for those with disabilities. The two most popular forms are target archery and field archery. Target archery involves shooting a specific number of arrows from a given distance at a target with 5 or 10 concentric circles. Scoring is completed by adding up the points for each arrow striking the target. This is the most popular archery activity taught in secondary school programs. Field archery involves 28 stationary targets of assorted sizes and shapes placed at varying distances. Field shooting requires a larger area and considerable safety procedures. It is especially appealing to those who hunt and bow fish. Archery seems to be quite popular with certain individuals. Many families enjoy participating together, for archery activities can be enjoyed by all family members.

Sequence of Skills

Bracing the Bow

Several methods are used for stringing or bracing the bow. One method involves using a bowstringer device made of a 5-foot rope with a leather cup on each end. The cups are put on both ends of the bow with the string hanging down toward the ground in front of the body. After placing 1 string loop in position, place 1 foot on the center of the bowstringer, and pull the bow straight up with 1 hand. Use the free hand to slide the free string loop into place. To unstring the bow, reverse the process.

Another stringing technique is called the step-through method. Start by placing the bottom string loop in position, then put the bottom curve of the bow across the top of the right ankle, and step between the string and the bow with the left foot. Use the left hand to bend the bow against the left thigh until the string loop can be moved into place with the right hand. Be sure to keep the face away from the bow tip.

Stance

The feet should straddle the shooting line and be shoulder width apart. The toes are in a direct line with the target. The knees should be relaxed, and a comfortable standing posture maintained.

Nocking the Arrow

Hold the bow horizontally in the left hand, and place the nock of the arrow on the nocking point of the string. The odd-colored feather should face away from the bow. Use the index finger of the left hand to steady the arrow on the arrow rest.

Extend and Draw

The string is on the first joint of 3 fingers of the right hand. The index finger is above the arrow, and the next 2 fingers are below the arrow. Rotate the bow to a vertical position with the left arm parallel to the ground. Extend the left arm and draw the string toward the body with the right hand. Keep the right elbow parallel to the ground. Be sure the fingers of the bow hand are loose and relaxed.

Anchor and Hold

The string should touch the nose, lips, and chin, while the index finger touches under the center of the chin. The anchor point should be the same for every shot.

Aiming

Target archery has 2 basic methods of aiming—point of aim and bowsights. The beginner should probably use the point-of-aim technique, which involves finding a spot somewhere on a vertical line drawn above, through, and below the middle of the target. This point of aim will vary according to the distance from the target. To locate the point, align the eye and the arrow with an object on the vertical line through the center of the target. Shoot several rounds and then adjust the point of aim up or down accordingly. A mechanical bowsight can be mounted on the bow and used by aligning the center of the target through the aperture. The aperture is then adjusted up or down, or left or right, depending on the pattern of the arrows for that shooting distance. The aperture position is then noted for each distance and is used in the future.

Release and Afterhold

As the arrow is released, the back muscles remain tight while the string fingers relax. The relaxed drawing hand moves backward slightly along the neck. The bow arm and head remain steady until the arrow hits the target.

Retrieving Arrows

Arrows in a target should be removed by placing the arrow between the index and middle finger of the left hand. The palm of the hand should be away from the target facing the archer. The right hand should be placed on the arrow close to the target. The arrow is removed by gently twisting and pulling at the same angle at which the arrow entered. If the fletching (feathers or plastic material used to stabilize the flight of the arrow) is inside the target, the arrow should be pulled through the target. Arrows should be carried with the points together and the feathers spread out to prevent damage.

Ideas for Effective Instruction

Equipment

The composition of bows is primarily wood, fiberglass, or a laminated combination of the 2. Both straight and recurved bows are available. The recurved bow has curved ends to provide additional leverage, which increases the velocity of the arrow. Bows also have different weights and lengths. Archers should select a bow based on their strength and skill. Starting with a lighter bow is best and then progressing to a heavier one as skill and strength are developed. In class situations, teachers should try to have a variety of bows available for different ability levels.

Arrow shafts are made of wood, fiberglass, or aluminum. It is important for the beginning archer to get the proper length arrow. A good method for determining proper length is to have someone hold a yardstick against the sternum, perpendicular to the body, while the individual extends the arms with the palms on either side of the yardstick. The point at which the fingertips touch the yardstick is the correct arrow length. For beginners, it is better to have long arrows. Many different types of points and feathers are available.

Many types of finger tabs and shooting gloves are also available for protection and to promote smooth release. An arm guard should be used to prevent the bowstring from slapping the bow arm and to keep long clothing sleeves snug to the body. Movable and stationary quivers are used to transport arrows and sometimes to support the bow while retrieving arrows.

General Rules

1. Archers must straddle a shooting line. Arrows should always be pointed down-range.
2. An end of 6 arrows is usually shot at 1 time. A round consists of a number of ends shot at several distances.

3. Values for rings in a target are as follows:

   Five-Ring Scoring
   Gold = 9
   Red = 7
   Blue = 5
   Black = 3
   White = 1

   Ten-Ring Scoring
   Gold = 10, 9
   Red = 8, 7
   Blue = 6, 5
   Black = 4, 3
   White = 2, 1

4. An arrow that bisects 2 colors scores the higher of the 2 values.
5. An arrow that bounces off a target or passes through a target is given 7 points if there is a witness.
6. The petticoat, or outside area of the target, counts as a miss.

Organization, Skill Work, and Safety

Beginning students can experience success quickly if the instructor moves the target close to them (10 yards or less). Students can then move away from the target as their skill level increases. A safe environment is important. Make sure that students follow strict rules for shooting procedures. Partner work is useful for checking form, reminding about safety procedures, and giving feedback. A form for a rating scale or checklist for shooting can also be useful and motivating to some students. Several checklists are available from the sources listed at the end of the unit.

Time should be spent with partners and observers to make sure that they are actively involved in the learning process and concentrating on the specific shooting skills. Make sure that all students are mentally involved, even when they are not shooting.

Lead-Up Games and Learning Activities

Relays

Each team has 1 target and each person has 1 arrow. The first person in line shoots and then goes to the end of the line. All team members shoot 1 arrow and then the team score is tallied. The team with the highest score is the winner.

Turkey Shoot

Each team draws a turkey about the size of a target on a piece of paper. The turkey is placed on the target. Each team tries to hit the turkey as many times as possible.

Tic-Tac-Toe or Bingo

Balloons or a target with squares are placed on the regular target—3 rows of 3 for tic-tac-toe, or 5 rows of 5 for bingo. The object is to hit 3 or 5 in a row vertically, horizontally, or diagonally. The game can be for individuals or for teams.

Target Work-Up

Start with 4 or 5 students on a target. Shoot an end of 4 arrows and tally the score. The highest scorer moves up 1 target, and the lowest scorer moves down a target. This can be an individual or partner activity.

Tape Shooting

Place 2 pieces of masking tape across the target, 1 vertically and 1 horizontally. The object is to hit either piece of tape. This can also be an individual or team event.

Suggested Performance Objectives

Core Objectives

Objectives 1, 2, and 3 should be completed before the student is allowed to shoot on the range.

1. On a written test covering safety rules, archery terminology, and scoring, the student will score at least 70% (2 attempts allowed).
2. The student will demonstrate how to brace and unbrace the bow. Grading is on a pass-fail basis.
3. The student will demonstrate the 9 steps of the shooting technique (that is, stand, nock, extend, draw, anchor, hold, aim, release, and afterhold). Grading is on a pass-fail basis.
4. At a distance of 10 yards, the student will hit the target at least 5 of 6 times and score a minimum of 28 points.
5. At a distance of 15 yards, the student will hit the target 4 of 6 times and score a minimum of 24 points.

6. At a distance of 20 yards, the student will hit the target 4 of 6 times and score a minimum of 24 points.
7. The student will participate in a minimum of 2 out of 3 novelty archery events.

Optional Activities (Extra Credit)

1. On a written test covering safety rules, archery terminology, and scoring, the student will score 100%.
2. At a distance of 10 yards, the student will hit the target 6 of 6 times and score at least 40 points.
3. At a distance of 15 yards, the student will hit the target 5 of 6 times and score at least 40 points.
4. At a distance of 20 yards, the student will hit the target 5 of 6 times and score at least 38 points.
5. The student will write a 2-page report on the history of archery, complete with bibliography.
6. The student will participate in all 3 days of novelty archery events.
7. The student will design and put up a bulletin board about archery.

Reinforcement Menu

1. Objectives 1, 2, and 3 must be met before students are allowed to shoot.
2. Post the checklist of objectives on the bulletin board.
3. Post on the bulletin board the high ends and high rounds for each class.
4. Post on the bulletin board the results of the class tournament for each distance.
5. Give ribbons to winners of novelty events.
6. Award extra-credit points for exceeding skill requirements.

Rainy-Day Activities

Discussion and practice can focus on these skills:

Eye dominance
Stance
Nock
Extend
Bow hand position
String hand and arm position
Draw
Anchor
Tighten-hold
Aim
Tighten-release
Afterhold

BOWLING

The game of bowling today is a form of kingpins, the first bowling game to use finger holes in the ball. The sport has changed from a simple game played outdoors to a complex mechanized game played in large modern facilities. Bowling has become one of our most widely enjoyed recreational activities. Any family member may participate because the game is suitable for all ages and both sexes. Bowling can be played in any season, and facilities are usually available at most times of the day. Leagues are popular, and many businesses sponsor employee leagues. Schools have intramural leagues, and many bowling establishments organize leagues for children. These leagues are usually sanctioned by the proper national organization.

The play in bowling consists of rolling balls down a wooden alley with the object of knocking over 10 wooden pins positioned at the far end of the alley. The bowler stands any distance behind the foul line and takes 3, 4, or 5 steps before releasing the ball down the alley. If the player touches the alley beyond the foul line, a foul is called, and the ball counts as 1 ball bowled. No score is made on a foul, and the pins knocked down are immediately replaced. In bowling and duckpins, the pins knocked down after the first ball rolled are cleared away before the next ball is rolled. In candlepins, knocked down pins are not cleared away. Each bowler has 10 frames in which to knock down as many pins as possible. If a bowler knocks down all of the pins in 10 frames of bowling, a perfect score of 300 is attained.

Sequence of Skills

Picking Up the Ball

If in an alley area, face the direction of the returning balls. Place the hands on opposite sides of the ball and lift the ball to a comfortable position in front of the body before placing the fingers and thumb in the holes. Avoid placing the thumb and fingers in the holes to pick up the ball, as this places strain on the bowling hand.

Gripping the Ball

Holding the ball in the left hand (if right-handed), place the 2 middle fingers in the holes first and then slip the thumb in the thumbhole. Do not squeeze the ball with the fingertips, but maintain contact by slightly pressing the palm side of the fingers and thumb toward the palm area of the ball. The little finger and index finger are relaxed and flat on the ball.

Stance

The stance is the stationary position that the bowler holds before approaching the foul line. The development of a stance, which varies among bowlers, is essential for consistency in bowling. To locate the starting position, stand with the back to the foul line, walk 4½ steps, stop, turn, and face the pins. The number of steps will vary with the 3-, 4-, or 5-step approach. Standing erect, place the feet parallel to each other, or the left foot may be slightly in front of the right foot. The feet should be about 1.5 inches apart. The weight is on the left foot, and the knees are slightly bent. The head is up, and the shoulders are level.

The ball is held at waist level and slightly to the right. The arm is straight from the shoulder to the wrist. The ball will be pushed out during the first step and will swing down directly below the shoulder. The wrist is kept straight and stiff during the pendulum swing. The elbow moves back alongside the body and should not be braced on the hip. The ball is supported by the nonbowling hand. The shoulders, hips, and feet are square with the pins when the stance is established.

After learning the basic stance, the bowler can develop a personal style. Some leading bowlers hold the ball approximately level with the chin and a few inches from the body. Proficient bowlers usually hold the ball at waist level and a few inches away from the body. The upper torso leans slightly forward. Taller bowlers sometimes use a half crouch and a shorter backswing.

Aiming

The method of aim should be decided after the footwork, timing, and method of rolling the ball have been established. The bowler should then experiment to find the preferable method of aim. Spot bowling is recommended.

1. *Pin bowling.* The bowler looks at the pins and draws an imaginary line between the point of delivery and the point on the pins at which the ball will be aimed. This line will be the route of the ball. The usual point to hit is the 1-3 pocket.

2. *Spot bowling.* The bowler draws an imaginary line from the point of delivery to some spot down the lane, usually at the division boards where the maple meets pine. Most lanes have triangular markings for spot bowlers.

Approach and Delivery

One-Step Delivery. One-step delivery should be learned before the 3-, 4-, or 5-step delivery. The stance for the 1-step delivery differs from the general stance discussed previously. The foot opposite the bowling arm is behind. Extend the bowling hand, and after extension, drop the hand slowly to the side and simultaneously lean forward, bending the knees. Keep the arm relaxed and the wrist straight. Swing the arm forward to eye level, back to waist level, and forward again to eye level. The stance for the 1-step delivery is assumed. The hands are at waist height as if gripping the ball. Push the arms forward, release the left hand, and complete the pendulum swing.

Repeat the push-away and the pendulum swing, but as the arm swings forward (at the completion of the swing), slide ahead on the foot opposite the bowling arm. Keep the shoulders straight and the body facing straight ahead. Practice the simultaneous movement of arm and foot. No ball is necessary when first learning the approach and delivery. When the timing is learned, then add the ball.

Four-Step Delivery. The 4-step delivery is the most popular. The stance is with the opposite foot forward, as presented earlier. Starting with the right foot, take 4 brisk walking strides forward. Repeat the 4-step walk, making the fourth step a slide. At the completion of the slide, the full body weight should be on the sliding foot, knee bent, and shoulders parallel to the foul line. The forward foot should be pointed toward the pins.

To coordinate the delivery, the bowler should assume the stance, start the 4-step walk, and push the ball out, down, back, and forward so that the arm movements coordinate with the steps (1, 2, 3, slide). As the foot slides, the ball comes forward and is released. At the release, the thumb is out, and the fingers and wrist are turning and lifting the ball. The right leg swings forward for balance, and the right arm, which was straight throughout the backswing, bends at the elbow for the follow-through. The body then straightens to get more lift on the ball.

Different types of balls can be thrown, depending on how the ball is released.

1. *Straight ball.* The wrist and forearm are kept straight throughout the entire delivery. The thumb is on top of the ball, at 12 o'clock position, and the index finger is at 2 o'clock.
2. *Hook ball.* The ball is held throughout the approach, delivery, and release with the thumb at 10 o'clock and the index finger at 12 o'clock. If the ball hooks too much, move the thumb toward the 12 o'clock position.

Ideas for Effective Instruction

Gymnasium Bowling Sets

Gymnasium bowling sets are available through many equipment dealers. They usually contain 10 plastic pins, a triangular sheet for pin setup, score sheets, and 1 hard plastic ball. Sizes of the finger holes will vary and so may the weight of the ball. The cost is approximately $60 per set.

Score Sheets

Score sheets can be drawn and duplicated. Sheets are included in gym sets, or an instructor can check with a local establishment about purchasing or a possible donation.

General Rules and Scoring

1. A game consists of 10 frames. Each bowler is allowed 2 deliveries in each frame, with the exception of the tenth frame in which 3 are allowed if a spare or strike is scored.
2. The score is an accumulated total of pins knocked down plus bonus points for spares and strikes.
3. If all 10 pins are knocked down on the first ball rolled, it is a strike. The scorer counts 10 plus the total of the next 2 balls rolled.
4. If all pins are knocked down with 2 balls rolled, it is a spare. The scorer counts 10 plus the number of pins knocked down on the next ball rolled.
5. If no pins are knocked down when a ball is rolled, the bowler is charged with an error. This includes gutter balls.
6. If pins left after the first ball constitute a split, a circle is made on the score sheet around the number of pins knocked down.
7. A foul results if the bowler steps across the foul line.

Etiquette

1. Take your turn promptly.
2. The bowler to the right has the right-of-way. Wait until the bowler on the right is finished before assuming stance.
3. Stay on your approach.
4. Step back off the approach after delivery.
5. Use your ball only, and use the same ball throughout.
6. Do not talk to a player who is on the approach.
7. Respect all equipment and the establishment.
8. Competition is encouraged, but be gracious in any case.
9. Return all equipment to its proper place.

Organization and Skill Work

Teach skills in sequence. Once the basic grip and stance have been taught (group situation), stations can be used for skill practice. Depending on the unit structure, students can work at stations on skills to be checked off, or they may be involved in lead-up games, engaged in mini-tournaments (using gym sets), or practicing skills at a bowling facility. Since bowling skills are perfected through constant practice, the unit should be designed for maximum activity.

If space is available, mock lanes can be made. Using mock lanes can enhance the number of students involved in activity while using a smaller space. Students are able to practice the approach, release, and spotting without pins. They can work in pairs, taking turns practicing and rolling the ball back. Team games with the mock lanes and gymnasium bowling sets can be enjoyable. Hand out score sheets and have students record their scores. Scorers sign their name, and score sheets are checked for correct scoring procedure. Games with mock lanes and gymnasium sets can be used as a lead-up to bowling at a nearby facility.

Lead-Up Games and Learning Activities

Red Pin

Use regulation alleys or lanes set up on the gym floor. One pin is painted red (tape may be substituted). The bowler rolls 1 ball in each frame. The bowler scores only if the red pin is upset. The pinsetter makes no attempt to specifically place the red pin. It will occur in random placement. Because only 1 ball is rolled, no spares are scored. Strikes are possible and should be scored as in regulation bowling. This activity can be used for team or individual competition.

Scotch Bowling

This activity can be played on regulation lanes or in a gym with marked lanes. Students choose a partner and decide who will roll the first ball. Partners then alternate throughout the game, which is scored like regulation bowling.

Shuffle-Bowl

The game is played on a shuffleboard court using shuffleboard cues, disc, and bowling pins or Indian clubs. The discs are slid at the pins. Play and scoring are carried out as in regulation bowling.

Skittles

Use an open area, wooden discs, and 10 small pins or Indian clubs. Slide or pitch the discs at the pins from a specified distance. Use regulation scoring.

Three Pins

Regulation equipment or the gymnasium with marked lanes can be used for play. The bowler attempts to knock down the 1-2-3 combination by hitting the 1-3 pocket (1-2, if left-handed). One ball is allowed for each turn. Players start with 20 points. Three pins down subtracts 3 points, 2 down subtracts 2 points, and 1 pin down subtracts 1 point. The first player to reach 0 points is the winner.

Soccer Bowling

Any open area, indoors or outdoors, is suitable for play. Soccer balls and wooden pins are used, and the game is scored like regulation bowling.

Basket Bowling

Play in an alley marked on the gym floor. Allow a 15-foot approach. Use 2 indoor softballs and a metal wastebasket propped up on its side with 2 bricks or similar objects facing the foul line. Five to 10 players and 1 retriever make up a team. Each player attempts to roll 2 balls into the wastebasket. Rotate and trade places with the retriever. One point is scored for each basket made, and the high scorer wins. If teams play against one another, use a time limit. Each player is allowed 5 turns. If the bowler steps over the foul line, 1 point is subtracted. If the ball is bounced on the alley, 1 point is subtracted. An official scorekeeper and judge are necessary.

Objectives, Tests, and Rating Form

Objectives

1. Bowl 6 games at any lane. Keep score and turn in the score sheet to the instructor. On a separate sheet, state the two basic rules for scoring. List and explain the symbols used in scoring.
2. Research and write a paper on the history of bowling using at least 4 sources. The paper

Name _____ Bowler										
Approach										
Push away on first step										
Push-away: out and down—elbow straight										
Backswing: straight—in line with boards										
Backswing: to shoulder level										
Steps: smooth, gliding, even rhythm										
Steps: increase in length and speed										
Slide on left foot										
Release										
Shoulders: parallel to foul line										
Shoulders: level										
Upper body: inclined forward										
Left foot: in line with boards										
Weight balanced on left foot										
Thumb in 12 o'clock position										
Ball first strikes alley 1.5 ft in front of left foot										
Follow-through: straight and to shoulder height										
Aim										
Approach: straight, in line with boards										
Release: proper dot or dots at foul line										
Crosses proper dart										
Where does ball strike pins? (e.g., 1–3, 1, 3, 1–2)										

Place a (3) in proper square if the item is performed correctly.
Place a (–) if it is not correct.

FIGURE 20.1   Bowling rating form

should be typed double-spaced and include a bibliography.

3. Learn the correct way to pick up and hold the ball. Be able to demonstrate the hand positions, footwork, and release. Be able also to demonstrate the hand position that creates a hook, a straight ball, and a backup ball. Performance is evaluated on the basis of an oral explanation to the instructor.

4. Watch at least 1 tournament, either live or on television, for an hour, or observe an hour of league bowling. Report in writing about how this type of bowling differs from open bowling.

5. Obtain a rule book from the Women's International Bowling Congress (WIBC) and find out what special prizes are awarded in sanctioned leagues. Illustrate and explain the patches and award procedures.

6. Visit a lane and ask the operator for an inspection of an automatic pinsetter in operation. Find out how to operate the ball clearer, how to turn on the teleprompter, and how to reset the pins. Discover where the trouble bell and the foul line indicator are located and how the foul line operates. When ready, take a short quiz from the instructor on this information.

7. Make a poster diagramming a lane. Enlarge and make offset drawings of the approach area and the pin-fall area. Write a short paper telling how one might use this information when bowling.

8. Compile a list of 15 bowling terms and a definition of each.

9. Take a written examination on bowling covering etiquette, scoring, handicaps, averages, techniques, terminology, history, and rules.

10. Demonstrate the proper stance, the 4-step delivery, and the position of the hands on each step.

11. Write a paper describing the following: moonlight bowling, headpin tournament, 3-6-9 tournament.

12. Practice spare bowling of a single pin until 4 out of 10 shots are made. (Have the proprietor take all but 1 pin out of the rack, and shoot at any set that the automatic pin spotter provides.) When ready, test yourself by trying 10 consecutive shots. Record the score as either a miss or a spare. Use any score sheet provided by the alley, and turn it in for credit.

Rating Form

A rating form (Figure 20.1) is useful for partner work and when facilities are limited. The form enables students who are not participating actively to be cognitively involved. The instructor should spend some time helping students learn to use the form correctly.

GOLF

Each weekend millions of golfers everywhere try to obtain a tee-off time to hit and chase a little white ball around an 18-hole golf course. Golf may appear to be a simple sport, but it is actually a complex activity made up of many different shots or strokes (such as woods, long irons, short irons, pitching, chipping, and putting). It is quite challenging and proves to be fascinating to people of all abilities and ages, from 8 to 80. Golf is truly a lifetime sport that can be enjoyed by all people.

Sequence of Skills

The two primary methods of teaching golf are the swing or whole method and the position or part method. Both approaches lead to the same result—square contact with good acceleration. Both teaching methods can be effective, but the whole method seems easier and faster to learn, which makes it better suited to the limited time available for a physical education unit.

The order of skills to be learned in a beginning class follows: grip; stance; alignment; iron shots—half swing, three-quarter swing, and full swing; wood shots—half swing, three-quarter swing, and full swing; putting; chipping; pitching; and the bunker shot.

Grip

Encourage students to use the overlap grip (80% of all golfers use this grip). Place the left hand on the club in the following manner: First support the club with the right hand and let the left hand hang naturally at the side, then bring the left hand in until it contacts the grip of the club and wrap it around. (Checkpoint: The V formed by the thumb and index finger should point directly to the center of the body, and 2 knuckles should be visible on the left hand when looking straight down at the grip.) Place the right hand by letting it also hang naturally at the side. Bring it in to meet the club and wrap the fingers around the club so the little finger of the right hand lies over the index finger of the left hand. The thumb of the left hand should fit nicely into the palm of the right hand. (Checkpoint: The V formed by the thumb and index finger of the right hand should point to the center of the body or slightly to the right of center.) A final check on the grip is to extend all fingers and let the club fall to the ground. If the grip is correct, the club will fall straight down between the legs and feet.

Stance

The golf stance should be both comfortable and relaxed. There is a slight bend in the knees and at the waist. The arms and shoulders are relaxed. The feet are shoulder width apart for the driver and closer together for the shorter clubs. The ball is positioned within a 6-inch span, starting inside the left heel for the driver and moving toward the center of the stance for the wedge.

Lift the club straight out in front of the body at waist level and swing it back and forth similar to a baseball bat swing. After 3 or 4 swings, return to a balanced position in the center. Bend forward from the waist until the club touches the ground. Now relax, and the club will move in slightly closer to the body. It is important that the waist bend lowers the club and not the arms. The relationship between arms and body remains the same until relaxation occurs. (Checkpoint: The preceding check can be applied to every club in the bag. It illustrates how far forward or back the ball must be played and the distance the student should stand from the ball.)

Alignment

A simple procedure for achieving alignment involves the following steps:

1. Stand about 10 feet behind the ball and draw an imaginary line from the flag to the ball.
2. Move to the side of the ball and set the club face square to the target line. Both feet should be together with the ball centered.
3. Grip the club first and then spread the feet apart on a line parallel to the target line. The ball should be on line with the target, and the feet should be on a parallel line just left of the target. The distance between the toes and the ball is approximately 1½ feet.

Half Swing

Each student's swing will vary according to the person's stature, degree of relaxation, understanding of the swing, and natural ability. The half swing is started by bringing the club halfway back to a position parallel to the ground and then letting the club swing forward to the same position in front. The swing should be similar to the swing of a pendulum, and the grass should be brushed in both the backswing and forward swing. When the club is parallel to the ground in the backswing, the toe of the club should point straight up, and the grip end of the club should match the line of the feet. At the end of the forward swing, the toe should be straight up again, and the far end of the club should match the line of the feet. After students can do a half swing, introduce the ball. Tell them to concentrate on swinging the club correctly and on the proper alignment procedures.

Three-Quarter Swing

The three-quarter swing is simply an extension of the half swing. The hands reach approximately shoulder height on the backswing and on the forward swing. Many students may be at this point already, because most usually swing longer than they think.

Full Swing

A full swing is characterized by a club shaft that is almost parallel to or parallel to the ground at the top of the backswing. The full swing is a further extension of the half and three-quarter swings. At the top of the backswing, the clubhead should point to the ground, and the shaft should point toward the target. The club face will thus be square, and the plane will be correct.

The golf swing actually begins at the top of the backswing. The backswing is simply preparation. Students should visualize the full swing as a circle drawn in the air with the clubhead. The circle starts at the top of the backswing and is completed at the finish of the forward swing. Students should watch the clubhead draw the actual circle 2 or 3 times, always keeping the circle out in front. This will help them maintain 1 plane throughout the swing.

At this point, students should have the feel of the full swing, and it is time to experiment with different irons. Try the 5 iron, 9 iron, and finally the 3 iron. Concentration is still on the swing, for the same swing is used with every club. Once patterns of error have developed (such as slicing), students can begin to focus on changing a specific aspect of the total swing.

Woods

The same progression should be used to teach wood shots from the half to the full swing. The first wood hit should be the 3 wood from the tee. Next, move to the driver, or 1 wood, from the tee, and then experiment with the 3 wood off the ground. Students should move halfway down the club's grip to begin swinging. Tee the ball so the top edge of the club comes one-quarter to one-half of the way up the ball. The stance will be at its widest (shoulder width), and the ball will automatically be positioned forward, inside the left heel.

Putting

Identical to the pendulum of a clock, the putter is an extension of the arms and shoulders, and swings as 1 unit an equal distance back and forward. The feel is best obtained by having students grip as far down the shaft as they can reach. Square the putter to the target line and stroke straight back and straight through. Have students try the following putting techniques:

1. Use a reverse overlap grip in which the index finger of the left hand lies over the little finger of the right. This allows the whole right hand to be on the club for control.
2. The stance may be wide or narrow, and the ball may be centered in the stance or forward, remaining inside the left heel. If the ball is forward, a slight weight shift to the left must accompany this stance.
3. Place the dominant eye directly over the ball to improve visualization of the target line.
4. Feel the putter accelerating through contact. This may require shortening the backswing slightly.
5. If the ball misses the hole, overshooting the putt is preferable.
6. Keep the putter blade low to the ground to assure good ball contact.

Learn to judge break, or the roll of the green, by standing behind the ball and looking at the line between the ball and the hole, and also at the slant of the entire green. Visualize throwing a pail of water toward the hole, and picture which way the water would run. For most putts (that is, 4 feet or less) play the ball to the opposite inside edge of the cup. If the putt is longer, gradually move to the edge of the cup and eventually outside the cup as a point of aim. The point of aim may be a spot on the imaginary line to the hole or a point even with the hole but to 1 side. In both cases, the break takes the ball into the hole.

Chip, Pitch, and Bunker Shots

A chip shot is used when the ball is slightly off the green and there is room to hit the ball approximately halfway to the hole. The ball must land on the green and roll close to the hole. If there is not enough room to roll the ball to the hole, then a higher trajectory pitch shot is used. The pitch shot should land at the target. The bunker shot is used for coming out of a sand trap.

A chip shot usually requires a 7 iron and a putting-type stroke. A good technique is to have the students stand off the green and toss the ball underhand so that it rolls to within 4 feet of the hole. Students then place a tee in the green where the ball hit. The tee becomes the target for the chip shot.

The pitch shot should be practiced at different distances with different sized targets (the greater the distance, the larger the target). Baskets, hula hoops, and parachutes are possibilities at 10, 30, and 50 yards. The 9 iron or wedge is used with a one-quarter, one-half, or three-quarter swing, depending on the distance and the circumstances. Students should learn to make a smooth swing and to let the loft of the club hit the ball. The ball should land at the target and roll slightly forward.

The long jump landing pit can be used for bunker shot practice. Students should use a wedge or 9 iron and concentrate on the following:

1. Open the club face at address.
2. Line up 2 inches behind the ball and focus on that spot, not on the ball.
3. Barely scrape the sand with a one-quarter through full swing, depending on the distance required to land the ball.
4. Always follow through with the club.

Ideas for Effective Instruction

Introduce and stress safety rules on the first day of class. A golf ball or club can cause serious damage, and thus strict adherence to safety rules must be demanded. If the class is large and space is limited, safety officers may be appointed who can help manage ball retrieving, changing from station to station, and other responsibilities assigned by the instructor.

The following are safety suggestions that may help in class organization:

1. Allow ample swing space between students for any group formation.
2. Do not carry clubs while retrieving balls.
3. If space is limited, take students back of the line for individual correction.
4. Do not retrieve balls until instructed.
5. Group the left-handed players together at the far end of the hitting line, facing the right-handed players.
6. Be certain that equipment is in top condition at all times, and tell students to notify the instructor if equipment needs repair.
7. Caution students never to swing toward one another, even without a ball.

Start students with a high iron (7, 8, or 9) so they will experience success quicker. Students need to un-

derstand that developing a golf swing takes a lot of practice and is not an easy skill to master. Make sure that students are not overloaded with information and that they receive ample practice time. Depending on the amount of equipment available, teachers may want to assign partner work and to use a swing rating form. This motivates students without clubs to be more involved cognitively and improves their observation skills.

Learning stations can be arranged in the gymnasium or in outdoor fields. An example of an indoor facility, including irons, woods, chipping, pitching, and putting, is shown in Figure 20.2. An outdoor area could be arranged in a similar manner (such as around a football or baseball field).

Learning Activities

Modified Courses

Many teachers set up a short golf course in the field space they have available. Broomsticks, traffic cones, and hoops can serve as pins, tees, and holes. A power

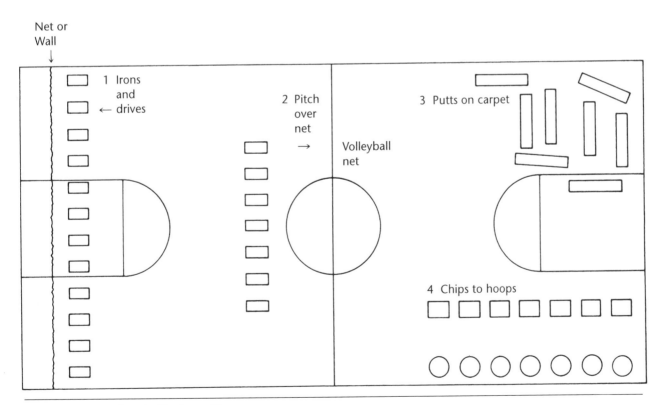

FIGURE 20.2 Indoor facility for golf

mower can be used to shape the fairways and greens. If it is impossible to dig holes, students can "hole out" when the ball strikes the target or when they are within a club's length of the target. Whiffle balls, plastic balls, or regular golf balls can be used, depending on what is available. All types of hazards can be set up using tires, hurdles, jump ropes, and cones. Specific course etiquette and rules can be taught with a modified course.

Putting

Miniature putting courses can be set up on smooth grass surfaces, carpeted areas, old carpet pieces, blankets, towels, mats, canvas, and even smooth floors if a whiffle ball is used. Paper cups, pieces of colored paper, shoe boxes, bleach containers, cans, and jars are possibilities for holes.

Partner Golf

Playing on a regular course or on a putting course, partners alternate hitting or putting toward the pin. If the class size is large, use groups of 3 or 4.

Target Golf

Establish a number of concentric circles and point values around a target. Rope, jump ropes, or chalk can be used to mark the circles. The distance and size of the circles can vary according to the club used. This activity can be done with individuals or teams.

Rainy-Day Activities

Rainy days are a good time to have a "spell down" with questions on rules, fundamentals, etiquette, and types of matches. Crossword puzzles and word searches are available in the suggested readings. Short putting courses can be set up in the indoor space available.

Skill Tests

Many of the drills and game situations already mentioned can be used for evaluation. Here are a few other possibilities:

1. *Parachute.* Count the number of 7-, 8-, or 9-iron shots that land on the parachute in 10 trials.

2. *Putting.* Play 9 holes on a practice green and keep score. Ideally, each student would score 2 per hole to par the course.
3. *Chipping.* Count the number of balls that end up inside the 4-foot radius circle.
4. *Pitching.* Pitch 10 balls at each station (10, 20, and 40 yards), and count the number of balls that land inside the target area.
5. *Bunker Shot.* Arrange a string in a circle with a 10-foot radius around 1 hole, and count the number of bunker shots that finish inside the circle after 10 trials.

A rating scale can be used as part of an evaluation scheme or as a part of the learning activities done with partners (Figure 20.3).

GYMNASTICS

Gymnastics refers to the performance of a routine on a piece of heavy apparatus or on a large mat. The routines are evaluated by a panel of judges on a 10-point scale. The gymnastics events for men include parallel bars, horizontal bar, long-horse vaulting, still rings, pommel horse, and floor exercise. Women's events include the uneven parallel bars, balance beam, side-horse vaulting, and floor exercise. In many major gymnastics competitions, the participants must perform a compulsory or set routine and an optional or original routine.

Varying forms of gymnastics were the most common activity in early physical education programs. These different forms of gymnastics were brought to the United States primarily from Germany and Sweden. Gymnastics became popular through clubs formed in the communities, YMCAs, and the public schools. Private gymnastics clubs and sport schools are still popular, and gymnastics is still taught in some secondary schools and colleges in the United States. Many adults continue to enjoy gymnastics as a lifetime recreational activity. In some geographic areas, competition is available through the private clubs for various age groups.

Instructional units in gymnastics and tumbling are an excellent way to achieve a balanced secondary physical education curriculum. Unfortunately, many school districts do not have the heavy apparatus. In these situations, an extensive unit on tumbling should be incorporated in the program. Gymnastics

Golf Rating Scale

1. Grip (4 points—1 each)
   _____ Right-hand V is straight up or slightly right
   _____ Two knuckles of left hand showing
   _____ Grip tension is correct
   _____ Hands completely on grip of club

2. Stance (4 points—½ each)
   _____ Feet proper width apart
   _____ Standing proper distance from ball
   _____ Weight even over feet (ask)
   _____ Knees bent properly
   _____ Proper bend from waist
   _____ Arms hanging naturally
   _____ No unnecessary tension in arms and hands
   _____ No unnecessary tension in legs

3. Alignment (3 points—1 each)
   _____ Not left of target
   _____ Not right of target
   _____ Proper sequence of address. (Draw imaginary line and pick a spot on the line. Set club square, feet together. Place right foot first on parallel line. Take last look at target.)

4. Swing (10 points—1 each)
   _____ One piece take away
   _____ Head did not move up and down
   _____ Head did not move back and forth
   _____ Left arm extended
   _____ A complete coil is present
   _____ Club toe up to target—backswing—at parallel level
   _____ Club toe up to target—forward swing—at parallel level
   _____ Club accelerates through ball
   _____ Club continues after contact
   _____ Facing target at the finish

Points	Performance
10	Good contact, good trajectory, good direction
9	Good contact, good trajectory, fair direction
8	Good contact, fair trajectory, fair direction
6	Fair contact, fair trajectory, fair direction
4	2 items fair, 1 item barely acceptable
2	1 item fair, 2 items barely acceptable
0	Miss or near miss

FIGURE 20.3 Golf rating scale

activities offer students an interesting variety of challenges and should be available for students to explore and experience.

Sequence of Skills

Each gymnastics event is a highly specialized area that incorporates many specific skills and techniques. A sequence of skills should be taught on each piece of apparatus and for floor exercise. In a coeducational class, 8 pieces of apparatus and 2 different floor exercise routines can be offered if the equipment is available. Comprehensive texts with in-depth information on the sequence of skills for each event are listed in the suggested readings. Gymnas-

tics teachers need to have an extensive background in the teaching strategies and safety procedures for all of the individual events. Teachers should analyze carefully the abilities and characteristics of their students, the time allotted to the gymnastics unit, and the pieces of equipment available for instruction. Safety is especially important because of the hazards posed by many of the gymnastics events.

Ideas for Instruction

Each piece of apparatus and the floor exercise can be arranged as a specific learning area for students. After students are introduced to each area and given introductory tasks to perform, they can be distributed evenly throughout the area. This ensures that students will have maximum opportunity to attempt the various skills. Each student can be given a performance card to record the completion of tasks. The tasks can be written as performance objectives or as simple cues. These objectives and the recording forms will help motivate students to use class time in a productive manner.

A gymnastics meet with student judges is an enjoyable culminating activity. Teams can be organized, and students can select their favorite events. Students work with a partner or in groups of 3 for safety purposes. One person performs and the partner spots. Spotting must be explained carefully to students, and the importance of spotting must be continually reinforced.

JOGGING

Joggers and road races are probably the most visible form of the fitness renaissance. Millions take to the road regularly for fitness and sport reasons. Various types of distances for running events have become popular with men and women of all ages. Marathons, triathalons, 15-k, 10-k, 5-k, and 2-mile fun runs are being offered virtually every weekend. People in all areas of the country run in all kinds of weather. Secondary students in physical education programs should have positive experiences with running because this is a potential lifetime activity that can contribute to fitness and be a form of play. Jogging is an easy, inexpensive activity that can be done individually or with a group.

Sequence of Skills

Jogging is simply slow running. It is different from walking in that both feet leave the ground during the flight or airborne phase. In walking, 1 foot is always in contact with the ground.

Running Form

Chapter 16 gives in-depth coverage to running form. Teachers should spend time working on running form, emphasizing 1 aspect of form with each drill. Students can overlearn the position of the head,

hands, arms, knees, feet, and body lean. In distance running, the stride is shorter than in sprinting, and the heel of the foot should strike the ground before the ball of the foot. Breathing should be natural, through both nose and mouth.

Designing a Program

Students need to understand how to design a jogging program to meet their individual objectives. Programs will differ according to those objectives. Some students want to lose weight, others may want to condition themselves for skiing, and others will want to improve their time in 10-k races. Program goals may vary, but students should all understand how the principles of frequency, intensity, and duration apply to a running program. Proper warm-up, cool down, and stretching and strengthening activities must be taught. These are covered in Chapter 16.

Equipment

Runners must obtain adequate running shoes. Many are available at prices ranging from $20 to over $100. They should have a well-cushioned, elevated heel, and a durable bottom surface. The toes should not rub the front of the shoe, and the tongue and lining should be padded. The sole must be flexible, with 2 layers for absorbing shock. An arch support should be built into running shoes.

The remaining equipment (shorts, socks, sweat suits, rain suits, jackets, hats, mittens, and so forth) is a matter of personal preference depending on the weather. Comfort is the key, with loose-fitting, non-irritating material. Extremely cold and warm weather can be dangerous. Students should understand how to prevent problems by dressing properly and avoiding certain weather conditions.

Ideas for Effective Instruction

Beginners should understand that jogging is an individual activity that can be noncompetitive. If students choose to be competitive runners, that is fine and is a personal choice. Teachers should reinforce this attitude by reducing the emphasis on running races in a jogging unit. The unit emphasis can be on personal improvement and accomplishing individual goals.

Jog-Walk-Jog

Beginners can be given a distance to cover by alternating jogging and walking. They progress by gradually reducing the walking and increasing the jogging. Various students can be assigned different distances, depending on their abilities. This technique can be used for jogging on a track. Students can jog the straightaways and walk the curves for 1 mile.

Timed Runs

Students can be given a set time of a certain number of minutes. They then try to jog continuously for the designated time. (Teachers blow a whistle every minute or half minute.)

Other Running Activities

Refer to Chapter 16 for descriptions of activities such as form running, file running, walk-sprint-jog, pace work, random running, and Fartlek. All can be modified for a jogging unit.

Group Runs

Divide students into small groups of similar ability. The group can run together for a certain time or distance. They should be encouraged to use the "talk test" during the run. This refers to the ability to comfortably carry on a conversation during a run as an indicator of proper jogging intensity.

Training Heart Rate

After students have learned about training heart rates (see Chapter 16), they can check their heart rates at rest before running, after running so many minutes, and again immediately after a run. This will help them to understand the concepts of training heart rate, recovery heart rate, and jogging at sufficient intensity.

Orienteering Runs

A jogging unit can include several orienteering meets emphasizing running from point to point on the school grounds. Draw a map with 10 checkpoints that must be found by the students. Each checkpoint has a secret clue, such as a letter, word, color, or team name. Students can work alone or with a partner. (See Chapter 22 for more orienteering ideas.)

Cross-Country Runs

Map out a cross-country course around the school grounds and in neighboring areas, and hold a meet with a chute for finishers and numbers distributed for the finishing positions. Arrange teams and establish categories for beginners, intermediates, and advanced runners. Set time limits, and allow students to run time trials to determine their category or team. Students can choose to be on a team or to run for individual improvement.

Exercise Trails

Set up an exercise trail around the school grounds with several stations for stretching and strengthening various muscle groups. Use a boundary cone with a sign to mark each station, and give students a rough map showing where each station is located. After completing a station activity, students should jog to the next station. The stations can be set up so the students get a total body workout. After a certain period of time, the trail can be modified.

Running with Equipment

Some students with special interests may want to run with a piece of equipment (for example, dribbling a soccer ball or a basketball). Others may want to carry a football or roll a hula hoop. Let students be creative, as long as they are engaged in a safe activity. Running with equipment adds variety to activities and is a good motivational device.

Mileage Cards and Maps

Many people enjoy keeping a record of the distances covered. Goals can be established for a given time period. Students can jog across the state by coloring in a route or moving a pin to a given point as they accumulate miles. Mileage cards or charts can be kept individually, or they can be posted in the locker room or on a bulletin board. Individual or group competitions can be set up based on number of miles accumulated.

Rainy-Day Activities

Many of these activities (rating forms, pace work, timed runs) can be modified for running in the gymnasium. If the gym is also not available, there are many interesting running topics that teachers can discuss with students. These include training methods, safety, injuries, equipment, health benefits, exercise and calories, marathons, Cooper's program, and the female runner. The suggested readings are filled with discussion topics.

RESISTANCE TRAINING

Various forms of resistance training have become extremely popular activities for general conditioning. Adults and students of all ages are lifting weights and working on resistance machines in schools, health clubs, YMCAs, and in their homes. Current research has made women aware of the misconceptions about and benefits of resistance training. Coaches and athletes involved in different sports are using extensive resistance training programs to improve performance. Resistance training is now well entrenched in the activity habits of society. A properly developed resistance training program can produce positive changes in the body composition and in a person's performance. People engaged in resistance training look better, feel better, and perform daily activities better. All of these results have contributed to the popularity of the sport.

Many different types of resistance training equipment are available. Machines such as the Universal Gym, Nautilus equipment, the Orthotron, and the Cybex II are used commonly for training programs. Each machine offers a number of different advantages. Free weights, including different types of dumbbells and barbells, are still quite popular and are available in most weight rooms. Physical education programs need to analyze carefully such factors as cost, space, objectives, and usage before purchasing resistance training equipment.

Sequence of Skills

Principles, Terminology, and Safety

Beginning resistance trainers need to understand the basic principles of training relative to their specific objectives. Students must understand the definitions of strength, endurance, flexibility, warm-up, cool down, sets, repetitions, frequency, rest intervals, and the various types of lifts for specific muscle groups. The type and number of lifts are determined by a student's objectives. Proper form must be understood in order to gain maximum benefits and to complete the activities safely. Spotting techniques are a necessity for certain lifts, especially with heavy weights. Safety in the weight lifting area must be stressed constantly. Chapter 16 gives general information on these aspects of resistance training. Additional specific information is available in the suggested readings listed at the end of this unit.

Spotting

Spotters are people who stand by a lifter to provide help when necessary. Spotters are concerned about preventing a weight from falling or slipping if the lifter cannot control the weight. All students should understand the spotting procedures for a specific lift. They can check the equipment for proper alignment, tightened collars, and so forth, and they can be aware of the position of other students in the area. Specific attention should be paid to each lift, especially with heavier weights.

Breathing

Lifters should try to be consistent and natural in their breathing. Most experts agree that breathing should follow a pattern of exhaling during exertion and inhaling as the weight is returned to the starting position. With heavy weights, many lifters take a deep breath before the lift and hold the breath until the final exertion. The final exhalation helps complete the lift. Care is necessary, because holding the breath too long can make a person light-headed and may even cause one to faint.

Grips

The three major grips are the overhand, underhand, and alternating. These grips are used with different types of lifts; for example, the overhand with the palms down is used for the bench press, the underhand with the palms up is used for curls, and the alternating with 1 palm up and the other down is used with the dead lift.

Body Position

With free weights, it is especially important to get the feet, arms, and body aligned properly for lifting and removing weights from power racks or squat stands. Carelessness in alignment can result in an unbalanced position, which can, in turn, result in dropping the weights or in poor lifting technique. Each lift requires a different position, depending on whether the bar is being lifted from the floor or from a rack. Spotters must understand the type of lift to be executed and their specific responsibility. For example, with a back squat, the following steps should be followed:

1. Check the collars to see that they are tightened.
2. Grip the bar and space the hands wider than the shoulders.
3. Align the middle of the back under the midpoint of the bar.
4. Use a pad or towel to cushion the bar against the back.
5. Bend the knees and align the body vertically under the bar.
6. Keep the head up and lift the weight straight up.
7. Move out from the rack and assume a comfortable foot position about shoulder width apart.
8. Perform the lift with a spotter on either side of the bar.

Upper-Body Lifts

Bench Press.   Use an overhand grip with hands slightly wider than the shoulders. Bring the bar down to the chest and press up over the shoulders (Figure 20.4). Exhale on the press upward.

Curl.   Use an underhand grip with the arms about shoulder width. Curl the bar up the shoulders and extend downward slowly to a straight arm position (Figure 20.5). A reverse curl can be used with an overhand grip.

Bent or Upright Rowing.   Both lifts use an overhand grip about shoulder width. The bent position starts with the barbell on the floor and the body bent at the hips (Figure 20.6). The knees are bent slightly. The bar is pulled to the chest while the back is stable. The upright position (Figure 20.7) starts with the bar across the thighs. The bar is pulled up to the chin area and returned slowly.

FIGURE 20.4   Bench press

FIGURE 20.5   Curl

FIGURE 20.6   Bent rowing

Military Press.   An overhand grip slightly wider than the shoulders is used in a standing or sitting position. The bar is pressed upward from the chest and returned (Figure 20.8). A variation brings the bar down behind the head and then back up.

Bench Pullover.   Lying on a bench, the bar is gripped overhand and is pulled straight up and over the face from the floor (Figure 20.9).

Shoulder Shrugs.   With a straight barbell across the thighs or with 2 dumbbells at the sides of the body (Figure 20.10), the shoulders are raised or shrugged as high as possible and then returned to the starting position.

Triceps Extension.   A barbell, 2 dumbbells, or a machine can be used. With the barbell, the weight bar is started overhead with an overhand grip and is then lowered slowly behind the head and extended back to the starting position. With a machine, the bar is brought down in front of the body.

FIGURE 20.7   Upright rowing

FIGURE 20.8   Military press

Lateral Raises. Lateral raises are done using an overhand grip with dumbbells. A standing or bent position can be used. The weights start at the sides or on the floor and are raised laterally with straight arms.

FIGURE 20.9 Bench pullover

Lower-Body Lifts

Front and Back Squat. Use an overhand grip with the bar across the front of the shoulders or across the upper-back muscles. The knees are bent to a position in which the thighs are parallel to the floor.

Dead Lift. Starting in a squat position with the weight on the floor, the feet are about shoulder width apart, and an alternating grip is used (Figure 20.11). The arms are kept straight and the back flat as the weight is lifted and the body comes to an erect position with the bar across the thighs.

Power Clean. The power clean is a complex lift that starts in the same position as the dead lift, but with an overhand grip (Figure 20.12). The lift includes a start, an acceleration, and a catch phase. The bar is pulled up, past the waist (Figure 20.13), and ends up above the chest. The lifter must control both the weight and the body as the weight moves through the starting position to the catch position.

Leg Curls and Extension. Equipment calls for a machine attached to a bench. The extension starts in a sitting position with the feet under a lower, padded section. The arms grip the sides of the bench, and the upper body is leaning slightly back. The legs are extended until they are parallel to the floor. The leg

FIGURE 20.10 Shoulder shrugs

FIGURE 20.11 Dead lift

FIGURE 20.12   Power clean—ready position

FIGURE 20.13   Power clean—intermediate position

FIGURE 20.14   Heel raises

curl uses the upper padded section of the machine. The lifter is on the stomach, and the heels are hooked behind the pad. The heels are then pulled up toward the buttocks and lowered.

Heel Raises.   Begin on the balls of the feet and the toes over a stable board or step. The lifter holds a weight in each hand at the sides (Figure 20.14). The heels are then raised and lowered.

Learning Activities

Circuit Training

An effective strategy for organizing the activities in the weight room is to set up a circuit with a number of stations. The students can be divided into groups and rotated after a certain number of minutes. Students perform a specific number of sets and repetitions at each station.

Each student should keep a daily log of the sets and repetitions and of the weights that were lifted. These records are important in organizing a progression and should help to motivate the students. Depending on the equipment and facilities available, a good approach is to develop a circuit for both lower-body exercises and upper-body exercises. Students can alternate days performing upper- and lower-body workouts. Aerobic conditioning activities can also be alternated with the resistance training. Many teachers like to add variety to the circuit routines by changing stations regularly.

Partner Resistance Activities

Chapter 16 describes a number of partner resistance activities that can be used to supplement and add variety to a resistance training unit. These can also be added to a circuit or can be scheduled as an entire day's lesson. They are useful in situations in which equipment is limited. For example, while students are waiting their turn to use a weight machine, they can perform several resistance activities. Isometric exercises can also be used in these situations.

Muscle-of-the-Day

Another good learning activity is to present students with information about 1 muscle at the end of each lesson. The name of the muscle and its functions are written on a card and placed on the wall of the weight room. A quick review of the muscles covered plus the addition of a new muscle takes place each day. This is a good concluding activity after each day's workout. Specific information on the muscular system is available in Chapter 17.

Motivational Devices

Resistance training offers tangible evidence of improvement in the various lifts. This improvement can be tied to many different motivational devices: T-shirts, certificates, and becoming a member of a club are popular examples of awards for lifting certain amounts of weight. These types of devices can be quite simple, yet are effective and meaningful for many students. Figure 20.15 is a good example of motivational club criteria used at Westwood High School in Mesa, Arizona. The club is available to students in the weight training classes.

Club Requirements

Requirements—To become a member, you must lift a combined total of 5.2 times your weight. The 3 required lifts are bench press, dead lift, and squat.

Weight Class		Required Total	Weight Class		Required Total
100–109	=	520	160–169	=	832
110–119	=	572	170–179	=	884
120–129	=	624	180–189	=	936
130–139	=	676	190–199	=	988
140–149	=	728	200–209	=	1040
150–159	=	780	210–219	=	1092
			220 and up	=	1144

Each participant is allowed 3 tries for each lift. Weight may be added to the previous lift, but may not be subtracted from the previous lift.

Name _____ Date _____ Class 10, 11, 12

Body weight _____ Required total lift _____

	1st	2nd	3rd	Best of 3 lifts
Bench press	_____	_____	_____	_____
Dead lift	_____	_____	_____	_____
Squat	_____	_____	_____	_____

Total _____

Coach's signature _____

FIGURE 20.15 Motivational club criteria for weight lifters

ROPE JUMPING

Rope jumping can be a demanding activity enjoyed by all ages and ability levels. The American Heart Association has endorsed rope jumping for years because of its positive effects on cardiovascular endurance. It is an inexpensive activity that can be done in a limited amount of space, indoors or outside. Through rope jumping, students develop rhythm, timing, and coordination, as well as fitness. The numerous jumping activities can challenge all ability levels. The rope can be turned many ways at varying speeds, and the jumper can use a variety of foot patterns. Individual, partner, and small group activities are available.

Rope jumping is a useful carry-over activity that can be enjoyed throughout one's life. Developing creative rope jumping routines and skills can be a challenge to students. Because of the rhythmic aspect of jumping rope, teachers should add popular music to enhance everyone's motivational level.

Body Position and Rhythm

Jumping rope requires proper body position and alignment. The head should be up with the eyes looking ahead. Good balance is a must, with the feet, ankles, and legs close together. The body is erect during the jump. The knees flex and extend slightly with each jump. The elbows are kept close to the body at approximately a 90-degree angle. The basic jump should be straight up and down and about 1 inch high. The rope should be turned primarily with the wrists and forearms. Effective jumpers land on the balls of their feet and stay in 1 spot.

The speed at which the rope turns is referred to as the rhythm. Slow-time (half-time) rhythm involves turning the rope 60 to 90 revolutions per minute. The student jumps, rebounds, and then jumps again as the rope comes through. A rebound is a slight bend at the knee in order to carry or keep the rhythm. The student does not actually leave the ground during a rebound. Slow time is the easiest rhythm for beginners. Fast-time rhythm involves turning the rope 120 to 180 turns per minute. There is no rebound because the rope and the feet must move faster. In double-time rhythm, the rope is turned at the same speed as slow time, but instead of using a rebound, the performer executes a different type of step while the rope is coming around. Dou-

ble-time rhythm is the most difficult to learn, because the feet and the turning of the rope must be coordinated. The feet must move quickly while the rope turns slowly.

Sequence of Skills

Several types of ropes are available that are useful for teaching the skill to secondary students. Sash cord and hard-weave synthetic ropes can be used, but the best jump ropes are made of plastic links with a plastic handle that turns. The rope should be heavy enough to maintain a rhythmic rotation. The length of the rope will vary according to the height of the student. Proper length can be determined by standing in the middle of the rope and pulling the ends up to the armpits or slightly higher. If the ends of the rope reach beyond that area, students can wrap the extra rope around the hands, or get a longer rope if the one tested is too short. Most secondary students will need a 8-, 9-, or 10-foot jump rope.

Individual Steps

The following are foot patterns that can be used with all 3 rhythm patterns—slow time, fast time, and double time. Students should try the patterns in slow time before moving on to fast and double time.

Two-Foot Basic Step.   The student jumps over the rope with both feet together. In slow time, there is a rebound in between each turn of the rope.

Alternate-Foot Step (Jog Step).   The student alternates feet with every jump. The unweighted leg is bent slightly at the knee. A variation can have students jump a consecutive number of times on 1 foot before switching feet. For example, a student might jump 5 times on the right foot and then 5 on the left foot. With a fast-time rhythm, this step looks like jogging.

Side Swings—Left or Right.   The student moves the rope to either side of the body and jumps off both feet in time with the rope. The student does not actually jump over the rope. This is a good technique to use to work on timing and cardiovascular fitness because it is demanding.

Swing Step Forward or Sideways.   Same as the jog step, except the unweighted leg swings forward or sideways rather than backward. The student can alternate the forward swing with the side swing on each foot.

Rocker Step. The student starts with 1 leg in front of the other. As the rope comes around, the weight is shifted from the front leg to the back leg and alternates each time the rope goes around. The student rocks back and forth, from front foot to back foot.

Legs Spread Forward and Backward (Scissors). The student starts with 1 leg forward and 1 leg back, similar to the starting position for the rocker step. As the rope turns, the front leg is shifted back and the back leg is shifted forward. The position of the legs shifts each time the rope is turned.

Legs Crossed Sideways (Jumping Jack). The student starts with the legs straddled sideways. As the rope is turned, the legs are crossed with the right leg in front. Another straddle position is next, and then the legs are crossed again with the left leg in front. This sequence is repeated. The jump can also be executed with the feet coming together, instead of crossing each time, similar to the foot pattern of a jumping jack exercise.

Toe-Touches Forward or Backward. The student starts with 1 foot forward. The toe of the forward foot is pointed down and touches the ground. As the rope turns, the feet trade places, and the opposite toe touches the ground. For the backward toe-touch, the foot starts in a backward position with the toe touching. The feet then alternate positions with each jump.

Shuffle Step. The student starts with the weight on the left foot and the toe of the right foot touching the heel of the left foot. As the rope turns, the student steps to the right and the feet trade places. The left toe is now touching the right heel. The step is then repeated in the opposite direction.

Ski Jump. The student keeps both feet together and jumps to the left and right sideways over a line. This motion is similar to that of a skier. The jump can be performed with the rope going forward or backward.

Heel-Toe Jump. The student jumps off the right foot and extends the left leg forward, touching the heel to the ground. On the next jump the left foot is brought back beside the right foot with the toe touching the ground. The pattern is then repeated with the right foot touching the heel, then toe.

Heel Click. The student starts by completing several sideways swing steps in preparation for this pattern. As the leg swings out to the side, the opposite foot is brought up and the heels are touched together. The heel click can be completed on either side.

Crossing Arms. Crossing the arms can be added to all of the basic foot patterns. In crossing the arms, the hands actually trade places. The hands must be brought all the way across the body and kept low. The upper body crouches forward slightly from the waist. Crossing can also be used for backward jumping. Students can learn to cross and uncross after a certain number of jumps.

Double Turns. A double turn occurs when the rope passes under the feet twice during the same jump. The student must jump higher and rotate the rope faster. The jump should be about 6 inches high, and a slight forward crouch is necessary to speed up the turn. Students should try consecutive double turns forward or backward. Various foot patterns can also be tried with double turns.

Sideways Jumping. The rope is turned sideways with 1 hand over the head and the other hand extended down between the legs in front of the body. As the rope is turned, the student jumps the rope 1 leg at a time. The weight is shifted back and forth between the legs as the rope turns around the body. Students can turn the rope either left or right, and either hand can be held overhead. Students should try the technique several ways.

Shifting from Forward to Backward Jumping. There are several ways to change jumping direction. The first way is to begin jumping forward. As the rope starts downward, the student executes a left or right side swing. A half turn should be made in the same direction as the rope. As the rope is coming out of the side swing, the student must bring it up in a backwards motion. This motion can be completed to either side, as long as the turn is toward the rope side.

Another way to execute the shift is to make a half turn while the rope is above the head with the arms extended upward. The rope will hesitate slightly and then should be brought down in the opposite direction.

A final shifting strategy is from a cross-arm position. As the rope is going overhead, the student uncrosses the arms and makes a half turn. This starts the rope turning in the opposite direction. The key is to uncross the arms and turn simultaneously.

Partner Activities

A wide variety of challenging combinations can be performed with partners using 1 rope. The partners can start jumping together, or 1 person can run into position after the other partner has started jumping. Partner activities can be fun with students the same size. They are more challenging when performed with students of varying sizes.

1. One person turns the rope forward or backward:
   a. Partner faces the turner for a specific number of jumps.
   b. Partners are back to back for a specific number of jumps.
   c. Partner turns in place—quarter turn, half turn, and so on.
   d. Partner dribbles a basketball while jumping.
   e. Partners match foot patterns (such as jog step, swing step).
   f. Partners complete double turns.
2. Two students turn the rope forward or backward:
   a. Partners stand side by side, facing the same direction.
   b. Partners face opposite directions.
   c. Repeat activities 2a and 2b with elbows locked.
   d. Repeat a, b, and c while hopping on 1 foot.
   e. Partners are back to back turning 1 rope with the right or left hand.
   f. Repeat variation e while turning in a circle—both directions.
3. Three students jump together with one turning the rope, one in front, and the third in back. This can be done forward and backward.
4. Two students, each with a rope, face each other. One student turns the rope forward, and the other turns backward, so the ropes are going in the same direction. Partners jump over both ropes on 1 jump. Students should then change their rope direction.
5. One student turns the rope. The partner comes in from the side, takes 1 handle of the rope, and begins turning. The partner's entrance must be timed so the rhythm of the rope remains con-

stant. The partner then leaves and enters from the other side. This stunt can be performed with a forward or backward turn.
6. Partners face each other, turning 1 rope with the right hand. One partner turns to the left and exits from jumping while continuing to turn the rope for the other partner. After several turns, the partner who was out returns to the starting position. A variation can be tried with the partner turning to the right one-quarter turn.

Ideas for Effective Instruction

Rope jumping is a good example of an activity that can be improved with practice. Remind students constantly that these skills will be perfected only with regular practice. Such reminders help keep students from getting discouraged quickly.

Students should first try new jumping techniques without the rope to get the basic idea. They can then try the stunt with a slow-time rhythm with a rebound in between each movement. As they improve, fast time and double time can be tried. Some students may need to practice turning the rope in 1 hand to the side of the body to develop the necessary rhythm. Students should practice timing their jump with the rope turning at the side. An instructor might do some partner jumping with a student who is having trouble with timing. Another effective instructional strategy is to use a movie, videotape, or loop film to give students a visual model of the skill. Several are listed in the suggested readings section of this chapter.

Students need plenty of room for practicing. Care should be taken because the ropes can be dangerous to a person's face and eyes. Horseplay with the jump ropes should not be tolerated.

Ropes can be color coded for various sizes. Students can help distribute and collect the ropes so they do not get tangled. Student helpers can hold their arms out to the sides, and the other students can place the ropes over their arms. Music with different tempos provides a challenge and motivates many students.

Learning Activities

In addition to the foot patterns, rhythms, turning patterns, and partner activities that have been mentioned, there are other effective learning activities that can be done individually, in small groups, or with the entire class.

Follow-the-Leader

Students can work with a partner, a small group, or the entire class—moving forward, backward, diagonally, or sideways—following a designated leader. Various foot patterns can also be used while moving.

Leader in the Circle

The students follow the leader who is in the center of a circle. This activity can be done with large or small circles. The leader calls the name of the next leader after a designated time period or after a certain number of foot patterns have been executed.

Relays

Many different jump rope relays can be played with boundary cones and various types of jumps. For example:

1. Jog-step down around the cone and back (forward turns).
2. Same as variation 1, but with backward turns.
3. Jog-step backward using forward turns.
4. Same as variation 3, but with backward turns.
5. Hop to the cone on 1 foot, and hop back on the other.
6. Ski-jump down, and forward swing-step back.
7. Jog-step through a series of 6 cones, do 10 sit-ups, and jog-step back.
8. Use a 2-foot basic step going down, do 5 rocker steps, 5 scissor steps, and come back with a two-foot basic step.
9. Partners (side by side with 1 rope, elbows locked, both facing forward) go down forward and come back backwards.
10. Partners (side by side with 1 rope, 1 person facing forward, the other facing backward) go down and back with a forward turn.

Routines

Various routines can be developed individually with guidelines for foot patterns, change of direction, crossing over, changing levels, rope speed, and routine length. Small groups can also make up routines, choose music, and perform together, and partner routines can be developed with 2 people using 1 rope. An example of the guidelines for a small group routine follows:

1. 2 minutes or less—5 members per group.
2. 2 changes of direction (such as forward, backward, diagonal).
3. 2 changes of floor pattern (such as circle, square, back to back).
4. 2 changes of levels (such as high, low).
5. 5 changes of foot patterns (such as rocker, basic 2-step).
6. 1 change of rope direction.
7. 1 double turn.

Rainy-Day Activities

All jump rope activities are good for rainy days because they can be performed indoors in a limited space. Hallways and gymnasium foyers are possible areas for jump rope activities. Students can work on individual skills if a limited space is available. A rotation schedule may have to be arranged so that some students are practicing while partners are observing and using a rating scale or checking off performance objectives. Students can also devote time to learning the appropriate terminology for foot patterns and rhythms.

TRACK AND FIELD

Track and field events consist of running, jumping, weight throwing, and vaulting. Running events include sprinting short distances, running middle and longer distances, and hurdling over barriers. Relay races with 4 team members are run over various distances. The jumping events include the high jump, long jump, and triple jump. The throwing events are the shot put, discus, javelin, and hammer throw. The vaulting event is the pole vault.

In the United States, instruction in track and field activities as part of the physical education program began in the late 1890s. Both men and women have been interested in pursuing these events for various reasons. The tremendous variety of skills necessary for running, jumping, throwing, and vaulting provides people with an exciting challenge.

Track and field should continue to be an important part of the secondary school physical education program. Students with different body types are able to find success in some track and field activity. All students should have the opportunity to explore and experience the wide variety of challenges of this unit.

Secondary schools have changed to metric distances for the running events. These distances vary some from state to state and from men's events to women's events. The men's running events usually include the following: 100, 200, 400, 800, 1600, and 3,200 meter; 400-, and 1,600-meter relay; 110-meter high hurdles, and 400-meter intermediate hurdles. The field events for men usually include the high jump, long jump, triple jump, pole vault, shot put, discus, javelin, and hammer (only in certain states). Women's running events are similar to the men's, but the women run only 1 hurdle race, which is 100 meters. The 1,600-meter relay race is sometimes replaced with a medley relay consisting of 100, 100, 200, and 400 meters. In the field events, the women do not pole vault, triple jump, or throw the hammer. It is interesting to note that women are finally being allowed officially to run longer distances (such as 1,600 and 3,200 meters). The 1984 Olympic Games in Los Angeles marked the first Olympic marathon for women.

Sequence of Skills

Since track and field is a highly specialized area that includes many specific skills and techniques for each of the running, jumping, vaulting, and throwing events, it is difficult to cover adequately all of these activities in a limited space. Several good texts are available with in-depth information about specific events and the skills involved. Much of what should be taught will depend on the abilities of the students, the length of time allotted to the unit, and the equipment available for instruction. Teachers developing units for track and field should refer to the suggested readings.

Ideas for Instruction

Each event in track and field can serve as a learning station for students. After students are introduced to the events, they can rotate from station to station and work on each activity. Keep a clipboard at each station with records of each day's best performances in an activity. The day-to-day records can be used for

motivation and as evidence of individual improvement. A class track meet is an enjoyable culminating activity. Teams can be organized and a regulation dual meet conducted.

REFERENCES AND SUGGESTED READINGS

Aquatics

American Red Cross. 1993. *Swimming and Diving*. St. Louis: Mosby.

Hallett, B., and Clayton, R. D. (eds.). 1980. *Course Syllabus: Teacher of Swimming*. Reston, VA: AAHPERD.

Mood, D. P., Musker, F. F., and Rink, J. E. 1991. *Sports and Recreational Activities for Men and Women*. 10th ed. St. Louis: Mosby.

Thomas, D. B. 1989. *Teaching Swimming: Steps to Success*. Champaign, IL: Human Kinetics Publishers.

Vickers, B. J., and Vincent, W. 1994. *Swimming*. 6th ed. Dubuque, IA: Brown & Benchmark.

Archery

Haywood, K. M. 1989. *Archery: Steps to Success*. Champaign, IL: Human Kinetics Publishers.

McKinney, W. C., and McKinney, M. W. 1994. *Archery*. 7th ed. Dubuque, IA: Brown & Benchmark.

Mood, D. P., Musker, F. F., and Rink, J. E. 1991. *Sports and Recreational Activities for Men and Women*. 10th ed. St. Louis: Mosby.

National Association for Girls and Women in Sport. 1979–1980. *Archery-Fencing Guide*. Reston, VA: AAHPERD.

Seidel, B. L. et al. 1980. *Sports Skills: A Conceptual Approach to Meaningful Movement*. 2nd ed. Dubuque, IA: Wm. C. Brown Group.

Sysler, B. L., and Fox, E. R. 1978. *Lifetime Sports for the College Student*. 3rd ed. Dubuque, IA: Kendall/Hunt Publishing Co.

Bowling

American Bowling Congress, Public Relations Department, 1572 E. Capital Drive, Milwaukee, WI 53211.

Martin, J. L., Tandy, R. E., and Agne-Traub, C. 1994. *Bowling*. 7th ed. Dubuque, IA: Brown & Benchmark.

National Association for Girls and Women in Sport. 1979–1981. *Bowling-Golf*. Reston, VA: AAHPERD.

Strickland, R. H. 1989. *Bowling: Steps to Success*. Champaign, IL: Human Kinetics Publishers.

Golf

Kennington, D. 1981. *The Sourcebook of Golf*. Phoenix, AZ: Oryx Press.

Owens, B. B. 1989. *Golf: Steps to Success*. Champaign, IL: Human Kinetics Publishers.

Owens, B. B. 1992. *Advanced Golf: Steps to Success*. Champaign, IL: Human Kinetics Publishers.

Mood, D. P., Musker, F. F., and Rink, J. E. 1991. *Sports and Recreational Activities for Men and Women*. 10th ed. St. Louis: Mosby.

Nance, V. L., Davis, E. C., and McMahon, K. E. 1994. *Golf*. 7th ed. Dubuque, IA: Brown & Benchmark.

Gymnastics

Cooper, P., and Trnka, M. 1982. *Teaching Gymnastic Skills to Men and Women*. Minneapolis, MN: Burgess Publishing Co.

Mood, D., Musker, F. F., and Armbruster, D. 1983. *Sports and Recreational Activities for Men and Women*. 8th ed. St. Louis: Mosby.

Zakrajsek, D., and Carnes, L. 1986. *Learning Experiences: An Approach to Teaching Physical Activities*. Champaign, IL: Human Kinetics Publishers.

Jogging

Fixx, J. 1977. *The Complete Book of Running*. New York: Random House.

Henderson, J. 1977. *Jog, Run, Race*. Mountain View, CA: World Publications.

Mood, D. P., Musker, F. F., and Rink, J. E. 1991. *Sports and Recreational Activities for Men and Women*. 10th ed. St. Louis: Mosby.

Resistance Training

Baechle, T. R. 1992. *Weight Training*. Champaign, IL: Human Kinetics Publishers.

Moran, G., and McGlynn, G. 1990. *Dynamics of Strength Training*. Dubuque, IA: Brown & Benchmark.

Rasch, P. J. 1990. *Weight Training*. 5th ed. Dubuque, IA: Brown & Benchmark.

Stone, W., and Kroll, W. 1980. *Sports Conditioning and Weight Training*. Boston, MA: Allyn & Bacon.

Westcott, W. L. 1995. *Strength Fitness: Physiological Principles and Training Techniques*. 4th ed. Dubuque, IA: Brown & Benchmark.

Rope Jumping

American Alliance for Health, Physical Education, Recreation, and Dance. 1992. *Jump Rope for Heart*. Reston, VA: AAHPERD. (Jump Rope for Heart materials can be obtained by contacting your local affiliate of the American Heart Association or by calling AAHPERD Special Events Office at 703-476-3489.)

American Heart Association. 1984a. *Jump for the Health of It: Basic Skills*. Dallas, TX: American Heart Association.

American Heart Association. 1984b. *Jump for the Health of It: Intermediate Single- and Double-Dutch Skills*. Dallas, TX: American Heart Association.

Melson, B., and Worrell, V. 1986. *Rope Skipping for Fun and Fitness*. Wichita, KS: Woodlawn.

Poppen, J. D. 1989. *Action Packet on Jumping Rope*. Puyallup, WA: Action Productions.

Sutherland, M., and Carnes, C. 1987. *Awesome Jump Rope Activities Book*. Carmichael, CA: Education Co.

Track and Field

Bowerman, W. 1972. *Coaching Track and Field*. Boston, MA: Houghton Mifflin Co.

Doherty, J. 1976. *Track and Field Omnibook*. 3rd ed. Los Altos, CA: Track and Field News Press.

Powell, J. 1971. *Track and Field Fundamentals for Teacher and Coach*. 3rd ed. Champaign, IL: Stipes Publishing Co.

21 Dual Sports

Dual sport activities usually require 2 to 4 players. They are often played by adults during leisure time. These activities are excellent for participation throughout life.

BADMINTON

Badminton is popular in schools from the middle and high school through college levels. Competition at the college level is popular nationally and internationally. The activity is considered a lifetime sport and can be enjoyed by all in a recreational setting. The game is played with a shuttlecock and racquet on a court with a net set at a height of 5 feet. The court is marked for both doubles and singles competition. A toss of a coin or a spin of the racquet determines service or court choice. The game begins with a serve from the right-hand service court to an opponent standing in the opposite right-hand service court.

Sequence of Skills

Grips

Forehand. With the racquet lying across the palm and fingers of the racquet hand, the index finger should be separated from the rest of the fingers. Wrap the thumb around the other side of the handle. The grip resembles a handshake and is called the "pistol grip." This grip is used for serving and forehand shots.

Backhand. Move the thumb to a straightened position and to the right of the handle. Rotate the rest of the hand one-fourth of a turn to the right (if right-handed). Regardless of the grip used, the player should make contact with the shuttlecock as early

and as high as possible. This gives the player a better angle for return and for more controlled shots and forces an opponent to move quickly.

Serves

Ready Position and Preparatory Action. Stand with the nonracquet foot forward and the weight mainly on the racquet foot. The feet should be approximately 12 to 15 inches apart. The nonracquet shoulder is toward the receiver, with the racquet held waist-high and behind the body. Keep the wrist cocked.

The shuttlecock must be contacted below the waist at the instant of the serve. Either a forehand or backhand shot may be used, but the forehand is most common. Until the serve is delivered, the server and receiver must be in their legal service courts. Part of both players' feet must remain in contact with the ground.

Singles Service. Review the ready position. Extend the nonracquet arm and drop the shuttle-cock before starting to move the racquet forward. As weight is shifted to the front foot, rotate the shoulders and hips. As contact is made below the waist, the wrist and forearm rotate. The racquet arm should follow through high and be extended over the left shoulder at completion of service. Most serves will be long and high. A short serve is, however, effective if your opponent is playing too deep.

Doubles Service. The stance is similar to the singles serve. Contact the shuttlecock closer to waist height and slightly more toward the server's racquet-hand side. Guide the shuttlecock instead of hitting it. The wrist does not uncock. Just prior to contacting the shuttlecock, shift the weight from the racquet foot to the nonracquet foot. Little follow-through or rotation occurs. The shuttlecock should peak in height just before the net and be descending as it clears the net.

Forehand Shots

Clear. Get in ready position with the feet and shoulders parallel to the net. Hold the racquet slightly to the backhand side, and bend the knees slightly. Contact the shuttlecock as high as possible and in front of the body. The racquet face should be tilted upward, and the shuttlecock should clear the opponent's racquet and land close to the backline.

Drop. When contact with the shuttlecock is made, the racquet face should be flat and pointing ahead or slightly downward. The shuttlecock is gently guided over the net. Remember to follow through. The shuttlecock should just drop over the net into the opponent's forecourt.

Smash. Extend the arm when the shuttlecock is hit in front of the body. Rotation of the wrist and forearm is performed quickly. The downward angle of the racquet face is more important than the racquet speed. The shot should only be attempted from the front three-fourths of the court.

Backhand Shots

Ready Position. From the forehand position, turn so that the racquet shoulder faces the net. The weight should be on the nonracquet foot, the racquet shoulder up, and the forearm slightly down and across the chest. While shifting the weight to the racquet foot, the body rotates toward the net. As the wrist leads, the racquet extends upward. The racquet arm and elbow should be fully extended at contact. The thumb should not point upward.

Clear. Hitting hard and upward, contact the shuttlecock as high as possible and hit it over the opponent's racquet. Contact should be made in front of the body with the racquet face flat to the target.

Drop. As the shuttlecock is guided over the net, the racquet should be flat and pointed ahead or slightly downward. The shuttlecock should land close to the net.

Underhand Shots

Ready Position. Place the racquet foot forward and the racquet face parallel to the ground. Cock the wrist and make contact as close to net height as possible.

Forehand Net Clear. The forehand net clear is a high, deep shot similar to the singles deep serve. Turn the shoulder slightly toward the net, and cock the wrist. An inward rotation of the wrist and a lifting of the forearm occur just before contact. Proceed to follow through with the elbow slightly bent.

Backhand Net Clear. The racquet foot is forward, and the racquet shoulder turned to the net. Contact the shuttlecock as close to net height as possible. As the player moves toward the net, the wrist should be cocked. An outward rotation is used for the backhand. The shot is high and deep into the opponent's court.

Forehand Net Drop. Review the forehand net clear. The net drop is guided over the net with a lifting motion. The shuttlecock should drop quickly.

Backhand Net Drop. This is the same motion as the forehand net drop, except that the backhand grip is used. The shuttlecock should be contacted close to net height.

Ready Position for Receiving

The feet should be parallel and positioned slightly wider apart than the shoulders. Bend the knees slightly with the weight forward. Hold the racquet with the head up and to the backhand side of the body.

Doubles Strategy

Up and Back. One player plays close shots while the partner plays deep shots.

Side by Side. Each partner plays half of the court and is responsible for close or deep shots in his or her half of the court.

Combination. Both side-by-side and up-and-back formations are used. Regardless of the strategy, partners should always call for the shot ("Mine!") to avoid accidental injuries.

Ideas for Effective Instruction

Racquets and Shuttlecocks

The racquet frame can be made of metal or wood. It is usually 26 inches long and weighs between 3.75 and 5.5 ounces. Nylon is commonly the choice of material for stringing the racquet. The metal frame racquets are desirable because they do not warp or require a press for storage.

The weight of the shuttlecock is between 73 and 85 grains, with 14 to 16 feathers. If authentic feathers are used, the shuttlecocks should be stored in a damp place. If nylon feathers are used, the shuttlecocks will be more durable and reasonably priced, which is desirable in the school setting.

Net

The top of the net is 5 feet from the floor at its midpoint. It is 5 feet 1 inch at the posts. The net is 30 inches in depth and 20 feet long.

Court

Figure 21.1 shows the dimensions of a badminton court.

Games and Match

Eleven points make a game in women's singles. All doubles and men's singles games are 15 points. A match constitutes 2 games out of 3. As soon as a side wins 2 games, the match is over. The winner of the previous game serves the next game. Players change courts after the first and second games. In the third game, players change after 8 points in a 15-point game and after 6 points in an 11-point game.

Scoring

Only the serving side scores and continues to do so until an error is committed.

Setting

If the score becomes tied, the game may be extended by the player or side first reaching the tied score. In a 15-point game, the set may occur at 13–13 (setting to 5 points) or 14–14 (setting to 3 points). In an 11-point game, the score may be set at 10–10 (setting to 2 points) or 9–9 (setting to 3 points). A set game con-

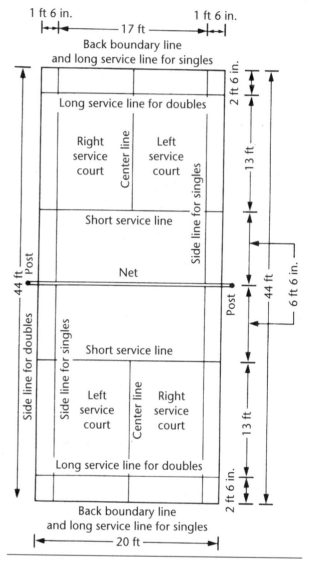

FIGURE 21.1   Badminton court dimensions

tinues, but the score called is now 0–0, or "Love all." The first player or side to reach set score wins. If a side chooses not to set, the regular game is completed.

Singles Play

The first serve is taken from the right service court and received cross court (diagonally) in the opponent's right service court. All serves on 0 or an even score are served and received in the right-hand court. All serves on an odd score are served and received in the left service court.

Doubles Play

In the first inning, the first service is 1 hand only. In all other innings, the serving team gets to use 2 hands. At the beginning of each inning, the player in the right court serves first. Partners rotate only after winning a point.

Even and odd scores are served from the same court as in singles play. If a player serves out of turn or from the incorrect service court and wins the rally, a let will be called. The let must be claimed by the receiving team before the next serve.

If a player standing in the incorrect court takes the serve and wins the rally, it will be a let, provided the let is claimed before the next serve. If either of the above cases occurs and the side at fault loses the rally, the mistake stands, and the players' positions are not corrected for the rest of the game.

Faults

A fault committed by the serving side (in-side) results in a side out, while a fault committed by the receiving side (out-side) results in a point for the server. A fault occurs in any of the following situations:

1. During the serve, the shuttlecock is contacted above the server's waist, or the racquet head is held above the hand.
2. During the serve, the shuttlecock does not fall within the boundaries of the diagonal service court.
3. During the serve, some part of both feet of the server and receiver do not remain in contact with the court, inside the boundary lines, until the shuttlecock leaves the racquet of the server. Feet on the boundary lines are considered out-of-bounds.

Organization and Skill Work

An effective way to add variety and skill work to classes is to create a series of stations. The stations can be arranged to use the space available in the gymnasium and can focus on badminton skills, conditioning activities, or a combination of both (Figure 21.2).

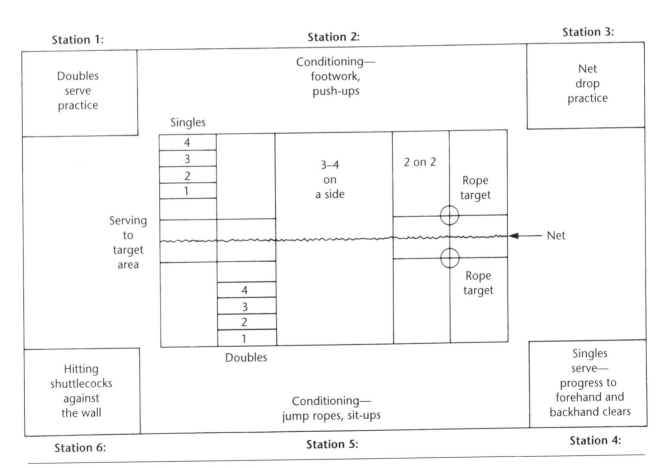

FIGURE 21.2　Station skill work—badminton

Partner activities are helpful with accompanying rating scales or checklists like the one following.

Partner Activities. Low doubles serve.

Equipment. One badminton racquet and 5 shuttlecocks per couple.

Procedure. One person is the server, and the other is the helper with a trained eye. The server follows the steps below, and the helper checks off the skills as they are completed.

1. Standing behind the 6-foot 6-inch line from the wall, drop the bird and hit it underhand against the wall. Repeat at least 5 times. The trained eye must be looking for and giving feedback on the following criteria:
   a. Keep both feet on the ground until after the shuttlecock is contacted.
   b. Hold the shuttlecock at chest height.
   c. Contact the shuttlecock below the waist level.
   d. Keep the racquet head below the wrist at point of contact.
   e. Keep the wrist firm, cocked throughout the stroke.
   f. Shuttlecock is guided, not hit.
2. From the same position behind the line, direct 3 of 5 serves above the 5-foot 1-inch line on the wall and below the 18-inch line above it. Switch positions, and if you were serving, become the helper. Help your partner, and remember that you are the trained eye who sees what your partner is doing. Partners repeat the first 2 steps.
3. Move to the court and take about 5 practice serves. Keep the serve under the 18-inch line. Now do 5 serves and have your partner record your score. This score is to help you determine your accuracy. Switch positions again and repeat step 3.
4. Now try step 3 using your backhand.

Tournament play works well for badminton. Ladder, pyramid, or round robin tournaments can add a competitive flavor to the class.

The use of marking tape on floor and walls, jump ropes on the court, fleece balls, and task cards can give the teacher more stations for a circuit. This enables the student to progress at a personalized skill level. Mini-games or lead-up games played on the courts allow for skill work, competition, and enjoyment. Regulation games and tournament play can gradually replace the lead-up games. Students should also be trained as scorekeepers and line or service judges.

Lead-Up Games and Learning Activities

Doubles Drop

After the short serve and underhand drop are taught, a "doubles drop game" can be played between the net and the short service line.

Overhead Clear

After the long serve and the overhead clear are taught, an overhead clear "rally" could be attempted. Try to keep the shuttlecock in play at least 5 times in a row; then try 10 times in a row, 15 times, and so forth.

Designated Shots

After the underhand clear is taught, work on a "designated shots rally." Start with a short serve, return with an underhand drop, return with an underhand clear, and return with an overhead clear. Keep clearing with overhead and underhand clears.

Server versus Receiver

After the "flick" serve and "push" return are taught, play a server versus receiver game. The receiver must try to return as many as possible of the server's 20 serves in a row, 10 from the right and 10 from the left. The server gets a point each time the receiver misses the return. The receiver gets a point if the server misses the serve. Reverse server and receiver roles.

Clear-Smash

After the smash is taught, play a long serve and overhead clear game. Start with a long serve, return with an overhead clear, and keep clearing until someone makes a short clear shot, then smash the short clear. Server is awarded 1 point if the smash is not returned, or loses 1 point if the smash is returned. Repeat the rally and try to make points by well-placed smashes.

Drive Rally

After the drive shot is taught, organize a drive rally with 4 players. Drive crosscourt and down the alley. If the drive shot is too high, smash return it.

Advanced Combination Drill

Start the rally with a long serve and return with an overhead drop, return with an underhand drop, return with an underhand clear to the opponent's backhand side, return with a backhand overhead clear, and return with an overhead clear unless the return shot is short. If the shot is short, use a smash.

Volleyball Badminton

Four players are on each team. Assigned positions rotate as in volleyball.

Three per Team

Alternate servers, and the "up" player plays the net shots.

Name the Shot

After 5 days of the badminton unit, challenge students to name the shots (Figure 21.3).

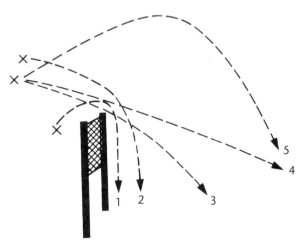

1. Net drop
2. Drop
3. Smash
4. Drive
5. Clear

FIGURE 21.3   Name the shot

Suggested Performance Objectives

Core Objectives

All directions given are for right-handed players.

Short or Low Serves

1. Standing 6 feet 6 inches from the wall, serve the shuttlecock 10 times in a row between the 5-feet and 6-feet marks on the wall.
2. Standing behind the short service line on the right side of the court, serve the shuttlecock crosscourt over the net 10 times and get 7 out of 10 in the court.
3. Repeat step 2 from the left side of the service court.
4. Standing behind the short service line, next to the center line in the right court, serve the shuttlecock crosscourt over the net, between the net and a rope 1 foot above it. Repeat 5 times in a row from the right, then 5 times from the left.
5. Standing behind the short service line, next to the center line in the right-hand court, serve 10 short serves in a row to the receiver's backhand side on the court.
6. Repeat step 5, standing in the left-hand court.

Long Serves

1. Standing to the right of and next to the center line, 12 feet from the net, serve 10 long serves in a row to the opposite court.
2. Repeat step 1 from the left service court.
3. Repeat step 1, but the serves must land in the backhand area marked on the court. Serve 5 long serves in a row to this area.

Underhand Clears: Forehand and Backhand

1. Standing between the net and the short service line, drop the shuttlecock and underhand clear on the forehand side, 10 clears in a row to the back 4 feet of the court marked for doubles.
2. Repeat step 1 on the backhand side.
3. Standing 6 feet behind the short service line, underhand clear on the forehand side 5 clears in a row to the back 4 feet of the doubles court.
4. Repeat step 3 on the backhand side.

Drops

1. Standing just behind the short service line on the right court, underhand drop on the forehand side a tossed shuttlecock from your partner. Return 10 drops in a row from the forehand side.
2. Repeat step 1 on the backhand side.

3. Repeat steps 1 and 2 from the left court.
4. Standing anywhere just behind the short service line, a partner tosses the shuttlecock barely over the net, alternating between your forehand and backhand on the toss. Underhand drop 10 in a row back between the net and a rope stretched 1 foot above the net.

Overhead Clears: Forehand

1. Standing within 12 feet of the net, a partner underhand clears the shuttlecock. Return 10 shuttlecocks in a row with an overhead forehand clear into the doubles court, at least 10 feet from the net.
2. Repeat step 1, returning 10 in a row to the back 4 feet of the doubles court.

3. Repeat step 1, returning 10 in a row alternating from right court to left court, at least 10 feet from the net.

Attendance and Participation

1. Arrive on time for class, dressed and ready to participate ($1/3$ of a point per day, up to 6 points maximum).
2. Participation in 15 games: 13 doubles and 2 singles.

Optional Objectives

1. Standing next to the center line on the right court and just behind the short service line, "flick" serve the shuttle 5 times in a row to the

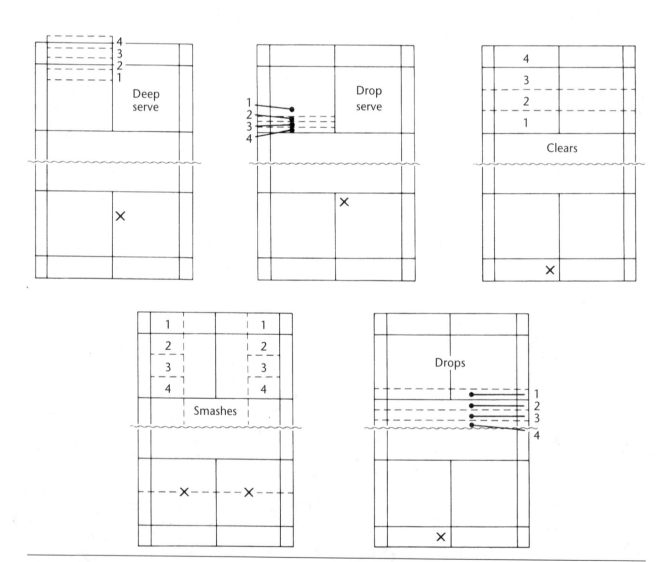

FIGURE 21.4   Badminton skills test

back 3 feet of the doubles service court. Repeat on the left.

2. Standing in the right receiving court for doubles, "push" return 5 short serves in a row either to the server's backhand side or down the side alley next to server. Repeat on the left.

3. Standing 6 feet from the short service line next to the center line on the right court, return 5 long serves in a row to the backhand side of the server with an overhead clear.

4. Repeat step 3, standing in the left court.

5. A server sets up short, high shots 6 to 8 inches from the net. Standing 6 feet from the short service line, smash 5 in a row within 15 feet of the net.

6. Repeat step 5, smashing 5 in a row down the left side of the court.

7. Repeat step 5, smashing 5 in a row down the right side of the court.

8. Standing within 10 feet of the short service line, return 10 of your opponent's smashes back over the net as smashes.

9. Standing within the last 5 feet of the back court, overhead drop opponent's clears to you. Drop 5 shuttlecocks to the right court side between the net and the short service line.

10. Repeat step 9 on the left court between the net and the short service line.

11. Stand on the center line, 6 feet from the short service line. Partner sets up low, flat serves down the forehand alley. Hit 5 forehand drives in a row down that alley.

12. Repeat step 11, hitting 5 backhand drives down the backhand-side alley.

13. Standing within 12 feet of the net, from a high clear set-up by a partner, backhand 5 overhead clears in a row to the back 6 feet of the doubles court.

14. Standing 15 feet or farther from the net, backhand 5 overhead clears in a row to the back 4 feet of the doubles court.

Skill Tests

Badminton courts can be marked in many different ways to provide students with a challenge in perfecting their skills (Figure 21.4). Using white shoe polish or masking tape, number portions of the target area in an ascending manner, from the easiest to the most difficult shots. Courts can be marked for deep serves, low serves, clears, drops, and drives. The teacher determines the number of attempts that each student is allowed.

FRISBEE

Frisbee is an exciting lifetime physical activity that can offer success and challenge at all ability levels. It can be played on almost any size field or gymnasium area and can be used with individuals, small groups, or teams. The International Frisbee Disc Association, which numbers over 100,000 members, has statistics showing that more Frisbee discs are sold yearly in the United States than footballs and basketballs combined. An annual World Championship held in the Rose Bowl draws large crowds to watch competitors focus on distance, accuracy, free style, and other games.

A number of factors make Frisbee disc sports an attractive new activity for physical education. A Frisbee costs only $4 to $8, depending on the type and quality of the disc. Frisbee provides excellent skills practice in throwing, catching, and eye-hand coordination, as well as offering many interesting individual challenges and team activities. The low injury risks and the attraction to students are positive factors. The sport can be effective in a coeducational environment and offers flexibility in terms of participants' ages and abilities and in terms of program space and time. Both team and individual skills can be learned with the Frisbee and used for a lifetime of enjoyment.

Sequence of Skills

Throws

Backhand Throw. The thumb is on the top of the disc and the remaining fingers are under the rim. The index finger can also be placed on the outside lip of the disc. Coil the wrist and arm across the chest. Step forward and release the disc (keeping it level) with a snap of the wrist .

Backhand (Across the Chest) Curves. Use the same technique as the straight backhand but release the disc at an angle, with the lower side being the desired direction. Throw curves both left and right by tilting the disc.

Underhand Throw. Use a backhand grip or put the index finger on the lip of the disc. Step with the opposite foot, bring the disc underhand past the body, and release level about waist height with a wrist snap.

Thumber Throw.   Hook the thumb under the disc and put the 4 fingers on top. Bring the disc down from the ear in a sidearm motion and release when the disc is even with the body. Avoid a follow-through with the disc.

Sidearm Throw.   Put the index and middle finger under the disc and the thumb on top. The 2 fingers can be together on the lip, or 1 can be on the lip and 1 in the middle of the disc. Release the disc in a motion similar to the thumber.

Overhand Wrist Flip.   Grip the disc with the fingers on top and the thumb under the lip. Cock the wrist backward and start the throw behind the back at shoulder level. Flip the wrist forward to a point in line with the body.

Catches

Sandwich Catch.   Catch the disc with 1 hand on top and the other on the bottom with the disc in the middle. Alternate hands from top to bottom on different occasions.

C-Catch.   Make a C with the thumb and fingers. Watch the disc into the C and close the fingers on the disc. Throws below the waist should have the thumb up, and those above the waist should have thumb down.

Additional Skills

1. *Skip-throw off the ground.* Tip the forward edge down and skip the disc to a partner.
2. *Tipping.* Use the finger, knee, head, toe, heel, or elbow. Watch the disc make contact with the various body parts and tip the disc in the air.
3. *Catches.* Catch with the finger, behind the back and head, between the legs, and 1-handed.
4. *Air brushing.* Strike the disc on its side to give it rotation.

Ideas for Effective Instruction

Frisbee discs are available from over 30 different companies. Avoid the cheapest discs because they will not fly without turning over. Whamo Company in San Gabriel, California, is the oldest and largest manufacturer of flying discs. They have an excellent World Class Series ranging from 97 to 165 grams. These discs are reasonably priced for secondary

schools. Many companies use discs for advertising, and it is often possible to acquire promotional discs at a discount.

Instruction can begin by having partners, positioned about 5 yards apart, work on the basic backhand and sandwich catch. As students improve, have them move farther apart and use the backhand curves with the C-catch and the 1-handed catch. Be sure to keep beginning students spread out and away from buildings, fences, and other obstacles, since the disc is difficult to control. Next, the underhand throw, thumber, and sidearm can be introduced with several fancy catches.

After students have the basic idea, create 4 stations that focus on accuracy, distance, accuracy and distance combined, and loft time. Many station variations can be designed to challenge students. Check the following section on activities for specific ideas. Frisbee golf is a particularly good activity for beginners with few developed skills.

Lead-Up Games and Learning Activities

Throw for Distance

Set up 5 or 6 cones at varying distances and let students experiment with different throws for distance.

Throw for Distance and Accuracy

Mark a line with varying distances and have students throw as far as possible on the line. Subtract from the total throw distance the distance of the Frisbee landing point away from the line. Students should develop both distance and accuracy.

Throw for Accuracy

Make a large circular target, about 9 or 10 feet in diameter, on the ground with rope or jump ropes. Set cones at 10-, 15-, 20-, and 25-yard distances. Let students have 5 attempts at each distance, and record the number of accurate throws. Another variation is to hang a hula hoop from a tree or goal post and have students throw through the hoop. Award 1 point for hitting the hoop and 2 points for going through the hoop.

Time Aloft

Record the time from disc release until it hits the ground.

Throw and Catch with Self

The object of this activity is to throw the disc as far forward as possible and then to run and catch the Frisbee. A starting line is designated at which the disc must be released, and distance is measured from that line. The disc must be caught.

Follow-the-Leader

One player makes a specific throw and the second player must try to make the same throw. The first player must match the catch of the second player.

Twenty-One

Players stand 10 yards apart and throw the disc back and forth. The throws must be accurate and catchable. One point is awarded for a 2-handed catch and 2 points for a 1-handed catch. A player must get 21 points and win by 2 points.

Frisbee Tennis

The same game as regular tennis, but the player must catch the Frisbee and throw from that spot. The serve starts to the right of the center mark and must go to the opposite back court, not into the service box.

Ultimate

Ultimate is a team game with 7 or more on a side. The object is to move the Frisbee down the field by passing and to score by passing across the goal line to a teammate. The person with the disc can only pivot and pass to a teammate. If the Frisbee is grounded not caught, intercepted, or goes out-of-bounds, the defending team gains possession.

Guts

Five to 7 players on a team stand behind a line 15 yards from the opponents' line. The goal line is 10 yards wide. The object is to throw so hard that the opponents cannot make a 1-handed catch. The Frisbee can be tipped by several people as long as a 1-handed catch is used. The receiving team gets a point if the throw is too high, too wide, or too low. The height is determined by having the team stretch their arms straight up, usually 7 to 8 feet high. The first team to score 21 points wins. Use extra caution with beginners and younger students. Move the goals back a bit and match ability levels.

Frisbee Soccer

The game is played like soccer, but the disc is thrown to teammates and at the goal. If the disc is dropped, the defenders play offense. Rules can be modified to include 2 goalies and limitations on the number of steps possible.

Frisbee Softball

The game is similar to regular softball. The pitcher throws the disc to the batter, who must catch the disc and throw it into play past the pitcher. If the batter drops the pitch, it is a strike. No bunting or stealing is allowed. The other rules of softball apply.

Frisbee Shuffleboard

Two players compete against 2 players. The game is played on a basketball court and the goal is to score by throwing the frisbee into the opponent's key. Throwers stand outside of the out of bounds line under the basket. The key is divided into 2 areas: the circular area around the free throw line is worth 2 points and the larger lane area is worth 1 point. Different colored frisbees are used to make scoring easier.

Frisbee Golf

Frisbee or disc golf is a favorite game of many students. Boundary cones with numbers can be used for tees, and holes can be boxes, hula hoops, trees, tires, garbage cans, or any other available equipment on the school grounds. Put the course together on a map for students and start them at different holes to decrease the time spent waiting to tee off. Regulation golf rules apply. The students can jog between throws for increased activity.

General Guideline.   Disc golf is played like regular golf. One stroke is counted for each time the disc is thrown and when a penalty is incurred. The object is to acquire the lowest score.

T-Throws.   T-throws must be completed within or behind the designated tee area.

Lie.   The lie is the spot on or directly underneath the spot where the previous throw landed.

Throwing Order.   The player whose disc is the farthest from the hole throws first. The player with the least number of throws on the previous hole tees off first.

Fairway Throws. Fairway throws must be made with the foot closest to the hole on the lie. A run-up is allowed.

Dog Leg. A dog leg is 1 or more designated trees or poles in the fairway that must be passed on the outside when approaching the hole. There is a 2-stroke penalty for missing a dog leg.

Putt Throw. A putt throw is any throw within 10 feet of the hole. A player may not move past the point of the lie in making the putt throw. Falling or jumping putts are not allowed.

Unplayable Lies. Any disc that comes to rest 6 or more feet above the ground is unplayable. The next throw must be played from a new lie directly underneath the unplayable lie (1-stroke penalty).

Out-of-Bounds. A throw that lands out-of-bounds must be played from the point where the disc went out (1-stroke penalty).

Course Courtesy. Do not throw until the players ahead are out of range.

Completion of Hole. A disc that comes to rest in the hole (box or hoop) or strikes the designated hole (tree or pole) constitutes successful completion of that hole.

Around Nine

A target is set up with 9 different throwing positions around it, each 2 feet farther away (Figure 21.5). The throwing positions can be clockwise or counterclockwise around the target. They can also be in a straight line from the target. Points are awarded based on the throwing position number (for example, number 7 means 7 points for hitting the target). The game can be played indoors or out.

One-Step

This game is a variation of Guts. Opponents stand 20 to 30 yards apart. The object is to throw the disc accurately so the opponent can catch it while taking only 1 step. If the throw is off target, the thrower receives a point. If the throw is accurate and the receiver drops the disc, the receiver is awarded 1 point. The first player with 5 points loses the match.

Suggested Performance Objectives

1. Throw 10 consecutive backhands through a hula hoop from 10 yards.
2. Same as objective 1, using underhand throws.
3. Same as objective 1, using sidearm throws.
4. Same as objective 1, using thumber throws.
5. Same as objective 1, using overhand wrist flips.
6. Throw a Frisbee 30 yards or more using two different throws.
7. Curve the disc around a tree and land it in a designated target area 3 of 5 attempts.
8. Same as objective 7, but use the opposite curve.
9. Catch 10 consecutive sandwich catches.

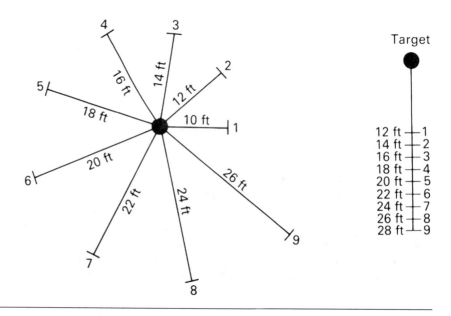

FIGURE 21.5 Around nine game

10. Catch 10 consecutive thumbs-down catches above the waist.
11. Same as objective 10, with thumbs up below the waist.
12. Catch 3 of 5 behind the head, behind the back, or between the legs.
13. Make 5 consecutive 1-handed catches, both left and right.
14. Throw 5 consecutive skips into a target area.
15. Score 30 or less on a round of Frisbee golf.

These are just a few of the possibilities for challenging students with Frisbee performance objectives. The objectives could be combined with a grading scheme or used with learning stations for skill development. Activities need to be field-tested in order to establish fair distances and criterion levels for various age students and ability groups. Figure 21.6 is a 3-week Frisbee unit for middle school students.

Rainy-Day Activities

1. Review and teach rules and strategies for the various Frisbee games.
2. Set up a short putting (Frisbee golf) course in the gym, hallway, or locker room.
3. Review grips, throws, releases, and so forth.
4. Discuss Frisbee literature, and have students read and report on specific information.
5. Discuss the various types and sizes of discs and the purpose of each type.

Introduction
What is Frisbee?
Types
Activities
Backhand throw
Sandwich catch
Backhand curves
C-catch
Underhand throw
	Review
	Backhands—curves
	Underhands
	Catches
	Teach
	Frisbee golf
	Activity
	Play 6 holes of golf
		Review
		Throws—catches
		Teach
		Thumber
		Sidearm
		Overhand flip
		Activities
		4 stations:
		   Distance
		   Accuracy
		   Curves
		   Partner work
			Review
			Throws—catches
			Teach
			Fancy catches
			Activities
			Follow-the-leader
			Twenty-One
			One-Step
				Review
				Fancy catches
				Teach
				Throw to self
				Activities
				Frisbee softball
				Frisbee soccer

Review
All throws
Teach
Skipping
Tipping
Brushing
Activities
4 stations:
   Distance with
     accuracy
   Self-catch
   Accuracy
   Partner work
	Review
	All catches
	Teach
	Free style
	Activity
	Ultimate
		Review
		Skipping, tipping,
		  brushing, free style
		Activities
		4 stations: skill work
		Frisbee tennis
		Frisbee golf
			Activity
			9 holes of Frisbee golf
				Activities
				4 stations:
				   Skill work
				   Evaluation
				   Around Nine
				   Follow-the-leader
				   Twenty-One
				   One-Step

Review Skills for station work *Activities* 4 stations Frisbee softball	*Activities* Ultimate Frisbee soccer	*Activities* Station work Evaluation Guts Around Nine Follow-the-leader Twenty-One One-Step	*Activities* 9 holes of Frisbee golf	*Activities* Station work Evaluation Ultimate Frisbee softball Guts

FIGURE 21.6 Frisbee block plan

6. Set up an indoor tossing accuracy test and let students work at improving their accuracy.

7. Develop a crossword puzzle or Frisbee word searches.

8. Assign a group of students to develop a crossword puzzle or a word search.

9. Devise and give a test on terminology.

10. Discuss with students the skills and activities of Frisbee and how Frisbee can fit into their lifestyles.

11. Have students develop rules and regulations for a new game that will be played when the weather clears.

12. Invite a local Frisbee club or expert to class to give a demonstration and instruction on Frisbee techniques and skills.

RACQUETBALL

The game of racquetball is a direct descendant from the game of paddleball, which was first played in the 1920s. In the 1940s, a racquet with strings was introduced and became known as "paddle rackets." This sport grew in popularity, and in 1969 the International Racquetball Association was established, and racquetball was born. Within the last 10 years, the game has grown tremendously in popularity. This growth has brought about a comparable increase in the number of facilities, changes in racquet style, and a livelier ball. A Neilson Company survey found that racquetball was the fastest growing participation sport from 1976 to 1979.

Racquetball can be played on a 1-, 3-, or 4-walled court. The most popular is the enclosed 4-wall court with a ceiling, but the other types of courts are more common at the middle and high school levels. The game can be played with 2 people (singles), 3 people (cutthroat), or 4 people (doubles). The object is to win each rally by serving or returning the ball so the opponent is unable to keep the ball in play. A rally is over when a side makes an error or is unable to return the ball to the front wall before it touches the floor twice. Note that one can score only when one is serving.

Sequence of Skills

Grip, Eastern Style

Forehand.   Form a V on the top bevel of the handle with the thumb and index finger. Rest the thumb on the knuckle of the middle finger on the left side bevel of the handle. The palm of the hand should be approximately level with the bottom of the racquet. The index finger should be in a pistol grip position.

Backhand.   Rotate one-quarter turn to the left (counterclockwise). The V is now on the upper part of the left bevel.

Ready Position

The feet should be shoulder width apart and the knees slightly flexed. The back is bent slightly forward, and the head is up. The weight is on the balls of the feet. The racquet should be in front of the body at about chest height. Stand in the middle of the court, approximately 4 feet behind the short line.

Forehand

From the ready position, pivot until facing the right sidewall with the left shoulder forward. Bring the wrist back beside the right ear, and point the racquet toward the ceiling. The weight is on the back foot. Start the forward swing with the racquet, and shift the weight from the back to the front foot. Rotate the shoulders and hips toward the front wall. Contact with the ball should be in line with the instep of the front foot. Keep the eyes on the ball and follow through across the body.

Backhand

Follow the same technique as the forehand, but contact the ball when it is about 6 inches from the lead foot.

Backwall Shot

Proper setup position is the key to any backwall shot. Watch the ball carefully and set up with the weight on the rear foot and the racquet by the ear. Step forward and stroke into the ball at the proper position, as stated in the previous discussion.

Serve

Drive.   Hit the serve low and hard to the back corner where the back and sidewalls join. This usually goes to the receiver's backhand.

Crosscourt Z.   Serve so that the ball strikes the front wall 3 to 4 feet from the sidewall and then rebounds to the sidewall and bounces deep in the opposite corner. The speed and height of the serve can be varied to create different angles for the opponent.

Lob. The lob is a change-of-pace serve that hits high on the front wall and stays close to the sidewall. It should land deep in the back court and drop straight down.

Ceiling Shot

The ceiling shot is a defensive shot to move the opponent back and to open up the front center court. The shot can be hit with a forehand, backhand, or overhead stroke, depending on the position of the ball. If the ball is above the head, an overhead shot can be used. A forehand or backhand can otherwise be used. The overhead shot is similar to a tennis serve. The elbow leads the movement, and the arm stretches overhead to contact the ball with an extended arm. The object is to place the shot close to the front wall on the ceiling. It is usually hit to the opponent's backhand side, tightly against the sidewall.

Passing Shot

The passing shot is an offensive shot that is hit low and hard to either side of the opponent, just out of reach. The object is to keep the ball close to the sidewall and low enough so the ball does not come off the back wall to any degree. The shot is a wise choice when the opponent is out of center position to either side of the court.

Kill Shot

The kill is an offensive shot hit low on the front wall. It is impossible to return if hit accurately. It can be hit straight into the front wall or can be hit off the sidewall into the front wall.

Ideas for Effective Instruction

Racquets are made of wood, fiberglass, aluminum, and various other combinations such as graphite and fiberglass. They have different weights, shapes, strings, and grip sizes. Wood racquets are cheaper but heavier; fiberglass racquets are lighter but less durable. Aluminum is lightweight and durable, but is quite expensive. Grips are usually leather or rubber. Leather seems to provide a better grip, but is not as durable as the rubber. Grip size is the circumference of the handle in inches (such as $4^{1}/_{8}$, $4^{5}/_{8}$).

Racquetballs are quite lively and will break after some usage, so having extras is a good idea. Eye guards are available as a safety measure, and some players may want to wear a glove to provide a better grip.

It is usually best to have 2 students working in 1 court with 1 student on each side of the court. If more students must be placed on each court, then designate partners and have 1 hitting and 1 chasing balls or throwing setups. Have 2 hitters and two nonhitters per court. The nonhitter can perform a variety of functions such as analyzing strokes, checking safety, or using a rating scale. Keep the hitters close to the sidewalls to give everyone more room.

Skill work can be accomplished easily by practicing performance objectives. It is best to start with a bounce-and-hit method and progress to a setup throw off the wall. Either of these methods can be done alone or with a partner. Some students need to practice bouncing the ball and throwing the ball off the wall. Take time to show students how to perform these skills.

Stress the importance of safety on the court because of the confined area and the dangerous implements. Players should be encouraged to wear eye guards, and should be reminded never to turn around and expose the face to a person hitting from behind them. All players must tie the wrist strings snugly around the wrist to avoid losing control of the racquet and injuring others. Finally, players should be reminded that the rules of racquetball stress safety. Whenever there is any chance of endangering the opponent either by hitting with the racquet or by bodily contact, let the ball go and play the point over.

Lead-Up Games and Learning Activities

Ceiling Games

This is a change-of-pace game that requires students to use the ceiling shot. After the serve, a certain number of shots must hit the ceiling before or after hitting the front wall. If the ball does not hit the ceiling, it is a point or side out. A useful variation is to change the required number of ceiling shots that a person must hit each time. For example, start with one and then increase the required number. Or, require all ceiling shots after the serve.

Five Points and Out

This modified game allows 5 serves or less each time the serve changes hands. After 5 points are scored, the opponents change positions (server to receiver).

The opponents change positions normally if a side out is forced before the 5 points are scored. This modification keeps opponents from dominating the scoring through an exceptionally strong serve.

Eight-Ball Rally

After the serve, each person must hit the ball 4 times before a point can be scored. This forces a longer rally and encourages work on different shots.

Backhand Rally

After the serve, a player must hit a certain number of backhand shots before a point is scored or a side out is forced. Start with 1 required backhand and then increase the number gradually.

Accuracy Drills

A challenging activity is to mark off the courts with targets on the floor and walls. Jump ropes, boundary cones, boxes, and masking tape are useful for constructing targets. Challenge the entire class to make 5 lob serves, 5 forehands, 5 backhands, 5 Z serves, and 5 drive serves to the target areas. Kill shots off the back wall and sidewalls can be practiced to marked areas on the front wall. Announce the winner in each category. Vary the size of the targets and the designated skills each day.

Cutthroat and Doubles

Cutthroat is played with 3 people. The server plays the other 2 players. Doubles is 2 players versus 2.

Rotation

Rotation involves students playing a 5-minute game. A whistle is then blown and students rotate to the court on the left if they are ahead and stay where they are if behind. The object of the game is to move up to the last court. Rotation is also enjoyable when playing doubles. Teammates move ahead a court if they are leading when the whistle blows.

Suggested Performance Objectives

These performance objectives can be used for skill work, as a motivational device, and as part of an evaluation scheme. Students can evaluate each other or evaluation can be a combination of peer and teacher observation. A checklist can be used daily or weekly, and students can be required to complete a certain number of checklists before entering the class tournament.

Beginning Skills

Forehand Drive

1. Standing 3 feet behind the short line and 3 feet from the sidewall, bounce the ball off the sidewall and execute a proper forehand drive, hitting the front wall below the 8-foot line, 4 consecutive times.
2. Standing 3 feet behind the receiving line and 3 feet from the sidewall, bounce the ball off the sidewall and execute a proper forehand drive, hitting the front wall below the 8-foot line, 4 consecutive times.
3. Standing 3 feet behind the service line and in the middle of the court, feed the ball to the front wall and then execute a proper forehand drive below the 8-foot line, 3 of 4 times.
4. Standing 3 feet behind the short line and in the middle of the court, feed the ball to the front wall and then execute a proper forehand drive below the 8-foot line, 3 of 4 times.

Backhand Drive

5. Repeat task 1 using proper backhand drive.
6. Repeat task 2 using proper backhand drive.
7. Repeat task 3 using proper backhand drive.
8. Repeat task 4 using proper backhand drive.

Backwall Shot

9. Standing approximately 10 feet from the back wall, bounce the ball off the floor and then off the back wall and execute a forehand backwall shot, hitting the front wall below the 8-foot line, 3 of 4 times.
10. Repeat task 9 using the backhand backwall shot.
11. Standing approximately in the middle of the court, feed the ball to the front wall so it bounces off the floor and the back wall, and execute a forehand backwall shot, hitting the front wall below the 8-foot line, 3 of 4 times.
12. Repeat task 11 using the backhand drive.

Serves

13. Hit 3 of 5 drive serves to the left court that land within 3 feet of the sidewall in the back court and are otherwise legal.

14. Hit 3 of 5 crosscourt serves to the left court that land within 3 feet of the sidewall and are otherwise legal.

15. Hit 3 of 5 lob serves to the left court that land within 3 feet of the sidewall, do not bounce out from the back more than 3 feet, and are otherwise legal.

16. Repeat task 13 to the right court.

17. Repeat task 14 to the right court.

18. Repeat task 15 to the right court.

Ceiling Shot

19. Standing in back court, bounce the ball high enough to execute a proper overhand forehand ceiling shot so the ball hits ceiling, front wall, floor, and hits low off the back wall 3 of 4 times.

20. Repeat task 19 using regular forehand stroke.

Pinch Shot

21. Standing at midcourt, bounce the ball and execute a proper forehand pinch shot so the ball hits the sidewall, front wall, bounces at least 2 times, and hits the other sidewall 3 of 4 times.

22. Repeat task 21 using backhand stroke.

Intermediate and Advanced Skills

23. Repeat task 1 hitting front wall below the 3-foot line.

24. Repeat task 2 hitting front wall below the 3-foot line.

25. Repeat task 3 hitting front wall below the 3-foot line.

26. Repeat task 4 hitting front wall below the 3-foot line.

27. Repeat task 1 using proper backhand drive and hitting front wall below the 3-foot line.

28. Repeat task 2 using proper backhand drive and hitting front wall below the 3-foot line.

29. Repeat task 3 using proper backhand drive and hitting front wall below the 3-foot line.

30. Repeat task 4 using proper backhand drive and hitting front wall below the 3-foot line.

31. Repeat task 9 hitting front wall below the 3-foot line.

32. Repeat task 9 using the backhand backwall shot and hitting front wall below the 3-foot line.

33. Repeat task 11 hitting front wall below the 3-foot line.

34. Repeat task 11 using the backhand drive and hitting front wall below the 3-foot line.

35. Repeat task 19 using backhand stroke.

36. Repeat task 20 using backhand stroke.

37. Repeat task 21 with feed off the front wall.

38. Repeat task 22 with feed off the front wall.

39. Repeat task 1 hitting the front wall below the 1-foot line (kill shot), 3 of 4 times.

40. Repeat task 3 hitting the front wall below the 1-foot line, 3 of 4 times.

41. Repeat task 14 using the backhand in the right court, 3 of 4 times.

42. Repeat task 15 using the backhand in the right court, 3 of 4 times.

Rainy-Day Activities

1. Review rules and strategies for serving, court position, passing shots, singles play, cutthroat, and doubles play.

2. Have students critique several racquetball articles or a chapter from an activity book.

3. Develop a crossword puzzle or word searches on racquetball.

4. Assign a group of students to develop a crossword puzzle or word search.

5. Work on serving against a wall indoors. Speed and distances can be modified according to the available space.

6. Have on hand a variety of racquets, balls, gloves, and eye guards, and discuss the advantages of each.

7. Show loop films on racquetball.

8. Devise and administer a test on terms and strategy.

9. Discuss caloric expenditure playing racquetball.

10. Point out the health-related benefits of playing racquetball.

RHYTHMIC ACTIVITY

The urge to express oneself rhythmically has been characteristic of the human race throughout time. Dances have been done as religious rituals, as national and cultural customs, and as declarations of war. Current dances are borrowed from many cultures and groups both ancient and modern. Since the United States is a melting pot of cultures, we have a broad and diverse range of folk dances representing many peoples.

Every generation dances. It is important that students learn the dances of the past as they develop new dances unique to their group. A wide variety of social skills can be learned through social dancing. Often, if people are not taught dance skills during the school-aged years, they are hesitant to participate in later years. The rhythmic program should thus be viewed as an integral part of the physical education program. If dance skills are not taught as part of the program, they probably will not be taught at all.

Sequence of Skills

The program should consist of 4 major parts: square dance, folk and round dances, social dance steps, and country swing and western dance. Such a large number of skills and dances can be taught that it is impossible to list all of the activities here. Instead, refer to *Dance a While,* by Harris, Pittman, and Waller (1988), which offers supplementary and comprehensive coverage. Another concern is that different geographic areas have favorite dances and rhythmic activities peculiar to each. The authors could not offer activities that would be comprehensive enough in the rhythms area to suit all readers.

Square Dance

The text *Dance a While* by Harris, Pittman, and Waller (1988) is an excellent source for square dancing. The basic movements of square dance are detailed in progression from Level 1A, beginner basics, to Level 5, intermediate basics. Fifty skills are listed and explained in clear and concise terms. A classified index of square dances is also provided, along with the basic skills that are developed in each dance and the level of difficulty. Each dance description contains the necessary performance instructions and recommended records.

Country Swing and Western Dance

Country swing and western dance is popular with middle and high school students. The number of dance moves is limited only by the imagination of the dancers. An excellent source for a step-by-step approach to the moves can be found in the text *The Complete Book of Country Swing and Western Dance* by Livingston (1981). The text is illustrated in a step-by-step fashion with photographs and is easy to follow. The shuffle step is also included.

Folk and Round Dance

There are many folk and round dances of varying difficulty. When the dances are presented, the background and history of the dance should be shared with students. The *Dance a While* text (1988) offers a rich repertoire of dances. A classified index detailing the basic steps, formations, and degree of difficulty is most useful. Directions for the dances are given, along with recommended records.

Social Dance Steps

Social dance steps should be developed in the rhythms unit. Steps most commonly taught are the waltz, fox-trot, swing, tango, rumba, samba, cha-cha, and bossa nova. Each can be presented with the basic steps taught first, followed by 1 or 2 variations. With middle school students, the dance steps can be learned individually and then with a partner. Emphasis should be placed on creating an enjoyable atmosphere since peer pressure to succeed is great. Instructors can develop a positive class attitude by demonstrating proper dance etiquette and by showing their enjoyment of the activity. The *Dance a While* text (1988) is recommended as a valuable source.

TENNIS

Developing from a crude handball game played in fourteenth-century France, the game of tennis became one of the most popular sports of the 1980s. Part of its popularity stems from the fact that it is truly a game for a lifetime. Children as young as 6 years old can learn to play. In fact, most of today's superstars began playing at very early ages. Chris Evert-Lloyd, one of the top female players of this era, still plays with a 2-handed backhand, a skill she acquired when she did not have sufficient strength to hit 1-handed as a child.

Tennis can also be played well by older age groups. The United States Tennis Association (USTA), which is the governing body for tennis in the United States, conducts national championships and has established national rankings for age groups beginning with the 12-year-old-and-under group, through the 70-year-old-and-over group. Another reason for the popularity of tennis is that men and women can compete on the same court at the same time (mixed doubles). Few other serious sports offer this possibility. The popularity of tennis is noticeable as one sees thousands of tennis courts across the country, usually with people waiting in line to play. The huge audiences at such classic tournaments as Wimbledon and the U.S. Open also attest to the game's popularity.

Although some tennis is played on grass courts (as at Wimbledon), and some is played on clay courts, most American tennis is played on hard surfaces such as asphalt or cement. The court is separated by a net, which is 3 feet high at the center and 3.5 feet high at the net posts.

In singles, 1 player is on each side of the net. In doubles, 2 players are on each side of the net. All players have a racquet. The ball is put into play with a serve. After the return of the serve, players may hit the ball before it bounces or may allow the ball to bounce once before hitting it. The object of the game is to legally hit the ball over the net into the opponent's court. Most coaches of the sport will say that to win, all you have to do is to hit the ball over the net 1 more time than the opponent does.

Sequence of Skills

Tennis skills fall into 5 basic categories. Some skills may not fit exactly into any 1 category, but for organizational purposes, these 5 will suffice: volley, ground strokes, lob, overhead, and serve.

Volley

The volley should be the first stroke learned because it is the simplest stroke. The eye-hand coordination involved is similar to that involved in catching a thrown ball, a skill most students have mastered by high school. The volley requires no backswing, and the ball does not bounce, so timing is simplified.

Ground Strokes

The forehand and backhand ground strokes are considered to be the foundation of a solid game. The forehand is the easier of the two for most people and should be learned first. The backhand is more difficult but not too difficult to learn with proper instruction.

Lob

After learning the ground strokes, the lob is relatively easy. It is basically a ground stroke, hit at a different angle. Backswing and body position are identical to those of the ground stroke.

Overhead

The overhead and serve are different from the other strokes and require learning new patterns. The overhead, or smash, should be taught first, as this stroke resembles a simplified service motion. When the skill of hitting an overhead has been mastered, students will find it easier to learn to hit a serve.

Serve

The serve is a complicated stroke, and some tennis coaches prefer to introduce it as soon as possible to give students the maximum amount of time to master it. If the serve is the last skill taught, however, students are by then more familiar with the equipment, have a better feel for the game, and may be more successful with this skill.

Ideas for Effective Instruction

The Court

The game of tennis is played on a court as diagrammed in (Figure 21.7). A working knowledge of the court areas is vital to the student, not only for its importance in playing the game, but also for the following instructions.

Singles Sideline. The singles sideline delineates the playing court for singles. A ball landing on the sideline is in play.

Doubles Sideline. The doubles sideline delineates the playing court for doubles. A ball landing on the doubles sideline is in play in doubles.

Doubles Alley. The doubles alley is the area of the court in play in doubles after the serve. It includes the doubles sideline.

Base Line. The base line delineates the length of the court for both singles and doubles. When hitting a serve, the player must stand behind the base line

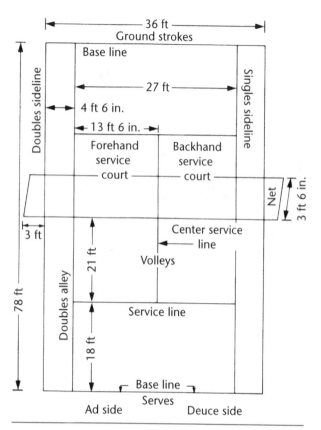

FIGURE 21.7 Tennis court markings

and may not touch it or step over it onto the court until the ball has left the racquet. A ball landing on the base line is in play.

Service Line. The service line delineates the length of the service court. A serve must land between the net and the service line or on the service line to be in play.

Center Service Line. The center service line divides the service court into deuce and ad sides. A serve hitting the center service line is in play.

Ad Court. The ad court is the service court to the receiver's left. Any time an odd number of points has been played, the serve is made to this court (that is, 15-0, 30-40, ad in, or ad out).

Deuce Court. The deuce court is the service court to the receiver's right. Any time an even number of points has been played, the serve is made to this court (that is, 0-0, 15-15, 40-15, deuce).

The Match

Most people play tennis to try to win the match. To win a match, a player must win a predetermined number of sets (usually 2 out of 3). To win a set, a player must win 6 games with at least a 2-game margin. If a set ties at 6 games each, a tie breaker is played to determine the winner of the set. To win a game, a player must be the first to win 4 points. Each of these terms is explained in the following discussion.

Points and Games

A player wins a point if the opponent fails to legally return the ball, or if the opponent, while serving, fails to legally put the ball into play. The opponent will be awarded a point in any of these situations: the ball is allowed to bounce more than once before it is returned, the ball is returned so that it does not cross the net or land within the playing court, the ball is hit twice while it is being returned, the player is touched by the ball while it is in play, or the net is touched while the ball is in play.

Two methods are currently used for scoring games. The conventional scoring progression is love-15-30-40-game. Both players start love (zero) and a player must win 4 points to win the game. The 1 exception is that a player must win by a 2-point margin. If the server leads 40-30 and the receiver wins the next point, the score is deuce. The next player who wins 2 consecutive points wins the game. At deuce, if the server wins the following point, the score is advantage in (ad in). However, if the receiver wins the point, the score is advantage out (ad out). When a player with the advantage wins the next point, that player also wins the game.

Another scoring system, called no-ad, or VASS, simplifies this process, speeds the game along, and is better suited for physical education classes in which time limits are a factor. In this system, points are counted 0-1-2-3-game. A 2-point lead is not required because the first player to win a fourth point wins the game. Using this system, there is no ad or deuce.

Sets

The first player (or doubles team) to win 6 games wins the set if they have a 2-game lead. A set might therefore last only 6 games (6-0), or might go to 10 or more games (6-4). If a set is tied at 5 games all, the winner of the next game would go up 6-5, and would not have the necessary 2-game margin to win the set. Should the leader win the next game, that player would also win the set, 7-5. If a set ties at 6 games each, however, a tie breaker is used. The winner of the tie breaker is the winner of the set, and the score is recorded at 7-6.

Tie Breaker

The USTA has established that the 12-point tie breaker be used at 6-all. This occurs in the following manner:

1. The player who served the first game of the set serves the first point.
2. The receiver of point 1 serves points 2 and 3, and the serve changes after every 2 points from that time.
3. Players change sides of the net at every 6 points (6-0, 3-3, 6-6).
4. The tie breaker is won by the first player to reach 7 points with at least a 2-point margin. If the first player to reach 7 does not have a 2-point margin, play continues until 1 player establishes a 2-point lead.

Match

In women's tennis and in almost all of men's tennis, the winner of a match is determined by the first player or team to win 2 sets. Some men's tennis is played to the best 3 of 5 sets, and thus if Smith defeated Jones (6-4, 3-6, 7-6, [9-7]), Smith won the first set 6-4, lost the second set 6-3, and won the third set in a tie breaker, the score of which was 9-7.

General Rules

The match usually begins with players spinning a racquet to determine who will serve the first game. The winner of the toss can choose to serve or to receive, and can also choose which side of the net to begin from, or can elect to have the opponent decide. After the initial choices are made, the opponent makes all other choices.

One player serves for a whole game. The first serve is hit from the right side of the court into the diagonal service area. The server has 2 chances to put the ball into play. If the serve is a fault, the second ball is served. If this serve is also a fault, the server loses the point. Any serve that touches the net but

still lands in the proper service court is a "let," and the serve is hit again. After the first point of the game, the following serve takes place from the left side of the court. The serve alternates back and forth on each successive point throughout the game.

An exception to this rule applies to no-ad scoring. At 3-3 in no-ad, the receiver chooses the side into which the serve will be made. The serve is not automatically made to the deuce side, as might be expected, but the receiver may choose to receive from either side. The opponent then serves the next game in the same manner. The serve alternates after each successive game for the entire match. In doubles, each team may choose which player serves first for that team, and this alternates each time it is that team's serve.

At the conclusion of every odd-numbered game, players change sides of the net—after the first, third, and fifth game, and so forth, there is a court change.

Tennis is governed by a strict set of rules, which cover every imaginable situation. A thorough knowledge of these rules is important for the tennis instructor. A copy of the rules of tennis can be ordered from the USTA (see the suggested readings at the end of this unit).

Etiquette

Rules of etiquette are a vital part of tennis. Except for large tournaments and professional matches, referees and ball retrievers are seldom present at tennis matches. Rules of etiquette must be followed for the game of tennis to be enjoyable to all.

Most rules of etiquette can be summed up in the motto: "Do unto others as you would have them do unto you." For instance, if a ball was not seen clearly as being out or in, play it over. When the point is over, try to return the balls to the opponent, not merely in the general direction.

Never enter a court (or walk behind one) while a rally is in progress. If one must walk through a court, wait until there is a court change.

A rule of tennis states that any interference during play shall cause a "let," and the point will be replayed. If the opponent claims that there was a distraction during play, do not hesitate to play the point over.

Minimize verbal outbursts on the court. Not only is it distracting to the opponent, but it may be bothering players on other courts. Never throw racquets or slam balls around in anger. This is dangerous and unsportsmanlike.

Organization and Skill Work

Most tennis classes are organized along traditional lines, that is, the instructor shows groups of students proper grips, stances, backswings, and so forth, at the same time. Another method of organizing the class is to allow students to progress at their own rate. This can be accomplished through the use of a unit with performance objectives. Each student knows exactly what is expected and moves from 1 task to the next when able.

Prepare a unit for each student in the class. As the students come to class, give them a unit, access to balls and racquets, and encourage them to get started.

When the entire class has arrived, call them together for an organizational meeting. These meetings might include a "tennis tip" for the day, some comment about the unit, or some skill analysis. The meeting should be short so that most of the class time can be devoted to practicing and mastering skills.

If stations are used, each court can be designated for a particular skill (that is, 1 court for volleys, 1 for ground strokes, and 1 for serving). Provide plenty of balls (beginners will fare as well with older balls as with newer ones) and racquets. Post the suggested skill tasks on the net or fence, and let the students progress at personalized rates. The instructor should be available for questions and feedback. Do not hesitate to intervene when a student is having difficulty.

Skill Work

The strength of the system is that it allows the teacher to help specific students with particular problems. Once the class has started, the teacher is free to roam the courts and to help students who are having problems. Key points to remember in teaching basic skills include the following:

Volley

1. Watch the ball hit the racquet.
2. Footwork—Step across to hit the volley (a volley to the right should have a final step with the left foot).
3. Minimize backswing—Swing no farther back than the shoulder.
4. Punch the ball and follow through.
5. Never drop the racquet head below the wrist. Bend the knees instead.

6. Squeeze the racquet grip when making contact with the ball.

Ground Strokes

1. Change grips for the backhand and forehand.
2. Early backswing—Get the racquet back as soon as possible.
3. Set up with the side of the body to the net.
4. Contact the ball even with the front foot; do not wait until the ball gets into the body.
5. Contact the ball with the racquet perpendicular to the ground.
6. Follow through.
7. Keep the knees bent throughout.

Lobs

1. Set up exactly like ground strokes.
2. Open the racquet face (approximately 45 degrees).
3. Lift up through the swing and finish with a high follow-through.

Overheads

1. Racquet is in "backscratcher" position; get it there as soon as possible.
2. Side of body is turned toward the net.
3. Contact the ball in front of the body. Do not let it float overhead.

Serves

1. First and foremost, control the toss.
2. Use continental or backhand grip (this will cause a slice serve, which is the most consistent).
3. "Throw" the racquet at the ball; use plenty of wrist and elbow.
4. Follow through; the back foot (from the stance) should end up on the court.

Safety

Tennis is a safe sport. Most injuries that occur are self-inflicted, such as ankle sprains, muscle sprains, or blisters. A few precautions can help prevent unnecessary injuries. For example,

1. Warm up properly before beginning play.
2. Never leave loose balls lying around the court.
3. Never hit balls (especially serves) when the player opposite is not ready.
4. Communicate. Both players on a doubles team going for an overhead can cost the team a point and cause an injury.
5. Wear appropriate footwear.

Lead-Up Games, Modified Games, and Rainy-Day Activities

Practice is often enhanced, especially for advanced players, when stroke practice is conducted under gamelike conditions. Many students find it enjoyable to compete. The following drills can be done competitively.

Twenty-One

In the game of 21, both players must remain behind the base line. The ball is put into play when either player drops the ball and hits a ground stroke. From that point on, the game uses the same rules as tennis, except that neither player may volley.

Advanced players can include the rule that any ball landing in front of the service line is out, or the ball may be approached from behind and volleyed. The first player to accrue 21 points wins.

Approach Game

To practice approaching the net, players use half of the court, from doubles sideline to center service line. After starting with a ground stroke, the first player moves halfway to the service line. After returning the first ball, player 2 moves halfway to the service line. After their next shots, players move to the service line and then continue to close in as far as possible, hitting volleys and half volleys. The game may be played to any total, usually 10 or 15.

Lob-Smash

Begin with 1 player at the net and the other at the base line. Base-line players hit a lob, which is returned with an overhead. They play out the point and begin again. After 10 points, players change positions. The winner is the player with the most points after these 20 points have been played. Lob-smash can also be played with doubles.

Short Game

Players begin at the service lines and hit soft ground strokes. The ball may not land behind the service line. Regular tennis scoring can be used, or a point total can be set.

Return Drill

The return drill can be used to improve a player's return. One player practices returns while 3 to 5 players alternate serves. The receiver returns from the court (either ad or deuce) for the entire time. Servers get 2 serves, just like the real game, and play the point. Only the server gets a point when a rally is won. When a server gets a designated number of points (usually 4 or 5), the receiver and server exchange places, and all servers' scores return to 0. Each receiver thus gets at least 12 to 15 returns before rotating off. The next time this same player becomes the receiver, returns are made from the opposite court. A variation is to have all servers serve and volley.

Half-Court Volleys

Divide the court into halves (as in the Approach game). One player begins at the net, the other at the base line. The volleyer puts the ball into play, and the player at the base line must hit a passing shot (ground stroke). The ball must be kept in the half-court. Play to 10 points, switch places, and continue for 10 more points. As a variation, after the initial shot, the groundstroker may hit lobs and may take the net if the opportunity arises.

Backboard Practice

If wall space is available in the gymnasium, ground strokes or volleys can be hit against the gym wall.

Service Practice

The gymnasium is an excellent place for beginners to practice the toss. Any line on the gym floor can be substituted for the base line. Soft foam-rubber tennis balls are excellent for practice of the entire service motion in the gym.

Volleys

Without a net, players can practice volleys indoors. Have them stand 10 to 20 feet apart and hit soft volleys to each other.

Suggested Performance Objectives

Students should work with a partner. When an objective has been mastered to specification, have a partner (or instructor, where indicated) initial the task. The tasks are designed to be progressively more difficult. A student should therefore not proceed to a new task until all preliminary tasks have been completed. The court markings in Figure 21.7 will aid in the comprehension of many of the tasks. Students should refer to the diagram as needed until the markings are learned.

Volley

1. Without a racquet, assume a ready position (feet shoulder width apart, knees bent, weight forward, hands in front of the body). Have a partner toss tennis balls to the dominant side. Stepping with the opposite foot, reach forward and catch 5 consecutive balls thrown from a distance of 15 feet.
2. From the ready position, gripping the racquet at its head, and using proper footwork (instructor will demonstrate), hit 5 consecutive forehand volleys to your partner who feeds the balls from a distance of 15 feet. (Balls may not bounce.)
3. Same as task 2, but grip racquet just above the grip (5 consecutive).
4. Demonstrate to instructor the continental grip—the grip with which volleys are hit.
5. Same as task 2, but use the continental grip, and grip the racquet on the grip (5 consecutive).
6. Same as task 2, but use the backhand side of racquet (5 consecutive).
7. Same as task 2, but grip racquet just above the grip and use backhand (5 consecutive).
8. Same as task 5, but use backhand (5 consecutive).
9. Stand halfway between the net and the service line. Partner or instructor will stand across the net at the base line and drop and hit balls at you. Volley 8 of 10 forehands across the net into the singles court.
10. Same as task 9, but use backhand (8 of 10).
11. Standing as in task 9, partner will randomly hit to your forehand and backhand side. Volley 8 of 10 balls into the singles court.
12. Same as task 11, but balls must land in the singles court behind the service line (8 of 10).
13. From a distance of at least 6 feet from a wall, hit 15 consecutive volleys above a 3-foot mark. The ball may not touch the ground.

Ground Strokes

1. Demonstrate to the instructor the eastern forehand and backhand grips.
2. Without a ball, practice 20 consecutive alternate forehand and backhand ground strokes, alternating the grip each time.
3. Standing behind the base line, drop and hit 10 consecutive forehands across the net into the singles court.
4. Same as task 3, but use backhand (10 consecutive).
5. Stand behind the base line. Partner stands 20 feet away and bounces balls to your forehand. Hit 5

of 7 forehands across the net into the singles court.
6. Same as task 5, but use backhand (5 of 7).
7. Standing behind the base line with a partner across the net, have partner hit or toss balls to your forehand. Hit 8 of 10 forehands across the net into the singles court.
8. Same as task 7, but use backhand (8 of 10).
9. Same as tasks 7 and 8, but have partner toss randomly to your forehand and backhand (8 of 10).
10. Standing behind a line 27 feet from the backboard, hit 10 consecutive ground strokes that strike the backboard on or above the white line, which is 3 feet above the ground.
11. Same as task 10, but hit 20 consecutive ground strokes.
12. With a partner (or instructor) at opposite base line, rally 20 consecutive ground strokes (ball may bounce more than once on each side of the net).

Lobs

1. From the base line, drop and hit 5 consecutive forehand lobs into the opposite singles court behind the service line. Balls must be hit high enough so that your partner, from volley position, cannot touch them with the racquet.
2. Same as task 1, but hit backhand lobs (5 consecutive).
3. With partner tossing or hitting balls from the other side of the net, hit 5 consecutive forehand lobs into the opposite singles court behind the service line.
4. Same as task 3, but hit backhand lobs (5 consecutive).

Serves

1. Demonstrate to the teacher the proper service stance and grip.
2. Using an overhead throwing motion, throw 5 consecutive balls into the service court from the base line on both deuce and ad sides (10 total).
3. Demonstrate proper toss technique to the instructor.
4. Lay the racquet on the ground with the face 6 inches in front of your front foot. Using the non-racquet hand, toss balls approximately 2 feet higher than your head, 3 of 5 must hit the racquet face or frame.
5. Make your normal toss into the air, and using the racquet hand, without a racquet, come

through the service motion and hit 5 consecutive balls with the palm of your hand.

6. With a racquet in the "back-scratcher" position, hit 5 of 7 serves into the proper service court.

7. Demonstrate to the instructor an acceptable full backswing for the service.

8. Same as task 6, but use the full backswing to hit 5 of 7 serves into the forehand service court.

9. Place 4 empty tennis ball cans in the outside corner of the forehand service box. Serve until you have knocked over 1 can.

10. Same as task 9, but place cans in the inside corner.

11. Same as task 9, but place cans in the backhand court.

12. Same as task 9, but place cans in the inside corner of the backhand court.

Overheads

1. Using the service grip and standing in service area (at the net), have a partner hit short lobs. Allow the ball to bounce. Hit 3 of 5 forehand overheads into singles court.

2. Same as task 1, but hit the ball before it bounces (3 of 5).

3. Same as task 1, but stand behind the base line (3 of 5).

4. Same as task 1, but hit 6 consecutive balls.

5. Same as task 2, but hit 6 consecutive balls.

6. Same as task 3, but hit 6 consecutive balls.

REFERENCES AND SUGGESTED READINGS

Badminton

Bloss, M. V. 1994. *Badminton.* 7th ed. Dubuque, IA: Brown & Benchmark.

Mood, D. P., Musker, F. F., and Rink, J. E. 1991. *Sports and Recreational Activities for Men and Women.* 10th ed. St. Louis: Mosby.

National Association for Girls and Women in Sport. 1982. *Tennis-Badminton-Squash Guide.* Reston, VA: AAHPERD.

Sysler, B. L., and Fox, E. R. 1978. *Lifetime Sports for the College Student.* 3rd ed. Dubuque, IA: Kendall/Hunt Publishing Co.

Frisbee

Caporali, J. M. 1988. The ultimate alternative. *Journal of Physical Education, Recreation, and Dance.* 59(9): 98–101.

Danna, M., and Poynter, D. 1978. *Frisbee Players' Handbook.* Santa Barbara, CA: Parachuting Publications.

Kalb, I., and Kennedy, T. 1982. *Ultimate: Fundamentals of the Sport.* Santa Barbara, CA: Revolutionary Publication.

Roddick, D., and Boda, T. (eds.). 1986. *The Discourse: A Manual for Students and Teachers of the Frisbee Disc Arts.* 2nd ed. San Gabriel, CA: Wham-O-Sports Promotion.

Tips, C. 1979. *Frisbee by the Masters.* Millbrae, CA: Celestial Arts.

Tips, C., and Roddick, D. 1979. *Frisbee Disc Sports and Games.* Millbrae, CA: Celestial Arts.

Racquetball

Allsen, P. E., and P. Witbeck. 1992. *Racquetball,* 5th ed. Dubuque, IA: Brown & Benchmark.

Brumfield, C., and Bairstow, J. 1978. *Off the Wall.* New York: The Dial Press.

Kittleson, S. 1993. *Teaching Racquetball: Steps to Success.* Champaign, IL: Human Kinetics Publishers.

Liles, L., and Neimeyer, R. A. 1993. *Winning Racquetball.* Dubuque, IA: Brown & Benchmark.

Pangrazi, R. P. 1987. *Racquetball, Sport for Life Series.* Glenview, IL: Scott, Foresman & Co.

Rhythmic Activity

Harris, J. A., Pittman, A. M., and Waller, M. S. 1988. *Dance a While.* New York: Macmillan Publishing Co.

Jensen, C. R., and Jensen, M. B. 1973. *Square Dancing.* Provo, UT: Brigham Young University Press.

Livingston, P. 1981. *The Complete Book of Country Swing and Western Dance.* Garden City, NY: Doubleday & Co.

Ray, O. M. 1992. *Encyclopedia of Line Dances: The Steps that Came and Stayed.* Reston, VA: AAHPERD.

Tennis

The following publications contain material pertaining to rules and regulations: *The Rules of Tennis, Rules of Tennis and Cases and Decisions, A Friend at Court (Rules, Cases, Decisions, Officials, and Officiating),* and *The Code (Unwritten Rules Players Should Follow in Unofficiated Matches).* All may be purchased from the United States Tennis Association Education and Research Center, Publications Department, 729 Alexander Road, Princeton, NJ 08540.

Braden, V., and Bruns, B. 1977. *Vic Braden's Tennis for the Future.* Boston: Little, Brown & Co.

Brown, J. *Tennis, Steps to Success.* 1989. Champaign, IL: Human Kinetics Publishers.

Johnson, J. D. 1993. *Tennis,* 6th ed. Dubuque, IA: Brown & Benchmark.

Mood, D. P., Musker, F. F., and Rink, J. E. 1991. *Sports and Recreational Activities for Men and Women.* 10th ed. St. Louis: Mosby.

22 Outdoor Adventure Activities

Many physical education programs have added popular adventure activities to the curriculum over the past 10 years. Rock climbing, caving, canoeing, orienteering, and backpacking are just a few examples. Many students are interested in these activities, which are challenging and provide a sense of risk and adventure. Activities that can be added to the curriculum in order to provide a degree of risk and adventure are ropes course activities, orienteering, and group initiative games.

ROPES COURSE ACTIVITIES

Ropes course activities involve obstacles that use ropes, cables, logs, trees, ladders, tires, swings, cargo nets, rings, and other equipment to present students with a challenge that usually has a degree of controlled risk. These obstacles require students to climb, swing, crawl, and balance themselves. Beneath many of the obstacles are water, mud, people, cargo nets, and trees. All of the activities are completed with student spotters or a safety belay line of some type under the direct supervision of the teacher. The activities can be linked together in sequence, or they can be utilized as separate challenges. Certain activities require strength and endurance, while others require balance and coordination. The ropes course activities can function as lead-up activities for rock climbing, caving, rappelling, or other adventure activities.

Teachers need to be certain that students begin with activities containing little risk. Student safety is always the most important factor. Generally, the beginning ropes course activities are situated close to the ground with many spotters available, thereby assuring students that little danger is involved. As they gain knowledge, experience, physical skill, and confidence, students can move to higher and more challenging obstacles. Teachers need to be aware of varying ability levels of students and not require all students to attempt the same activities unless they are ready for the obstacle. Some students will display fear of these types of activities and should be encouraged rather than pushed.

Ropes course activities, just like any other adventure activity, can be risky and have the potential for physical injury if safety factors are overlooked. The authors recommend that teachers seek the advice of experienced ropes course builders before constructing any of these activities (see the suggested readings at the end of this section). Ropes course activities can be built into the existing environment, or posts and logs can be placed in the ground. The following are examples of ropes course activities that could be utilized in a program.

Commando Crawl

In this activity, the student crawls across the top of a 2-inch manila hawser rope by placing the chest on the rope and passing the rope under the body (Figure 22.1). One foot is hooked over the top of the rope and the other leg hangs down for balance. The student slowly pulls his or her way across the rope by using the arms and the top leg. The student should be spotted on both sides of the rope in case of a fall. If a fall does occur, the spotters should catch the stu-

FIGURE 22.1 Commando crawl

dent and slowly lower him or her to the ground. The rope should be secured to 2 trees 4 to 5 feet high above the ground. A bowline knot can be used on 1 side of the rope, and the opposite side should be wrapped around the tree and tied off with 2 half-hitches. Wooden blocks may be secured to the trees below the rope to prevent the rope from slipping.

Tire Swing

Students swing across a set of tires that are secured to a top rope or cable (Figure 22.2). The tires are set at varying heights above the ground anywhere from 3 to 4 feet high. The tires should be 3 to 4 feet apart. The top cable should be 10 to 12 feet above the ground. To prevent a fall, spotters should be placed on both sides of the student as they proceed.

Kitten Crawl

Students crawl along 2 parallel inclined ropes that are secured at 5 feet high at 1 end and at 2 feet high at the other end. Students should be on all fours and can slowly crawl up or down the rope (Figure 22.3). Spotters should be aware that the participants can

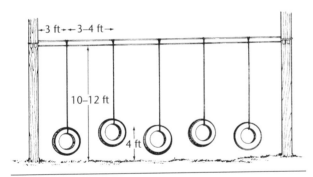

FIGURE 22.2 Tire swing

FIGURE 22.3 Kitten crawl

fall through the middle of the 2 ropes as well as over the sides. Wooden blocks can be used to prevent the rope from slipping down on the secured ends. The height of the ropes can be varied according to ability levels of the participants.

Two-Rope Bridge

Two parallel ropes about 5 to 6 feet apart are secured to trees or posts. The students stand sideways on the bottom rope and hold on to the top rope with their hands. They slowly slide their way across the rope (Figure 22.4). The height of the bottom rope should be less than 5 to 6 feet for beginners. If the height of the bottom rope is higher than 6 feet, then a belay or safety system should be used. A 15-foot swami belt or waist loop of 1-inch tubular nylon flat rope can be wrapped around the student's waist and attached with a carabineer to a belay line. The top of the belay line can be attached with a carabineer to the top rope of the bridge. Spotters can be used for lower bridges, and they should follow the participant across the rope and be ready for a fall.

Three-Rope Bridge

The 3-rope Burma bridge has been used in many areas for crossing various ravines, rivers, and mountain passes. It consists of two parallel ropes about waist high for handholds and a bottom rope to walk on (Figure 22.5). A number of V-shaped ropes should be placed about 2 feet apart along the bridge to support all 3 ropes. A rope or cable across the top of the bridge should be constructed for attaching a safety line. A swami belt can be attached to the student and

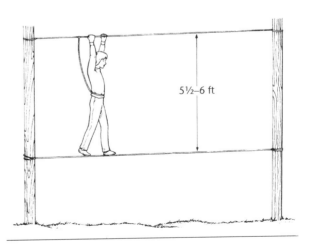

FIGURE 22.4 Two-rope bridge

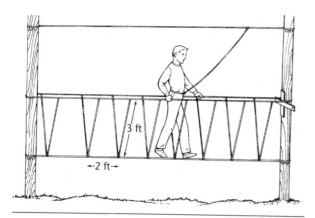

FIGURE 22.5   Three-rope bridge

then clipped to the top line with carabineers and a piece of nylon webbing. The height of the bridge can vary; it can be low or high depending on the local area. It is exciting to place the bridge over a natural obstacle if possible. It is important to use wooden blocks to prevent the ropes from slipping in order to assure that the ropes are kept tight.

Tension Traverse

The student balances and moves across a rope suspended between 2 trees. A top support rope is attached to 1 tree and the student applies tension on this rope for balance while sliding across the rope. The student should slide sideways across the rope. One hand should hold the support rope at the waist and the other hand should hold the rope above the head (Figure 22.6). The bottom rope is 2 to 3 feet above the ground and should always be taut. Again, wooden blocks should be used to prevent the rope from slipping down. Spotters should be used for

safety, and the students should be instructed to let go of the support rope and jump off if they are going to fall. If they hold on to the top rope while falling, they will swing into the tree or post.

Triangle Tension Traverse

This activity is similar to the tension traverse and adds 2 more sides to the activity. The bottom rope is placed in a triangle and the student starts at one intersection of the triangle (Figure 22.7). The student balances and moves around the triangle with a top support rope similar to the straight tension traverse. Spotters should be used for safety as the students move around the triangle. The height of the bottom rope should be 4 to 5 feet and it should be taut and blocked to prevent slipping.

Balance Beam

The balance beam is a log attached between 2 trees or posts anywhere from 5 to 10 feet high (Figure 22.8). It is a good obstacle that can be used as a bridge between 2 other rope activities. The students simply walk across the beam. If several beams are used in a course, they can be constructed at varying heights. If the beam is higher than 5 feet, a top safety belay line should be used. If the beam is lower than 5 feet, then student spotters are necessary for safety.

Inclined Log

The inclined log is simply a balance beam that is placed at an angle (Figure 22.9). It is effective for beginners to walk on an obstacle that moves from the

FIGURE 22.6   Tension traverse

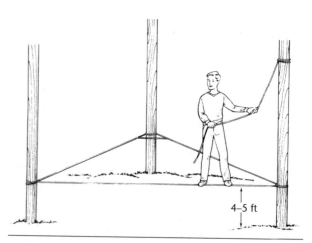

FIGURE 22.7   Triangle tension traverse

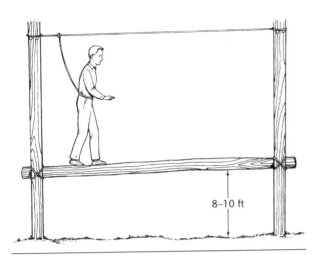

FIGURE 22.8   Balance beam

FIGURE 22.10   Swinging log

FIGURE 22.9   Inclined log

vent any slipping. Rubber tires can be nailed to the trees to prevent damage from the moving log. Participants need to move carefully to avoid falling on the log itself. Spotters can be used to help the students keep their balance.

Cargo Net Jump

Students move up an inclined log to a jumping platform and then jump into a cargo net in the tucked position. The cargo net should be 1-inch manila rope with a small mesh (Figure 22.11). A rope ladder could

ground to a higher level. Students can walk up the log, bear crawl on all fours, or hug the log as they move up, depending on their comfort level. A moving belay should be set up slightly off-center from the log so that students will not fall into the log. As students move up the height of the log, the belay person or spotters should move with them. The log should be notched to enhance the footing and nailed and lashed to the trees or posts for support.

Swinging Log

Students walk along a moving log that is suspended from trees by ropes (Figure 22.10). The log should never be more than 1 foot above the ground because falls will be frequent in this activity. All rocks, stumps, and objects should be cleared away from the area. The log should be notched where the ropes are attached to hold them in place. The upper attachment of the ropes should be blocked in order to pre-

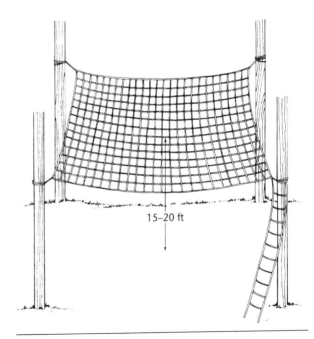

FIGURE 22.11   Cargo net jump

be used to exit the net. The net can be secured 15 to 20 feet above the ground or less, and the jumping platform should be about 5 feet higher than the net. The corners of the net should be secured and blocked to avoid slipping. These secured corners should be inspected regularly before each use. The instructor needs to be careful with students on a jumping platform. Students should be instructed to jump into the center of the net, and only 1 student should be allowed in the net at a time.

Giant's Ladder

The students balance, jump, and swing up a giant ladder that is made of logs. The ladder encourages development of balance, strength, agility, and endurance. Students stand and balance on the first rung and then jump to the next rung and land on the chest or abdominal area (Figure 22.12). The feet swing free below the rung; students then pull upward onto the rung and get ready to move up to the next rung. The rungs get farther apart as the student moves higher on the ladder. The second rung is 4 to 5 feet from the first, and the third rung is 5 to 6 feet up the ladder. Students must be belayed throughout the climb. A top cable should be used to attach the

belay rope. The instructor should keep a tight belay on students so they do not swing into any of the logs.

GROUP INITIATIVE ACTIVITIES

Group initiative activities are physical and mental challenges that require the cooperation and joint efforts of a group of students. They require the group to think, plan, and execute a strategy for solving the challenge. Teamwork and cooperation are necessary. These activities force students to work together. Some of the activities involve risk, excitement, and adventure; thus, proper safety and supervision strategies must be implemented. These activities can be completed indoors or outdoors. They can be conducted in conjunction with ropes course activities or as totally separate activities. Many of them require a few special props in order to be effective.

Electric Fence

The object is to get a group of students over the "electric fence" without touching the fence (Figure 22.13). A piece of rope is stretched between 2 trees. The rope should be 5 feet off the ground. The students should

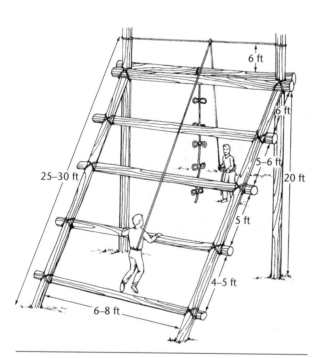

FIGURE 22.12　Giant's ladder

FIGURE 22.13　Electric fence

be given a 4 by 4 beam that is about 8 feet long to help them. Students are not allowed to use the support trees, nor are they allowed to reach under the rope. They can reach over the top of the rope. There are many solutions. A good procedure is to have the group hold the beam on their shoulders and get a few stronger people over first. Then they can hold the beam on the opposite side for the others.

Boardwalk

This involves the use of four 2 by 4 boards that are 10 to 12 feet long. Two sets of 2 boards are connected by ropes and eye bolts. About 10 students stand on 2 of the boards and then hold the other boards at about waist level (Figure 22.14). Working together, the stu-

dents alternate lifting the boards and move forward as a group. All must keep their feet on the boards. It can be a race or just a challenge to work together.

Platforms

A group of 6 to 8 students stands on the first of 3 platforms. The platforms are 14 feet apart in a straight line. The students are given a 12-foot board and a 4-foot board. The challenge is to move the group from platform to platform without touching the ground with either the boards or any person in the group (Figure 22.15). The best solution is to extend the smaller board out from the platform about 2 feet and get the entire group to stand on this board. Then, a smaller person can walk out on the board and place the 12-foot board to the next platform and walk across. After 3 or 4 people have reached the second platform, the boards need to be switched so the smaller one is now on the second platform. This process continues until all students are on the third platform.

Nitro Crossing

The object is to get each member of a group to swing across an area with a bucket of "nitro" (water) without spilling it. The swing rope must be attached to some type of tree limb or cross board that provides a good swinging area. Two trip boards need to be placed about 1 foot off the ground on either side of

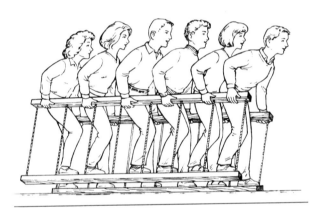

FIGURE 22.14   Boardwalk

FIGURE 22.15   Platforms

FIGURE 22.16   Nitro crossing

the swing area (Figure 22.16). The trip boards can be on top of cones or blocks of wood. Half of the group starts on 1 side and half starts on the other side. They try to swing their group members to the opposite side without spilling the nitro.

The Beam and the Wall

The object of this activity is to move a group of students over a log beam (Figure 22.17) about 8 feet above the ground or a solid wooden wall (Figure

FIGURE 22.17   The beam

22.18) that is 12 to 14 feet above the ground. The group cannot use the support trees or posts. They must work together to support each member up and over the obstacle. The wall can be built with a walkway on the back side for the students to stand. Once students get to the top, they can reach down and help others up.

Faith Fall and Trust Dive

The individual falls backward into the arms of a group of students. The individual stands on a balance beam or similar elevated object. The group lines up shoulder to shoulder in 2 opposite and facing lines (Figures 22.19 and 22.20). The arms are extended and alternated with the arms of the person directly across wrists. Do not allow students to lock wrists because the partners may bump heads. The individual falls when the catching line is ready.

Human Circle Pass

The group forms a tight circle about 6 feet in diameter, with the arms up in a catching position. One person is put in the middle and closes his or her eyes.

FIGURE 22.18   The wall

When ready, the person falls backward, forward, or sideways into the hands of the group members. They support and pass the individual around the circle. Everyone takes a turn being in the center of the circle.

Human Line Pass

Students sit in a line on the ground with legs straight out, feet touching the person in front of them. The first person in line stands and sits back into the hands of the sitting people who pass the person backward over their heads. The process continues until all people have been passed. Spotters can be placed on each side of the line to ensure safety.

Lightbulb Change

The group is in the dark and cannot proceed until the lightbulb is changed. The goal is to form a pyramid high enough to reach the ceiling (13 to 15 feet) to change the bulb (Figure 22.21). A piece of tape can be used to show the highest spot reached by the group. A wall with no windows or protruding objects should be used. Spotters can also be used to make sure that no one falls backward.

FIGURE 22.19   Faith fall

FIGURE 22.20   Trust dive

FIGURE 22.21   Lightbulb or high water

High Water

This is similar to the lightbulb change, but the groups compete against one another to see which can make the highest mark on the wall with a piece of chalk or tape.

Sasquatch Race

Two groups are formed and are instructed to make a moving object with a specified number of feet and hands on the ground. Everybody must be part of the group and joined to the others. After the sasquatch is built, the 2 groups race to a finish line.

Platform Stand

A platform with 20- to 24-inch sides can be used as the base of support. The object is to get as many people as possible standing on the platform simultaneously (Figure 22.22). The pose must be held for 8 seconds.

Stream Crossing

Students must move from 1 side of the area to the other without touching the floor. They are given small carpet squares on which to move across an imaginary stream. Fewer than the necessary number of squares are handed out, however, so students have

FIGURE 22.22   Platform stand

to pass the squares back and forth in order to get their team across. The first team to move all members across the stream is declared the winner.

Height Alignment

Members of the group keep their eyes closed and are instructed to align themselves in a single-file line from shortest person to tallest person. The students cannot talk and can use only their hands to figure out the arrangement.

ORIENTEERING

Orienteering is a challenging outdoor adventure activity that combines cross-country running and the ability to read a map and use a compass. It has been called the thinking sport because rapid decisions need to be made in determining which route to follow so that a minimum of time and energy is used. Ideally, the orienteering competition should take place in a wilderness area that is not familiar to the participants. Orienteering events can be set up for beginners, novices, and experts, thus enabling people of all ages and abilities to take part and find success in these activities. The need for both physical and mental skills can result in an enjoyable experience for all students and members of a family.

Orienteering activities can be easily modified and adapted to secondary physical education programs. Many activities can be completed in a classroom or gymnasium or on the school grounds.* Teachers can use compasses and homemade maps of the school grounds to develop a challenging unit. A nearby park or a vacant lot can add great variety to orienteering courses.

Sequence of Skills

The basic skills involved in orienteering include reading a topographical map, using a compass, and pacing various distances. Since many students have had little experience with these skills, it is important to

*Special thanks to John W. Horstman, Meadow Lake School, Robbinsdale, Minnesota, for many of the orienteering activities.

introduce new information and terminology slowly. Students can perform many of the activities with a partner, so there will be two heads working together on a problem. Teachers can include a variety of maps, a compass, and new pacing activities each day to keep the students challenged. Many activity types and hands-on experiences should be incorporated in the unit. Competitive events can be added after students begin to understand the basic map and compass skills. The block plan at the end of this unit will provide some ideas for the sequencing of learning activities.

Learning Activities

Compass Activities

Parts of the Compass.   Make the students aware of the basic parts of the compass and how the instrument works (Figure 22.23).

Compass Bearings and Directions.   Have the students complete the directions and degrees in Figure 22.24.

Following a Bearing.   Discuss how to hold the compass properly. Give students a bearing to find and follow. Have them stand in 1 line facing the instructor. Call out a bearing and have them rotate their bodies in place until they are facing the bearing direction.

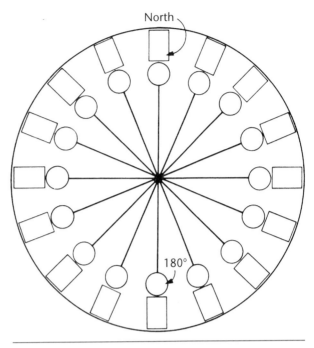

FIGURE 22.24   Compass bearings and directions

Landmarks.   The teacher calls out various visible landmarks, and students shoot a bearing from where they are standing to the landmark.

Forming a Triangle.   Place a penny or other small object on the ground. Set any bearing less than 90 degrees. Walk 10 paces on that bearing. Add 120 de-

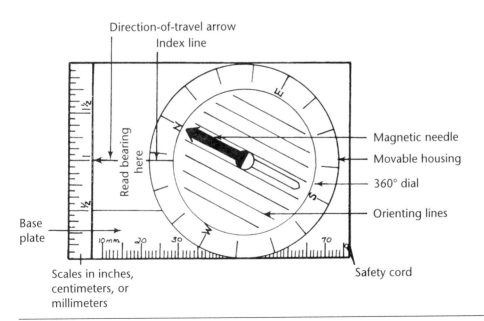

FIGURE 22.23   Parts of a compass

grees and walk another 10 paces. Repeat the procedure again and end up where you started. This drill can be repeated with another bearing and a different number of paces.

Forming a Square. This is basically the same as "Forming a Triangle" except that 90-degree bearings are added each time, and 4 sides are formed. The distance must be the same each time.

Numbers and Numerals. Tape the numbers 1 to 10 on the floor in scattered positions around the gymnasium (Figure 22.25). Next, tape the Roman numerals I to X in scattered positions on the gymnasium walls. The students begin by standing on any of the numbers on the floor and shooting a bearing to the corresponding numeral on the wall. This drill can be made competitive by trying for the fastest time and correct bearing.

Forming a Christmas Tree. On a piece of graph paper, have students place a dot in the southeast quadrant of the paper. From this starting dot, have them draw a line the distances shown in Figure 22.26 and on the appropriate bearing.

Map Bearings. Students learn to determine the bearing between points on a map. The teacher puts several points on a map and then tells the students to

Bearing	Distance (cm)		Bearing	Distance (cm)
1. 269	2.2			
2. 2	2.7		9. 136	6.3
3. 266	4.9		10. 293	1.9
4. 30	6.5		11. 141	5.2
5. 246	2.6		12. 284	2.4
6. 34	5.0		13. 125	5.2
7. 244	2.0		14. 271	5.1
8. 37	4.6		15. 179	2.7

FIGURE 22.26 Forming a Christmas tree

find the bearing and distance between the points. Ten numbered points might be shown, and students can find the bearing and distance from 1 to 2, from 2 to 3, and so forth. Advanced orienteering can include a discussion of magnetic declination and the addition or subtraction of declination.

Destination Unknown. Divide the class into 4 teams. Each team follows the given bearings and paces (Figure 22.27). All teams should end up at the same destination.

Schoolyard Compass Game and Competitive Compass Game. These are two challenging com-

FIGURE 22.25 Numbers and numerals

Scorecard

Number	Bearing
1–I	_____
2–II	_____
3–III	_____
4–IV	_____
5–V	_____
6–VI	_____
7–VII	_____
8–VIII	_____
9–IX	_____
10–X	_____

Divide students into four groups. Each team should follow the given bearings and paces, which will bring them all to the same destination.

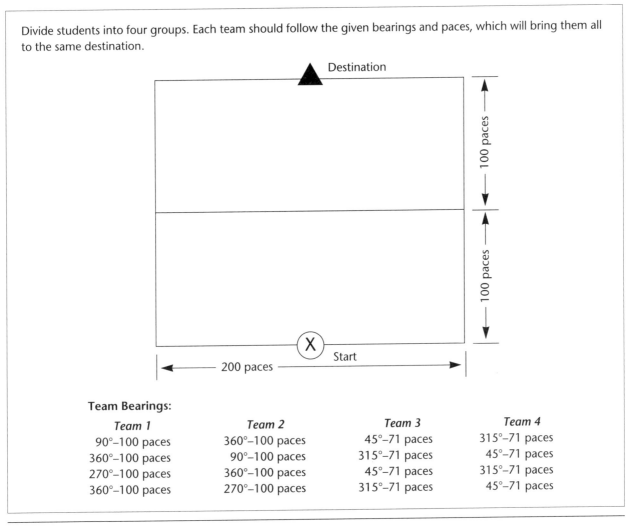

FIGURE 22.27 Destination unknown

Team Bearings:

Team 1	Team 2	Team 3	Team 4
90°–100 paces	360°–100 paces	45°–71 paces	315°–71 paces
360°–100 paces	90°–100 paces	315°–71 paces	45°–71 paces
270°–100 paces	360°–100 paces	45°–71 paces	315°–71 paces
360°–100 paces	270°–100 paces	315°–71 paces	45°–71 paces

pass games that are available from The Silva Company.* The games are inexpensive and can be set up easily in a school situation.

Map Activities

Mapping the School. Students draw up rough maps of the school grounds with all of the various buildings, fields, and identification points. These maps can later be used in orienteering competitions.

Map Squares. Cut up several topographical maps of the local area into small squares. Students try to locate the cut squares on an uncut map. Have the stu-

dents identify points of interest, symbols, distances, contour lines, vegetation, roads, water, and so forth.

Map Symbol Relay. Draw a map symbol on 1 side of an index card and write the name of a different symbol on the back of the card. A duplicate set of cards is necessary for each team in the relay (4 teams means 4 sets of cards). The game begins with the cards on 1 side of the gym and the teams on the opposite side. The teacher calls out the first symbol, such as a school. The first member of the team runs to the cards, finds the symbol, and then runs back to the team. The name of the next symbol to be found is on the back of the card with the school symbol. The game continues until all of the cards are played. Students waiting in line can be reviewing symbols. Students who select the wrong symbol must run back and find the correct symbol.

*The Silva Company, 2466 State Road 39 North, LaPorte, Indiana 46350.

Taking a Trip. Label 10 to 15 points on several topographical maps, and have students calculate the actual distance between a certain number of points. They can calculate map distance and actual mileage. Next, have the students estimate how many days would be necessary to complete the trip. They should be able to describe what the terrain is like and where the water stops are located.

Contour Identification. Have students identify various mountainous and hilly areas from the way those areas look on a contour map. Figure 22.28 is an example of contour problems.

Map Problems. Map activities, such as Figure 22.29, can be made up for a local situation.

Dot-to-Dot Hike. Students start at the X in the northwest corner (Figure 22.30) and draw in the figure by following the directions. Students can develop their own dot-to-dot hike making other figures.

Pacing Activities

Distance by Pace. Orienteerers must be able to judge distance by their pace. One pace equals 2 steps. A good drill for determining the length of pace is to set up a course that is 100 feet long. Students walk, jog, or run the course, and count the number of times that the right foot hits the ground. The length of the course (100 feet) is then divided by the number of paces in order to determine length of pace. Pace is usually rounded off to the nearest 6 inches. Pace will vary with walking, jogging, and running.

Contour Identification Problem

Have the students compare some actual terrain contours with the map representations. Training models are available from Silva, and the teacher can develop a number of contour representations for learning activities. The following are a few examples:

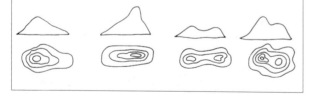

FIGURE 22.28 Contour problems

Distance by Time. One-mile courses can be set up in a variety of terrain, such as open road, open field, open woods, vegetated areas, dense woods, and mountainous areas. Students cover these areas by walking or jogging and record their times. The ability to cover a given distance at a consistent pace can be used later for competitive meets.

Competitive Orienteering Events

After students have received instruction in the use of the compass, maps, and pacing, competitive events can be introduced. Students should understand that they can compete against the environment, themselves, their peers, and elapsed time. It is not necessary to win the event to be successful.

Cross-Country or Point-to-Point Orienteering

Ten checkpoints are set up over the entire school grounds or park area. Teachers develop a map of the area to be covered, and duplicate maps are made up for all participants. Each participant uses a map and compass to find the checkpoints as quickly as possible. The compass is not necessary if unavailable. Decisions about the best route must be made quickly as participants begin. Several master maps should be set out with the locations of the checkpoints. Participants copy the checkpoints from the master map onto their own map. The time spent in copying down the checkpoints can be included in the overall accumulated time.

Each checkpoint should have a secret letter, word, or name that students must record on some type of card to show that they actually visited the checkpoint. In regulation meets, a coded punch with a number or letter is used at each control site. These punches are available from The Silva Company, but they are not a necessity. Checkpoints can be a boundary cone, an index card, an envelope, or something similar.

Score Orienteering

In score orienteering, each checkpoint has a designated point value. The checkpoints that are hardest to find and farthest away from the starting point are assigned the highest point totals. The object of the event is to accumulate the most points within a set time. Students are given a map of the area on which they copy the locations of the checkpoints from a master map. Students must visit as many sites as pos-

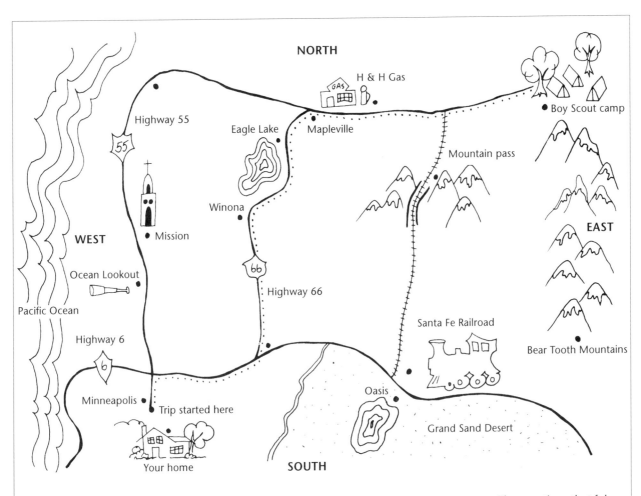

The dotted line on the map shows how you drove from your home to the Boy Scout camp. The questions that follow are about the map. Circle the best answer on this sheet.

1. When you started your trip, in what direction did you go first?
   North   South   East   West

2. If you had walked west of Minneapolis, what would you have come to?
   Great Sand Desert   Ocean Lookout   Pacific Ocean

3. When you got to Highway 66, what town did you pass first?
   Mapleville   Winona   H & H Gas

4. The mission is _____ of the Pacific Ocean.
   North   South   East   West

5. The Santa Fe Railroad runs _____ and _____ .
   North   South   East   West

6. The Scout camp is _____ of H & H Gas.
   North   South   East   West

7. The oasis is _____ of Highway 6.
   North   South   East   West

8. From the ocean lookout, what direction is the Bear Tooth mountain range?
   North   South   East   West

9. The first town west of the Scout camp is:
   Winona   H & H Gas   Mapleville

10. In the winter the birds fly
    North   South   East   West

FIGURE 22.29 Map problems

451

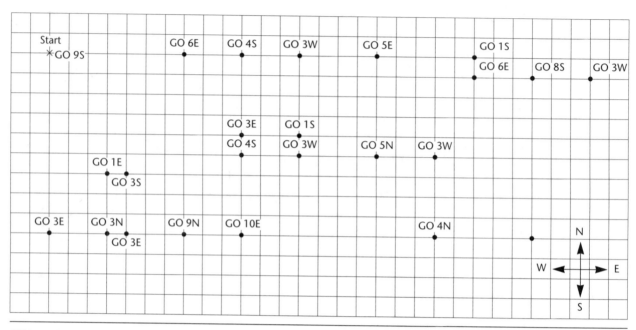

FIGURE 22.30 Dot-to-dot hike

sible within the time limit and then return to the starting point. If they are late, they can be disqualified or assessed a penalty. Students use some type of standard card to record the clue at each checkpoint that they visit.

Descriptive Orienteering

This type of event requires a compass and pacing skills instead of a map. Students attempt to find the

checkpoints as quickly as possible by following a bearing (90 degrees), a distance (50 yards), and a descriptive clue (small tree). The descriptive clue can be eliminated with more advanced participants. Students start at a designated master point and return to that point each time before starting toward the next point. In this way, teachers at the master point can monitor student progress throughout the meet. The checkpoints can all have letters, words, or team names. Each student is given a sheet similar to the

---

Orienteering 1

In the Answers column, fill in the key word or letter that you find at each checkpoint.

Checkpoint	Bearing	Description	Distance	Answers
1	90°	Backstop	50 yd	
2	180°	Goal post	100 m	
3	230°	Cottonwood	200 ft	
4	160°	Irrigation	35 yd	
5	341°	Hoop	75 m	
6	45°	Palo verde	400 ft	
7	106°	Trash barrel	150 yd	
8	270°	Power pole	250 ft	
9	78°	Fence post	350 yd	
10	200°	Jumping pit	40 m	

FIGURE 22.31 Descriptive orienteering sheet

one shown in Figure 22.31. A more challenging variation is to give students only the bearing and distance to 1 checkpoint. When they find that checkpoint, they will find the bearing and distance posted for the next checkpoint. Students must find each checkpoint to get directions to the next point. Students can be started at different checkpoints.

Block Plan

Figure 22.32 is a sample block plan that offers a suggested 15-day unit for orienteering. The activities recommended in the block plan are available in this section or in Darst and Armstrong (1991).

Suggested Performance Objectives

These objectives could be used in a middle school unit on orienteering.

1. Identify the compass points.
2. Name the parts of a compass.
3. Find a compass bearing on a map.
4. Follow a compass bearing on the ground.
5. Shoot bearings on key points.
6. Identify map symbols.
7. Identify map distances.
8. Determine pace for 100 yards.
9. Form a triangle using 3 bearings.
10. Form a square using 4 bearings.

1.	2.	3.	4.	5.
Introduction	*Review*	*Review*	*Review*	*Review*
What is orienteering?	Directions and degrees	Maps, symbols, etc.	Compass and bearings	Map bearings
Brief history				Map symbols
Directions and degrees	*Teach*	*Teach*	*Teach*	
Dot-to-dot problems	Maps, symbols, scales,	Parts of compass	Landmark bearings	*Teach*
Compass rose activity	contours	How to hold	Map bearings	Pacing
	Activities	*Activities*	*Activities*	*Activities*
	Map the school	Taking a bearing	Boy Scout map	Distance by pace
	Map squares	Dial a bearing	problem	Triangle game
	Contour identification	Magnetic influence	Sea adventure	Square game
			Christmas tree	Map symbol relay
6.	**7.**	**8.**	**9.**	**10.**
Review	*Review*	*Teach*	*Review*	*Review*
Pacing	Orienteering	Magnetic declination	Pacing	Declination
			Bearings	
Teach	*Activity*	*Activities*	Orienteering	*Activities*
Orienteering	Descriptive meet—	Declination problems		Descriptive meet
Point-to-point	Have students return	Meridian map and	*Activity*	(short)
Score	to master table each	compass fun	Point-to-point meet	Clues picked up at the
Descriptive	time for the next	Point-to-point activity		next control
Relay	bearing, clue, and	Schoolyard compass		Competitive compass
	distance.	game		game, or pacing by
Activities				time and distance
Taking a Trip				
Numbers and				
Numerals				
Destination Unknown				
11.	**12.**	**13.**	**14.**	**15.**
Review	*Activities*			
Materials for written	Relay orienteering	Written examination	Final score orienteering	Final point-to-point
exam	meet		exam meet	orienteering meet
	Schoolyard compass	Pacing—distance by		
Activities	game and competi-	time	(Off-campus if	(Off-campus if
Score orienteering	tive compass game		possible)	possible)
meet (20 min)	for skill test			
Landmark bearings for				
skill test				

FIGURE 22.32   Orienteering block plan

11. Complete an orienteering course in a time designated by the teacher.
    Standard no. 1 = 5 points
    Standard no. 2 = 3 points
    Standard no. 3 = 1 point
12. Take a 10-question exam on orienteering.
    Score: 100% = 5 points
             90% = 4 points
             80% = 3 points
             70% = 2 points
             60% = 1 point

REFERENCES AND SUGGESTED READINGS

Darst, P., and Armstrong, G. 1991. *Outdoor Adventure Activities for School and Recreation Programs*. Prospect Heights, IL: Waveland Press.

Fluegelman, A. (ed.). 1976. *The New Games Book*. Garden City, NY: Doubleday & Co.

Fluegelman, A. 1981. *More New Games*. Englewood Cliffs, NJ: Prentice-Hall Publishing Co.

Gilchrist, J. 1973. *Teaching Orienteering*. Willowdale, ON: Canadian Orienteering Service.

Houchalk, D. J., Samm, Jr., B., Hugglestone, A., and Howard, J. 1993. Orienteering. In Dougherty, N. (ed.). *Physical Activity and Sport for the Secondary School Student*, Reston, VA: AAHPERD.

Ibrahim, H. 1993. *Outdoor Education*. Dubuque, IA: Brown & Benchmark.

Kjellstrom, B. 1975. *Be Expert with Map and Compass*. New York: Charles Scribner's Sons.

Orlick, T. 1982. *The Second Cooperative Sports and Games Book*. New York: Pantheon Books/Random House.

Rohnke, K. 1984. *Silver Bullets: A Guide to Initiative Problems, Adventure Games, and Trust Activities*. Dubuque, IA: Kendall/Hunt Publishing Company.

Rohnke, K. 1989. *Cowstails and Cobras II: A Guide to Games, Initiatives, Ropes Courses, and Adventure Curriculum*. Dubuque, IA: Kendall/Hunt Publishing Company.

Simpson, B. 1974. *Initiative Games*. Butler, PA: Encounter Four, Butler County Community College.

Webster, S. 1989. *Ropes Course Safety Manual: An Instructor's Guide to Initiatives and Low and High Elements*. Dubuque, IA: Kendall/Hunt Publishing Company.

Index